INFINITE SPACE

CONTEMPORARY RESIDENTIAL
ARCHITECTURE AND INTERIORS
PHOTOGRAPHED BY JAMES SILVERMAN

gestalten

THE VIEW FROM THE WINDOW

On James Silverman's approach to architectural photography in the age of the globalized residence.

Text: ALAN RAPP

The window is still the humblest plane. It did not start out as that magic surface that generously permitted a vista out to the world. As early as the Republican era, before piped water, Roman houses had angular cutouts in the roof of a central living space that vented smoke from the hearth fire. A depression under this opening also gathered rainwater into the house's cistern. Aperture, skylight, and chimney: the earliest of what we would consider modern houses were adept at multitasking.

The windows eventually crept down to the wall surface, but they remained high for security's sake. Metal or wooden frameworks held small glass panes. Cast and blown glass on the industrial scale provided glazed windows for more houses, villas, and public and religious buildings, though primarily for the higher classes. They permitted light, but due to their irregularities they were not used for looking out. The invention of view tropism, designing around a vista, was still a ways off.

Covered with various materials–skins, cloth, flattened horn, slices of marble or crystal, or parchment–windows permitted soft light and some measure of insulation. Glass panes were not for the masses in the medieval era, but they became prevalent even before the Age of Reason and the invention of plate glass technology. It is hard to estimate the effect that the window had on the development of the modern interior, but what became clear is that developing the position, size of aperture, and technology of opening and securing windows had a two-way effect. The resident inside could see out–but anyone outside could see in. With the privileged view from the interior came the possibility of the equal-opportunity gaze from without. The siting of residences could still be bound primarily to ideas of territory and security, and the visual scan from that defensive position could also, it turned out, take in all of that landscape. The paradox of the window view was established.

Long before orthodox modernism, the modest window was the element through which one could bring the outdoors–light, air, or that ineffable, multisensory feeling of *atmosphere*–into the home. As sash, mullion, muntin, and pane glazing technologies became more refined, the overall concept of the "window" turned into a composite construction technology unto itself. The development of this technology permitted another modern innovation: the residential lifestyle. More indoor activities were possible at all times of day. By the time the first truly modern houses debuted in the early twentieth century–with their startling new qualities of factory aesthetics, the demotion of architectural and interior decoration, and the new imperative to design without servants (or their quarters) in mind–the modern window made them sunnier than what came before.

So what can be said about the contemporary house that goes beyond the most familiar framings? We have to acknowledge that however refined the design, assembly of materials, and sensitivity to site and climate is, and however increasingly technologized the modern house has become, in the end, it is a shelter and base for domestic life. The archetypal hearth-home, version 3.0. The notions of comfort and safety that those primal redoubts provided have undergone endless stylistic interpretations and variations, but it is a given that the modern house, even in sun-challenged climates, is flooded with as much daylight as possible.

What photographer James Silverman takes as his subject is the globalized residence. Whether in Brazil, in Sweden, or in Morocco, the houses in this volume have a lot in common—modernist tropes extruded to their utmost degree of geometric clarity, a sense of spatial openness, and again the light, the light, the light. Somewhat dependent on the climate and local building traditions, the primary materials can be wood, stone, or metal, but the various methods of dissolving the boundary between exterior and interior are what allow residents to experience the full potential of modernism's promise. The level of articulation of spaces is extraordinary. Elements coexist in complicated planar schemes, but at base is still the goal of exploring this age-old relationship between inside, representing civilization, and the natural world outside. There are a number of domestic spaces that are mostly exterior, or at least are not entirely constrained by interior walls, yet are very much a part of the house. Terraces, balconies, and porches—all are platforms for not just framing, but being part of the site, the environment, and the vista.

Seen in succession here through the lens of a photographer who is attuned to these formal and ambient qualities, it is as if the domestic sphere is undergoing a vast iterative process that somehow reflects and augments the effects of globalization. Contemplating the allusive phrase *infinite space,* we might imagine a concept for an impossibly vast structure, such as the radical design collective Superstudio's ultra-conceptual earth-spanning conjecture, *Continuous Monument.* But this is not the age when megastructural schemes that encircle the globe, critiquing the limits and nature of architectural agency in any context, are routinely proposed.

We retrench in the home, even today. But the difference now is that what I see out of my window extends much further than the eye's reach. The global house is knit together with every other in a skein that blends old and new. Old in its attempt to refine—if not perfect—a space that is a residence in the service of what is seen as its era's ideal lifestyle. New, in that its geographic sprawl is not contiguous or continuous in Superstudio's sense of vast and leveling spatial dynamics.

In the age of late globalization, of pocket-sized telepresence and mass migration, the house is inherently nodal. The concept of *home* takes on a special meaning. It is not just where we are, in the sense of staying put, but is now often also, in many changing and evolving senses, where we might be: ensconced in media, surrounded by a menagerie of goods produced around the world, and halfway in or out the door. Where we are is always someplace else.

The globalized residence creates a set of challenging conditions for the contemporary architectural photographer. If architecture as an applied practice is about designing space, then the architectural photo is volume made visible. Yet for all the power of the photograph to reveal, portray, and depict (all those words that still demonstrate the constant striving after, but never arriving at, the *real*), what we cannot see is at least half as important as what we can.

Global modernism emerged at roughly the same time that photomechanical reproduction flourished. In the early 1900s, architecture magazines such as ~

Architectural Forum and *American Architect* enjoyed the same color covers and photographic reproduction as popular American magazines such as *McClure's* and the *Saturday Evening Post.* For an extended period during modernism's heroic era, when buildings were meant to signify iconic singularity, the image became the primary currency of the movement. The clarity of form and purpose that undergirded the movement broadcast this architecture globally. In the trade press, lifestyle publications, monographs, and exhibitions that nourished different aspects of the industry, the foursquare of the photographic image conveyed the visual rhetoric that derived from a rational idea of composition. The architectural image had annexed space.

Silverman belongs to the proud pedigree of photographers who communicate global architecture through global media. When his images are reproduced in magazines, they need to work in their editorial context. He eschews some of the trendier conceits of architectural and interior photography today, chiefly the inclusion of the human habitant. It is a commonplace that classical architectural photography eschewed the human figure—and therefore the sense of programmatic use, residential comfort, and the basic sense of human belonging to space—but this was rarely absolute. There is always the balance of how to stage an interior as well; the space must look broken-in and not sterile or static. But it cannot look *too* lived-in or cluttered.

The photos in this volume manage to project the personality of the inhabitants as well as the character of the architecture by investigating the rooms and byways that are not typically part of the canon of interior photography: bathrooms, play rooms, the areas that are always just around the corner, and so on. The places where a good deal of family life actually happens, rather than just the idealized living room and most up-to-date kitchen. The sense of human presence is acute, even if the inhabitants are not visible. An idiosyncratic but effective gesture that Silverman employs is to show a tap running, as if the owner just stepped out of the frame for a moment.

The residences that Silverman photographs largely diverge from each other in terms of site condition, climate, dominant material, and almost every resulting aspect that combines these toward their design—but the similarities they embrace are more illustrative. The architects of global residential modernism seek to position their projects in as close to a natural context as possible. These houses are largely nestled into the landscape in a way that prioritizes the integration of site and structure, and as a secondary effect seems to distance or separate them from neighbors. The real kinship of these ideal residences, be they voluminous or not, is to the land.

But reading these photos, it is clear that contemporary house design casts this relationship in a more dynamic way than the stereotypical green building strategy of "sitting lightly" on the land. Even in a still photograph depicting immobile architecture, the dynamism of form and the legibility of program distinguish these houses. They do not sit so much as reach across the land, stretching out to demonstrate the exuberance of global architecture today.

In great photographs of great houses, we see a twofold ideal. The demonstration of a current pedigree of high design, but also the ongoing training that sharp and lovely photographs can impart to train the viewer's eye to seek out more. James Silverman shows us the view out the window, from whichever hemisphere we may find ourselves in, and we can see the corners of the world folding toward each other. In the end, this expansive, free-ranging modernism is really modernism that has come home.◆

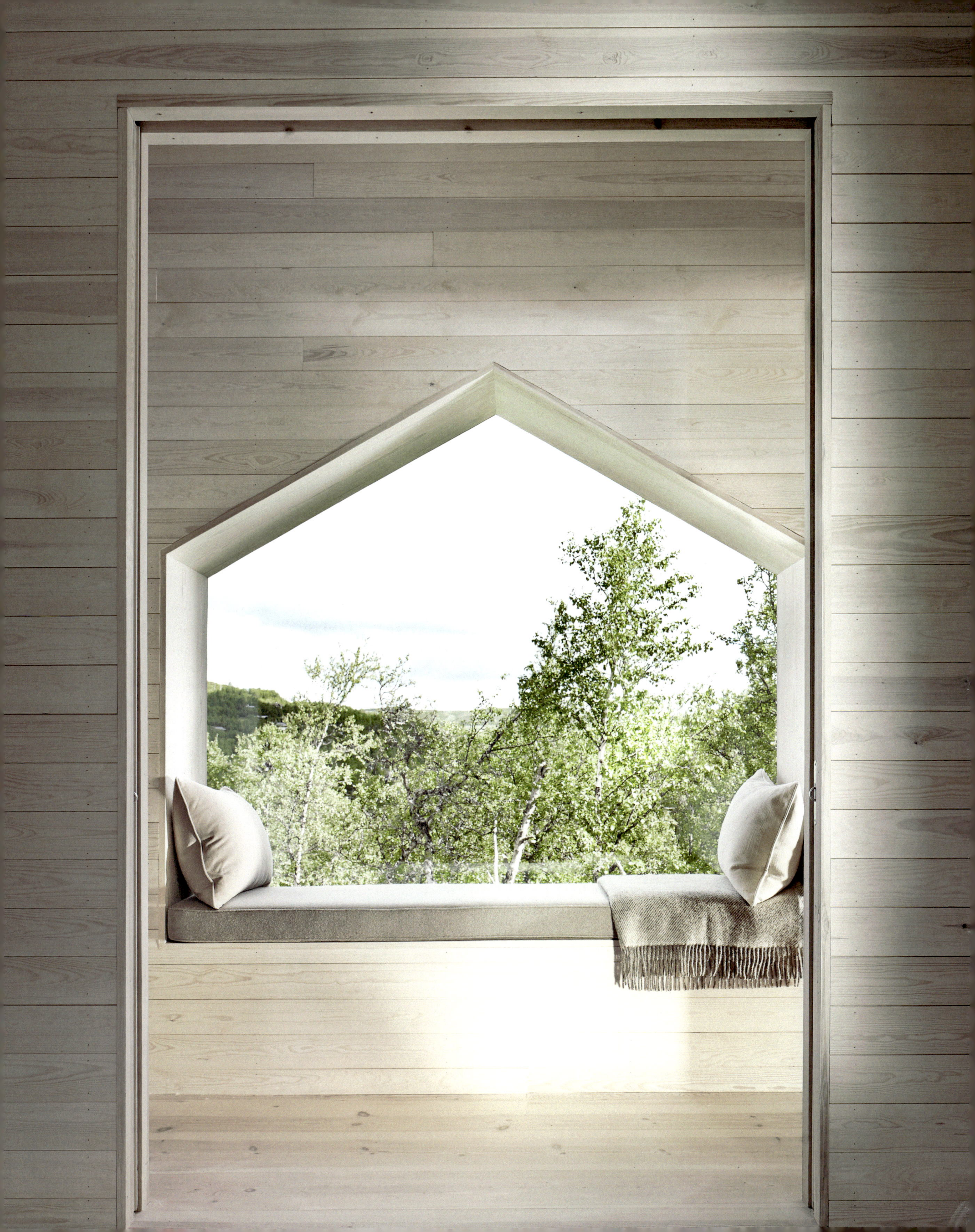

PUUTOSSALMI, FINLAND

VILLA BRUUN

SEPPO HÄKLI
OF HÄKLI ARCHITECTS

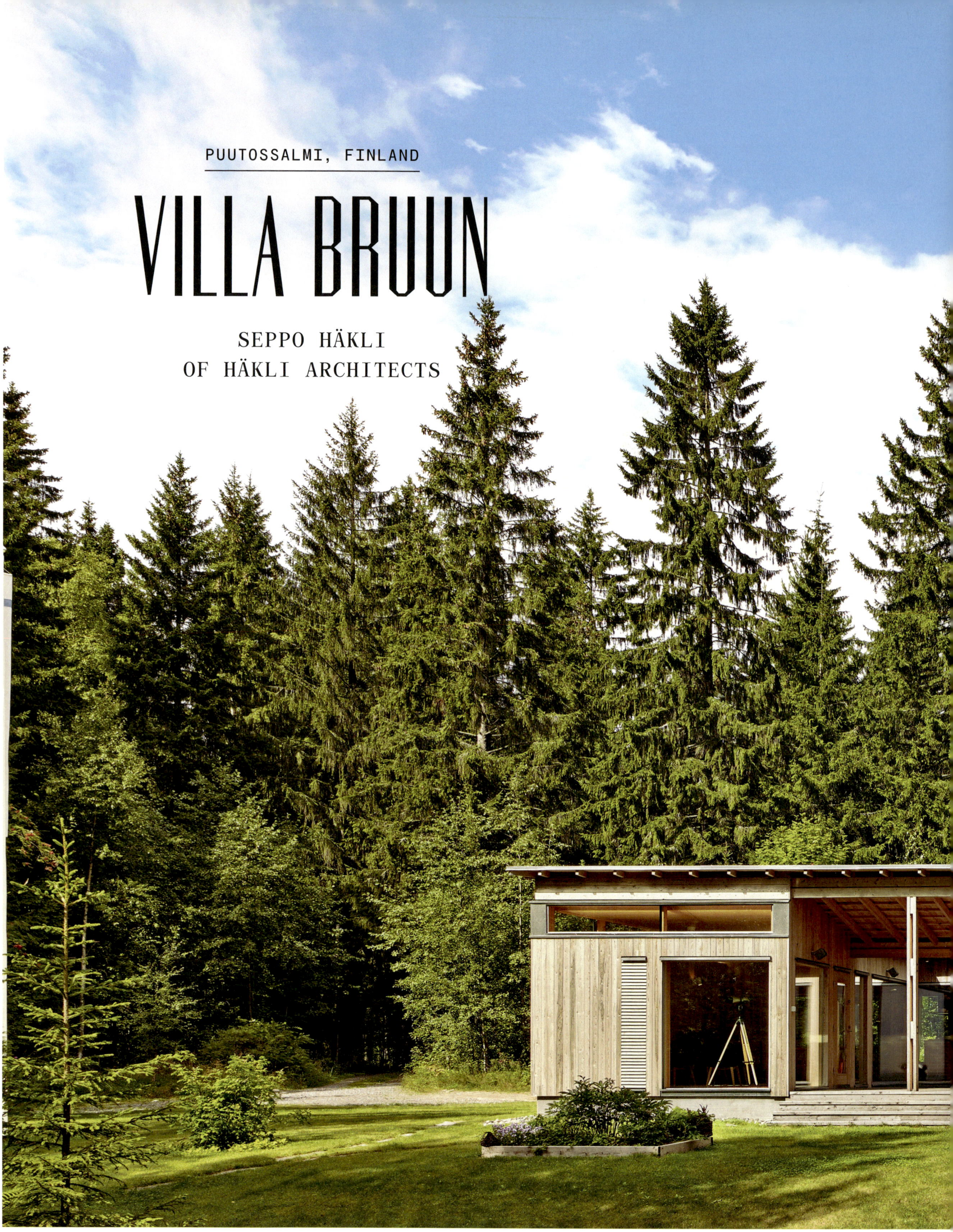

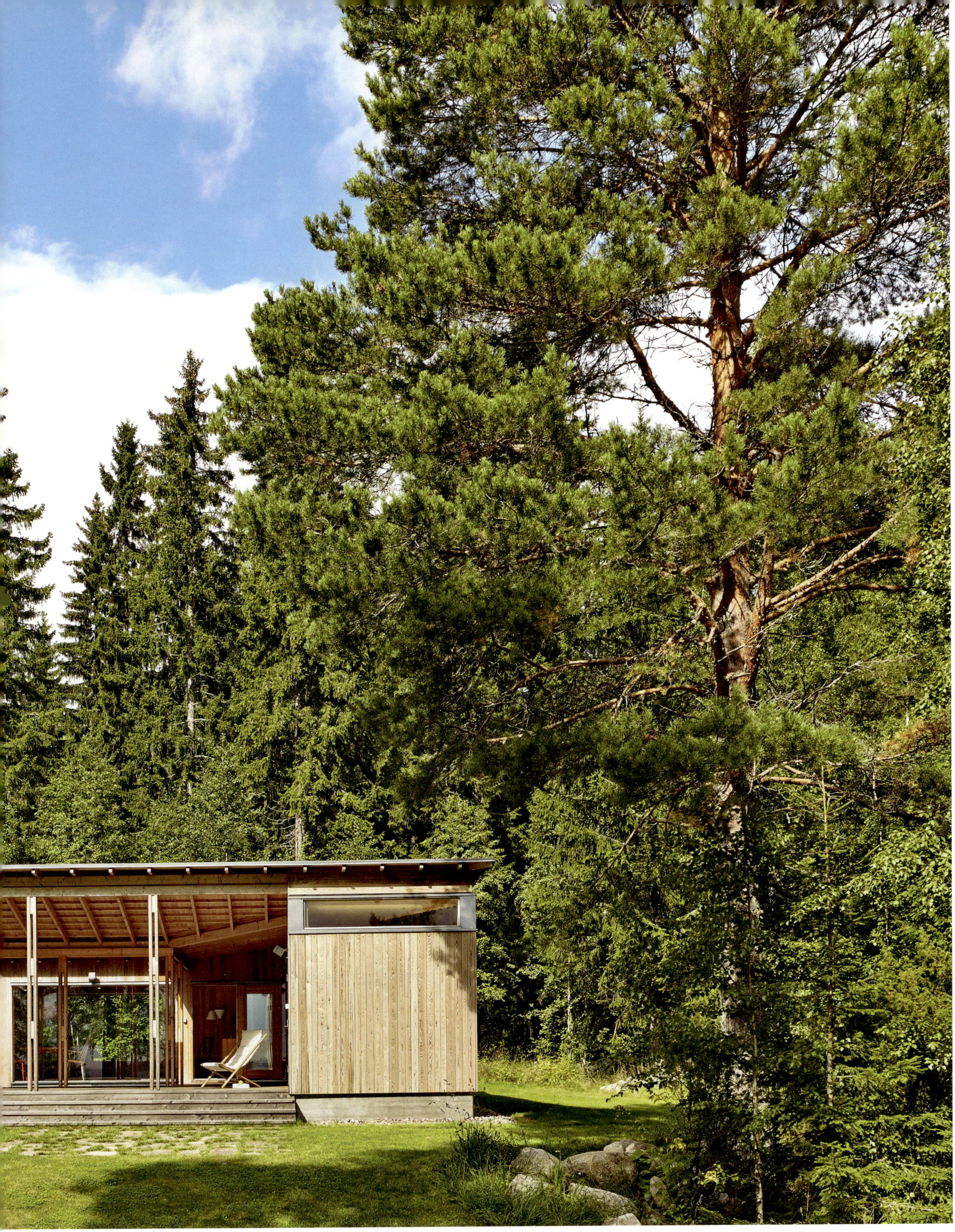

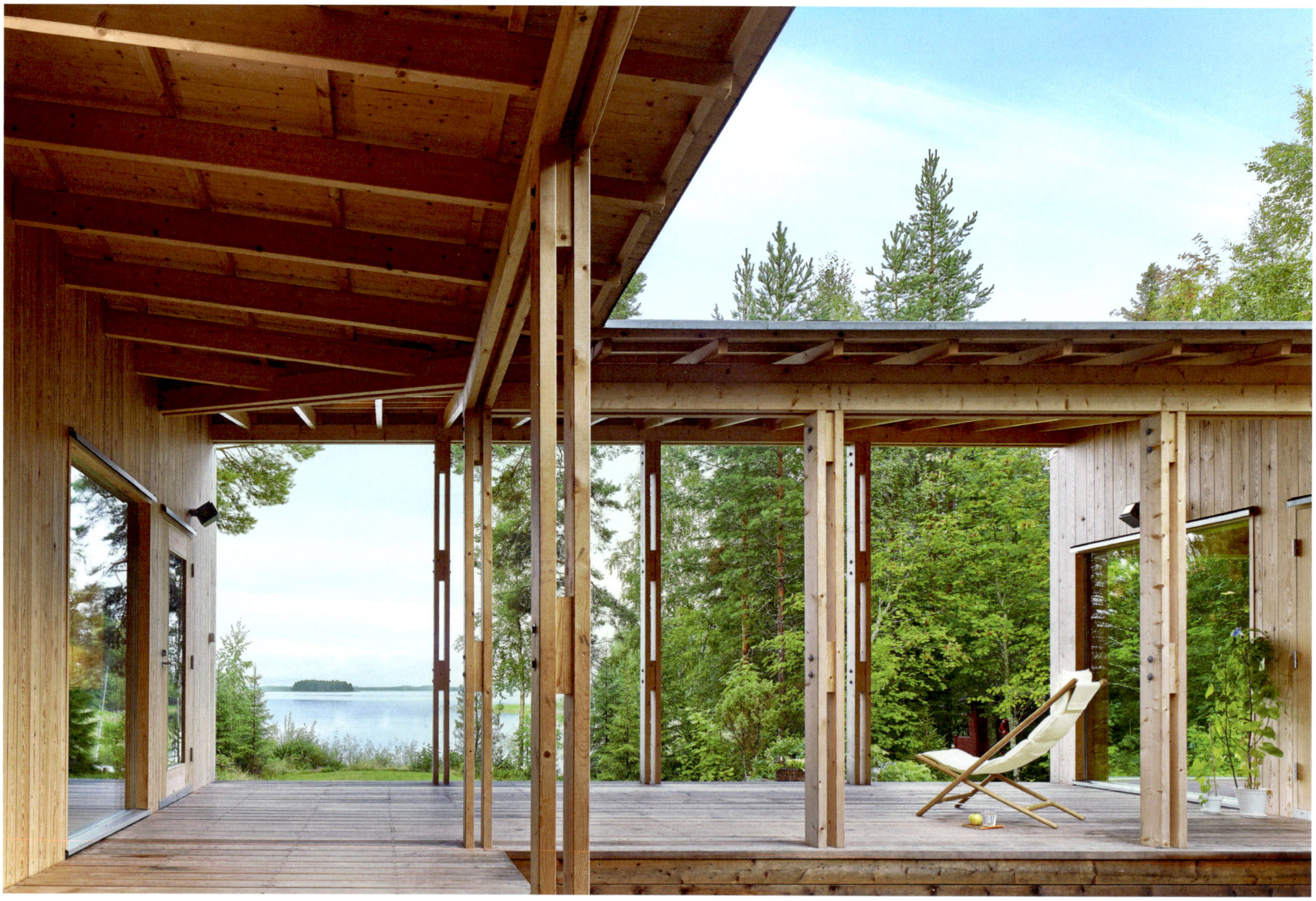

VILLA BRUUN Except for its clean brick floor and fireplace, Villa Bruun is all wood. White aspen, pale and rigid pine, and dark heartwood come together in an example of immaculate architecture and craftsmanship. The wood will mature with its surroundings as the cabin endures through the decades.

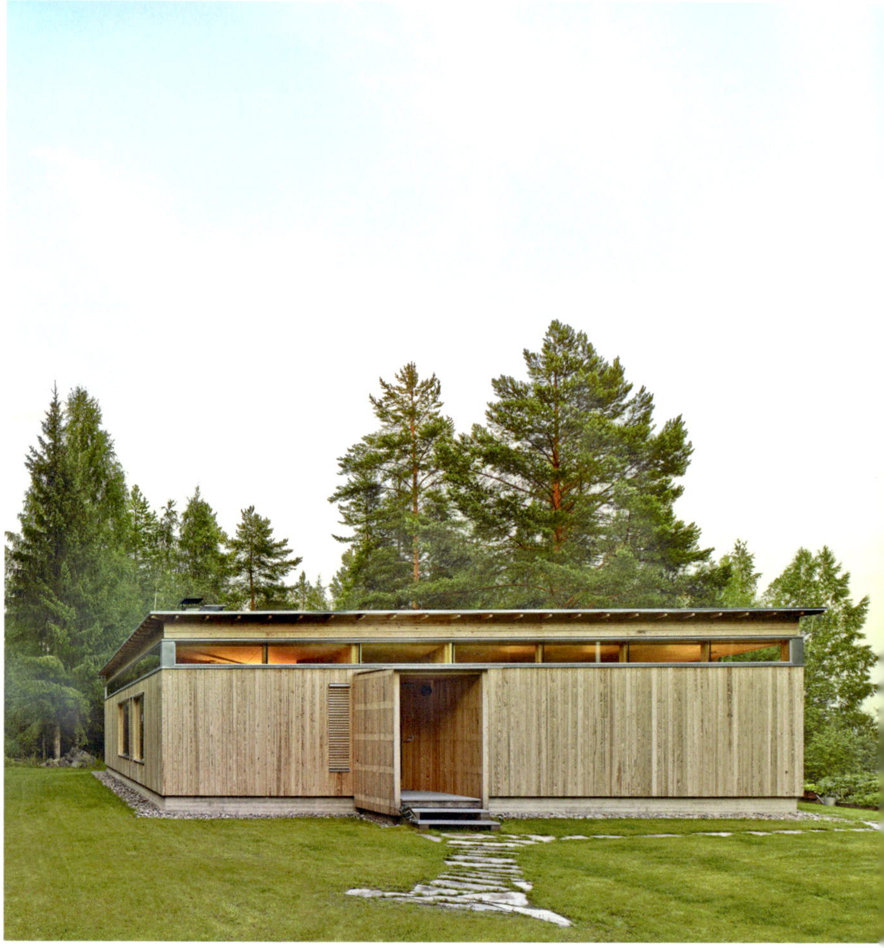

Nature is a vital base for the Bruun family. Since they live only 25 kilometers away from this lakeside site in Finland's Kallavesi region, Villa Bruun acts as a sanctuary where they and their relatives can convene throughout the year. Successfully contending with the region's varied climate, the villa is an open and accommodating guesthouse in the summer and a snug escape during colder months.

The new house replaced a cabin that had been in the Bruun family for nearly half a century, so hospitality was as central to the project as the lake itself. To integrate both the scenic and social aspects, award-winning architect ~

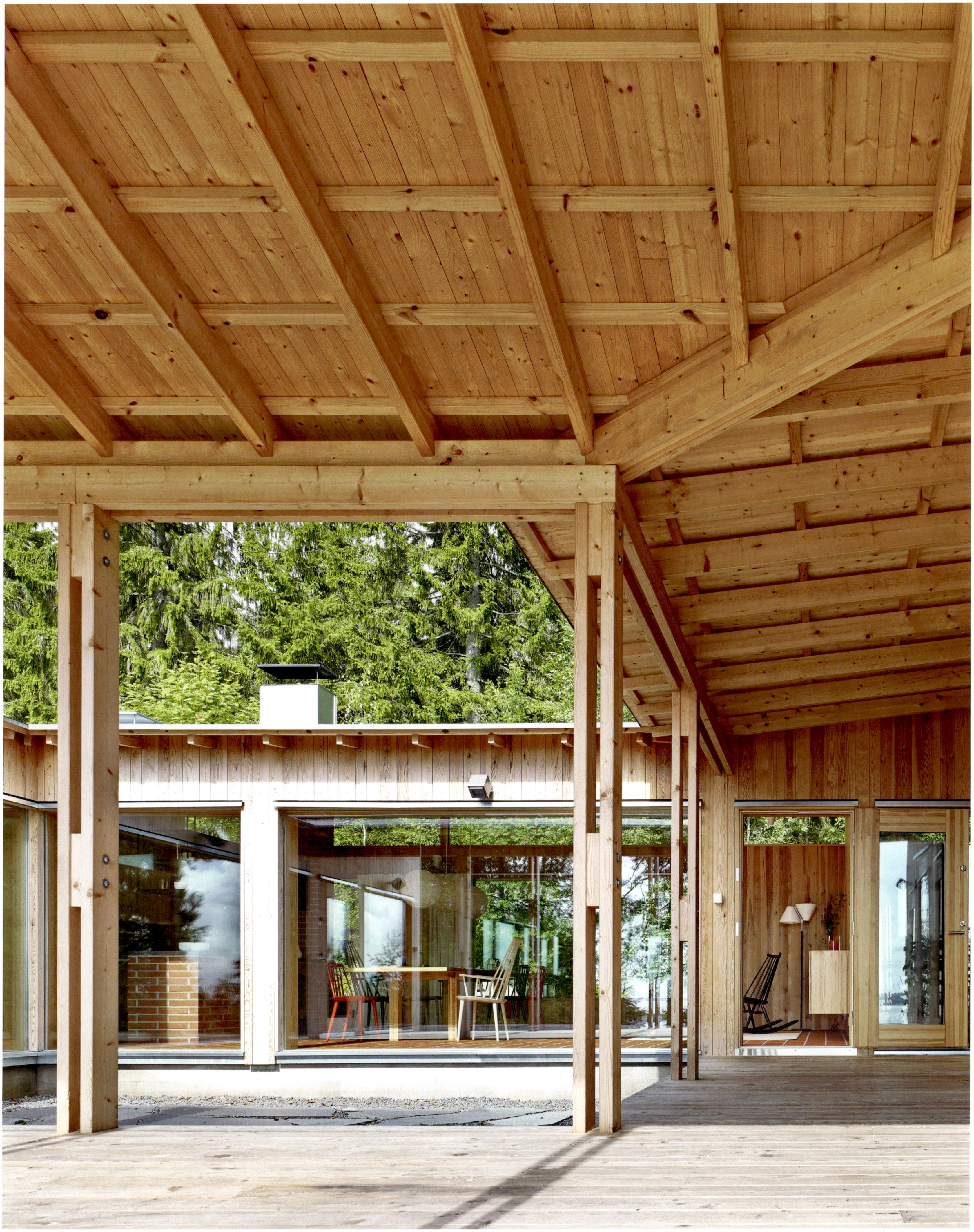

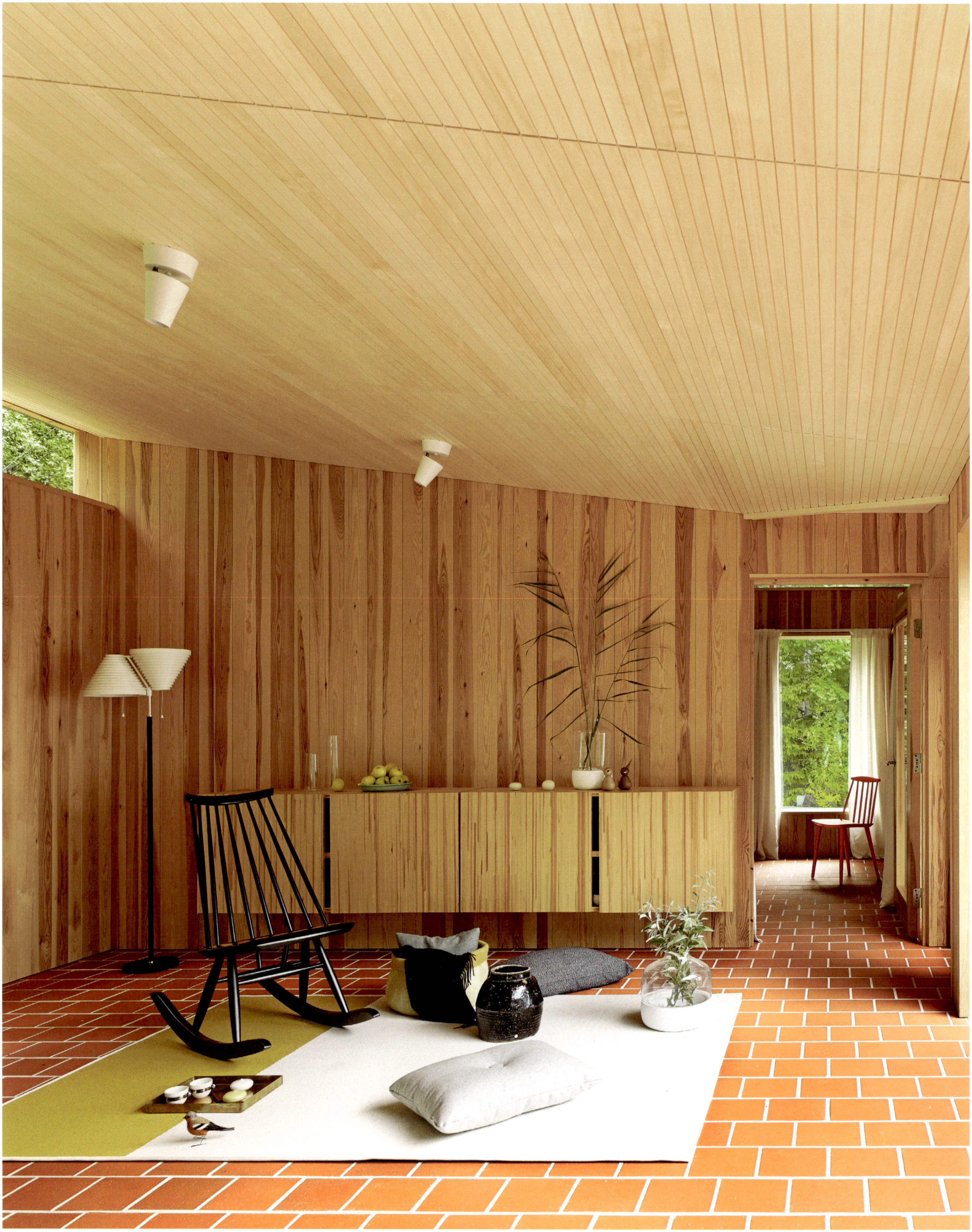

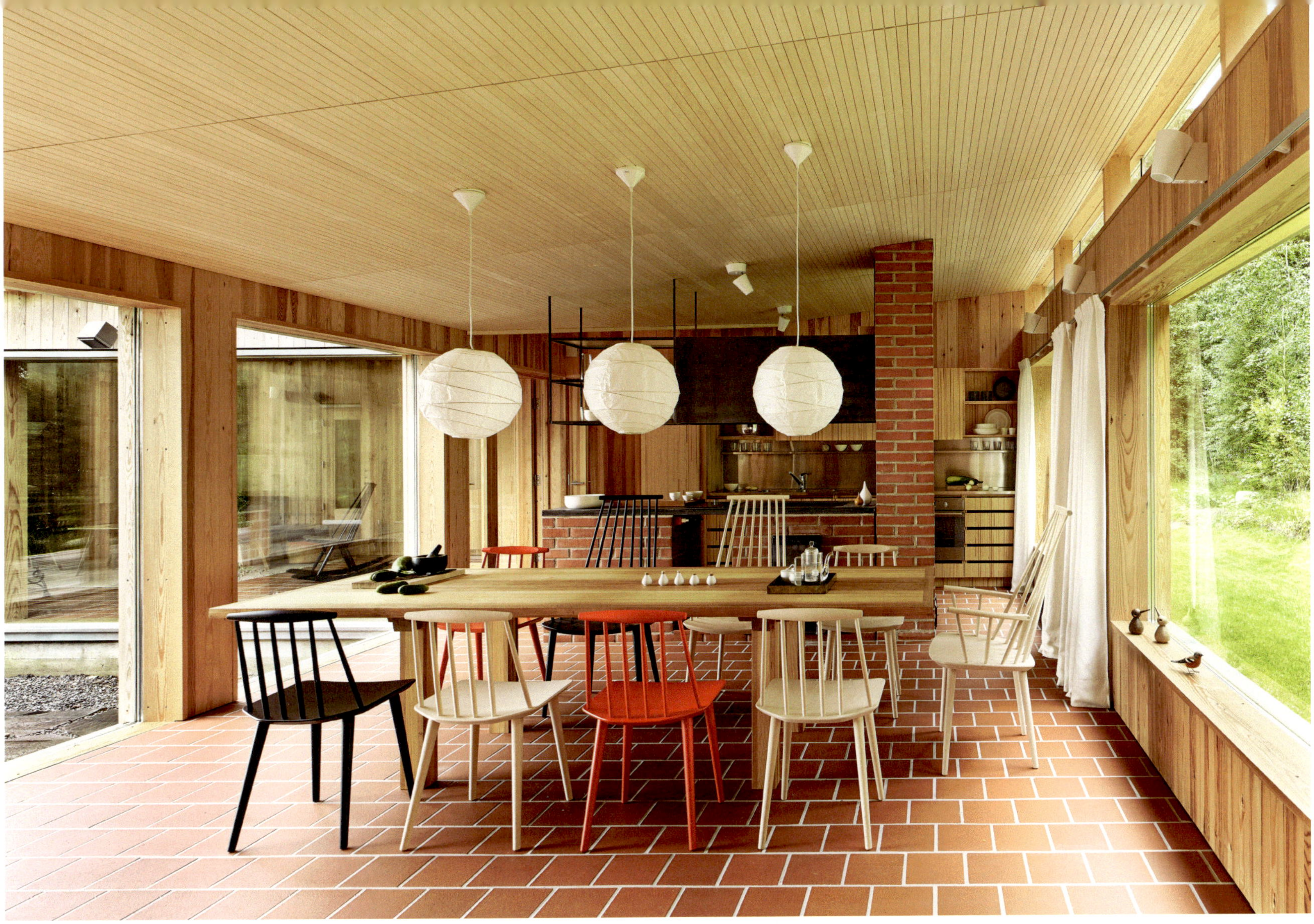

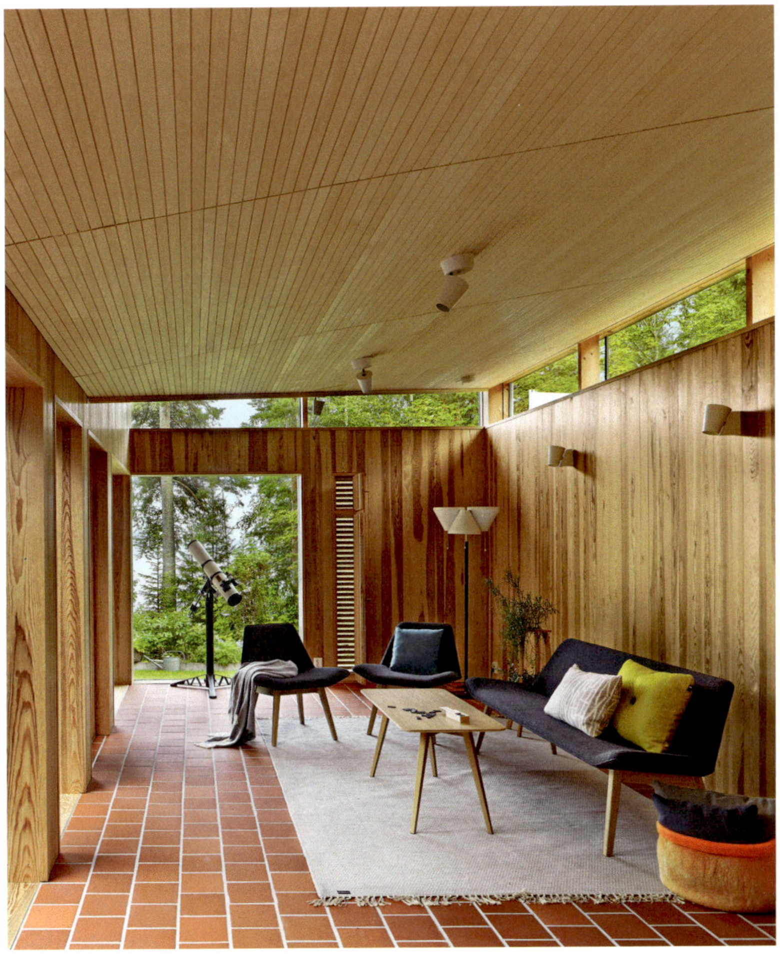

Seppo Häkli designed a pavilion-like structure that ensures clear views of the lake while opening the villa up for the family to socialize. A traditional Finnish tupa—a room that combines kitchen and living spaces—occupies two sides of the pavilion. Pale tongue-and-groove pine boards are offset by darker heartwood, and the brick fireplace and floor blend their warm, welcoming tones. When temperatures drop to -20 or even 30 degrees Celsius in the winter, underfloor heating can be remotely activated, ensuring that the villa is warm on arrival.

On the other side of the pavilion, across a small rock-garden courtyard, externally accessible cabins provide extra sleeping space for the Bruuns' extended family. Clerestory windows trace their way around the whole villa, casting light beneath the white aspen roof as the sun arcs through the day. Since the majority of the villa is made of wood, the building will weather with the climate, becoming a gray-silver that will harmonize with the forest.

Häkli says, "The family feel that it meets their needs perfectly. The dining area with a view to the lake is a special feature for them, and in summer the house is a perfect base for sailing, fishing, swimming, and socializing with their grown-up children and friends." ◆

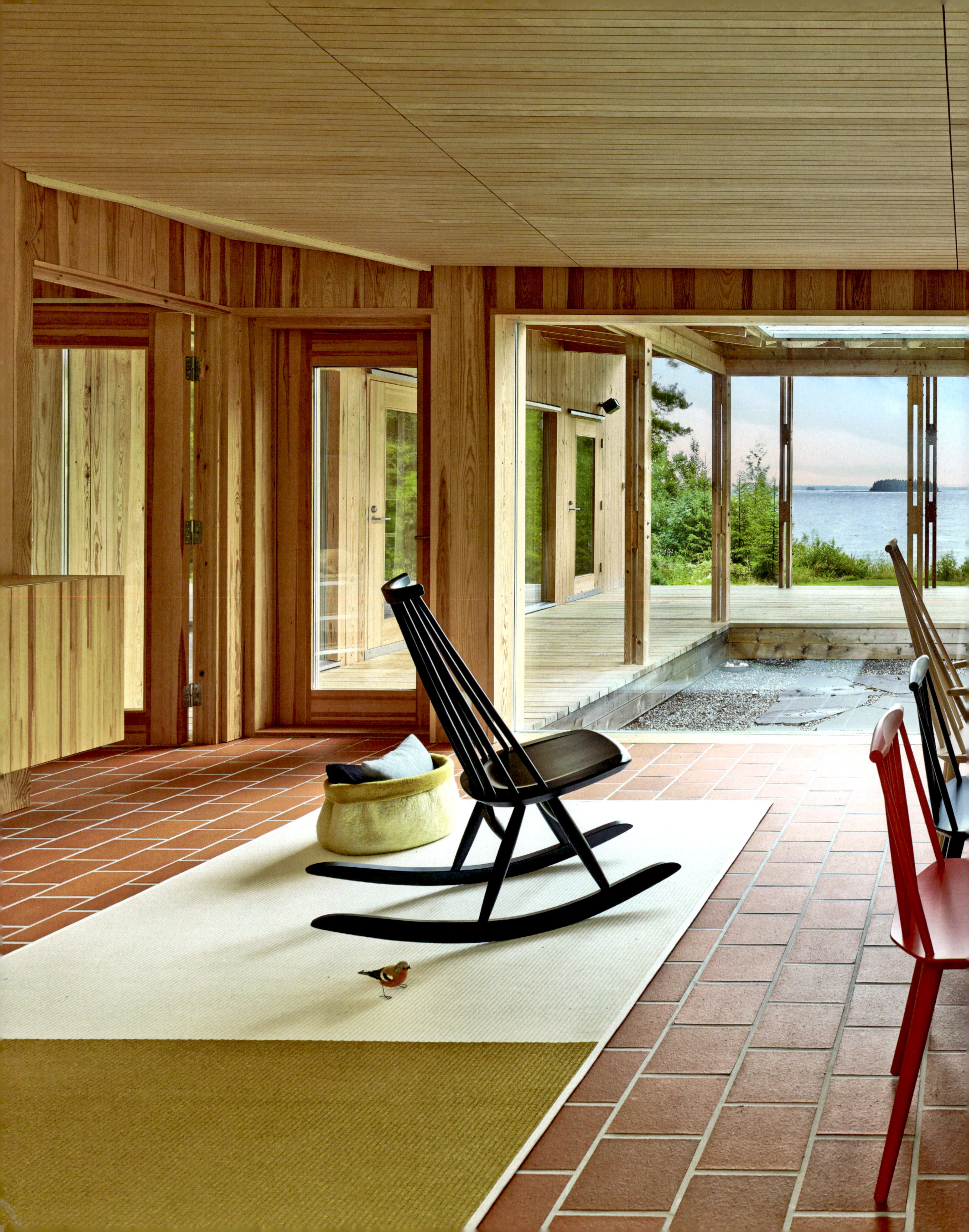

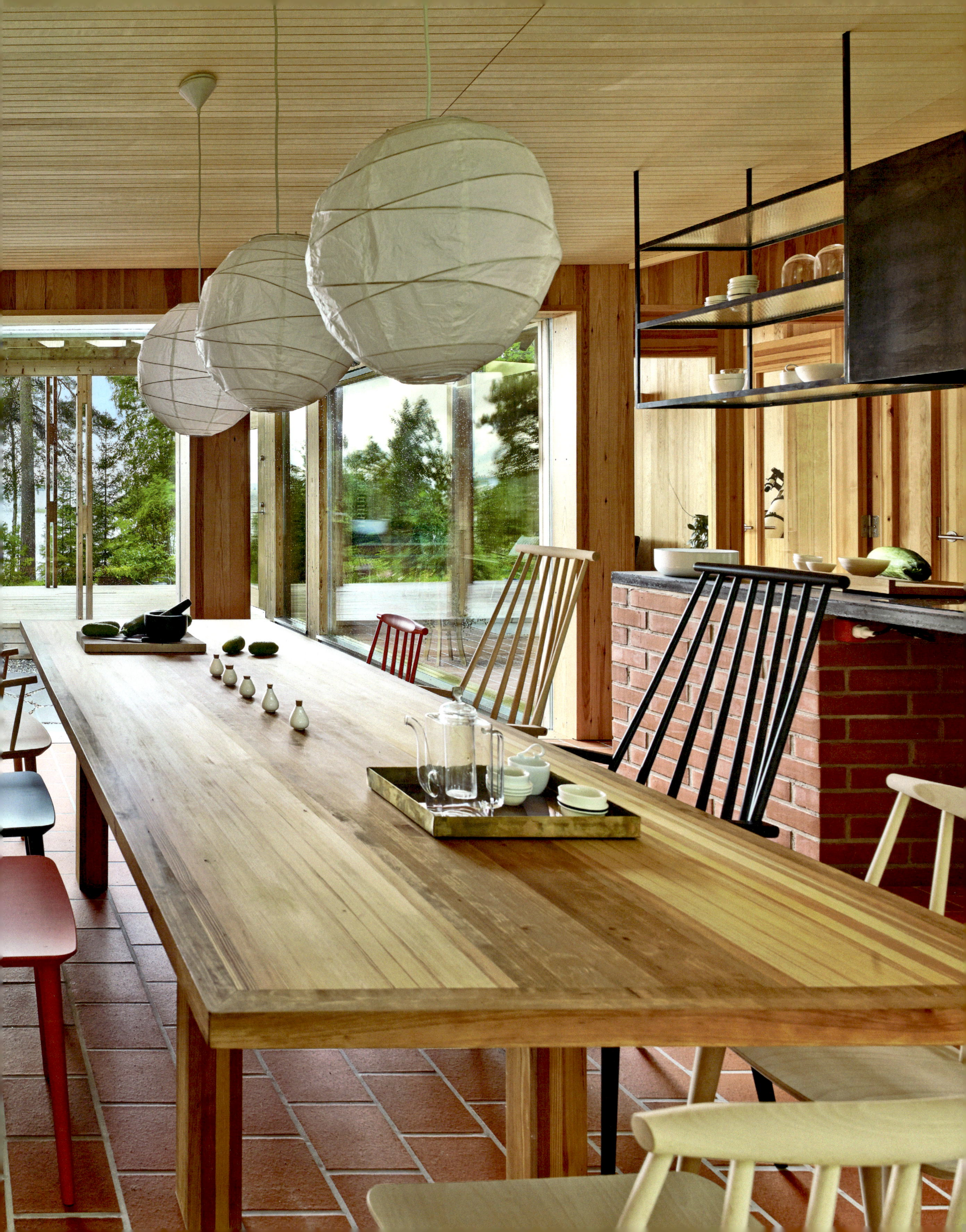

KARUIZAWA, JAPAN

N HOUSE

IIDA ARCHISHIP STUDIO

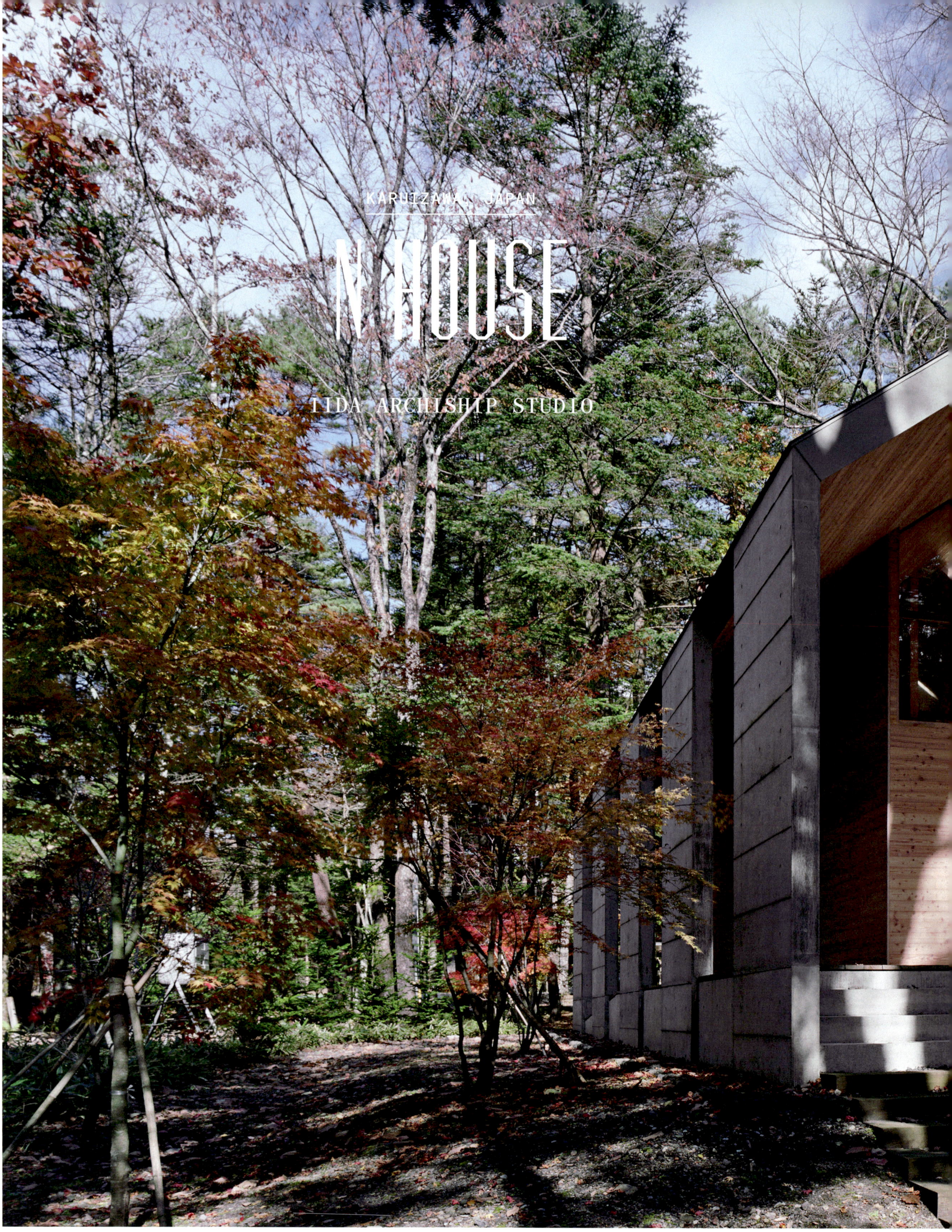

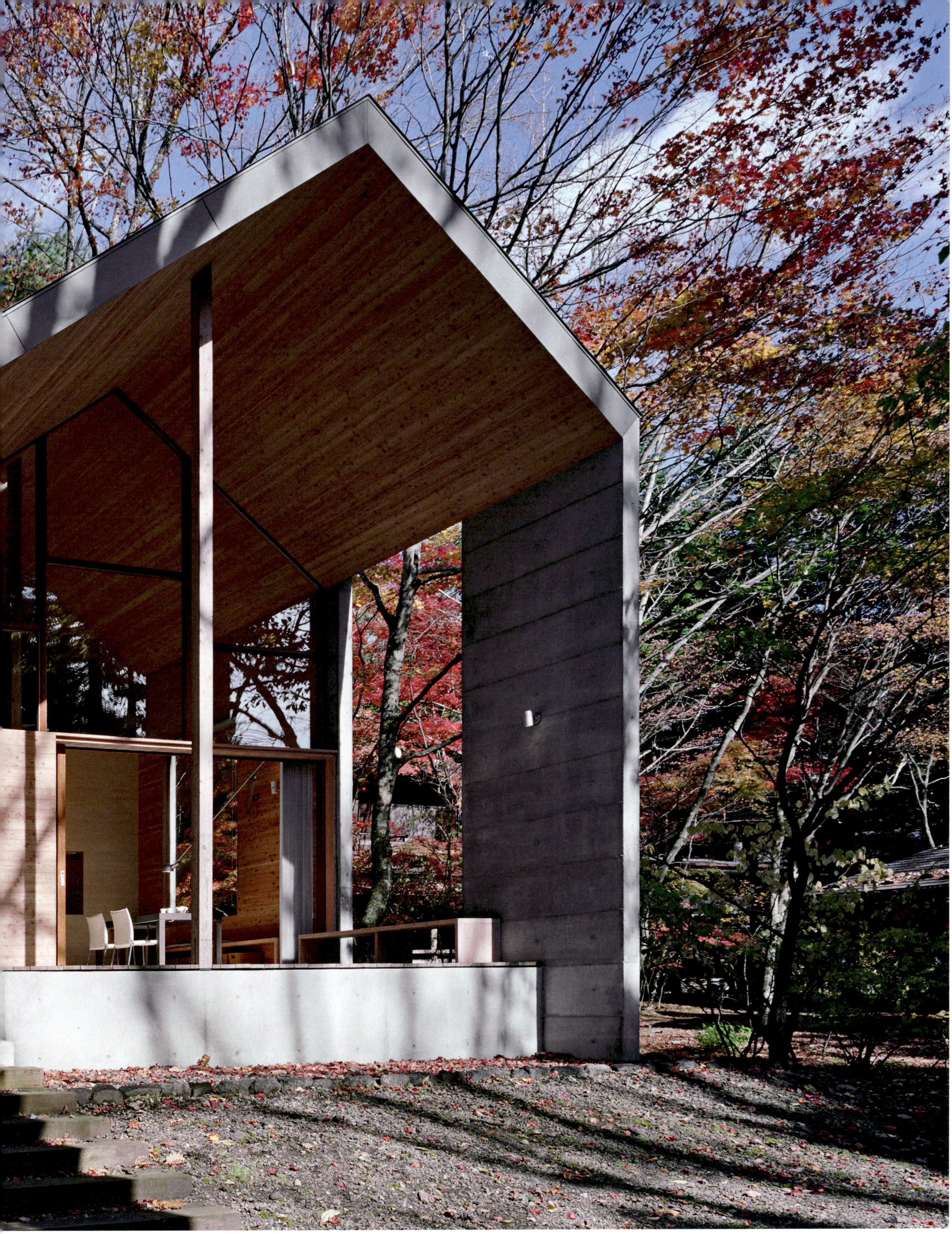

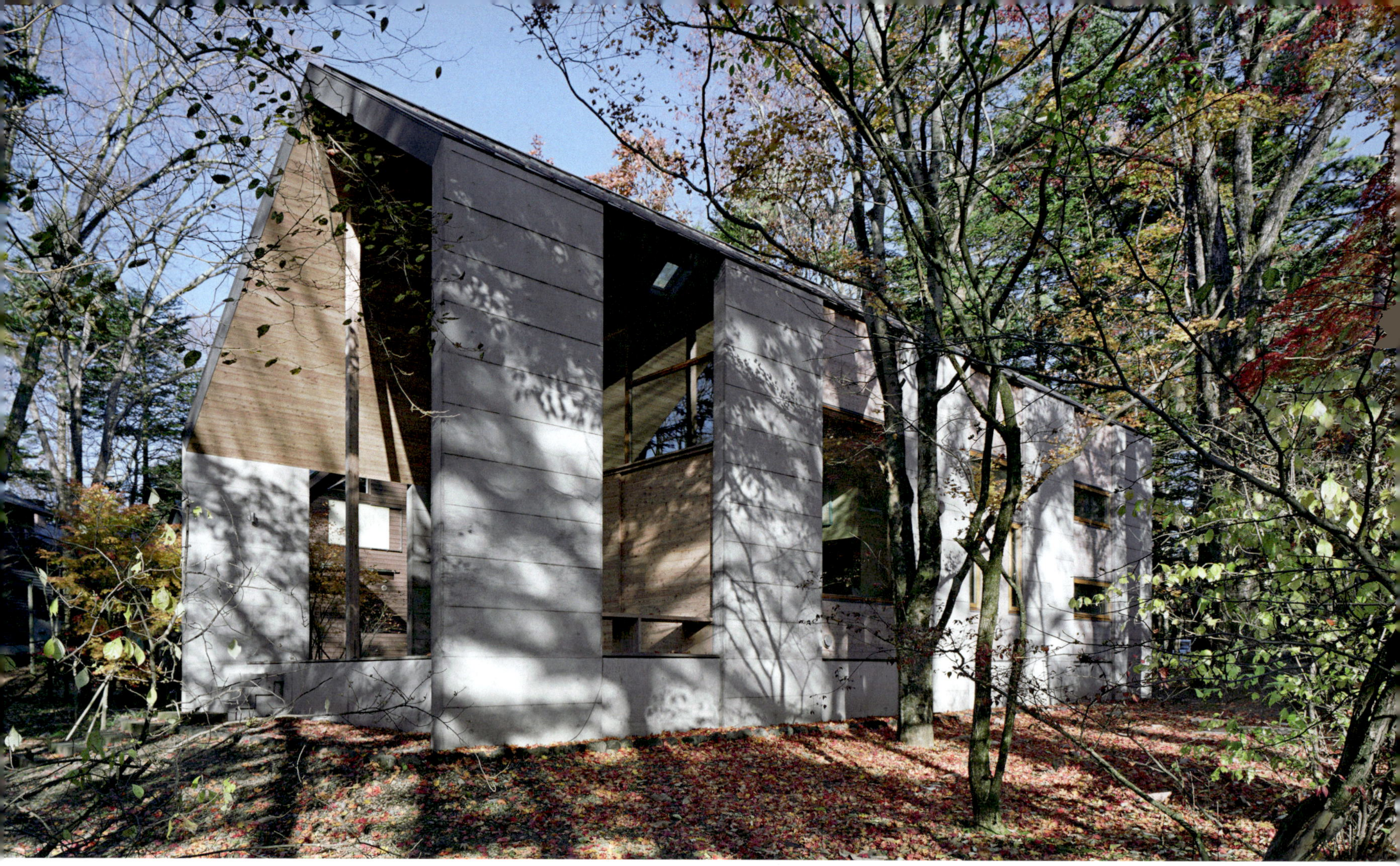

N HOUSE is located in Karuizawa, a popular vacation destination in Japan. In recent years, the mountainous region's popularity has soared and, sadly, many new developments have damaged the once pristine forest. By working with its precious environment, N House bucks the trend.

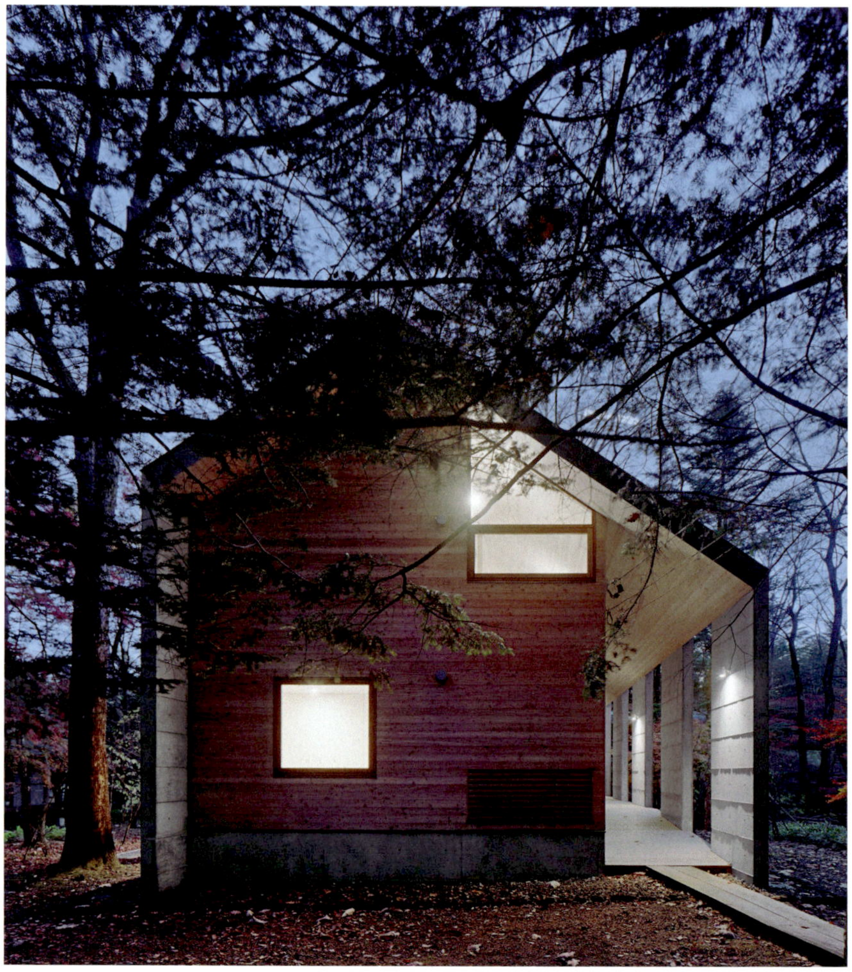

Ryoji Noyori's memories of Karuizawa stretch back to childhood visits to his grandparents' house. His wife, Hiroko Oshima, did not visit the area until her early 20s, but was instantly enchanted by the sylvan landscapes. Eventually, the two met and discovered that they shared more than a love of Karuizawa. 40 years later, the married couple returned to build a vacation home where Noyori's grandparents once lived.

They commissioned Yoshihiko Iida for the project based on his work on the Noyori Materials Science Laboratory—a facility built to honor Noyori's Nobel Prize in 2001. The architect was acutely aware of the negative impact of recent developments on Karuizawa's lush forests. "They're cutting down trees at an alarming ~

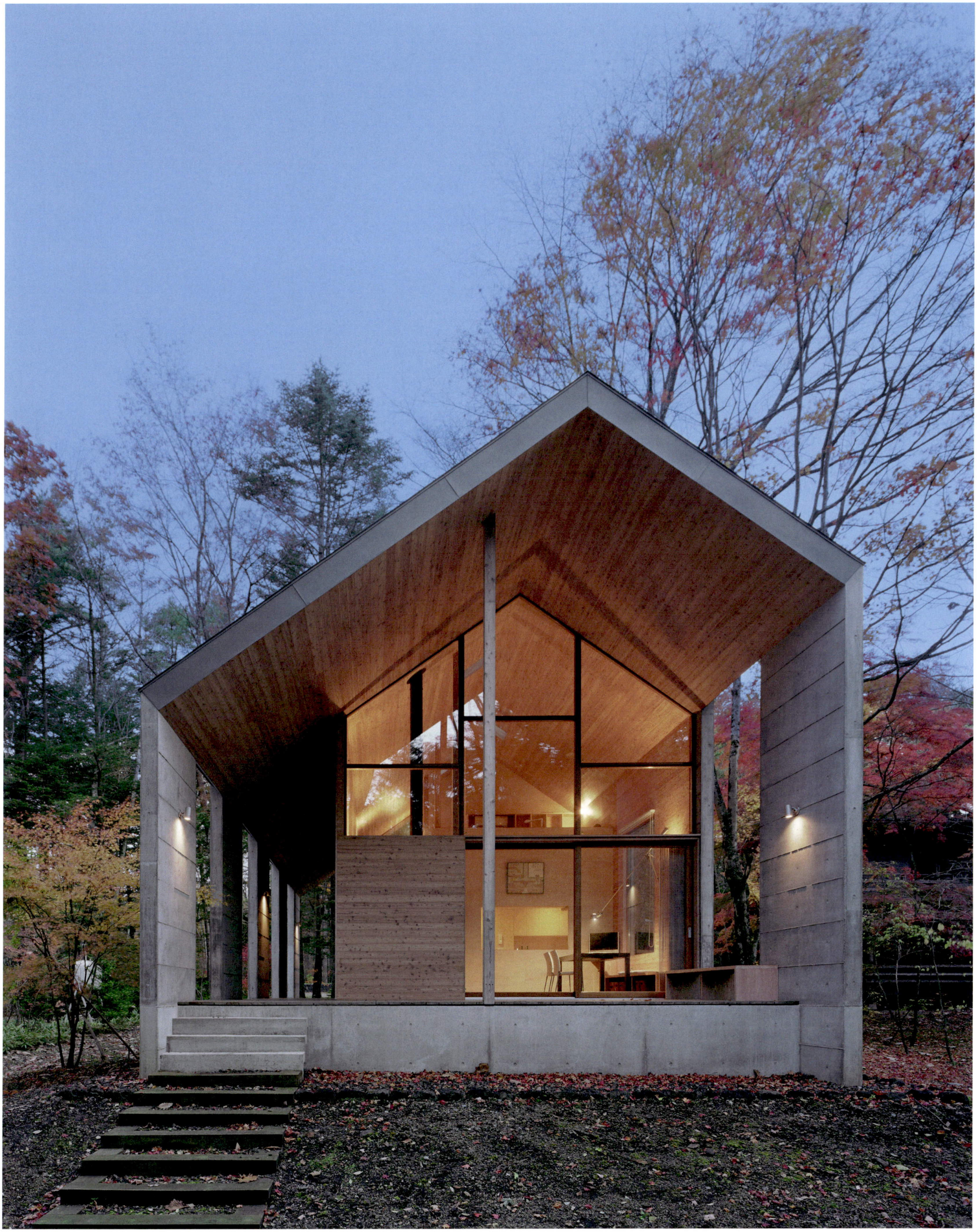

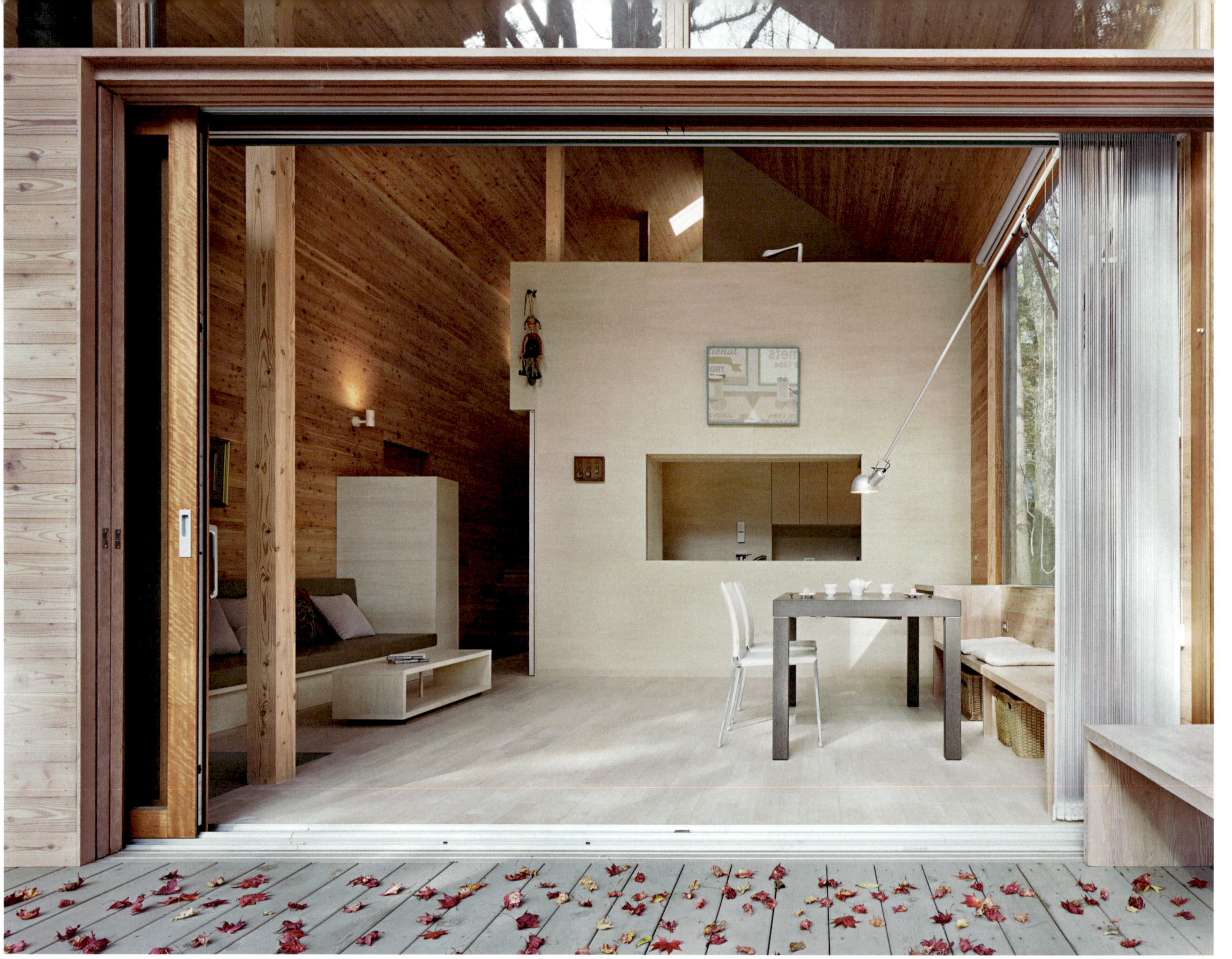

"THE PREDOMINANCE OF WOOD AND GLASS, AND THE CABIN'S PROXIMITY TO THE FOREST, SUGGEST A SCANDINAVIAN INFLUENCE, BUT IIDA DESIGNED THE HOUSE AROUND JAPANESE PRINCIPLES."

rate," he said, in a process that is "carving away the very soul of the place." To counter this trend, Iida did not cut down any trees during the construction of N House. In fact, he planted more.

The cabin itself is similarly sensitive to its environment. A room-spanning glass wall frames the forest to the south, expressing admiration for the beauty of the local trees. In the central space, kitchen, and bathroom, wooden panels coated with a low-gloss white complement the rich larch walls and ceilings while yielding a modern finish that resembles marble. The predominance of wood and glass, and the cabin's proximity to the forest, suggest a Scandinavian influence, but Iida designed the house around Japanese principles. The 6.6-meter sliding glass doors, the terraces, and the contact between inside and outside are modern manifestations of Japanese architecture that privilege suppleness and simple transitions. ◆

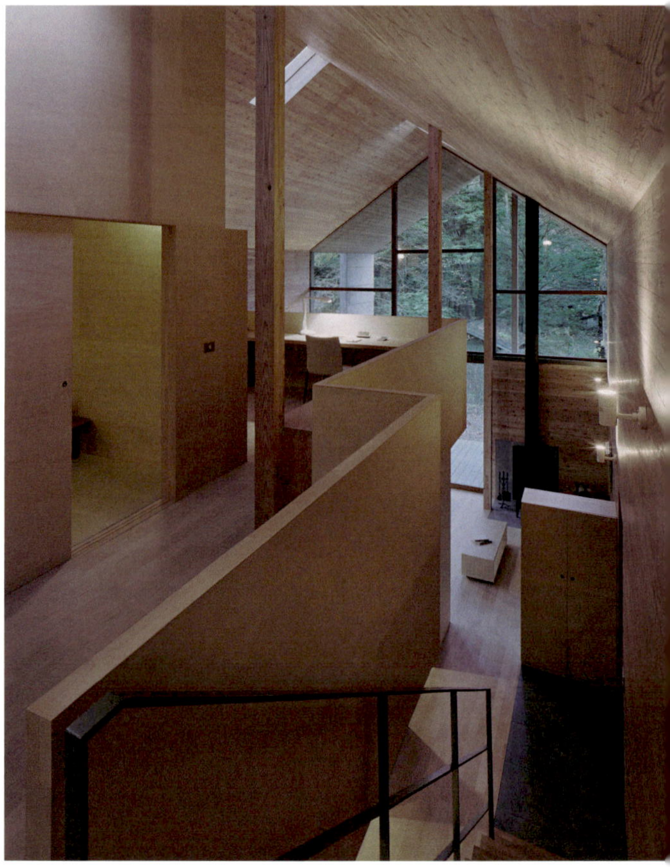

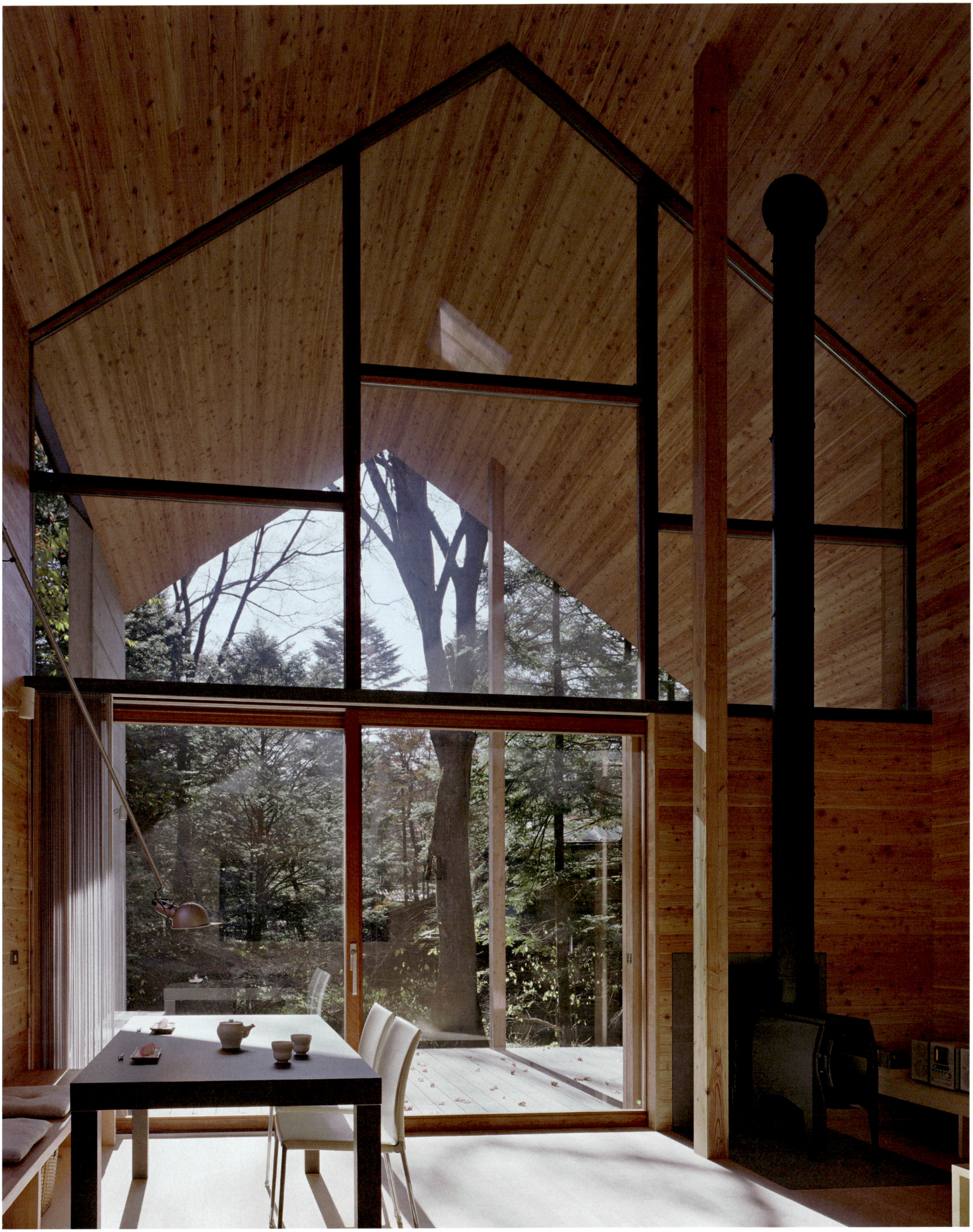

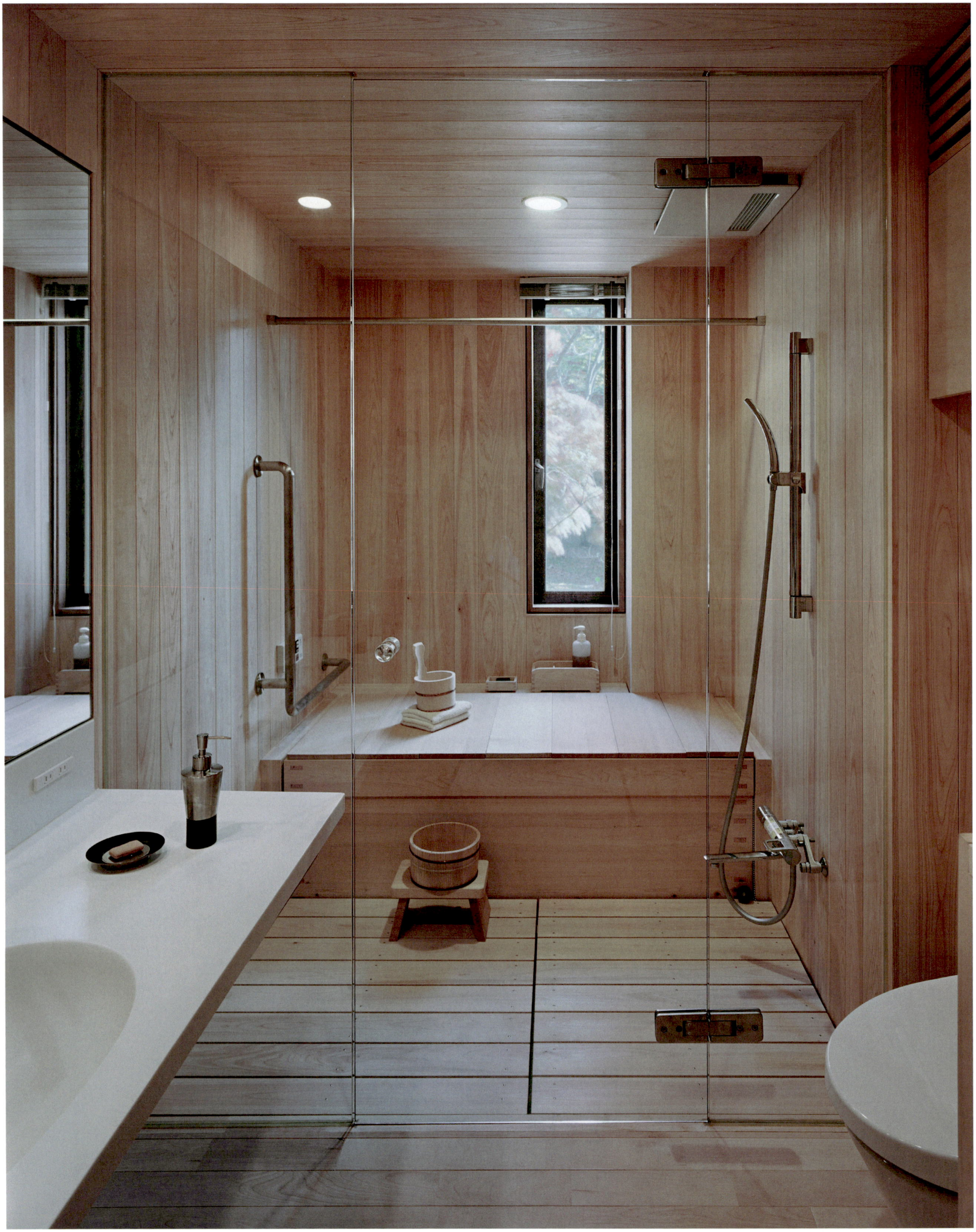

"Not a single tree on the property was touched in the building of this house—in fact, we planted more. I even took pains to protect the natural mosses on the site." — *Yoshihiko Iida*

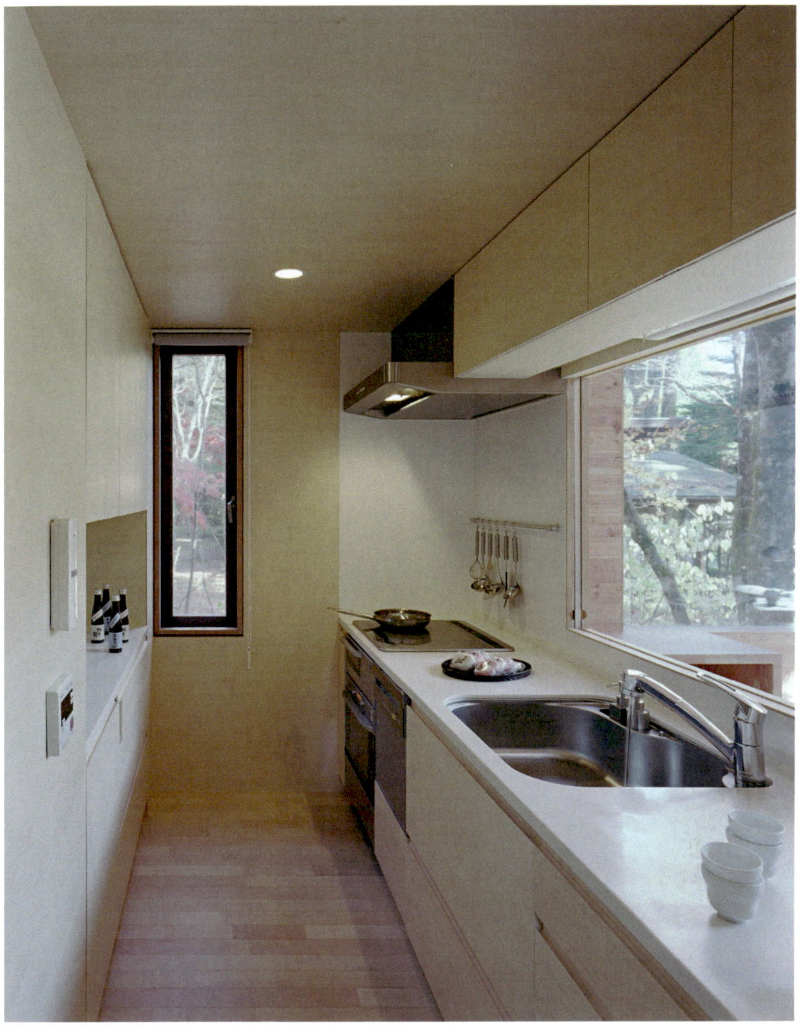

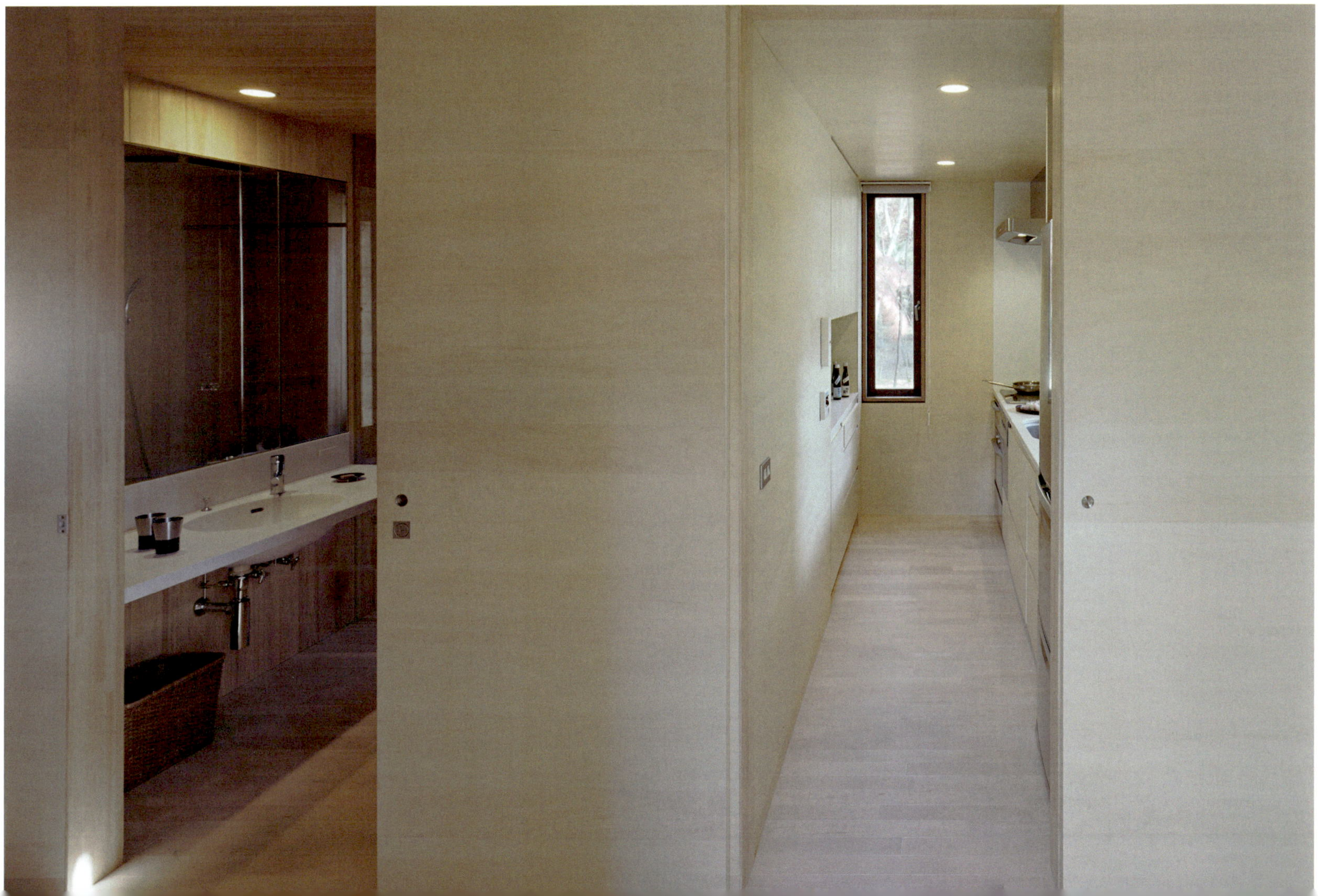

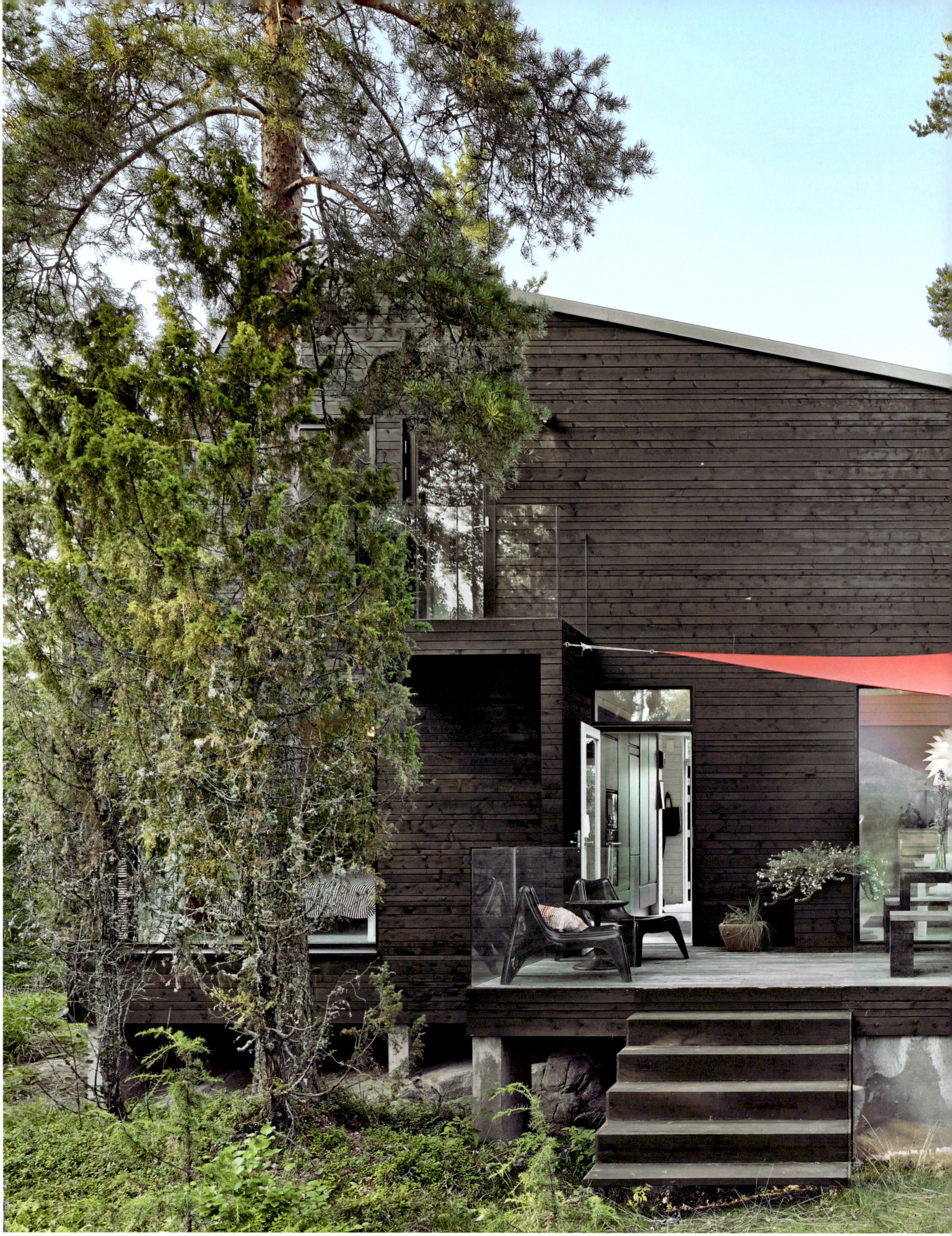

LAMMI, FINLAND

HOUSE LEHTIKIVI

LEHTINEN OF
ARKKITEHTUURI OY LEHTINEN MIETTUNEN

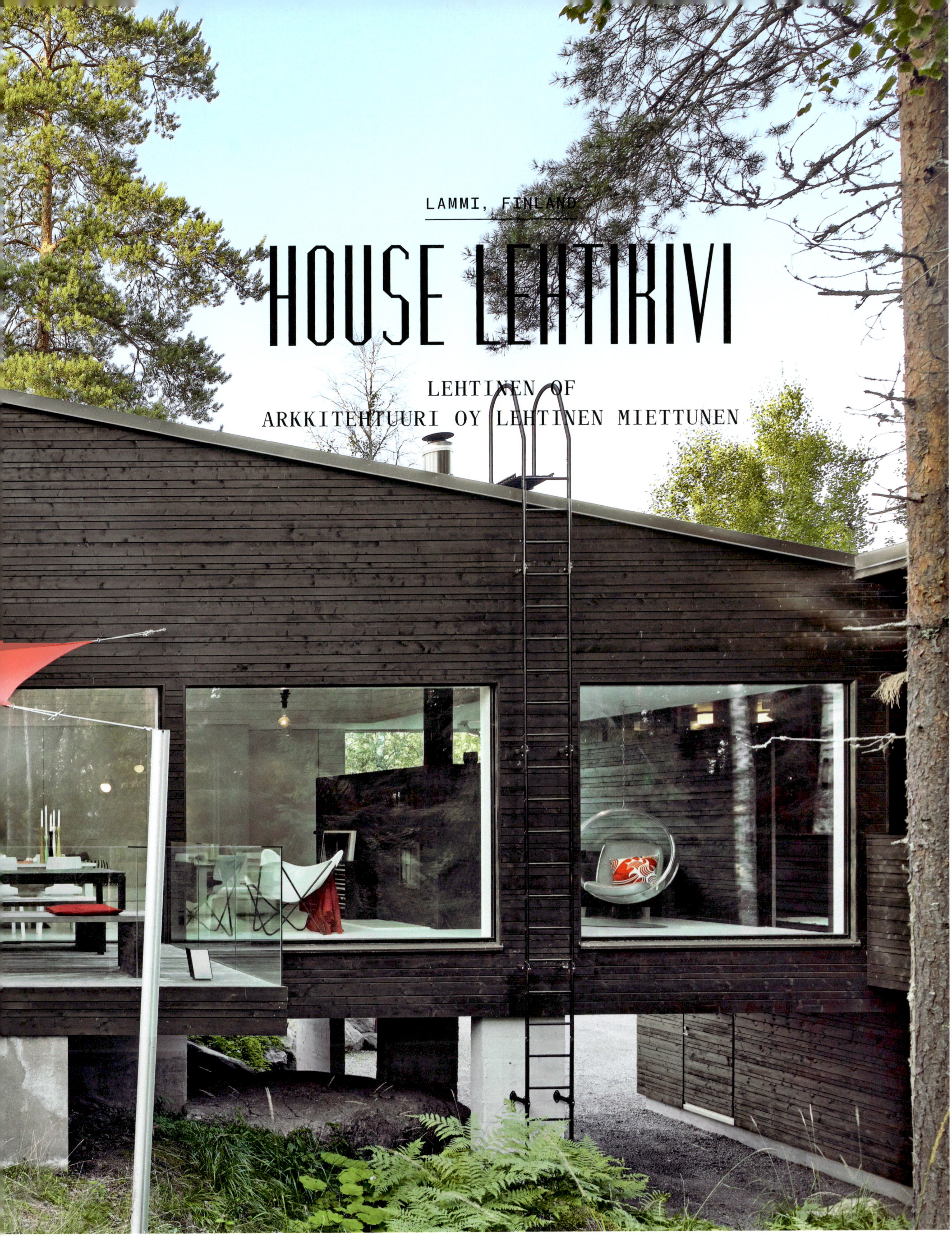

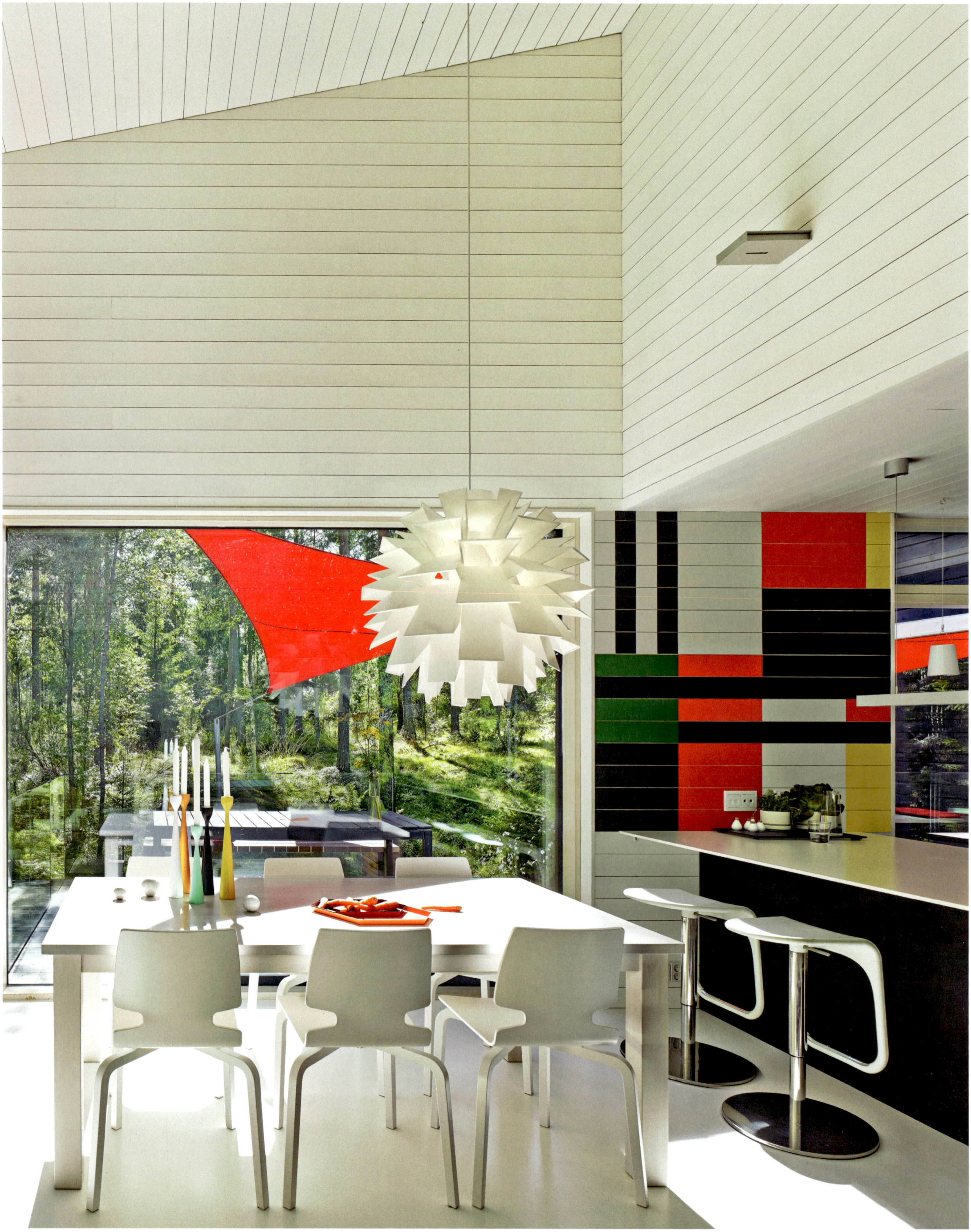

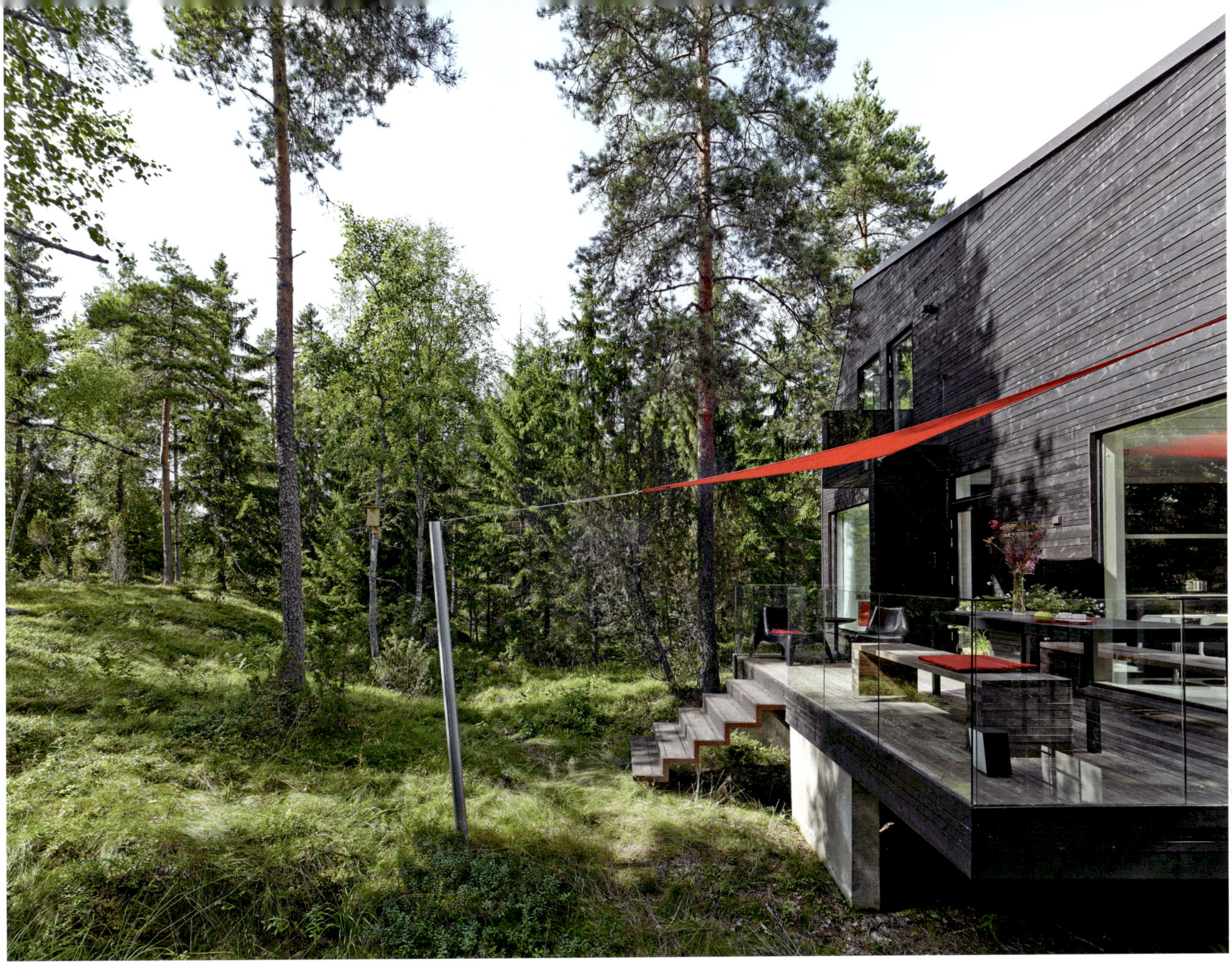

HOUSE LEHTIKIVI Lasse Lehtinen is a Finnish architect who pays careful attention to the traditional building methods of his homeland. Made almost entirely of timber, House Lehtikivi is forged from its sylvan environment, but what really makes this cabin unique is its robust, rock-like form.

Finland's Salpausselkä is a vast ridge system left over from the glaciers of the Ice Age. As a region inhabited for over 10,000 years, many of the houses that now grace the grandiose landscape remain in close contact with the environment as testaments to that enduring heritage. As with traditional Finnish cabins, much of that history is reflected in the use of wood, a material that merges seamlessly with the verdant setting.

House Lehtikivi is a cabin steeped in this tradition. Constructed of wood paneling, with a warmly finished interior complimented by the darker, black tar exterior, it pays homage both to its environment and to traditional carpentry methods. However, House Lehtikivi does not stop there. Considering the rocky environment in conjunction with the timbered surroundings, architect Lasse Lehtinen of Arkkitehtuuri Oy Lasse Lehtinen decided to integrate the stone element in the cabin's form. As he explains, "The main idea was to create a building as if it was created out of the rock, yet made of wood." In the realization of this idea, the cabin took on a sculptural form. Characterized by decisive angles, jagged intersections, and sheer surfaces, the bulky volume appears to be a chiseled extension of its rocky foundation.

The entrance to the main space is accessed via a gravel path that leads up to a wooden stairway and terrace. This section of the cabin is home to the master bedroom and the open-plan kitchen and living areas. A dramatic palette shift is achieved there by using white oil-based paint to coat the walls. Light spills in from full-height windows on the cabin's northern face, illuminating the living room, which is further complimented by a matte black fireplace. The upstairs area provides additional living space and room for guests, and features ~

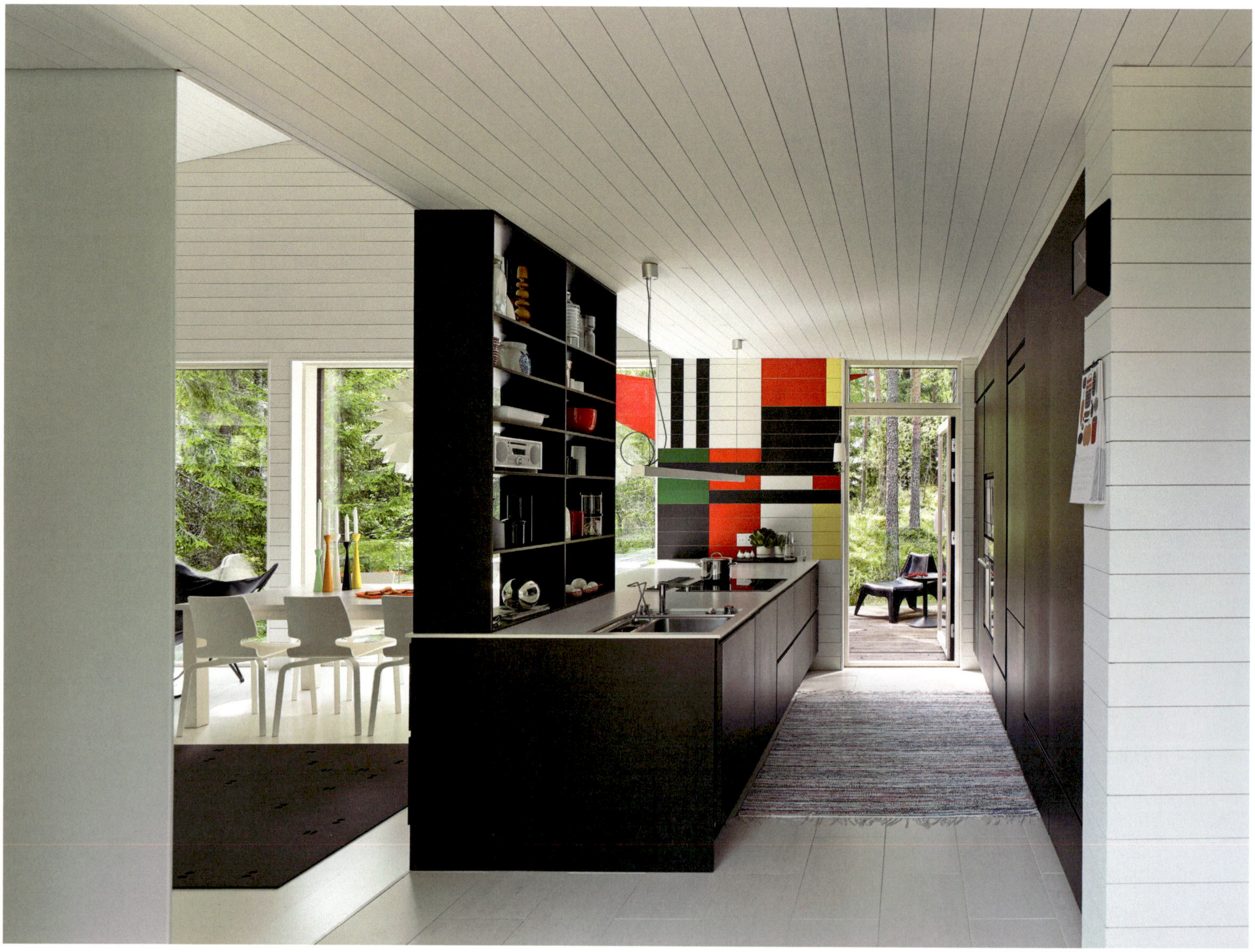

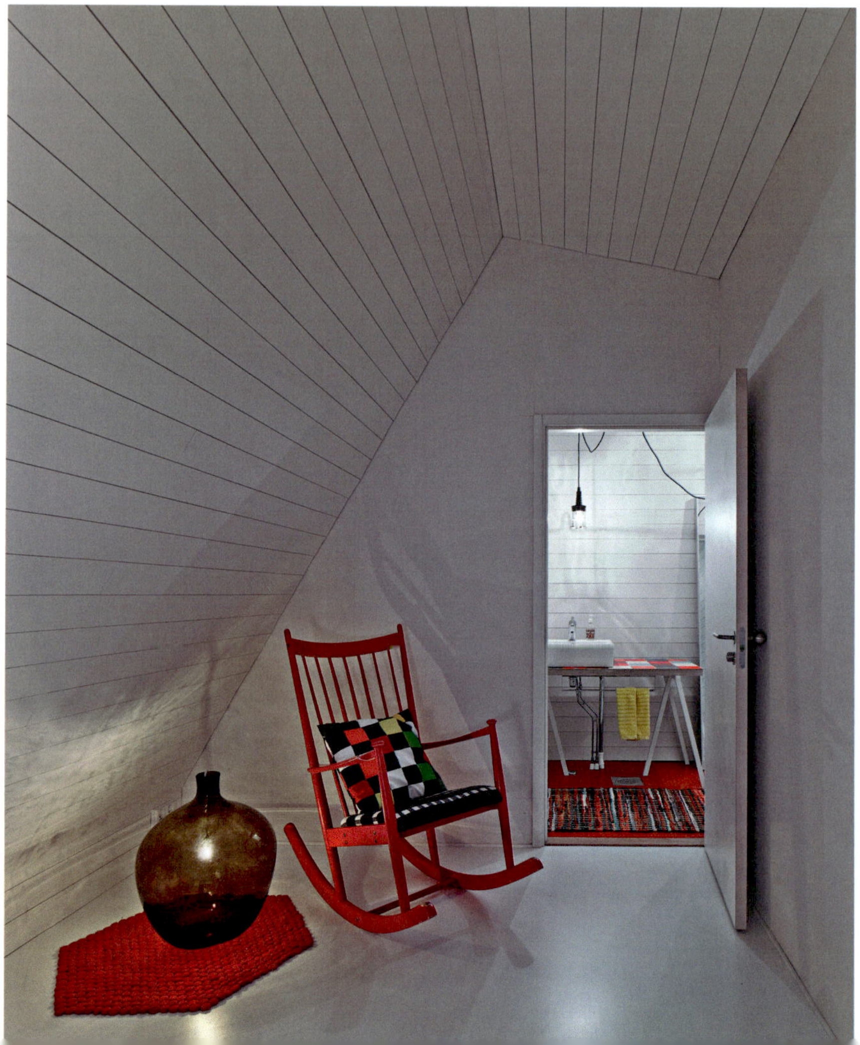

"The main idea was to create a building as if it was created out of the rock, yet made of wood." — *Lasse Lehtinen*

windows that afford views of the surrounding forest. Summing up his work, Lehtinen says, "It's so close to nature and is perfect for tracking the seasons and the constantly changing colors of the forest." ◆

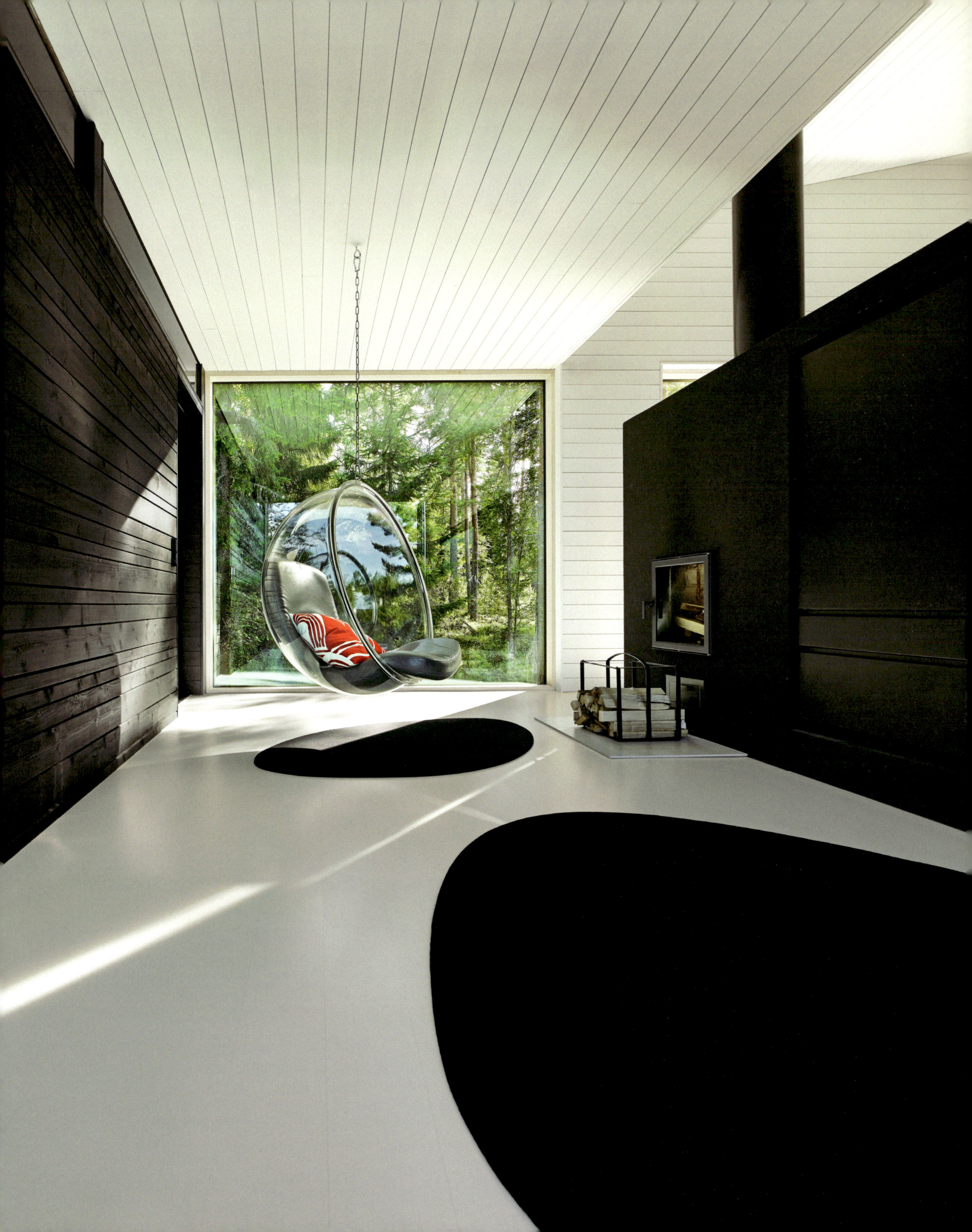

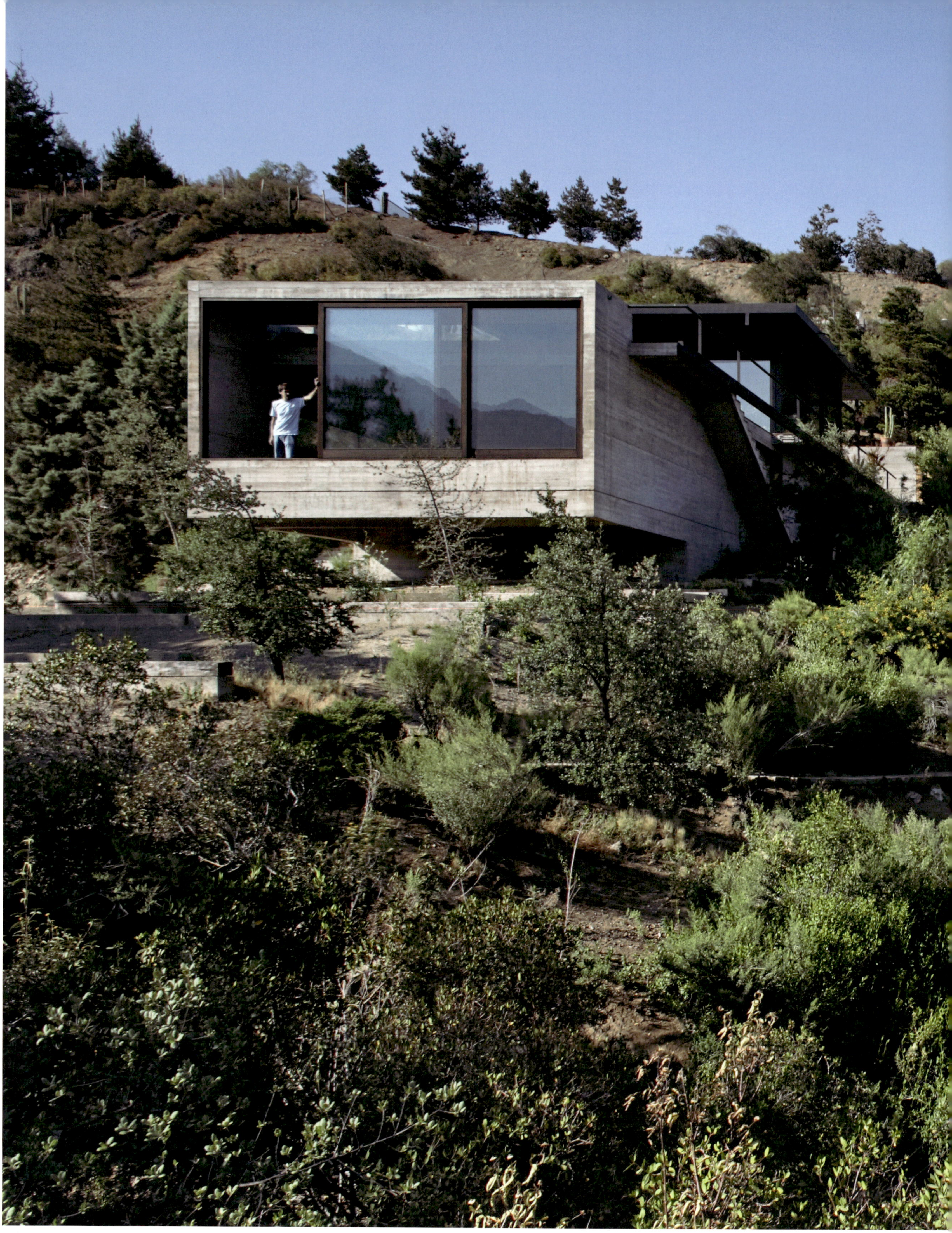

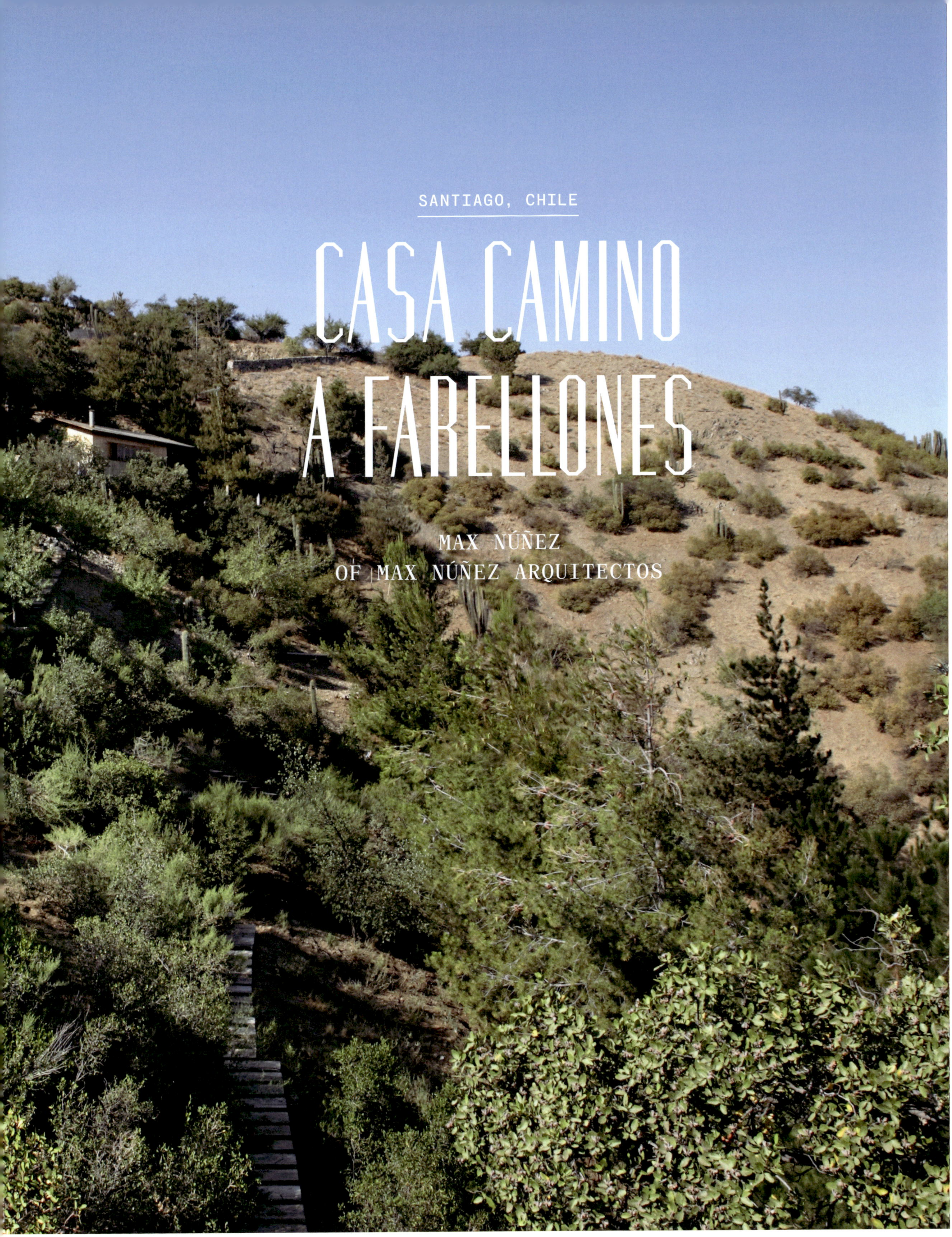

SANTIAGO, CHILE

CASA CAMINO A FARELLONES

MAX NÚÑEZ
OF MAX NÚÑEZ ARQUITECTOS

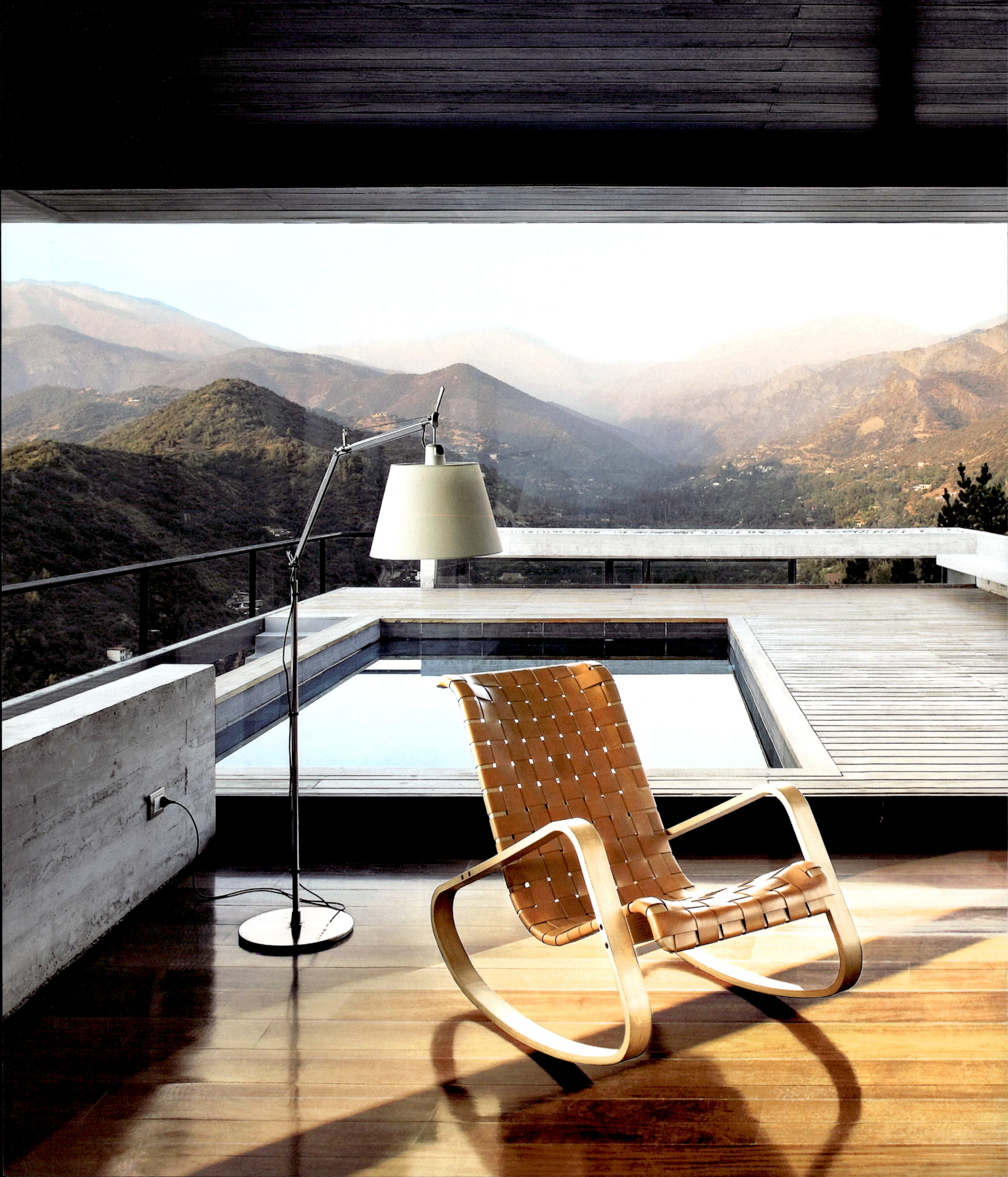

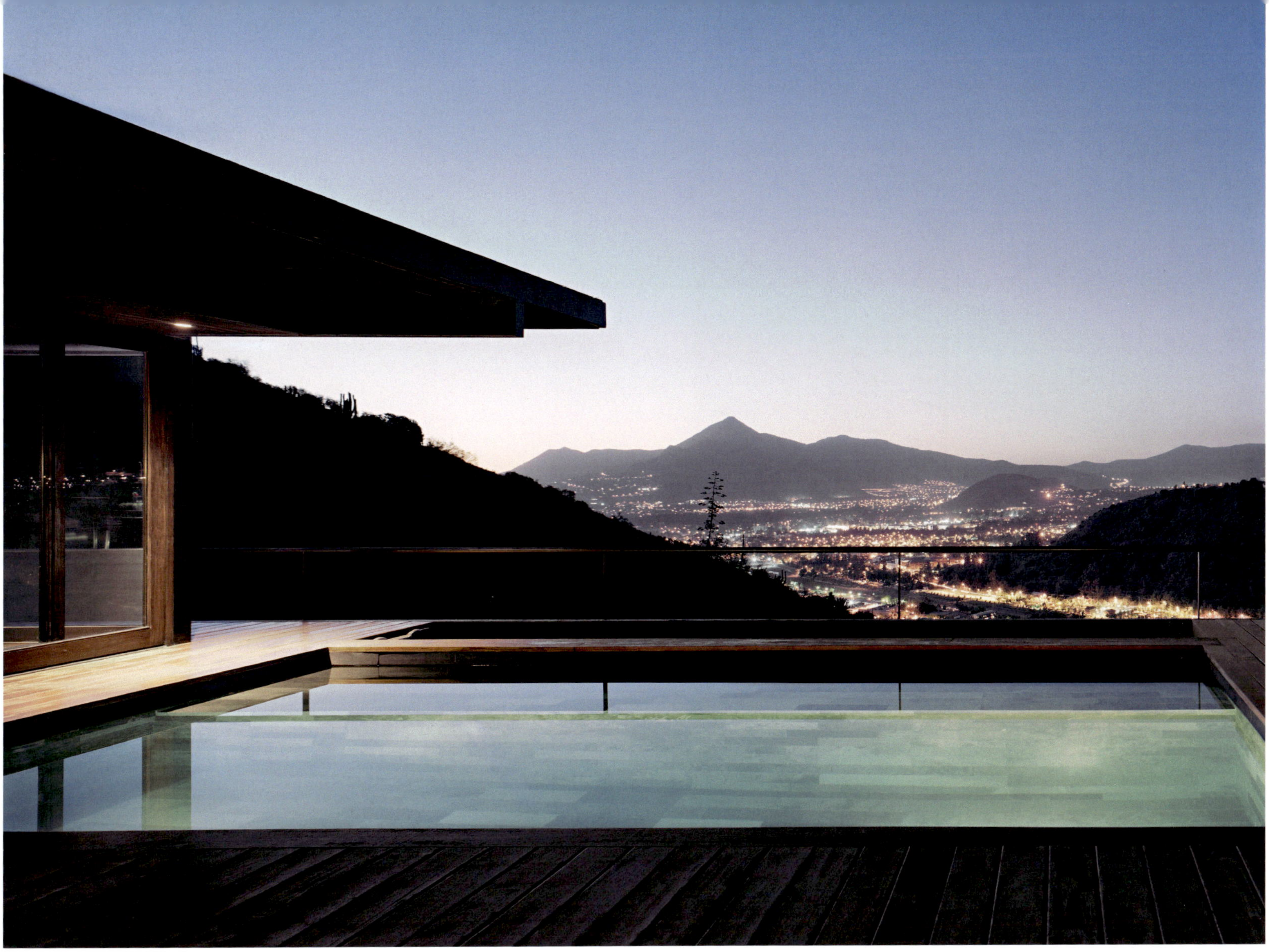

CASA CAMINO A FARELLONES Nature has always played a major role in the life of the owner of Casa Camino a Farellones. With an intimate knowledge of his client's lifestyle, Max Núñez designed a home that captures the multifaceted qualities of nature, a space that alternates between quietude and the loud spectacle of the environment.

Max Núñez of dRN Arquitectos first met his client in the early years of his nascent architectural career. They later reunited to turn what Núñez describes as a "dilapidated wood shack that was literally falling apart" into the concrete, timber, steel, and glass sanctum it has become. A mountain climber and skier, his client is a man at home outdoors. Since Núñez has known his client for years, he brought a sympathetic understanding to the project, constructing a home that captures the many dimensions of an adventurous life. The client's decision to live so close to nature suggests more than a simple love of flora and fauna. The location on the fringes of bustling Santiago, with views of the La Paloma and El Altar glaciers, also hints at the client's desire to live beyond the limits imposed by urban life. Reflecting that yearning, the lower story, which is home to the master bedroom, bathroom, and library, is cavernous and composed, inviting alpine light to stream in and the resident to gaze out. Concrete walls reassuringly mediate between interior intimacy and the world beyond. The bedroom enjoys a room-spanning view, with a generous glass wall to the front and narrow window gliding across the wall to its right.

The upper section is a glass cube hosting the living room and kitchen. Núñez says, "We wanted a panoptic situation up there. That's where the most direct relationship with the landscape occurs." Minimal furnishings and the use of wood and glass reduce the interior to a footnote commenting on the expansive vista. Free of impediments, the space dissolves the barrier between house and nature, creating a view that "is like being on top of a mountain," as the architect says. In opposition to the subdued and introspective lower quarters, this area sparkles with natural brilliance, ensuring that the house reflects the solitary yet spectacular qualities of the wilderness. ◆

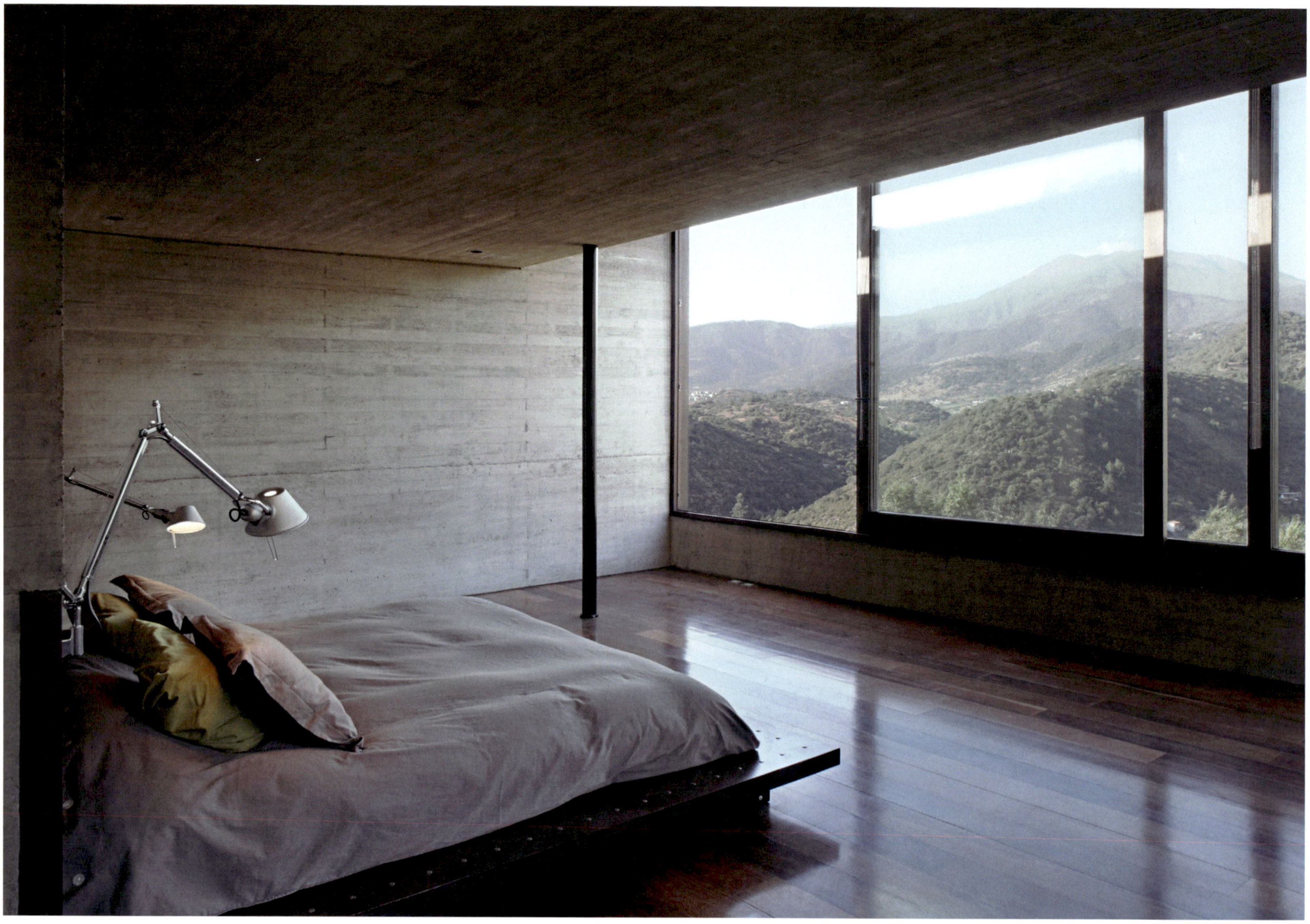

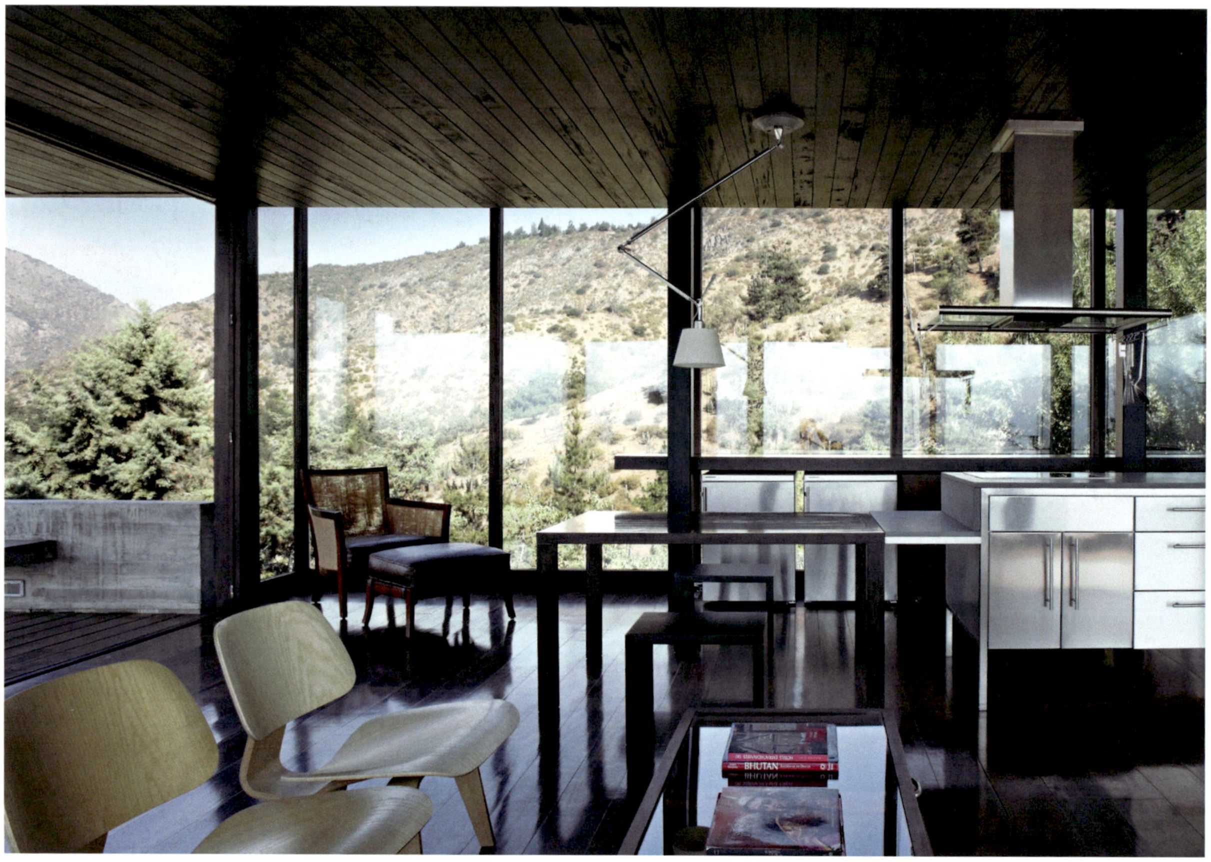

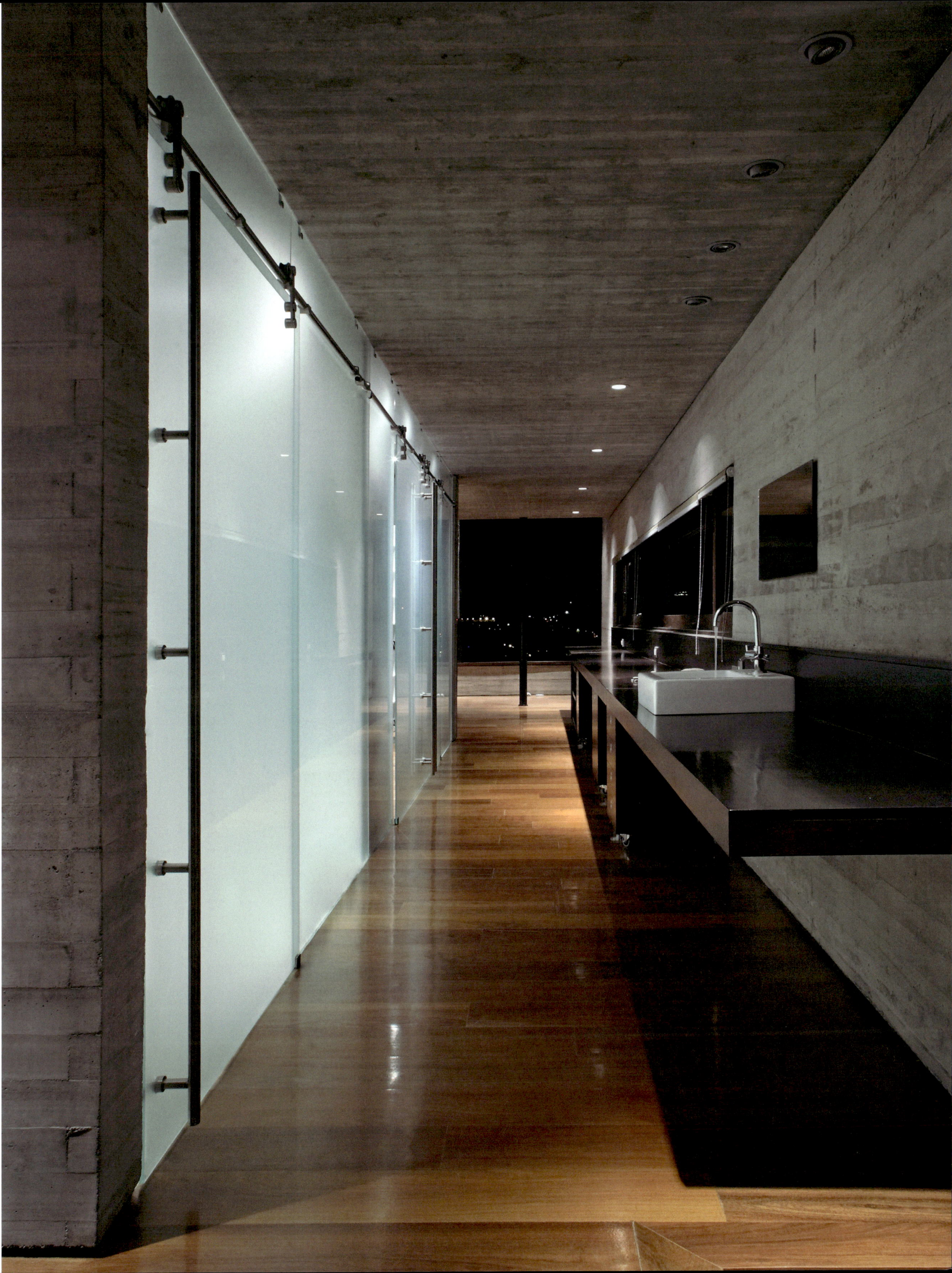

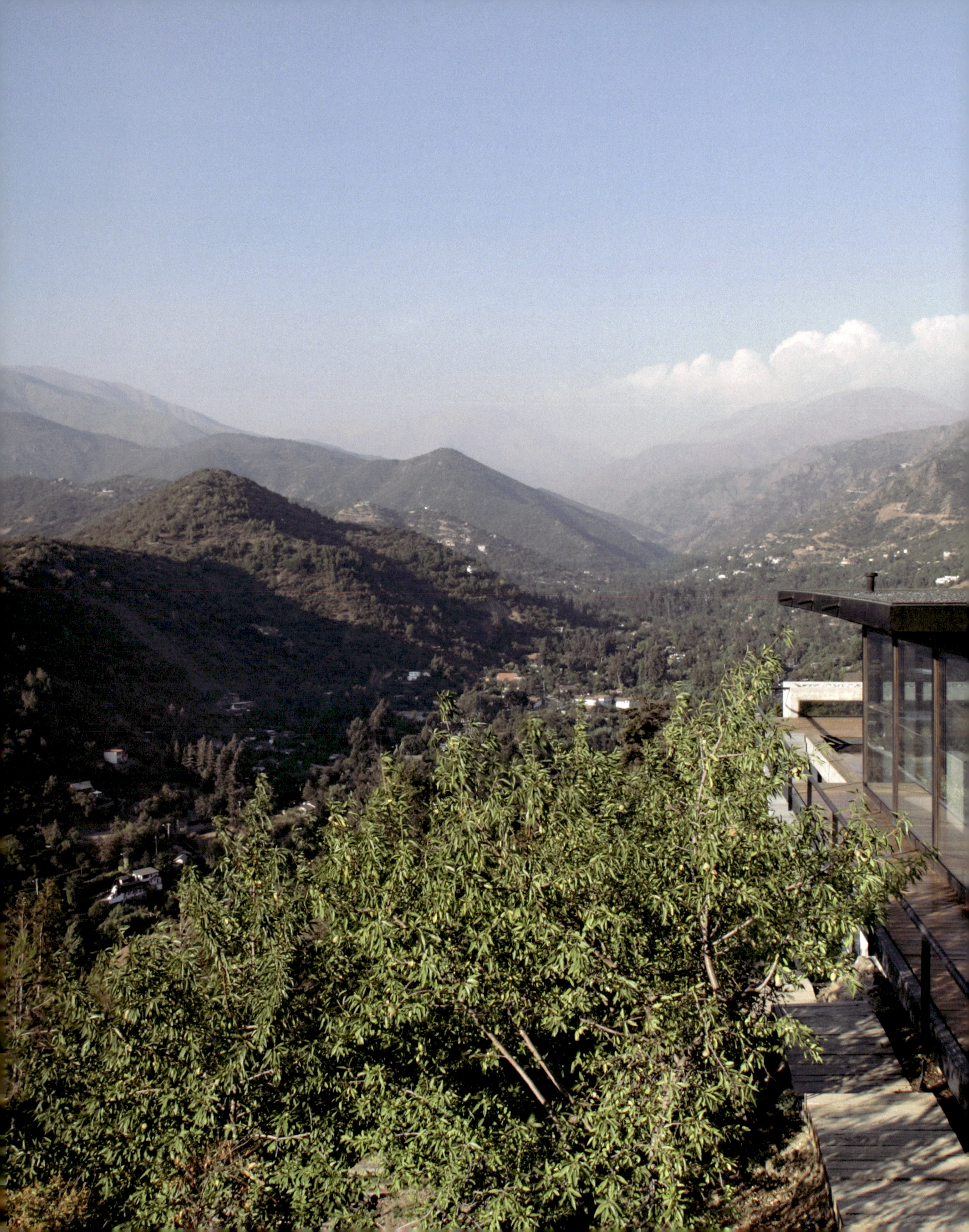

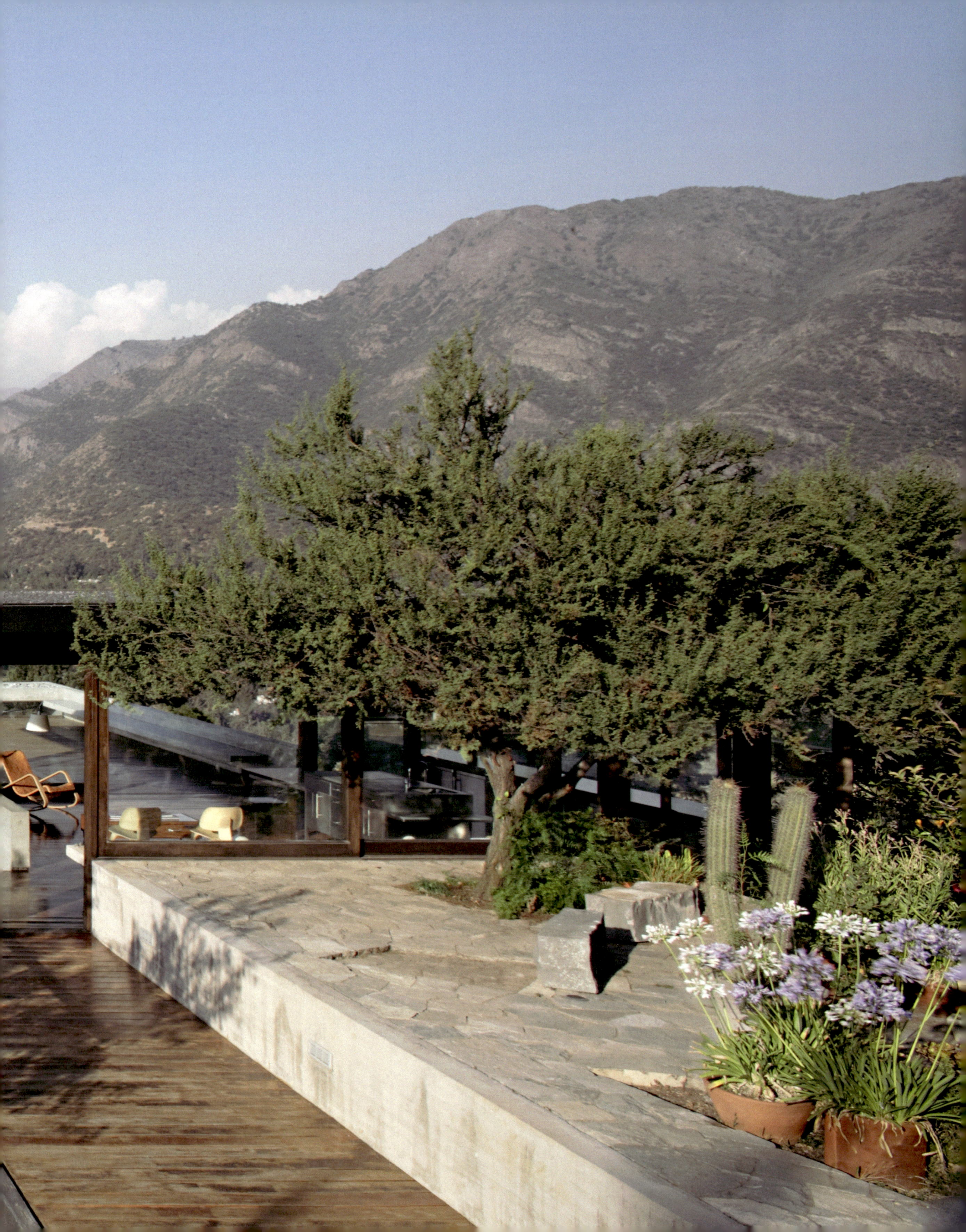

MONTERREY, MEXICO

CASA MONTERREY

TADAO ANDO

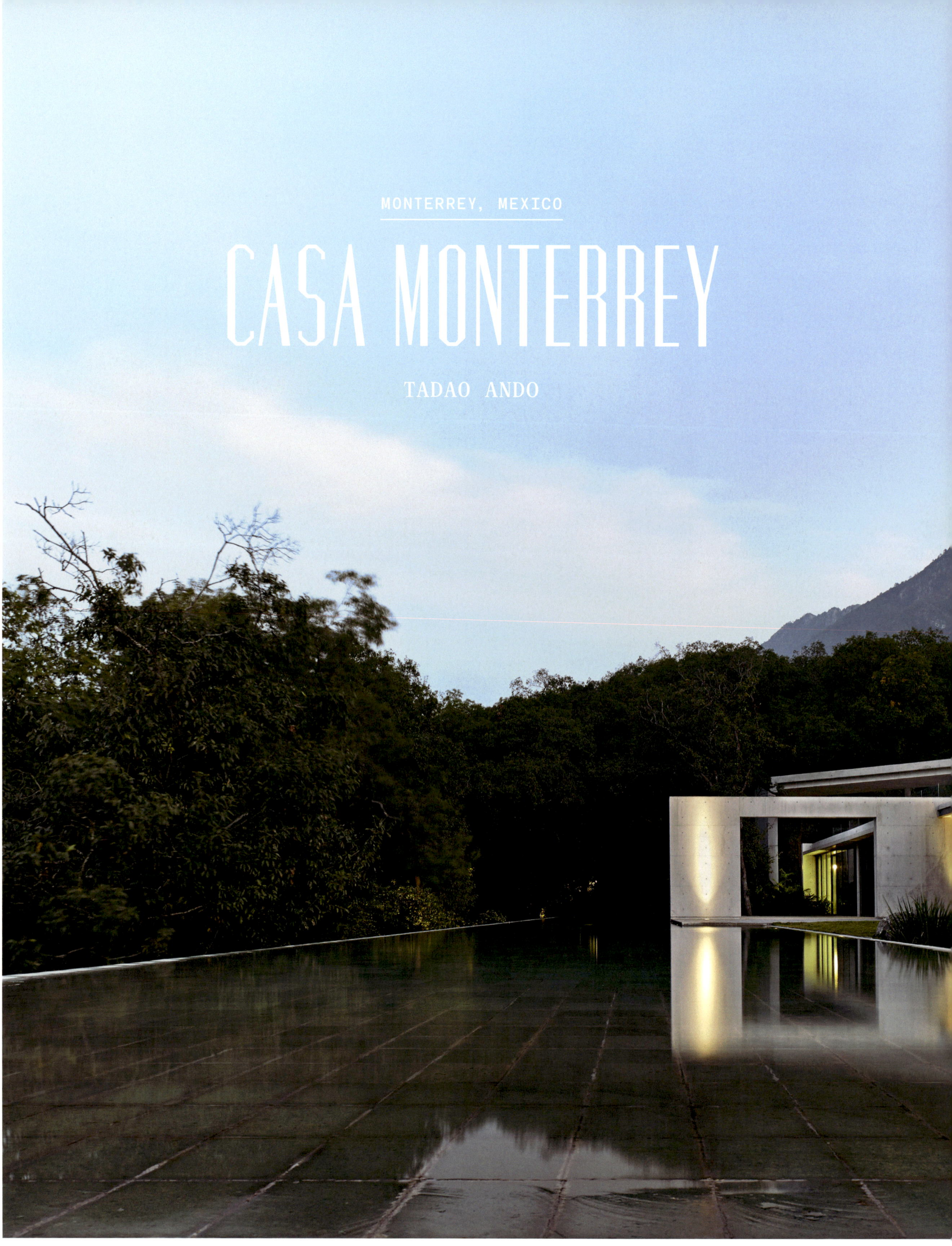

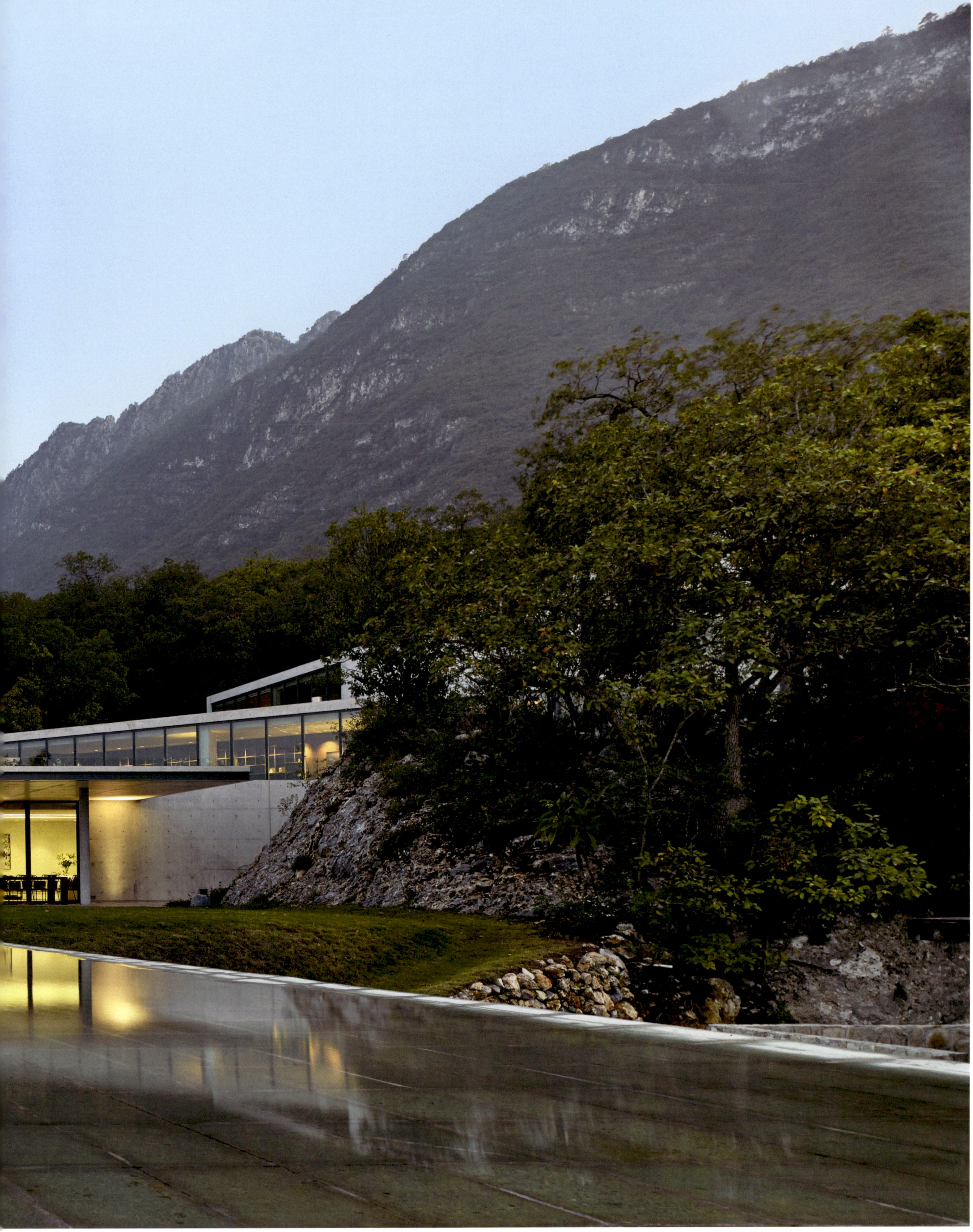

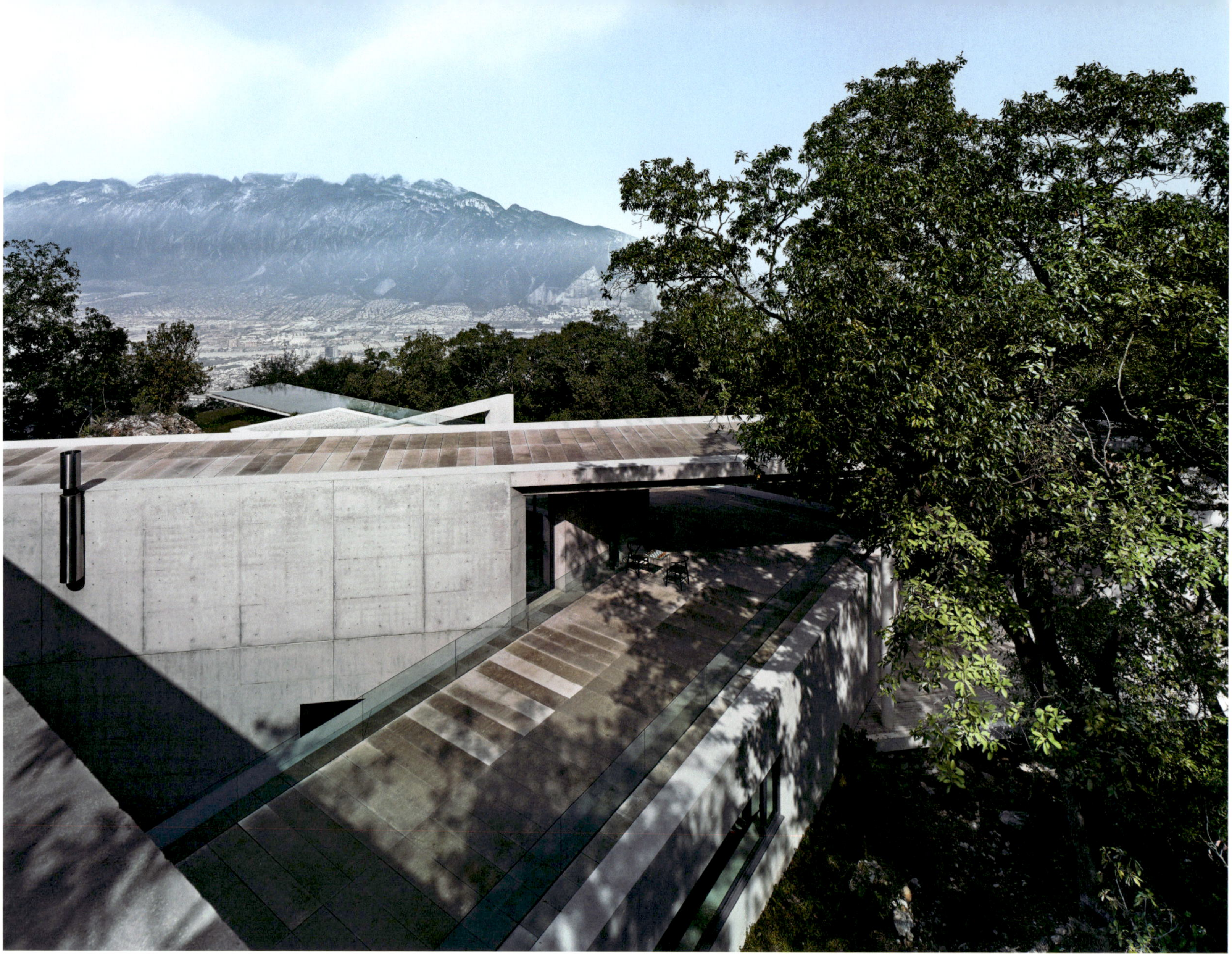

CASA MONTERREY Tadao Ando transplants his architectural approach from Japan to Mexico in this cross-sectional work of poured-in-place concrete. A composition of linear and orthogonal intersections, Casa Monterrey has all the rigidity typical of Ando's work, but also features an emphasis on the manipulation of light.

Initially, guests visiting this Monterrey home are denied the rich vista it affords. The driveway has a wall bracketing off the view of San Pedro Garza Garcia and Monterrey, the two cities that sit below this house perched on a Sierra Madre hillside. A playful move from Tadao Ando, this diversion tempers the site's boundless visual potential with controlled openings. The conflict between obscuration and revelation recurs inside the home as poured-in-place concrete walls intersect straight planes at 45 degrees. Spaces are opened up by glass façades and then pinched closed in tight corners. For the most part, Ando's architectural mode rests very close to the buildings he designed in Osaka in the 1970s. However, this mountainside site afforded him new options for manipulating light and vision. Shifting down the slope, concrete and glass enter an austere dialogue, yet sound calm, reassuring notes. The comforting aspects of this property are further reinforced in the main part of the house. There, an oak floor ascends one side of the double-height room, forming a compartmentalized bookcase spanning the length of the space. It faces a wall of glass, sectioned off into cubes that mirror the bookcase's geometric pattern. Light is reflected in from the enclosed water feature just outside, playing off the dark wooden hallway and bookcase, imbuing the area with a vibrant luminosity.

The outdoor space is split into two sections. Divided by a concrete wall that juts out of the main building, a timber deck acts as an informal place to relax and a concrete platform holds a sheltered dining table and seating area. Another pool extends past the decks and turf, cantilevered over the hillside. The view from the outdoor area is the ultimate reveal—a reward for those patient enough to discover it. ◆

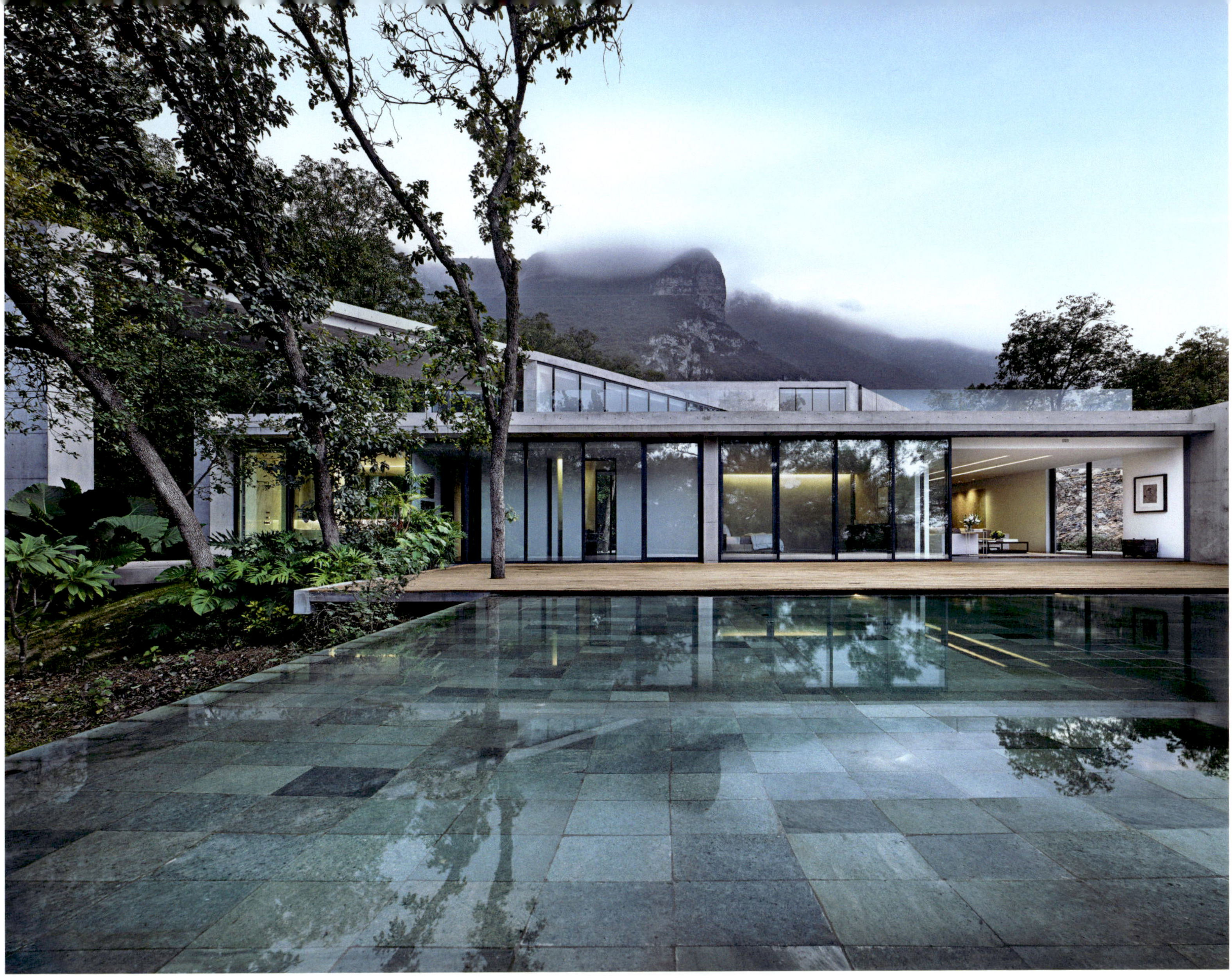

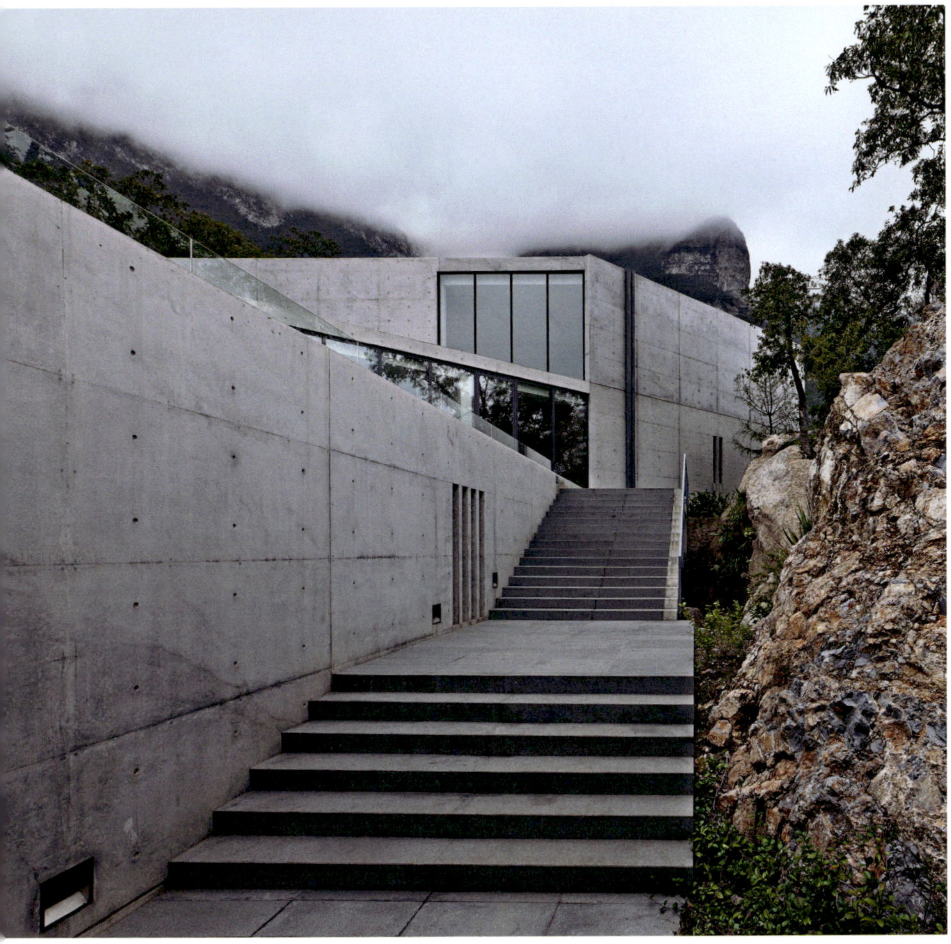

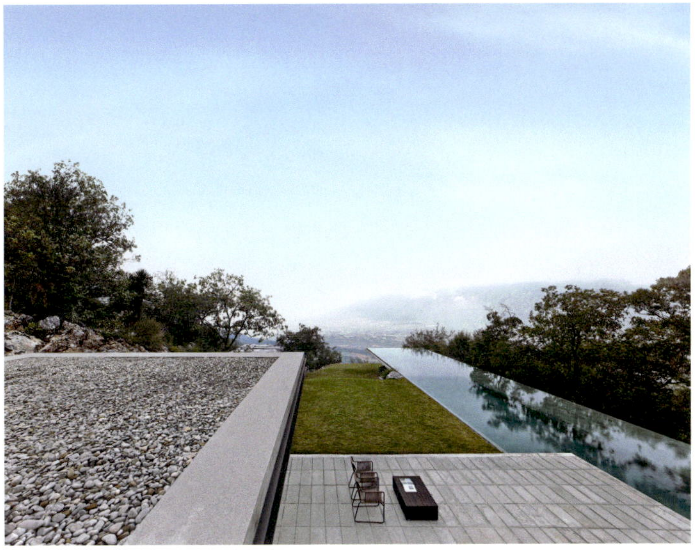

"SHIFTING DOWN THE LANDSCAPED SLOPE, CONCRETE AND GLASS APPEAR IN AN AUSTERE DIALOGUE, YET SOUND CALMING AND REASSURING NOTES."

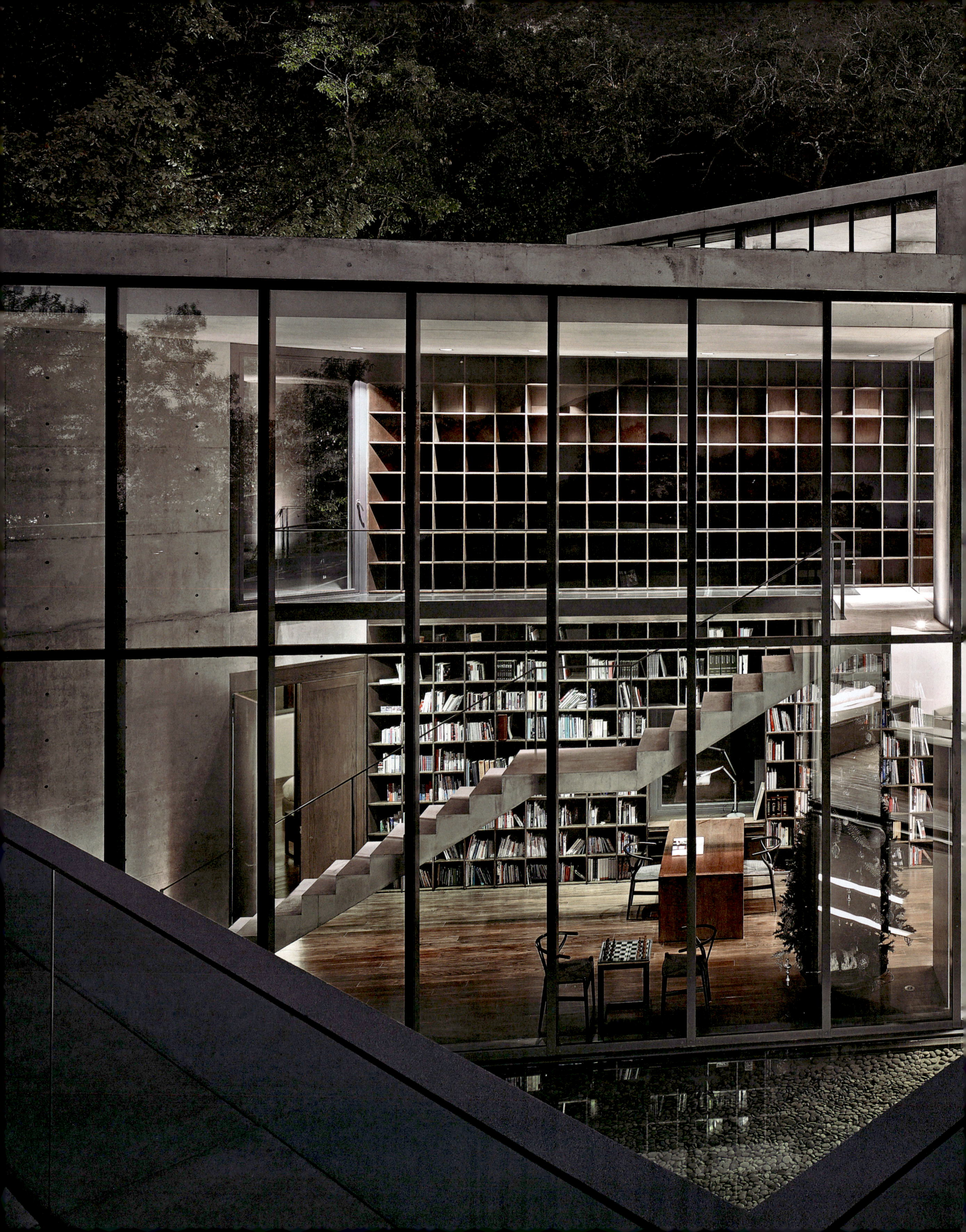

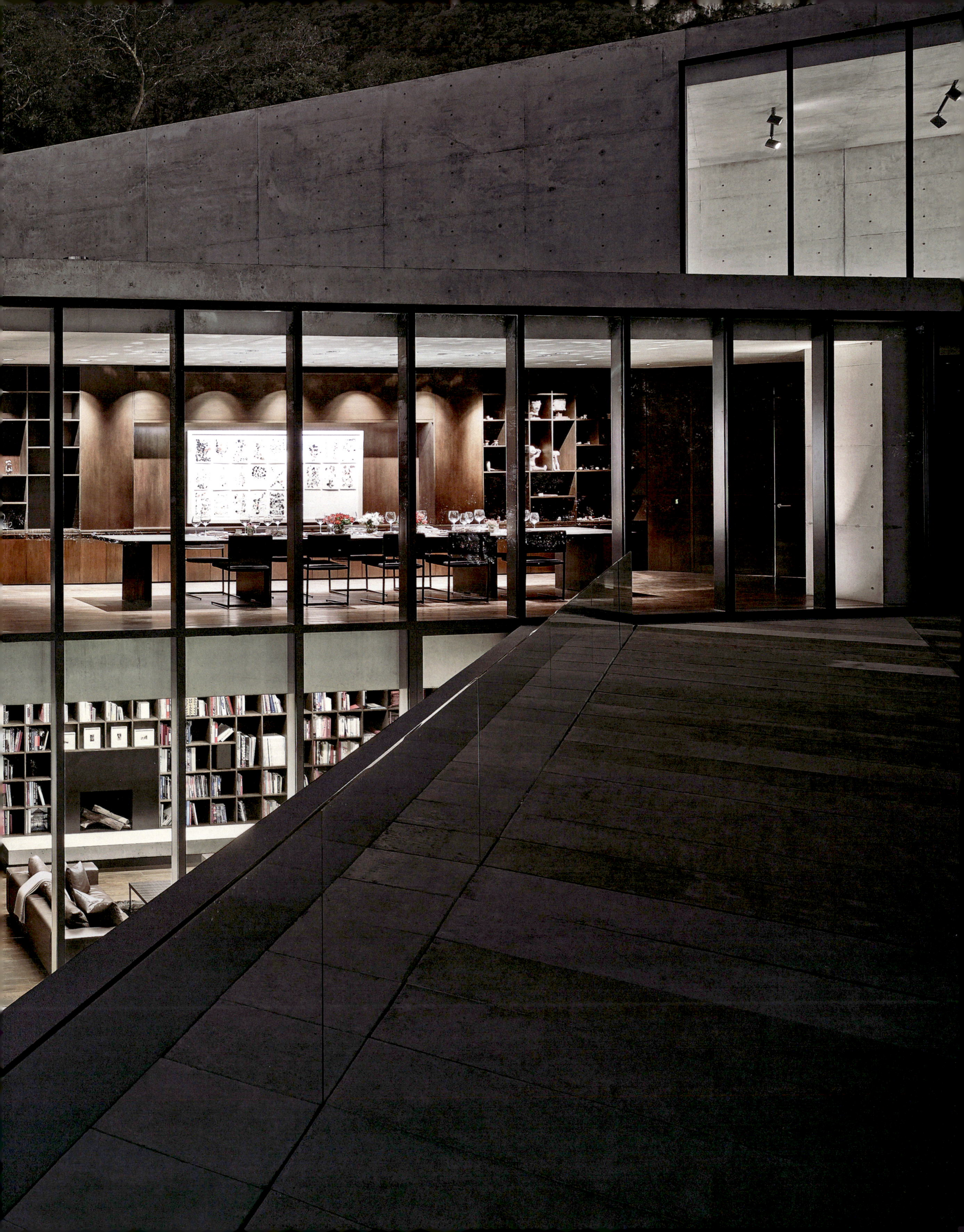

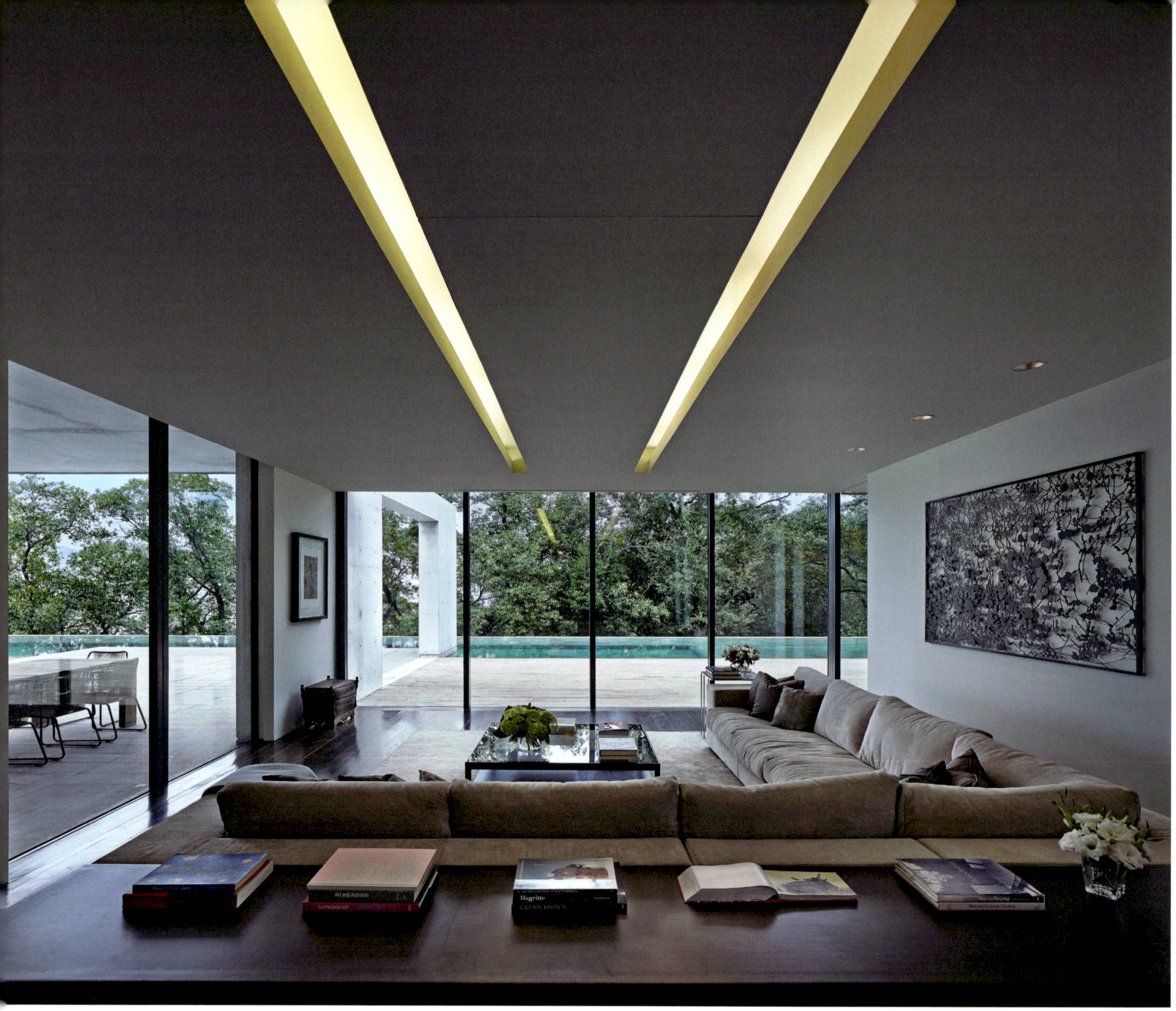

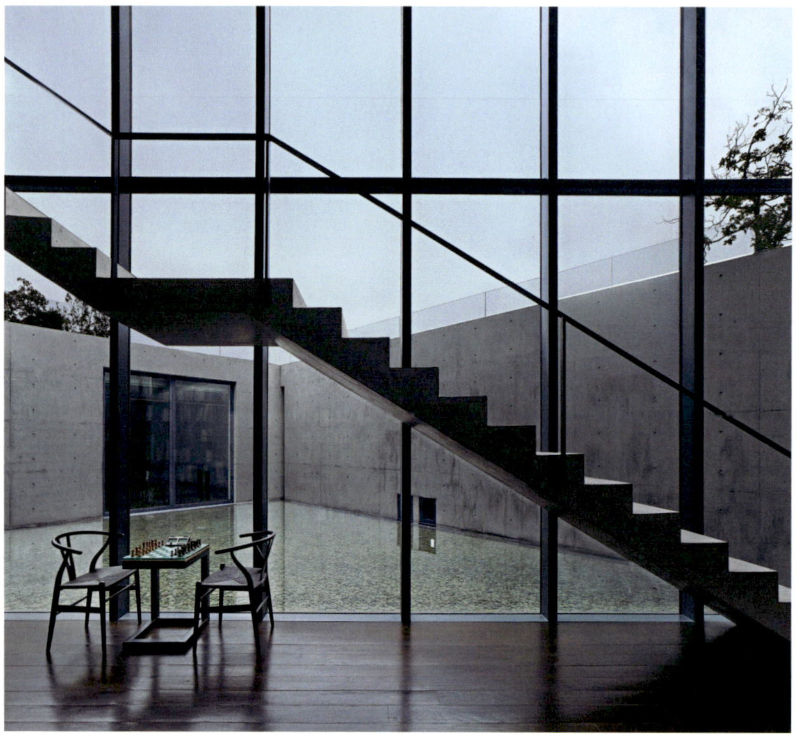

"THE VIEW FROM THE OUTDOOR AREA IS THE ULTIMATE REVEAL– A REWARD FOR THOSE PATIENT ENOUGH TO DISCOVER IT."

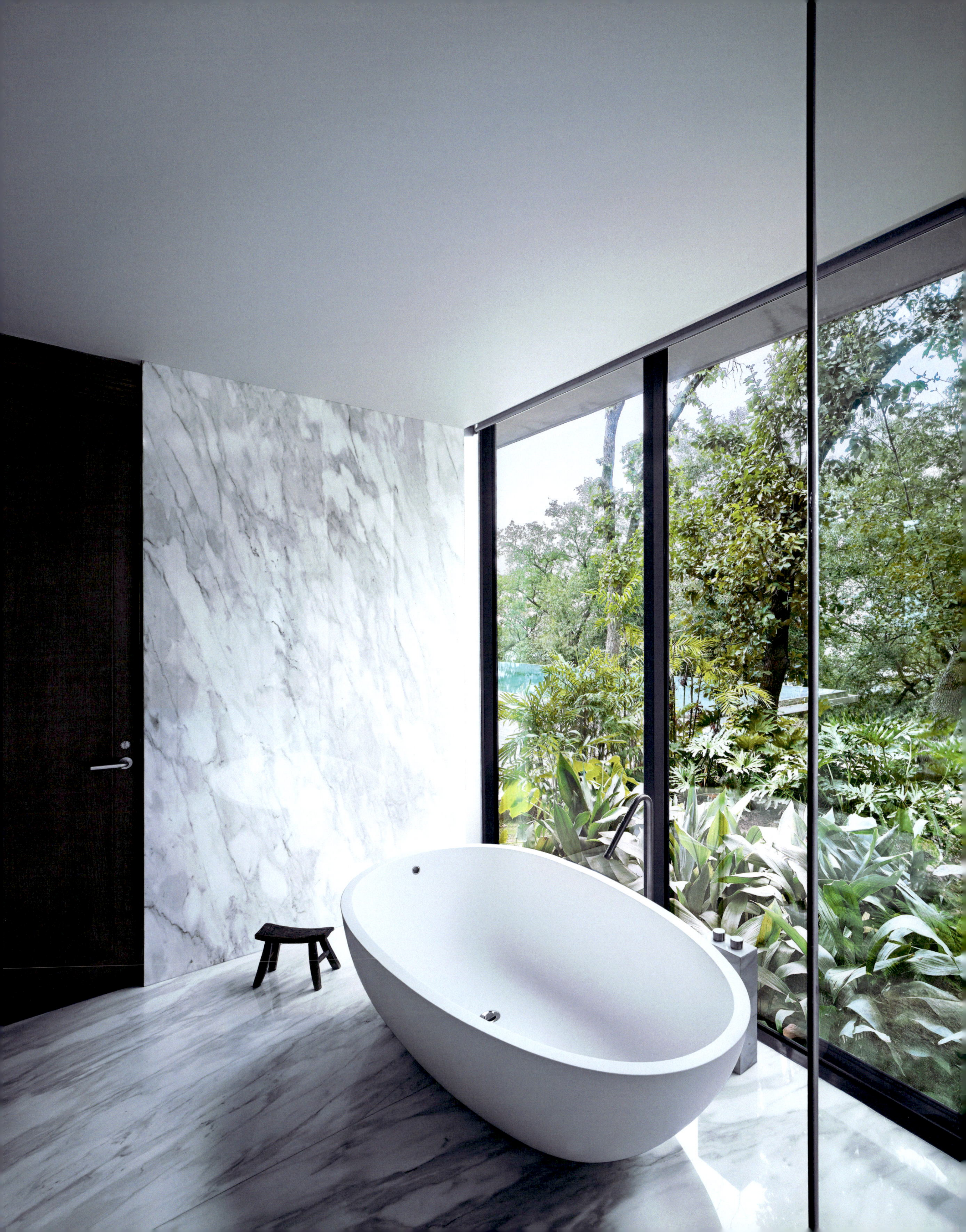

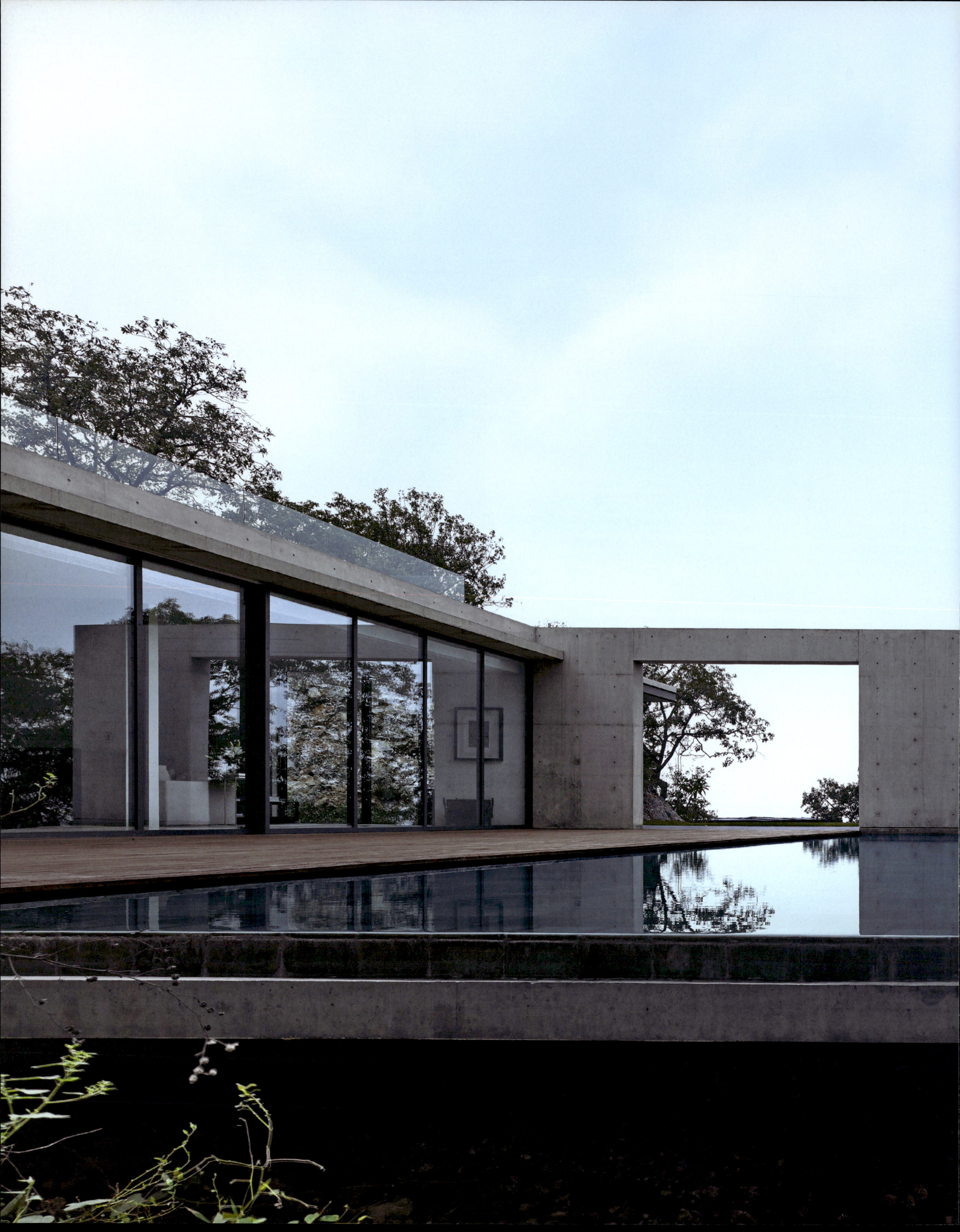

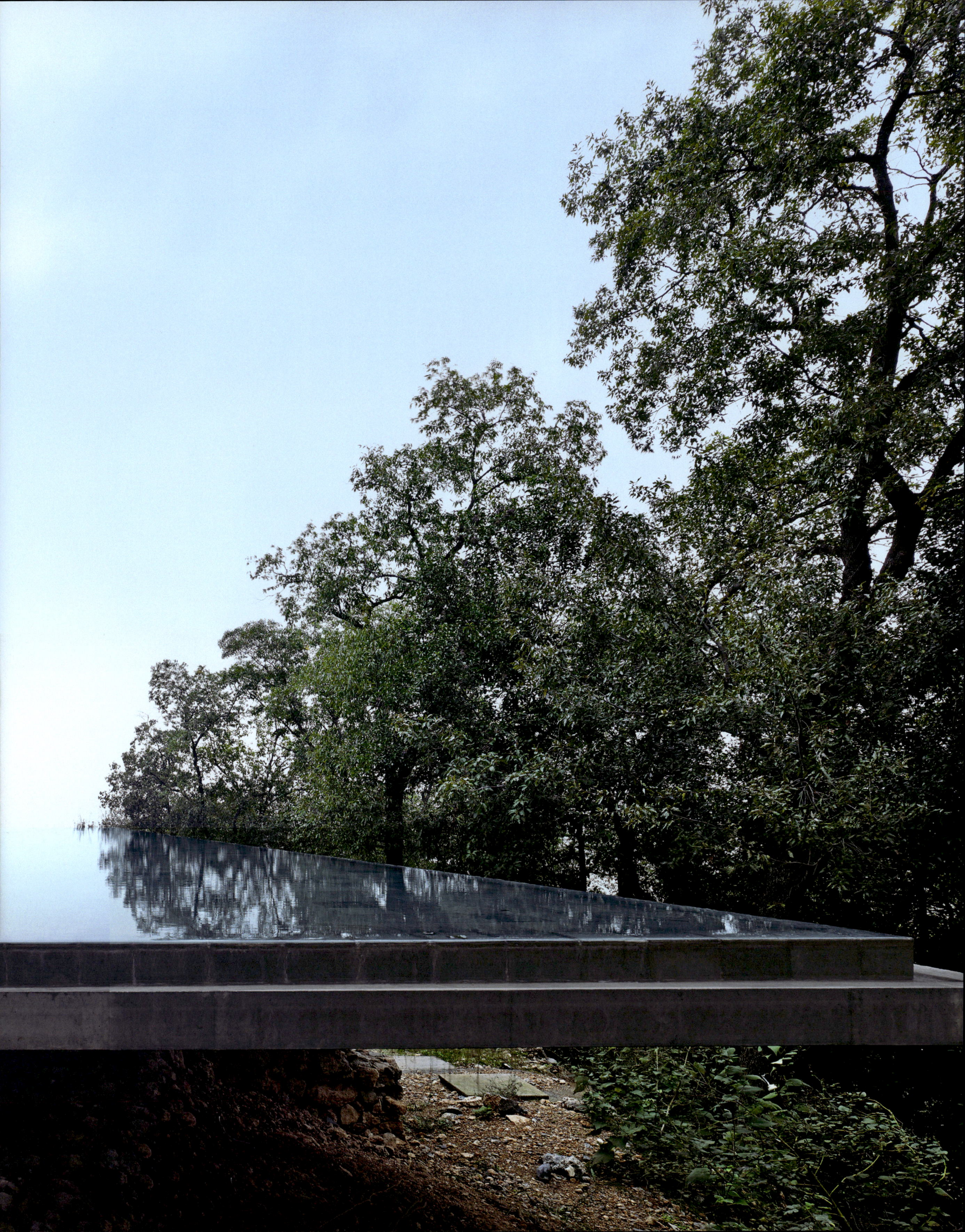

GLASKOGEN NATURE RESERVE, SWEDEN

DRAGSPELHUSET

MAARTJE LAMMERS AND BORIS ZEISSER

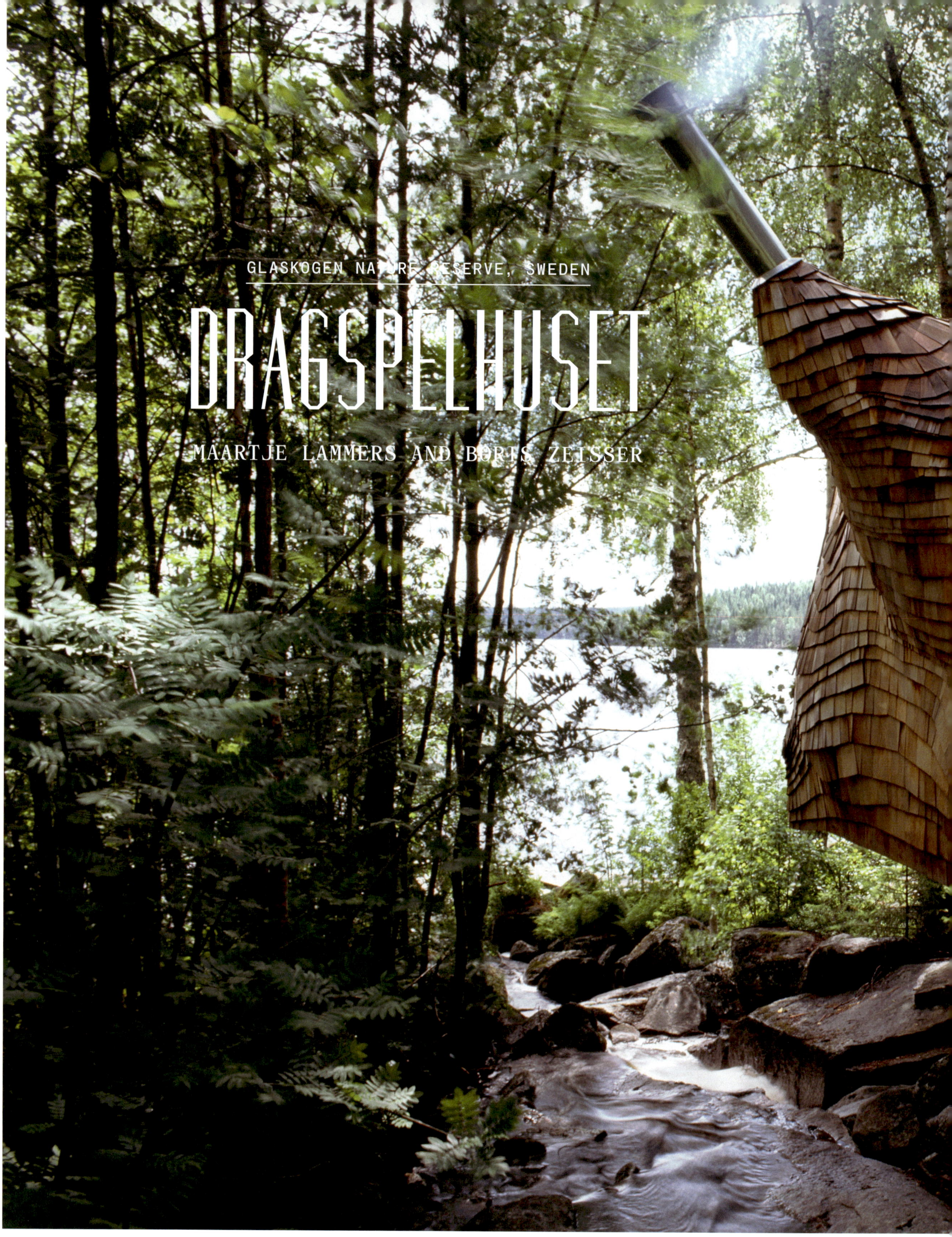

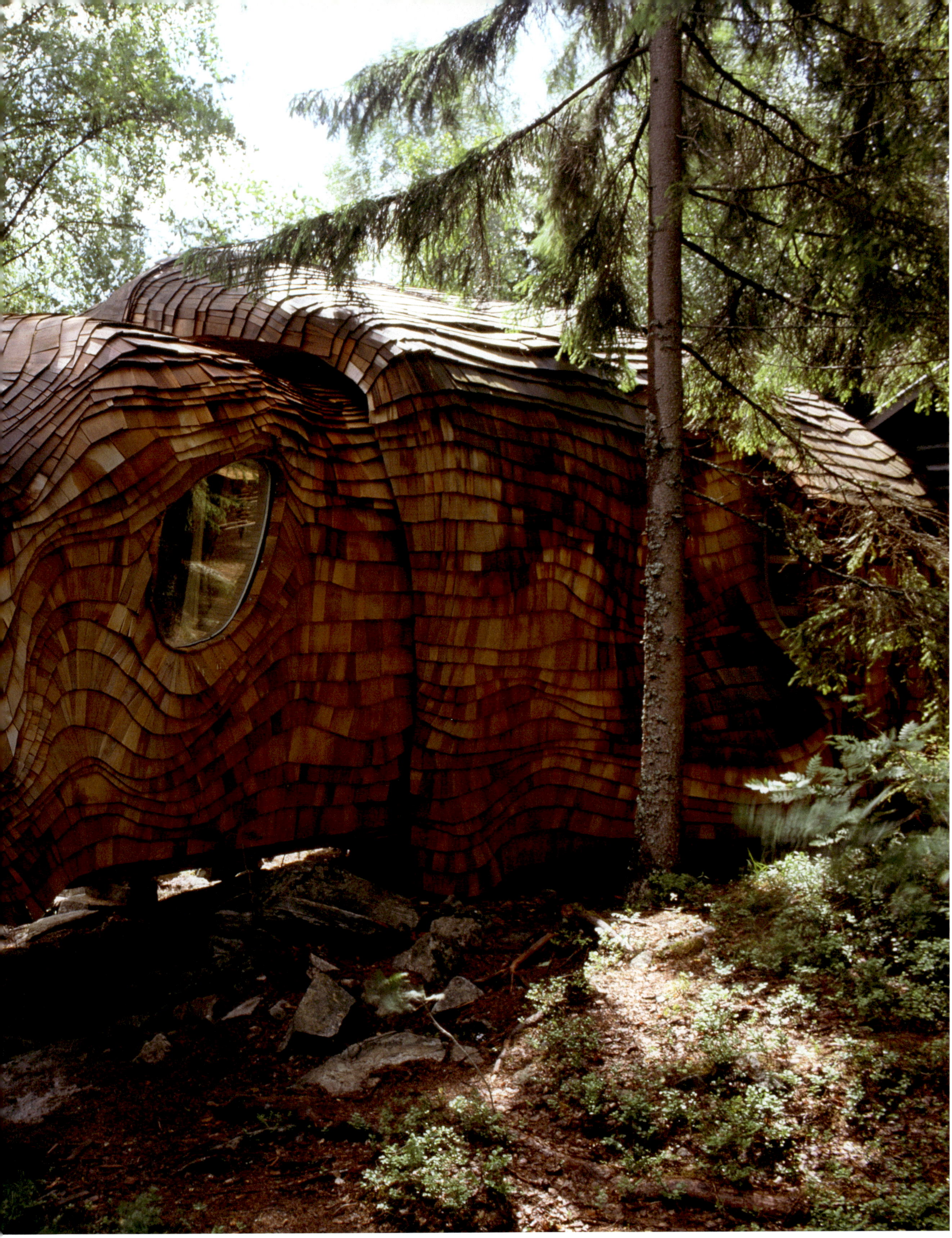

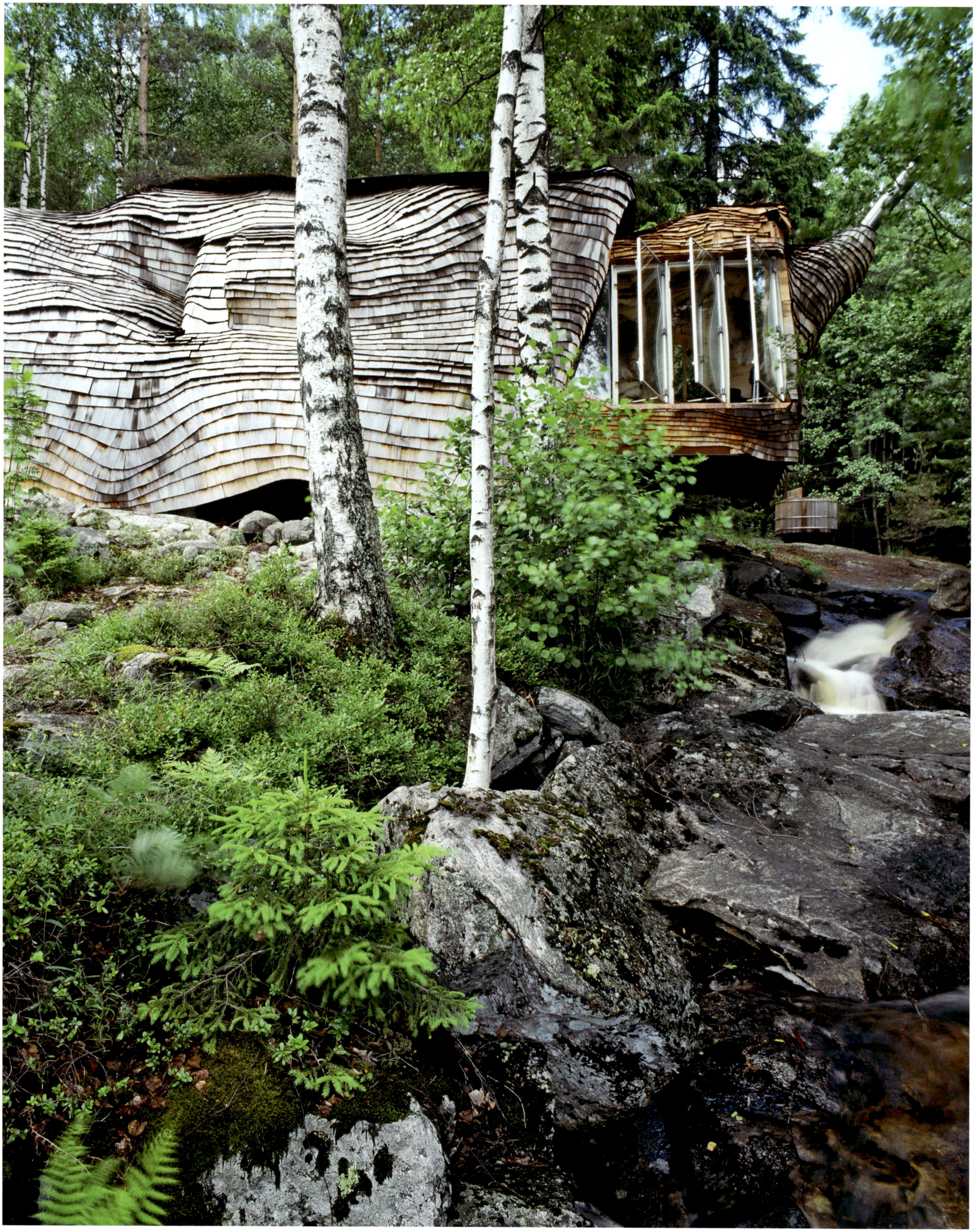

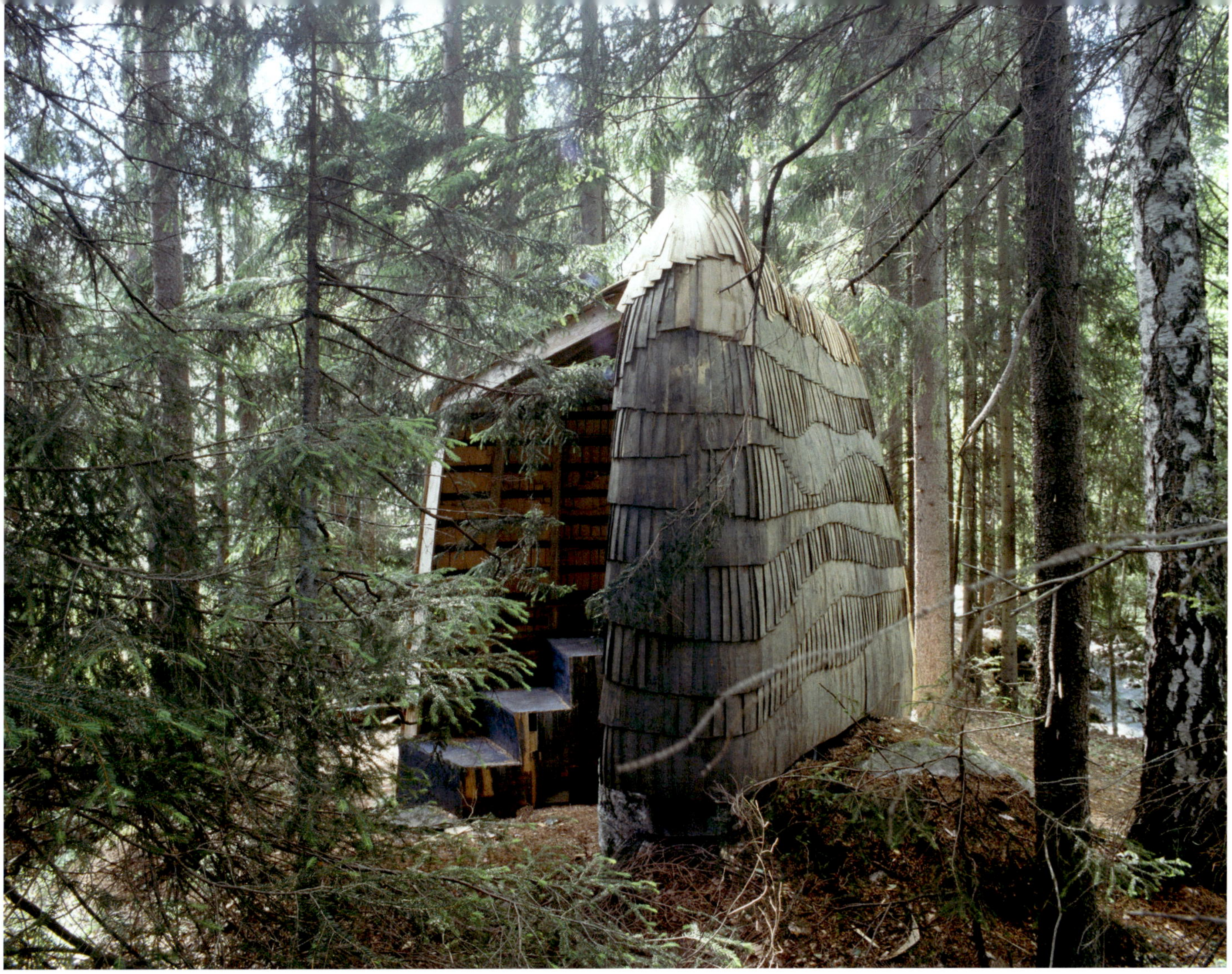

DRAGSPELHUSET After each dark winter, life reawakens on the shores of a Swedish lake. Caught up in the natural cycle, Dragspelhuset emerges from hibernation, extending its walls like an insect's wings. Its embrace of the properties of adaptability and physicality make this transition through the seasons possible.

On a Swedish lakeshore, one cabin is not like the others. Veiled by the dense forest and further camouflaged by its insect-like form, Dragspelhuset mimics both the appearance and function of its environment.

During the winter months, the cabin remains dormant, awaiting warmer weather—then, like a butterfly emerging from a chrysalis, it becomes the holiday house of architects Maartje Lammers and Boris Zeisser. The transitional quality of the cabin is made possible by the extendable living space that, come summer, stretches out over the nearby stream.

A practical feature as well as an aesthetic one, the extendable section was incorporated into Lammers and Zeisser's plans as a response to strict building codes in the surrounding Årjäng Municipality. At the time, additions to existing structures were restricted to 30 square meters. Cleverly negotiating this limit, the retractable living space adds 27 square meters of extra floor space.

Speaking of their design, Lammers says, "We very much wanted to work with architecture that could adapt itself to different circumstances, logical or problematic. To be able to adapt itself to the number of people, weather, and time of year."

Despite the extra floor area provided by the retractable living room, space in the refurbished cabin is limited. To maximize the cabin's potential, the kitchen area features a large countertop that doubles as a dining table, while in the bedroom, a hanging bed has been set up for their daughter Maria.

Dragspelhuset, meaning accordion house, takes its name from its distinctive exterior wood paneling as much as it does from its extendable living space. Canadian cedar cloaks the cabin in a reptilian formation. A durable wood that hardens with age, the choice of material further demonstrates the cabin's adaptability.
Drawing inspiration from its natural setting in form as well as function, Dragspelhuset morphs with the seasons, alternating between warm winter cocoon and adaptable summer haven. ◆

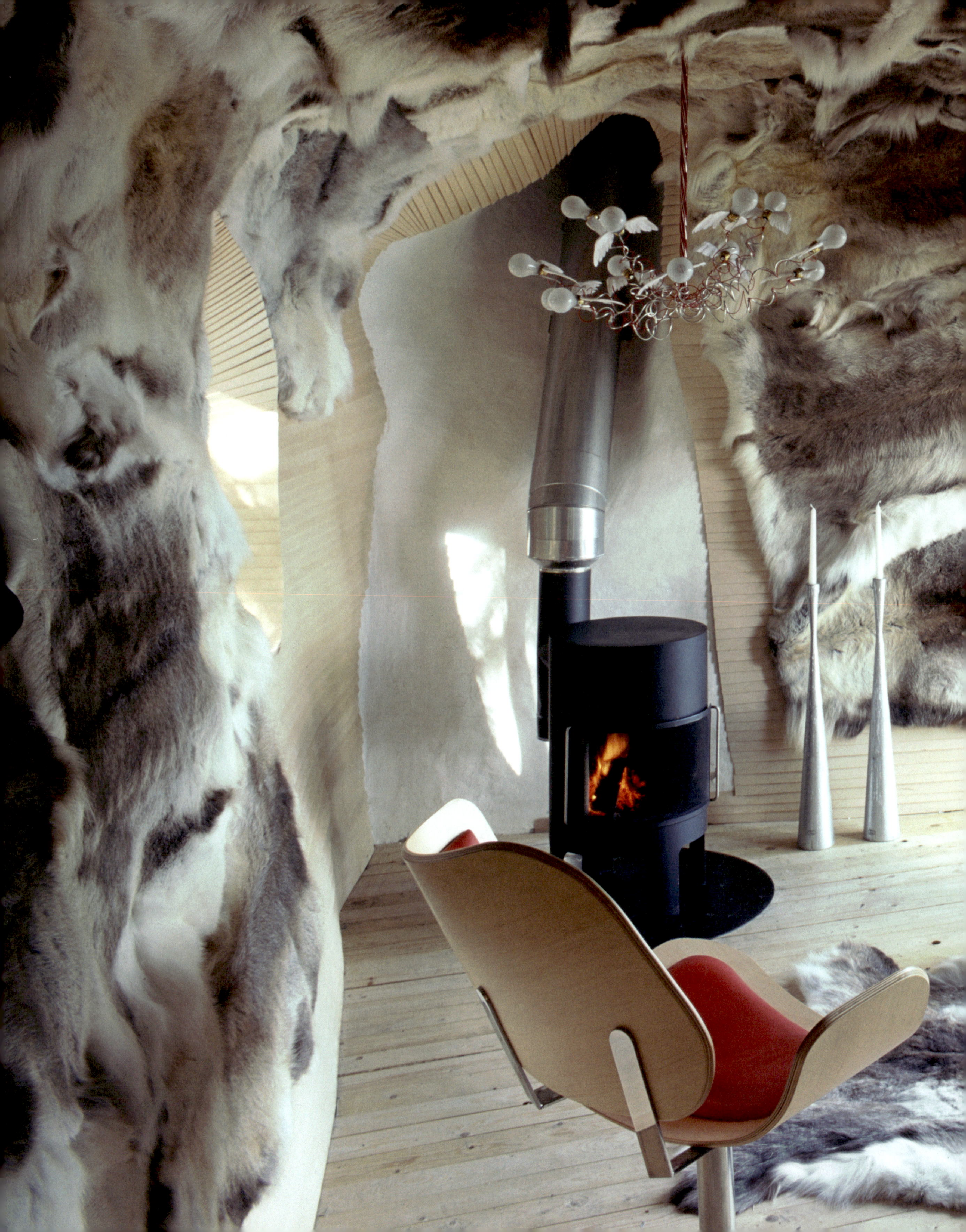

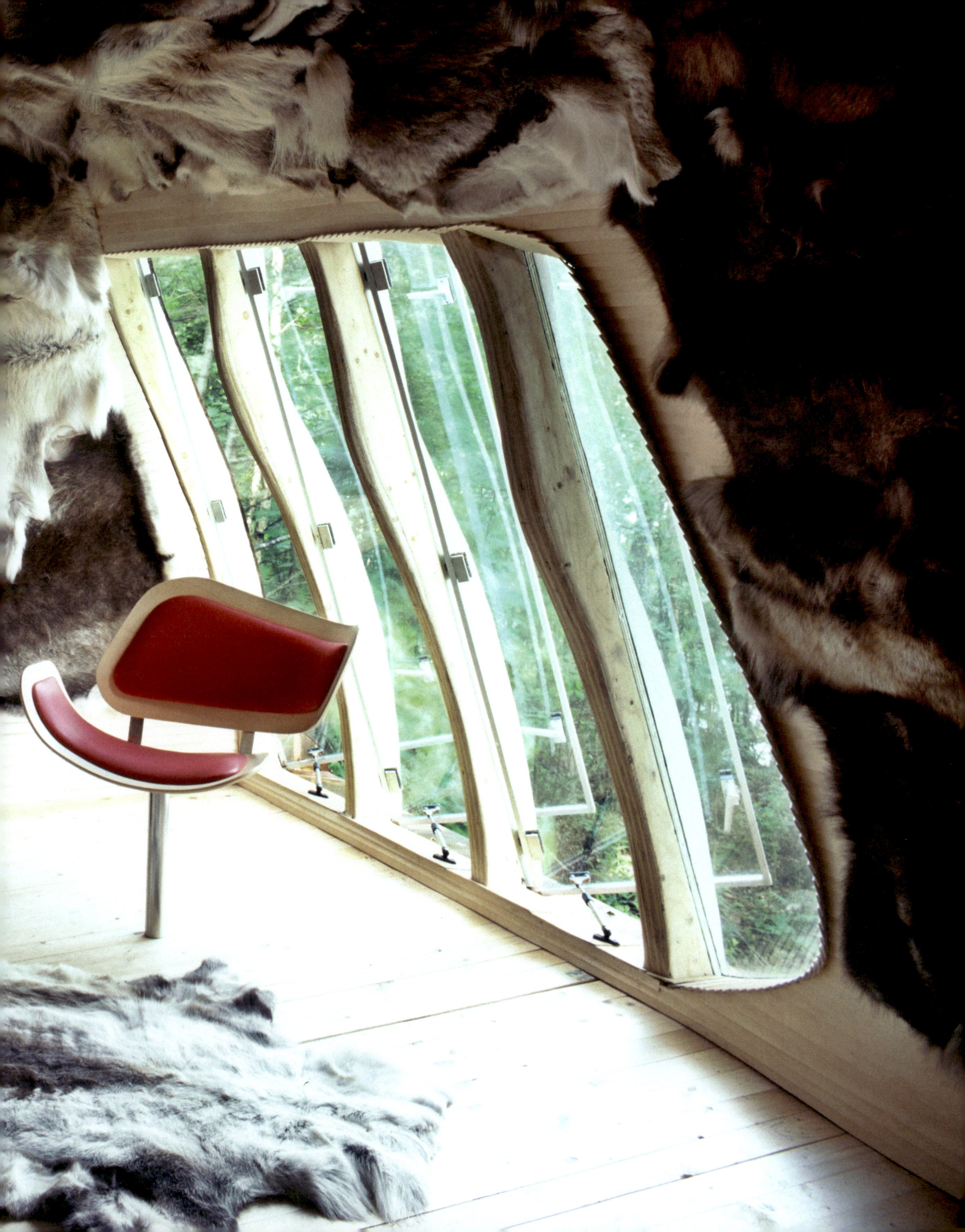

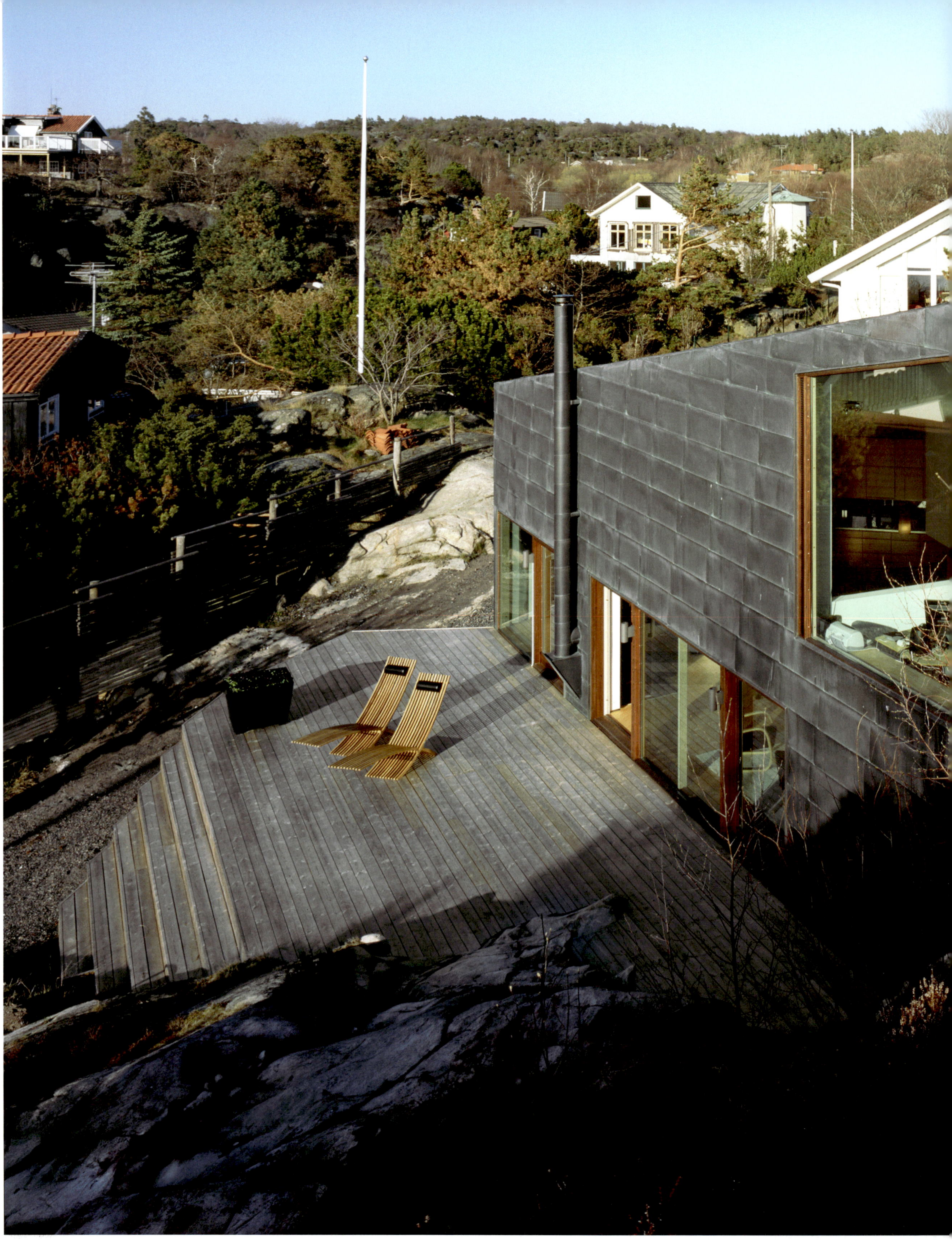

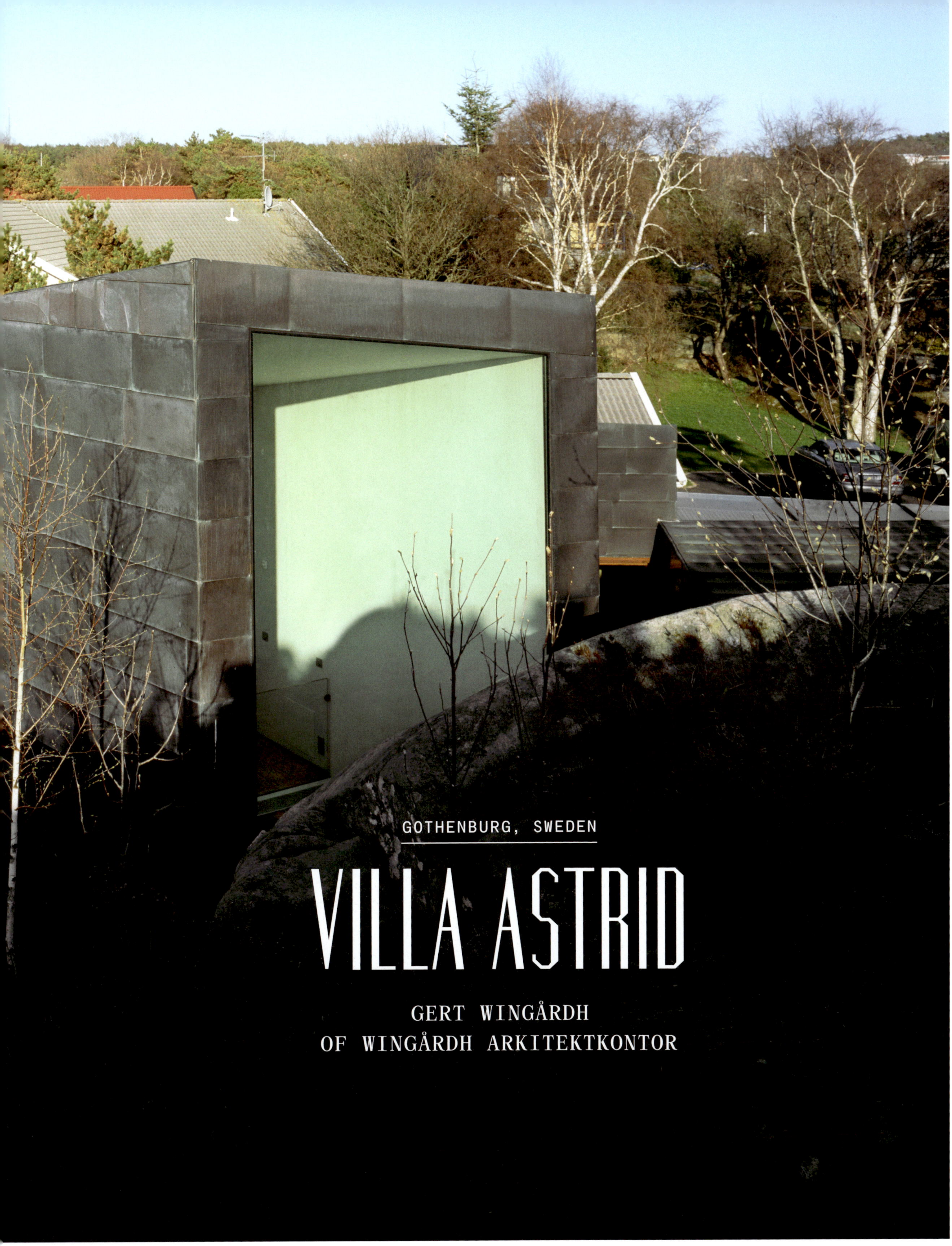

GOTHENBURG, SWEDEN

VILLA ASTRID

GERT WINGÅRDH
OF WINGÅRDH ARKITEKTKONTOR

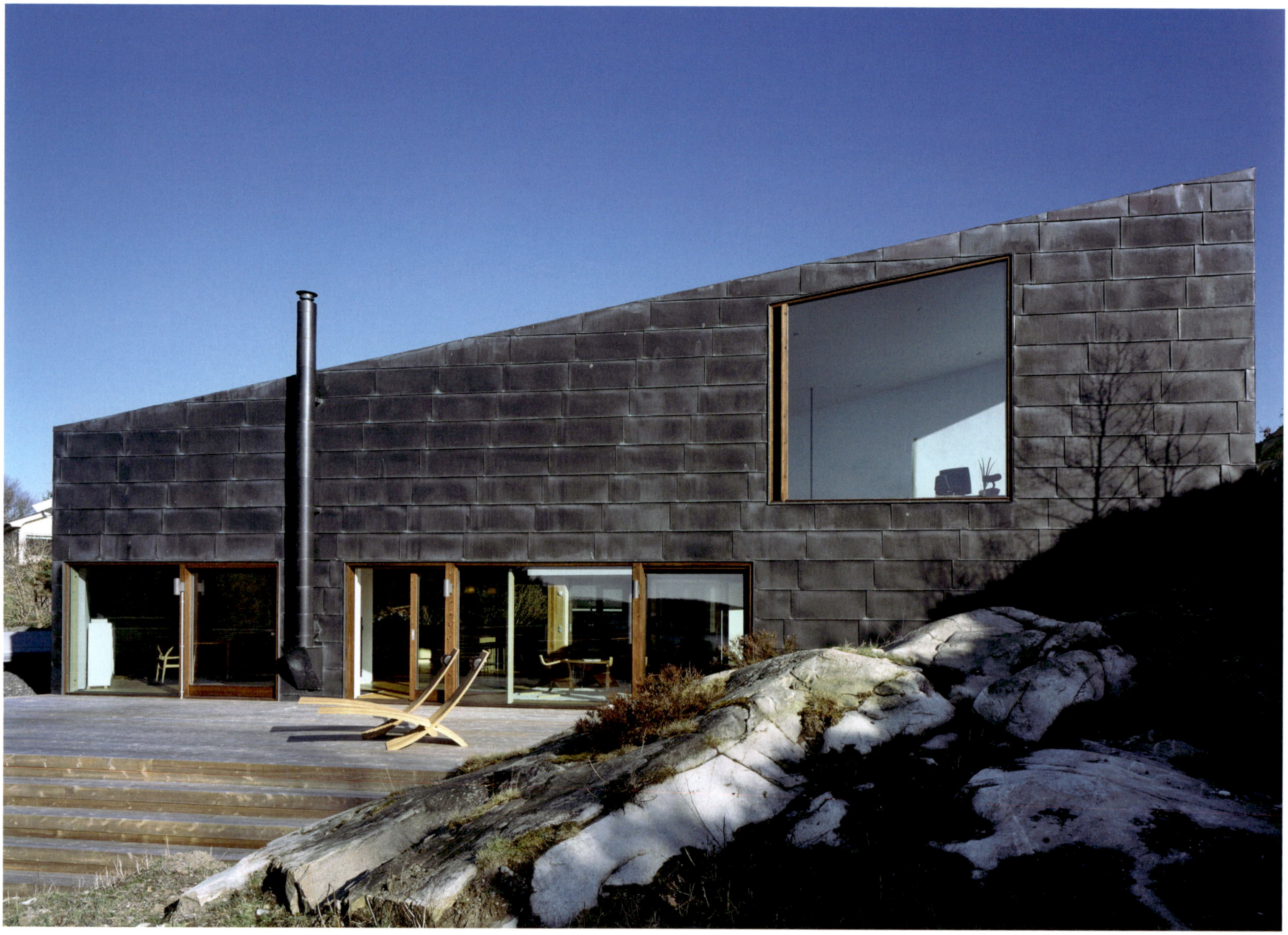

VILLA ASTRID began with a bang. Since the Gothenburg site was dominated by obtrusive rock, special blasting equipment had to be brought in to clear a nook for the home. But much of the original stone remains, some of which forms walls inside the home while massive boulders frame an outdoor courtyard.

Villa Astrid's plot was rocky, awkward, and altogether problematic. But that was not all that stood in the way of progress. Building regulations are strict in Gothenburg, restricting new structures to a maximum height of 3.5 meters. In an effort to circumvent the decidedly bleak outlook, the owners sought the help of Gert Wingårdh, whose solution, it turned out, was a simple one. "The owners wanted two stories," Wingårdh explains, adding, "My solution was to blast into the rock with dynamite." Wingårdh designed a V-shaped structure to be sunk in place of the much-reduced outcropping. At its widest point, the outer walls join the remaining rock, forming a small courtyard that also serves as one of the house's focal points. Sliding glass doors adjoin this area and lead to the bedrooms. But that is not the only use that Villa Astrid makes of its rocky ground. Rock also emerges through the structure to compose one of the walls in the main bathroom.

Above the bedrooms, the entrance floor is home to an open kitchen and living area. In keeping with the house's palette, the kitchen is made from ash wood and concrete. Suspended over one side of the living room, a mezzanine has been set up as a workspace. "This house is interesting because from the outside you can't see what it is. It's only once you get inside that it reveals its three-level structure, if you include the hanging mezzanine," explains Wingårdh.

Aside from concrete and ash wood—the latter material also serving as the flooring—huge windows, glass doors, and plain white walls account for the rest of the interior. The combination of the large windows and ~

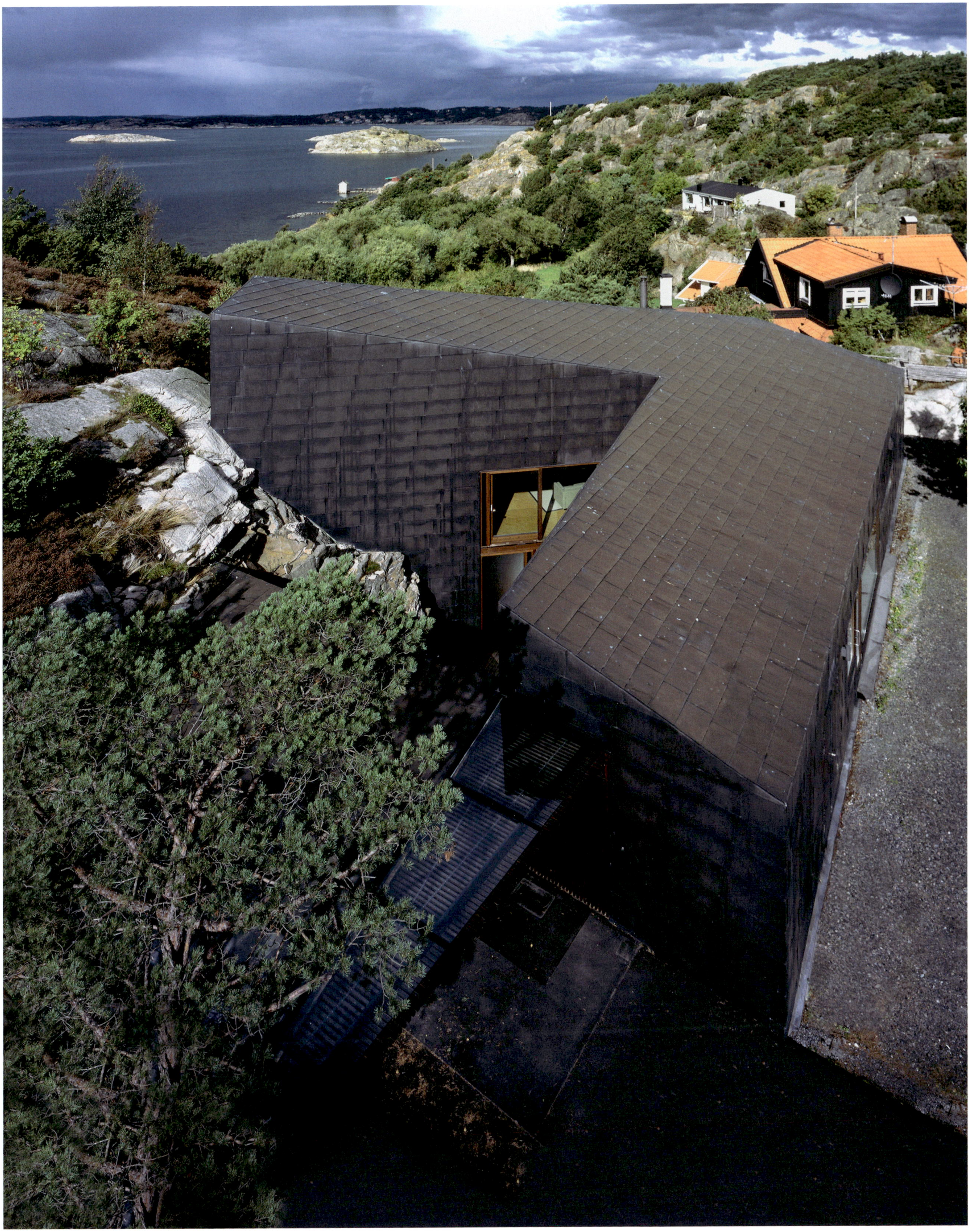

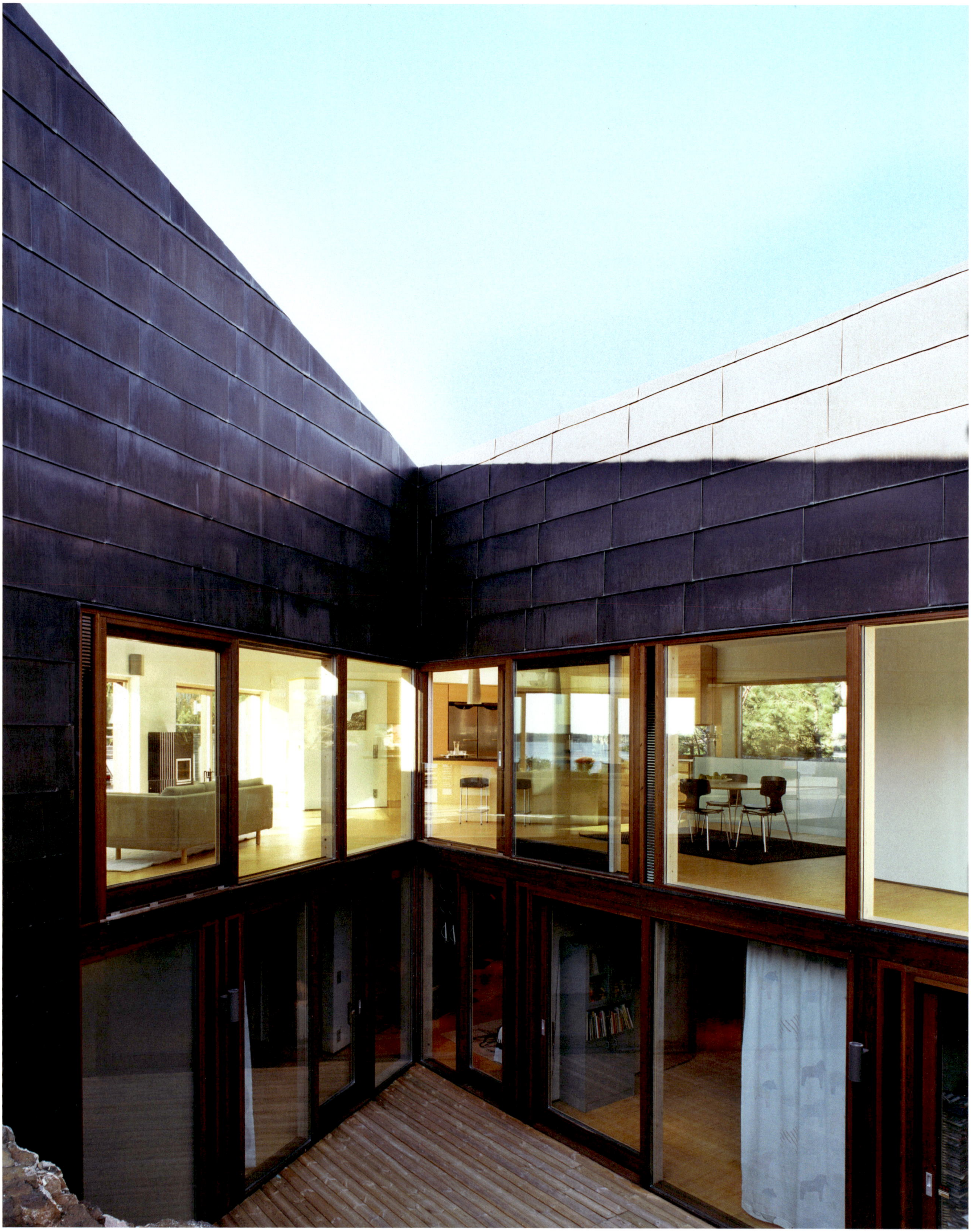

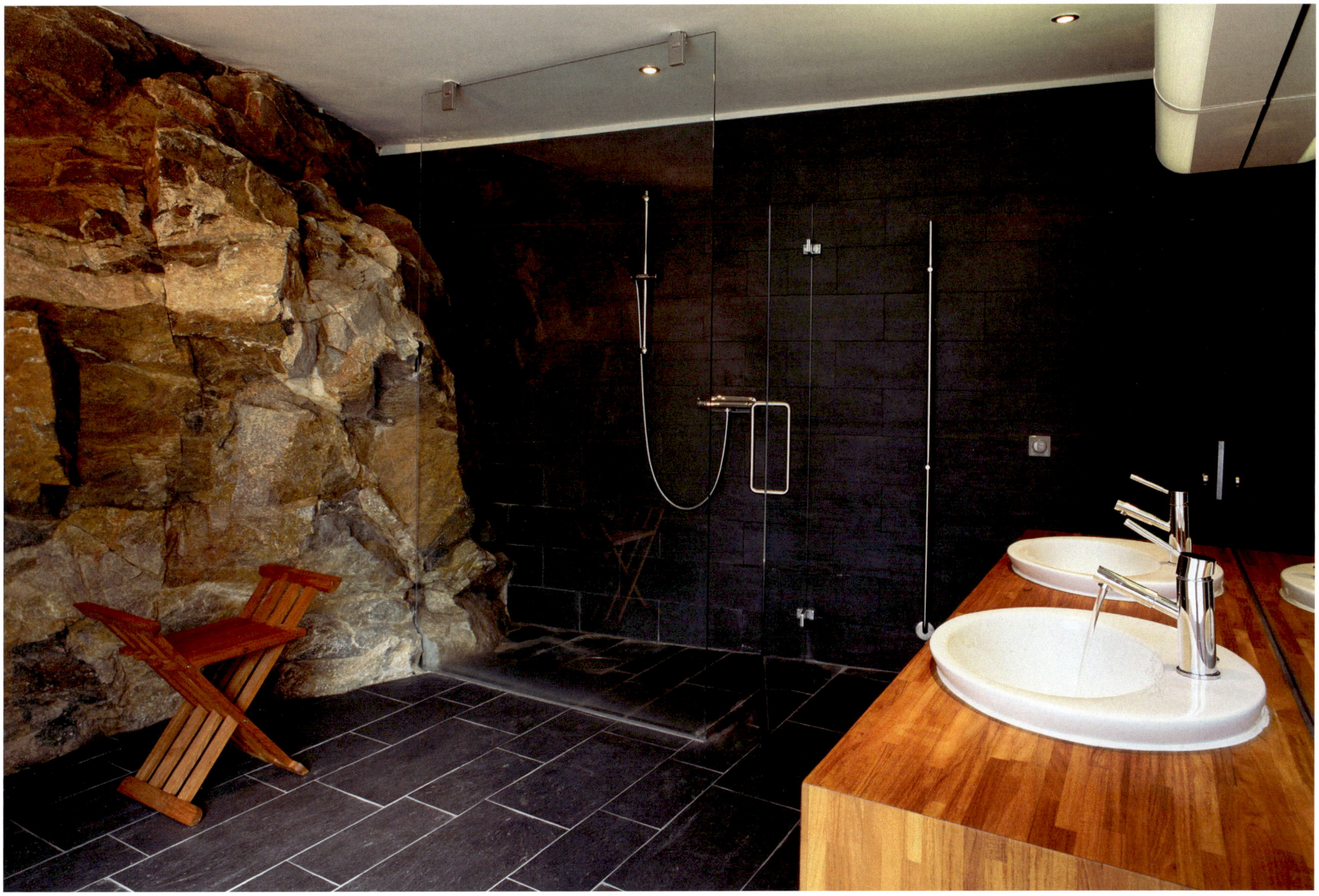

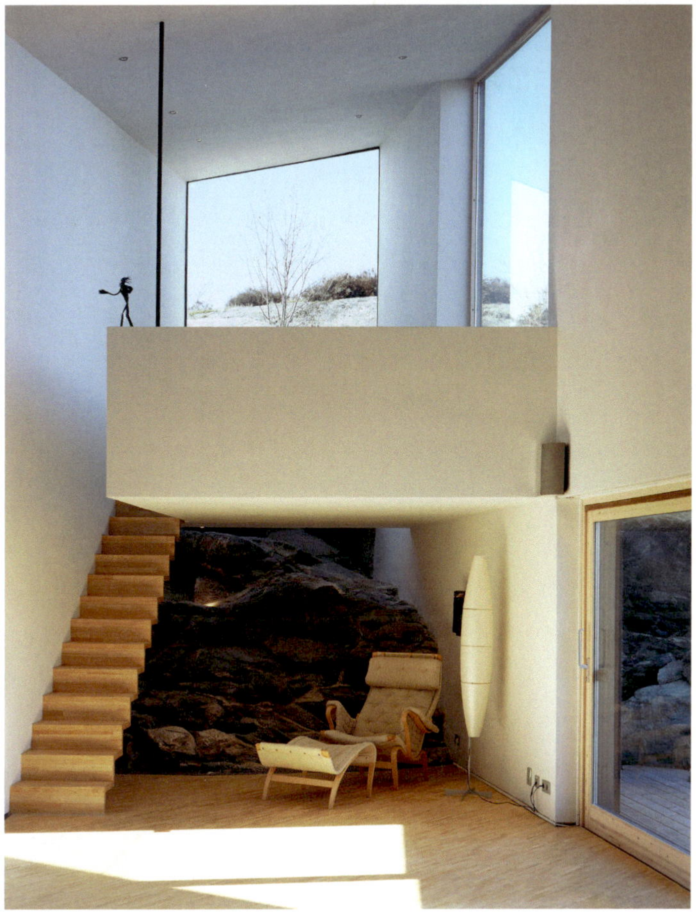

"AT ITS WIDEST POINT, THE OUTER WALLS JOIN THE REMAINING ROCK, FORMING A SMALL COURTYARD THAT ALSO SERVES AS ONE OF THE HOUSE'S FOCAL POINTS."

the building's shape creates captivating shadows on some walls in low light. The exterior of Villa Astrid is clad in pre-weathered copper plating, a durable material that will acquire a natural green patina over time, after which the house will appear to be in even closer contact with its surroundings. ◆

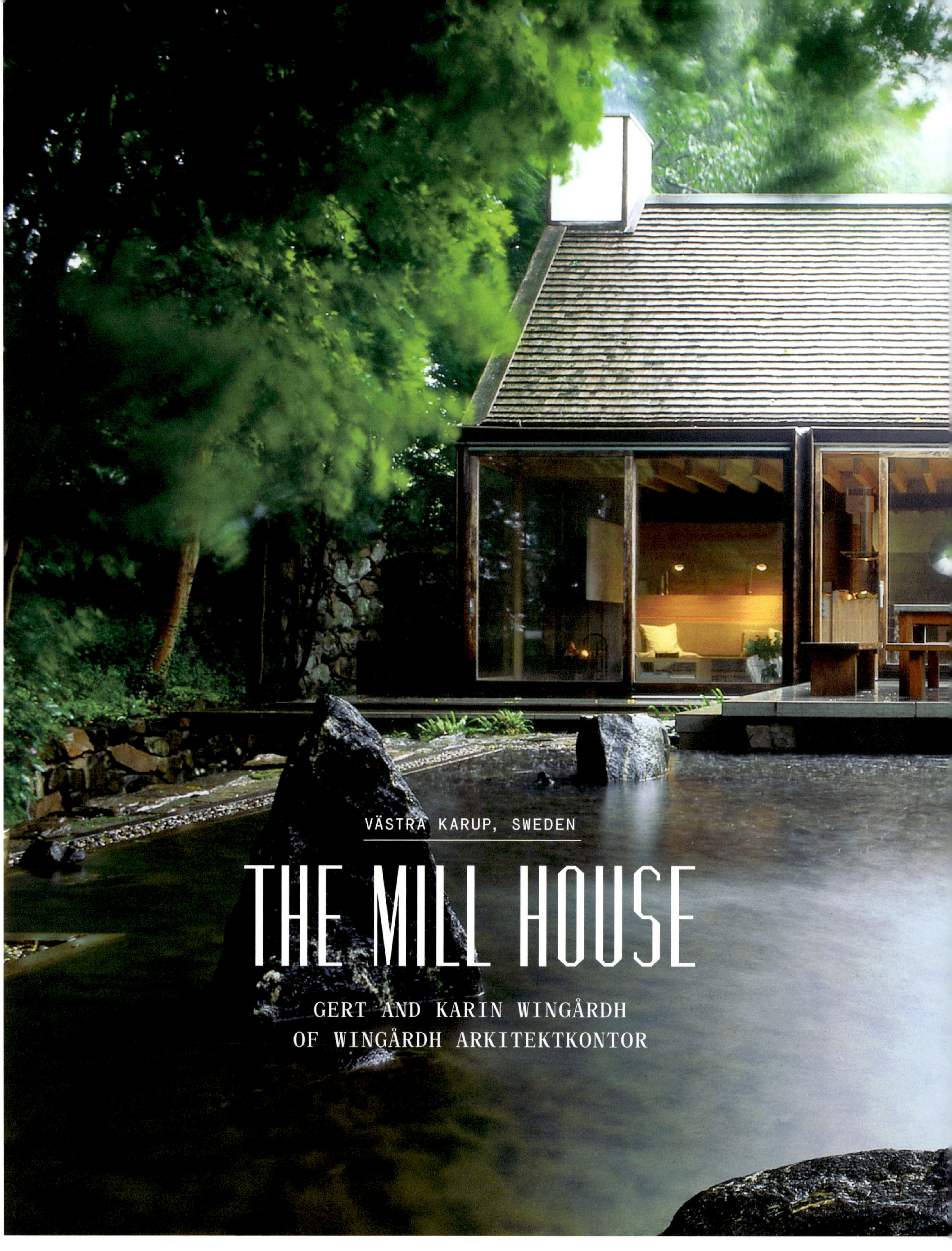

VÄSTRA KARUP, SWEDEN

THE MILL HOUSE

GERT AND KARIN WINGÅRDH
OF WINGÅRDH ARKITEKTKONTOR

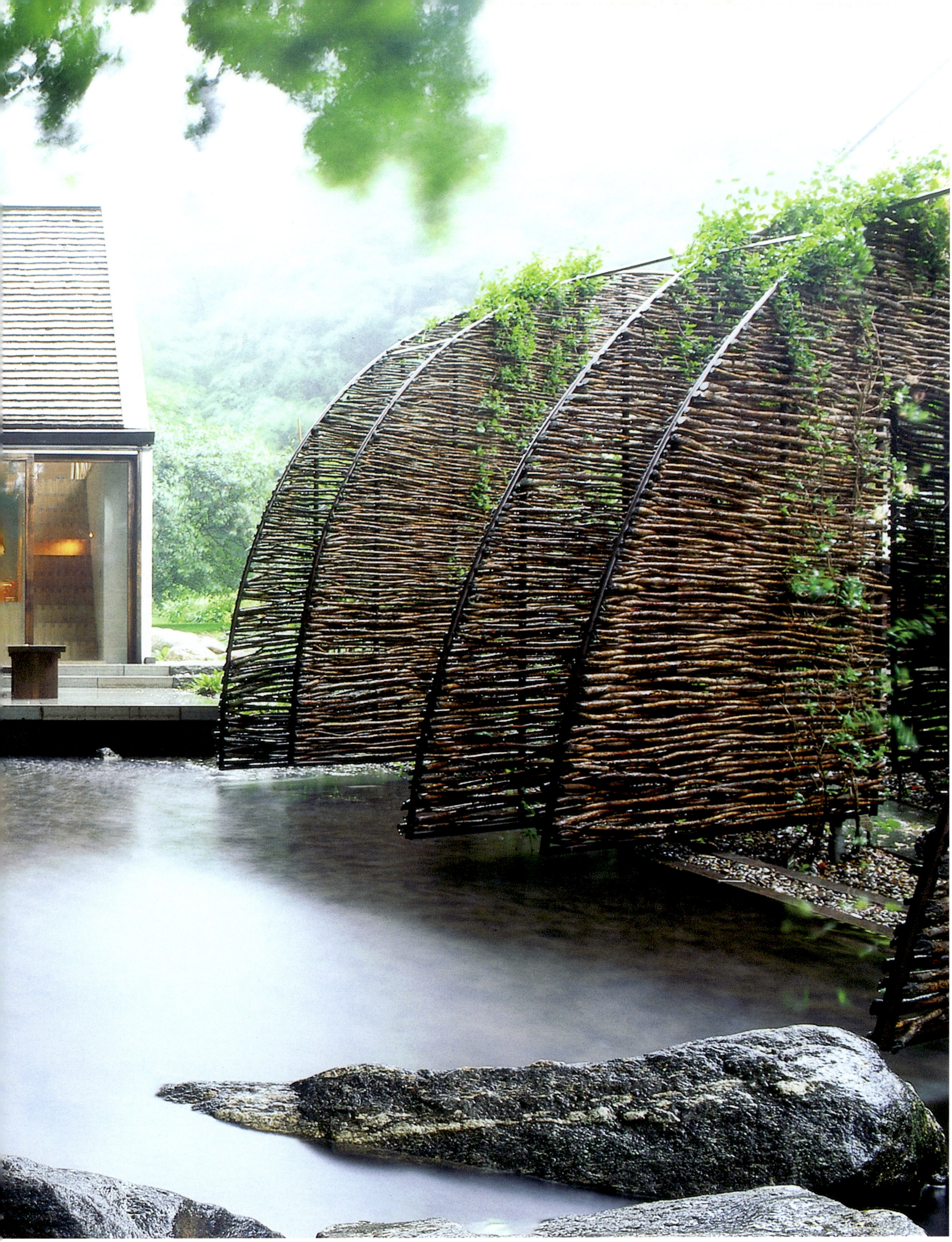

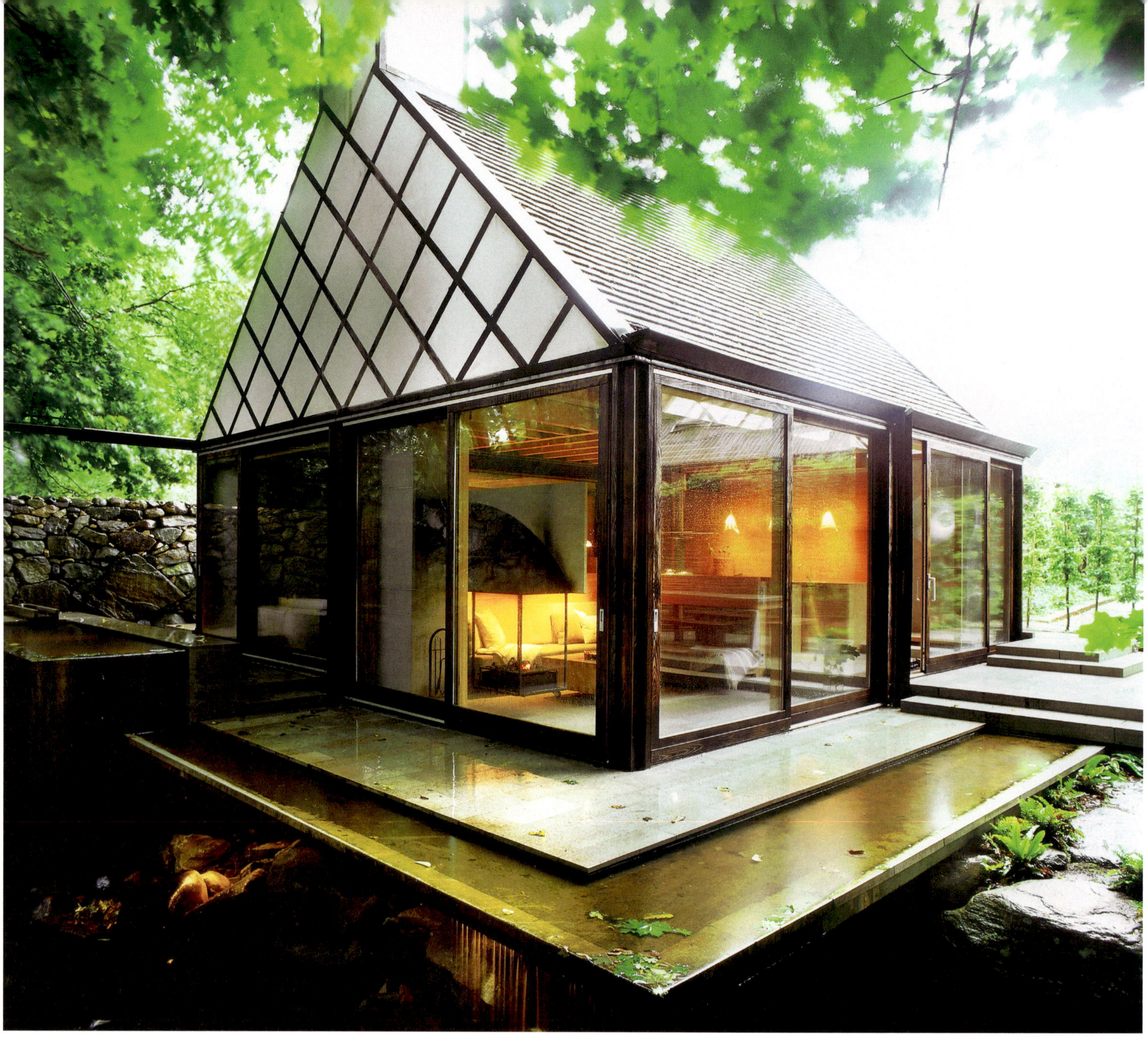

THE MILL HOUSE Simple, fresh, and close to nature, the Mill House is suffused with restorative power. From the oak and limestone sauna to the maple-clad living space, the cabin eschews a rigid distinction between outside and in, reflecting and elevating the revitalizing aspects of its tranquil setting.

Architects Gert and Karin Wingårdh were first recommended to the horse breeder Johan Dieden in the 1980s. Since then, they have created a series of structures on Dieden's farm in southern Sweden, with the Mill House being the latest result of that longstanding partnership. Speaking like an architect who has earned the unwavering trust of his client, Gert Wingårdh says that Dieden "gave us a free hand in this project." The Mill House, then, is a pure illustration of the Wingårdhs' organic architectural style.

The Wingårdhs centered the design on what they describe as a "relationship between inside and out, and a simple balance of materials." The Mill House's sauna, itself a balanced combination of oak and limestone, is the key feature governing the seamless transition demanded by that relationship. In addition to a source of heat, a sauna traditionally requires a source of cold water as well—an essential element of the ritual for cooling down after the sweltering heat. To address this necessity, the Wingårdhs, with the help of Nature Oriented Design, redirected an existing stream to flow to an outdoor bath that constantly brims over and eventually pools in a reflecting pond in front of the cabin. The steady trickle of the stream can be heard in quiet moments and is a constant reminder of nature even when one is indoors.

The interior never strays far from the two natural tones of gray limestone and light maple wood. From the sunken living room to the raised kitchen, the two colors

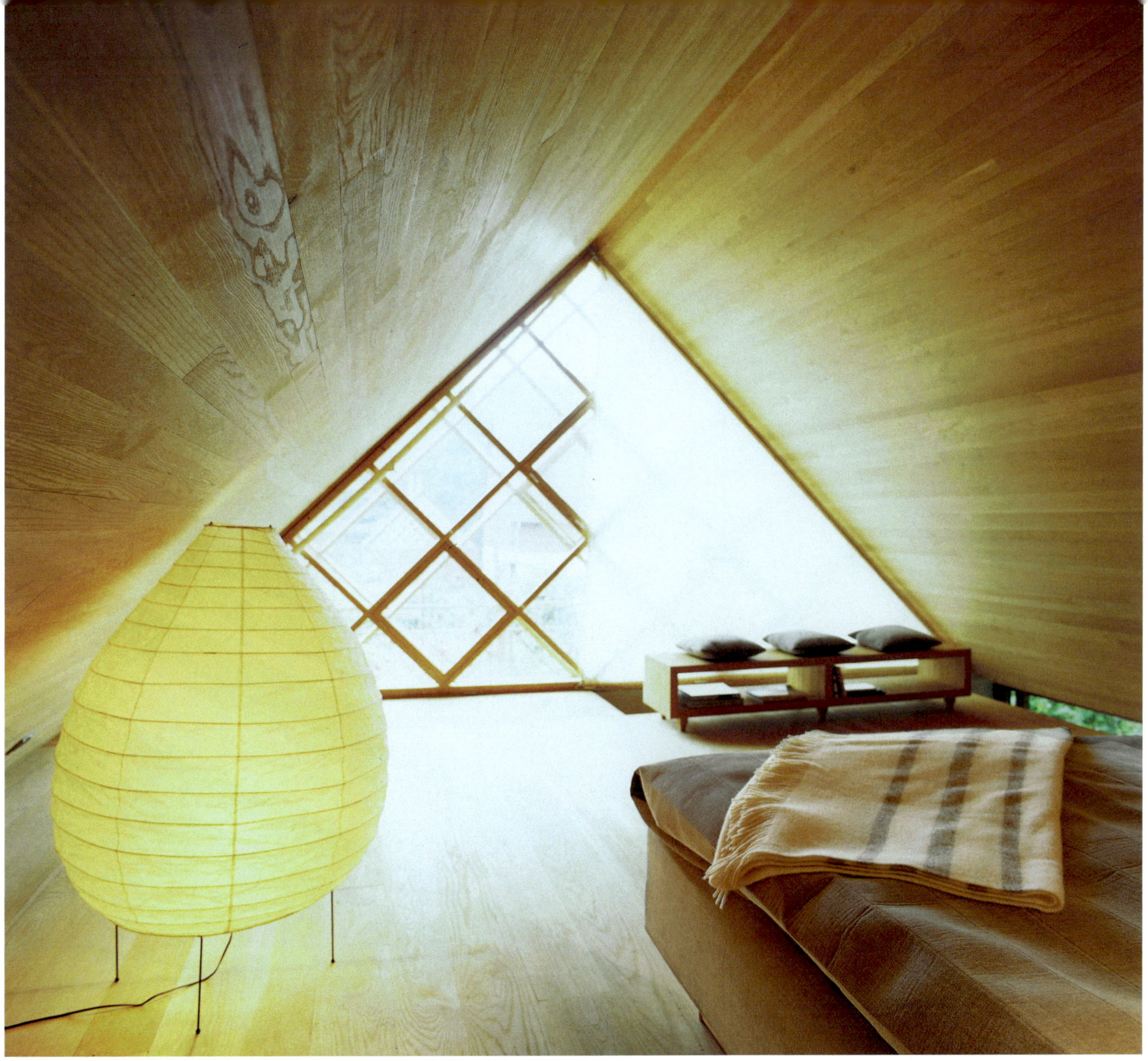

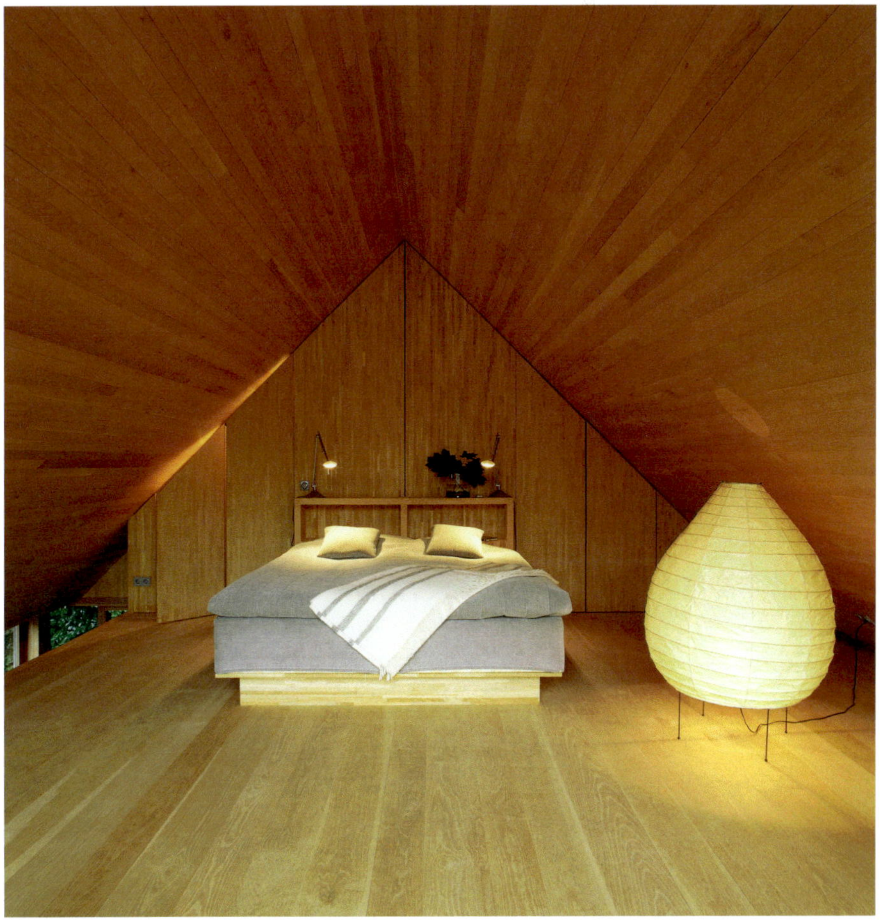

exist in easy dialogue, and their warmth, along with the large glass-encased hearth, helps carry some of the sauna's heat into the main area. Here, large sliding glass doors reiterate the fine balance achieved between the natural and manmade worlds, as visitors can sit and gaze out at the pool just beyond the lip of the terrace. There is something effortless and yet precise about the Mill House, which may be what Gert Wingårdh means when he says, "I allowed the environment to guide my planning." ◆

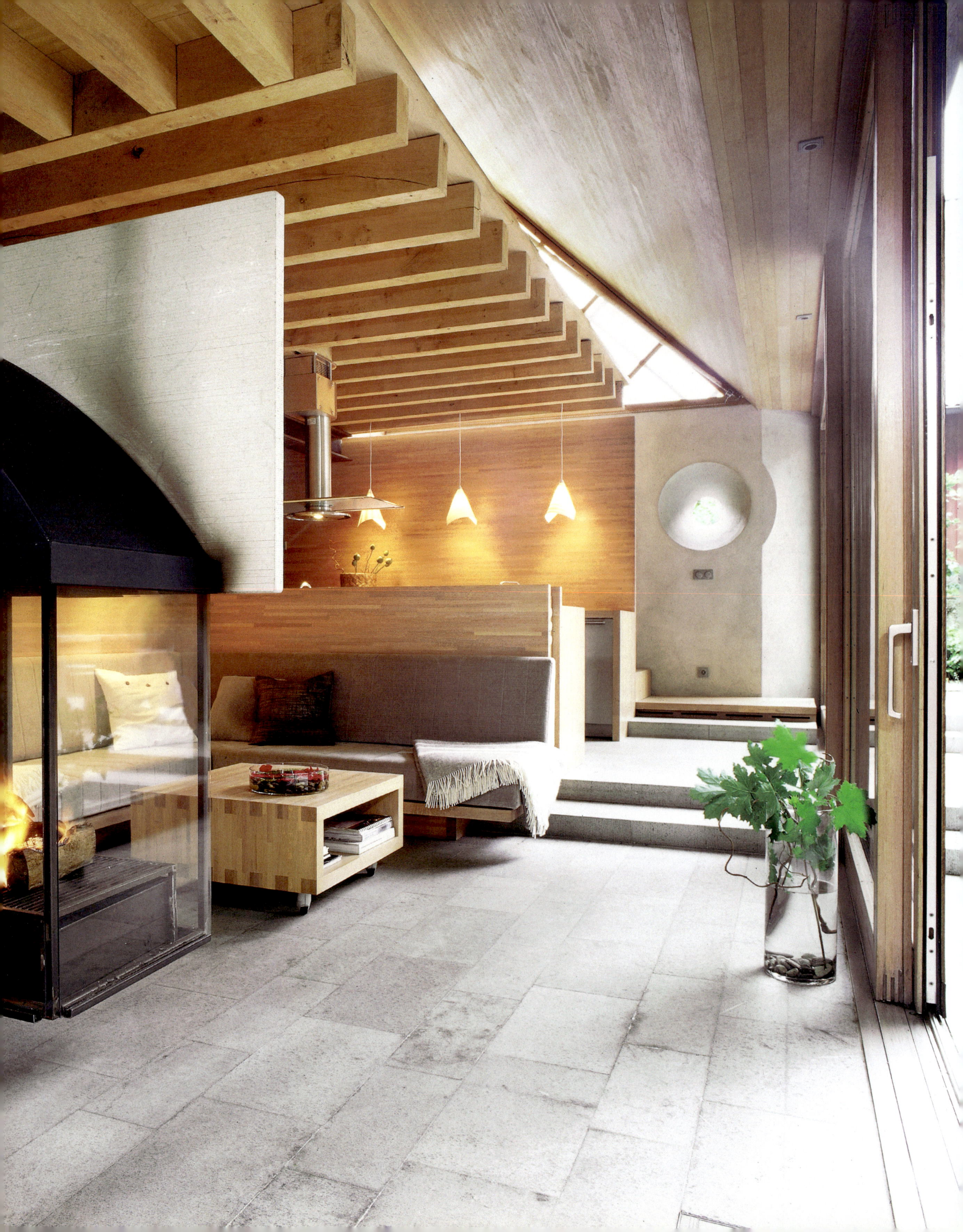

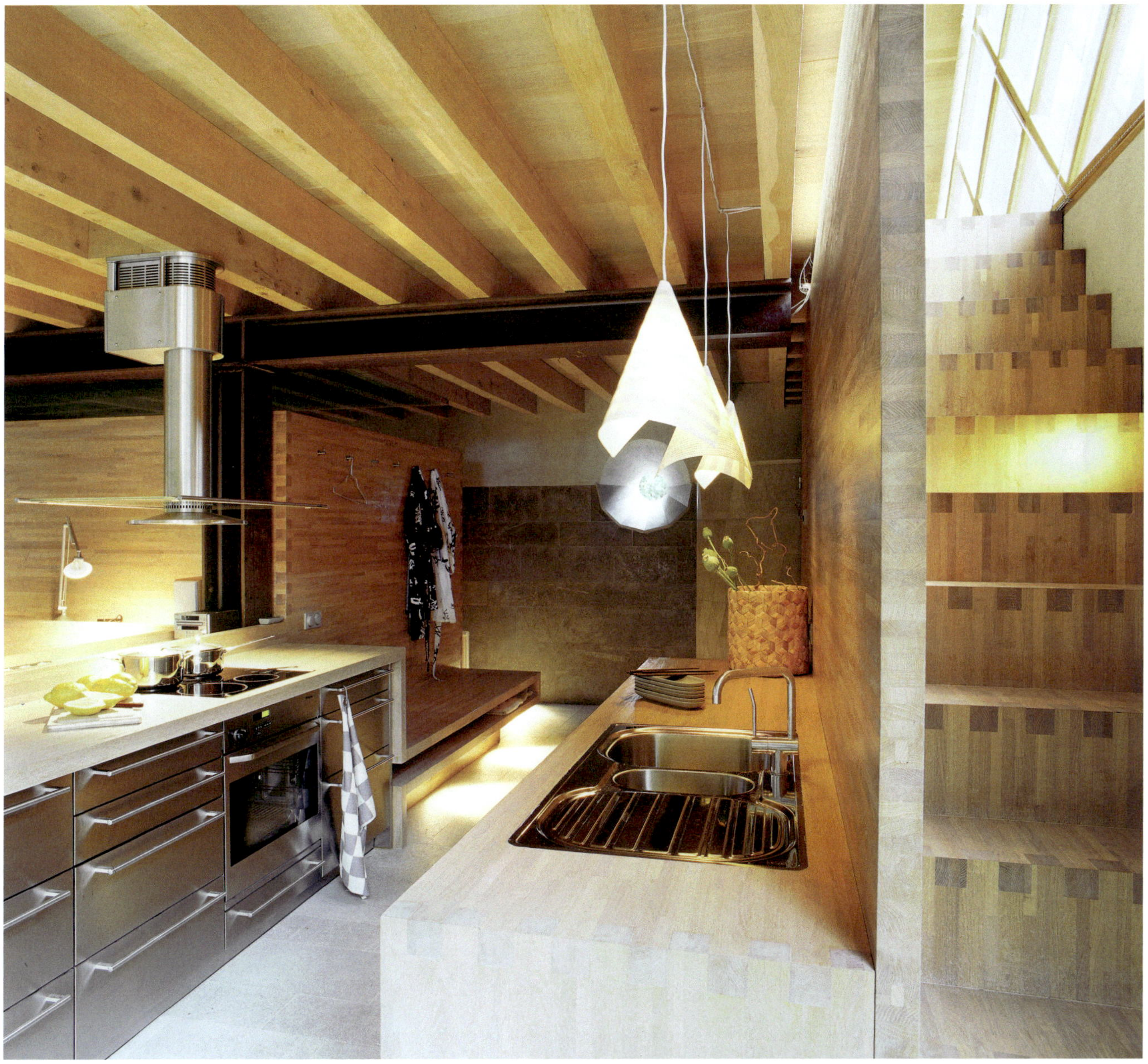

“THERE IS SOMETHING EFFORTLESS AND YET PRECISE ABOUT THE MILL HOUSE, WHICH MAY BE WHAT GERT WINGÅRDH MEANS WHEN HE SAYS, ‘I ALLOWED THE ENVIRONMENT TO GUIDE MY PLANNING.’”

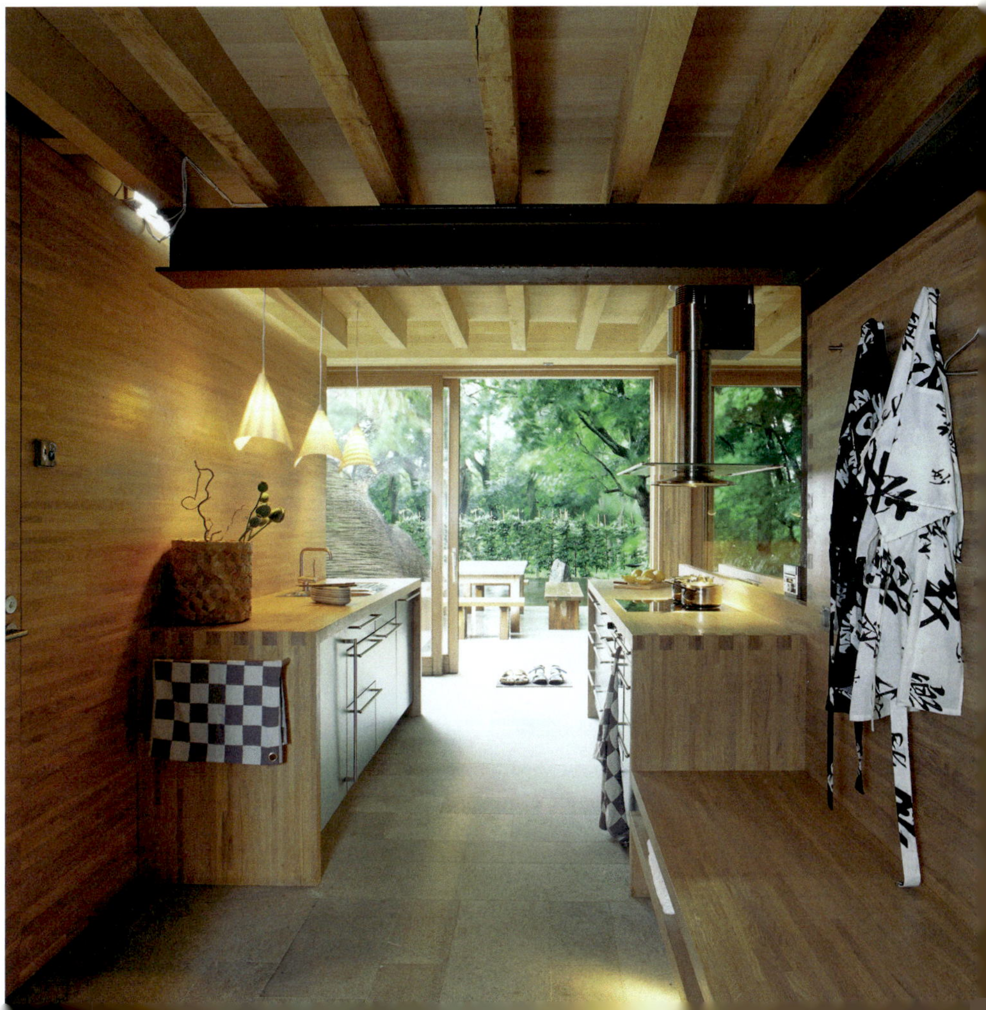

VAME

STEFAN ANTONI OLMESDAHL
TRUEN ARCHITECTS (SAOTA)

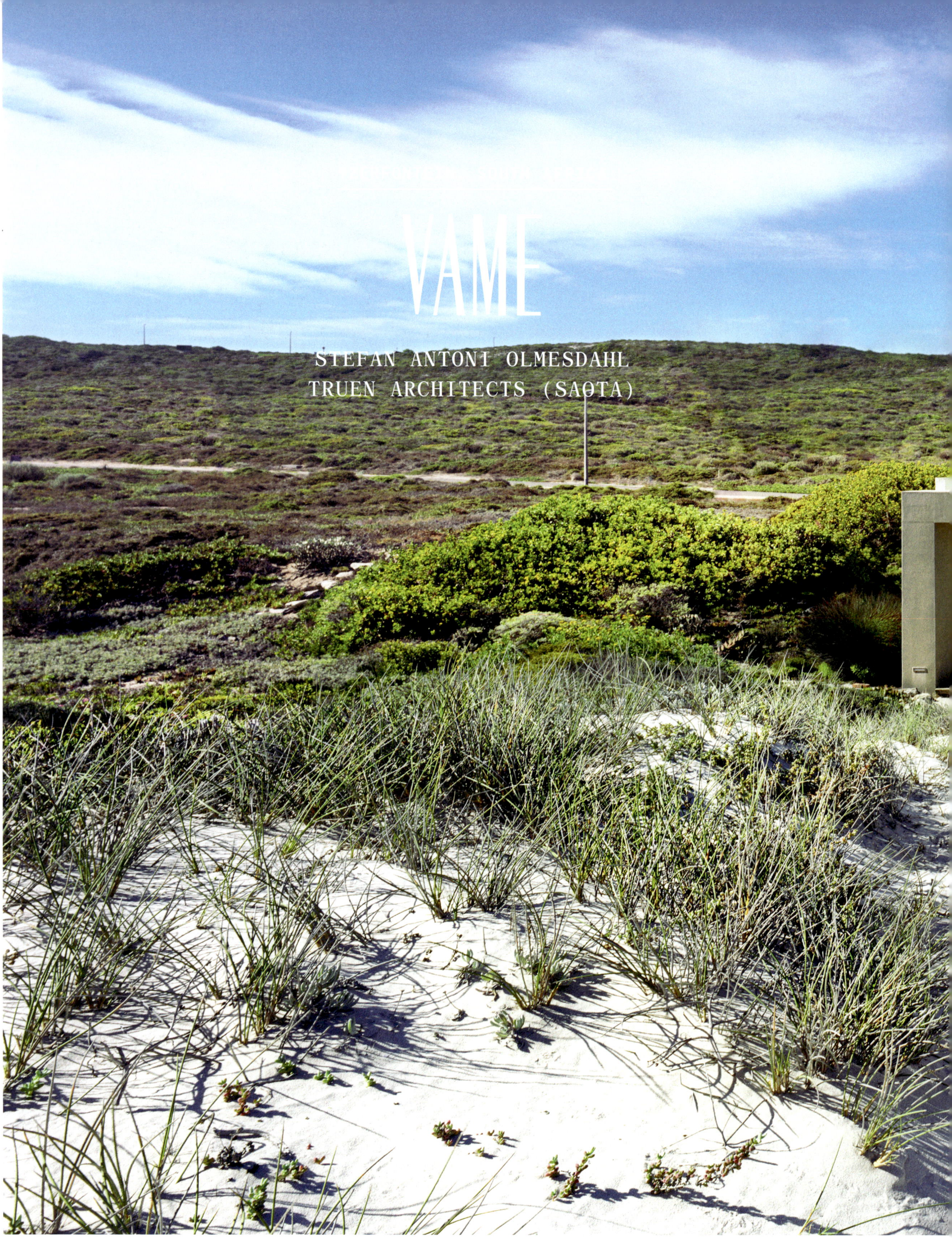

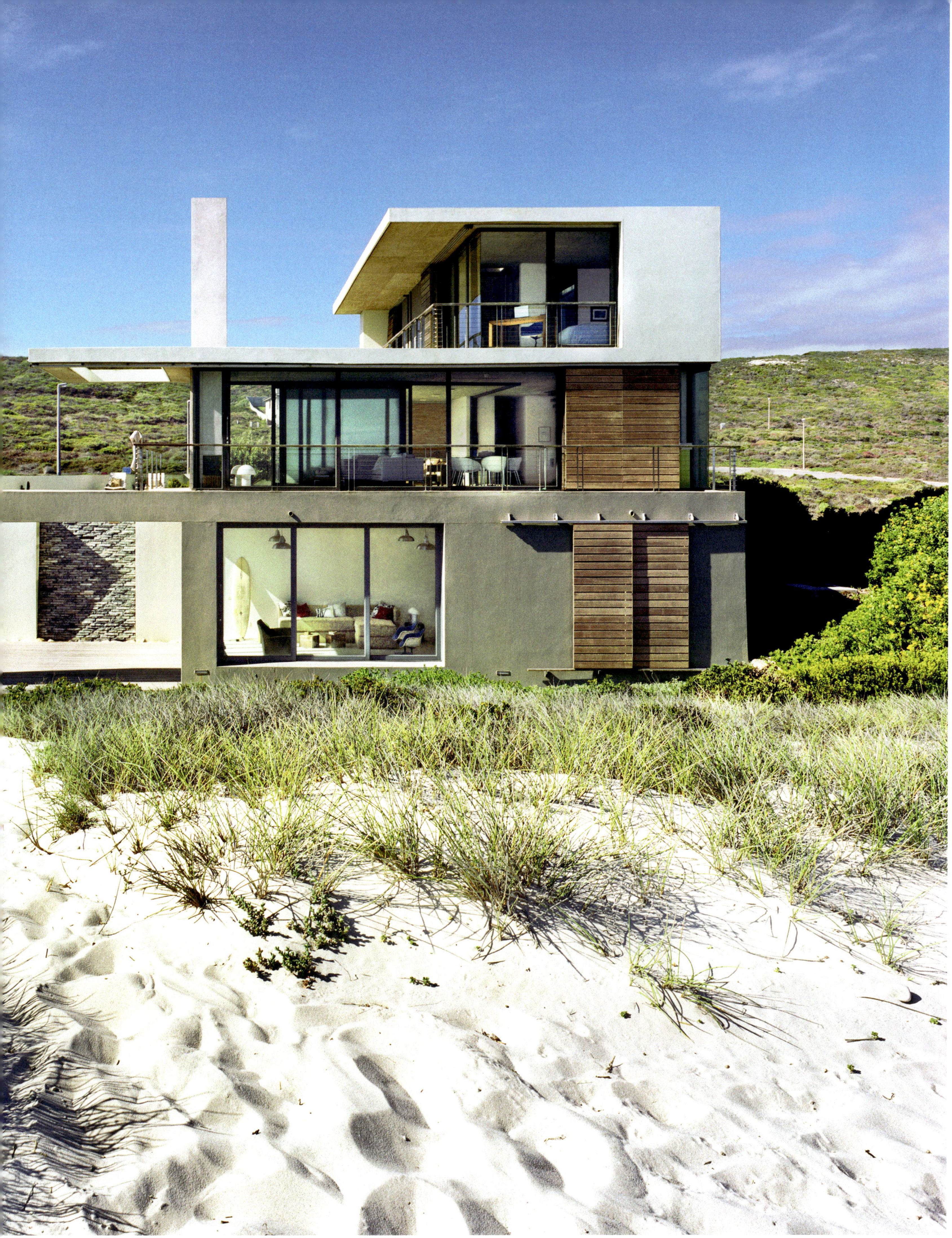

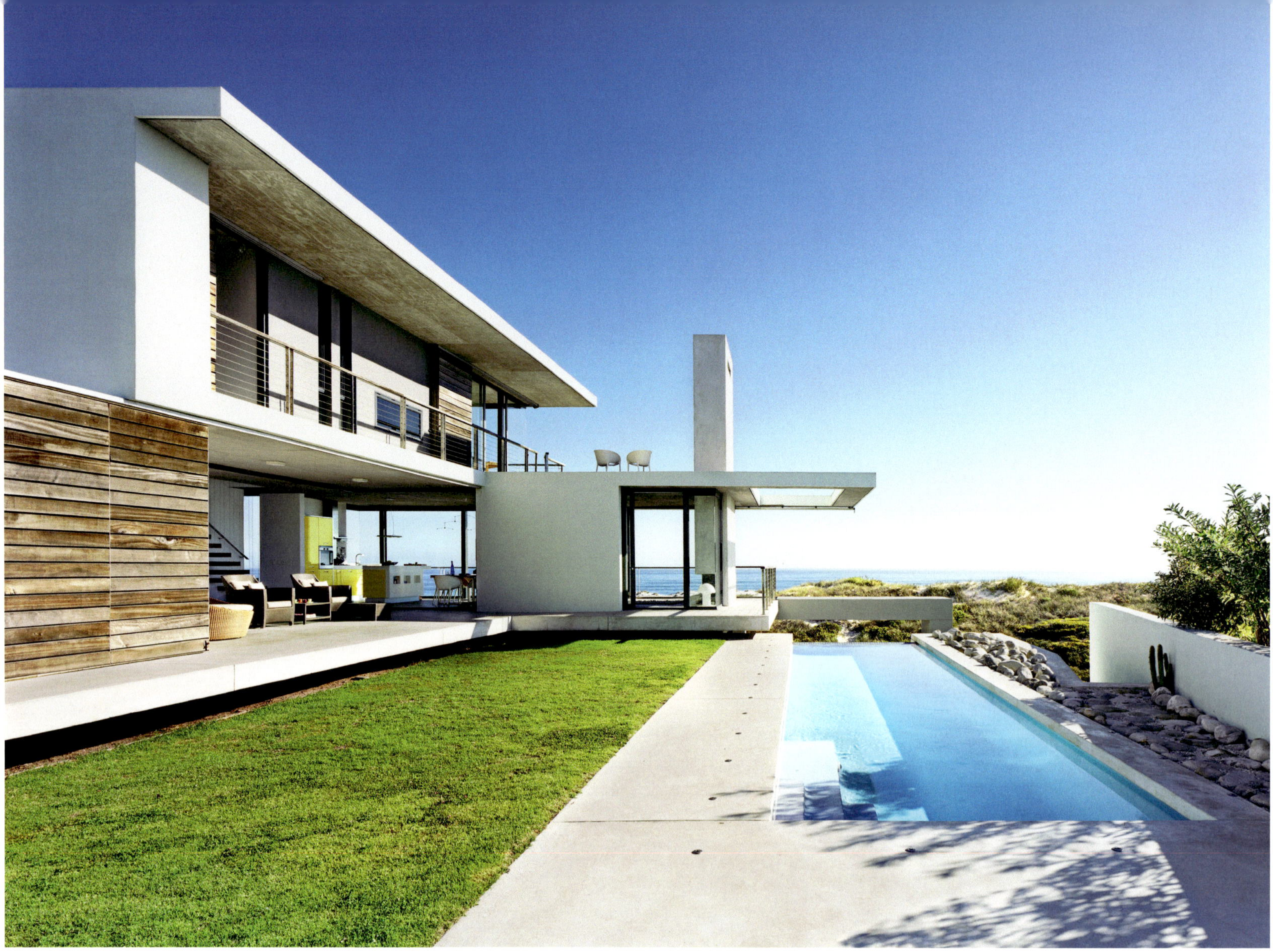

VAME Perched on white sand dunes, VAME absorbs the totality of its serene location. A frameless image of the dunes and the deep blue ocean enters through full-height glass windows, merging with the home's neutral color palette, textured materials, and well-designed water features.

Yzerfontein is a small town 90 kilometers to the north of Cape Town, South Africa. The area is a haven for tourists and the original owners of this house, who wanted to create an "open, yet private" home, were fortunate to secure an isolated site. Inspired by the backdrop of rolling sand dunes and endless ocean, the architecturally minded couple wanted to erect a distinct stand-alone dwelling. Describing their commission, the SAOTA team explains, "The client gave us a very simple brief and total freedom. We aimed to create a very simple composition playing with the juxtaposition of rectangular elements."

A prevalent sculptural inclination can be glimpsed throughout VAME. From a distance, its austere volumes appear in sharp contrast to the gently undulating landscape. Two rectilinear forms intersect in an L-shape; their elongated faces—composed almost exclusively of glass—open up to the infinite vista while also acting as windbreakers for the seaside courtyard. Here, a rectangular length of lawn mirrors the form of the slim pool, and cubic volumes, employing a cutout technique in places, protrude from the structure's body in precisely considered dimensions. The architects say this is their favorite feature because it provides "great views of the garden, pool, and the living spaces, as well as the sea through them."

Off-shutter concrete ceilings, white plaster walls, and polished concrete floors are the ideal interior complements to VAME's sculpted exterior. Giving defintion to large open spaces, the subtle tones of these materials intensify the presence of nature. The middle floor, for example, features a joint dining, kitchen, and living area where the view takes center stage. The house exemplifies such a nuanced understanding of proportions that it is no surprise that SAOTA's Stefan Antoni, when asked if he would change anything in hindsight, says, "When you come up with such a simple and effective solution, there is not much that one would want to change." ◆

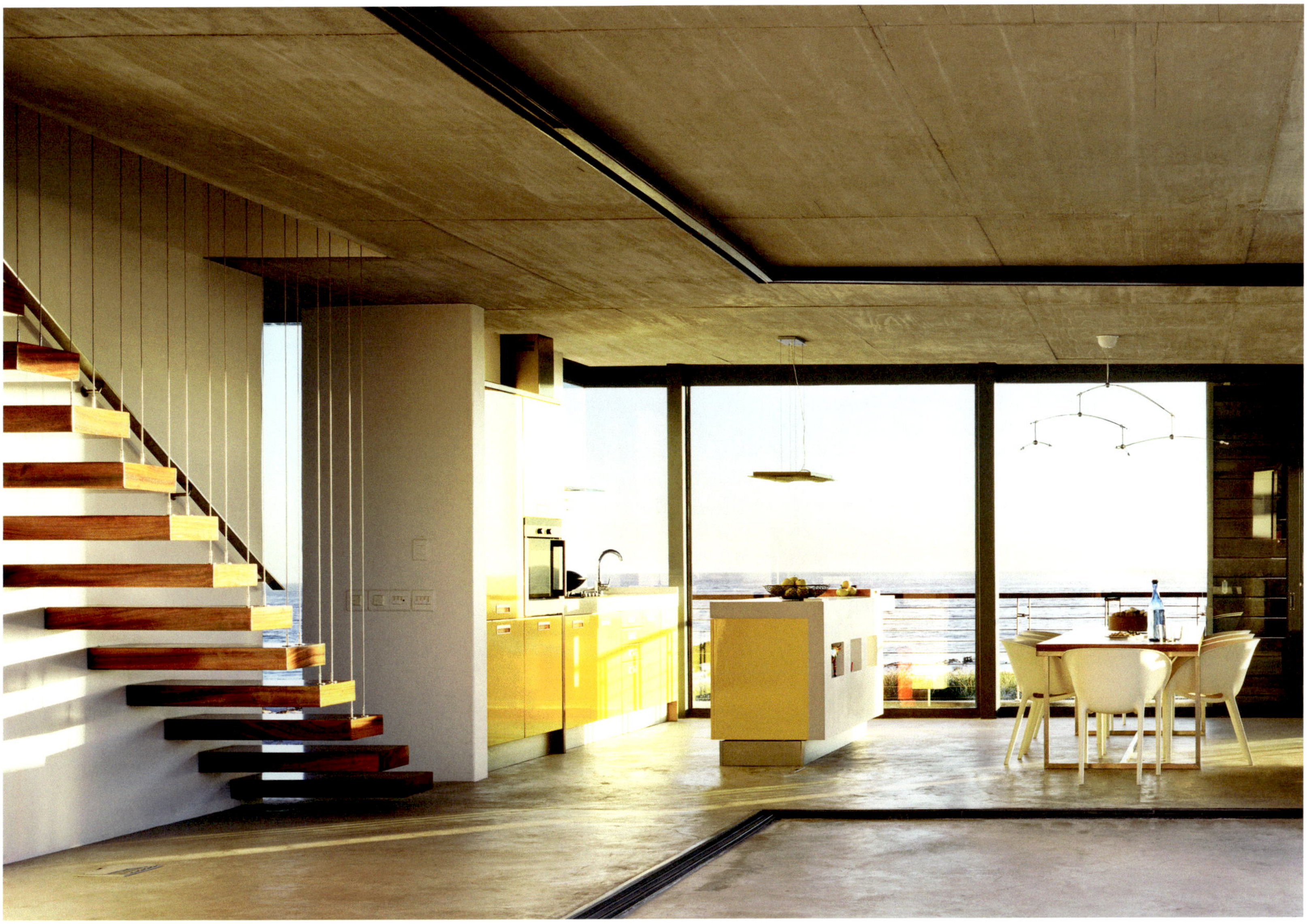

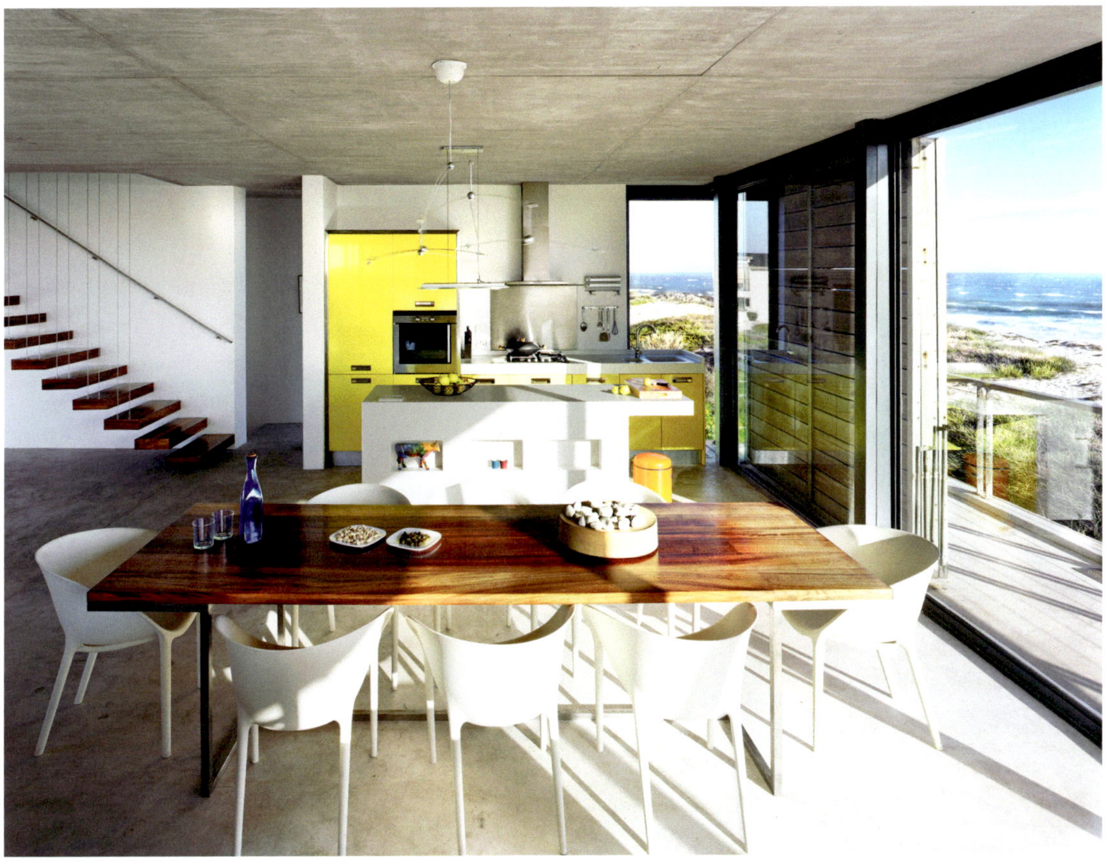

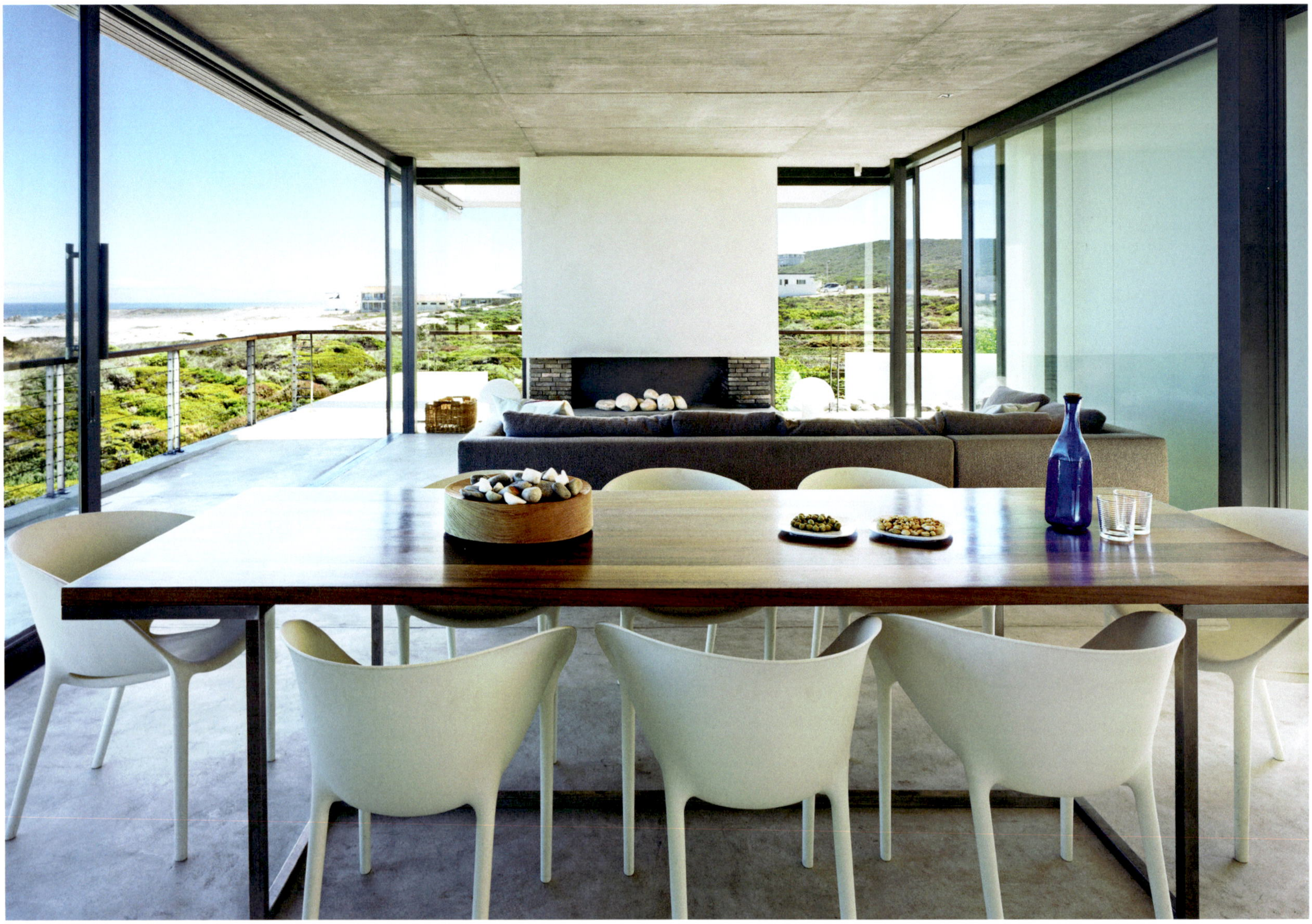

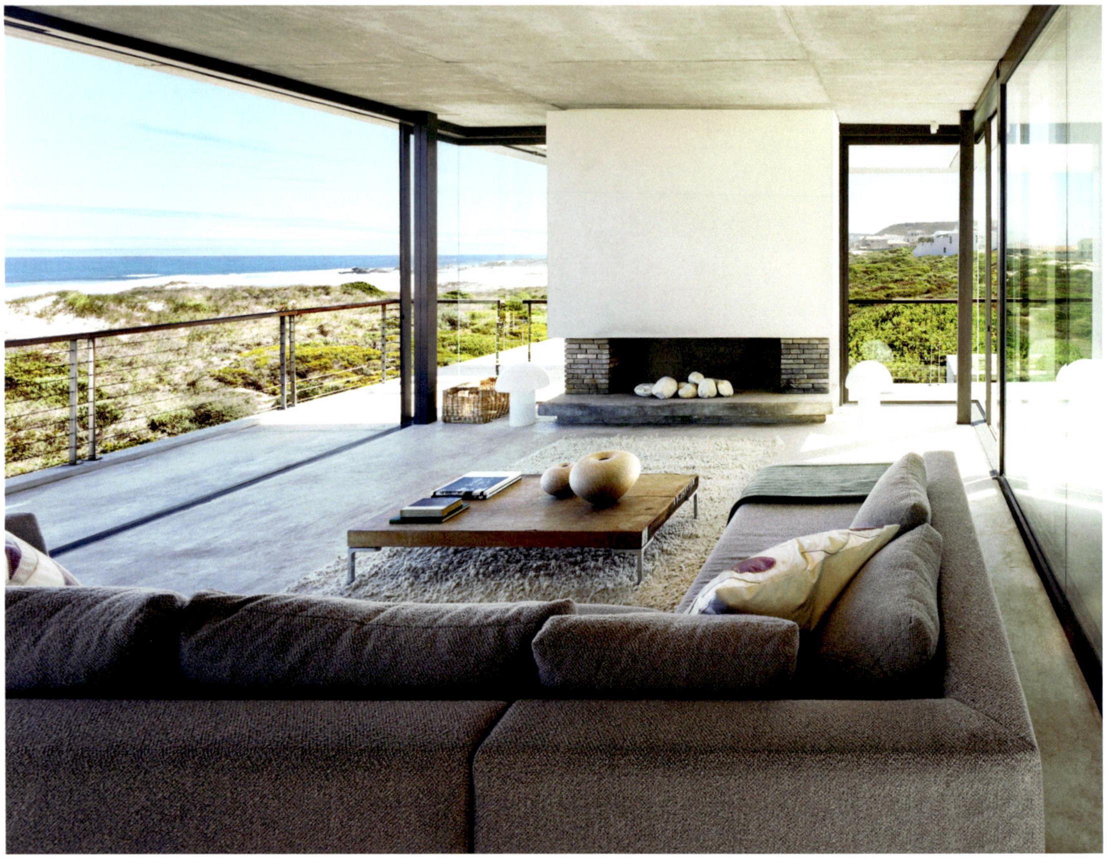

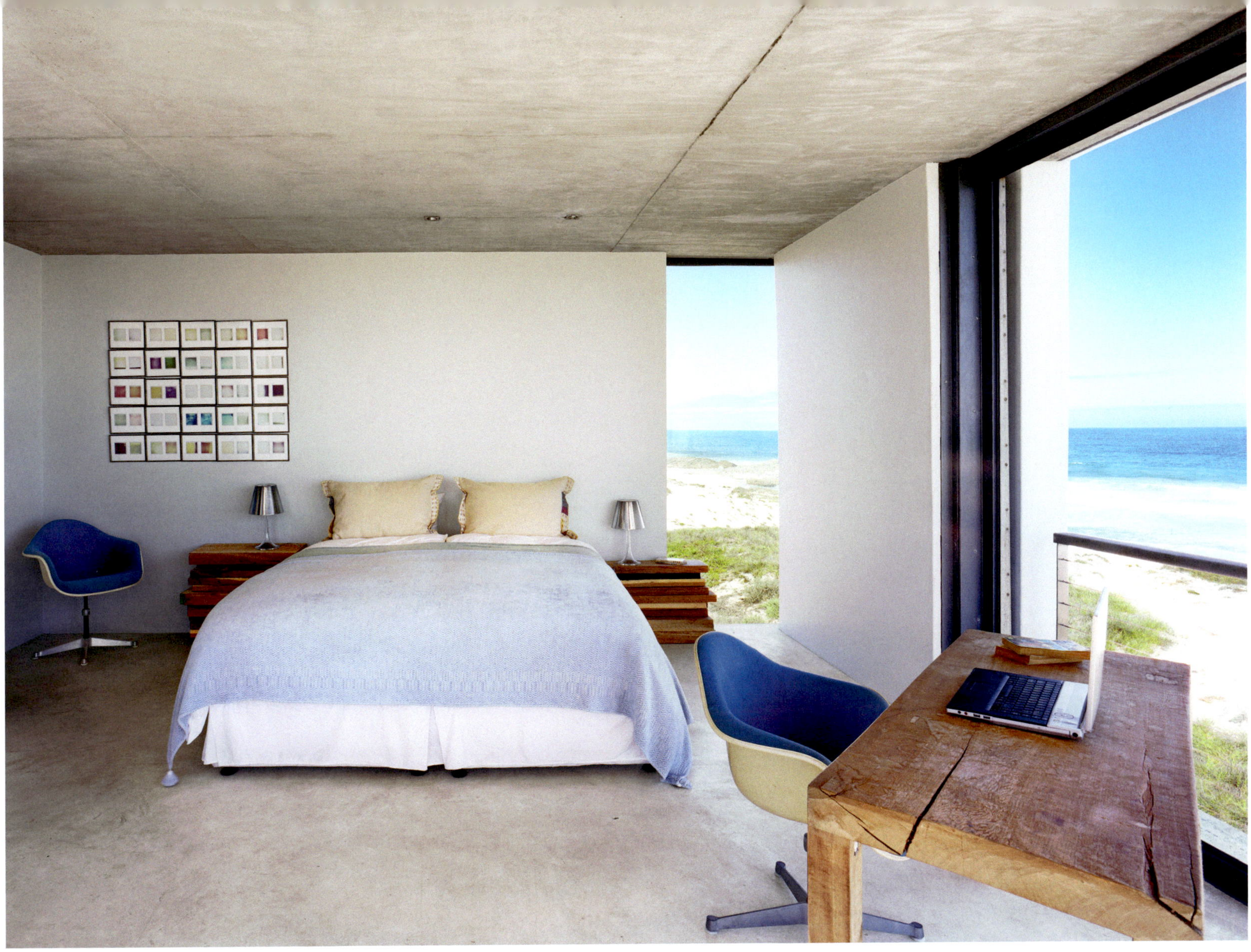

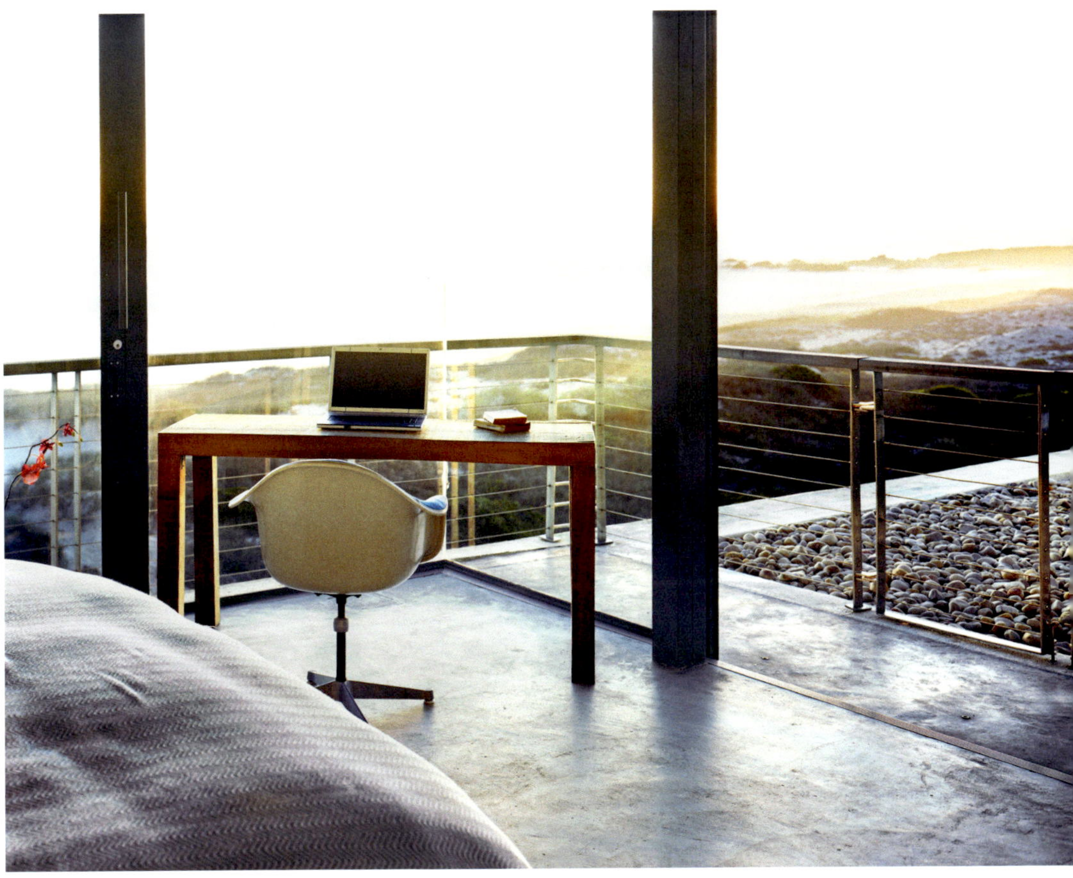

"OFF-SHUTTER CONCRETE CEILINGS, WHITE PLASTER WALLS, AND POLISHED CONCRETE FLOORS ARE THE IDEAL INTERIOR COMPLEMENTS TO VAME'S SCULPTED EXTERIOR."

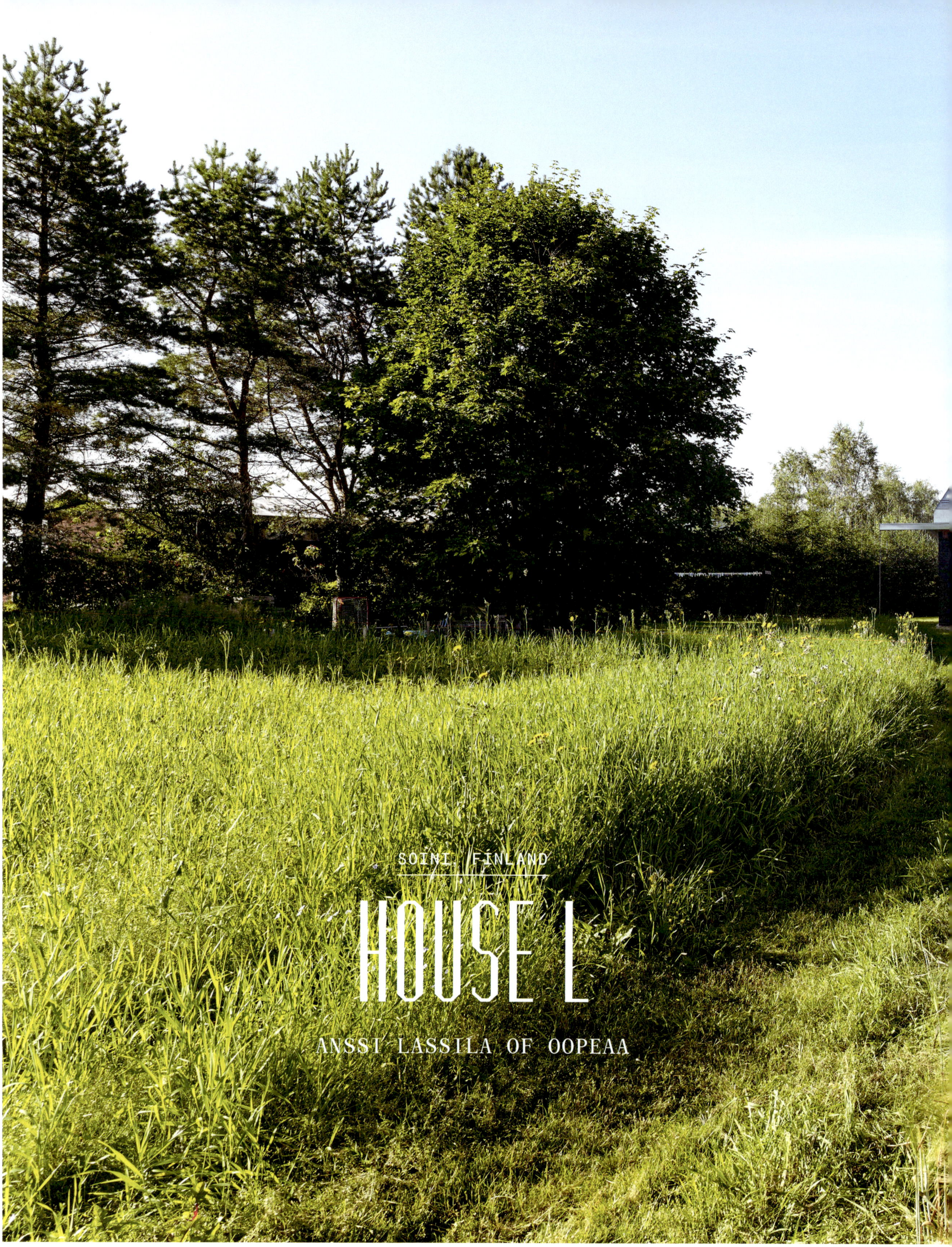
SOINI, FINLAND
HOUSE L
ANSSI LASSILA OF OOPEAA

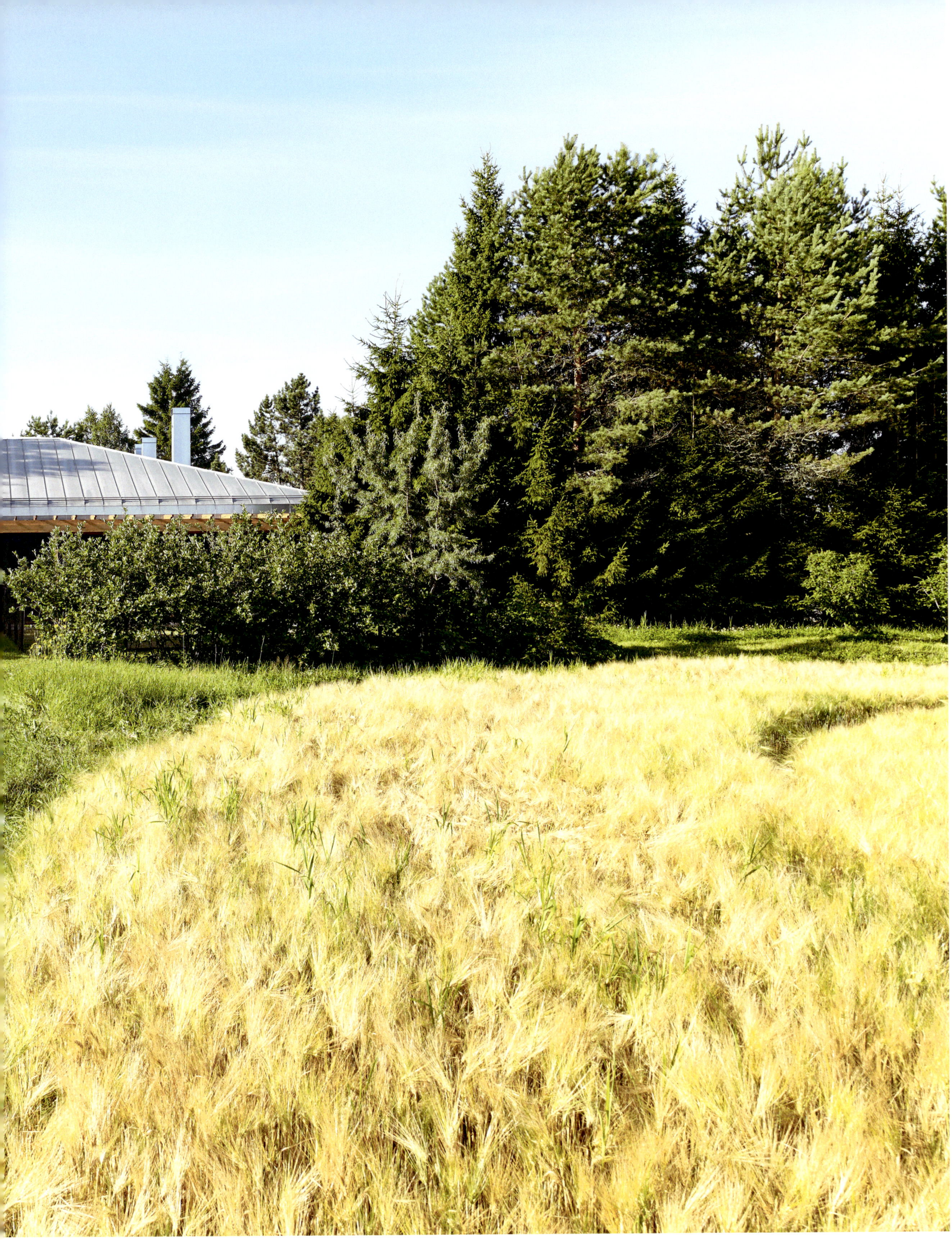

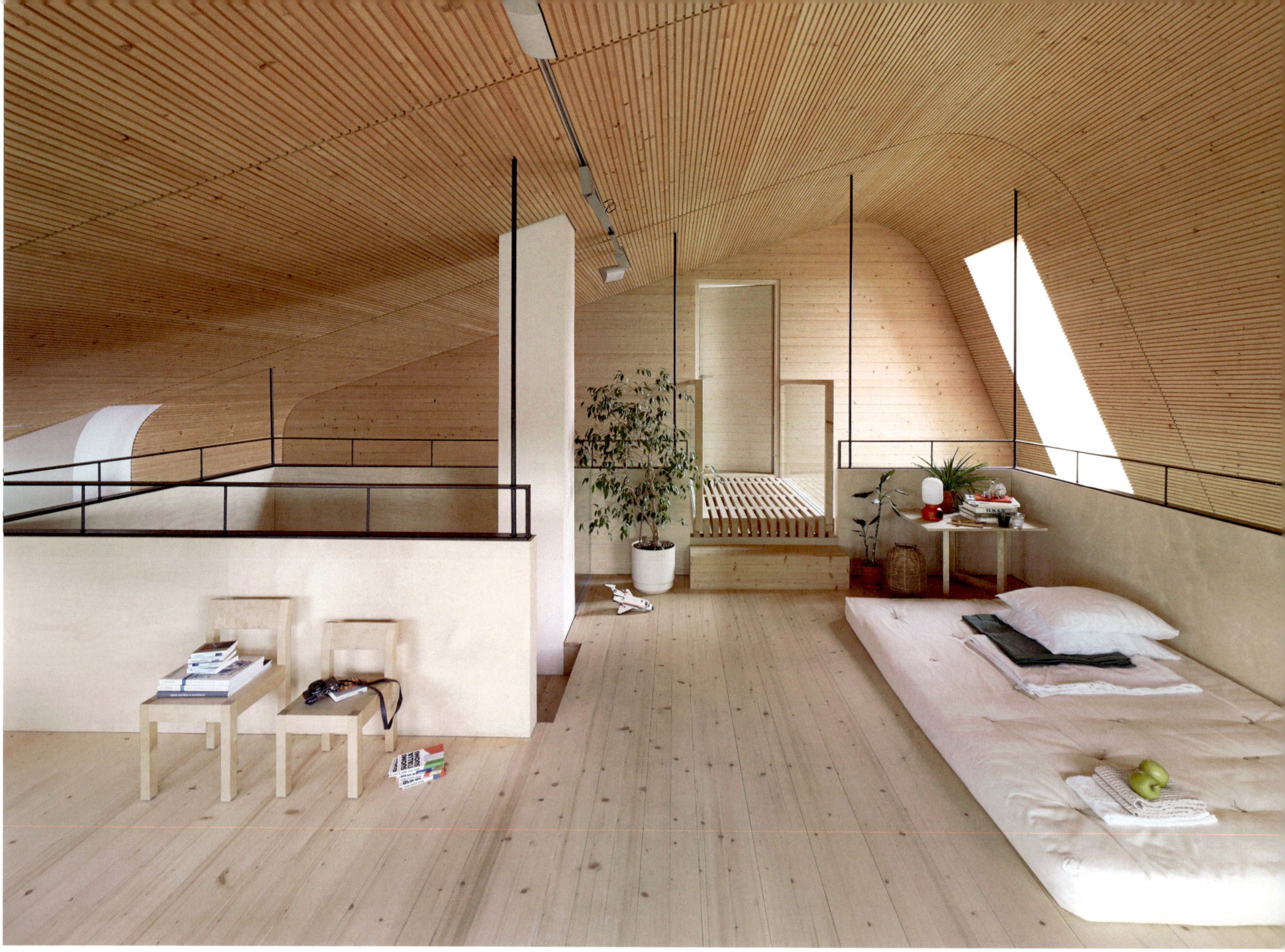

HOUSE L is a surprising mix of old and new. The ultra-modern black brick and reflective zinc exterior contrast with the timeless wooden interior, creating a robust cabin that will endure through many generations of the Lassila family and continue their long history in the remote Finnish woodlands.

Anssi Lassila's family has lived in the Soini region of Finland since the 16th century and on this particular site for over 200 years. The owner and architect had planned to renovate an old family-owned cabin there, he says, but "when we looked closer at the house we realized it was in a very bad state of repair."

While the new cabin utilizes the old foundation, House L is an entirely new structure that makes its most notable departure from its ancient predecessor in the exterior zinc cladding. "My main idea was that the house should have a long lifespan, that's why I've used zinc for the cladding and roof," Lassila explains. The zinc shell is not only durable, it also reflects sunlight and the surrounding greenery, clothing the house in a vibrant mirror of its woodland setting.

Clean arrangements of spruce run through the interior. The walls are clad in thicker cuts that taper to thinner lengths at the junction with the ceiling, emphasizing the openness of the double-height living and dining room. Three bedrooms are accessed via a narrow hallway that can be closed to the living area, allowing the heat generated from the central fireplace to be concentrated when the climate is at its coldest. The spacious kitchen, with a cooking island and cabinets washed in a white oil paint, occupies a middle ground between the natural wood of the ground floor and the stark white of the central staircase. The stairs are partially hidden within this austere volume, and cutouts in the base provide room for the fireplace to breathe.

The meticulous wood finish continues upstairs. There, an open multipurpose room sits on top of the stairwell, and a small office can be accessed via a slatted wooden walkway. This space sometimes serves as guest ~

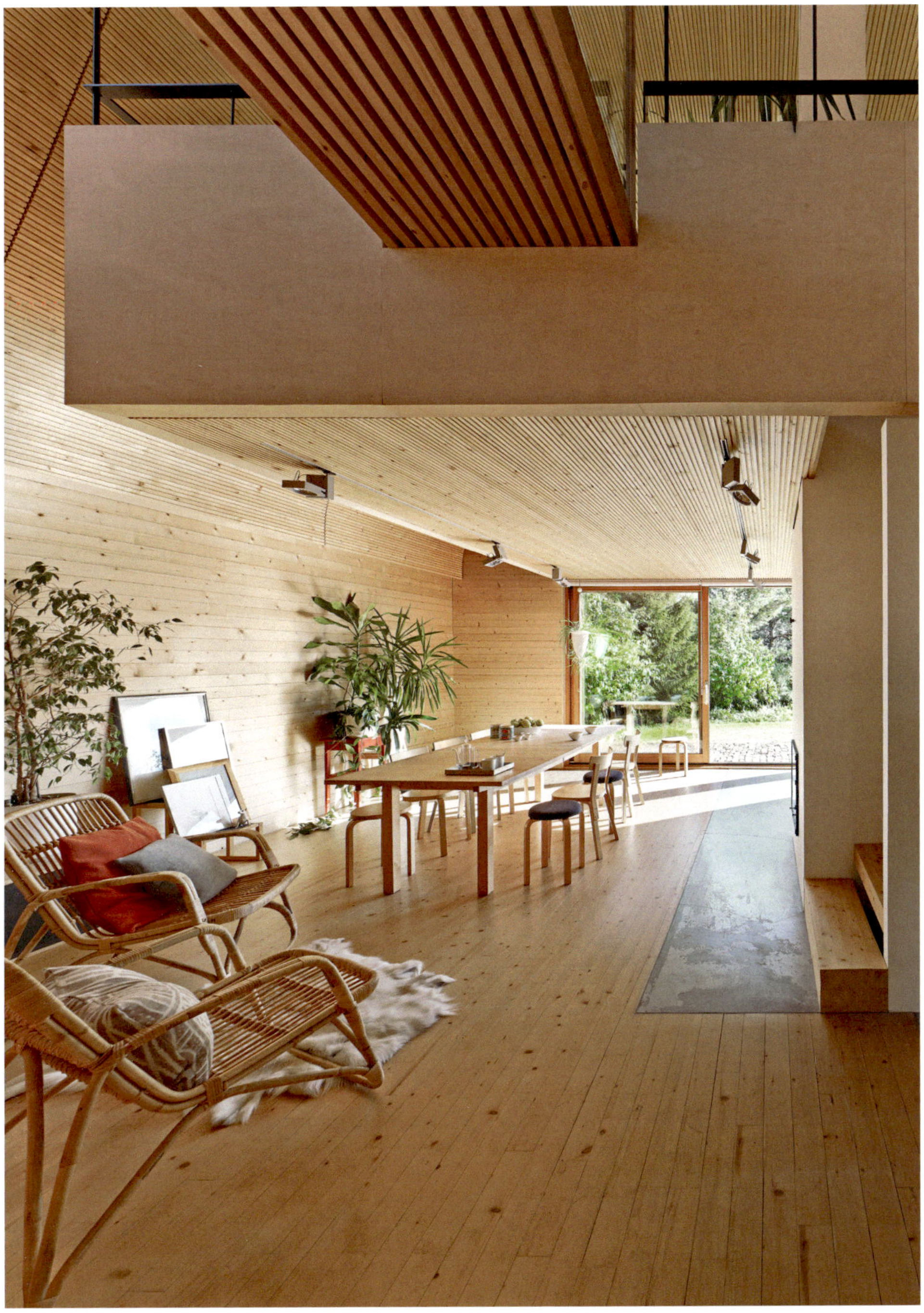

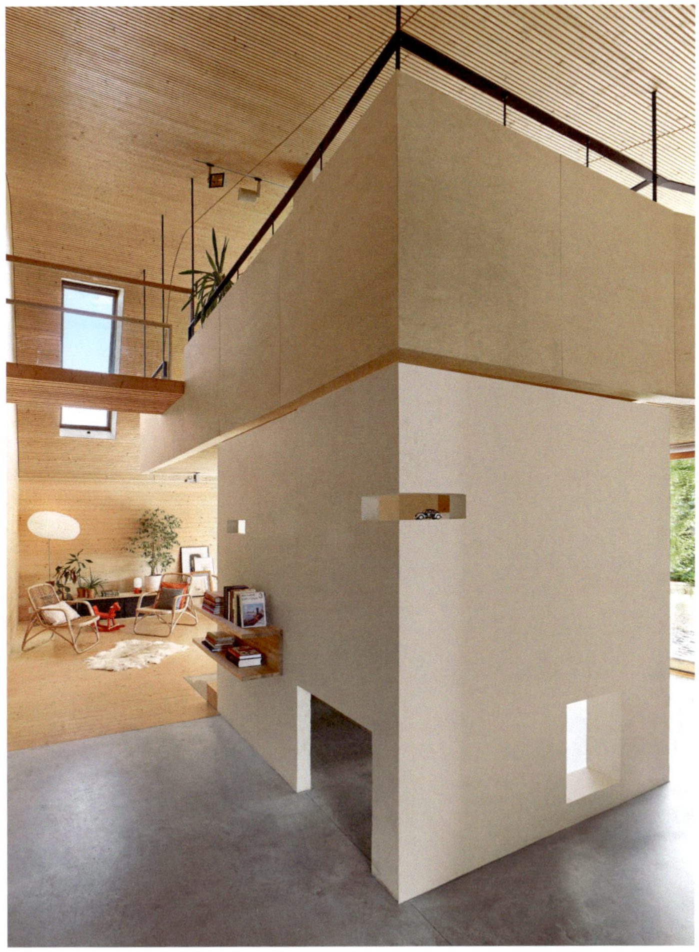

“My main idea was that the house should have a long lifespan, that’s why I’ve used zinc for the cladding and roof.”
— Anssi Lassila

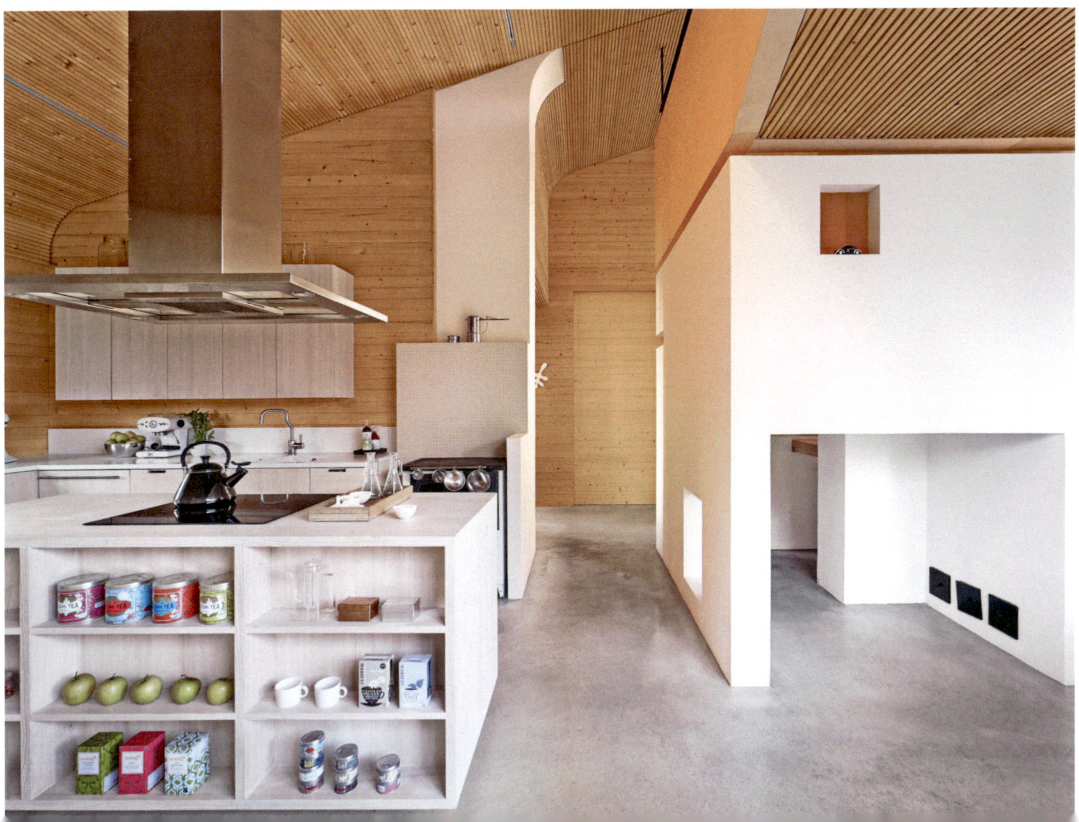

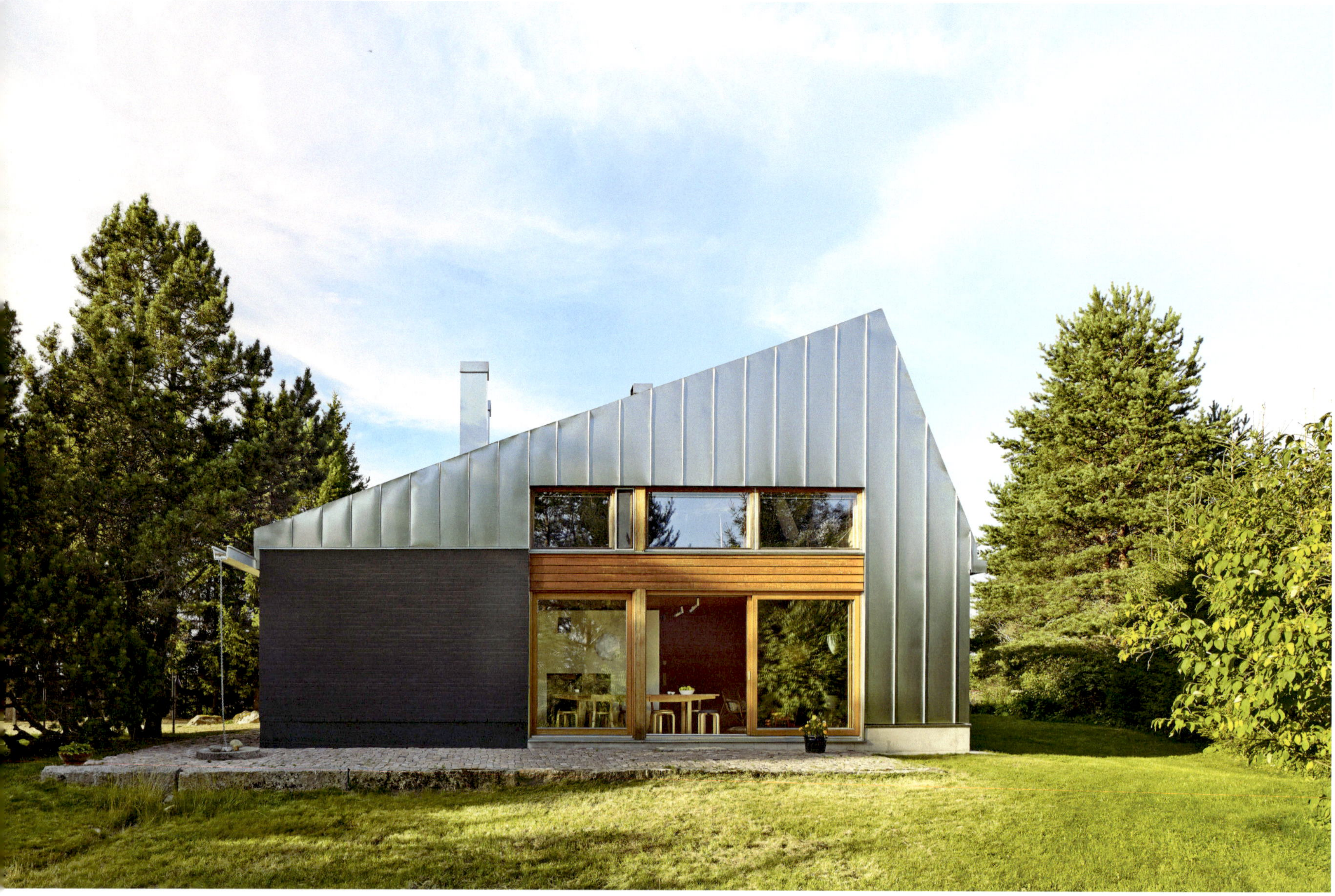

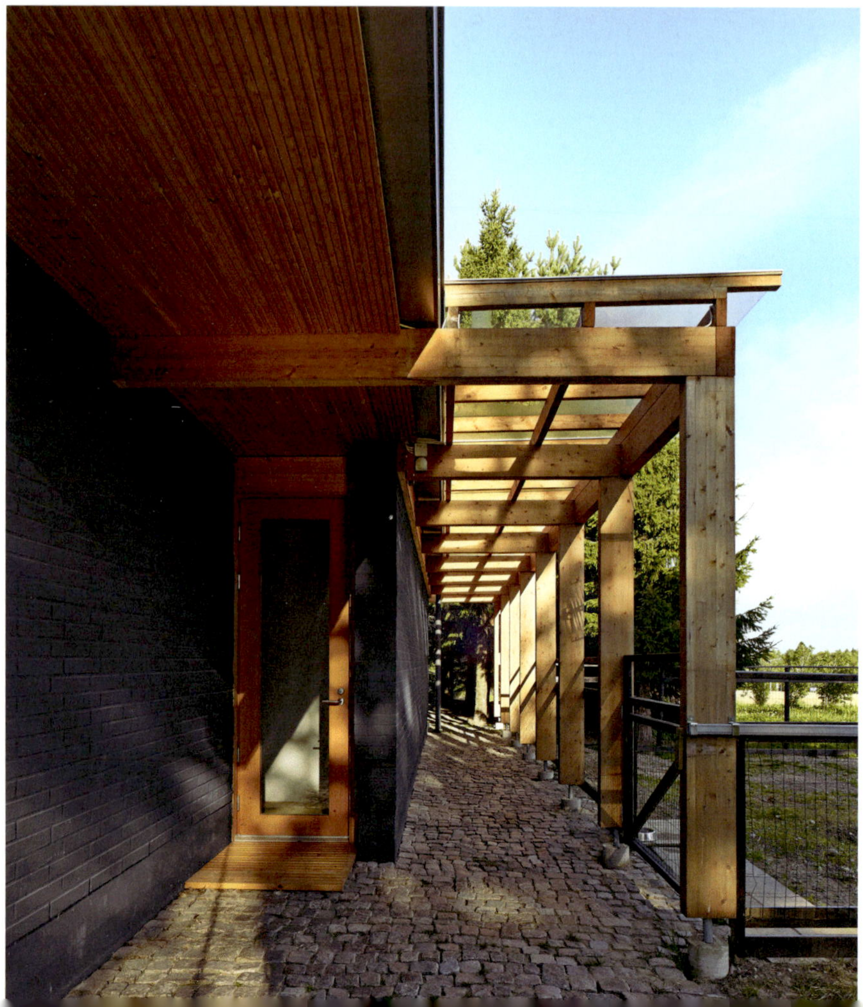

quarters, but it is also a favorite spot for Lassila's son, who uses it as his play area. There is no doubt that House L's robust zinc exterior and Lassila's attention to detail will preserve the house for many generations to come. ◆

"THE ZINC SHELL IS NOT ONLY DURABLE, IT ALSO REFLECTS SUNLIGHT AND THE SURROUNDING GREENERY, CLOTHING THE HOUSE IN A VIBRANT MIRROR OF ITS WOODLAND SETTING."

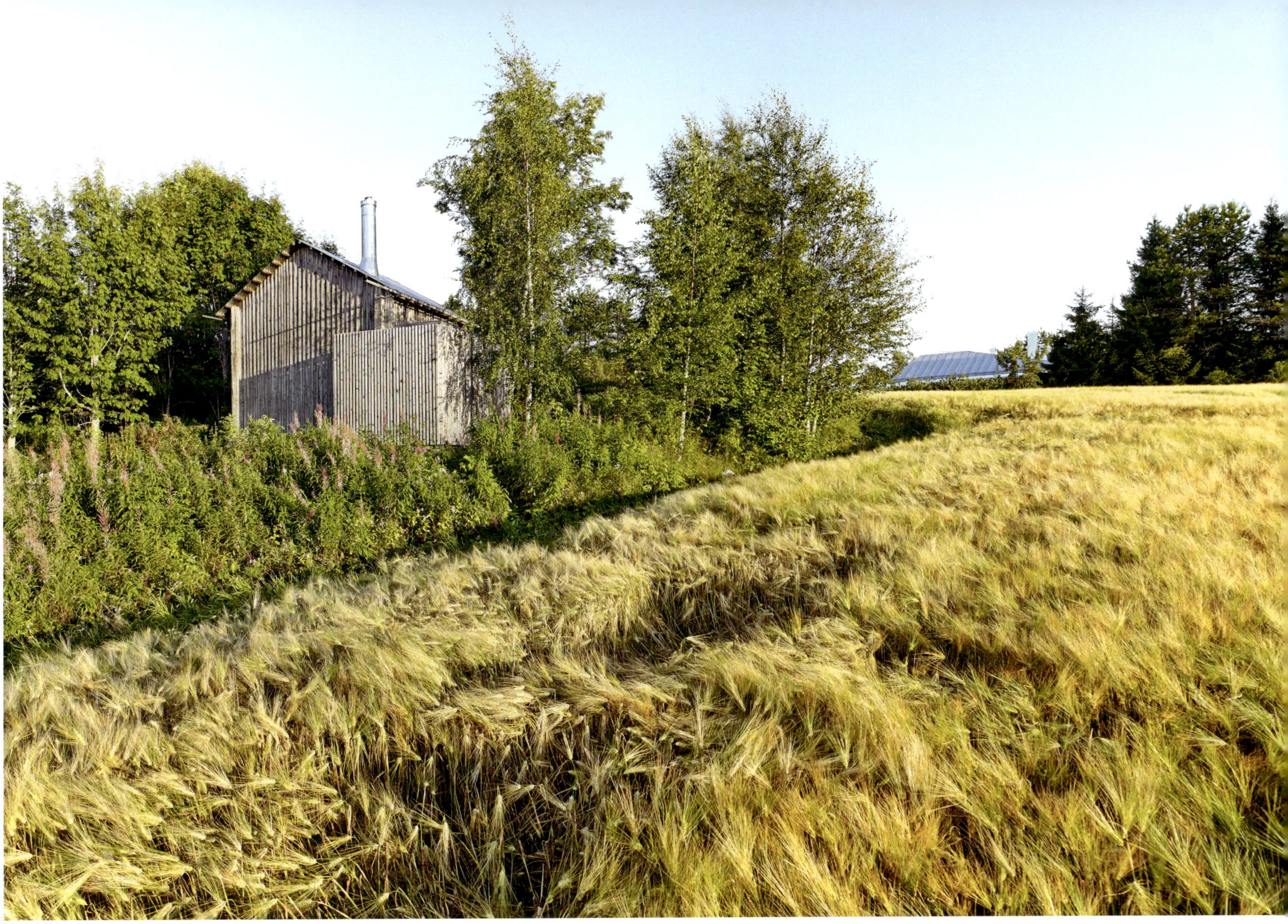

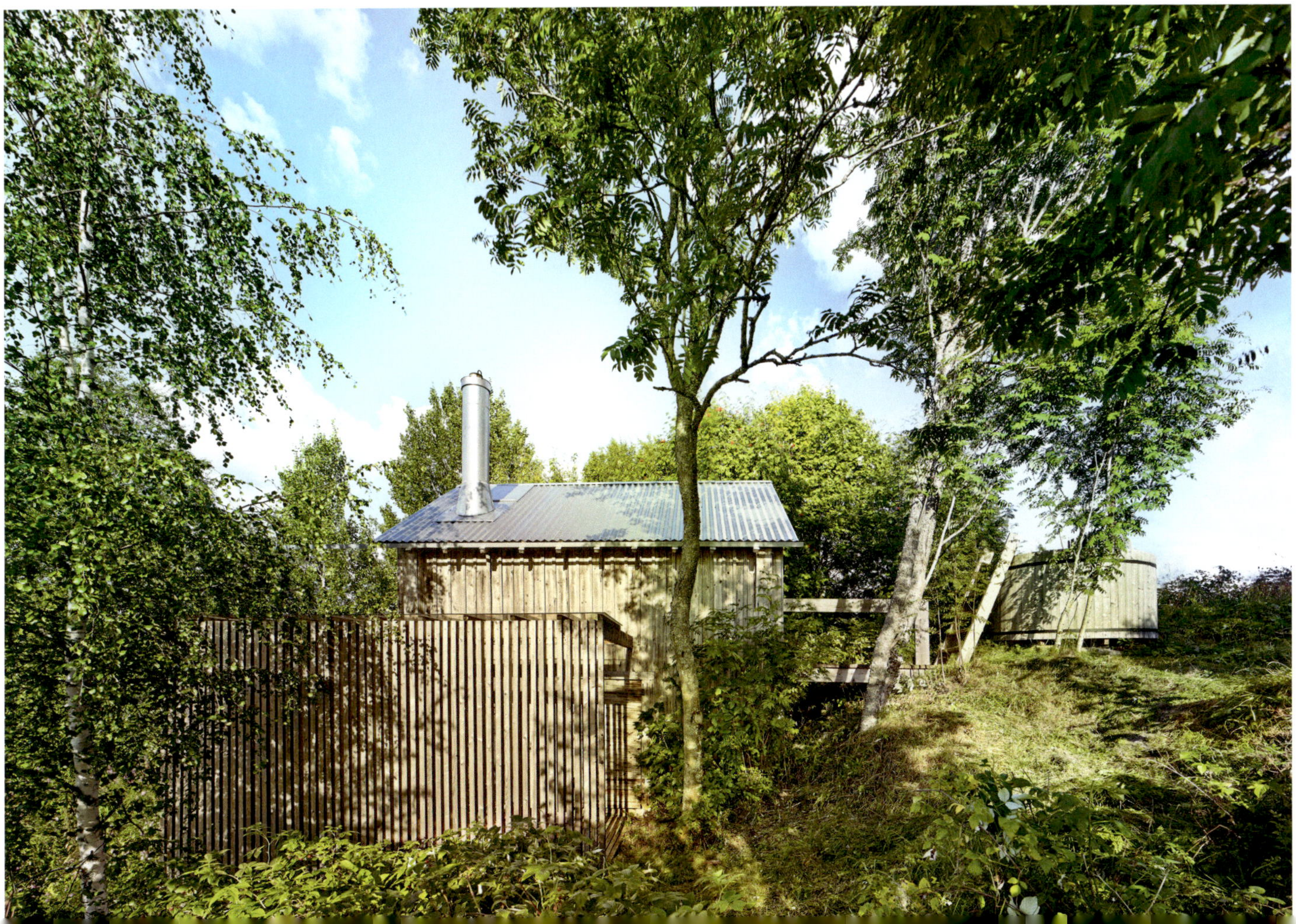

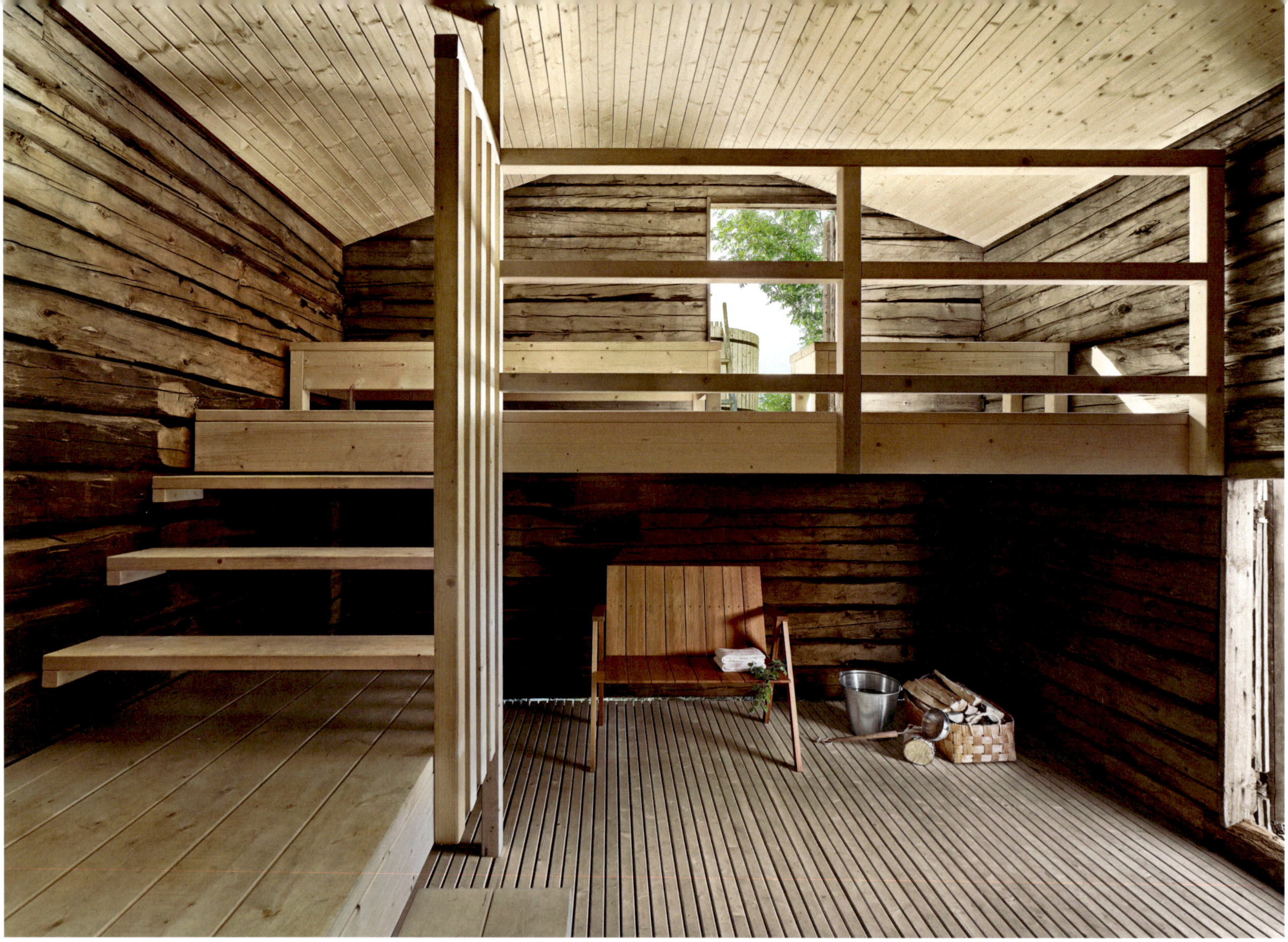

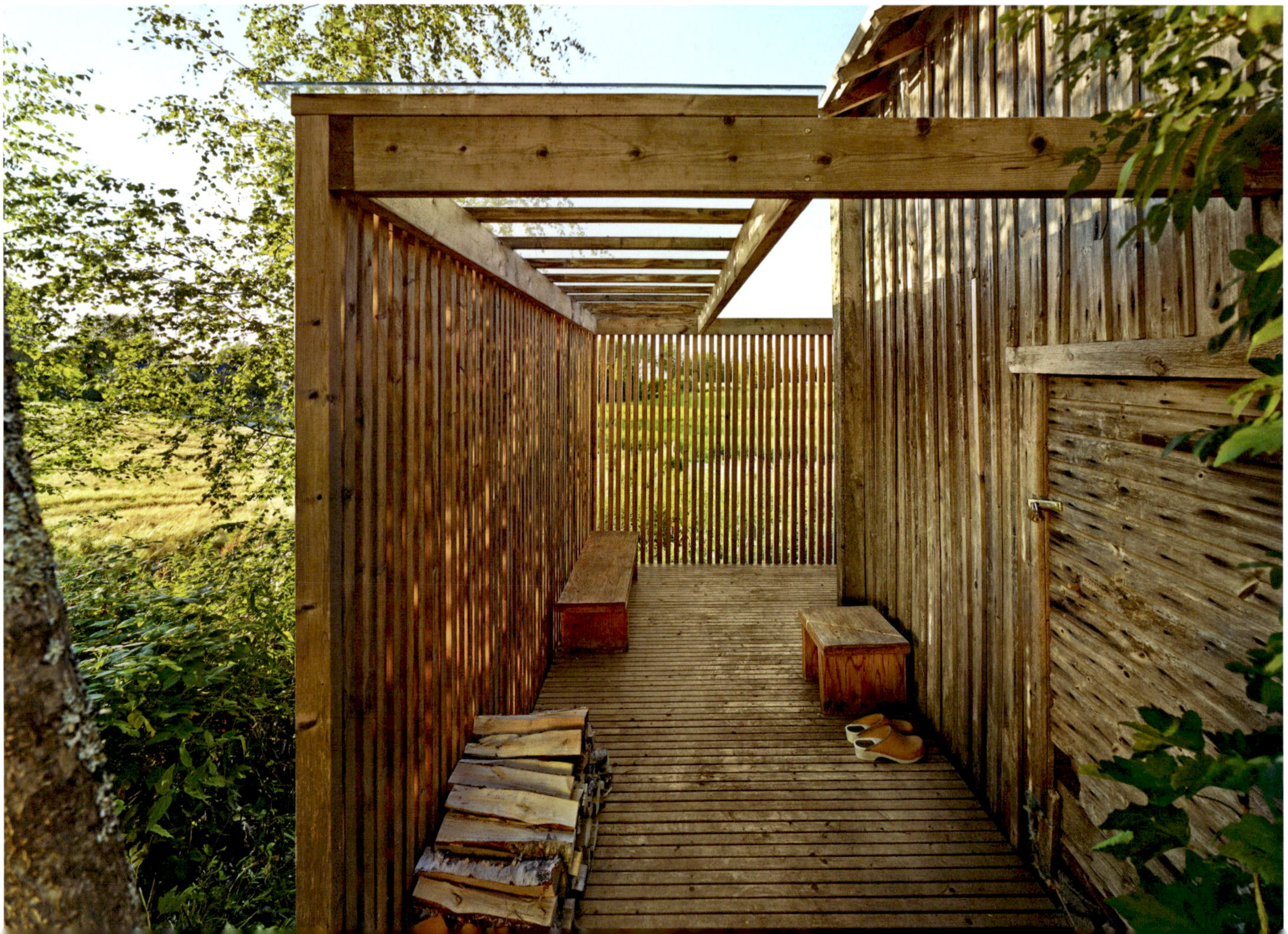

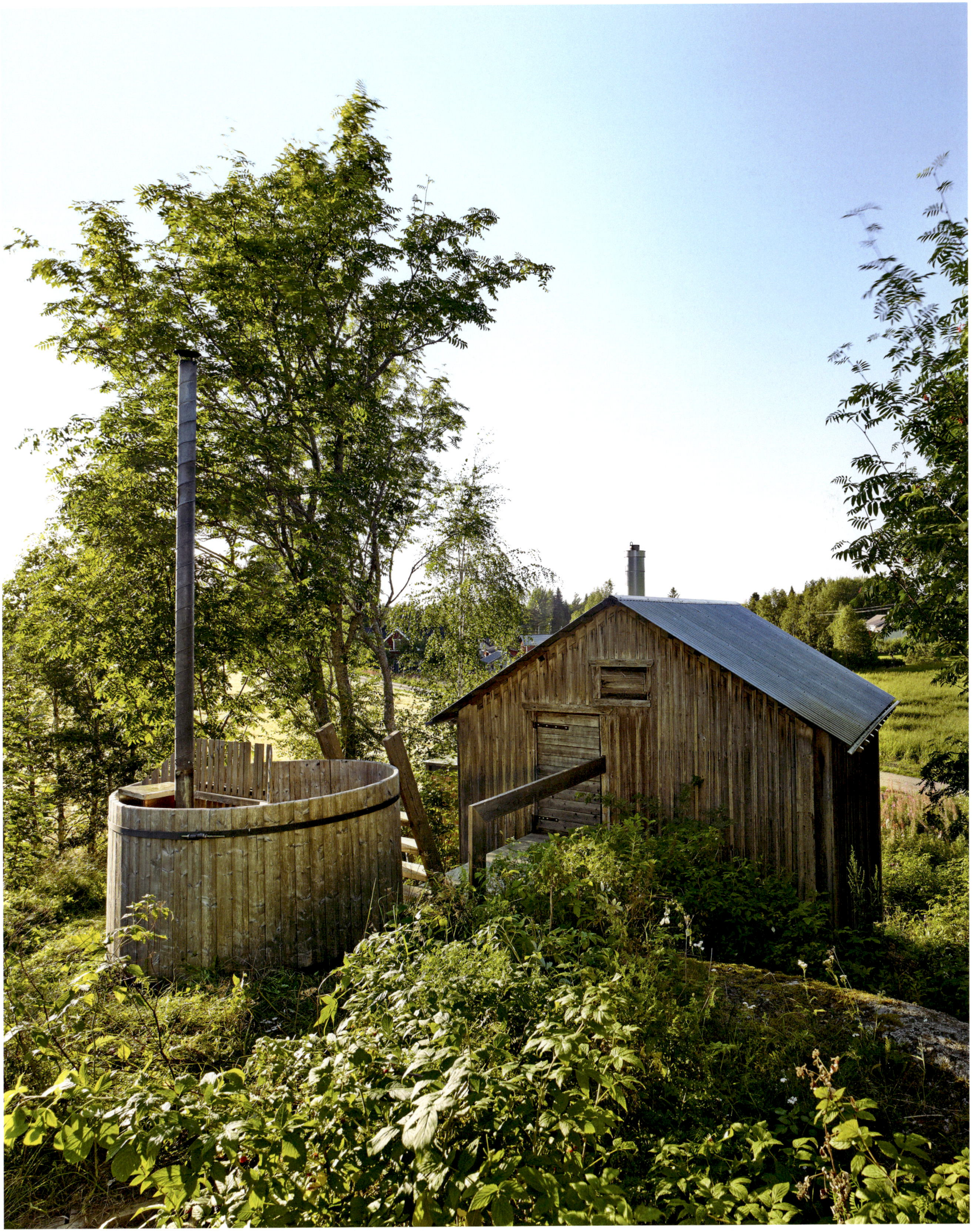

SANT VICENÇ DE MONTALT, SPAIN

CASA DEL LABERINTO

OSCAR TUSQUETS BLANCA

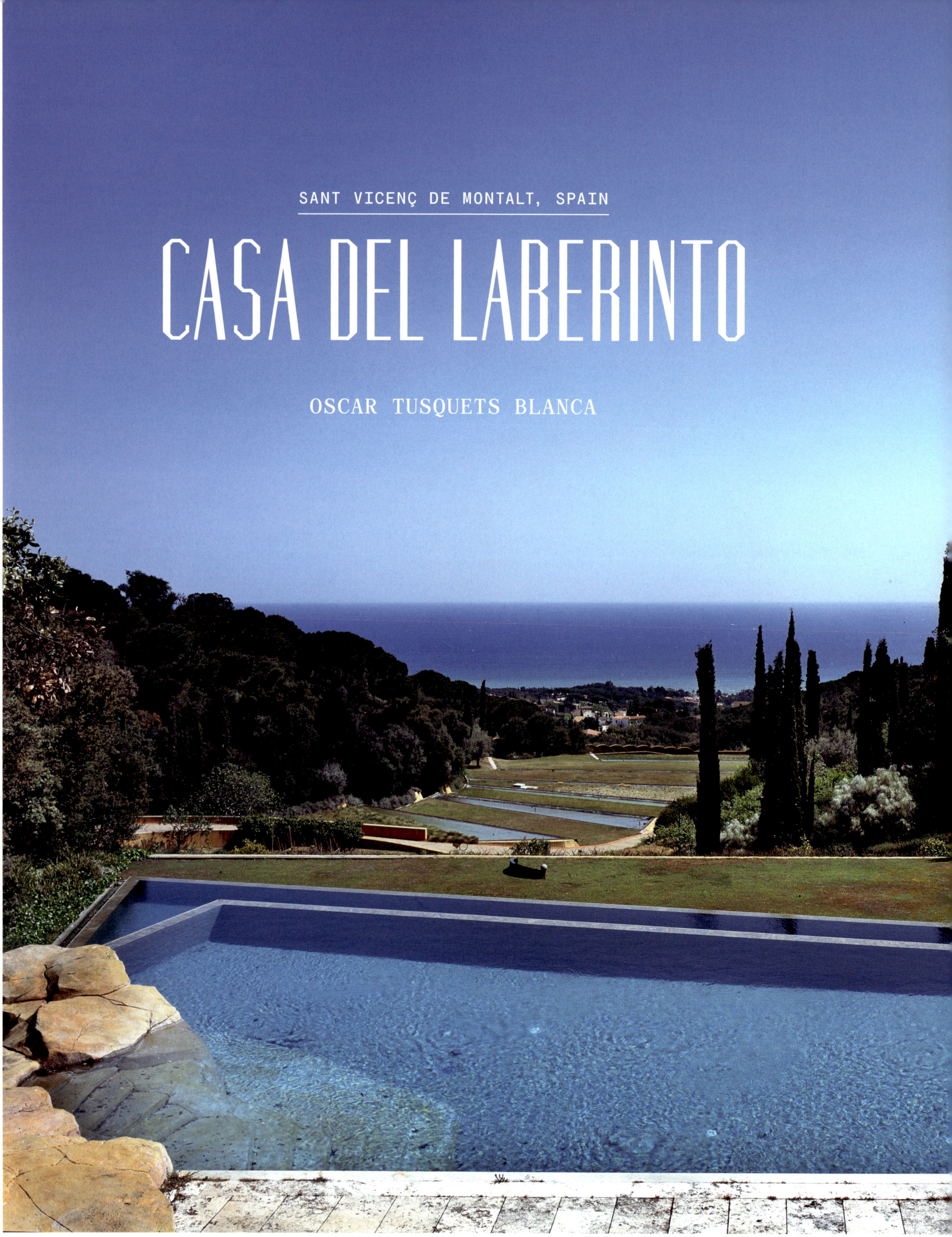

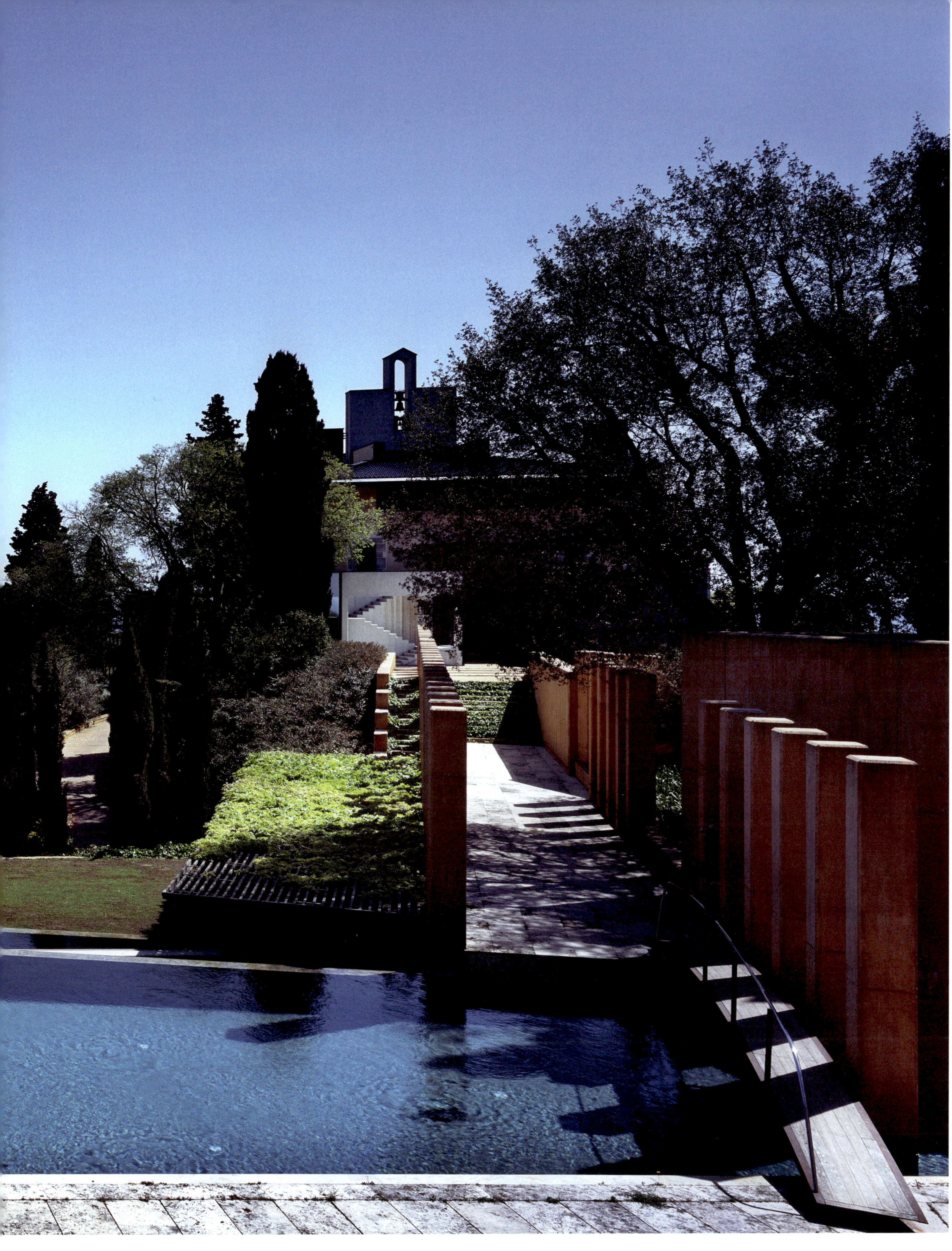

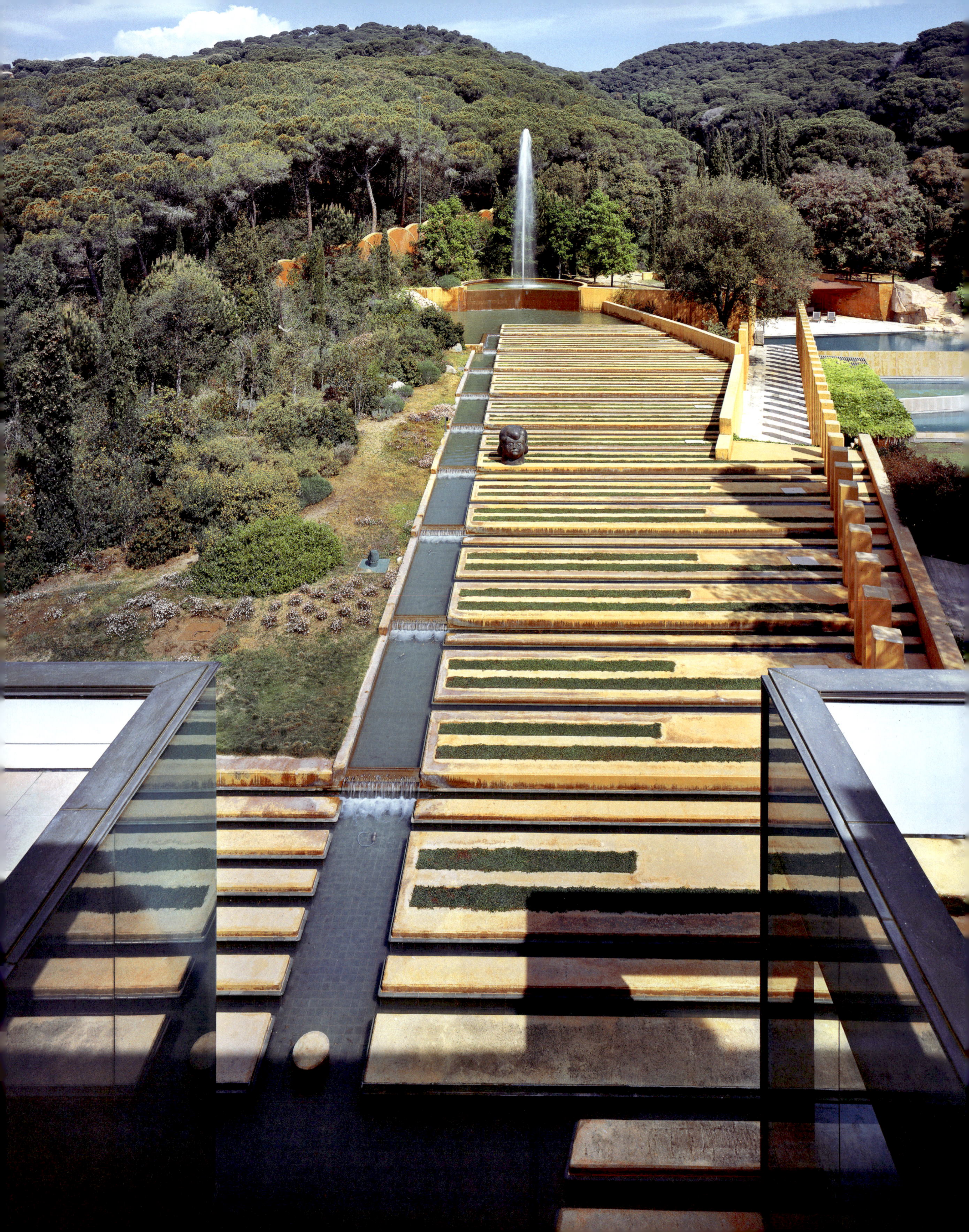

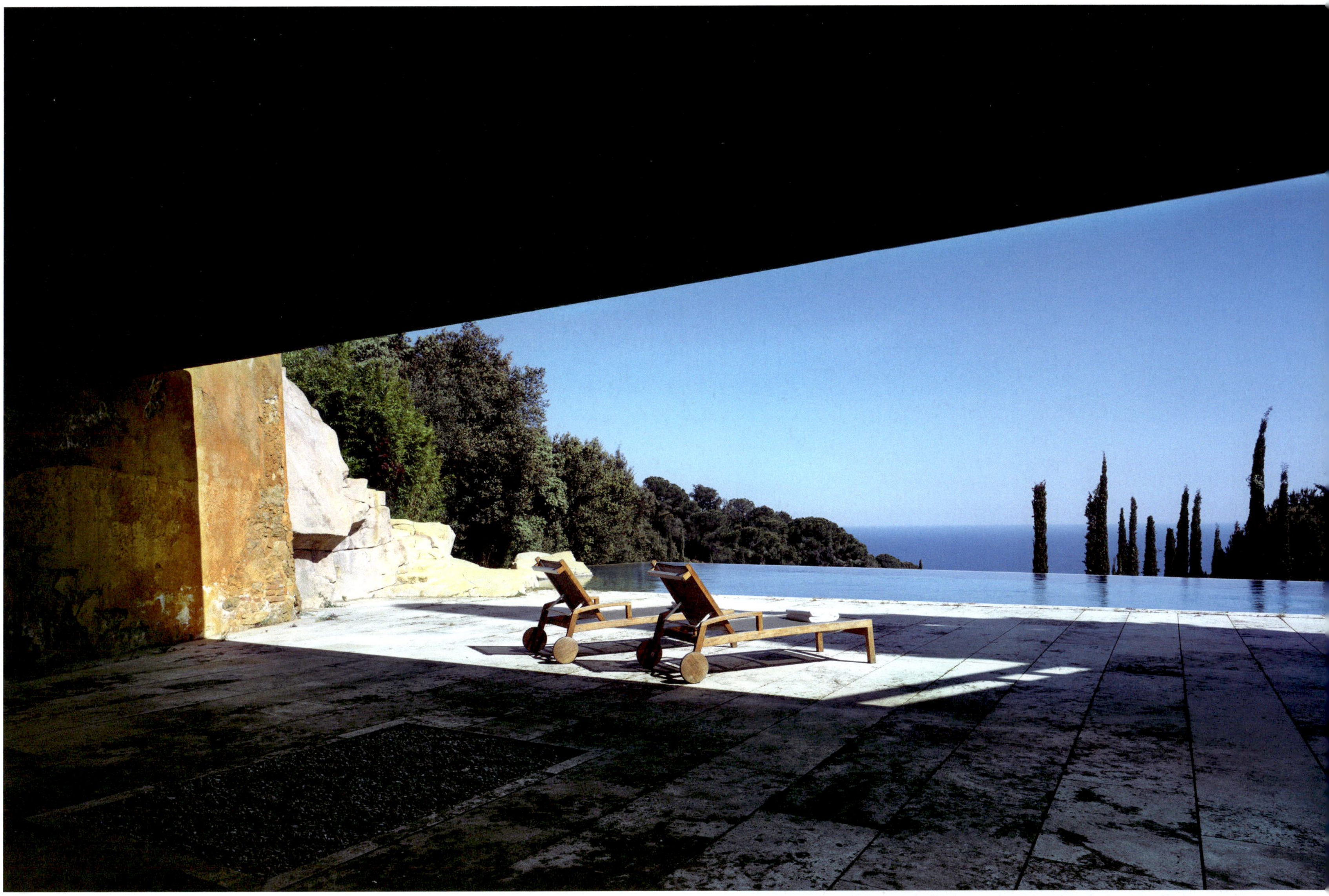

CASA DEL LABERINTO Old structures present problems as well as possibilities for renovation and renewal. In working with the original form, architect Oscar Tusquets has revealed the timeless quality of the earlier building while at the same time adding modern elements that shift the architectural terrain to the 21st century.

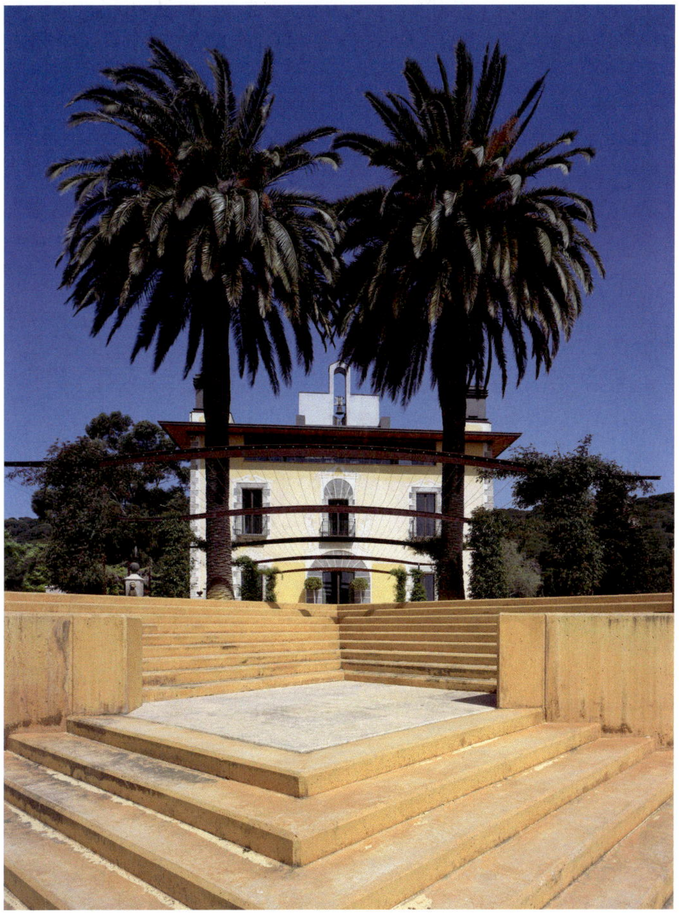

Located north of Barcelona, Casa del Laberinto crowns an expansive 22-hectare site in the Maresme region. The labyrinth in its name is partly a reference to the classic hedge maze that constrains one side of the property, but the sense of wonder and bafflement does not end there.

The project began somewhere between the renovation and restoration of a house that was over 400 years old. The architect, Oscar Tusquets Blanca, followed the original shape of the building, gently simplifying the southern face with what he calls "rounded geometry."

On the northern side, Tusquets stripped away a dull exterior and replaced it with two cubes made of ~

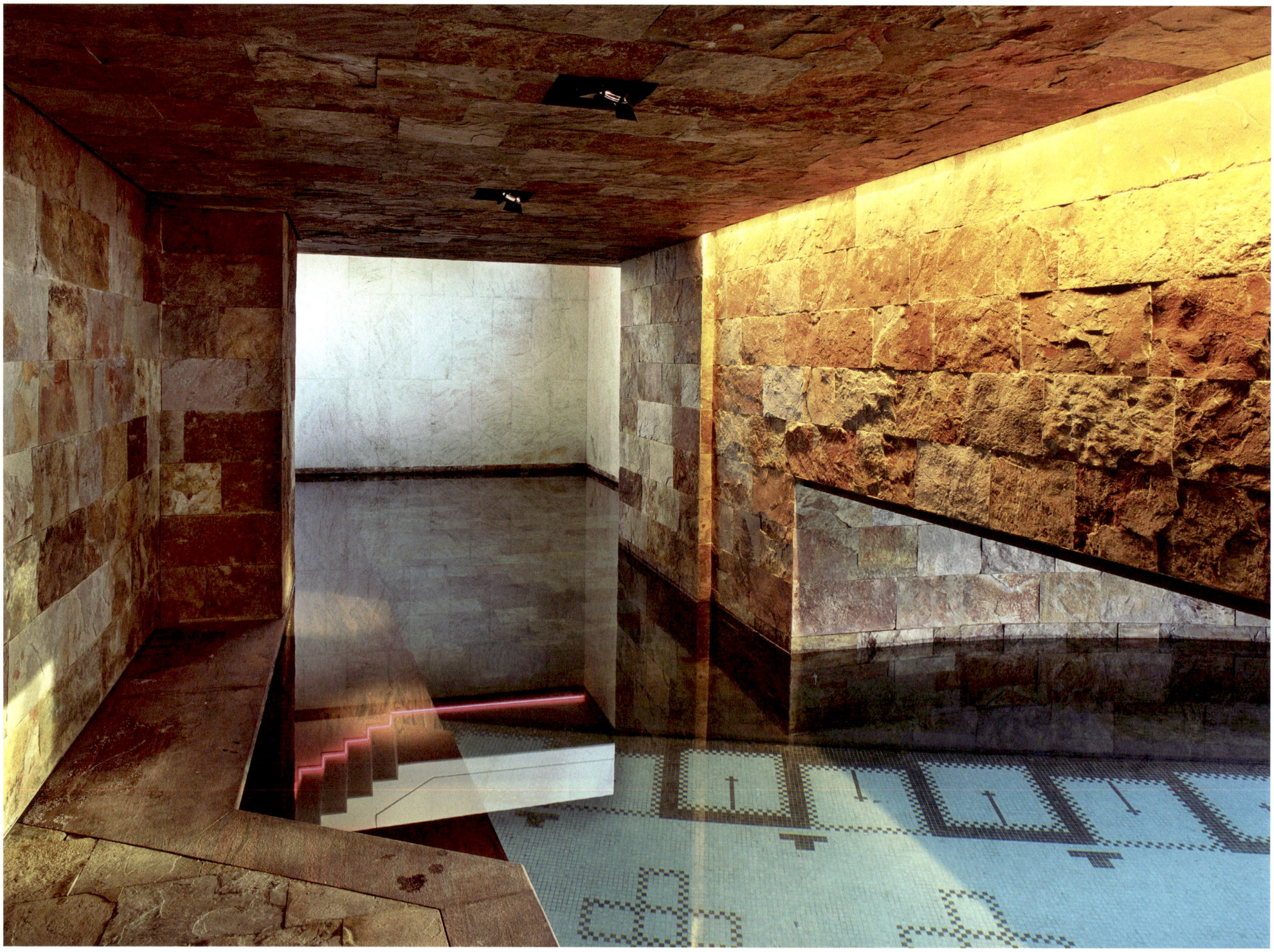

concrete and glass separated by a central corridor. One of the boxes is a dining room with a wraparound window affording picturesque views of the garden. The other is a creatively lit external staircase.

In addition to the challenges these astute modern adjustments posed, Tusquets had to overcome the darkness that gripped the central space. He designed a reflective

"OSCAR TUSQUETS BLANCA AIMED TO REVEAL AND REINFORCE ASPECTS OF THE ARCHAIC APPEAL BY FOLLOWING THE ORIGINAL LINES AND SHAPES OF THE BUILDING."

internal waterway that runs throughout the length of the ground floor. He also removed some of the older rooms that were too narrow and redirected the light to shine on a stone wall that was part of the original foundation.

Overall, the project has maintained the historical integrity of the ancient house while adding interesting modifications, primarily through its creative use of light. ◆

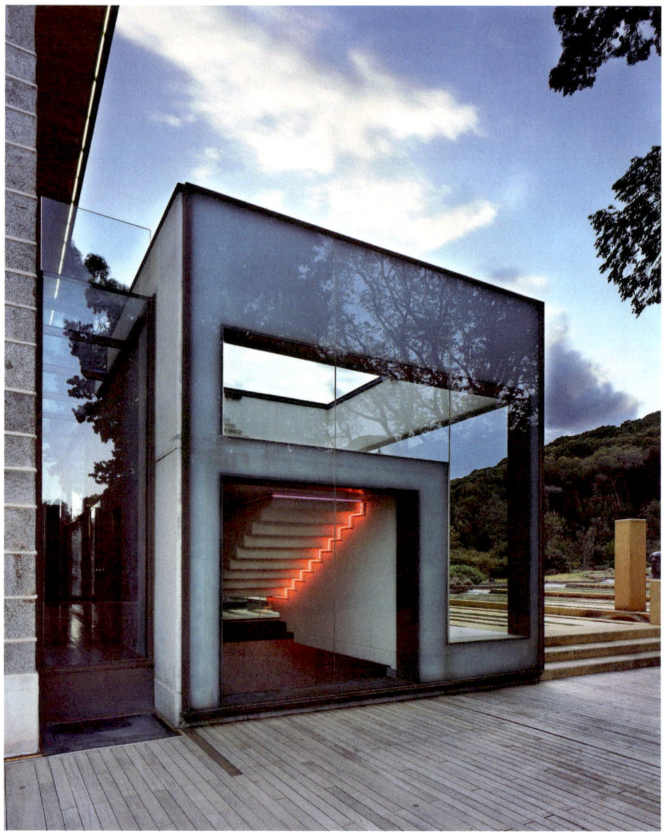

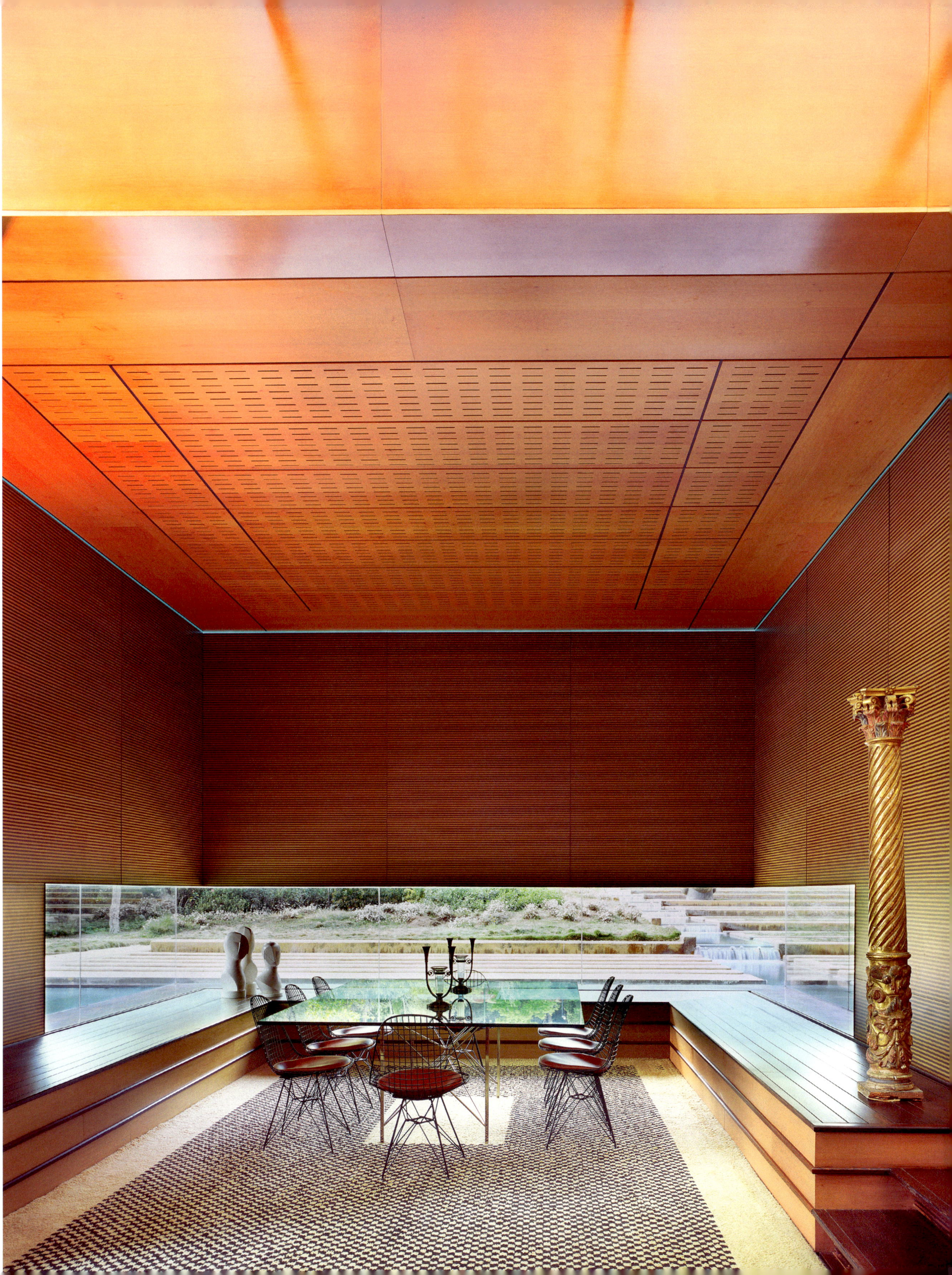

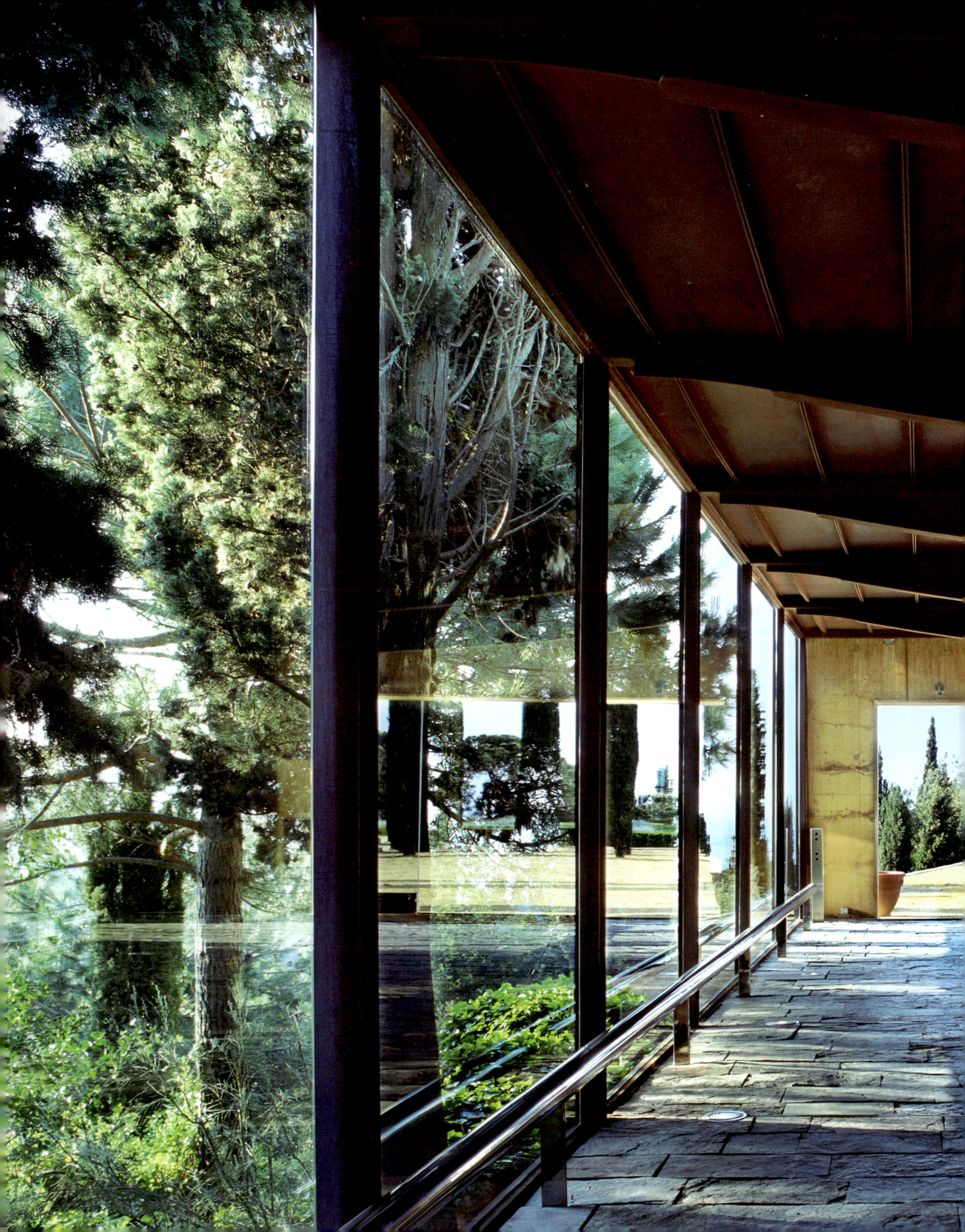

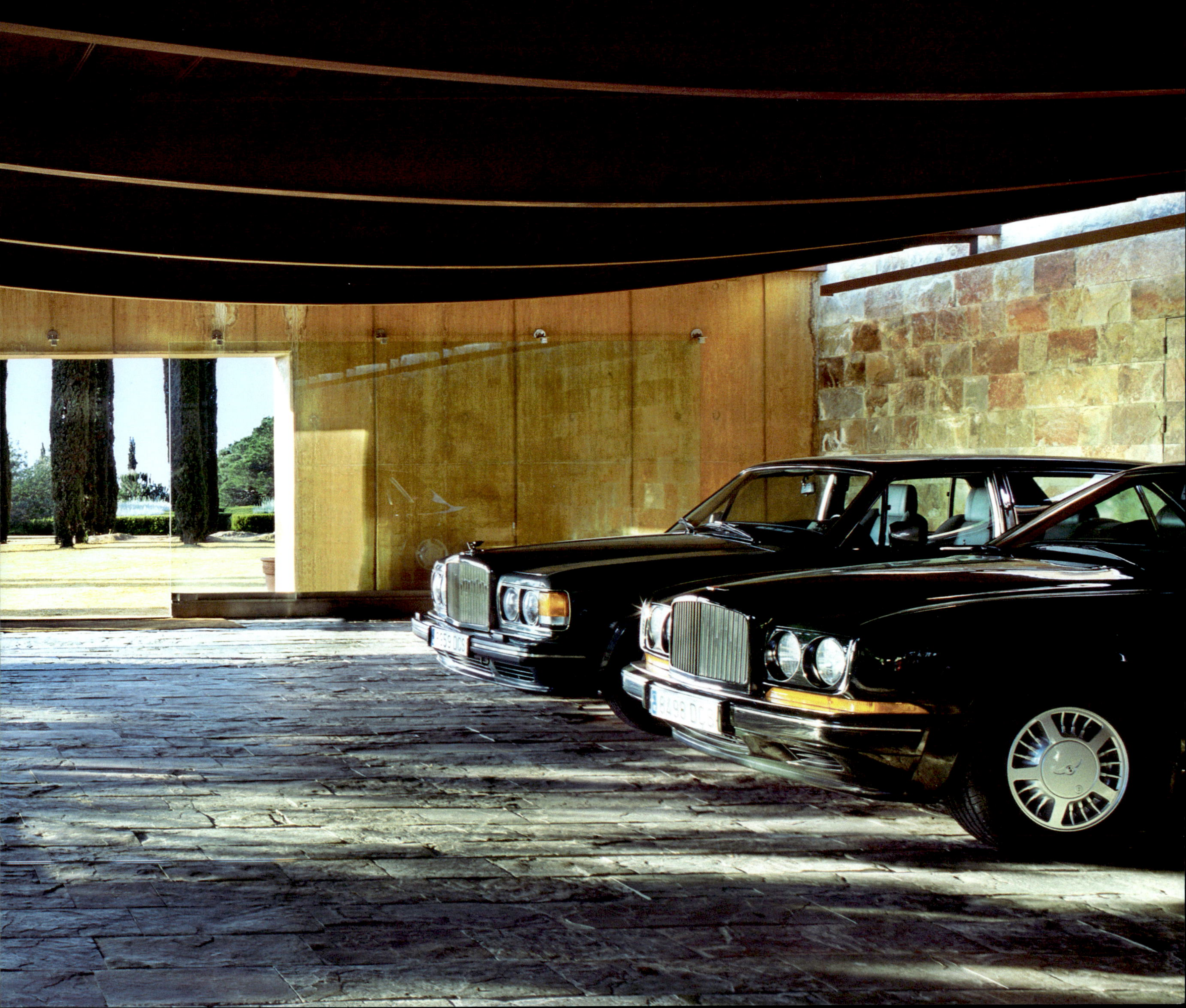

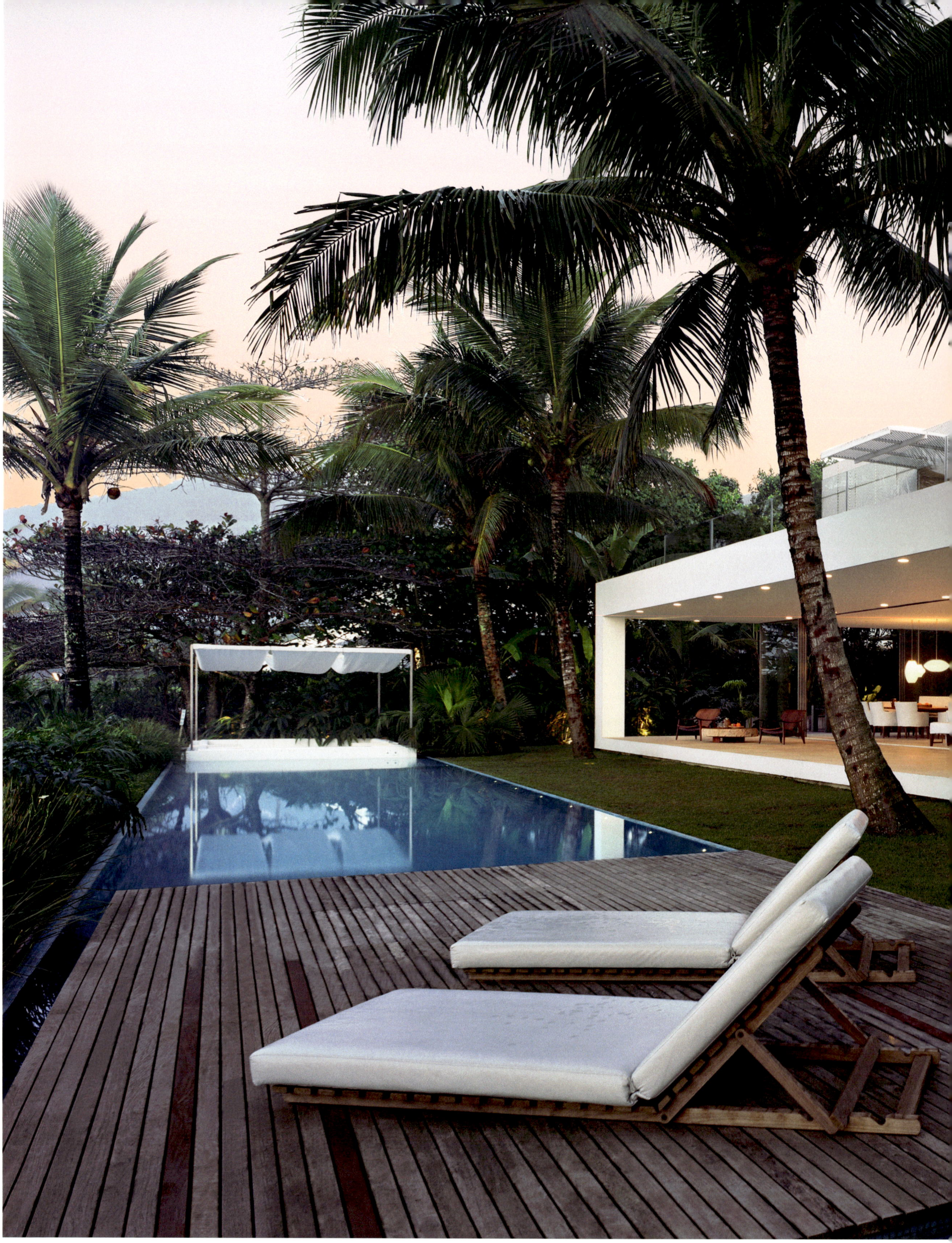

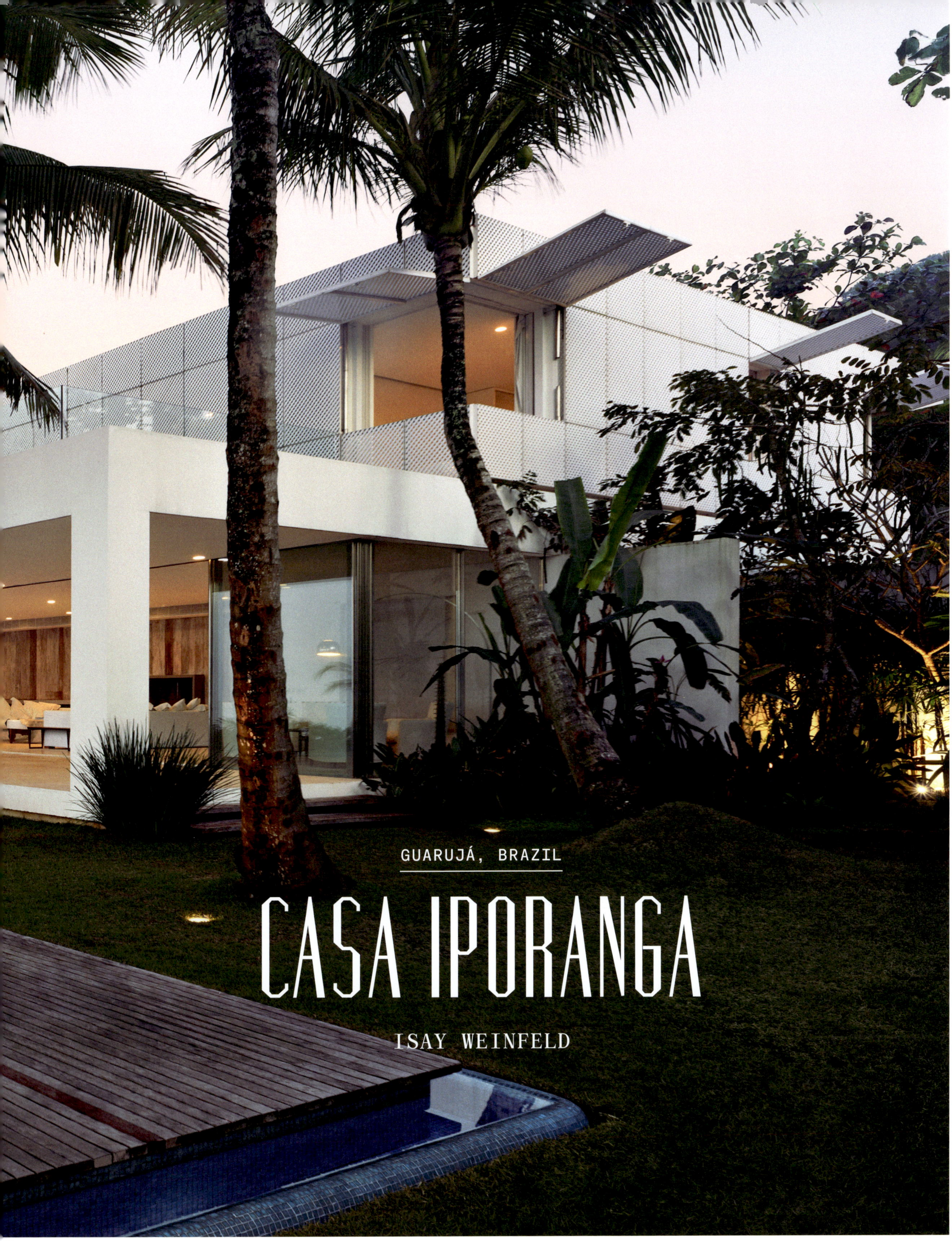

GUARUJÁ, BRAZIL

CASA IPORANGA

ISAY WEINFELD

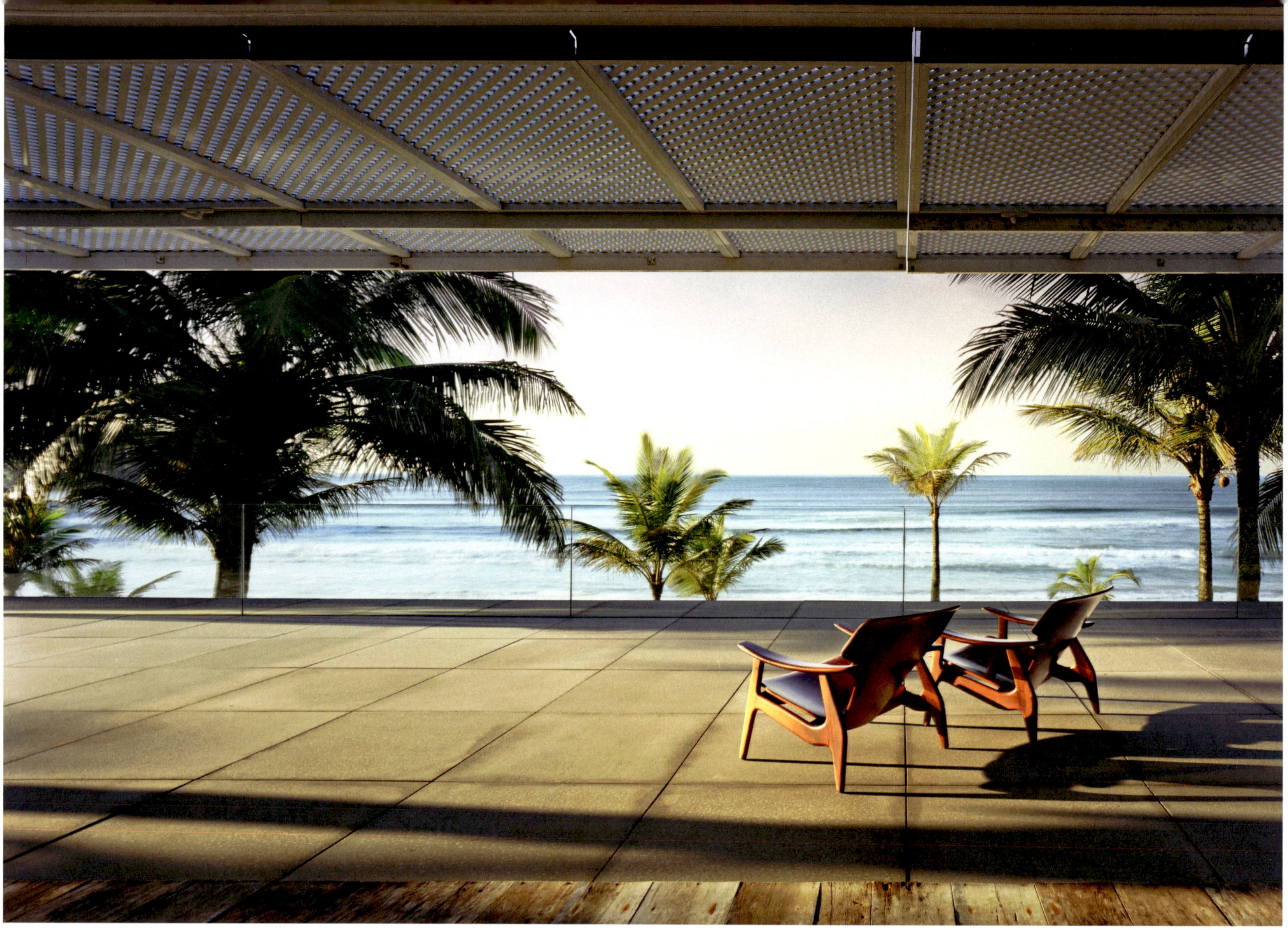

CASA IPORANGA The Brazilian architect Isay Weinfeld constantly finds new ways to modify his characteristic rectilinear forms. For Casa Iporanga, he incorporated his client's identity into the build via the latticework on the first level. These mashrabiya-like screens are a tribute to the owner's Syrian heritage.

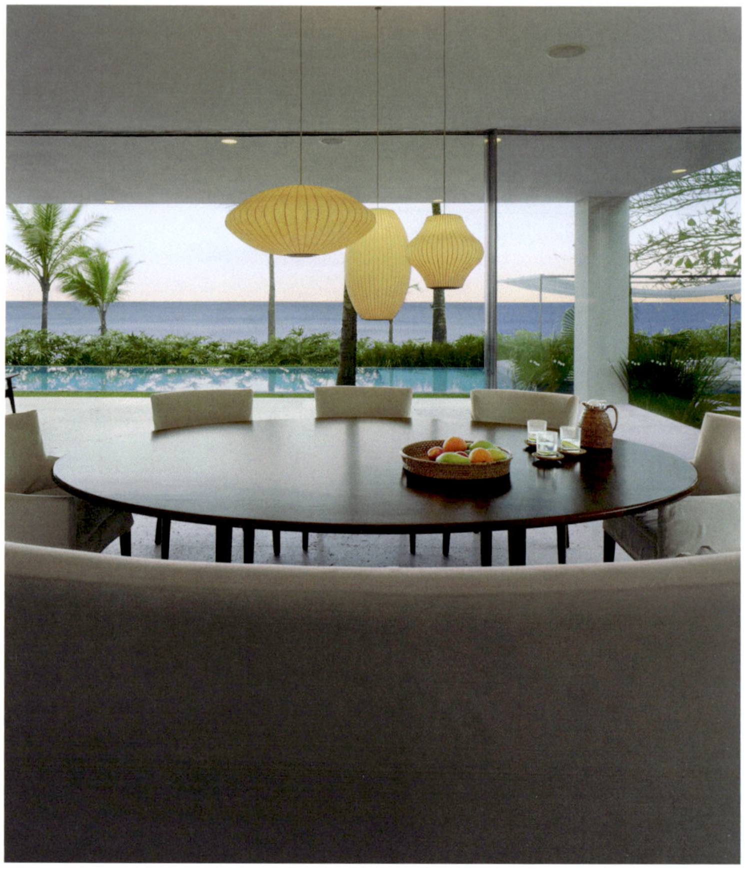

Casa Iporanga is the third project that the homeowners have commissioned from the award-winning Brazilian architect Isay Weinfeld. This time, Weinfeld set to work outside the humming cosmopolitan hotbeds of New York and São Paulo—the locations of their two prior collaborations—turning instead to the Brazilian beach town of Guarujá, a place known for its chic houses and natural beauty.

The relationship between Weinfeld and the family is one based on trust and mutual enjoyment. The family says, "We chose to work with Isay because he loves what he does and does it with such passion and soul. You learn and enjoy the process with him. If possible we'd ⌁

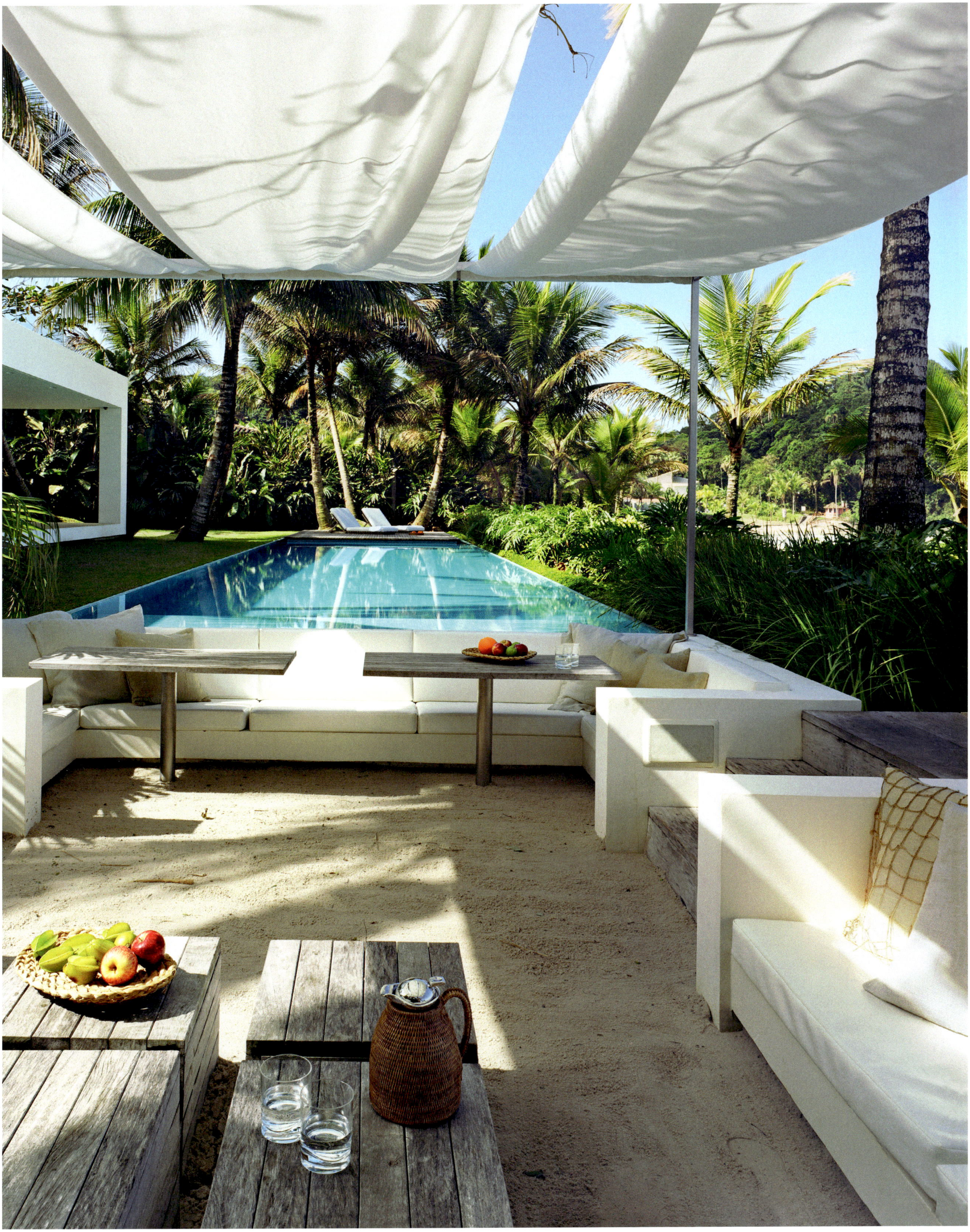

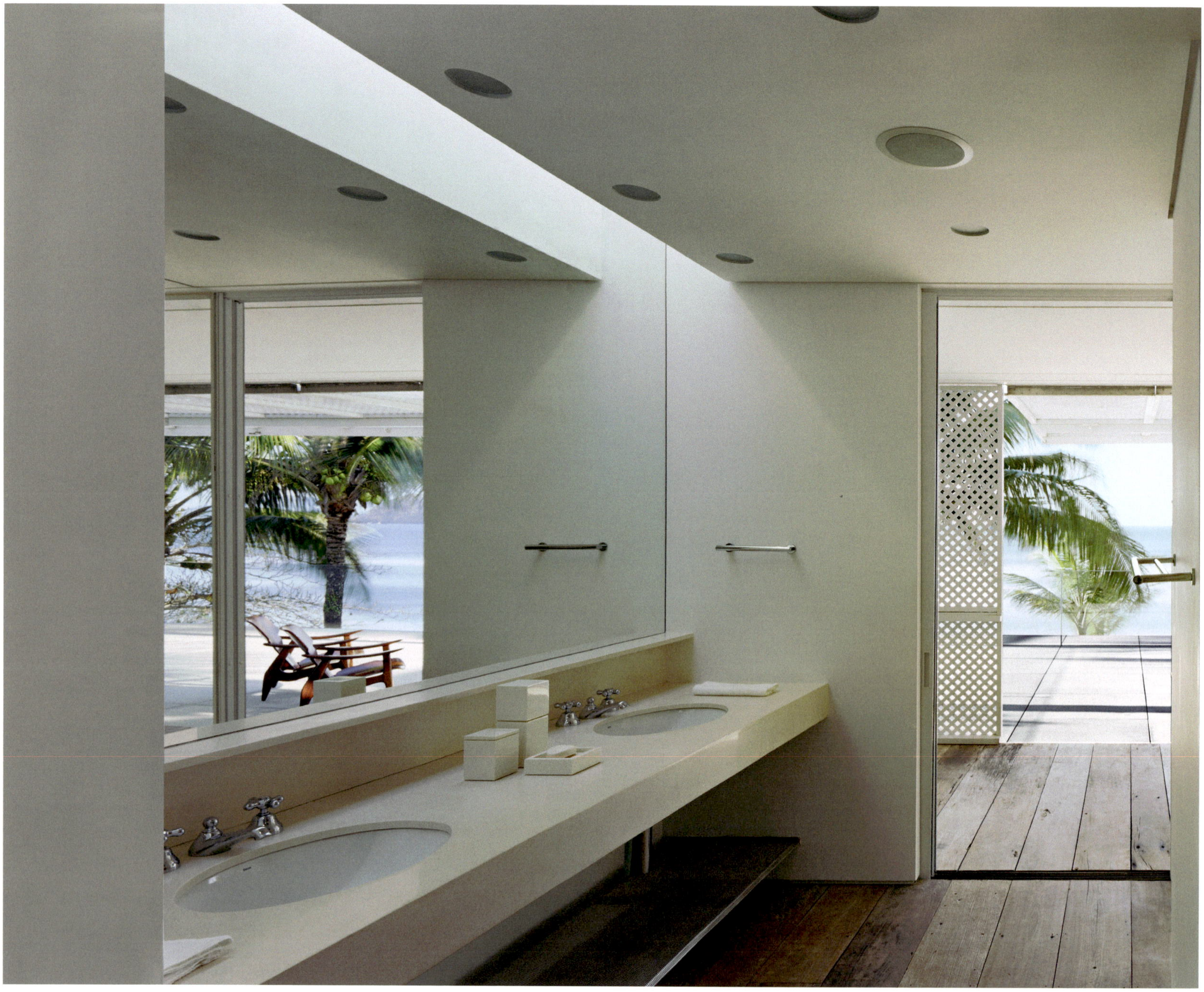

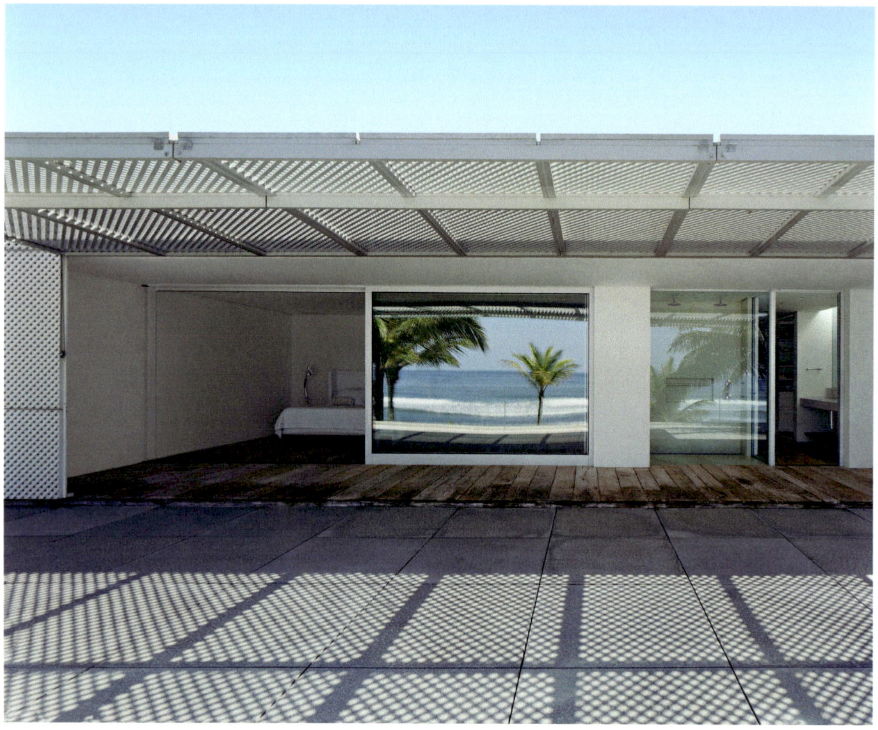

keep building houses and apartments just to spend more time with him." Such honest enjoyment can be glimpsed in Weinfeld's ability to replicate his favored forms—orthogonal, open, and weightless spaces—with seemingly infinite variations.

Speaking of his creative method, Weinfeld says, "When I create residential properties I always try to include some reference to my client's roots, but without compromising my style." In the case of Casa Iporanga, his clients' Syrian heritage is most visibly manifested by the building's mashrabiya-style façade. The aluminum screen cloaks the upper story of the house, allowing only slivers of light through to pattern the walls of the master bedroom and en-suite bathroom. The play of light continues when the mashrabiya is opened, clearing the view to the ocean while casting a crisscross shadow onto the spacious upper deck.

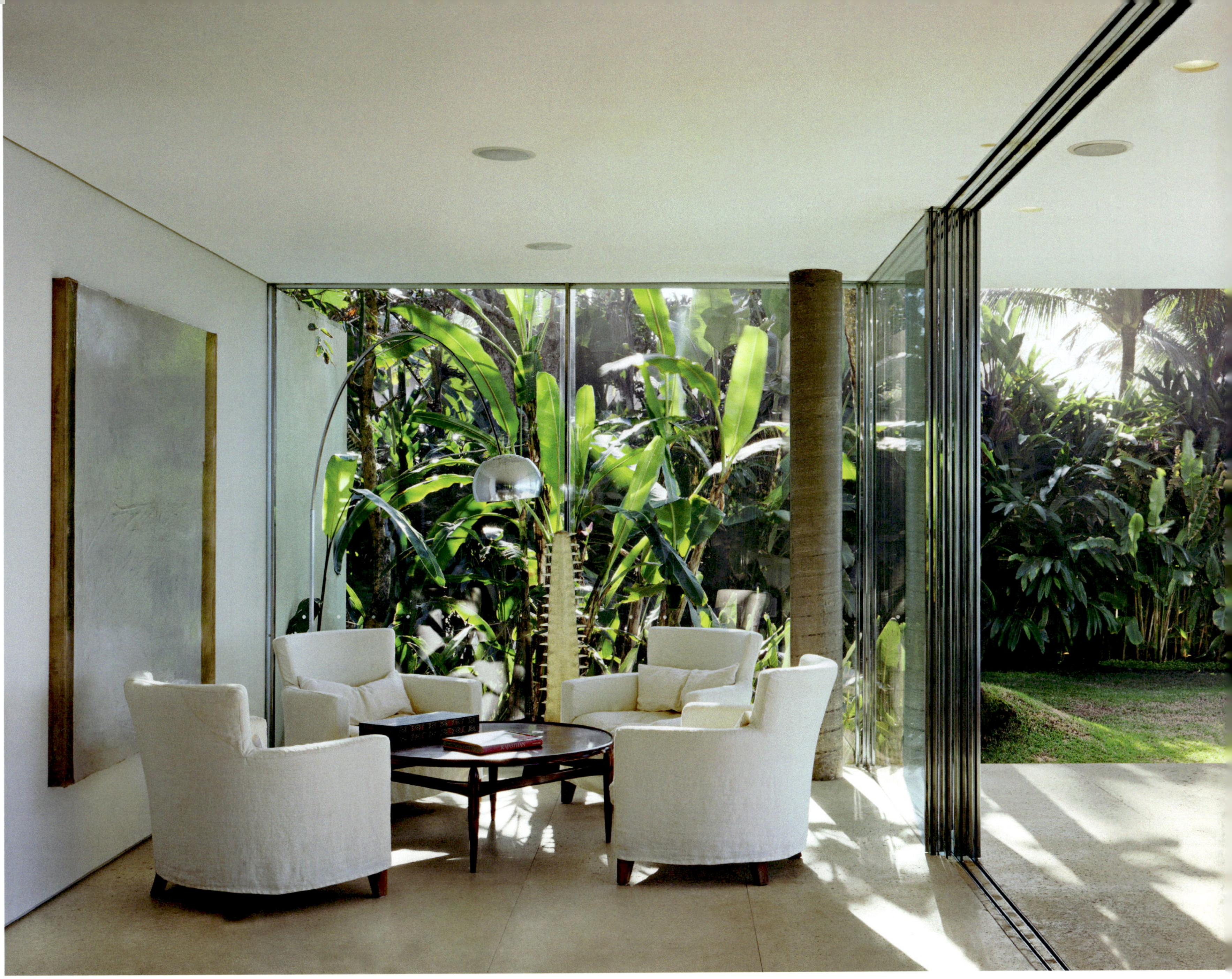

"THE ALUMINUM SCREEN CLOAKS THE UPPER STORY OF THE HOUSE, ALLOWING ONLY SLIVERS OF LIGHT THROUGH TO PATTERN THE WALLS OF THE MASTER BEDROOM AND EN-SUITE BATHROOM."

The ground floor is completely open. The full-height glass face can be discretely drawn away, removing all barriers to the pool and beach. The family are especially pleased with this feature, saying, "You feel like you're outside and part of the garden and beach." Casa Iporanga seems to be a perfect collaboration that fulfills the wishes of both the architect and the family. ◆

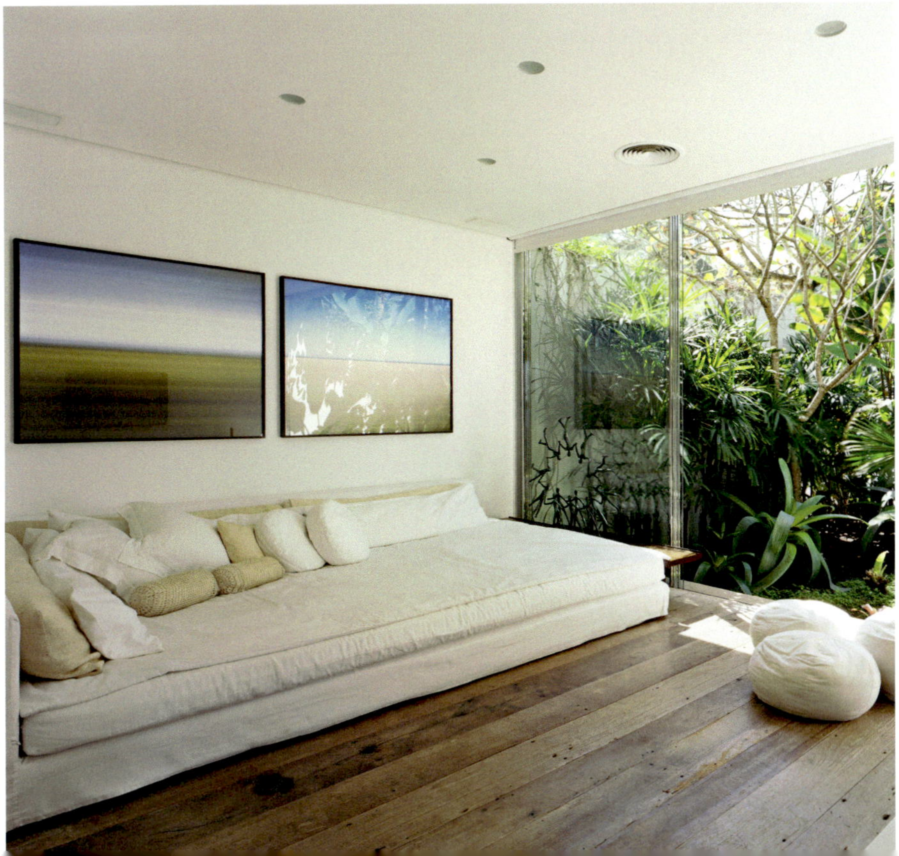

LAHTI, FINLAND

KOTIRANTA

LASSE LEHTINEN
OF ARKKITEHTUURI OY LEHTINEN MIETTUNEN

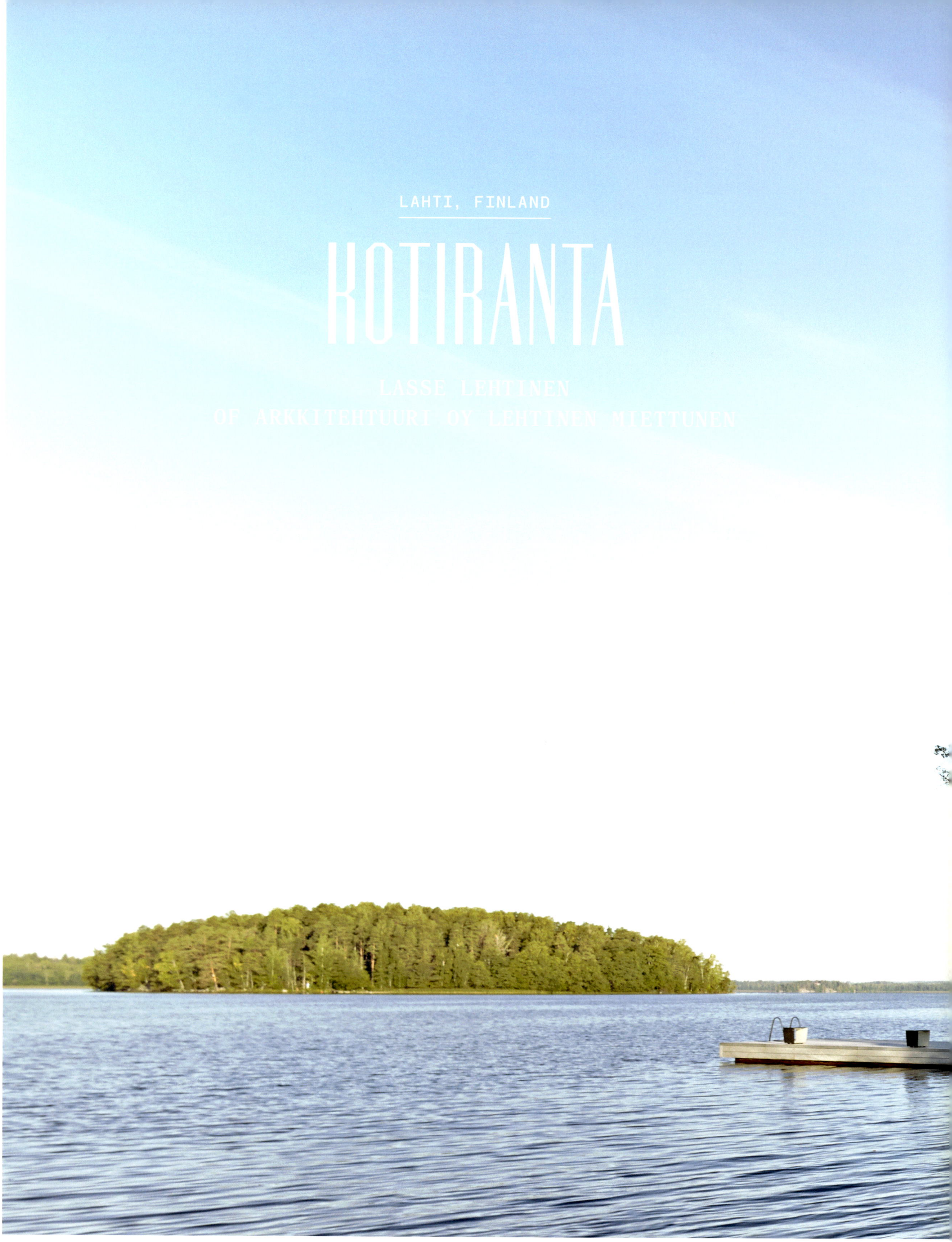

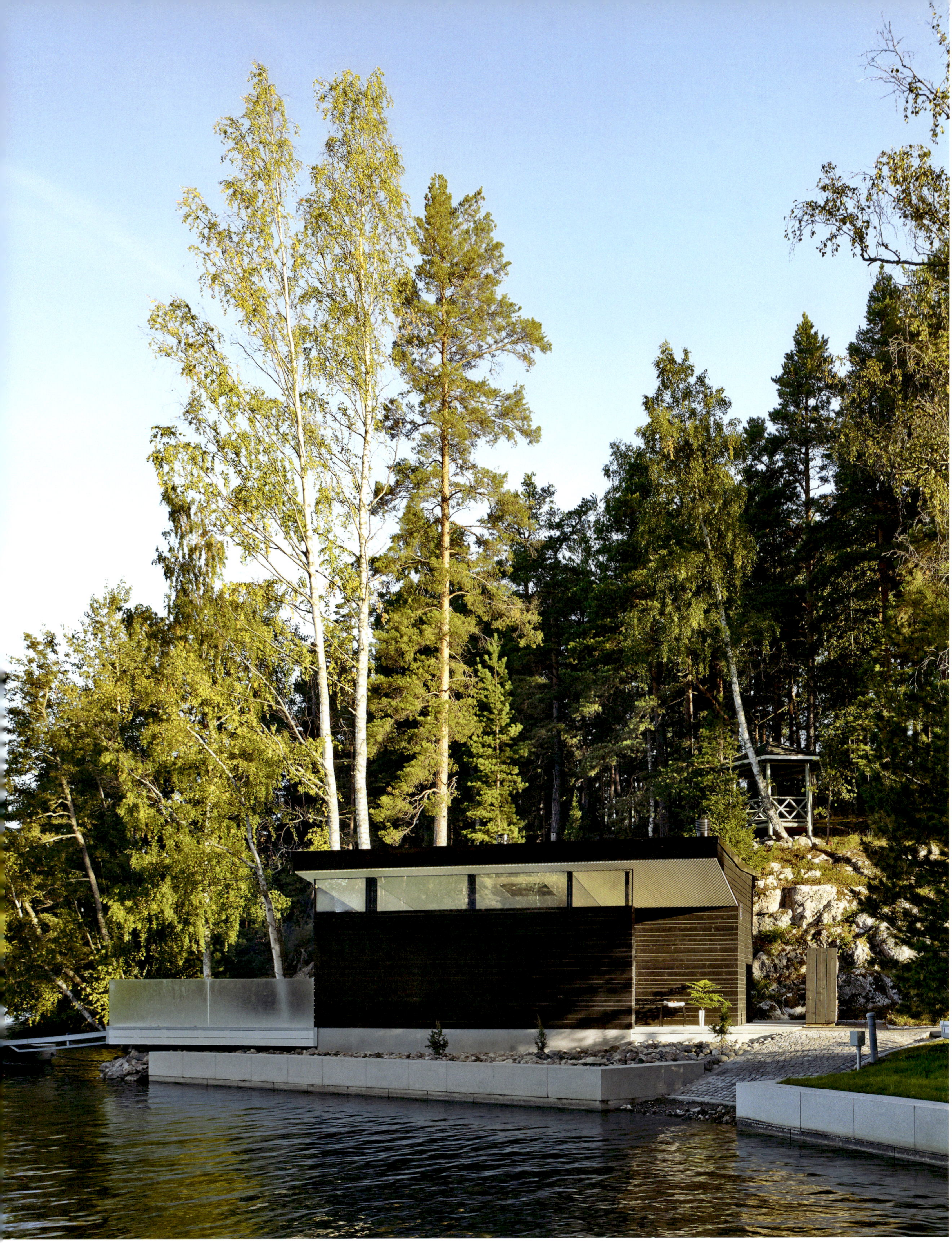

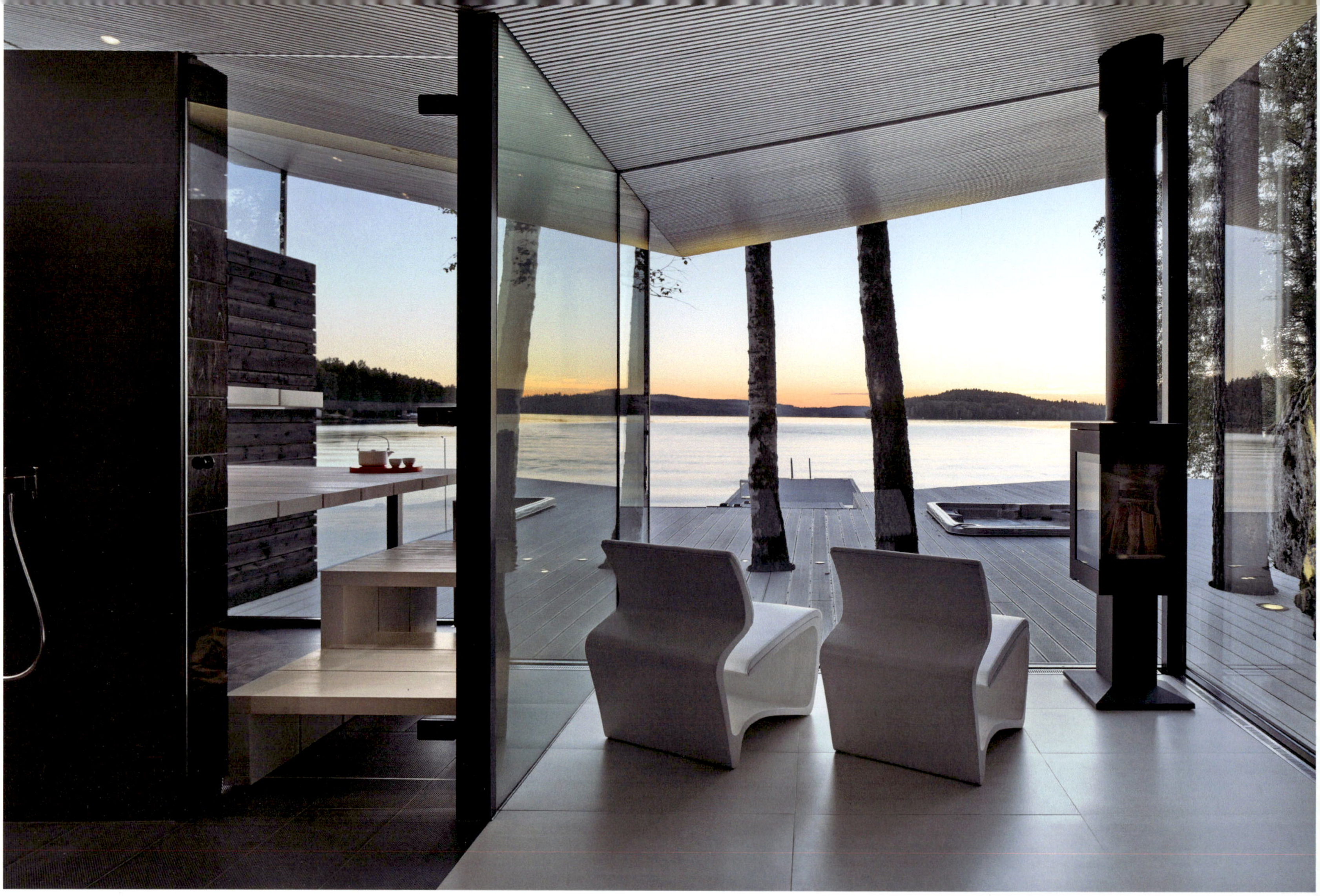

KOTIRANTA As a standalone sauna, Kotiranta condenses Finland's enduring passion for steam in an artful masterstroke. Conceived as a sculpture rather than a construction, it works with the land and the lake, creating a space that not only respects its surroundings, but is also inspired by them.

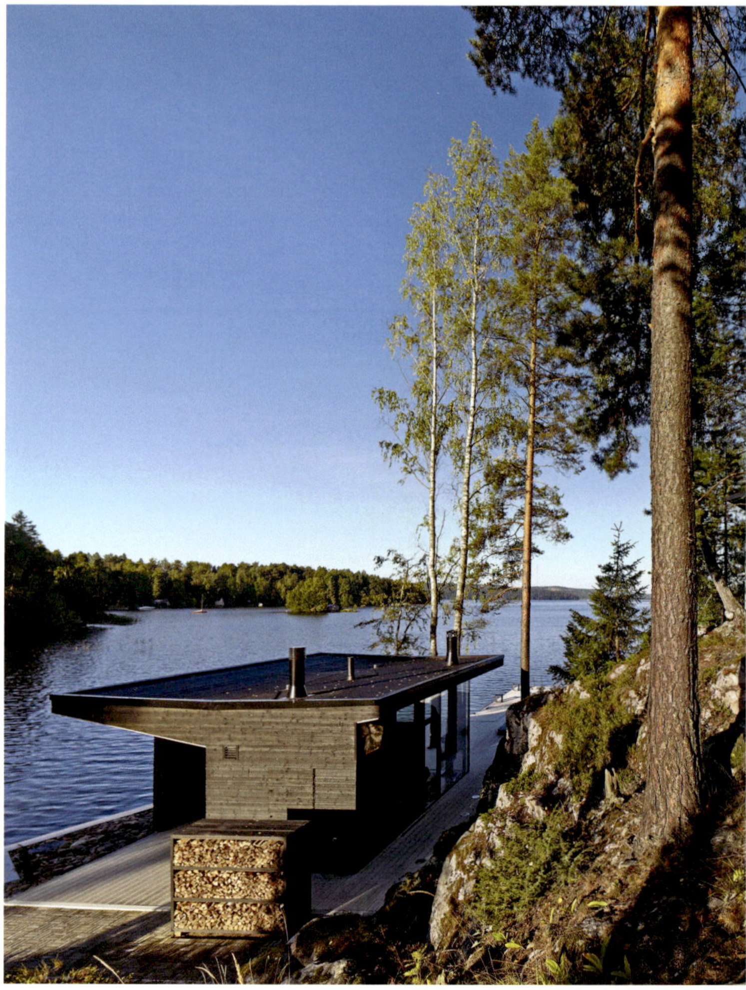

Nearly every Finnish household has a sauna. However, what distinguishes this version is the fact it is only a sauna. Without a house dictating form, architect Lasse Lehtinen of Arkkitehtuuri Oy Lehtinen Miettunen had an ocean or, rather, a lake of possibilities to explore.

Given the site's proximity to the lake and the cliff face, Lehtinen had the perfect opportunity to implement his personal design method, which he describes as weaving an "interface between architecture and nature that is as narrow as possible." Interestingly, he looked at the project not as a construction, but as a malleable work of art: "The sauna has been perceived as a sculpture, not as a traditional house, where the functions of the rooms and the requirements of the environment dictate the design solution." The sculptural aspect is apparent in the incongruity between the ~

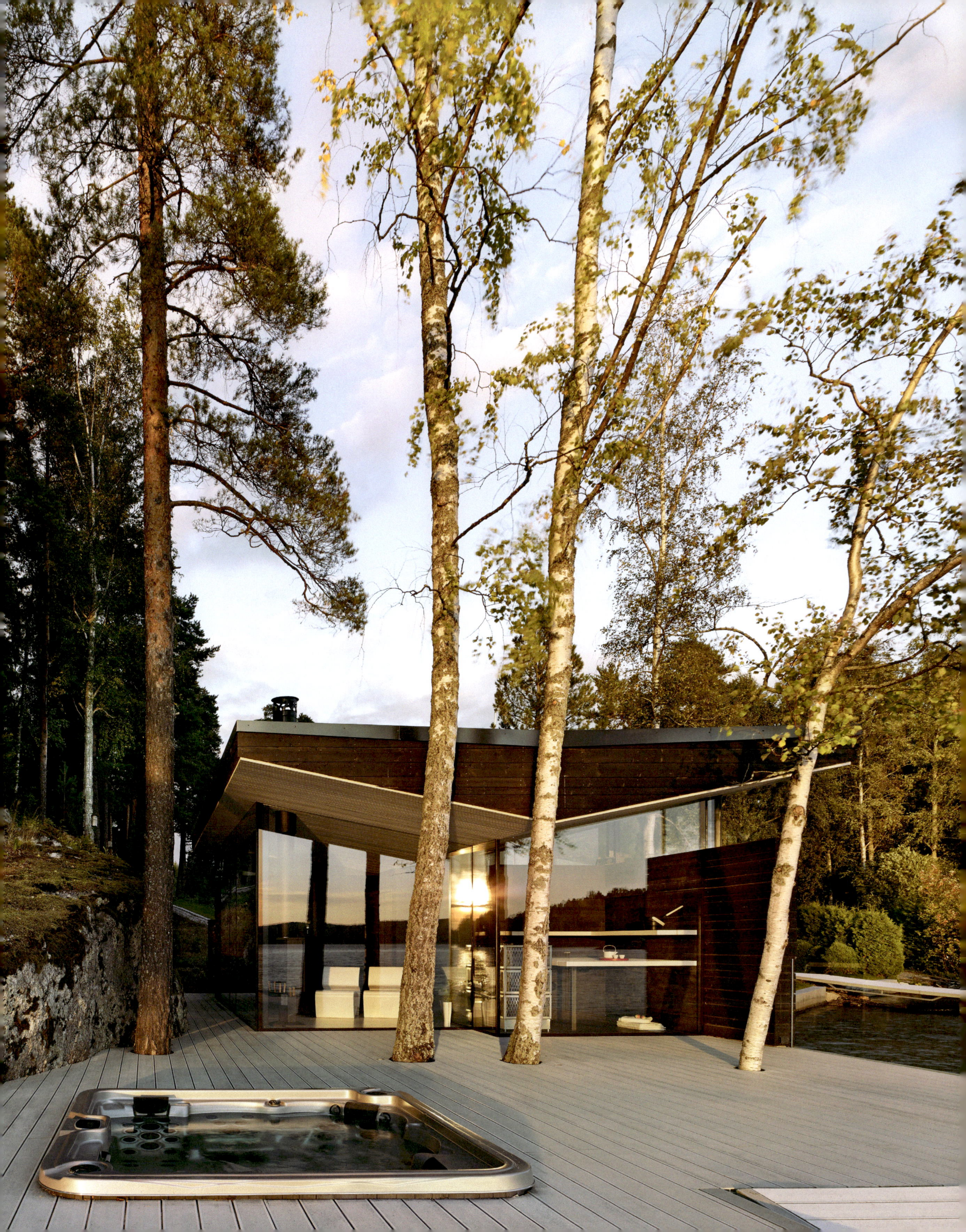

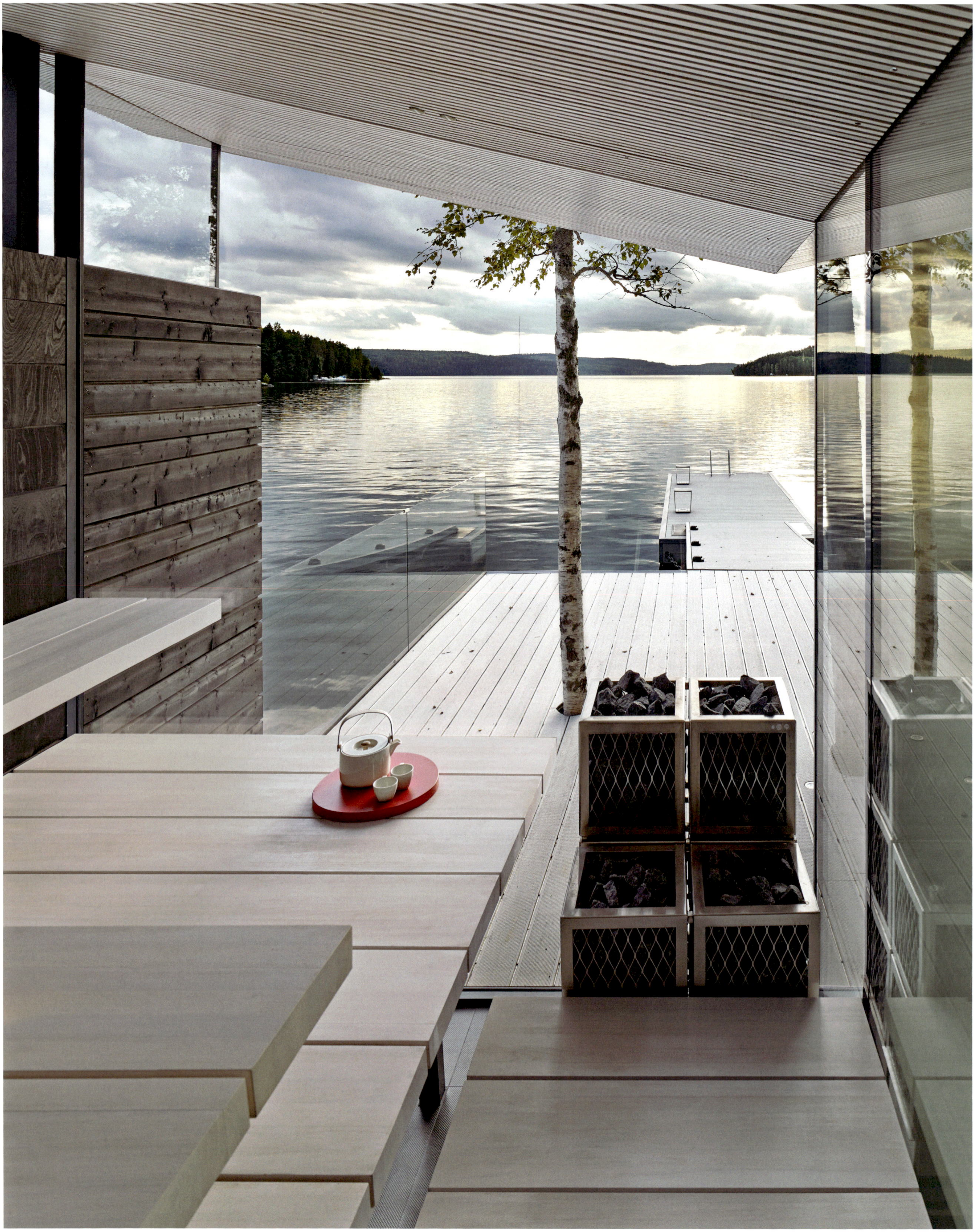

sauna's darkened timber walls and the lighter decking on which it sits. Since the tone of the platform blends with the surrounding cliff, the sauna appears to have been carved out of stone.

The view out to the lake is unhindered by any structural compromise, as full-height windows span the sauna's entire face. In a further embrace of the serene environment, mature trees protrude from the deck. Owner Juha Toivonen, who, along with his entire family, was integral to the sauna's sculpting, is extremely proud of the respect for nature that was maintained during construction—only one tree had to be cut down.

The sauna's interior consists of modern materials. Some, like the stereo system, have been artfully hidden to maintain the natural aesthetic. Other features include underfloor heating, LED lights, heated windows, and ventilation with a heat recovery system to reduce winter frost.

Sitting in the steam room, dissolving into a contemplative state, it is easy to imagine how the boundary between inside and outside might evaporate. A sculpture that echoes its surroundings with masterful ease, this sauna is as much a work of art as it is a retreat. ◆

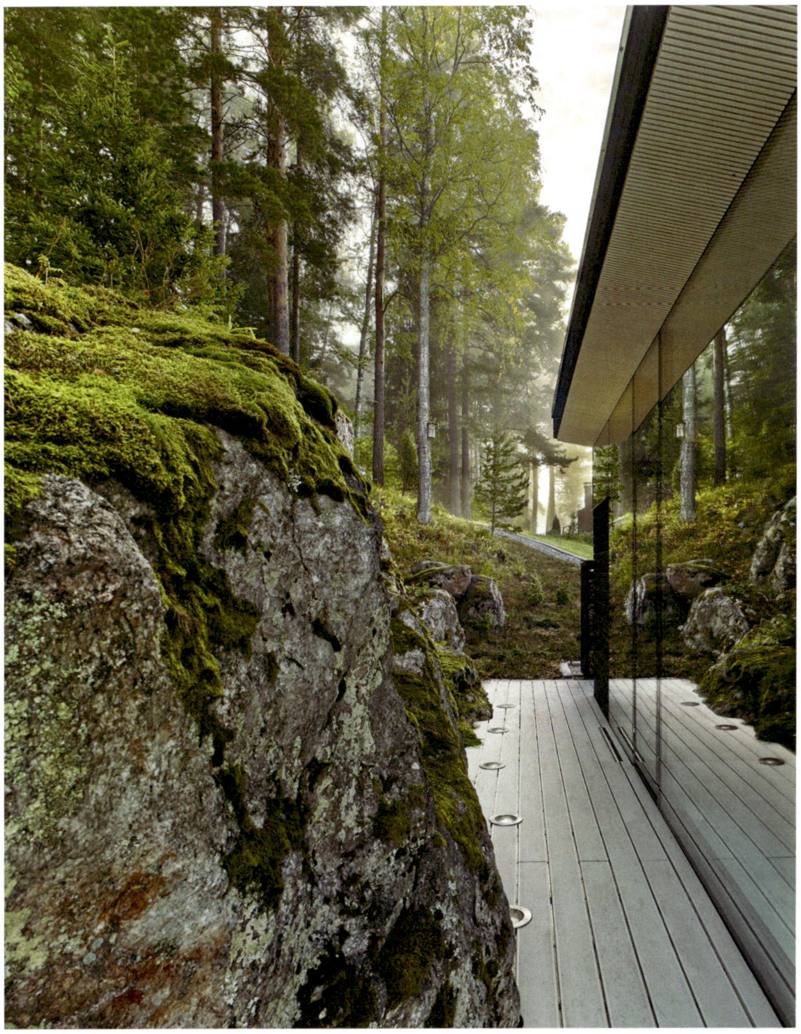

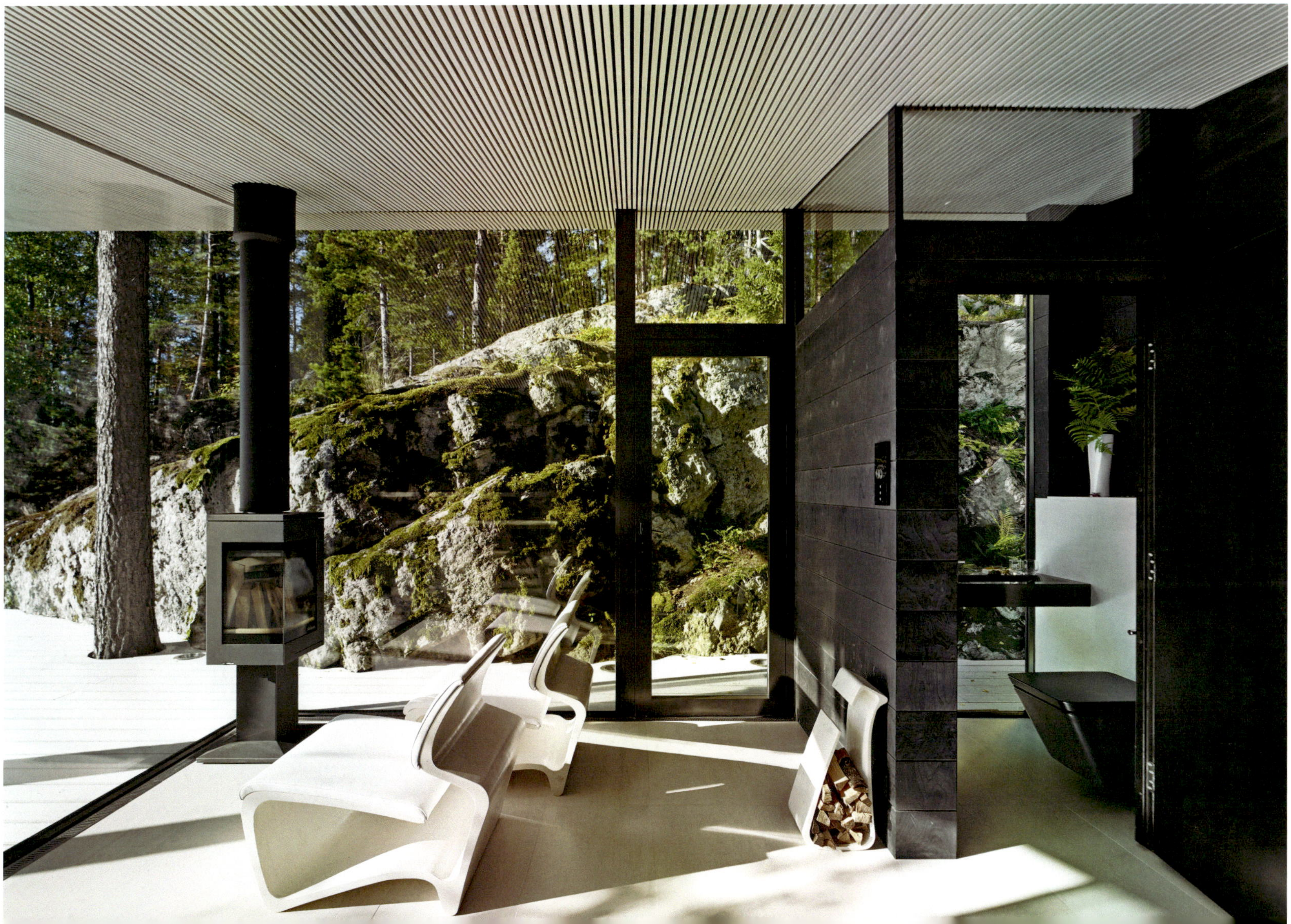

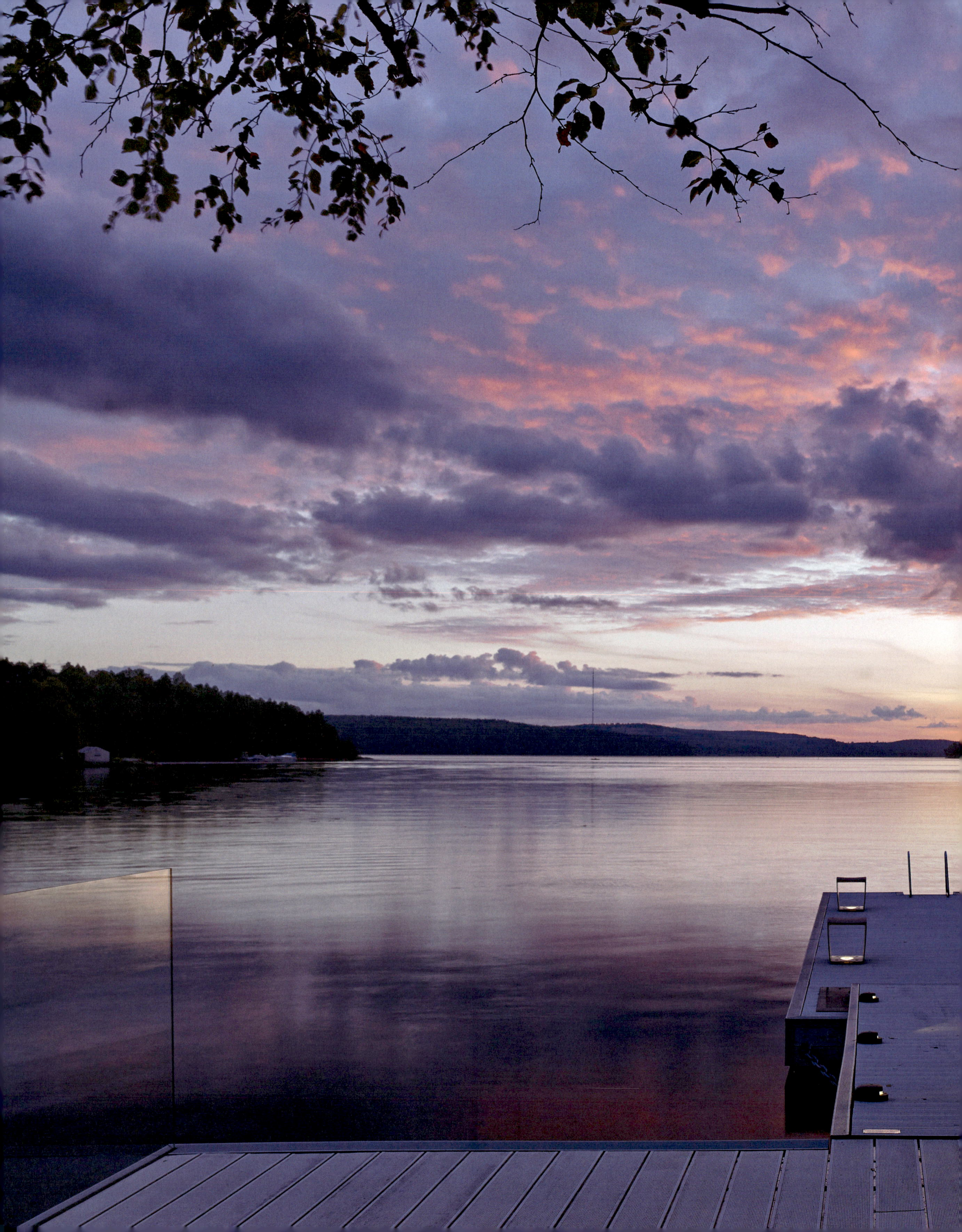

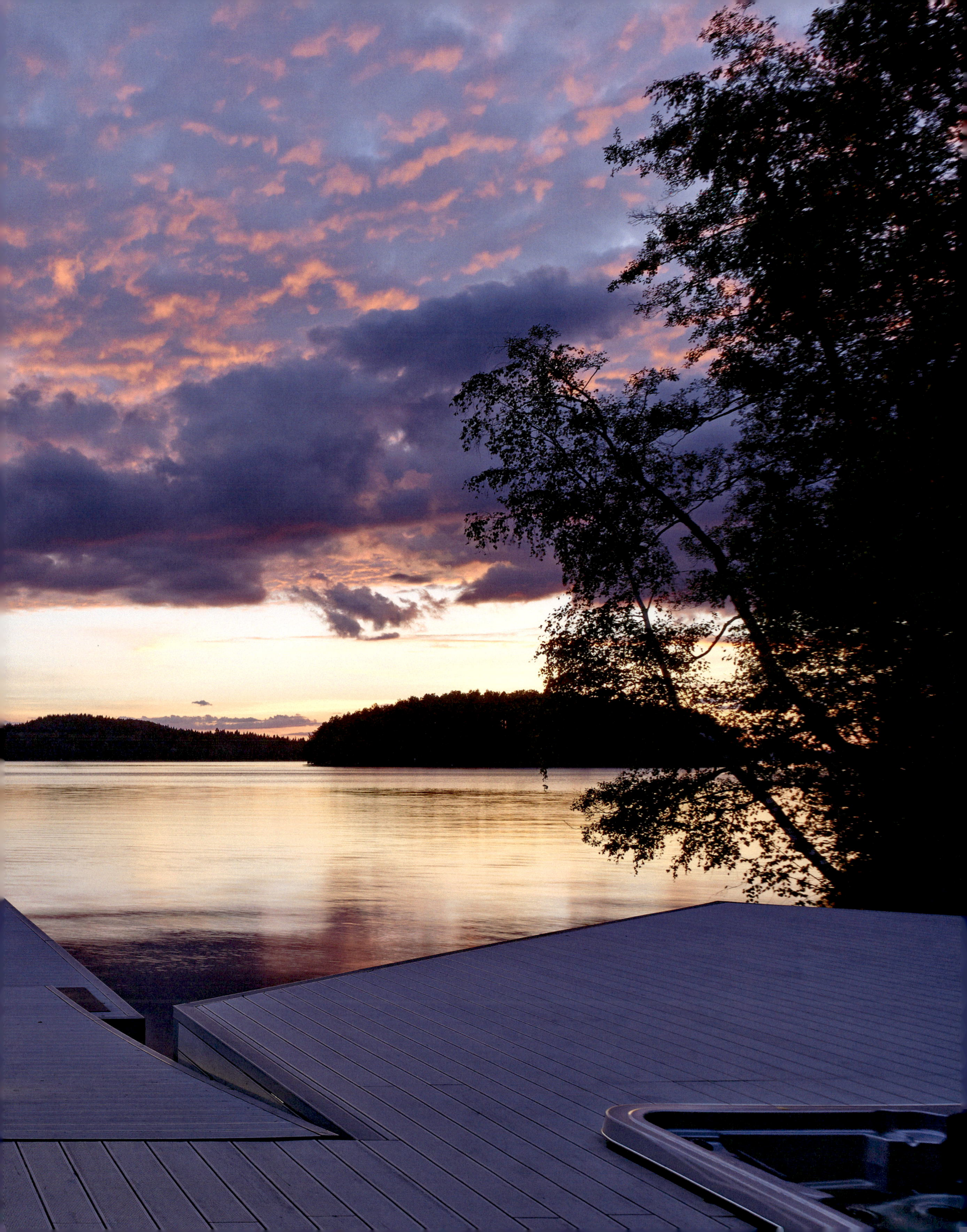

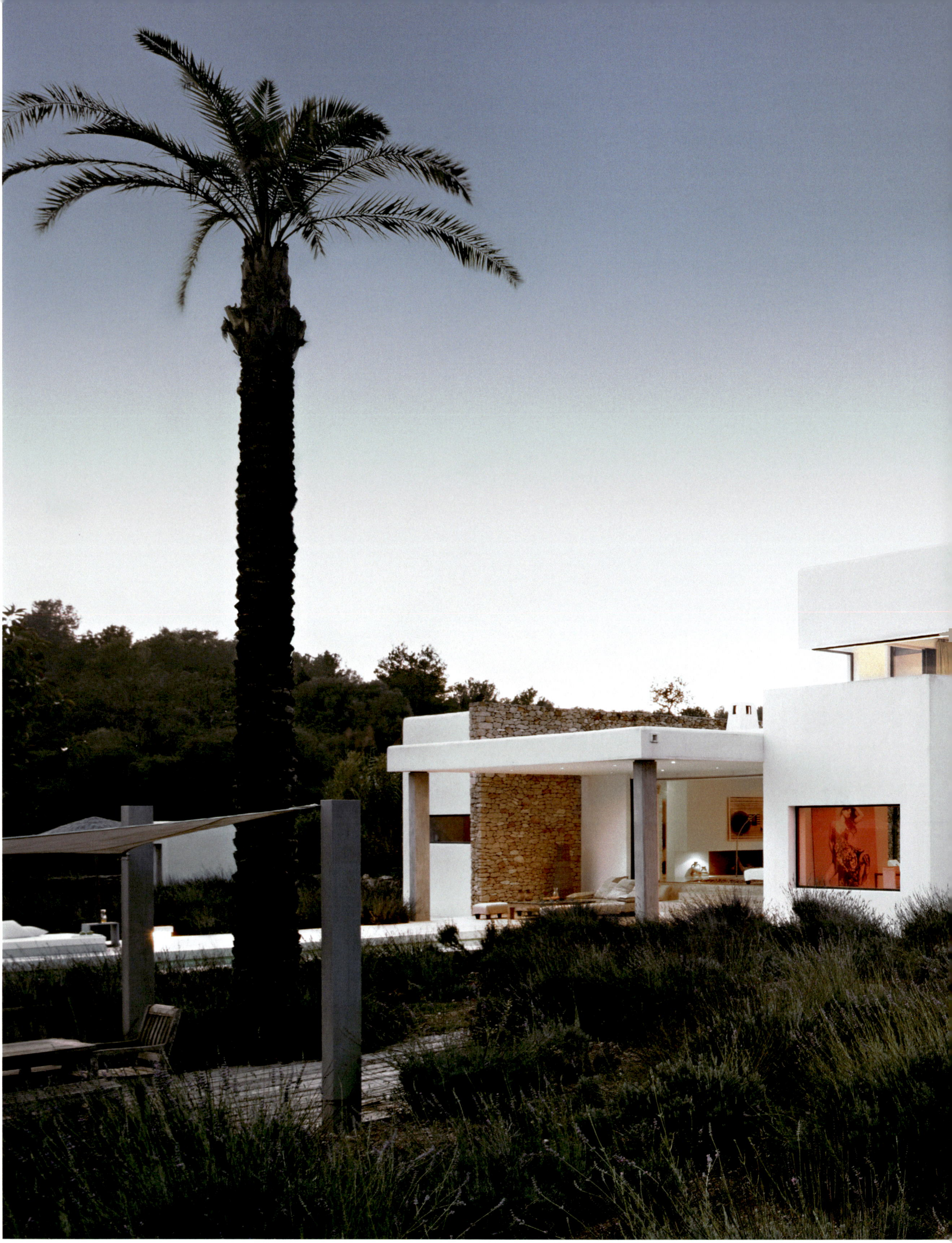

IBIZA, SPAIN

CAS PATRÓ

JAIME SERRA OF
ATLANT DEL VENT (ADV)

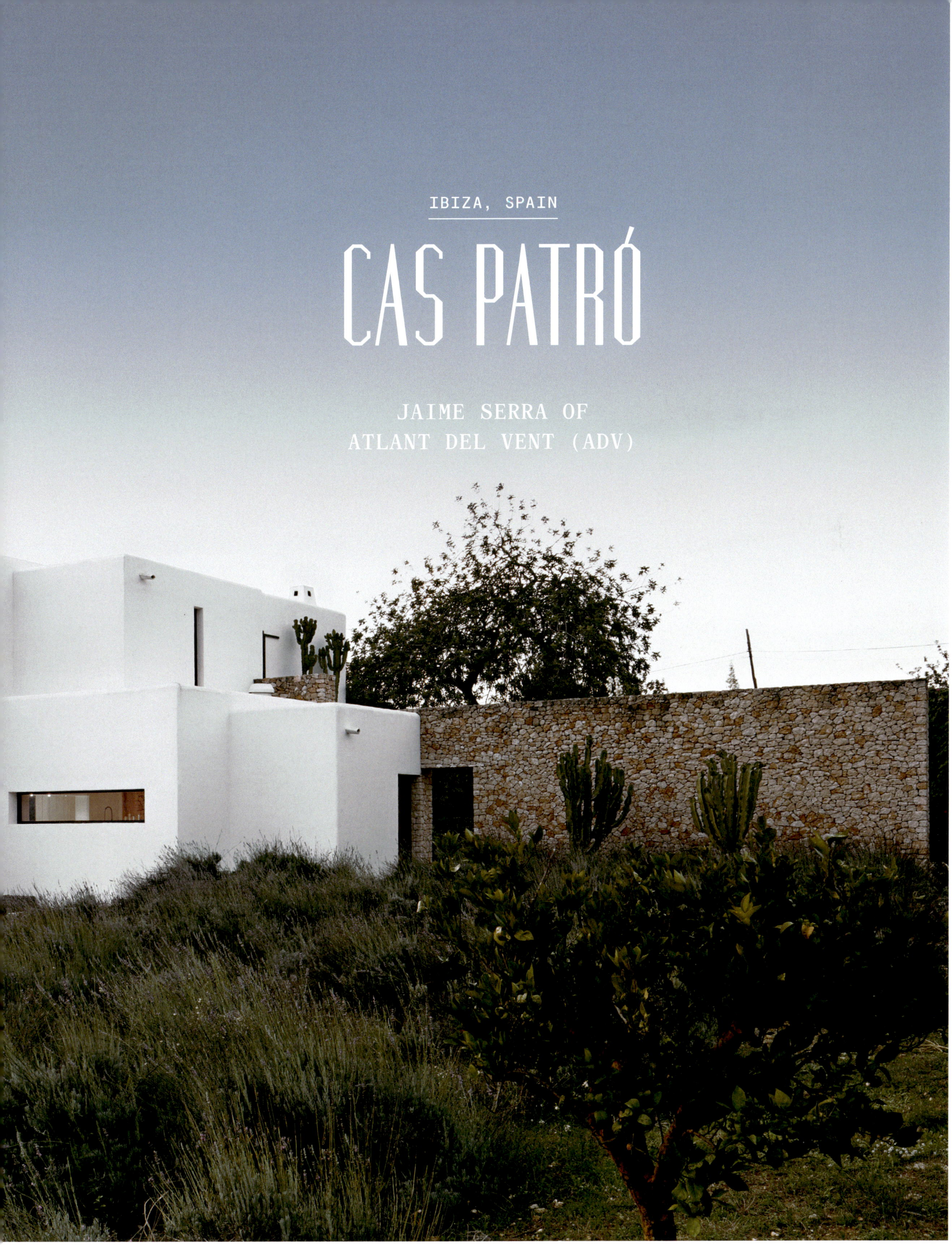

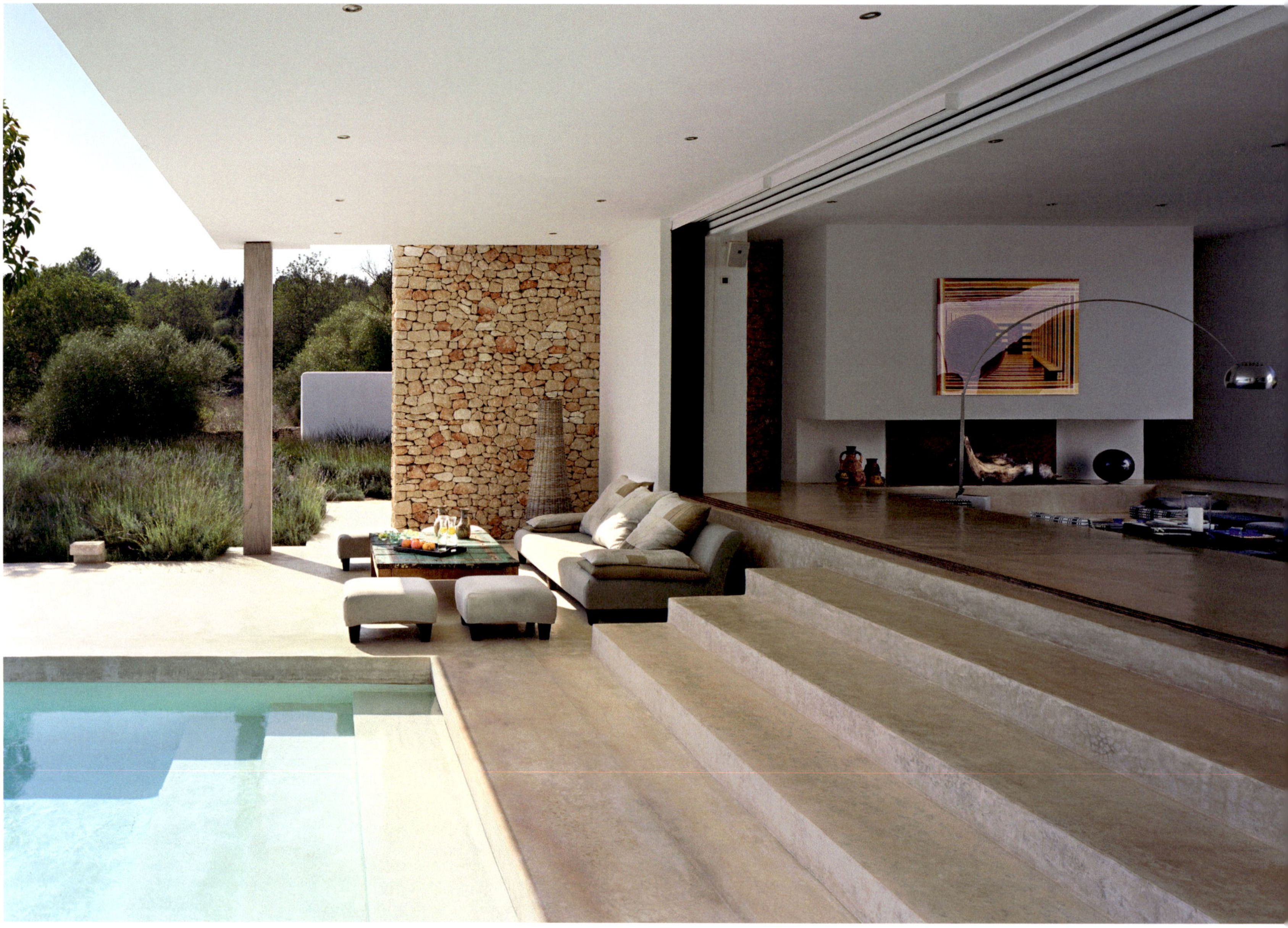

CAS PATRÓ In regions with extreme climates, it pays to be attentive to traditional construction methods. Embracing this methodology, Cas Patró builds upon ancient techniques, adding a few modern touches that accent its conventional characteristics.

Without deserts there would be no oases. In a similar sense, it was Cas Patró's arid foundation that created the possibility of its vital and brilliant finish.

Architect Jaime Serra of Atlant del Vent (ADV) created this idyllic yet resolute escape crowning a scorched hill near Dalt Vila in Ibiza, Spain by embracing certain aspects of the environment. Speaking of his methods, the Catalan architect says, "I tell my clients that there should only be three materials per room—the end result is guaranteed to be neutral, clean, and minimal." Employing white plaster, concrete, and rusted steel, Cas Patró hews a hospitable retreat out of the unforgiving landscape.

Serra says the owners wanted "a traditional look with a touch of contemporary architecture, a home that could be usable for all-year-round living, rather than just the summer months." His solution: doors that retract within the walls. In the winter they provide necessary insulation, while in the summer the building retains the clean doorways and open-plan flow of traditional Spanish villas.

Cut into polished concrete floors and softened by a fireplace and neutral cushions, the sunken living room preserves a place of rest and quietude. Floor-to-ceiling windows frame two slices of desert paradise. Looking over a sprawling vista, a pool contrasts with the dry wilderness, while on the other side, a concrete irrigation system splits a native garden in two. The lines of the pool, irrigation channel, and house combine to form sharp compliments to the stackedstone walls that reappear throughout Cas Patró's interior.

By working with the landscape, respecting traditional building styles, and adding a few modern elements, Serra has created a hideaway that can be used year-round. ◆

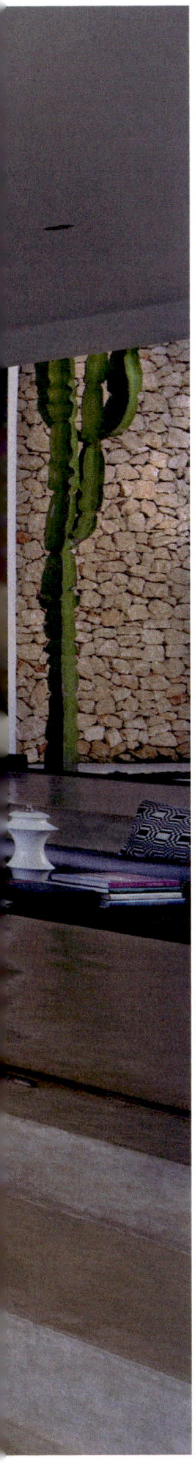

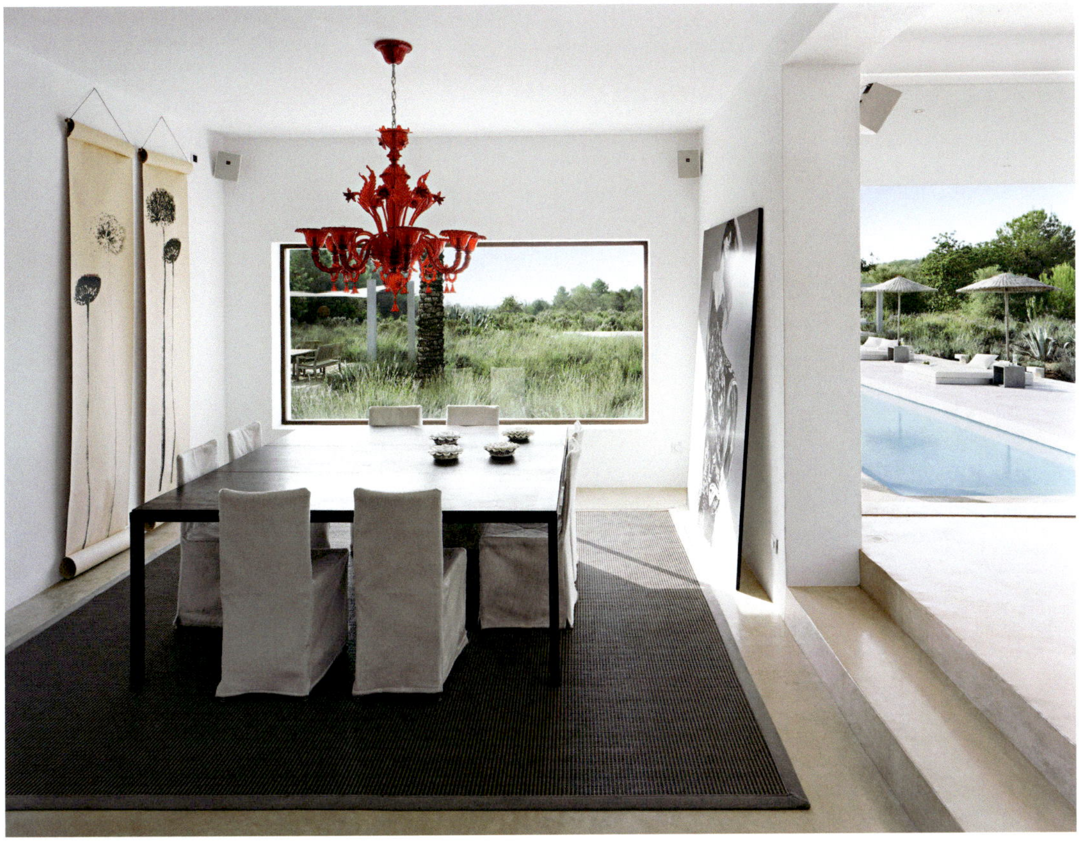

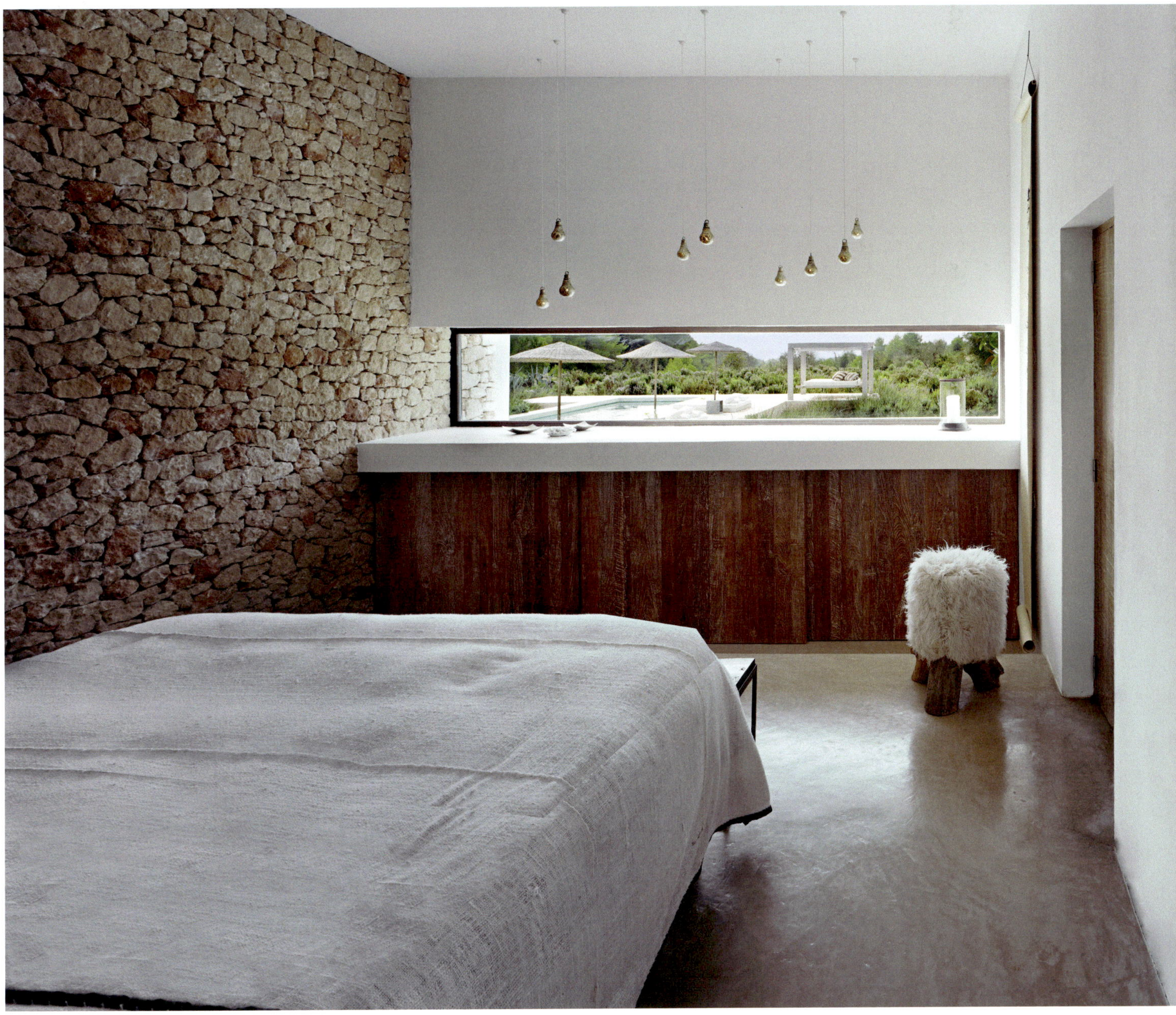

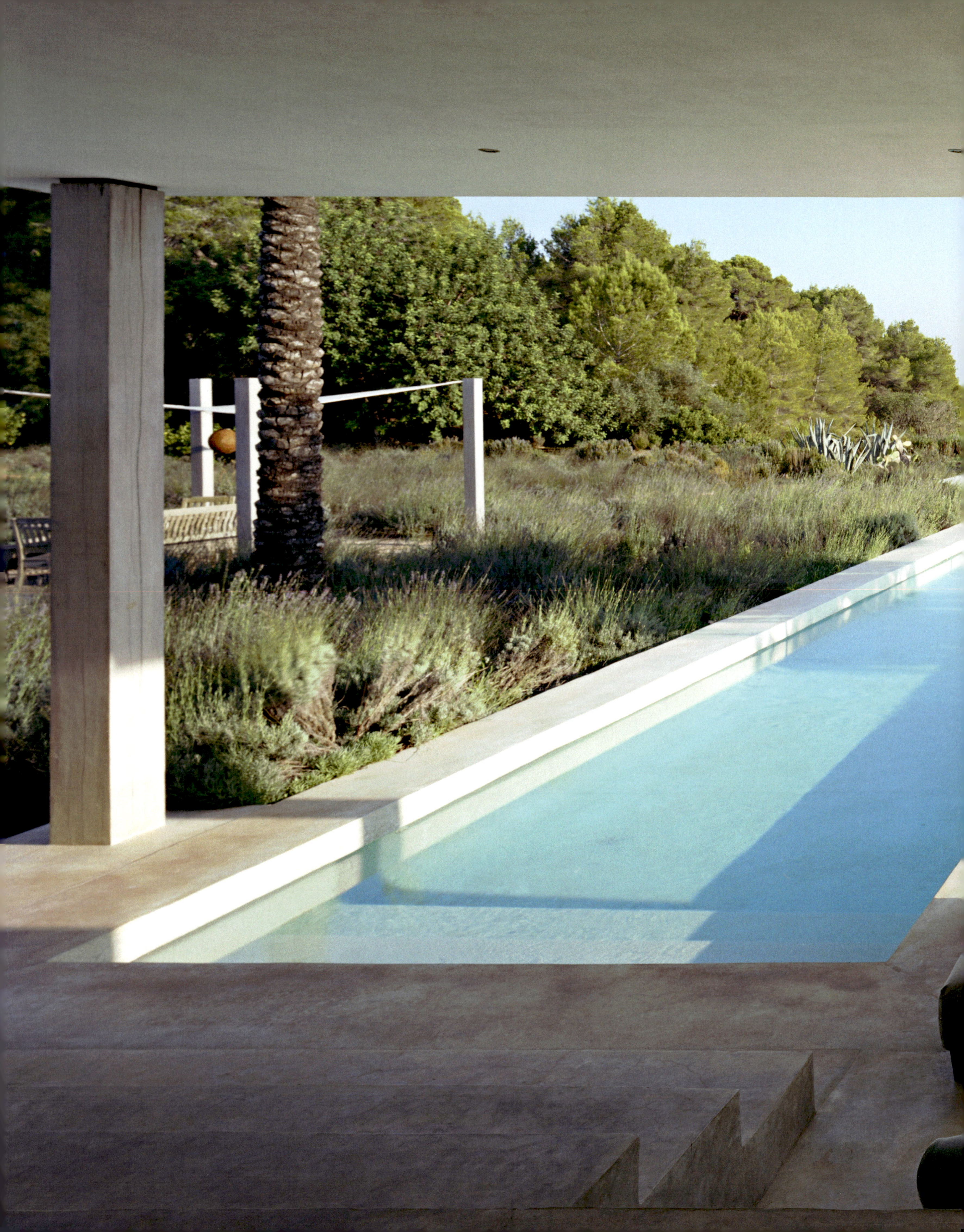

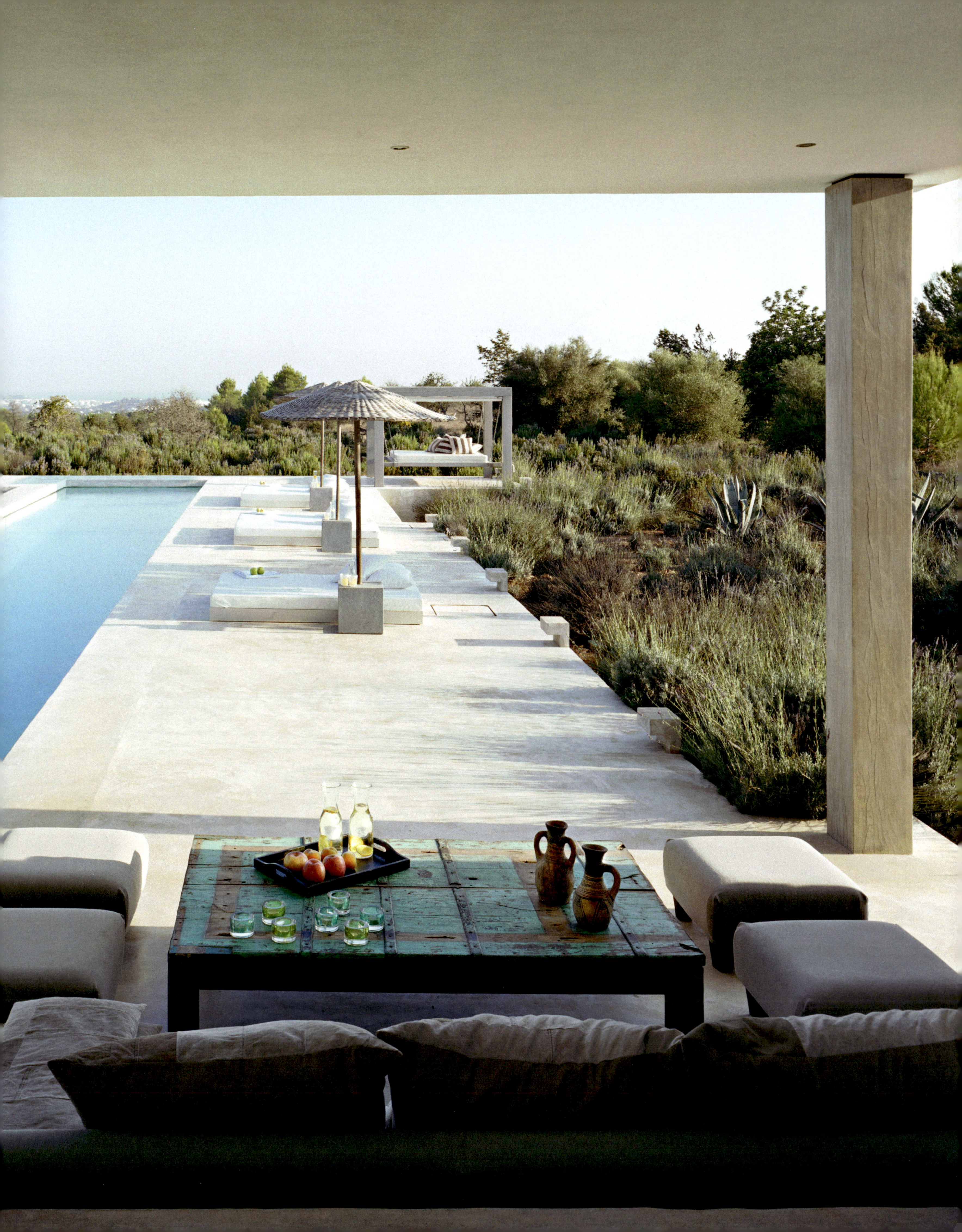

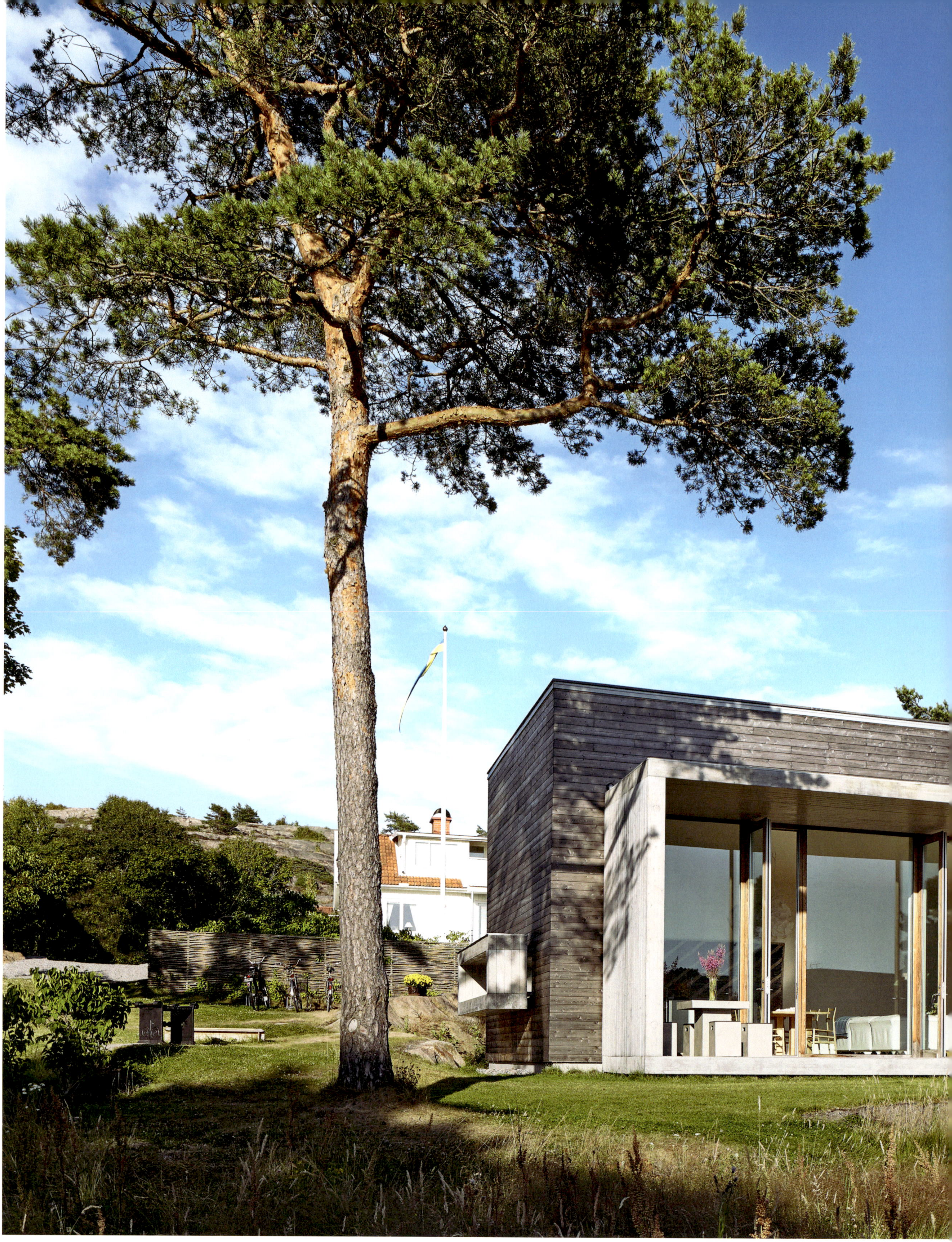

FJÄLLBACKA, SWEDEN

VILLA PINEUS

GERT WINGÅRDH
OF WINGÅRDH ARKITEKTKONTOR

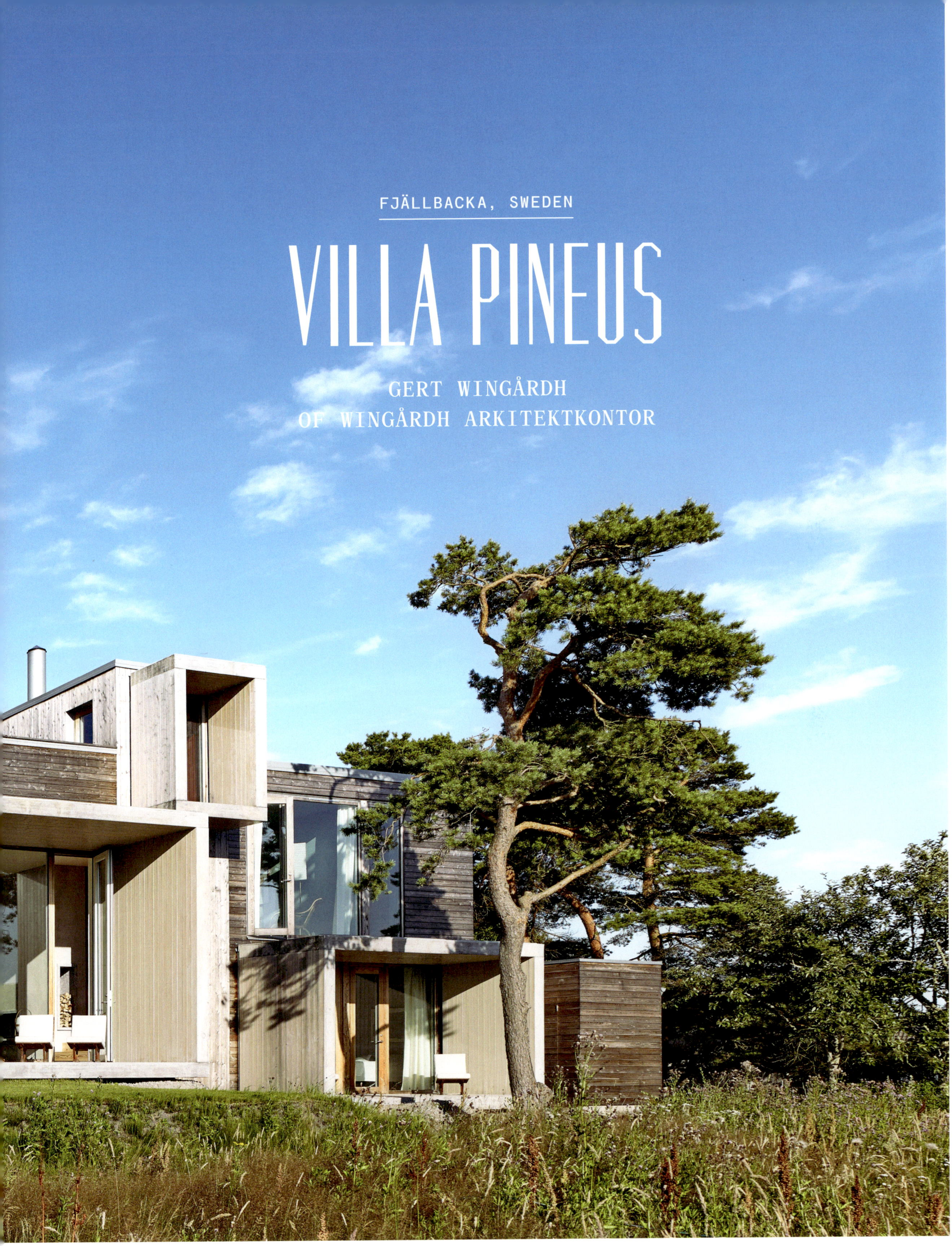

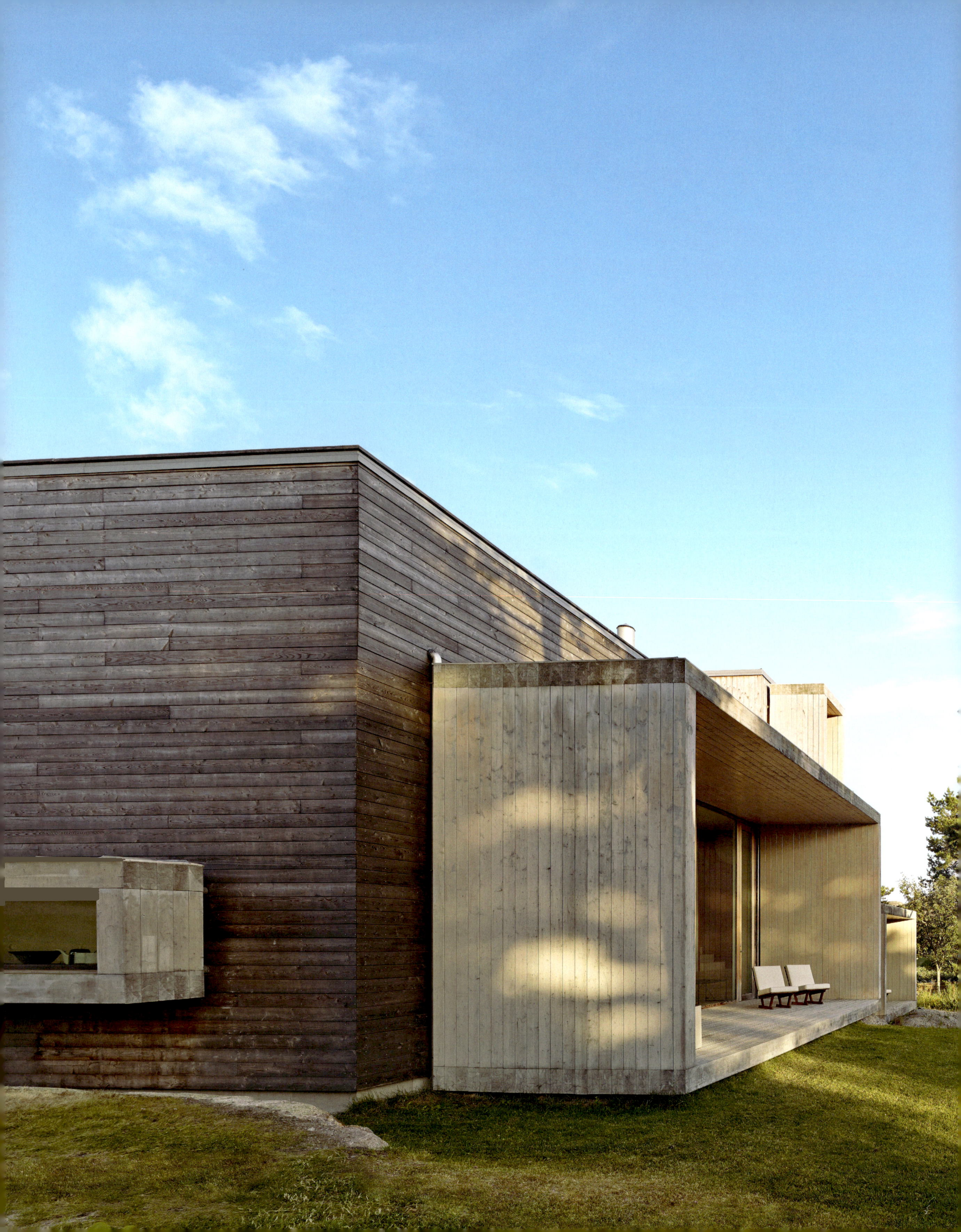

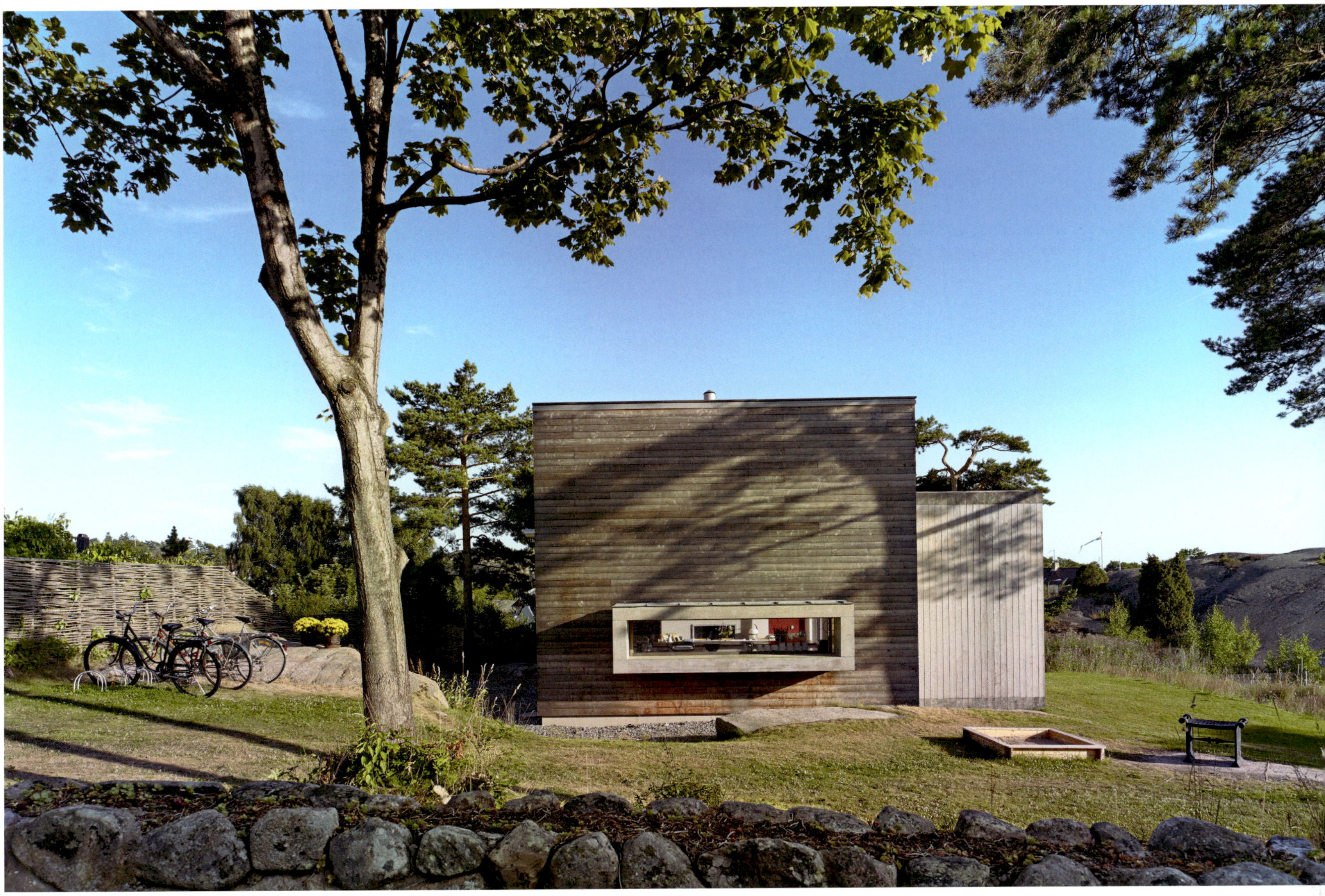

VILLA PINEUS Although the owners of Villa Pineus trade in antique goods, their home is nothing like a museum. Vibrant and suffused with light courtesy of its towering glass doors, the house revolves around hospitality. With this home, architect Gert Wingårdh has added another Swedish gem to his portfolio.

Isaac Pineus and Andrew Duncanson had bright ideas for their Swedish holiday home. As the owners of Modernity, a renowned Stockholm gallery specializing in furniture, ceramics, and jewelry from Scandinavian designers of the 20th century, the interior was always going to be immaculately furnished. Pieces by the likes of Giò Ponti, Enzo Mari, and Vico Magistratti decorate the home, historicizing what is otherwise an abode that adheres to an overtly contemporary design.

Besides being situated in the quaint fishing village of Fjällbacka, the site held special significance for Pineus because of his family's history there. He says, "My grandparents bought the site in 1945. The two houses next door belong to my parents and the other belonged to my grandparents." And while the house may not fit in with its neighbors in a straightforward visual sense, Pineus has ensured that it feels like a welcoming and family-friendly space. "An important part of the house is that it is boundaryless," he explains.

Gert Wingårdh was tasked with the project. He kept the interior minimal and spare, primarily utilizing cement and woods that retain neutral tones, with the exception of the almost obligatory inclusion of falu red—a deep shade of red that is used in many Swedish homes. He is particularly pleased with the way the larch has weathered to look like concrete, and the way the north façade unconsciously echoes some of Le Corbusier's modernist designs. Against this subdued backdrop, the rare objects sourced by Pineus and Duncanson are presented in a light that draws out the useful properties of each piece more than their precious and antique natures.

The home achieves its hospitable quality mainly through the huge 3.5-meter-high glass doors that lead out to the ground floor terrace. Pineus says, "In the summer the doors are open all through the day and the kids can ~

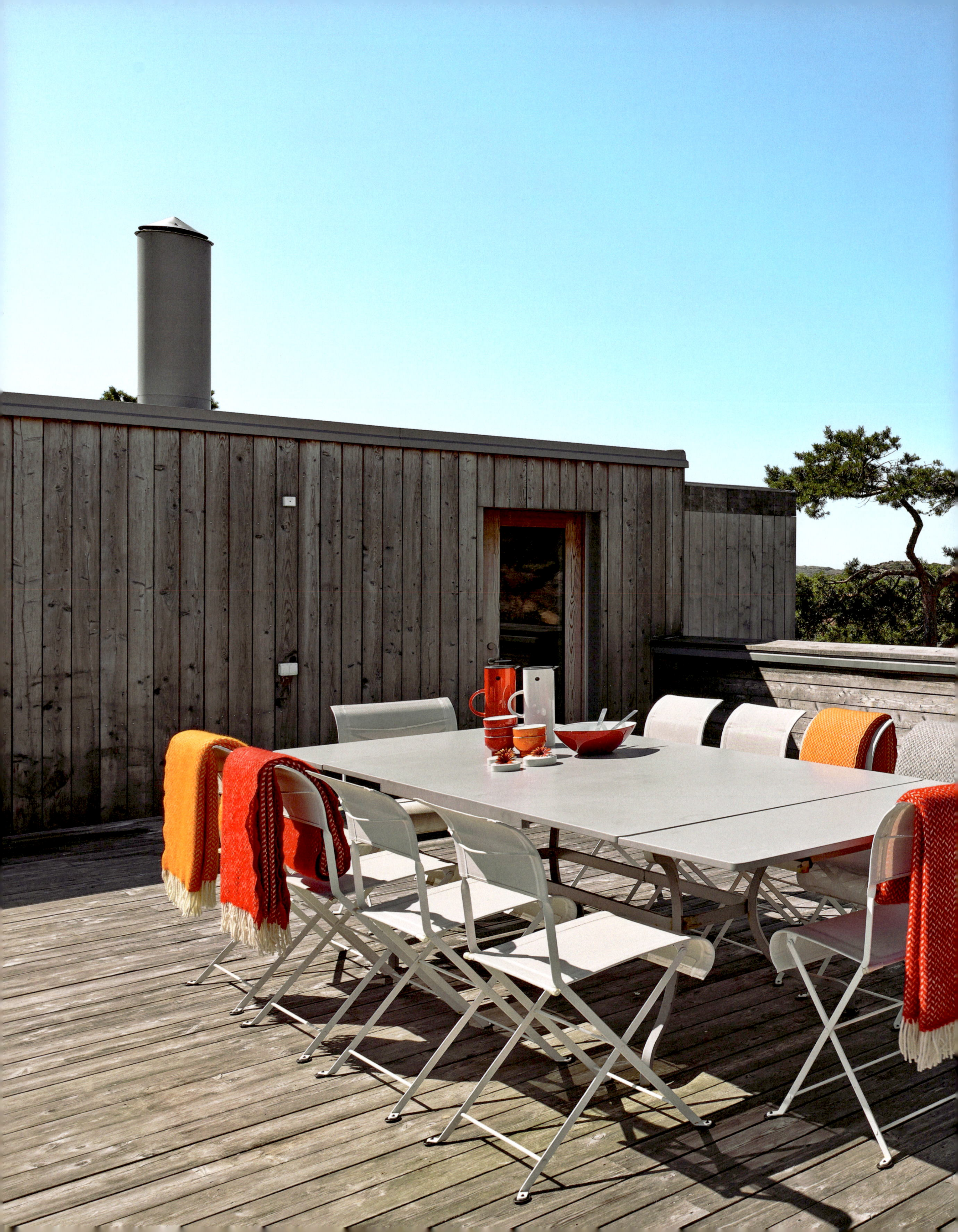

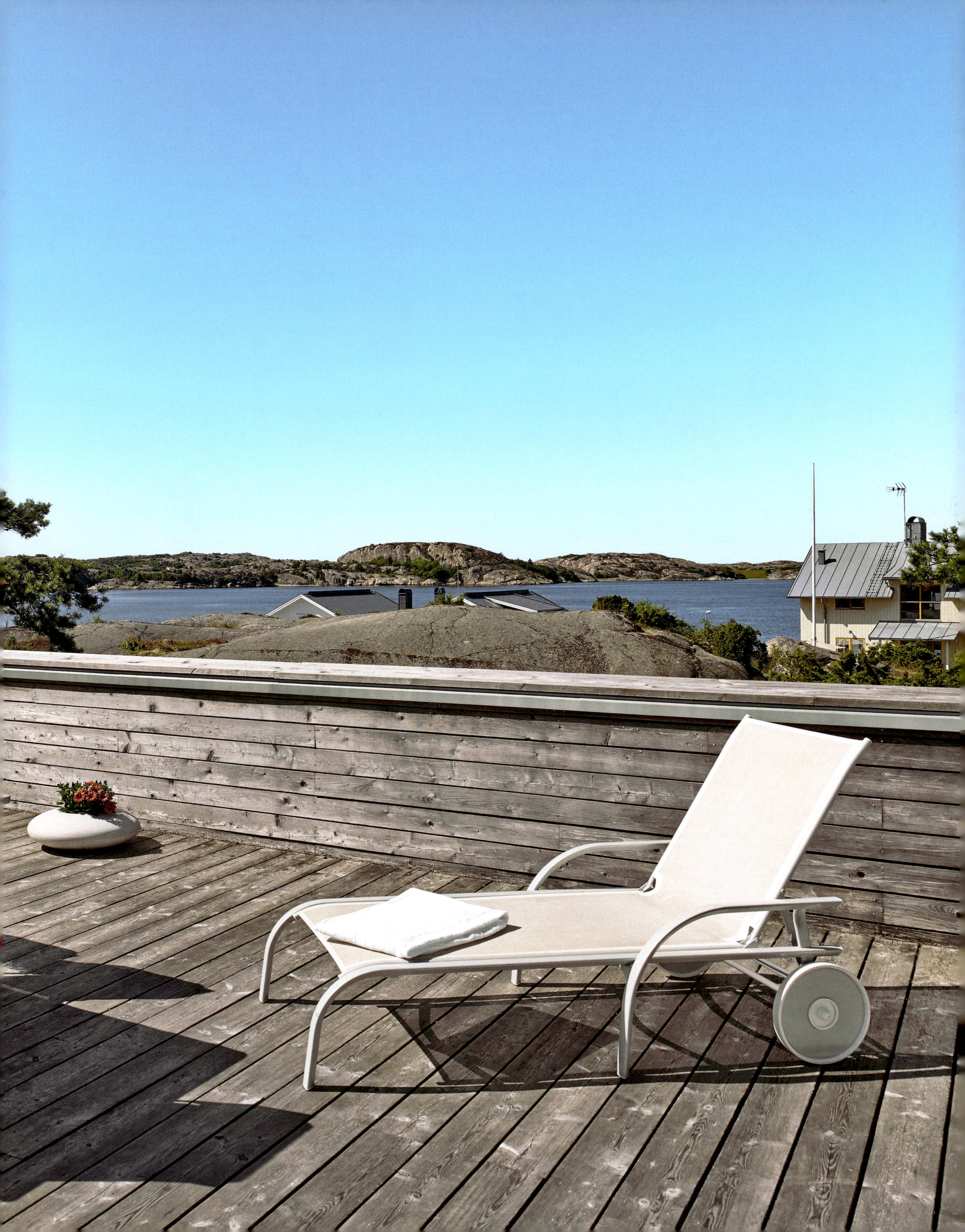

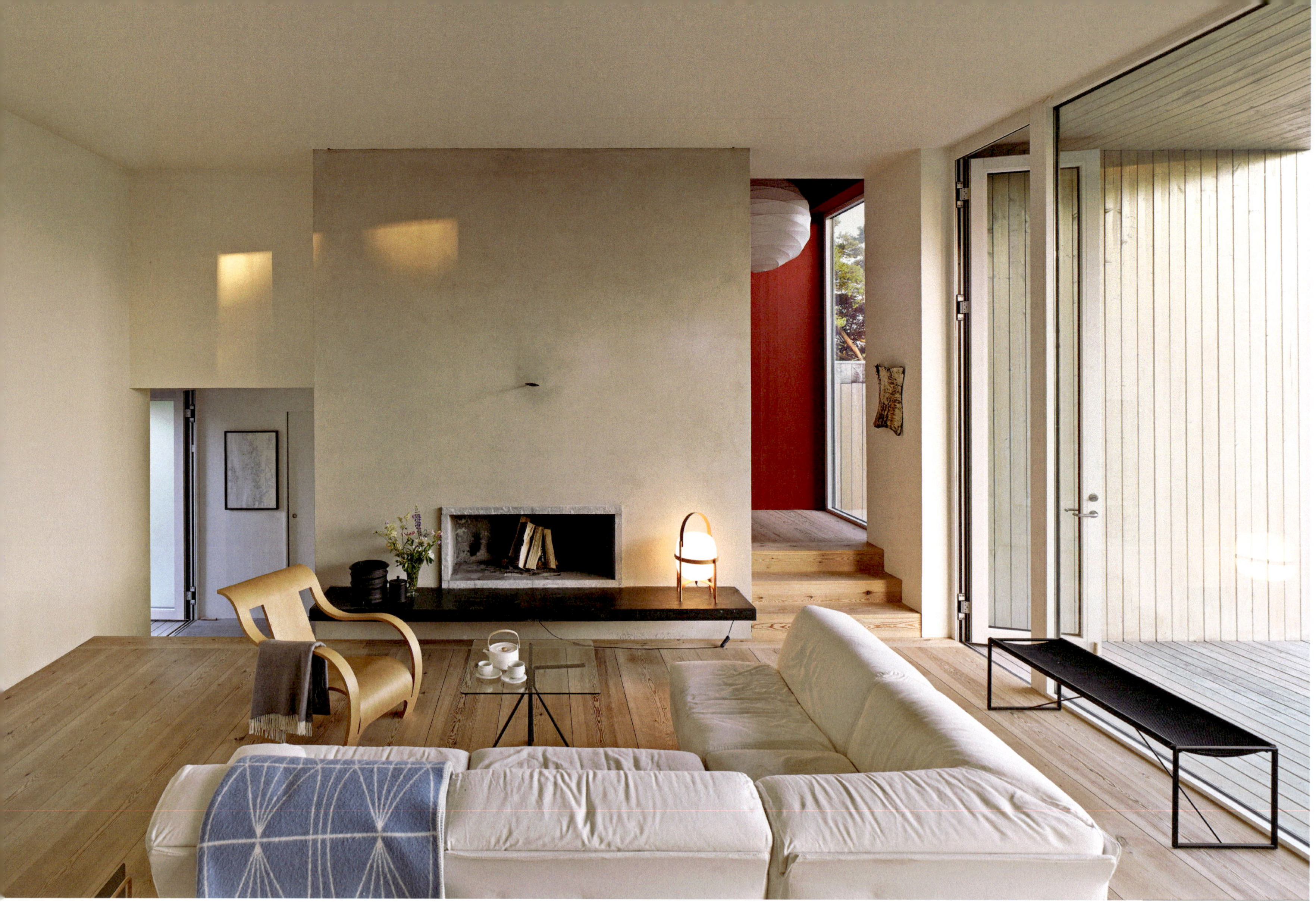

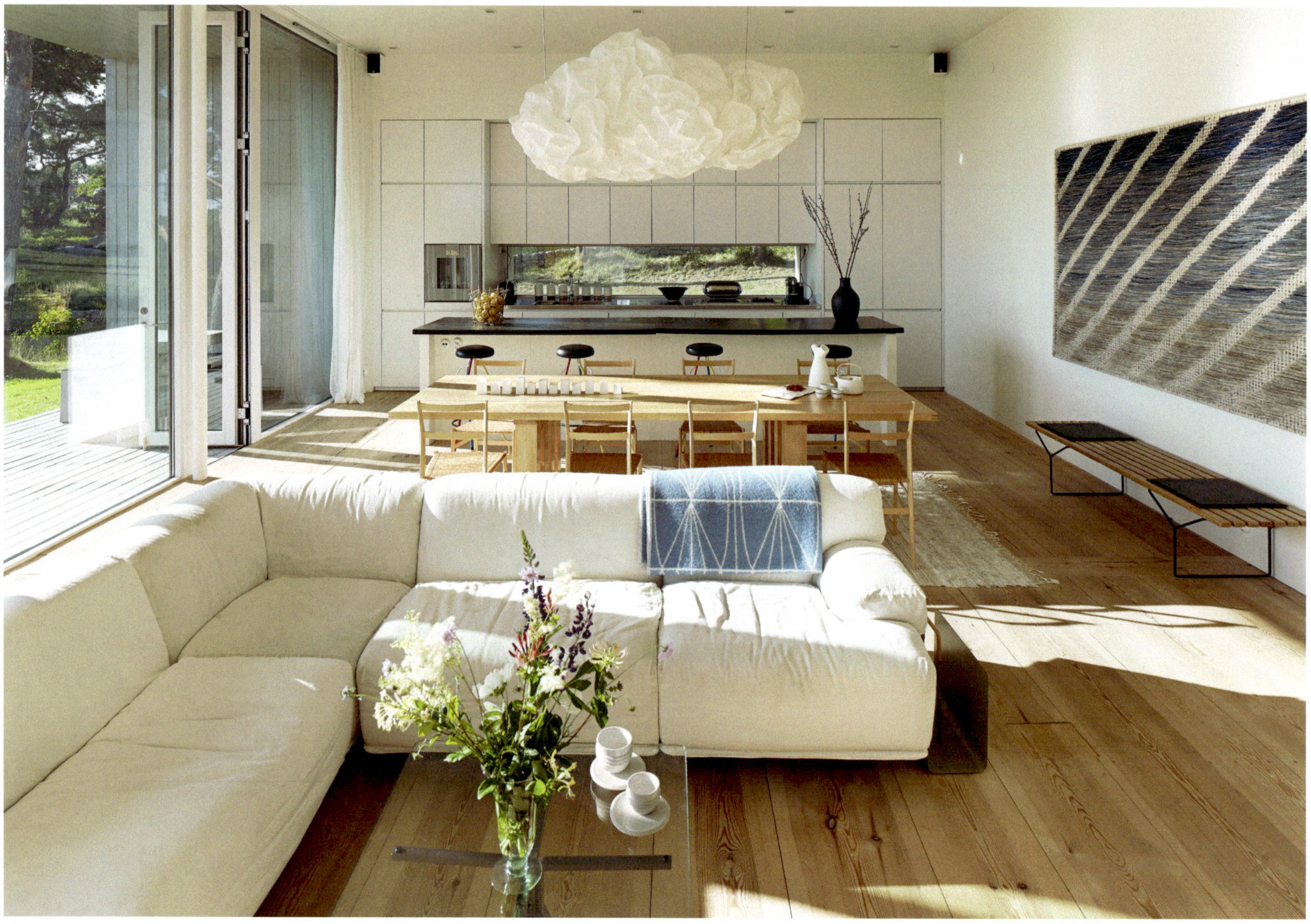

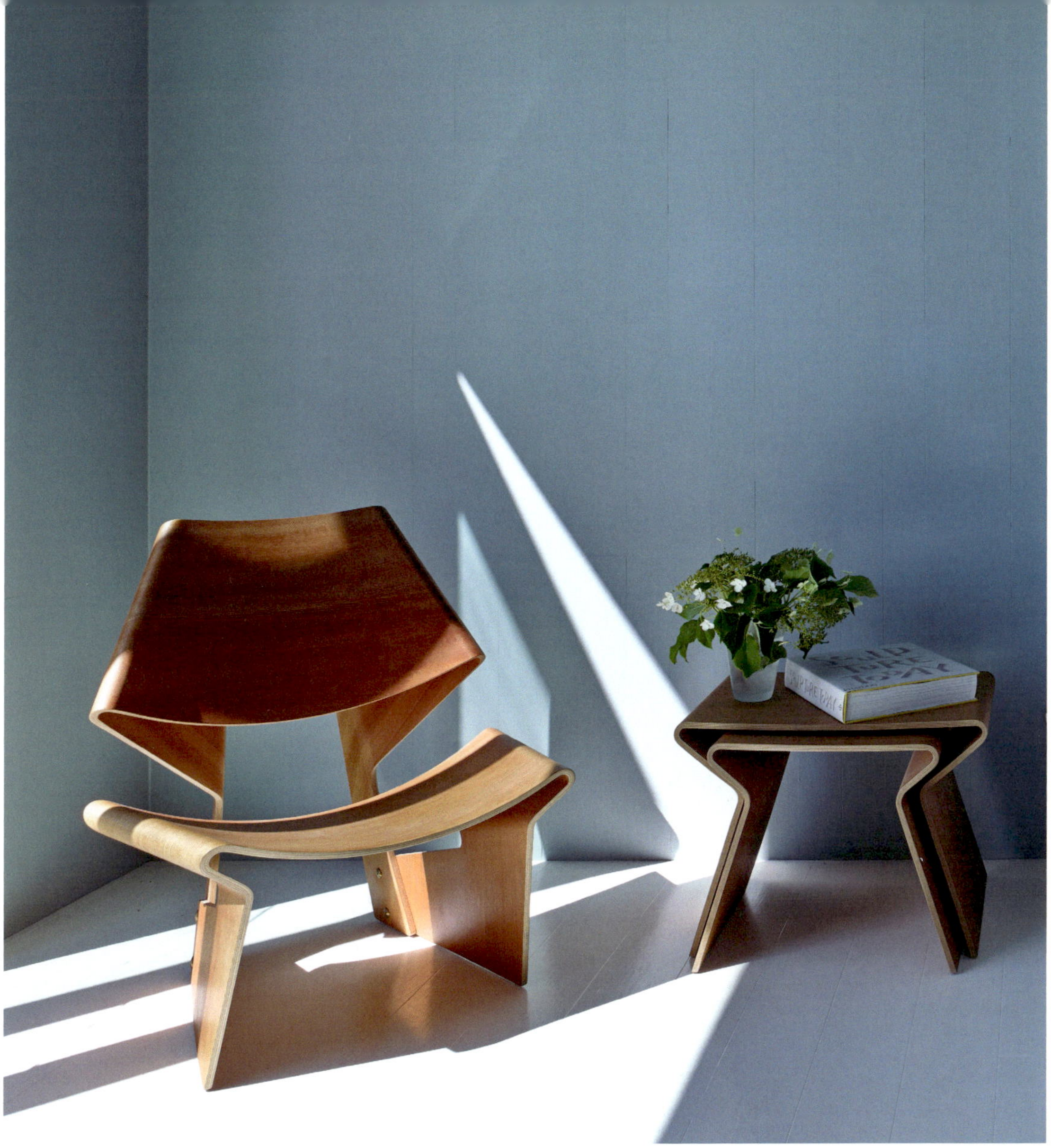

"PIECES BY THE LIKES OF GIÒ PONTI, ENZO MARI, AND VICO MAGISTRATTI DECORATE THE HOME, HISTORICIZING WHAT IS OTHERWISE AN ABODE THAT ADHERES TO AN OVERTLY CONTEMPORARY DESIGN."

run in and out. And my sister and her kids can come and go as they please." There is also plenty of room for more visitors, with the guest rooms situated upstairs along with the master bedroom, children's bedrooms, and sauna. Despite the modern appearance of the villa, it references an openness and warmth that can be traced back to Isaac's grandparents' era and beyond. ◆

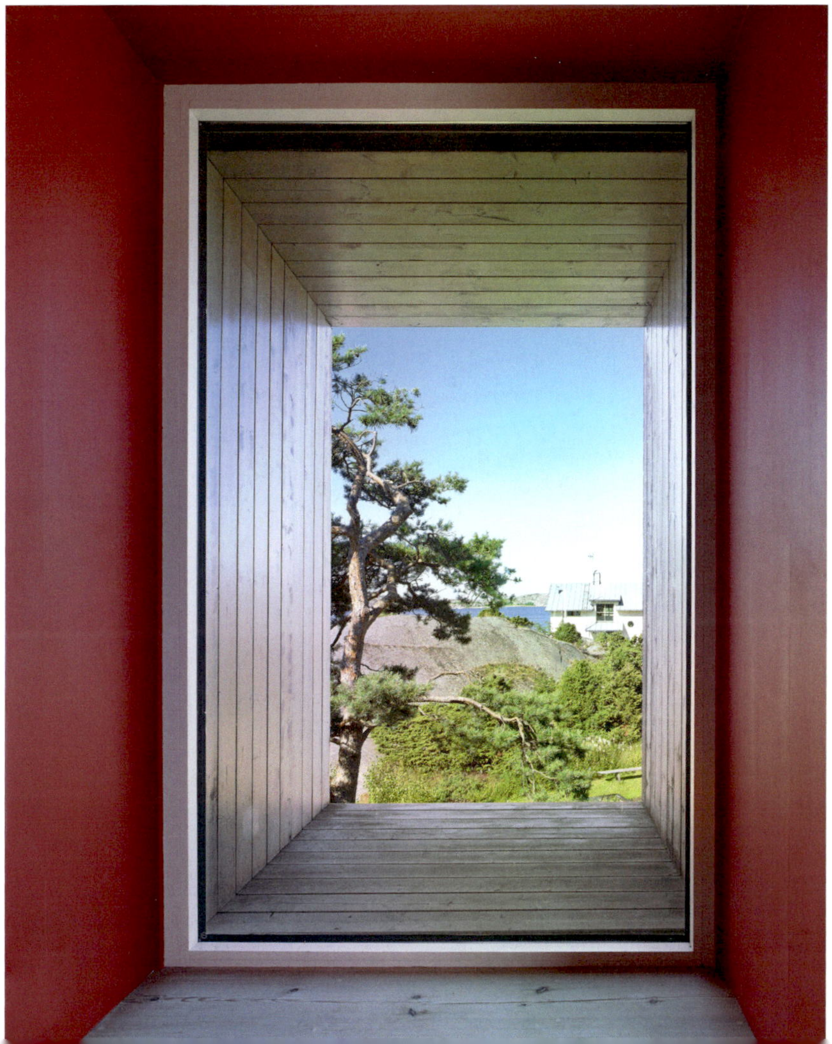

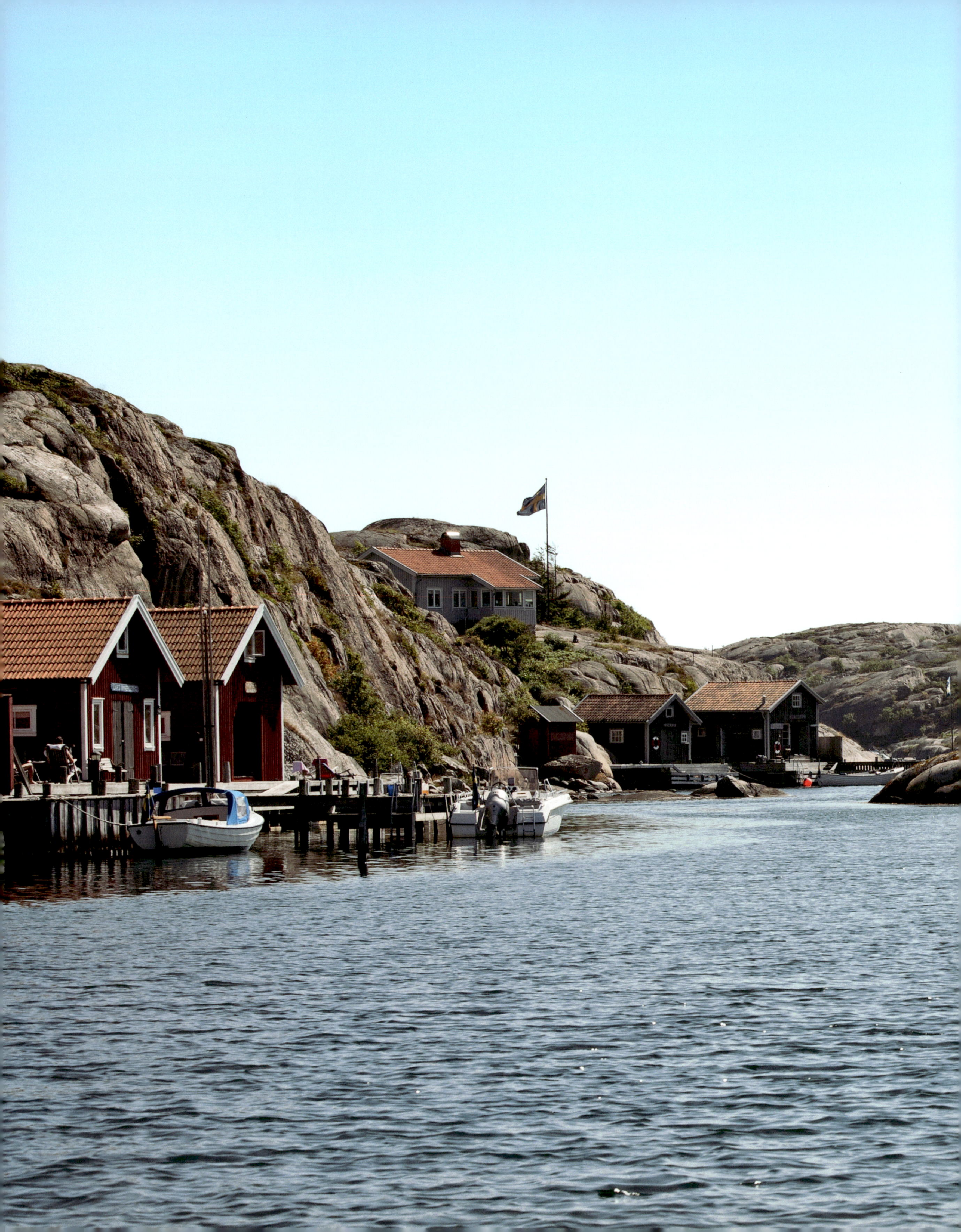

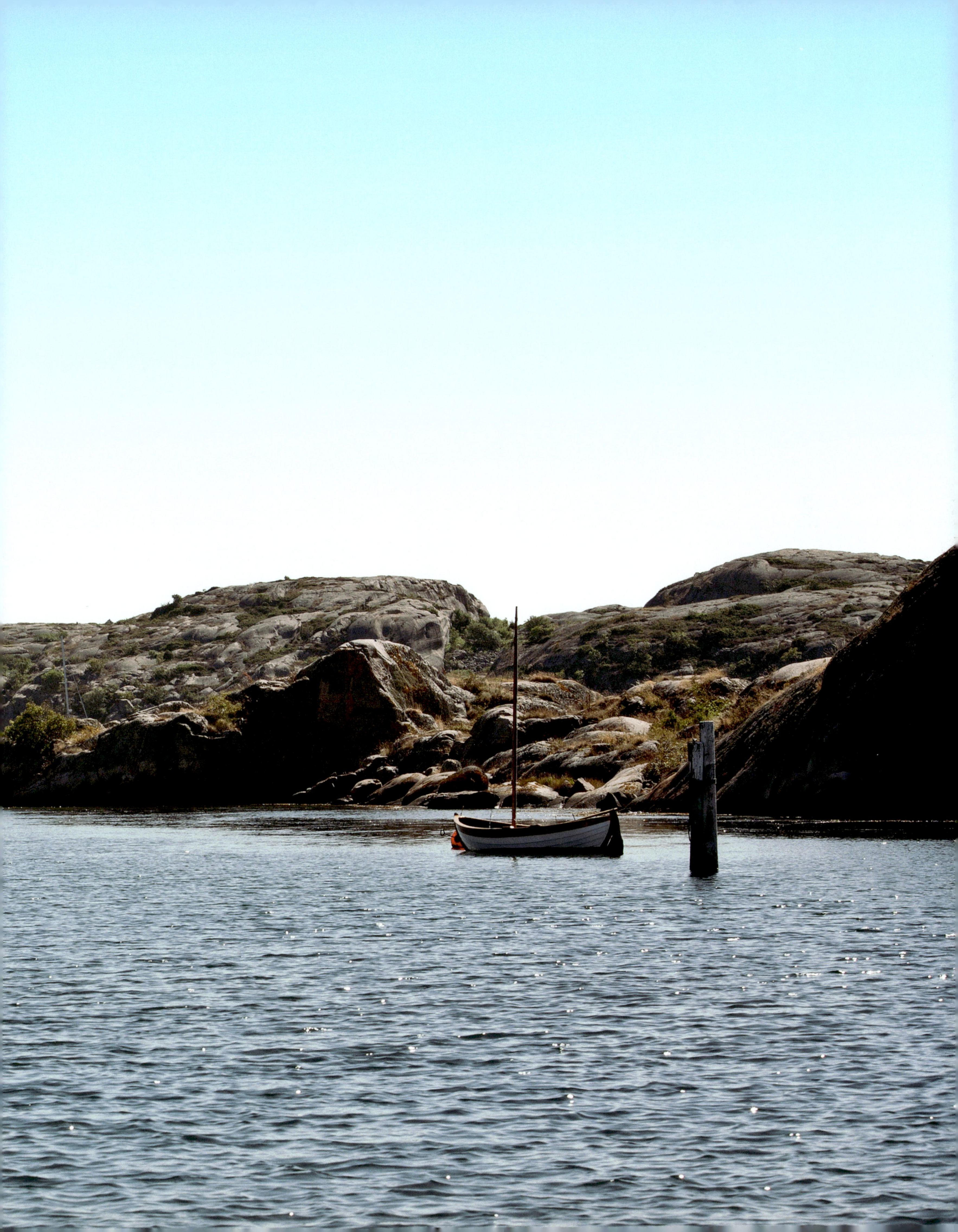

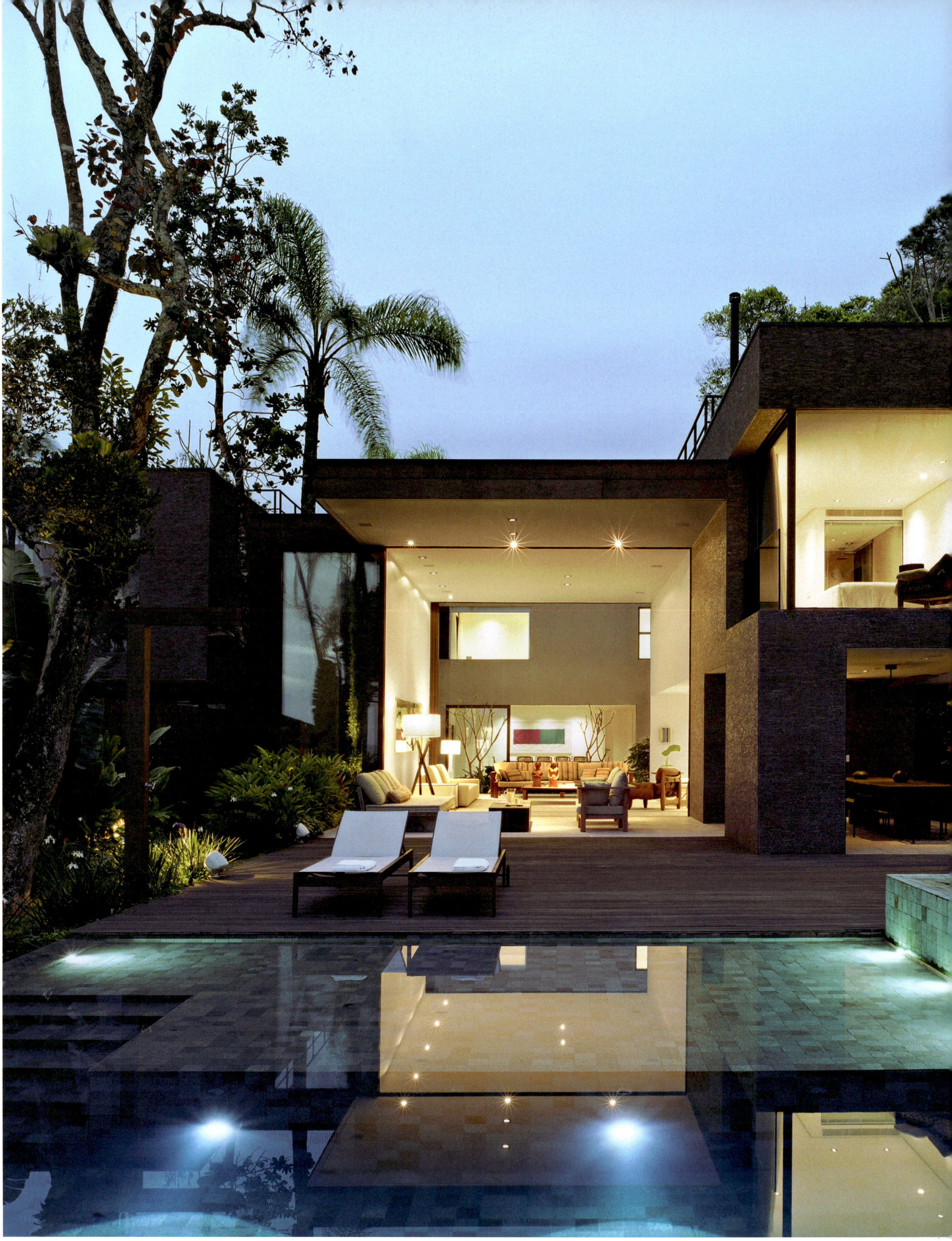

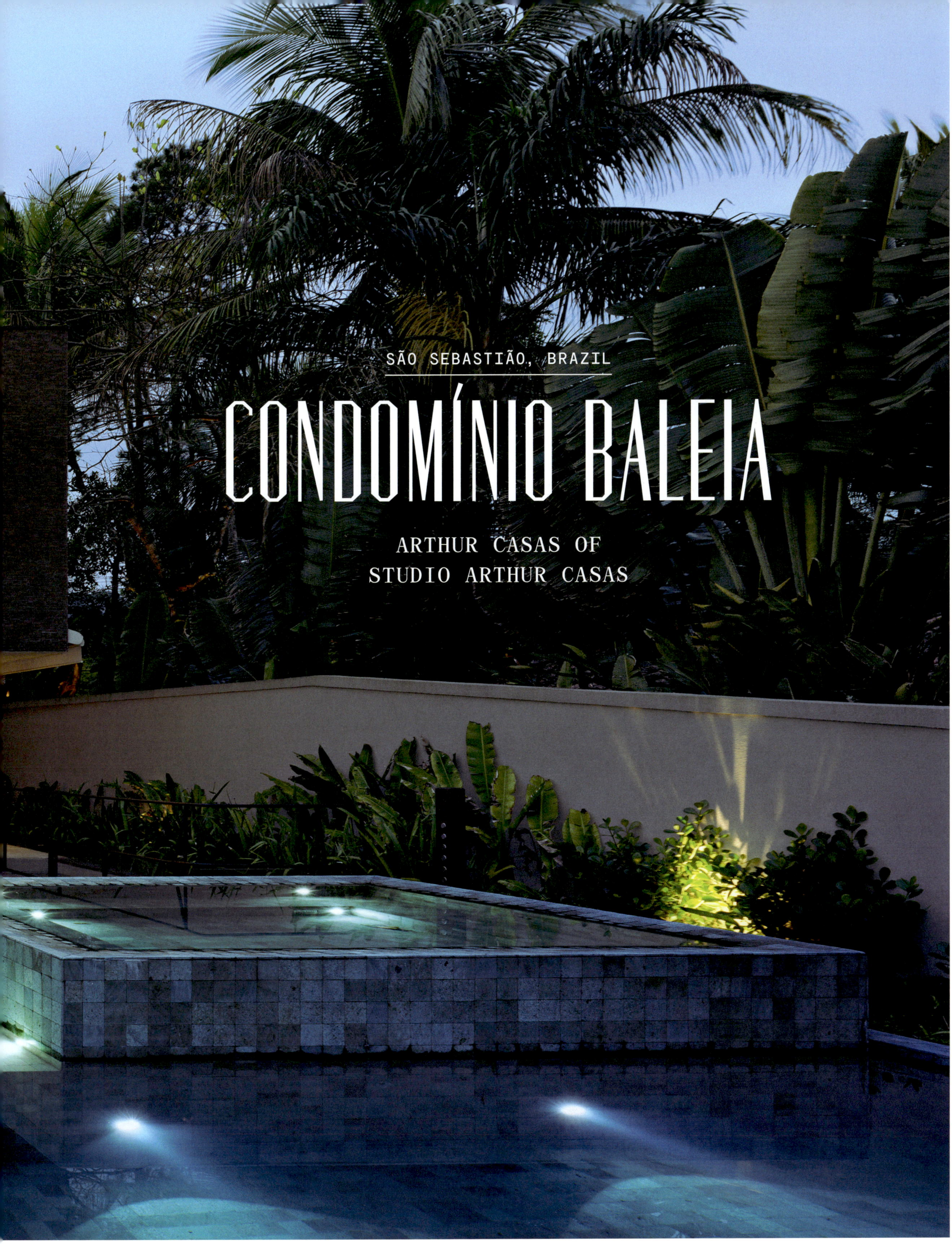

SÃO SEBASTIÃO, BRAZIL

CONDOMÍNIO BALEIA

ARTHUR CASAS OF
STUDIO ARTHUR CASAS

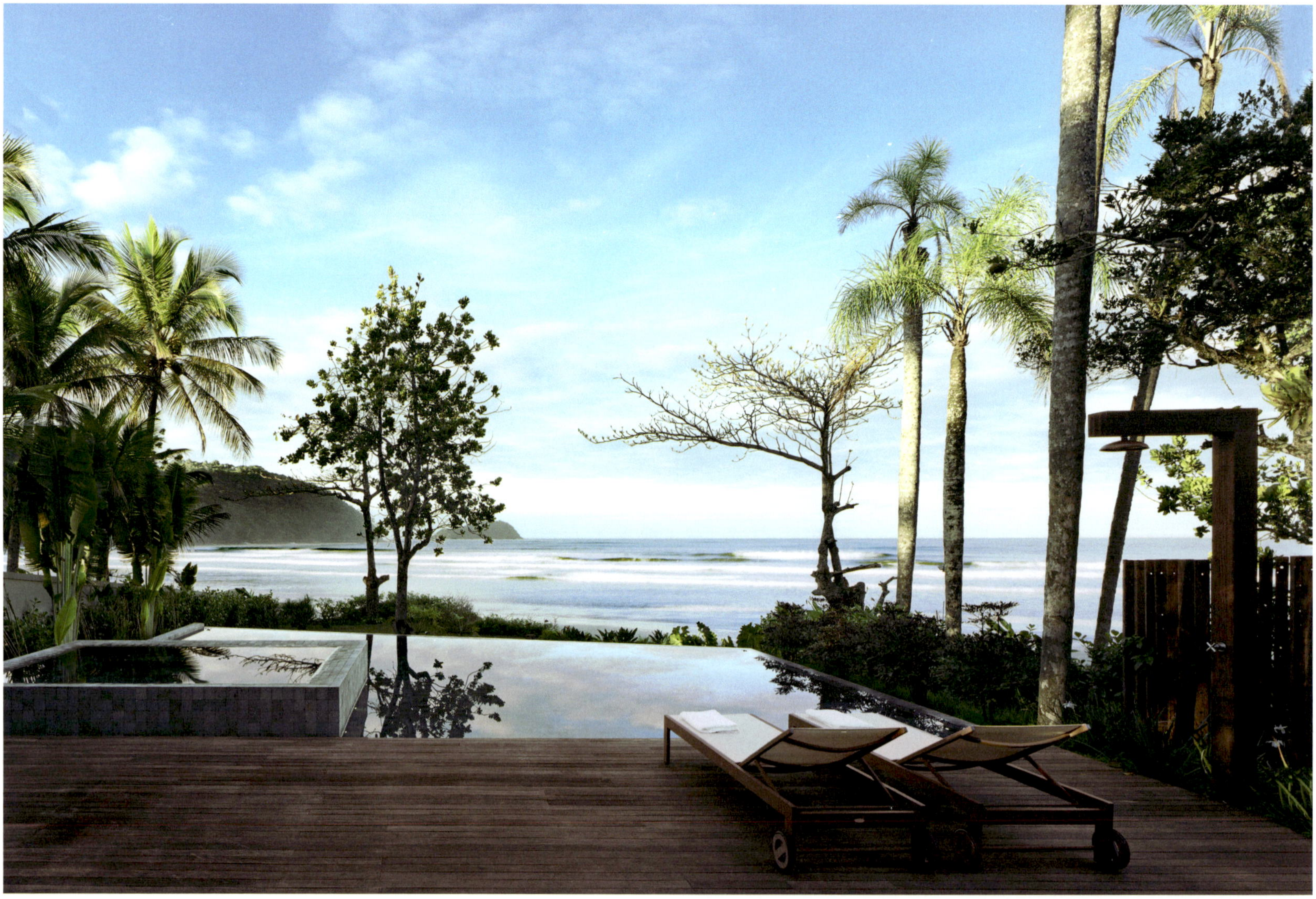

CONDOMÍNIO BALEIA Bold, geometric architecture does not necessarily have cold and isolating effects. Communicating with the verdant garden and nearby ocean, Condomínio Baleia interweaves simple materials and natural forms to create a cohesive and changeable space that is both comfortable and private.

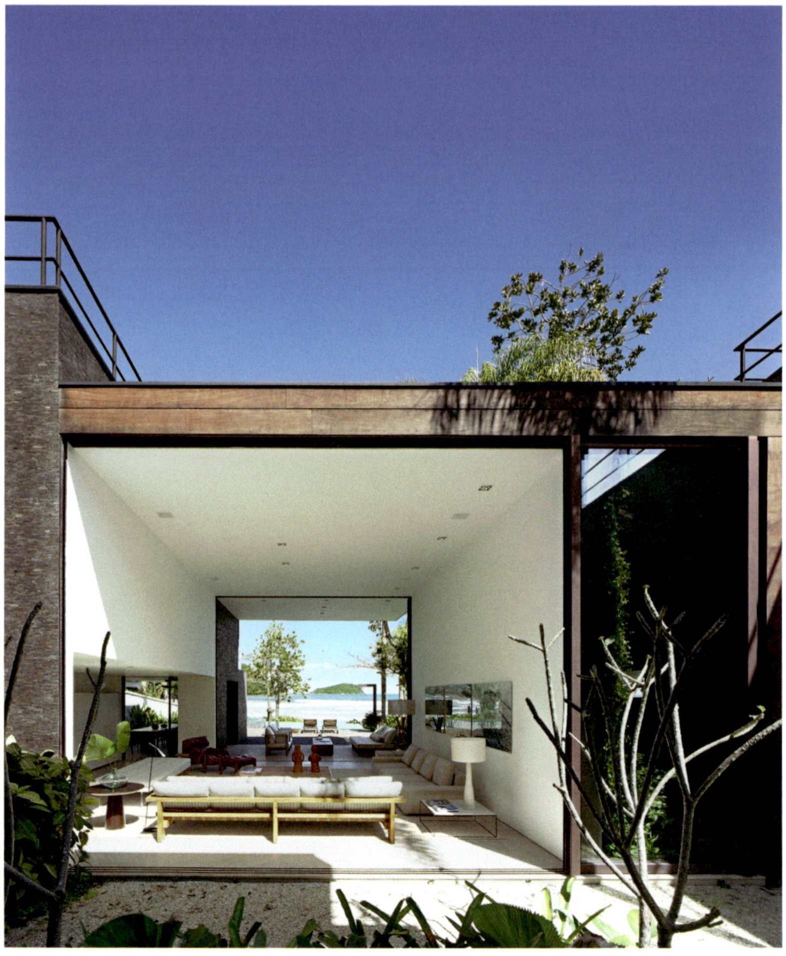

Condomínio Baleia is meant to be a dream come true for the Marcondes family. High ceilings, warmly toned hardwood, and an inspired deployment of glass usher the family and their guests through rooms both grand and humble.

In the realization of this home, architect Arthur Casas says he was "concerned with the way that the spaces can be experienced and shared, and how they can be used for comfort and leisure." On the ground floor, sliding glass screens partially disrupt the flow between an interior garden, a living space, and a beachside patio. Outside, the turquoise-tiled pool mediates

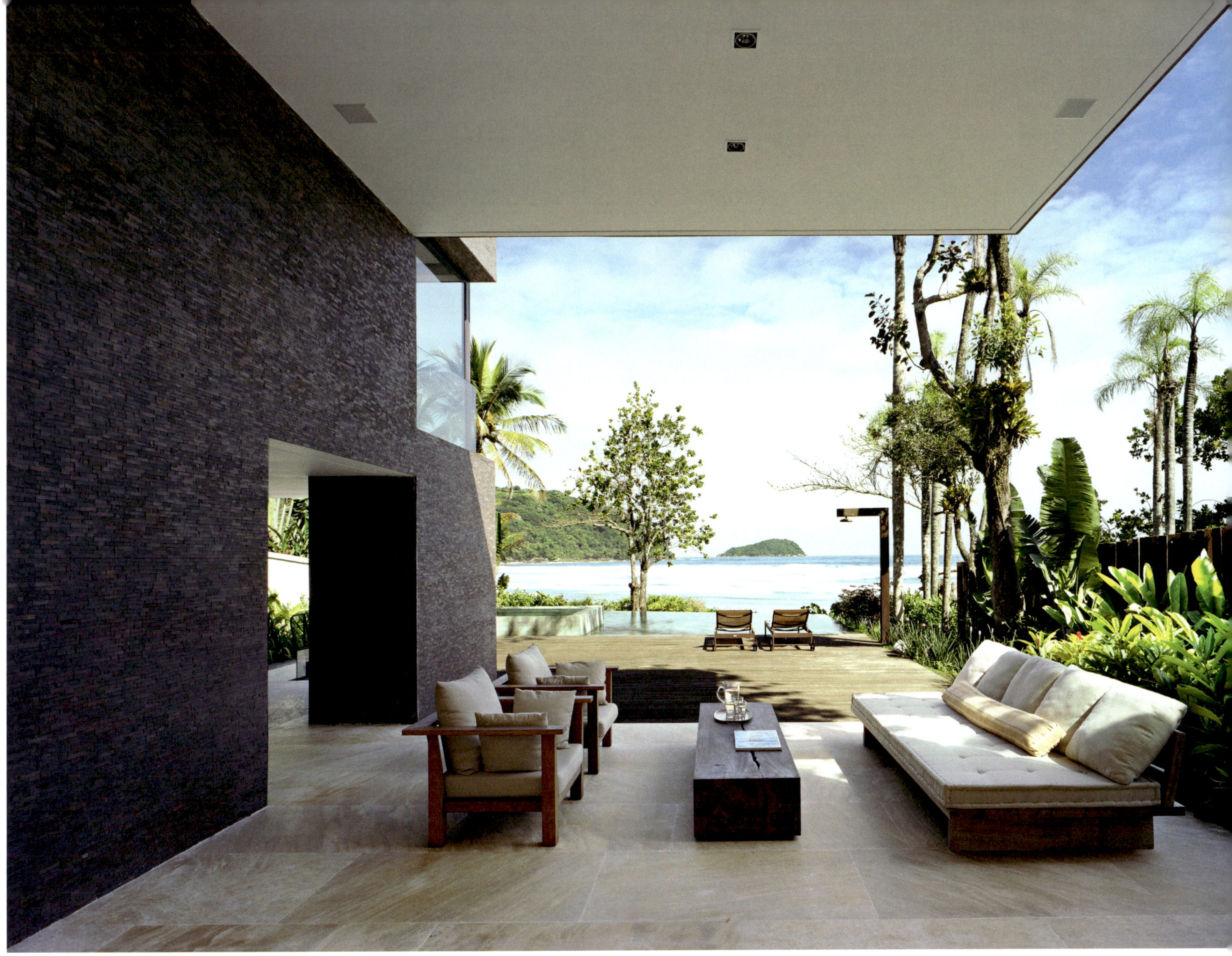

light reflected by the sea and garden. Trees provide privacy; the grass roof highlights a respect for the environment. Rather than obtrusive air-conditioning, wooden louvers channel breezes through the house.

> "HIGH CEILINGS, WARMLY TONED HARDWOOD, AND AN INSPIRED DEPLOYMENT OF GLASS USHER THE FAMILY AND THEIR GUESTS THROUGH ROOMS BOTH GRAND AND HUMBLE."

Transitioning between social and private spaces while celebrating the majestic location, Condomínio Baleia is ideal for savoring seclusion or for socializing. Ana Marcondes says, "This is a place where we like to rest and recharge the batteries. Yet at the same time we love having friends to visit, enjoying the house and the surrounding landscape." ◆

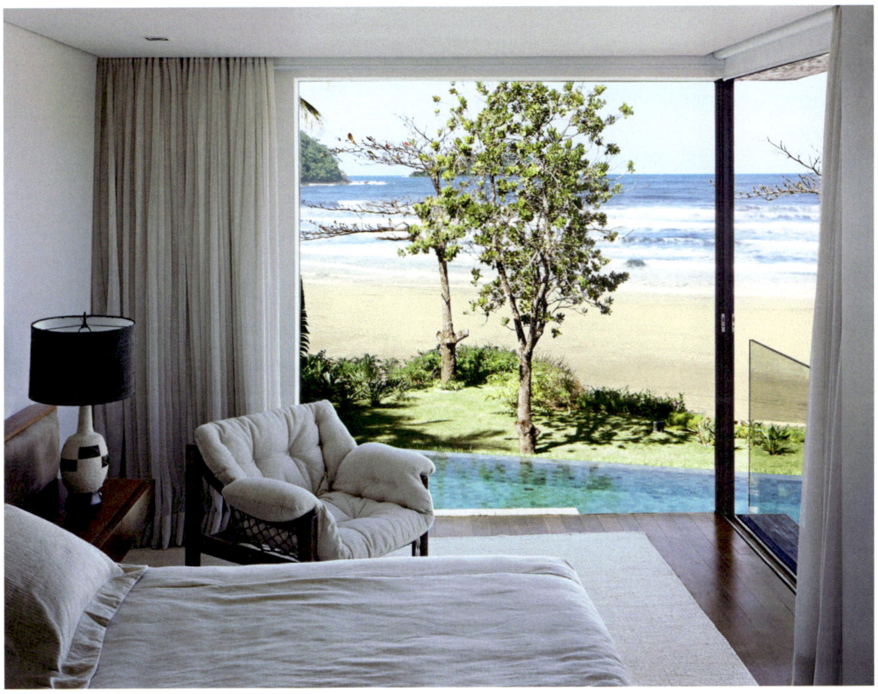

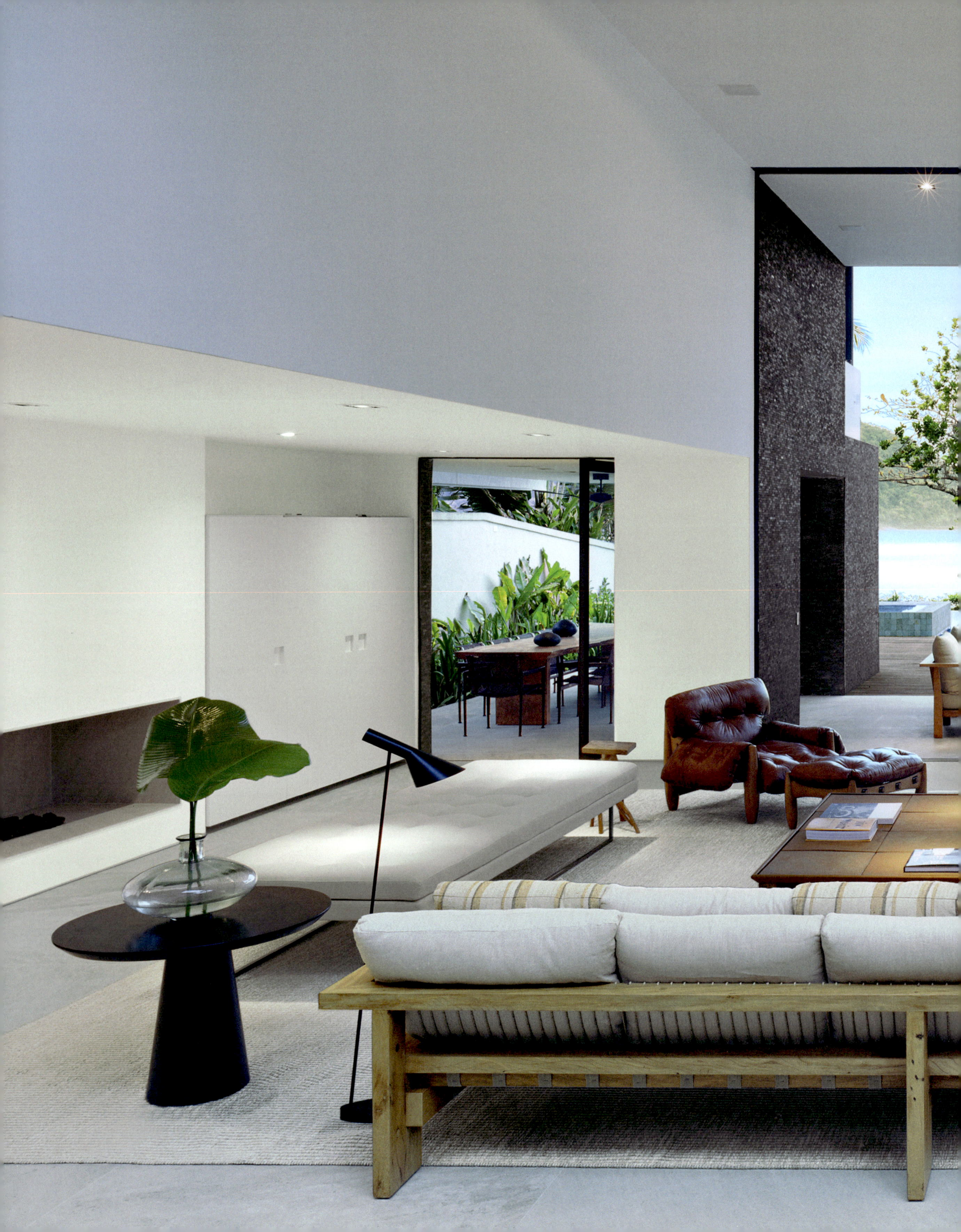

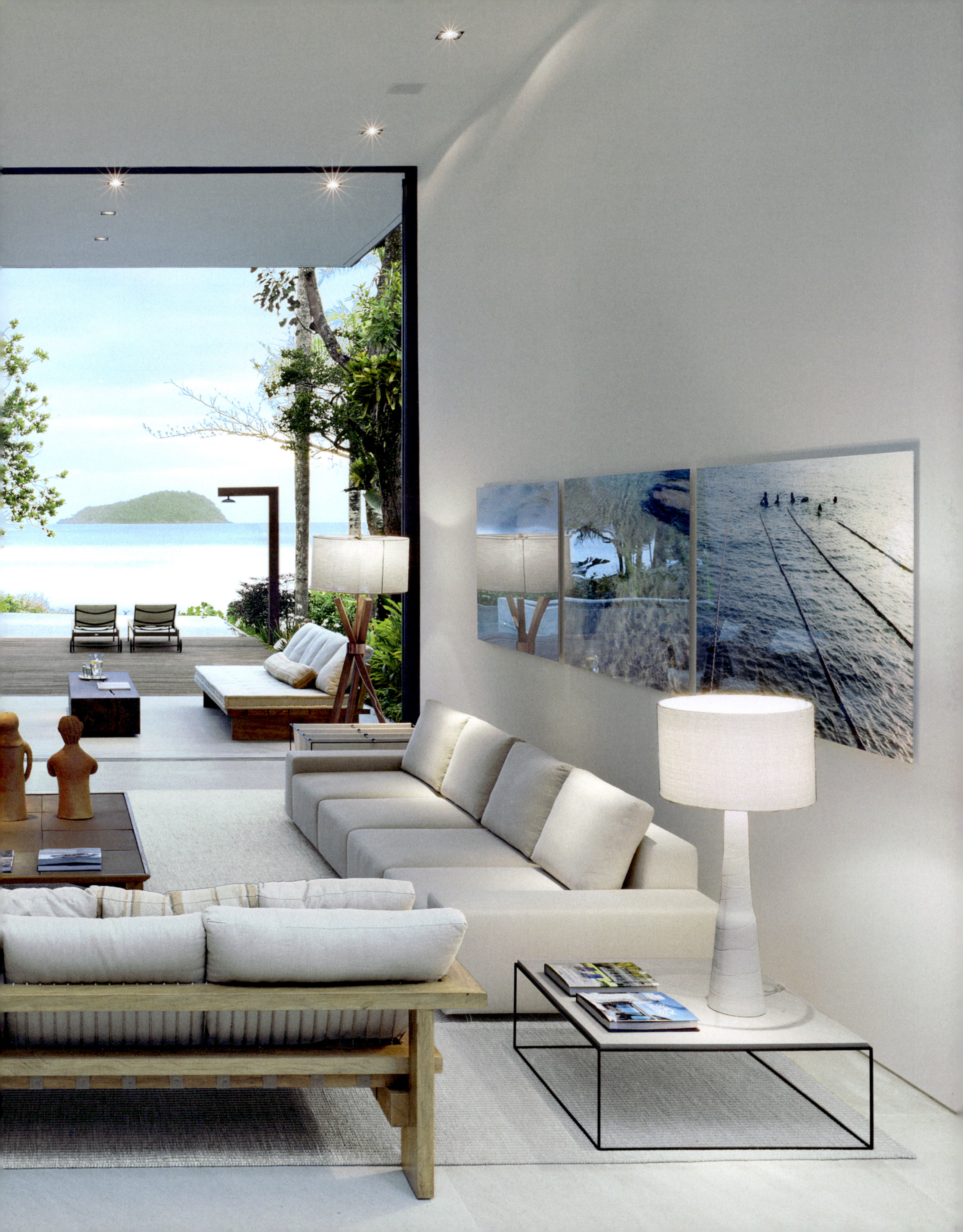

ILHABELA, BRAZIL

CASA ILHABELA

MARCIO KOGAN AND DIANA RADOMYLSER
OF STUDIO MK27

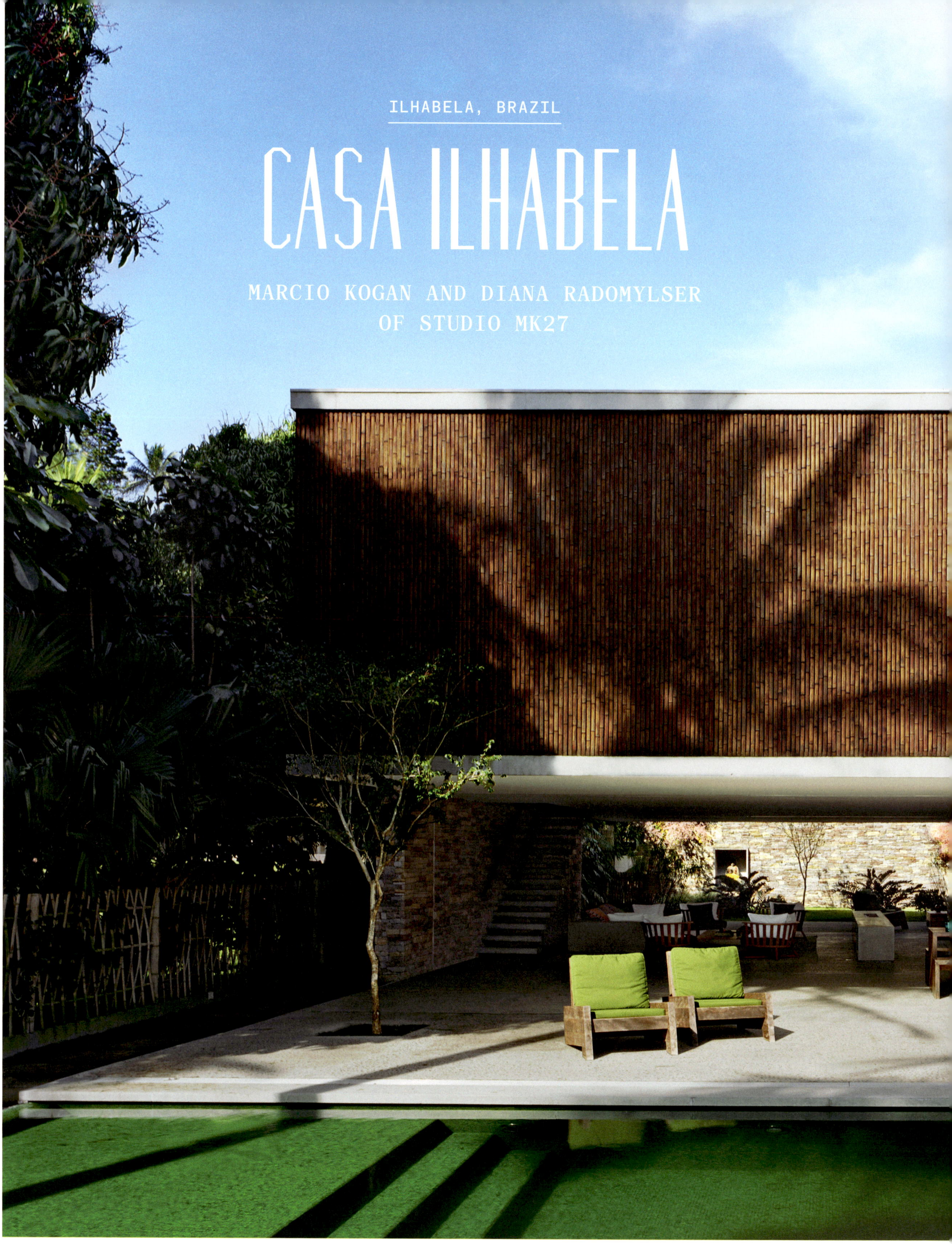

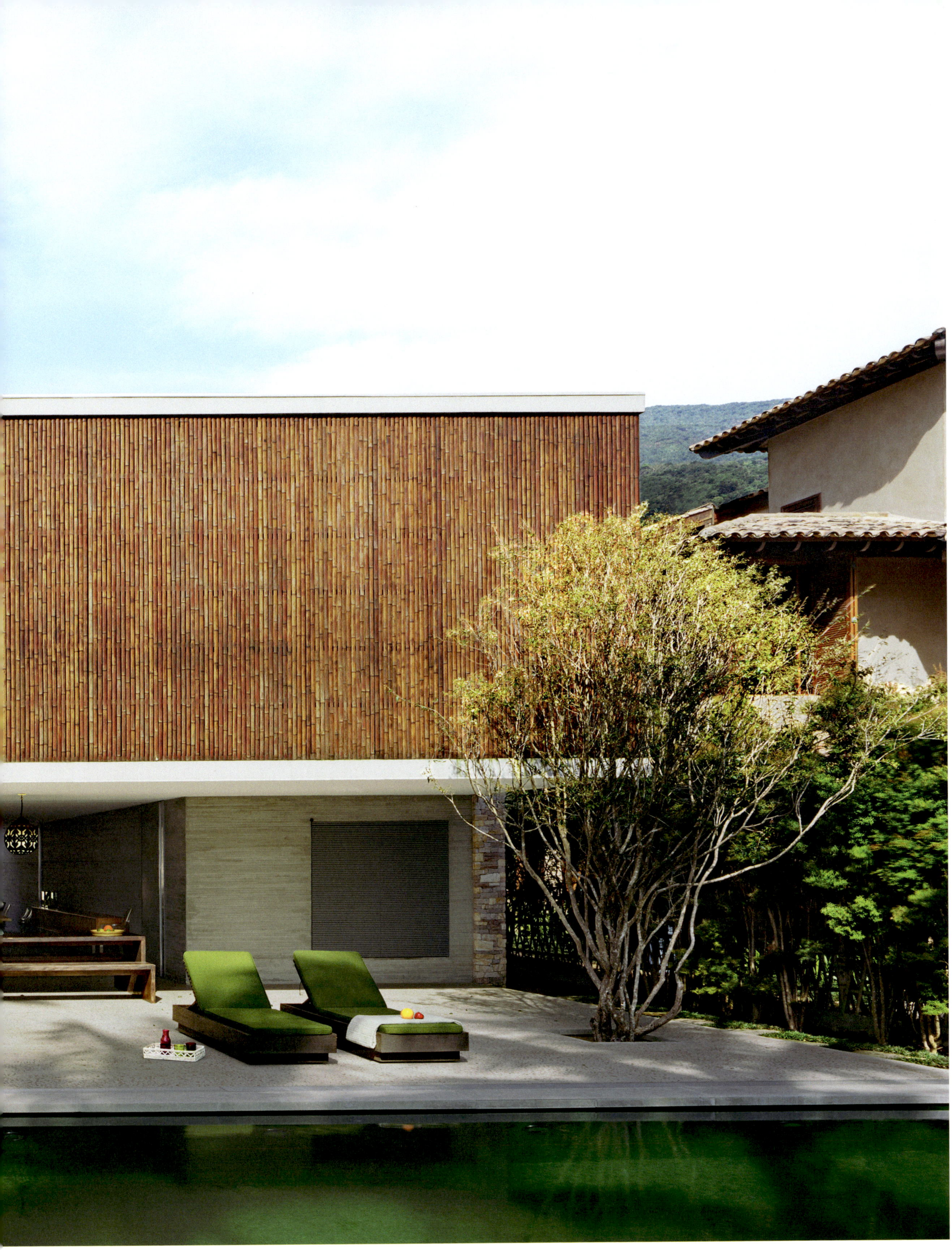

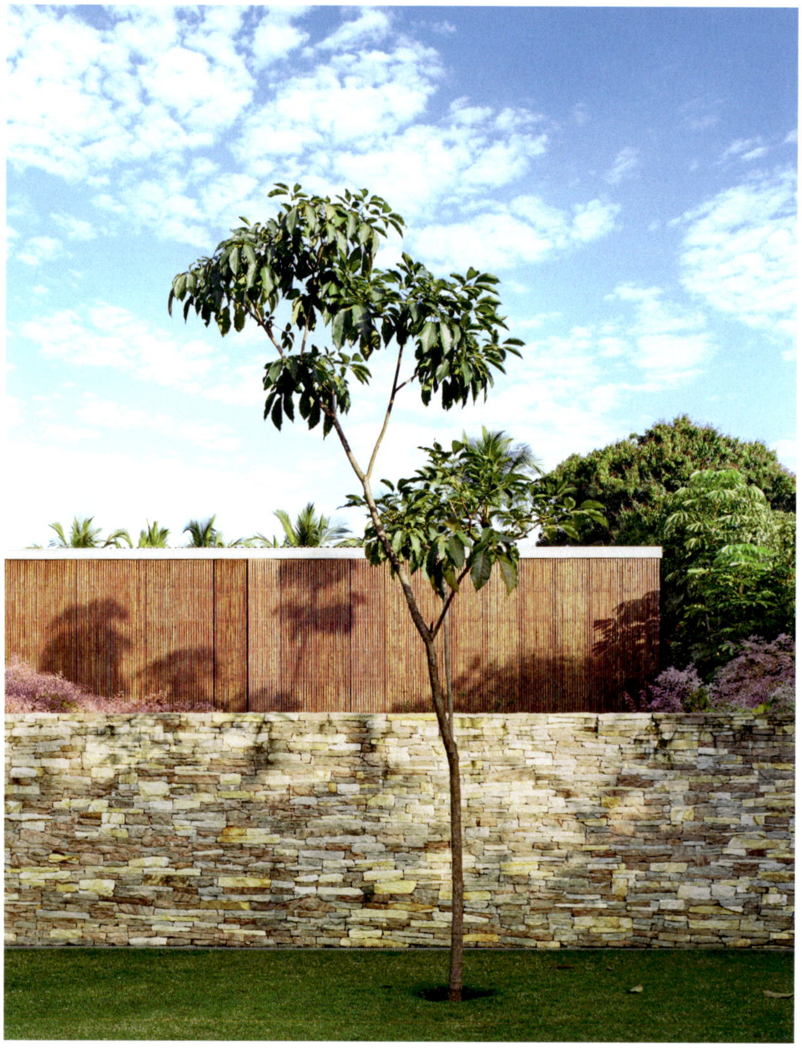

"A VERDANT OUTDOOR AREA BRIDGES THE SPACE BETWEEN HOUSE AND BEACH TO THE REAR, WHILE A GREEN POOL DISSOLVES THE DIVISION BETWEEN WATER AND GRASS."

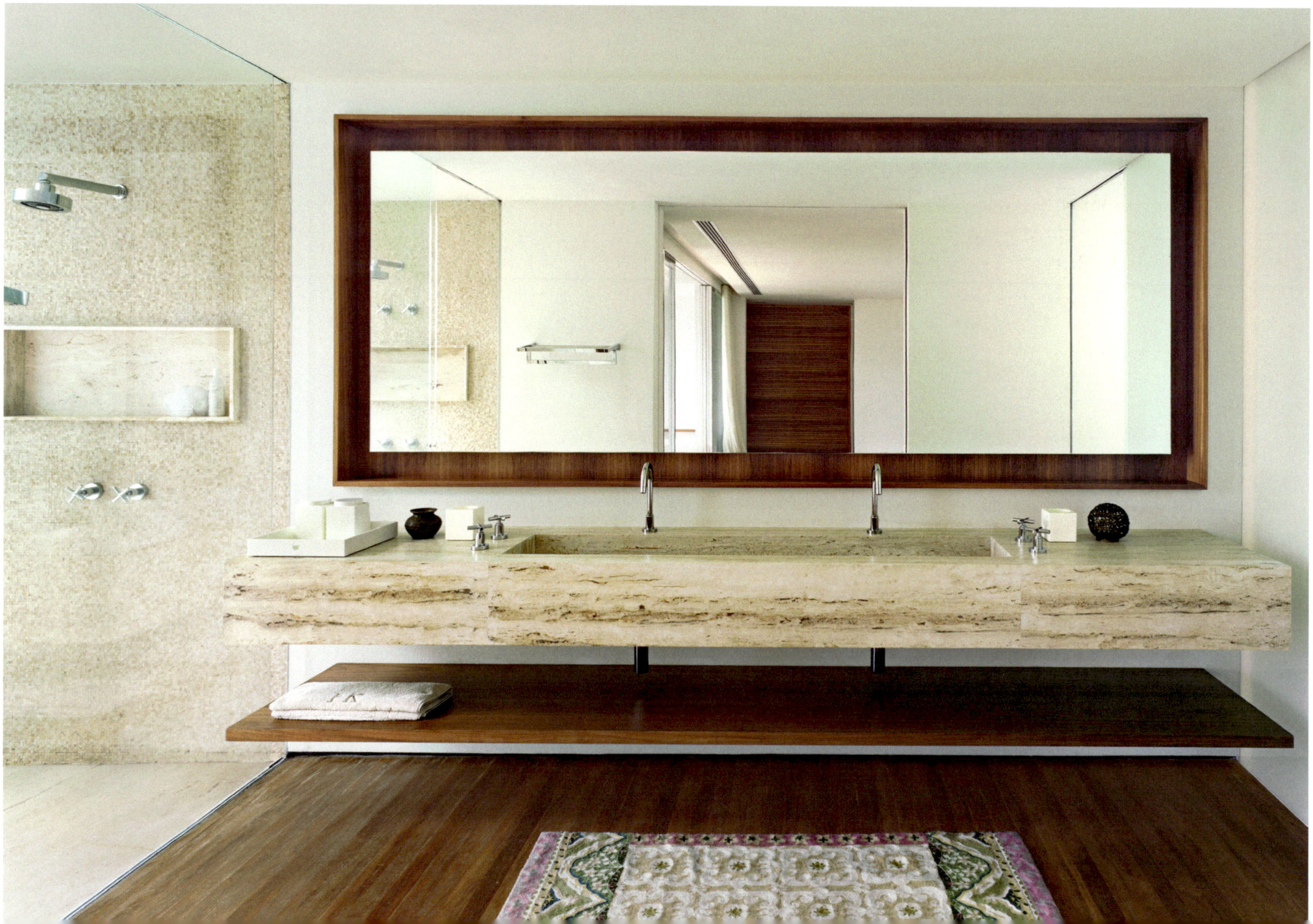

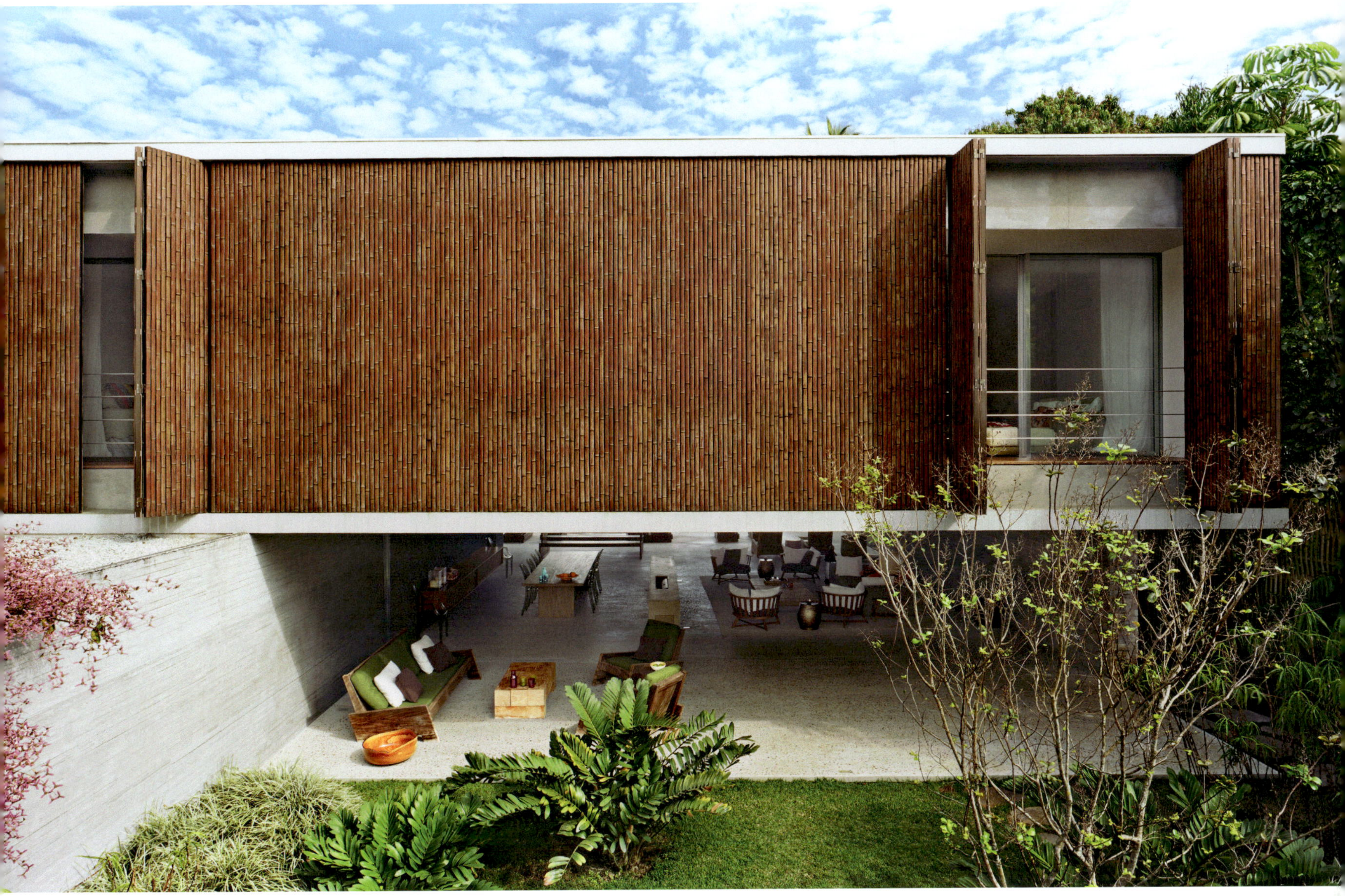

CASA ILHABELA Using local materials and taking design cues from the landscape, Marcio Kogan and Diana Radomylser of Studio MK27 have paid respect to the Ilhabela region. But they have also shaped the raw forms of Casa Ilhabela with references to Asian aesthetics, creating a neutral, muted, and flowing home.

The owners of this family home vacationed at Ilhabela many times before finding the perfect building site. They were drawn to this Brazilian island because, as they explain, "It offers the best of nature, the ocean is quiet and clear, with beautiful mountains and waterfalls, and all the water and wind sports there are to enjoy." Already attuned to the local environment, they knew precisely how their home should feel. So when they met principal architect Marcio Kogan and co-architect Diana Radomylser of Studio MK27, the brief was clear: to create a space with "clean lines, a mix of textures, and a house that integrates perfectly into [the] setting."

Casa Ilhabela is designed over two flowing levels. The living area on the lower level features a concrete floor that subtly blends with a stacked stone wall; the color palette never strays far from neutral shades. Another stone wall eclipses the road and encloses the front yard. A verdant outdoor area bridges the space between house and beach to the rear, while a green pool dissolves the division between water and grass. Radomylser explains that the openness of the lower level "allowed for total spatial and visual integration with the exterior and, as a result, the pool, the external deck, and the veranda become an extension of the living room's large open doorway."

Upstairs, there are five bedrooms and a TV room. All of the bedrooms are simultaneously shaded and lit by the distinct, porous bamboo shutters. Made from a locally sourced material, the folding shutters not only resonate with the house's Asian theme, but also let cool air flow through the entire home. The owners could not be happier with the result, saying, "With a small and almost private beach to the front of the house, and an amazing waterfall just around the corner, it fits perfectly to our lifestyle." ◆

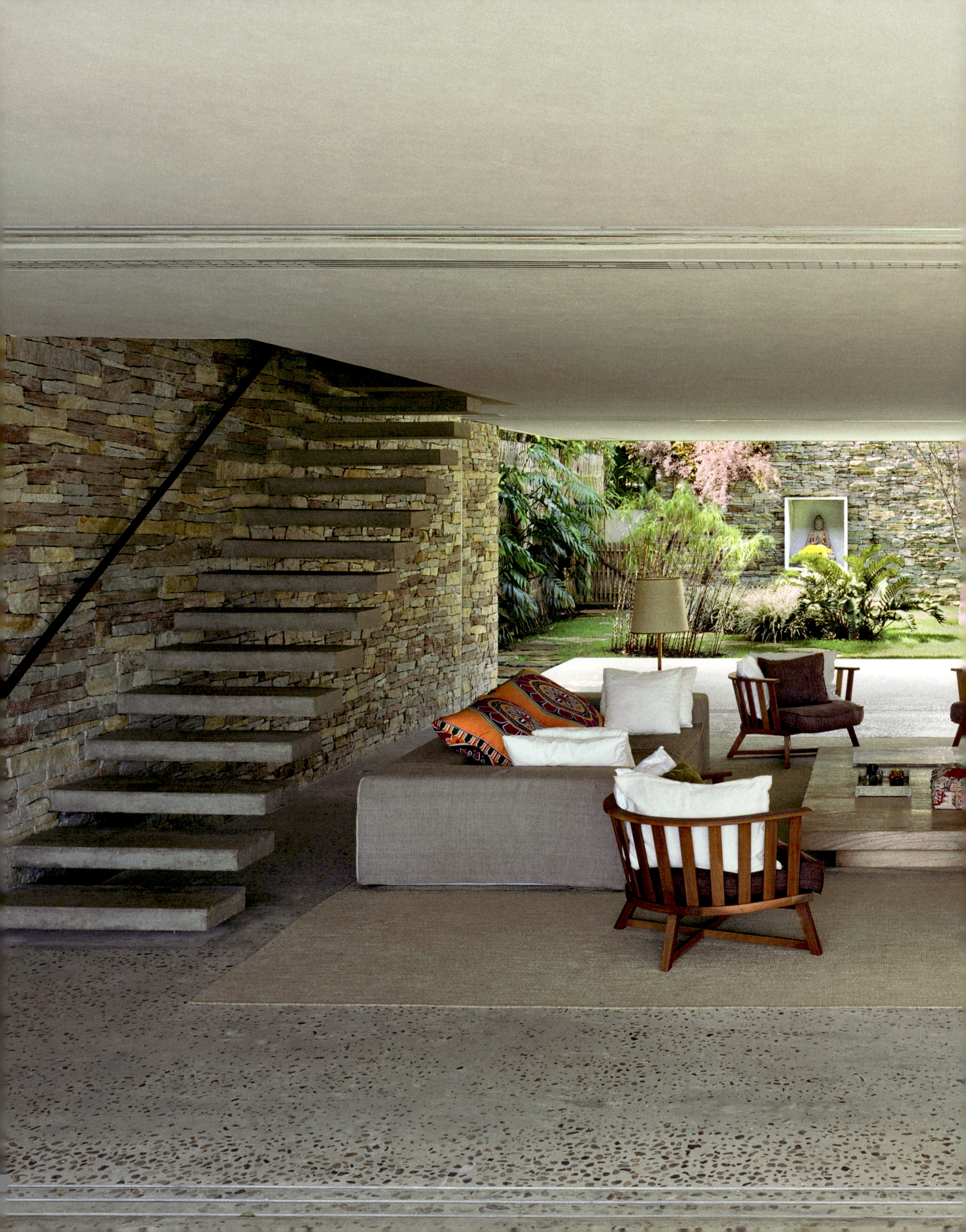

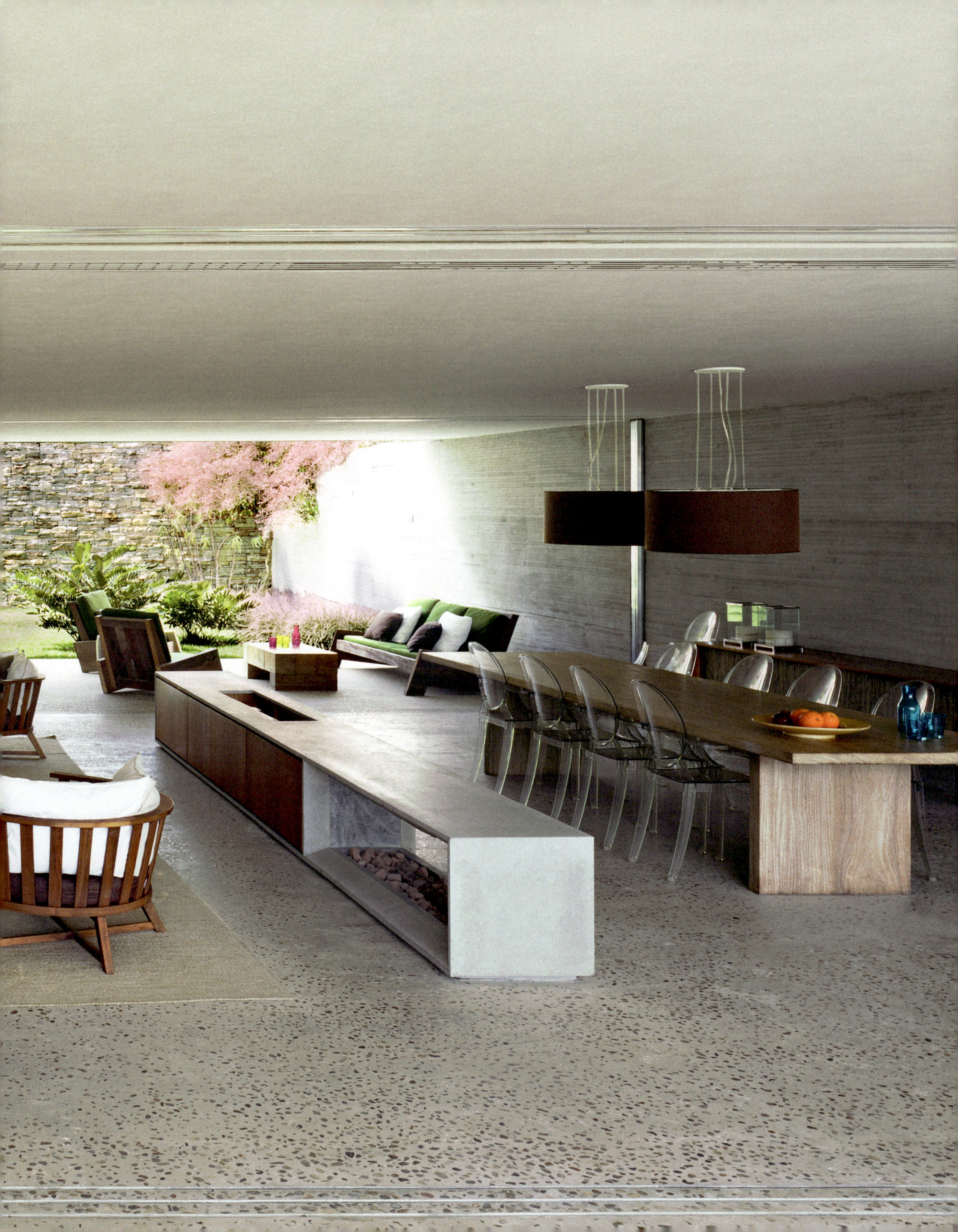

CAREYES, MEXICO

CASA LUNA

MANOLO MESTRE

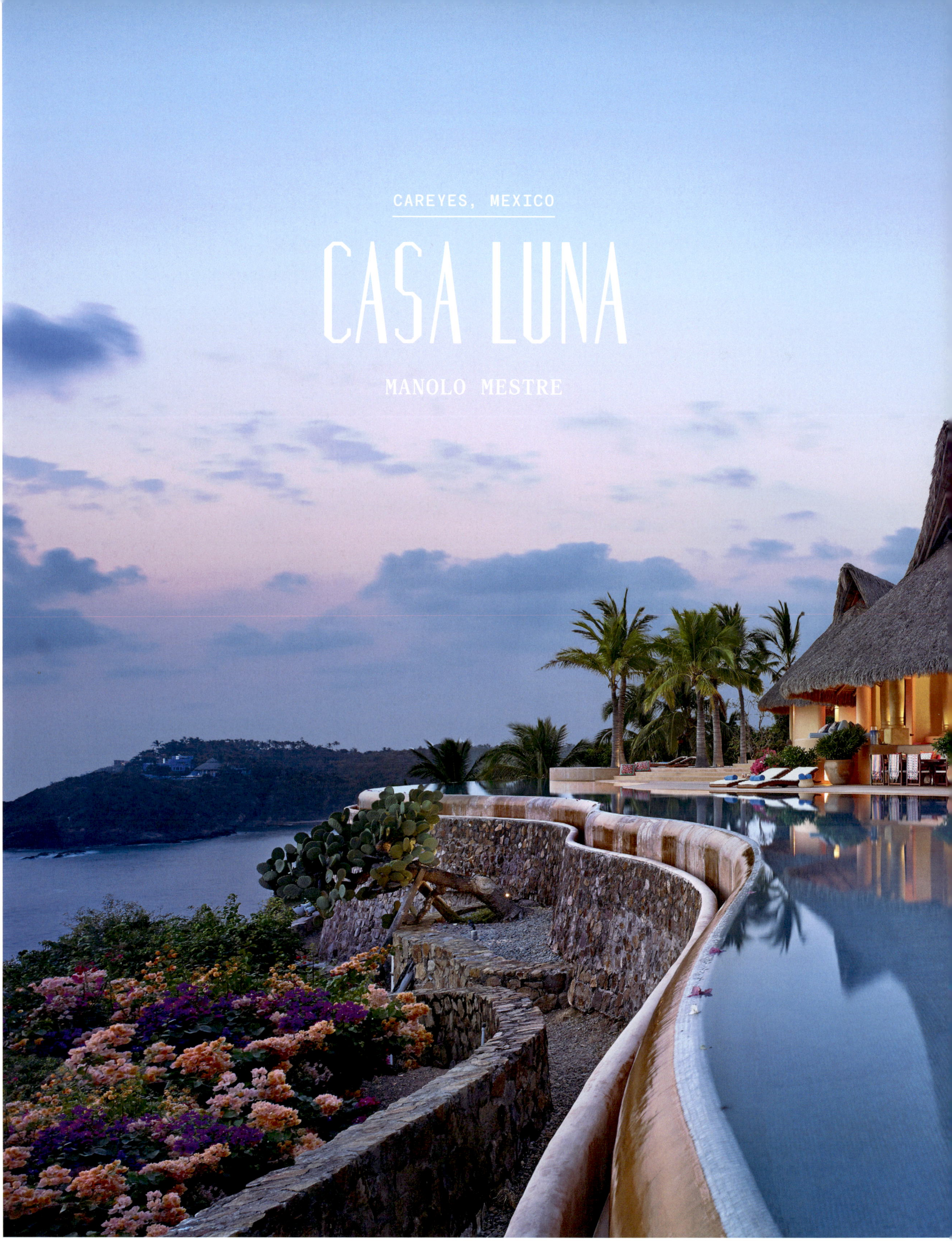

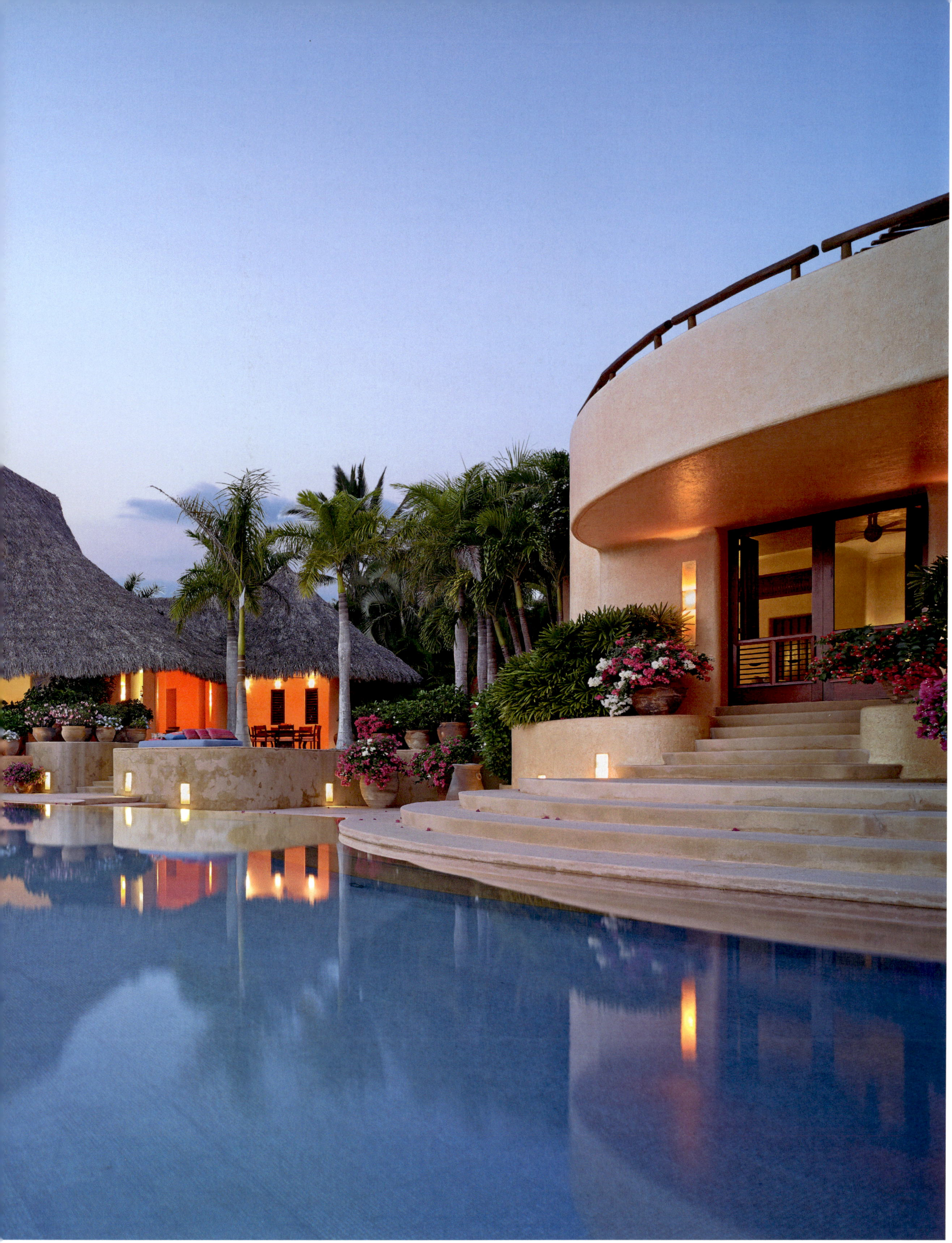

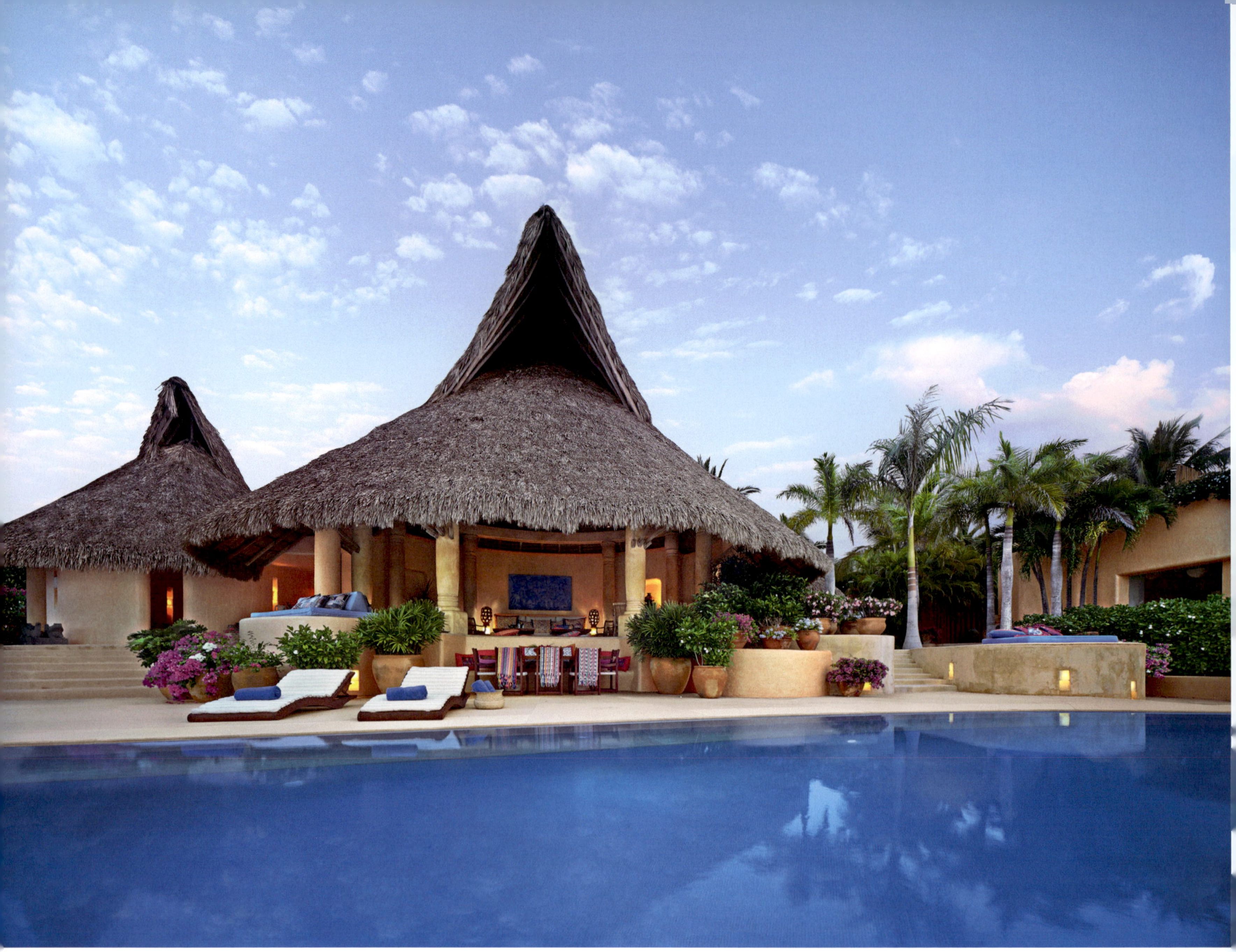

CASA LUNA The Careyes region of Mexico is known for the surreal buildings that protrude from the landscape. Casa Luna is no exception. The structure is grounded in the history of Mexican architecture, and while its ancient forms retain their mystical elements, they have also been refined with modern details.

Casa Luna was born out of a journey shared by the owner, Chris Tribull, and the architect, Manolo Mestre. Not content with relying on discussion alone as a means to realize their project, they actually toured Mexico together before work began, gaining the kind of mutual understanding that comes only through experience. Mestre introduced Tribull to the artists and craftsmen he knew as they traveled. The German-born businessman thus became acquainted with Mexican building techniques and, in turn, with the possibilities and limits of his own project. Tribull says the trip "was all a great adventure."

Much of Casa Luna was inspired by parts of their journey. While in Oaxaca, for instance, Mestre showed Tribull a cloister dating back to the 1500s where a mixture of crushed limestone and nopal cactus formed the stucco walls. Impressed by the smooth beige finish, Tribull decided to employ 12 artisans from Oaxaca to replicate these traditional walls in his own home.

In another tribute to Mexican architectural history, a sparely furnished living area and main dining room are nestled beneath the ancient form of the palapa. Since Casa Luna has no air conditioning, the fact that palapas draw air currents under their triangular roofs is essential for cooling the spaces.

Mestre refers to his style as "healing architecture," saying, "This house is all about happiness." His favorite ~

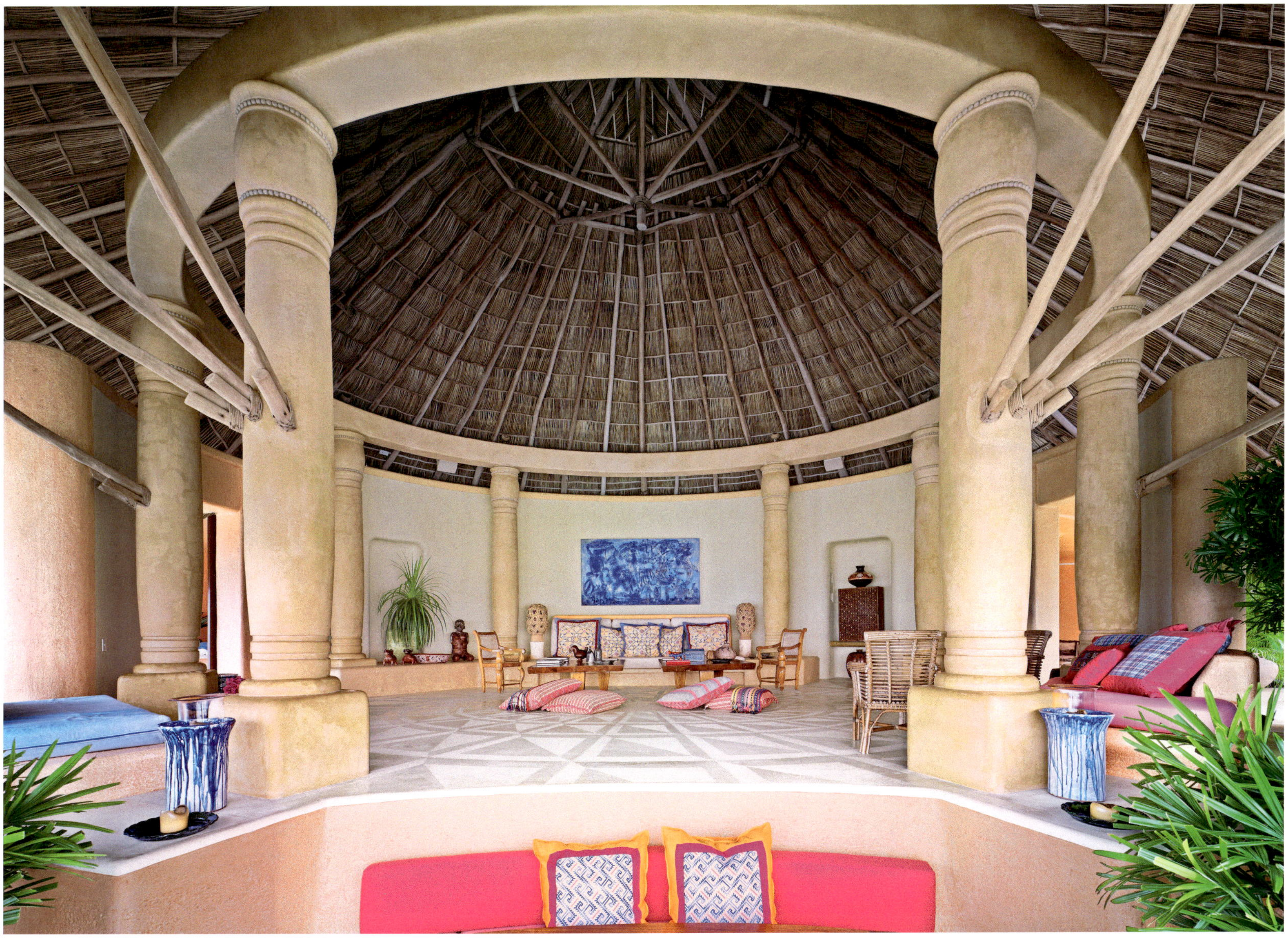

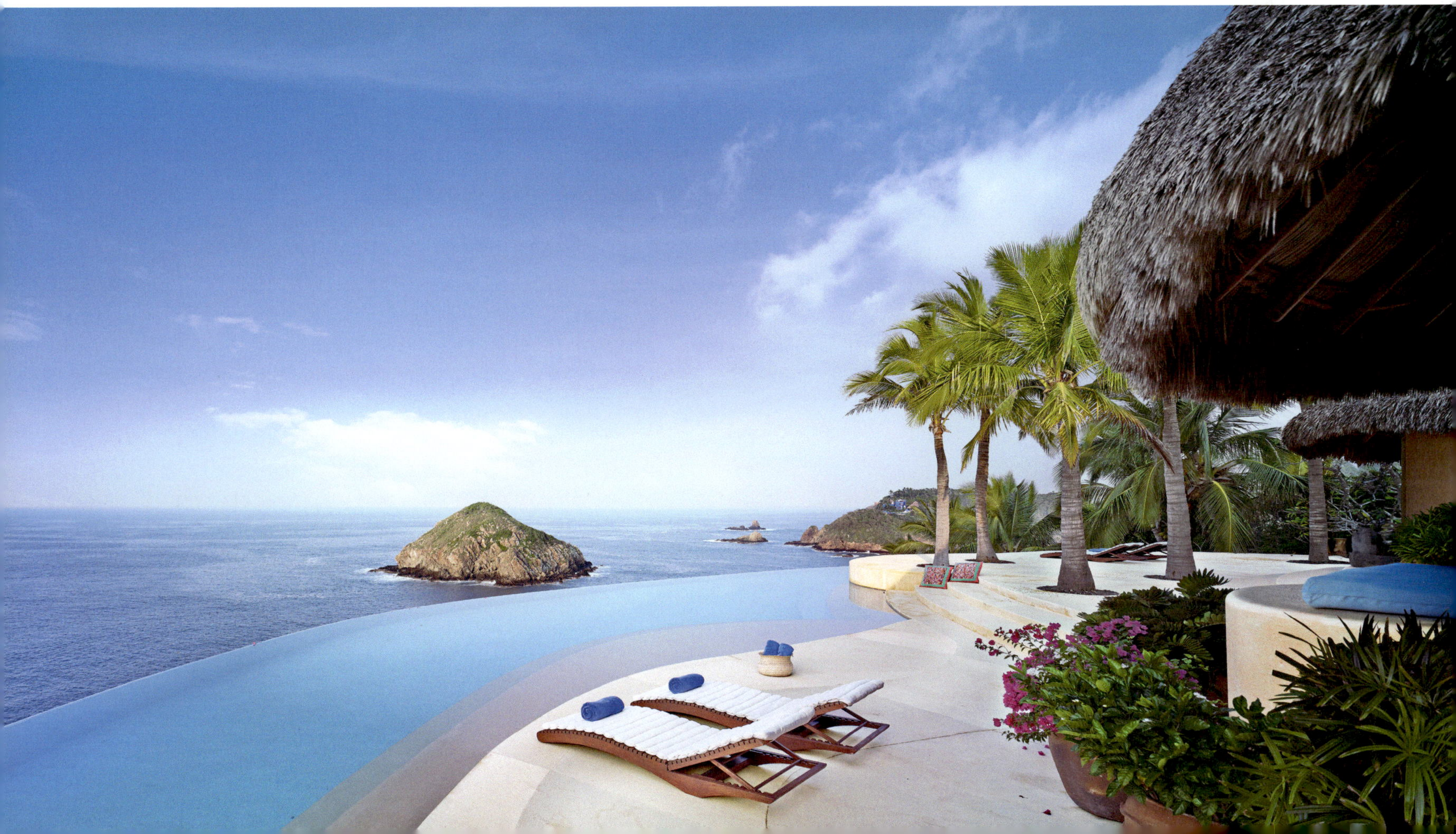

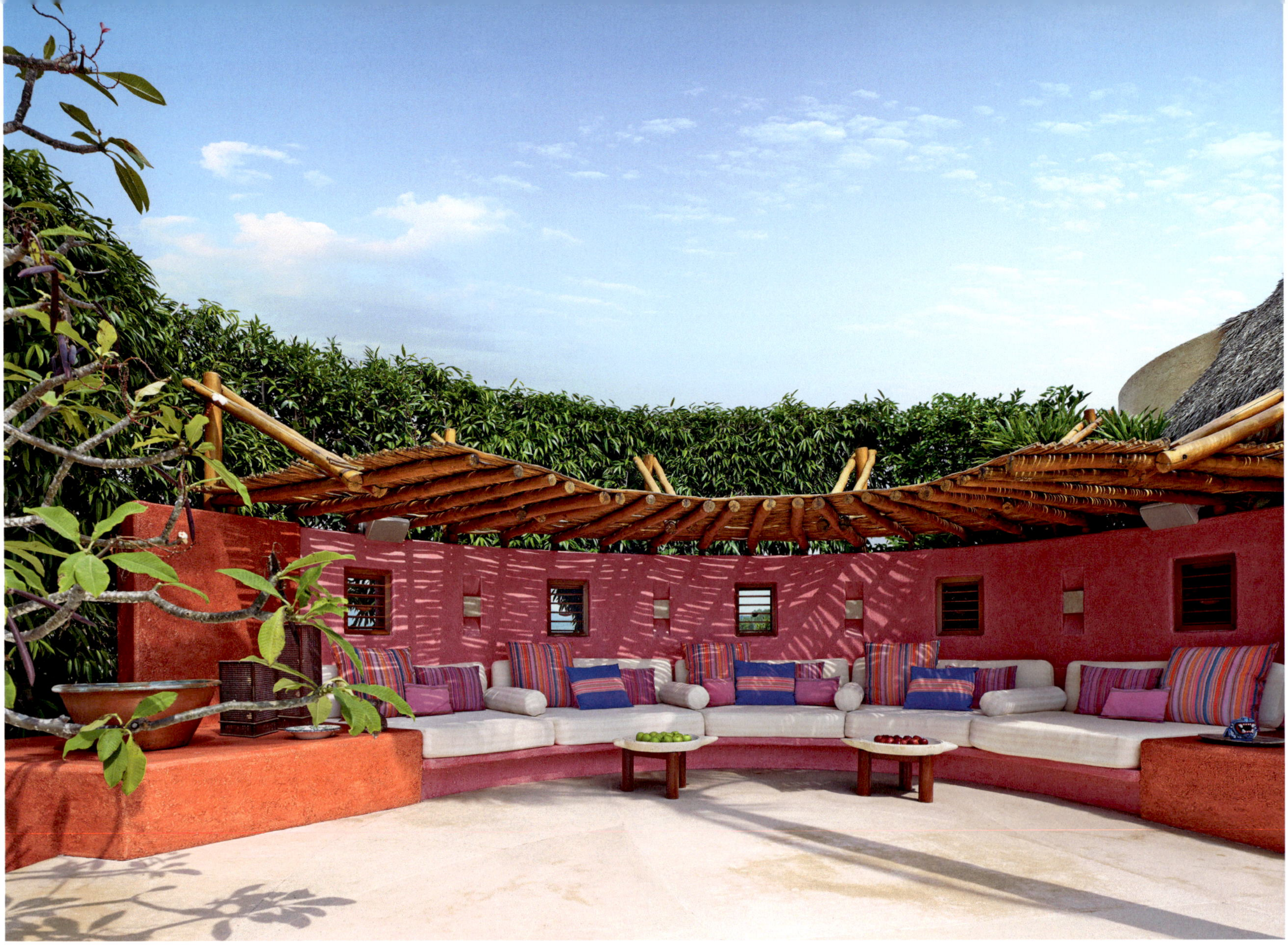

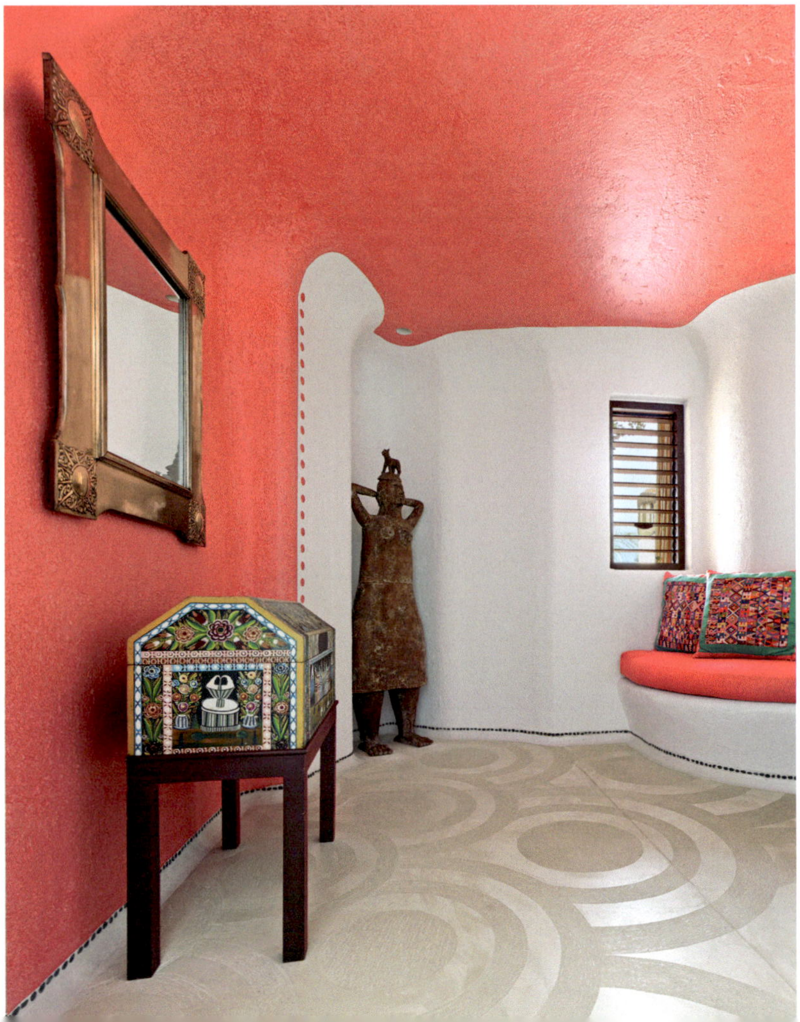

room, and the one that best represents this aesthetic, is the cozy and restful space to the side of the patio. Here, sheltered by a weave of guabillo hardwood and vines, guests can sit on brightly colored cushions and gaze out at the ocean.

> "IN ANOTHER TRIBUTE TO MEXICAN ARCHITECTURAL HISTORY, A SPARELY FURNISHED LIVING AREA AND MAIN DINING ROOM ARE NESTLED BENEATH THE ANCIENT FORM OF THE PALAPA."

With so many pieces of Mexican architectural history in one place, and a healing theme binding everything together, it is no wonder that Tribull thinks that Casa Luna is something special. As he says, "It's more like a piece of Mexican art." ◆

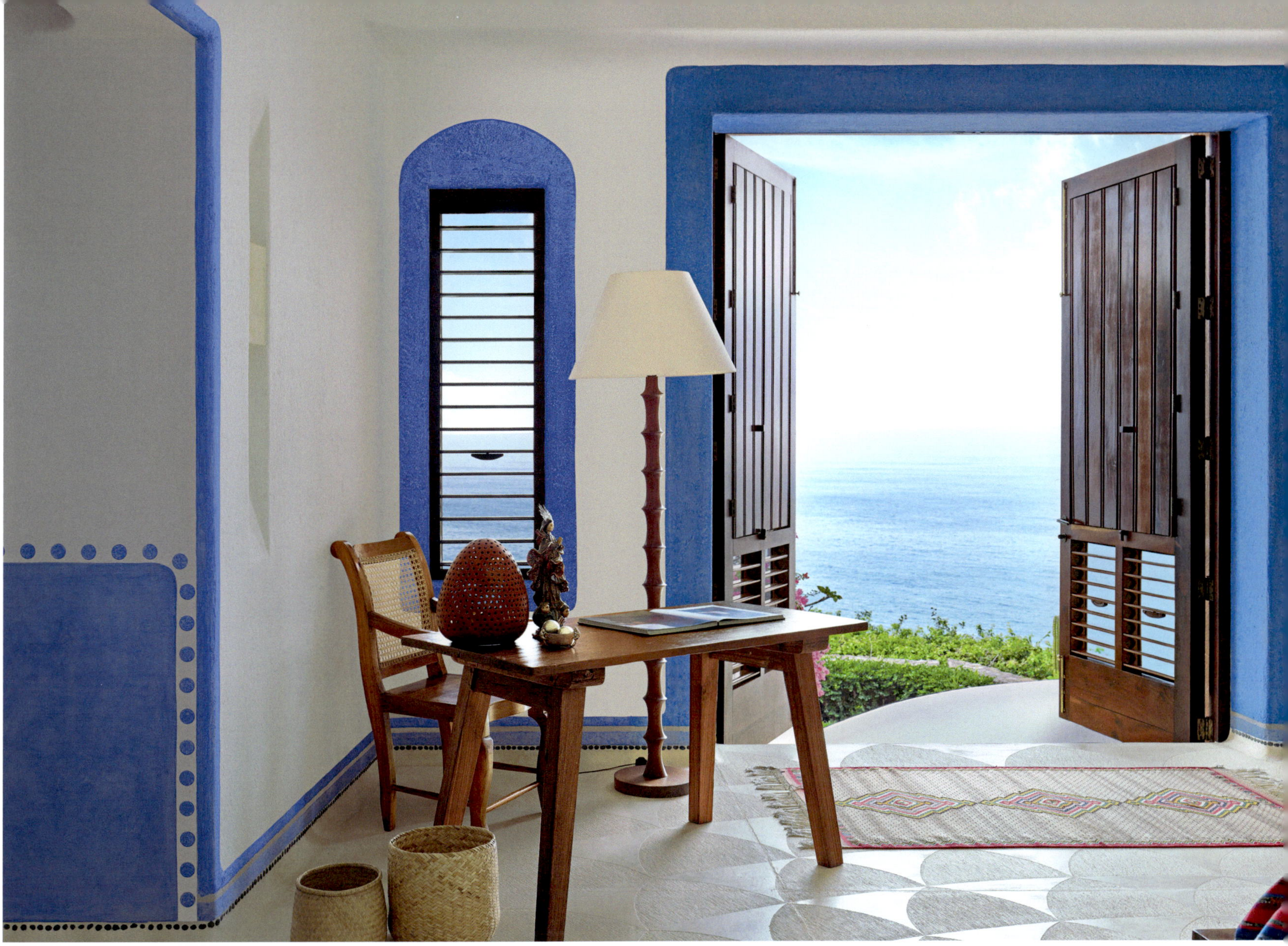

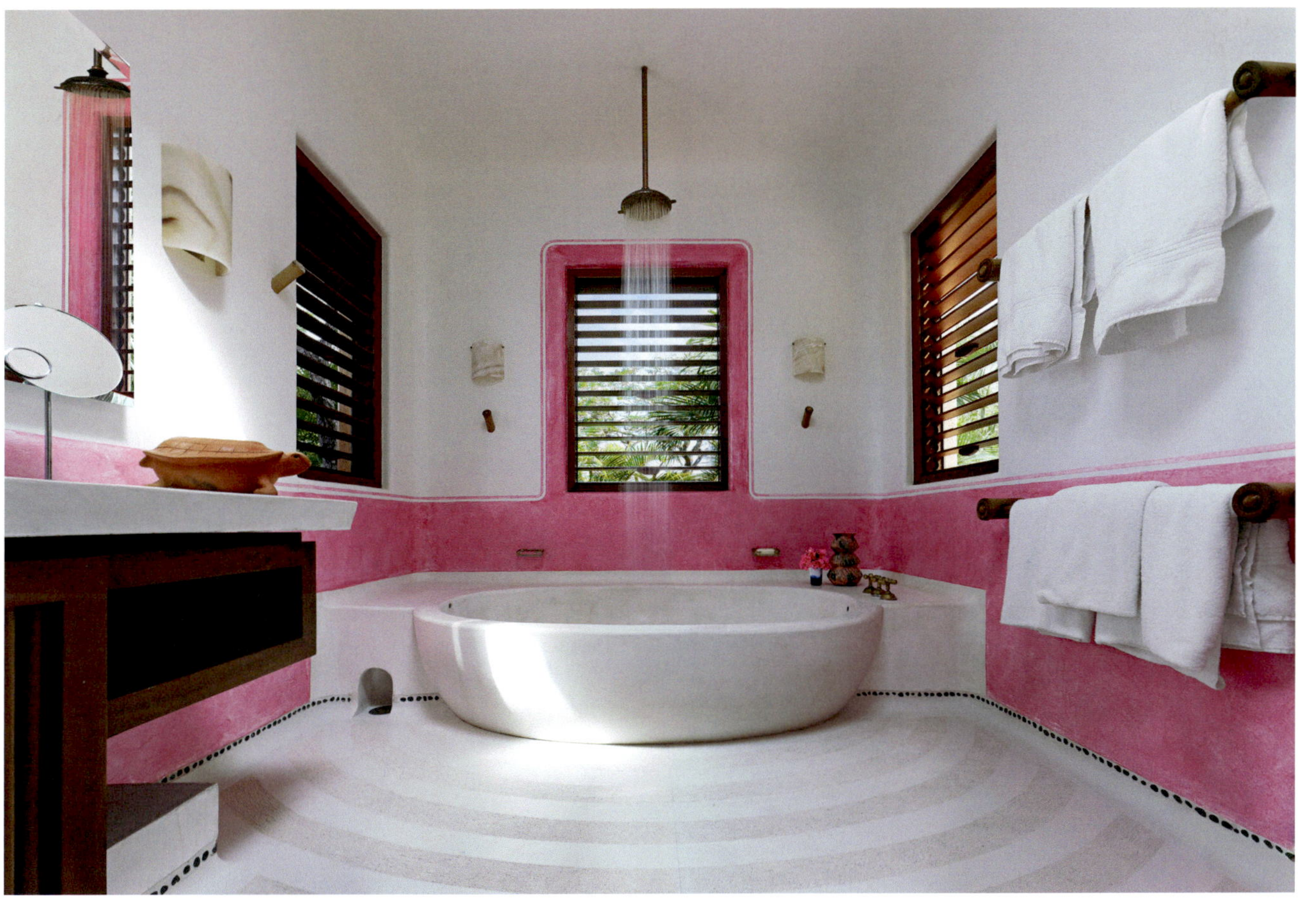

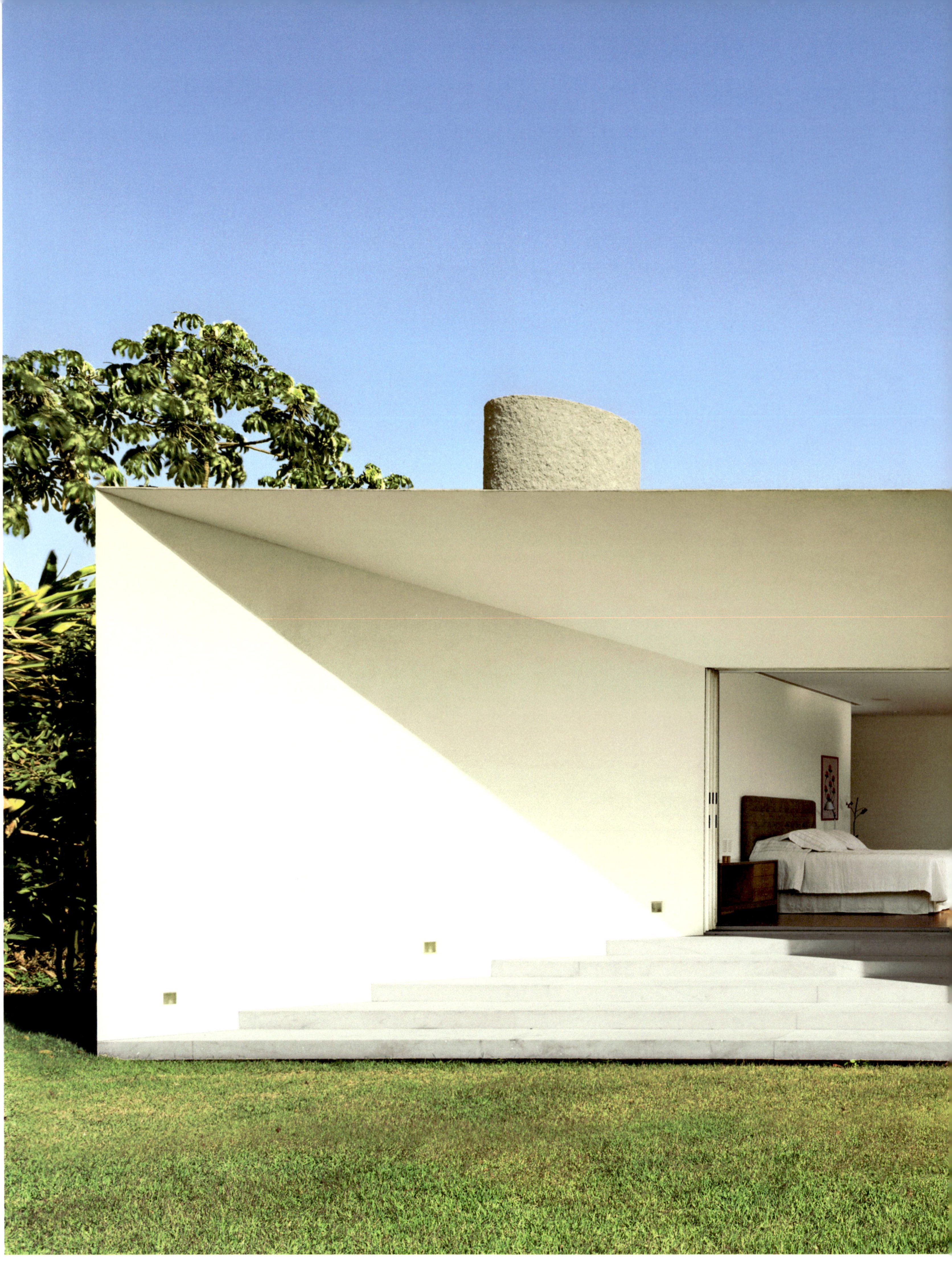

PIRACICABA, BRAZIL

CASA PIRACICABA

ISAY WEINFELD

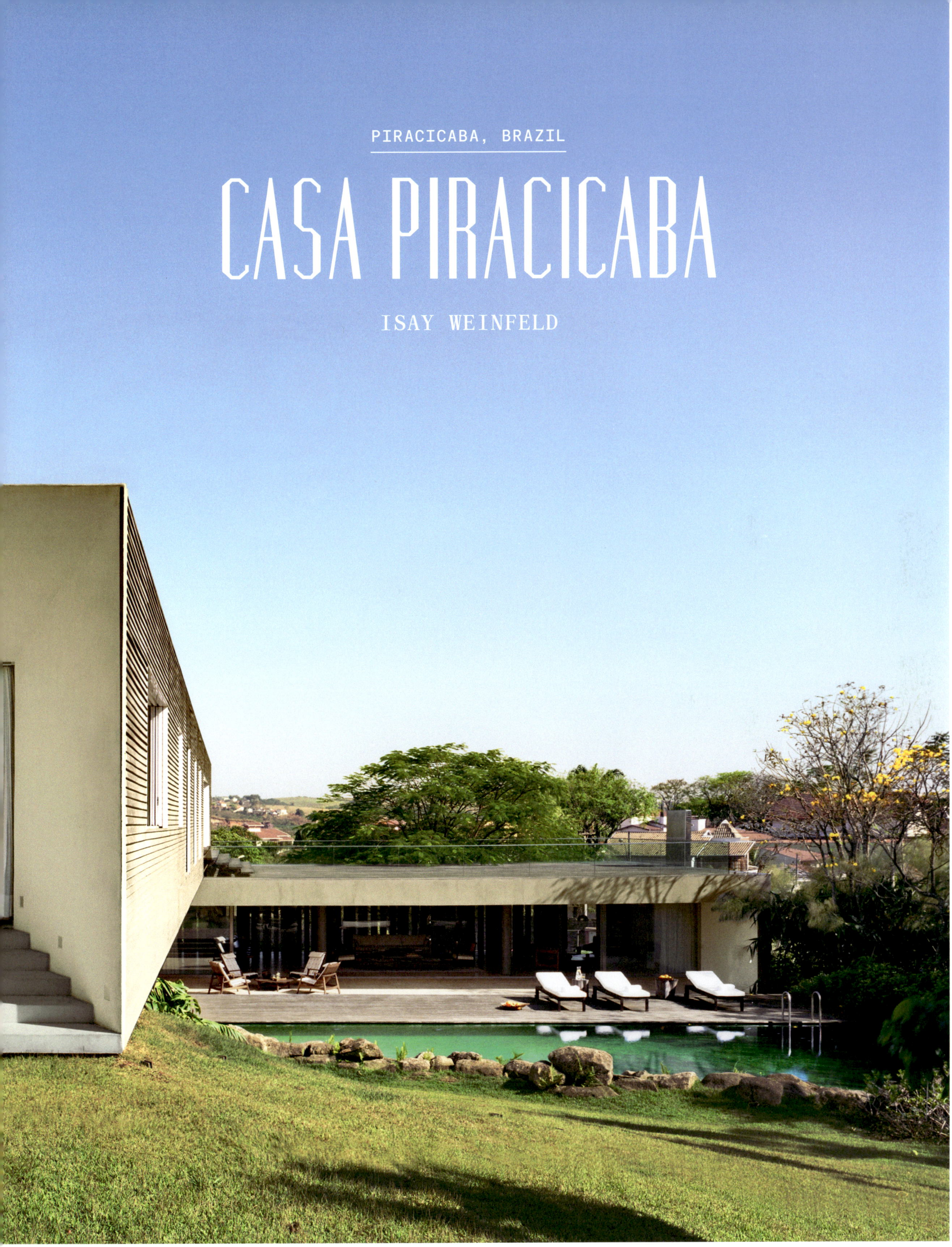

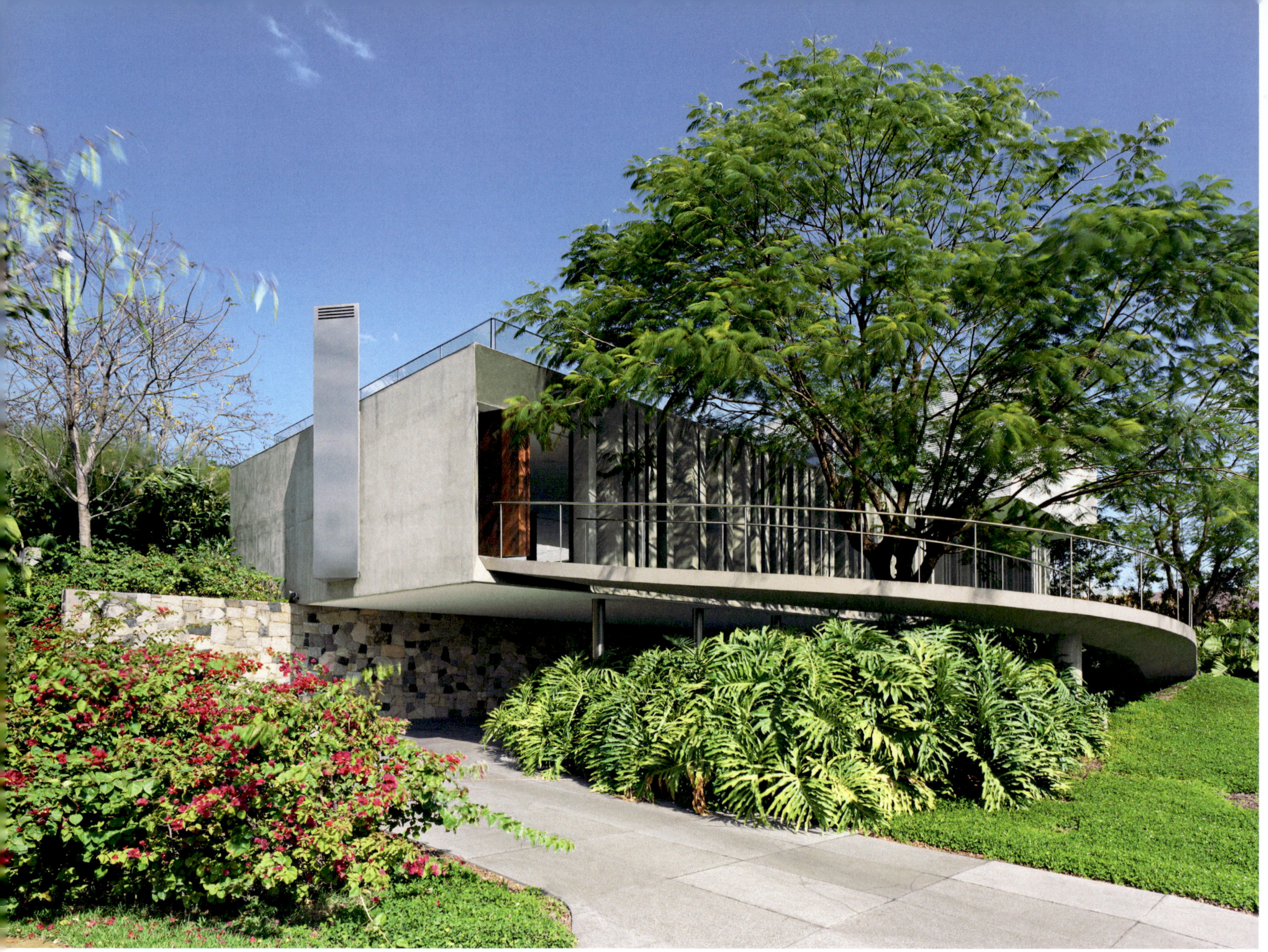

CASA PIRACICABA is a home away from home for a scattered Brazilian family. Whenever possible, three generations escape the frantic streets of São Paulo to congregate here. Isay Weinfeld's clean forms negotiate a leisurely flow between spaces—an ideal foundation for the family's cherished gatherings.

Isay Weinfeld's characteristic motifs converge with sharp clarity in Casa Piracicaba. Rectilinear forms, streamlined surfaces, open spaces, and a light, floating quality meet at subtle intersections. As with his work on hotels and bars, Weinfeld puts a Brazilian spin on the International style with this home.

Before Weinfeld could begin calculating the proportions of this intricate composition, he had to take the requirements of a large family into account. "The Piracicaba House was commissioned by a client with two grown-up kids and grandchildren," he explains, adding, "It was her wish to have a house where they could all gather and meet comfortably." Since the family lives 250 kilometers away, dispersed in different areas of São Paulo, Casa Piracicaba serves as a homey outpost where they can reunite under the tranquil ambience of Weinfeld's design.

However, the architectural process itself shared little of the house's final simplicity. The steep gradient of the land was the major problem to overcome, which Weinfeld did in his favored style, by stacking the three volumes on top of one another. The lower, partially subterranean section has space for storage, a mechanical room, and a garage. Accessed by a curved pathway, the second tier on the ground floor is home to the kitchen and dining areas. Enclosed by glass, the family can dine with a view of the emerald green pool at the edge of the ipê wood deck and the sweeping garden that slopes up the property. On the other side of the room, eccentrically placed concrete pillars obscure the view to the road and provide privacy. ~

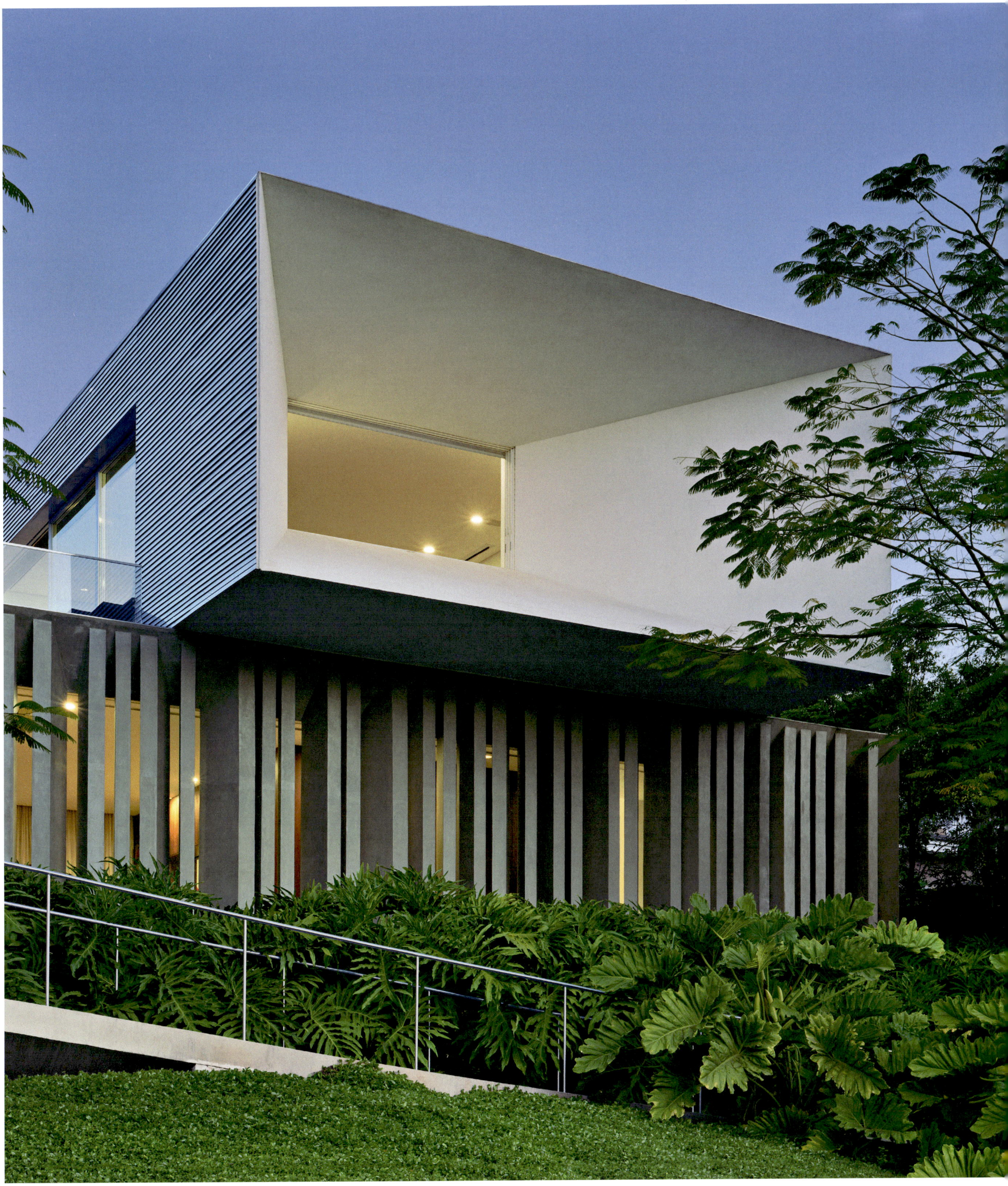

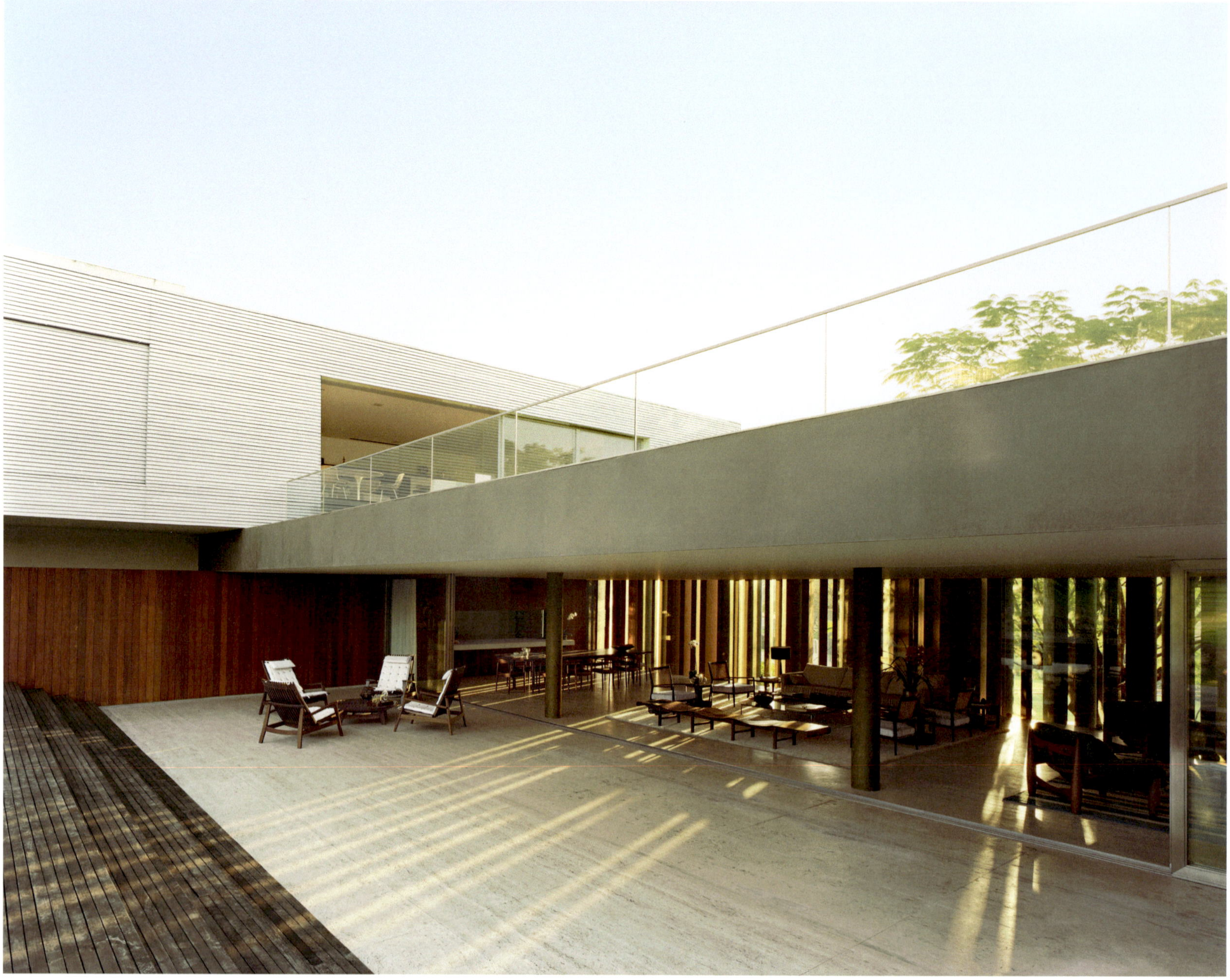

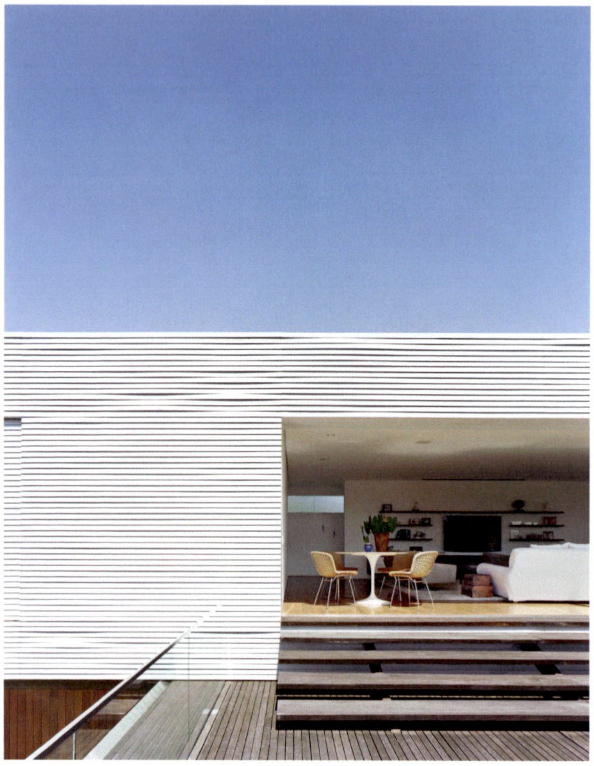

"WHILE THE MAIN STRUCTURE IS MADE OUT OF CONCRETE, IT BOASTS A LARGE VARIETY OF MATERIALS RANGING FROM STONE, ALUMINUM, AND MACCHIA ORO MARBLE TO NATURAL IPÊ WOOD DECKS AND CEDAR CLADDING."

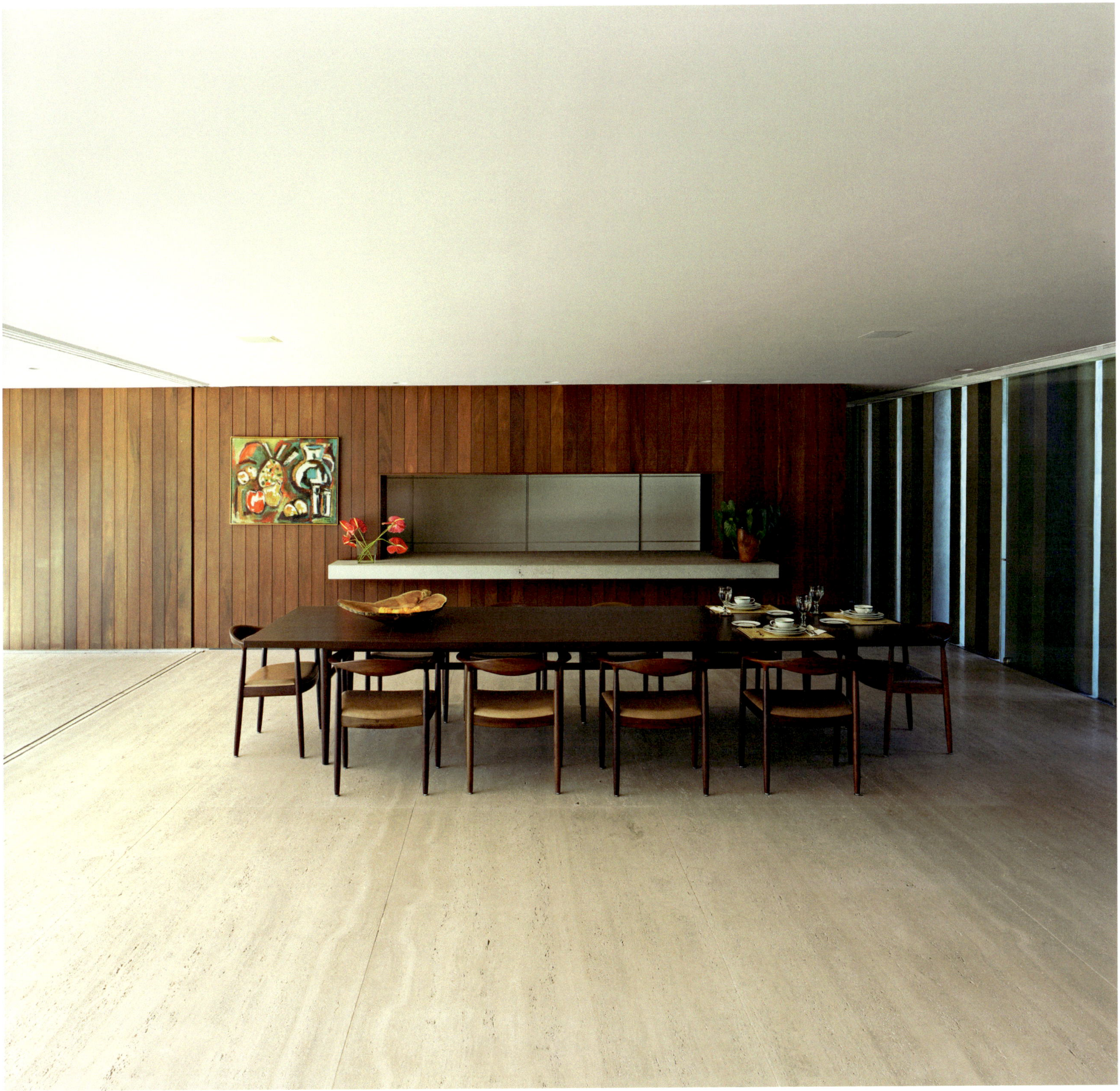

The top level meets the ground floor at a perpendicular intersection and is clad with white concrete. All the family's bedrooms are in this section, and there is also another living room that has a large deck covering the roof of the ground floor. All in all, Casa Piracicaba is the ideal place for the family to come together and fill the weightless, open spaces with joy. ◆

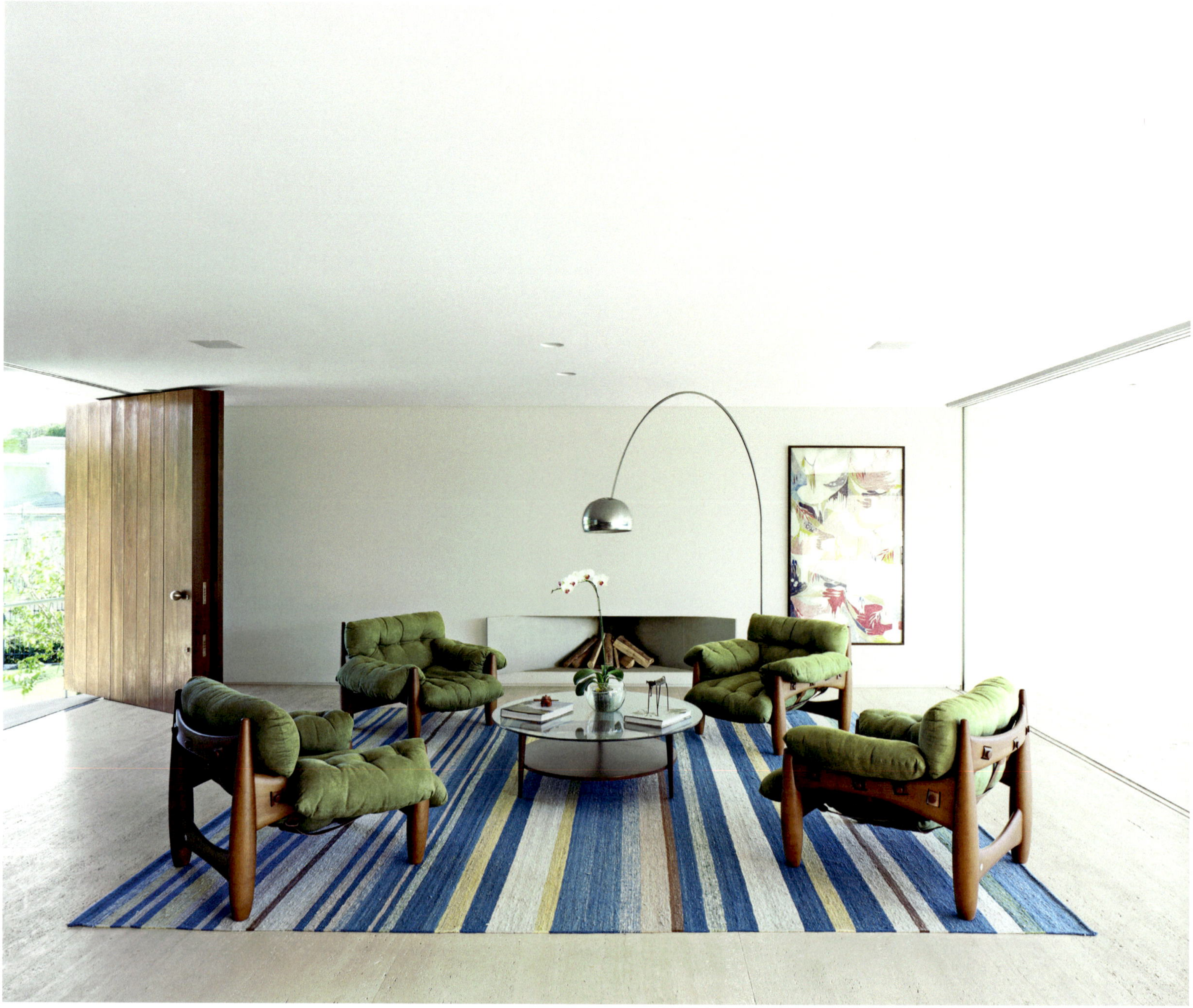

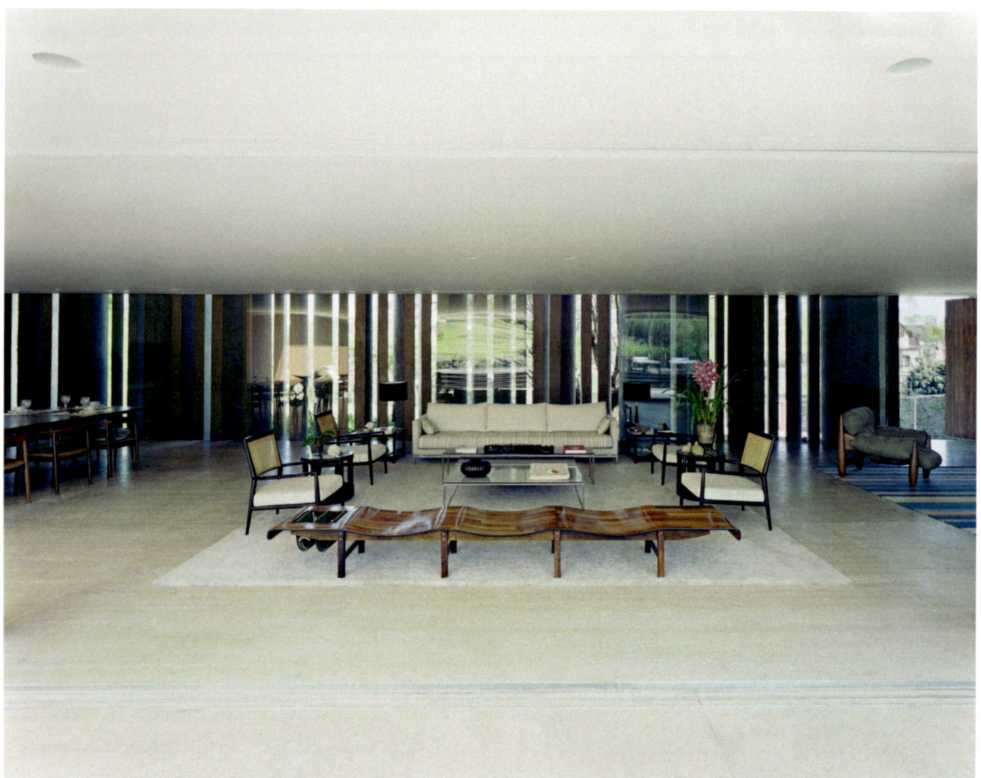

"RECTILINEAR FORMS, STREAMLINED SURFACES, OPEN SPACES, AND A LIGHT, FLOATING QUALITY MEET AT SUBTLE INTERSECTIONS."

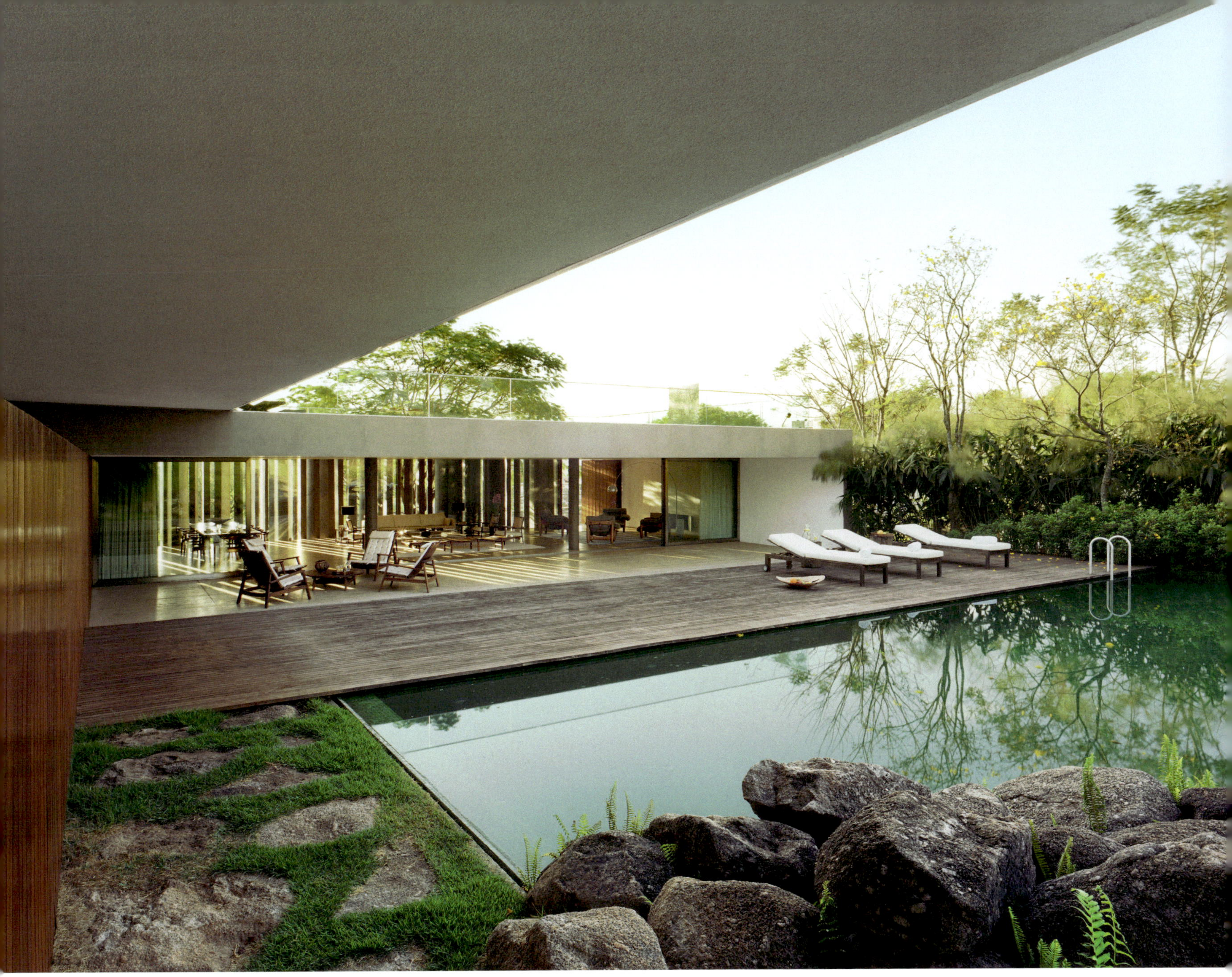

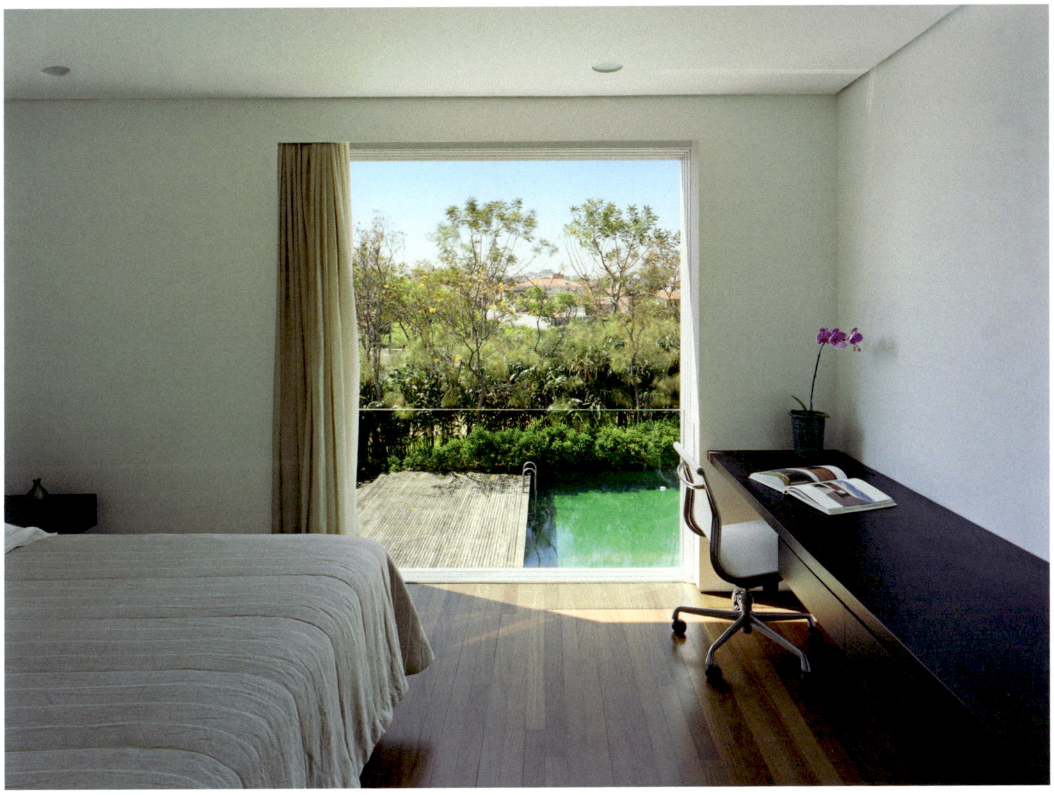

LAKE GENEVA, SWITZERLAND

CASA 26

MARC DIE, MICHAEL WIDRIG,
AND DANIEL KAUFMANN

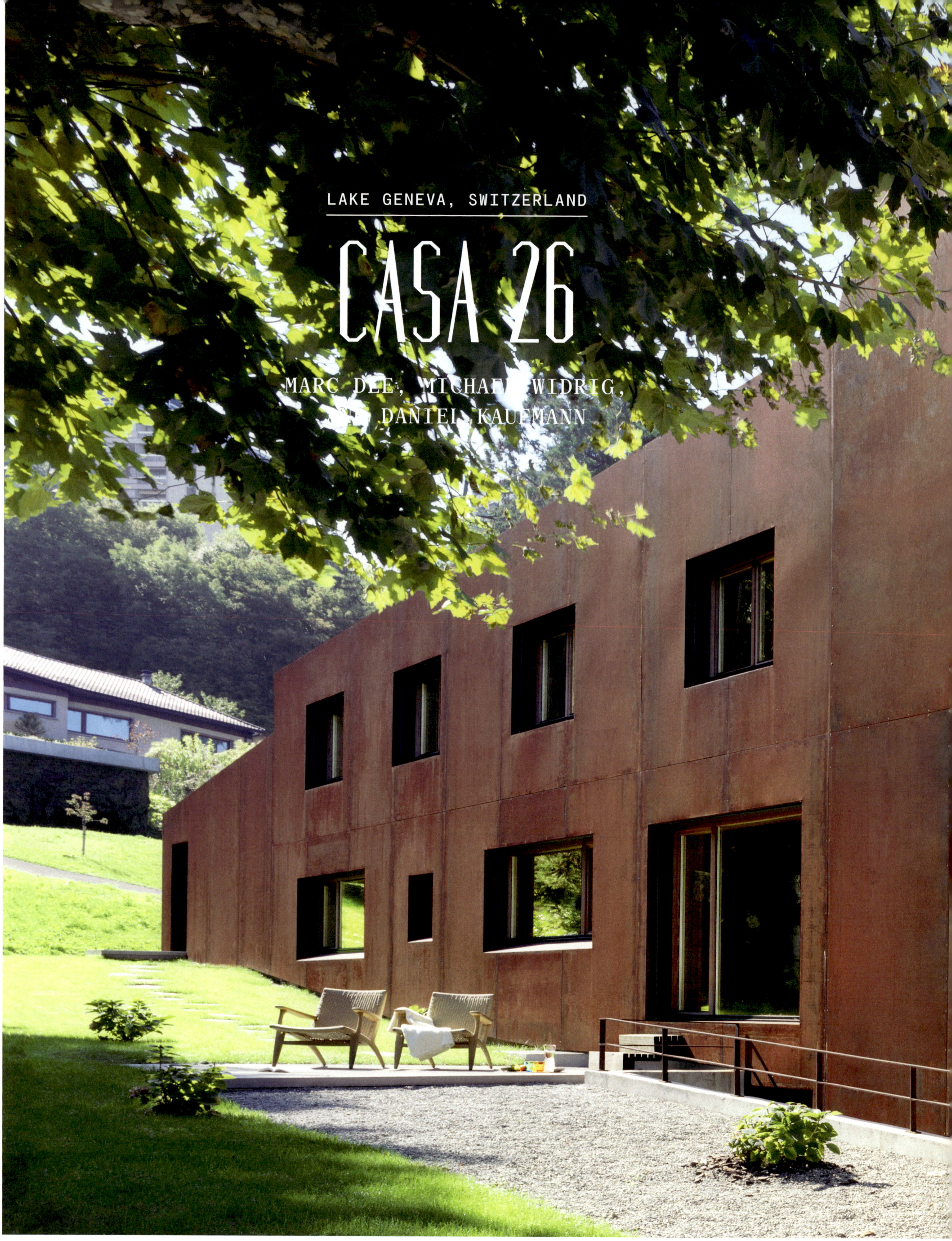

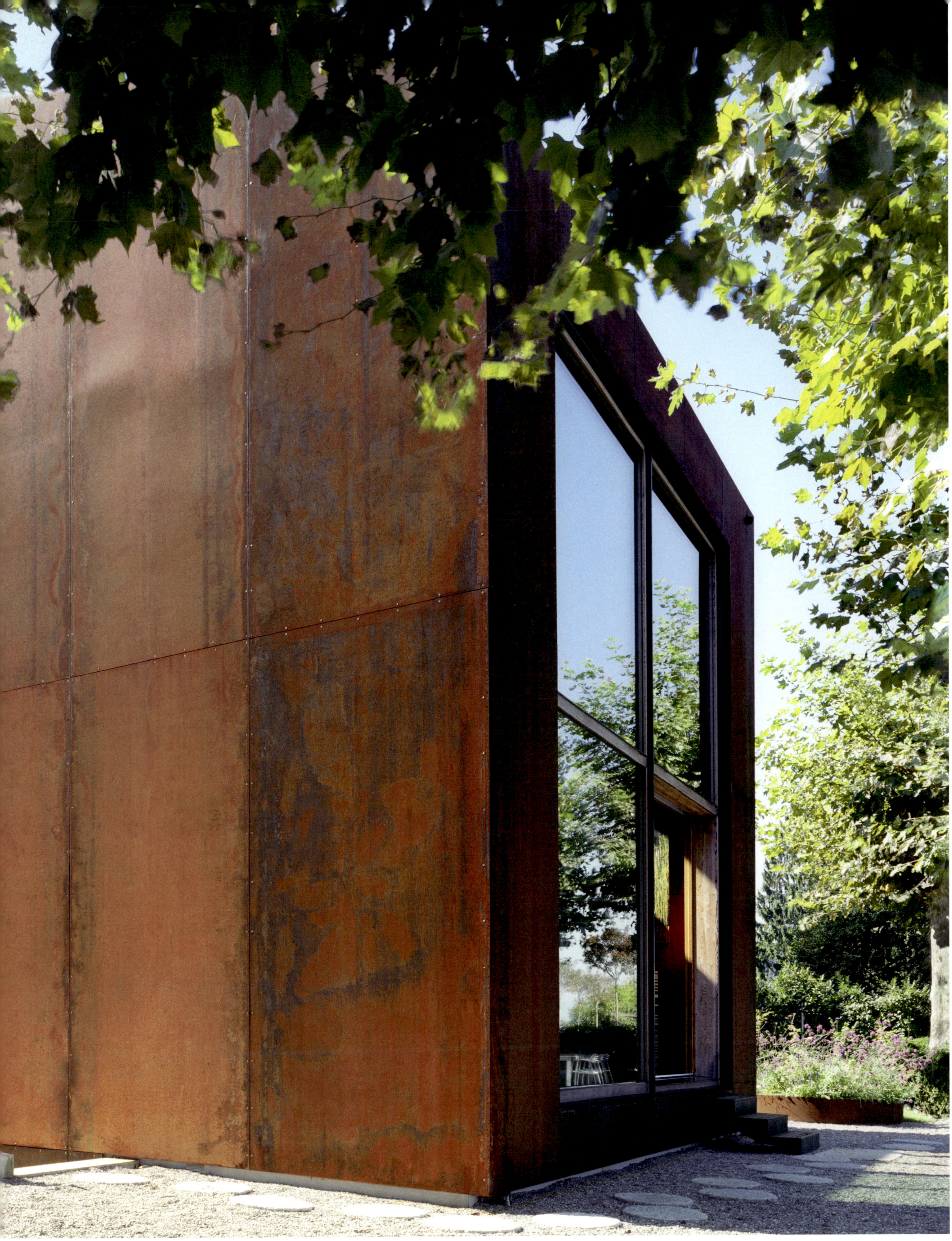

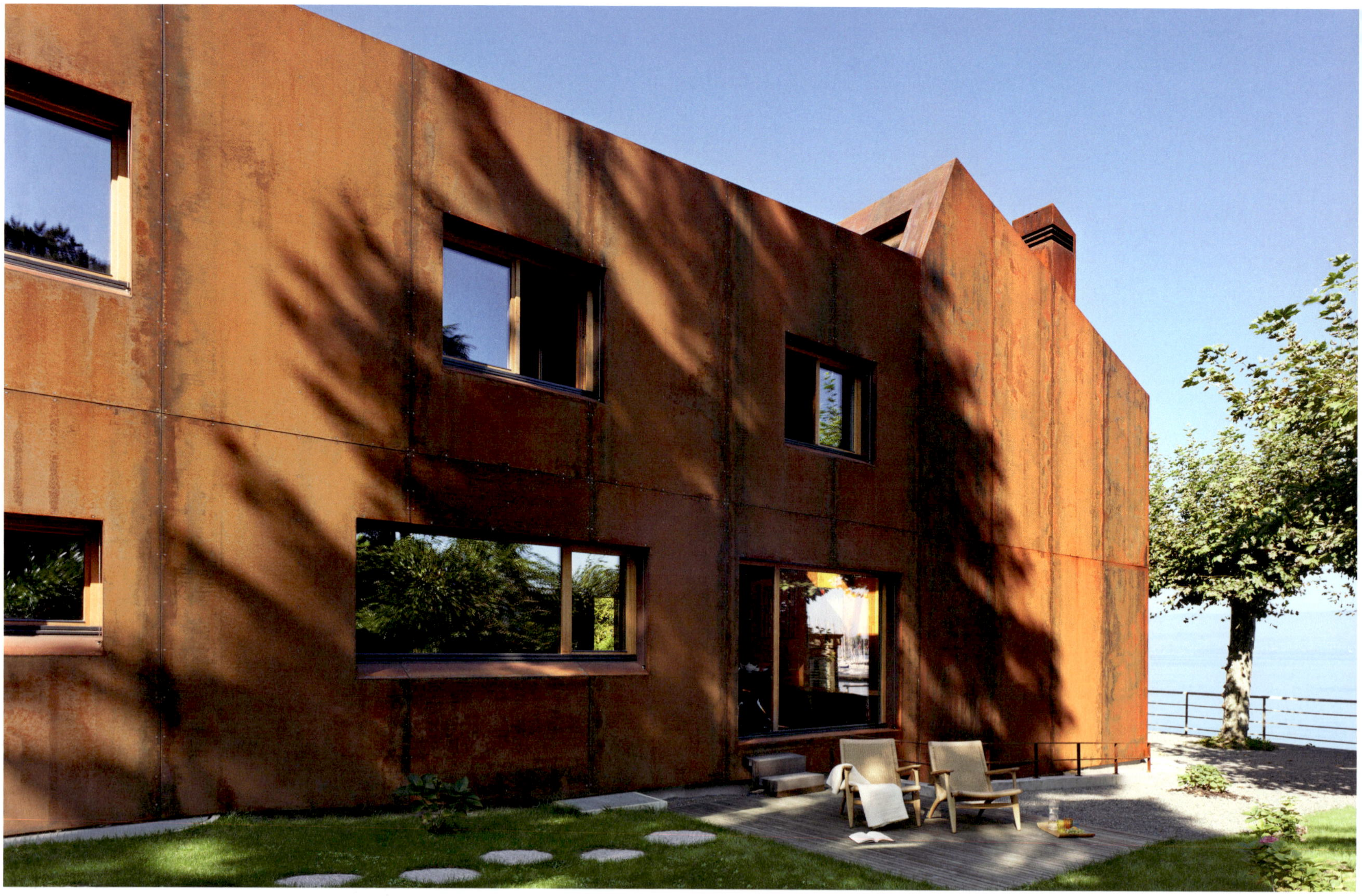

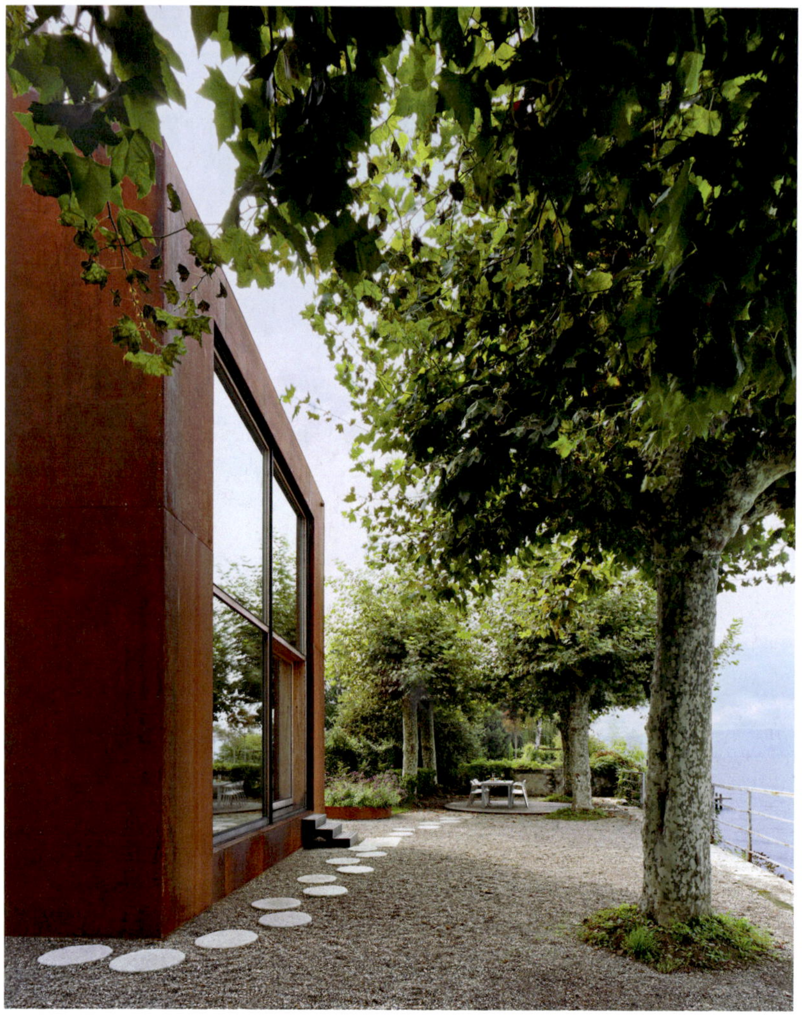

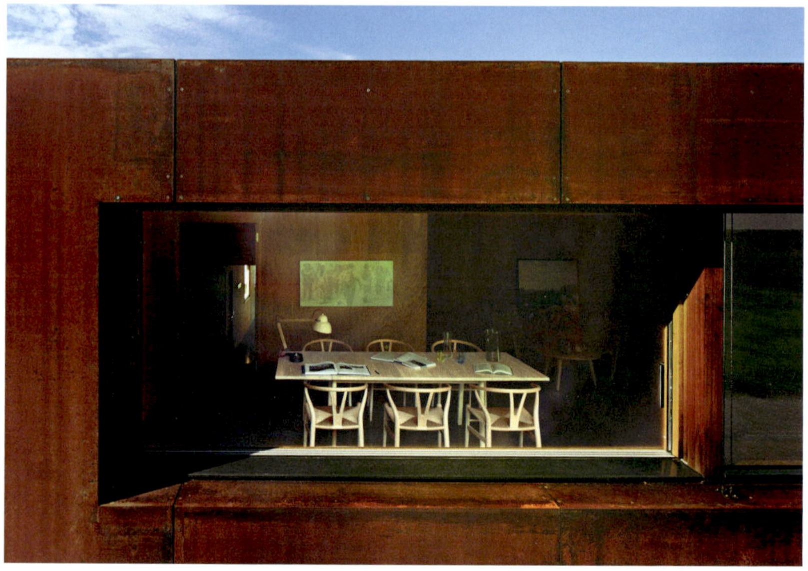

"THE HOUSE'S BLACK STEEL SHELL HAS RUSTED TO A COPPER COLOR, MAKING IT SEEM LIKE IT HAS BEEN DRAPED IN GOLD VELVET."

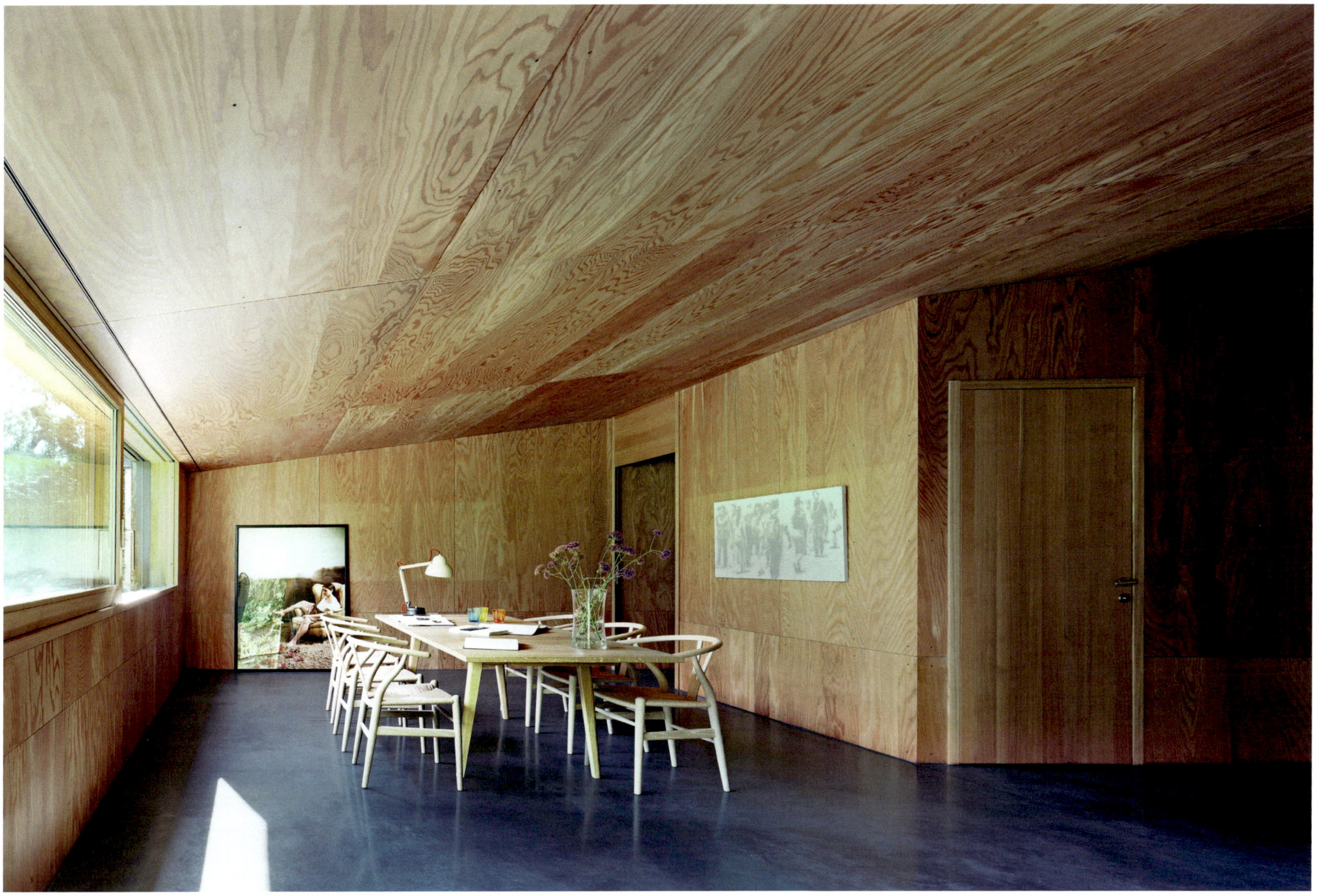

CASA 26 Built on an awkward site, Casa 26 is a product of enthusiasm and persistence. Going far beyond the standard holiday home, the house, which features a rusted façade that gives way to a dark larch wood interior, draws its influence from the kind of fluid and adaptable architecture found in boatbuilding.

Initially, Casa 26's site did not seem to hold abundant building prospects. Wedged between two properties, the extremely narrow strip of land was further hampered by a sewage line that cut the section in half. Despite these limitations, the site, located on the shore of Lake Geneva, transfixed Marc Dee of Menta Group. "I knew it was exceptional because it was the last plot which hadn't been built on," he explains. Pitting his enthusiasm against the site's evident shortcomings, Dee, along with architects Michael Widrig and Daniel Kaufman, set about turning the narrow patch of land into his personal holiday home.

The first step was to devise a way to best utilize the problematic space. Widrig and Kaufman decided not only to make the building long and narrow, but also to extend it over two levels. Dee says, "The idea was to create a simple country house for a family of four, minimal but homely." Having crafted a five-bedroom home that includes a sauna in the basement and a gallery, Dee seems to have worked the inhospitable land into all that and more.

Calling on the tradition of alpine housing, larch wood paneling dominates the interior. Varnished with dark oil, the rich tint of the wood is a deliberate reference to boatbuilding, an allusion that is furthered by the black steel shell that has rusted to a copper color, making the house seem like it has been draped in gold velvet. The gigantic nine-meter-high living space is illuminated by huge windows facing north toward the lake and by a series of skylights piercing the roof to catch the southern sun. Waxed concrete has been utilized as flooring, harmonizing nicely with the vintage furniture and spire-like fireplace that adorn the room.

Dee is pleased with the result and says, "We wanted everything to be visible; there are virtually no doors hidden in the wood paneling; none of the lighting is integrated, and we used plain or painted steel rather than stainless steel. It's a reaction against sleek, urban, minimal design." ◆

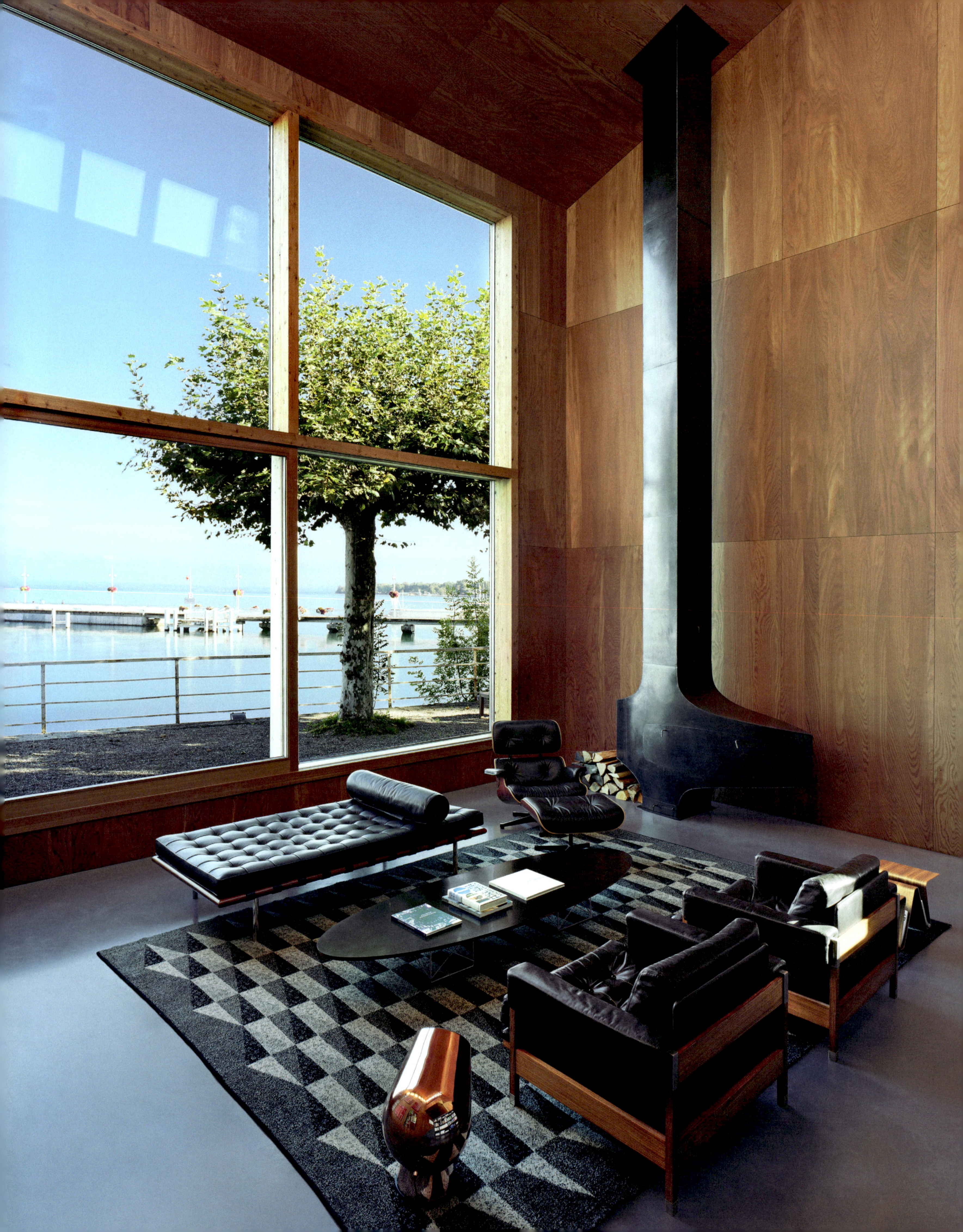

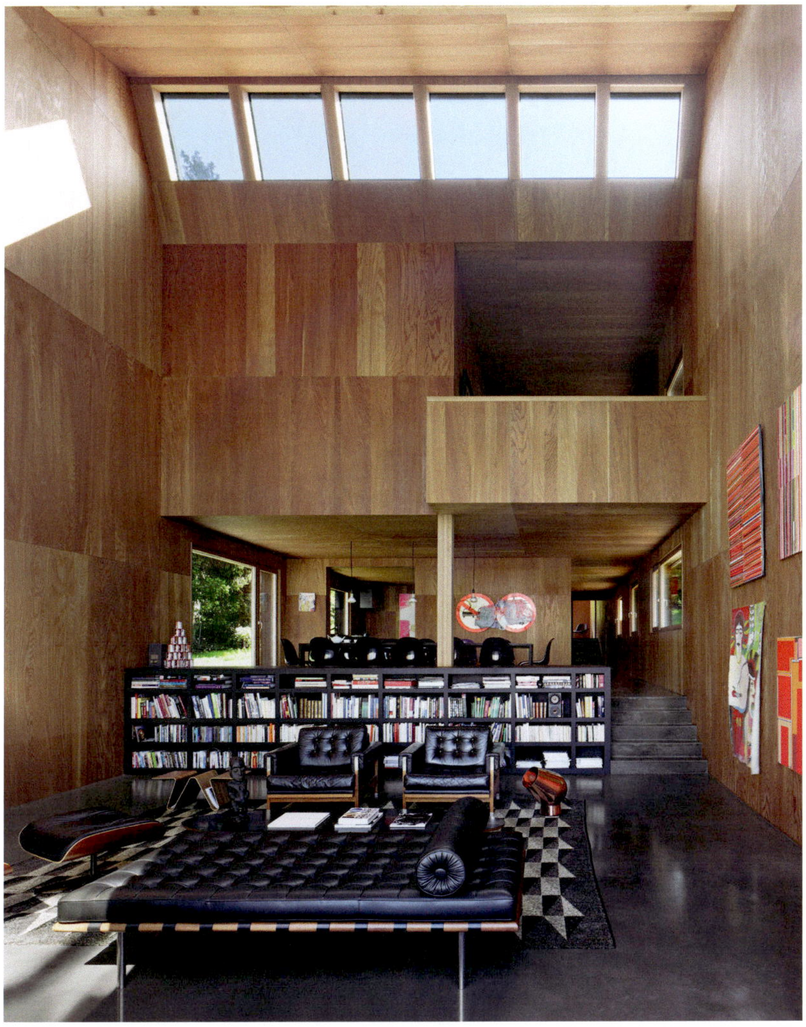

"THE NINE-METER-HIGH LIVING SPACE IS LIT BY HUGE WINDOWS FACING THE LAKE AND BY SKYLIGHTS PIERCING THE ROOF TO CATCH THE SUN."

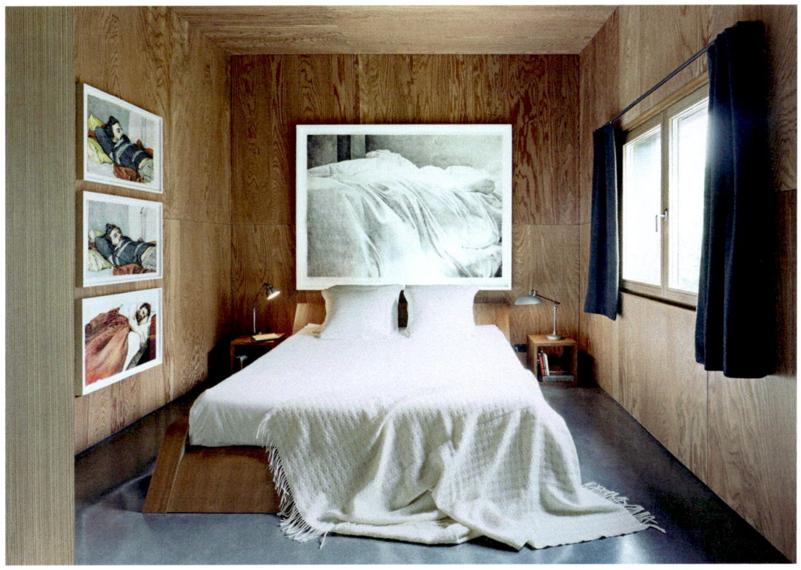

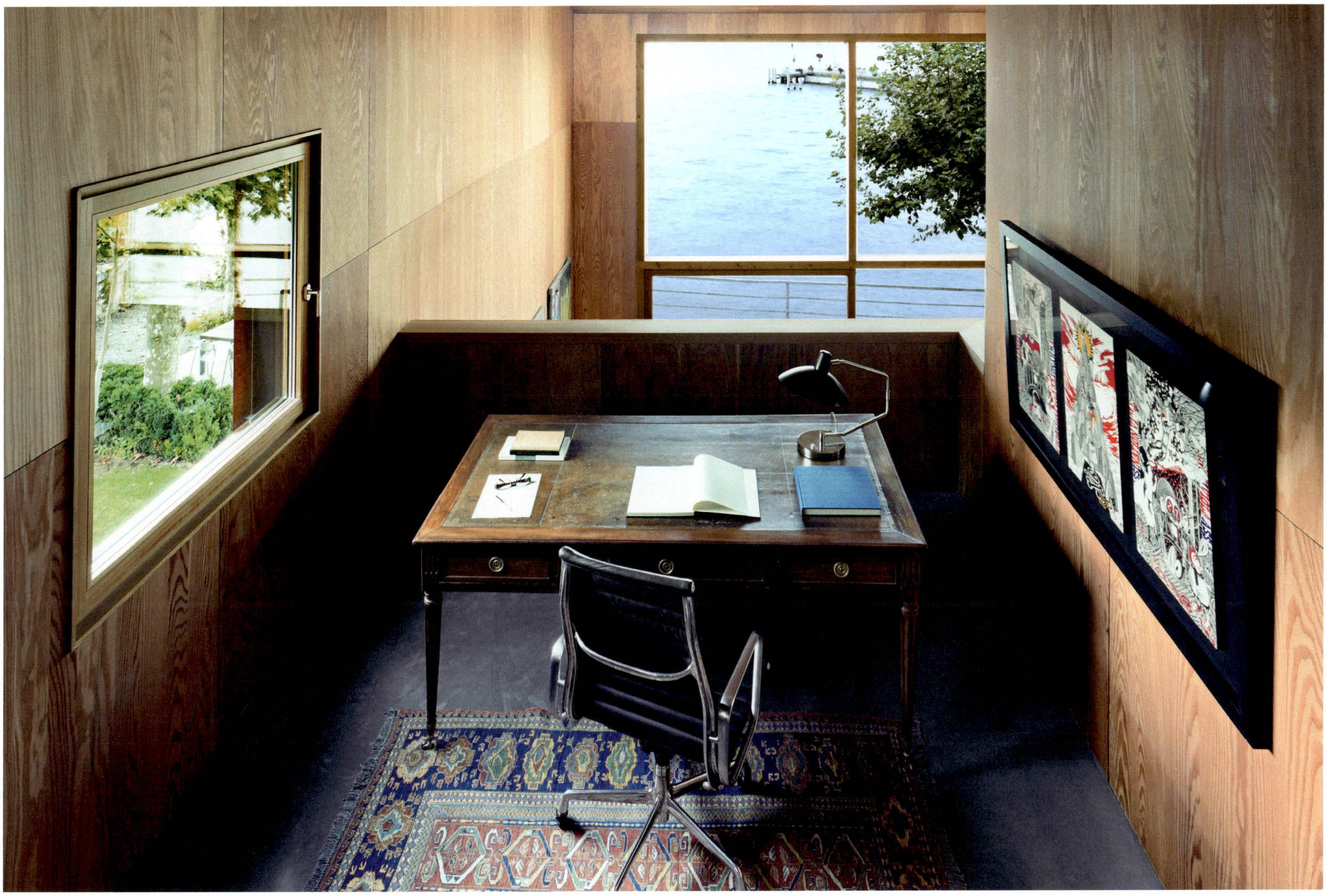

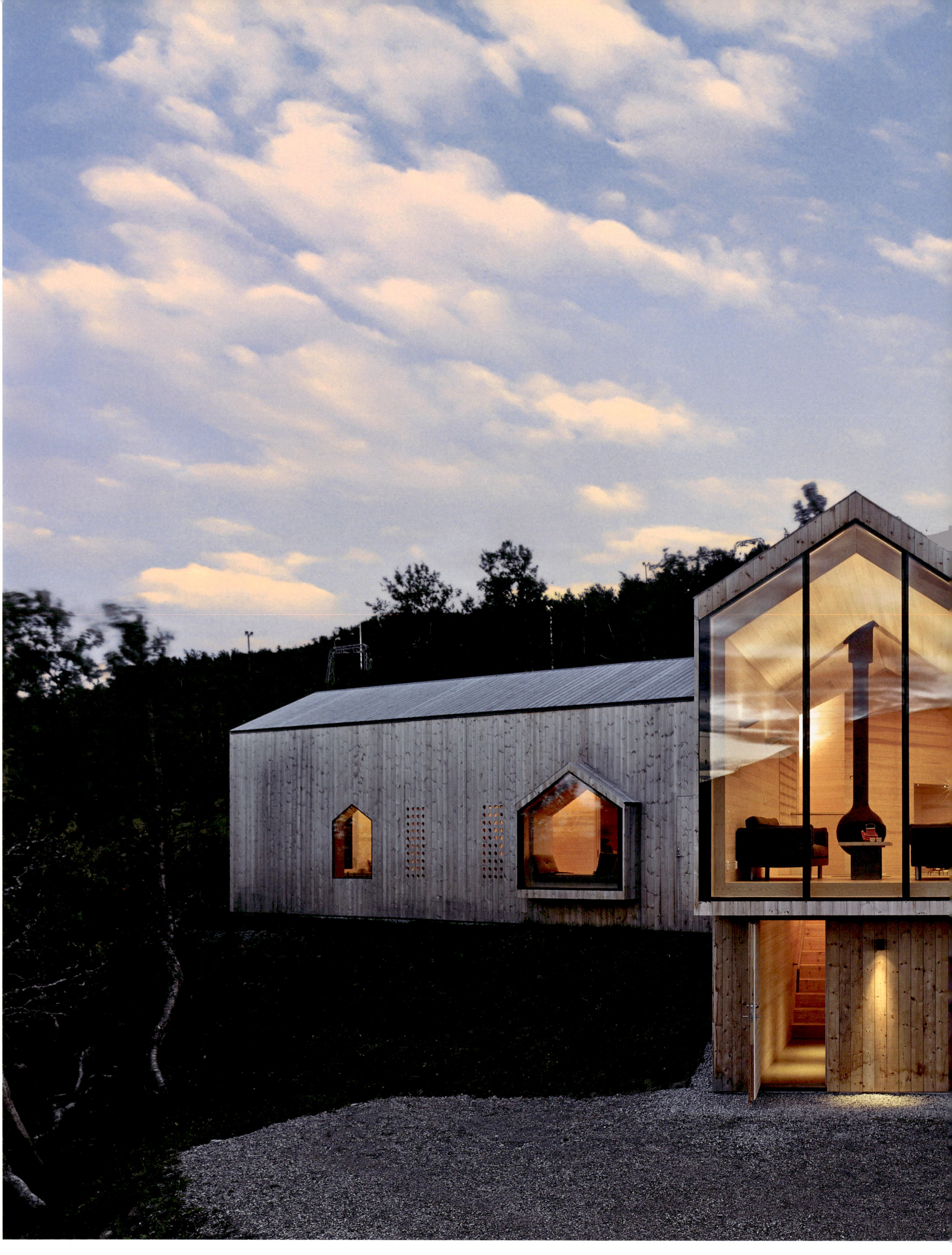

BUSKERUD, NORWAY

SPLIT VIEW MOUNTAIN LODGE

REIULF RAMSTAD ARKITEKTER

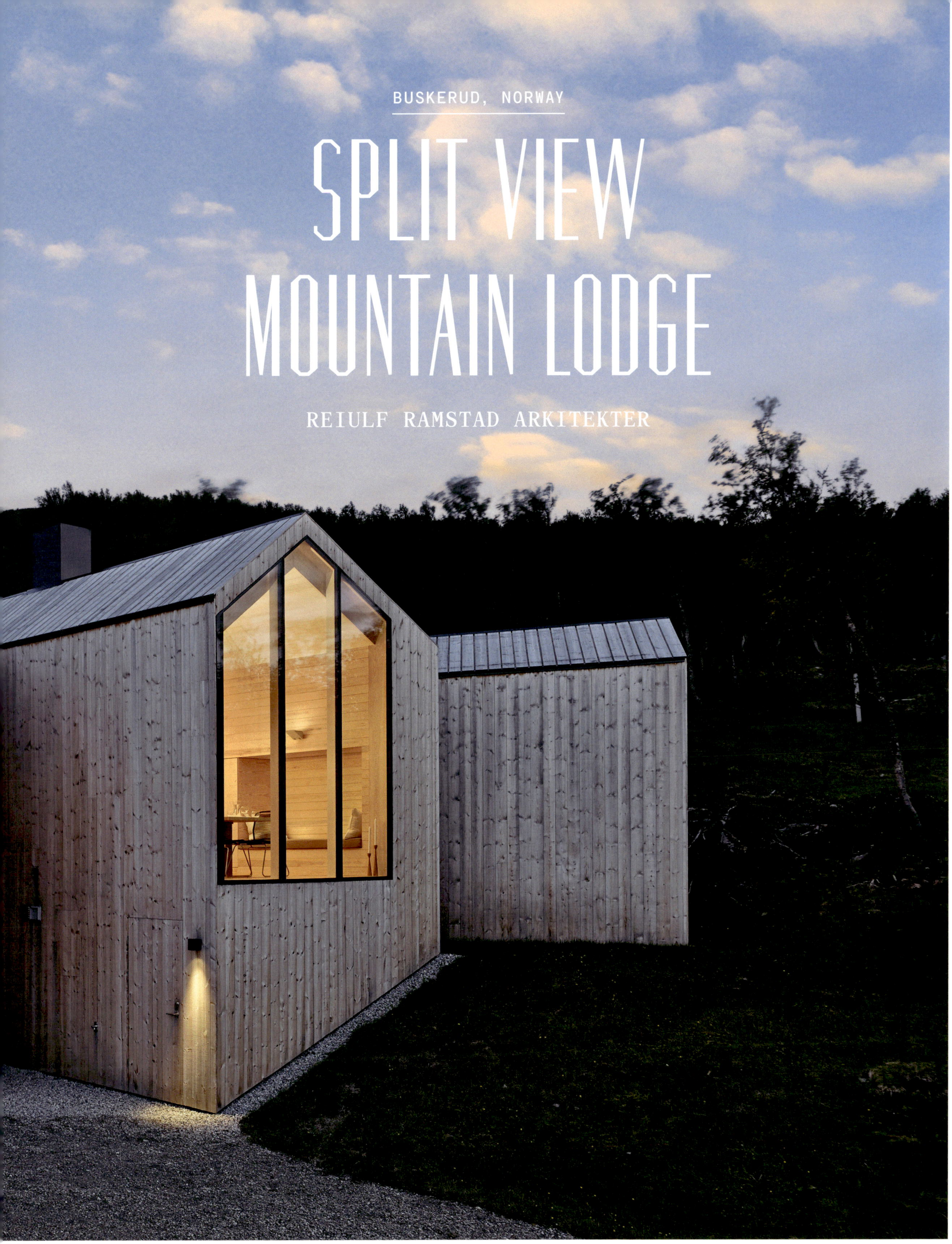

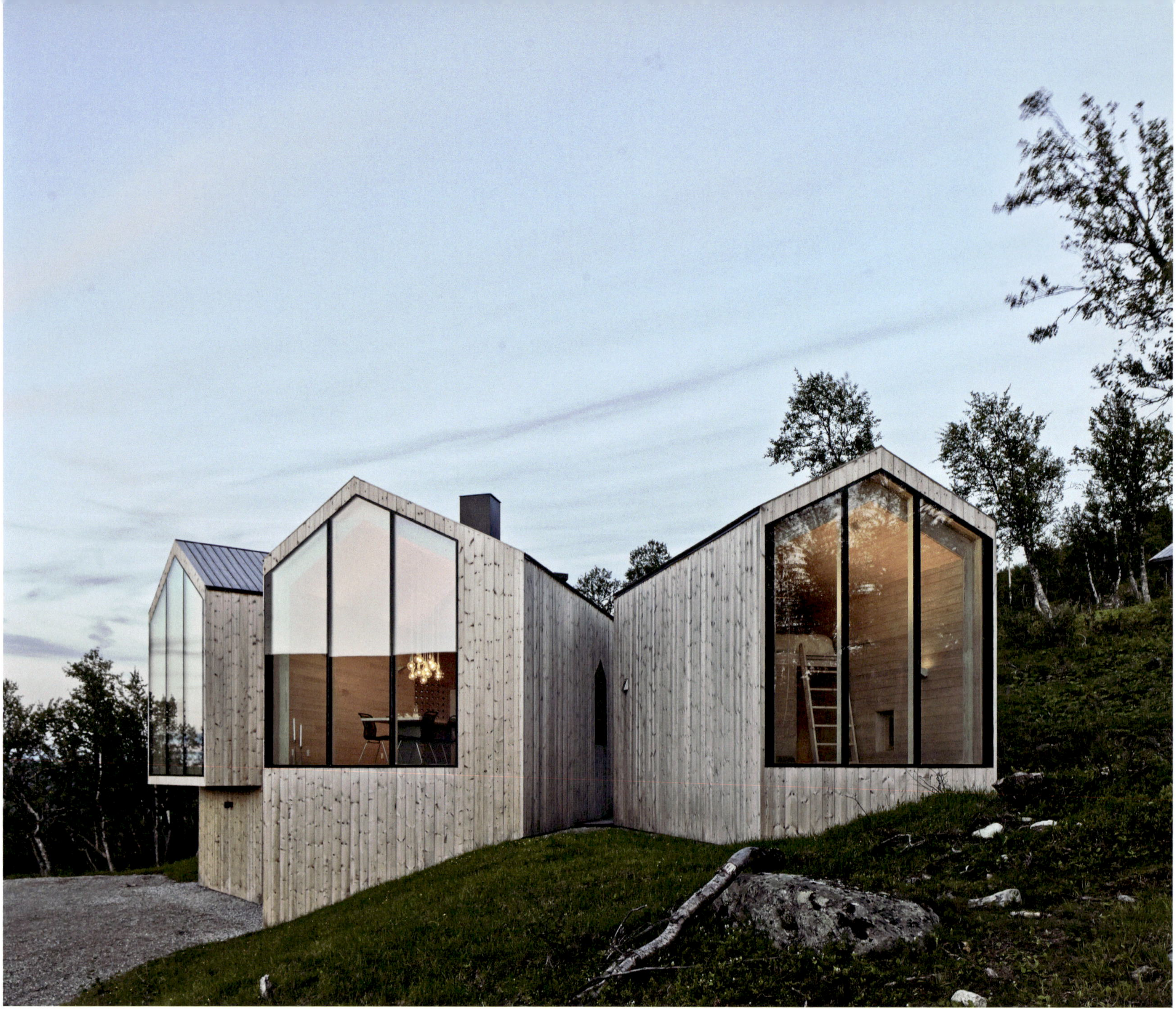

SPLIT VIEW MOUNTAIN LODGE An intimacy with nature is achieved through Split View Mountain Lodge's deployment of pale Norwegian pine and triple-glazed windows. This dialogue with the natural surroundings forms the basis of the house, which is a fine example of modern Norwegian carpentry.

The family that owns Split View Mountain Lodge handed Reiulf Ramstad Arkitekter a specific list of requirements for their cabin. Space for children's activities, a separate guest room, a split living and kitchen area, and four bedrooms were essential for their holiday home. According to Sigurd Nørsterud, one of the architects who assisted with the project, to meet all these requirements, the family had envisioned a large house that would have required a great deal of maintenance. However, Nørsterud and his colleagues were able to convince the family to opt for a more modest proposal, with the final house occupying a mere 130-square-meters. "Luxury isn't necessarily about having a lot of things, or a very big cabin. It's about finding beauty in simplicity and the quality of the finish," he explains.

Constructed from high-grade Norwegian pine, the finish is immaculate. A local carpenter has masterfully hidden the major beams of the house. "Part of the idea of using wood was to carry forward this Norwegian tradition of timber construction and connecting with the outside," Nørsterud says. The kitchen is set at the heart of the house, between three wings that branch off at unusual angles. A quaint fireplace serves as both stove and heater, and is connected to a bespoke countertop made ~

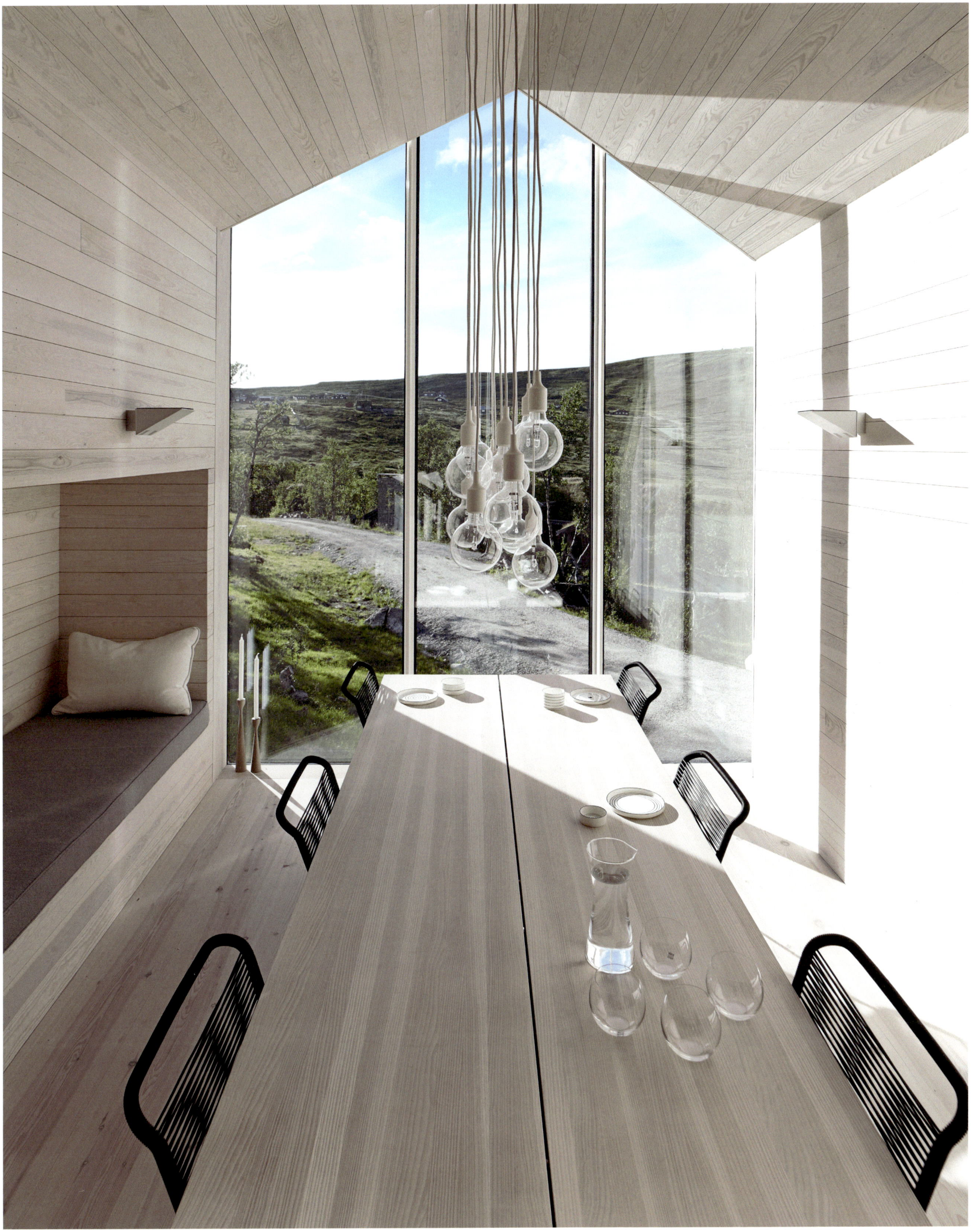

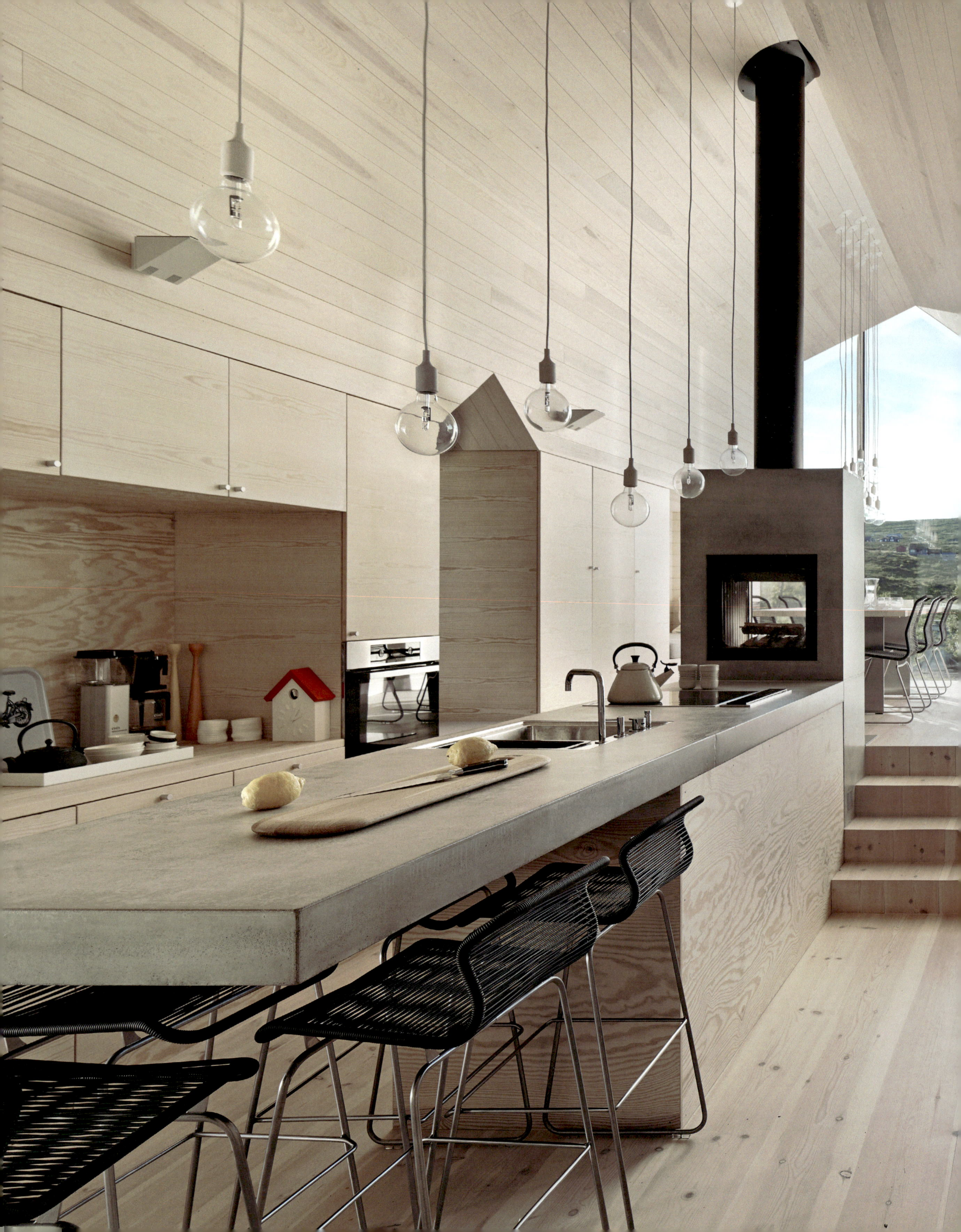

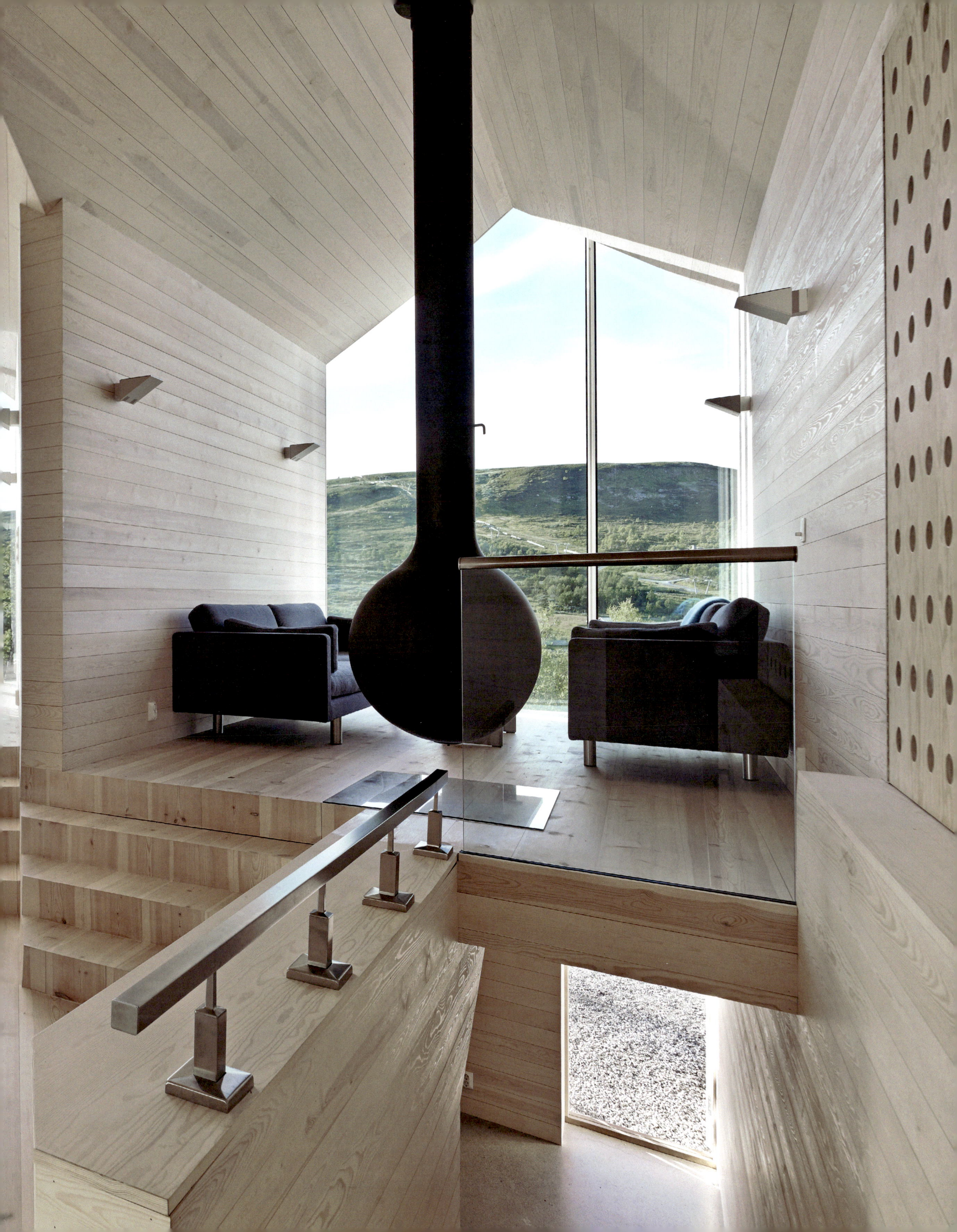

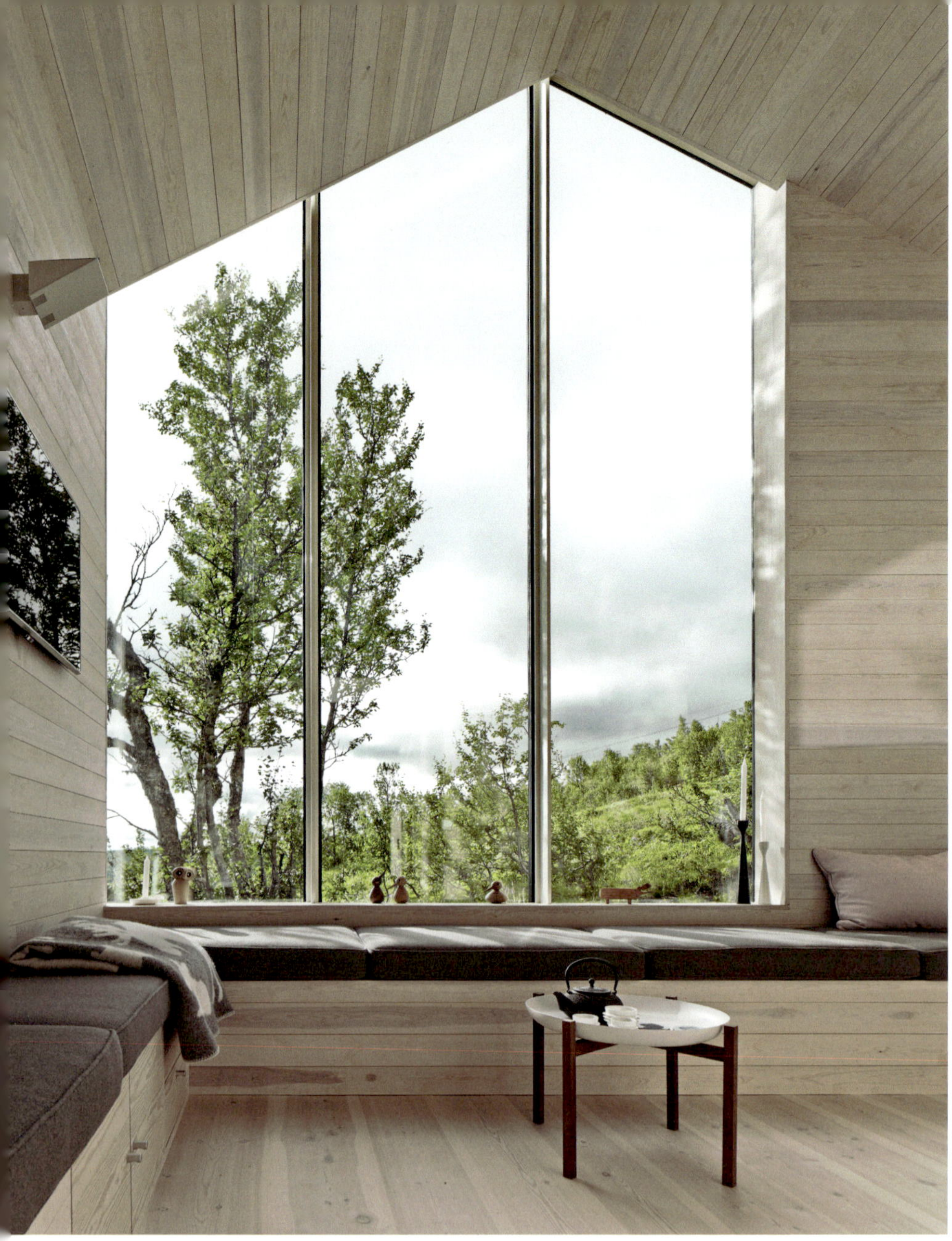

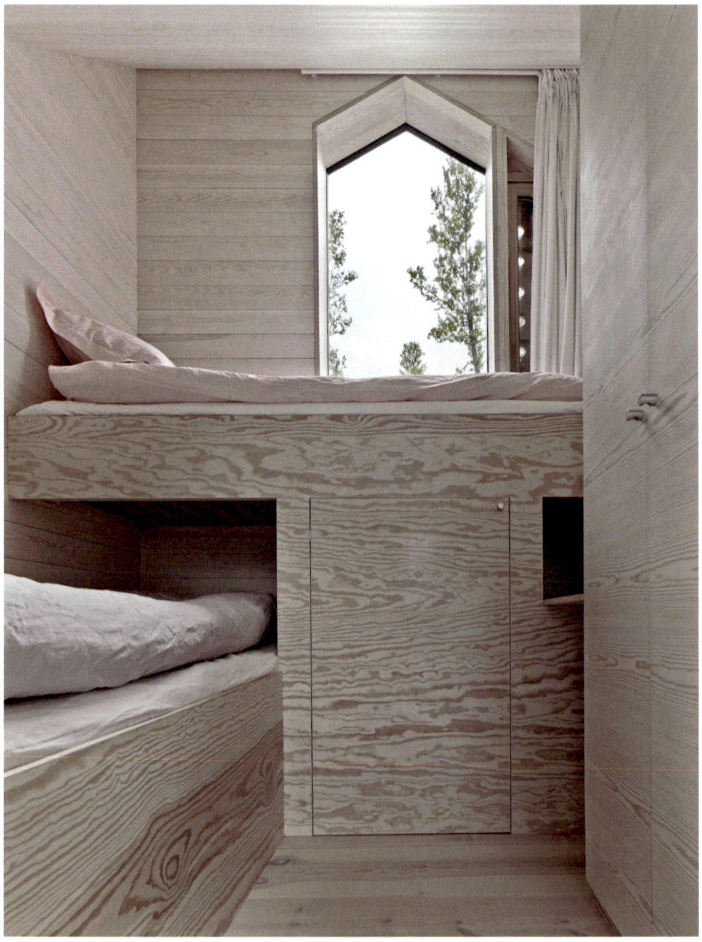

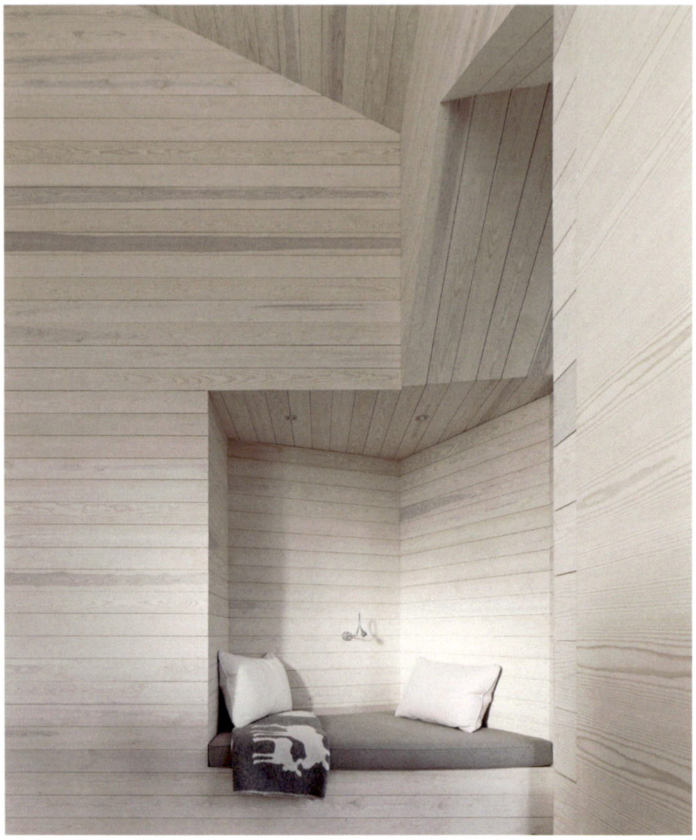

from reinforced concrete. Bedrooms for the children line the main corridor, each fitted with a bunk bed in case friends come to visit. In the master bedroom, like the living space, a window traces the line of the roof, offering

"IN THE MASTER BEDROOM, LIKE THE LIVING SPACE, A WINDOW TRACES THE LINE OF THE ROOF, OFFERING A BREATHTAKING VIEW OF THE RUSTIC LANDSCAPE."

a breathtaking view of the rustic landscape. Speaking about this feature, Nørsterud says, "Older cabins wouldn't have these kinds of views. That was one of the client's wishes, to have a good relationship with the outside." Split View Mountain Lodge certainly establishes a visual relationship with the landscape via the deployment of its windows, but it furthers this intimacy in its very materials. And as the cabin's pine gradually weathers to a silvery shade, it will only grow closer to its surroundings. ◆

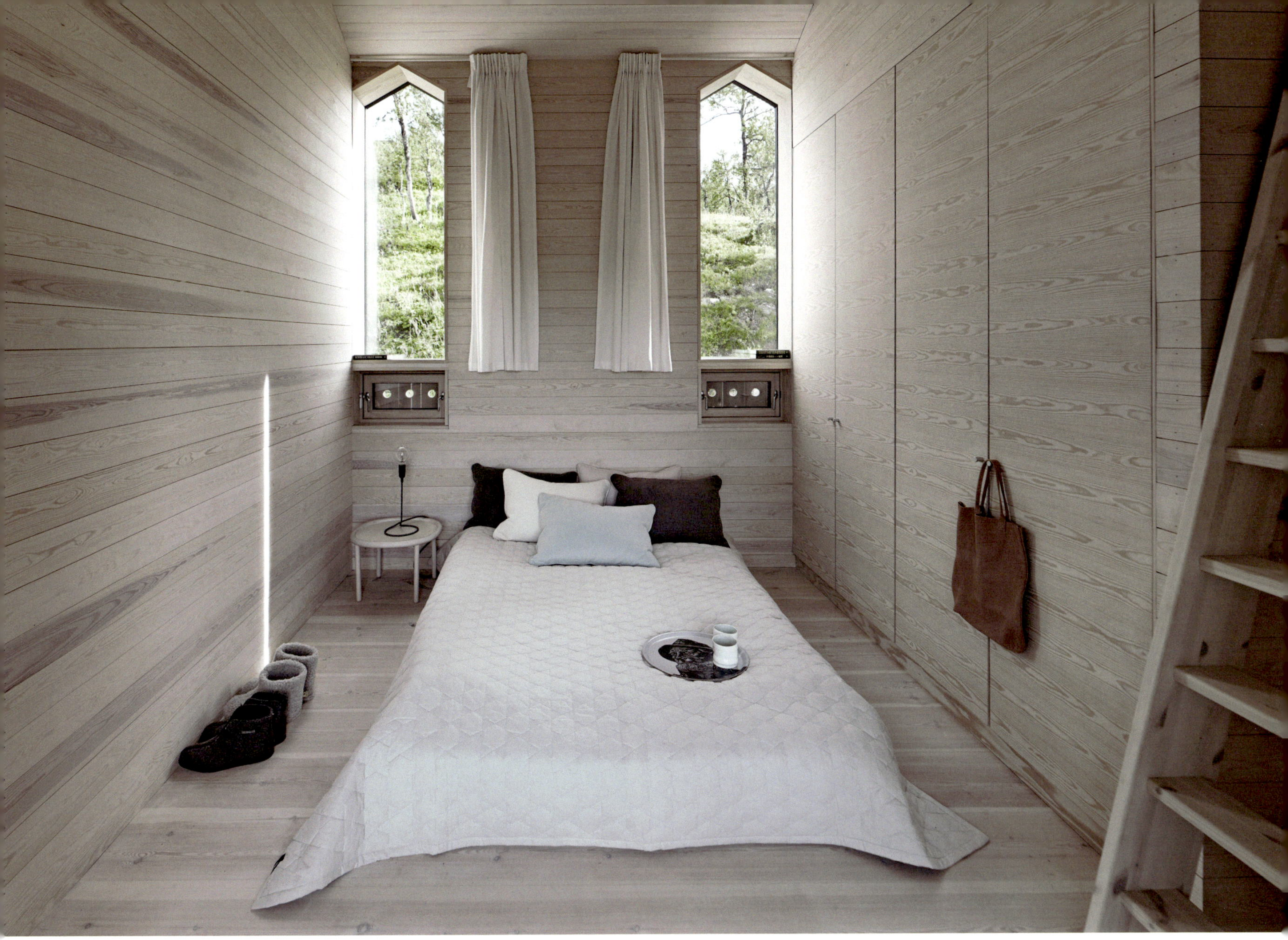

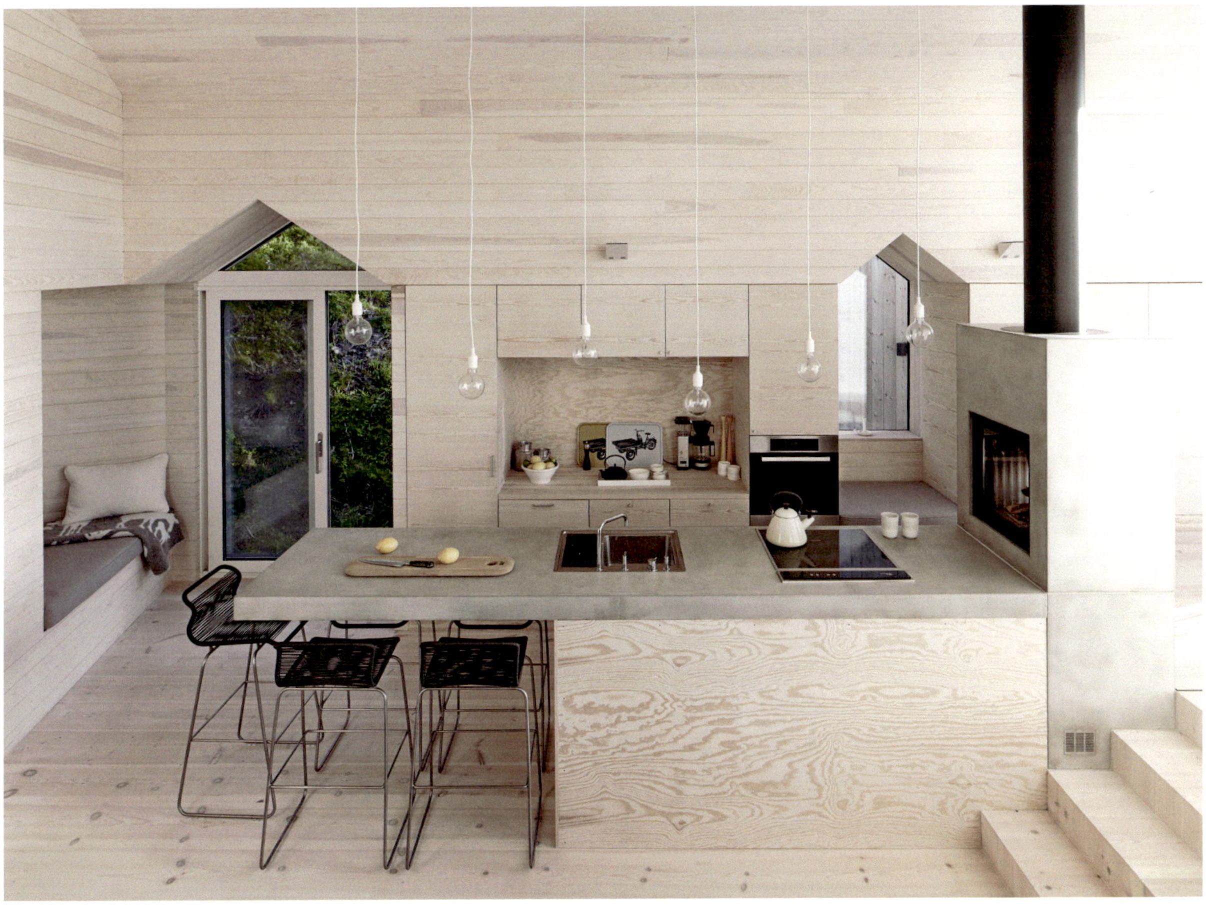

YAMAGATA, JAPAN

RSH 3

KAZUHIKO KISHIMOTO OF ACAA

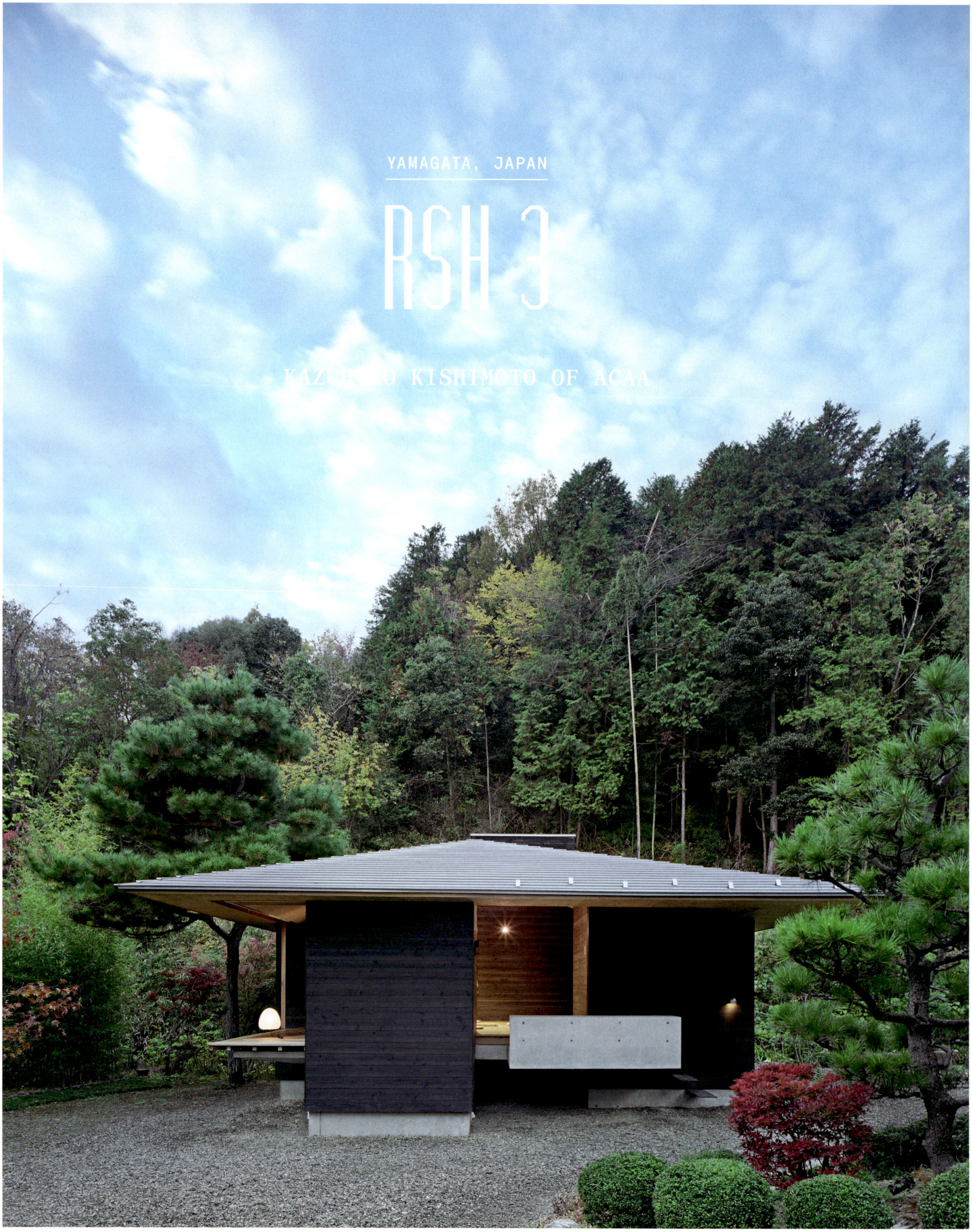

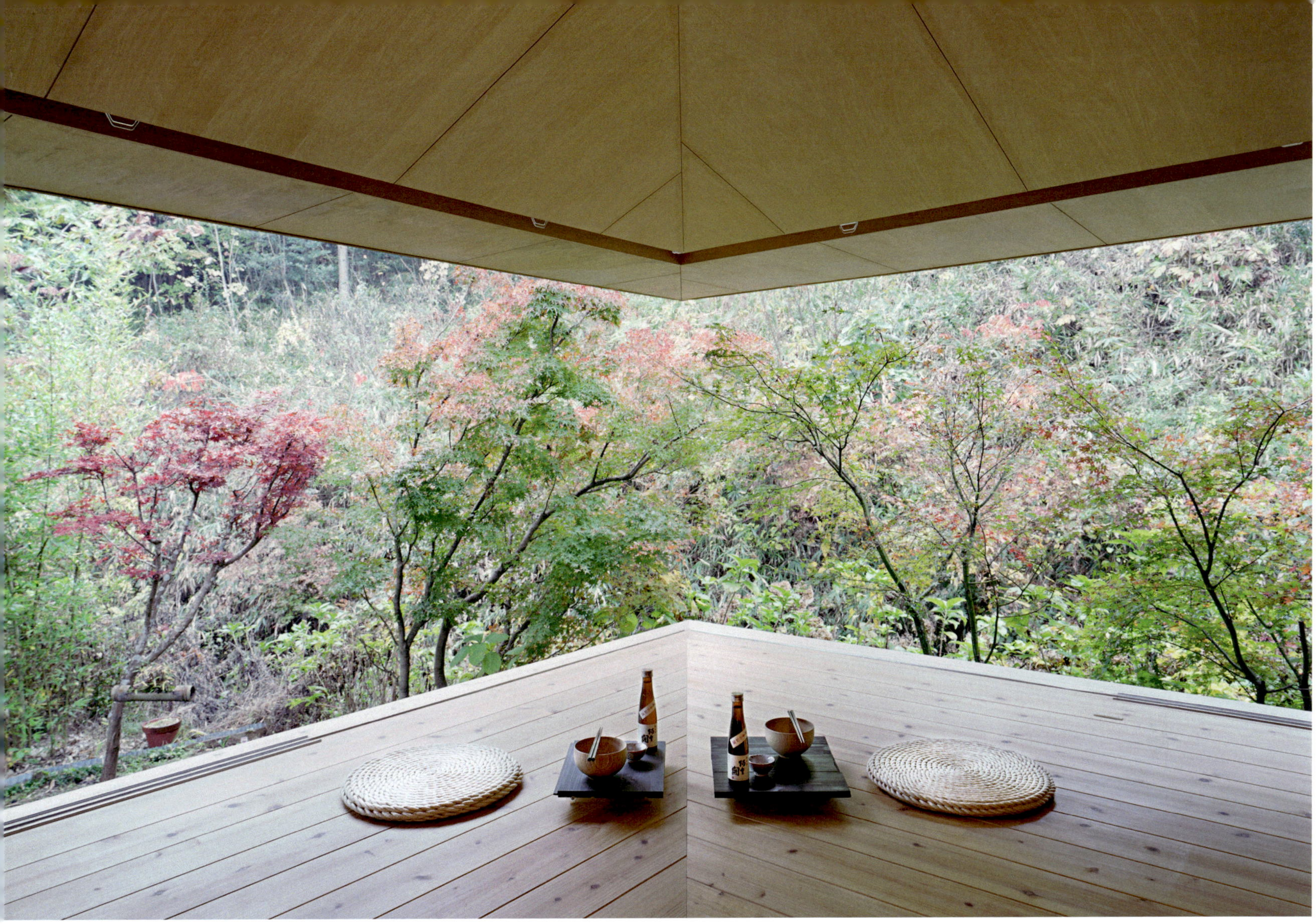

RSH 3 For a 39-square-meter space, this backyard retreat achieves a great deal. By changing the scale of the gazebo and compressing and expanding the partially divided sections, architect Kazuhiko Kishimoto was able to shape the way guests respond to it. The result is an emotive space that glides between open and closed areas.

RSH 3 is a compact gazebo-like structure that breezes over the chasm between public and private spaces. Calm nooks, shaded terraces, and an open interior—its center pierced by a sunken hearth—flow together in social arrangements, counterbalancing the punctuated zones of privacy. Planning an addition to the their property in Gifu Prefecture, the Itoh family asked architect Kazuhiko Kishimoto for a shelter where their visiting daughters and friends could sleep, as well as for a retreat for entertaining and relaxing. Speaking of how he managed to shape the 39-square-meter space to satisfy these two different requirements, Kishimoto says, "The solution is all about proportion—compressing space in some places and expanding it in others. These shifts in scale define one's relationship to the space and one's emotional experience of it."

Kishimoto was able to play with proportion through the introduction of the four "black boxes." These modules extend through the gazebo and anchor it to the ground while taking the full weight of the galvanized steel roof and cedar ceiling, subverting the need for a clutter of columns. For the Itohs and their guests, the black boxes provide storage space while also housing a bathroom, washroom, and kitchen. Their placement at the fringes of the gazebo also serves to open the interior and control the views of the crisp garden setting.

The open interior, in traditional Japanese style, is free of furniture, and the central hearth provides a warm point of orientation for social gatherings. At night, the guests can place a futon on the floor near the fire or find a more secluded spot on one of the nooks found on either side of the bathroom. The Itohs are understandably enthused about RSH 3, and it seems that the compact gazebo pleased its guests as much as its owners. Mieko Itoh says, "Most people don't want to leave," and her husband Shoichi adds, "Everybody loves this place." ◆

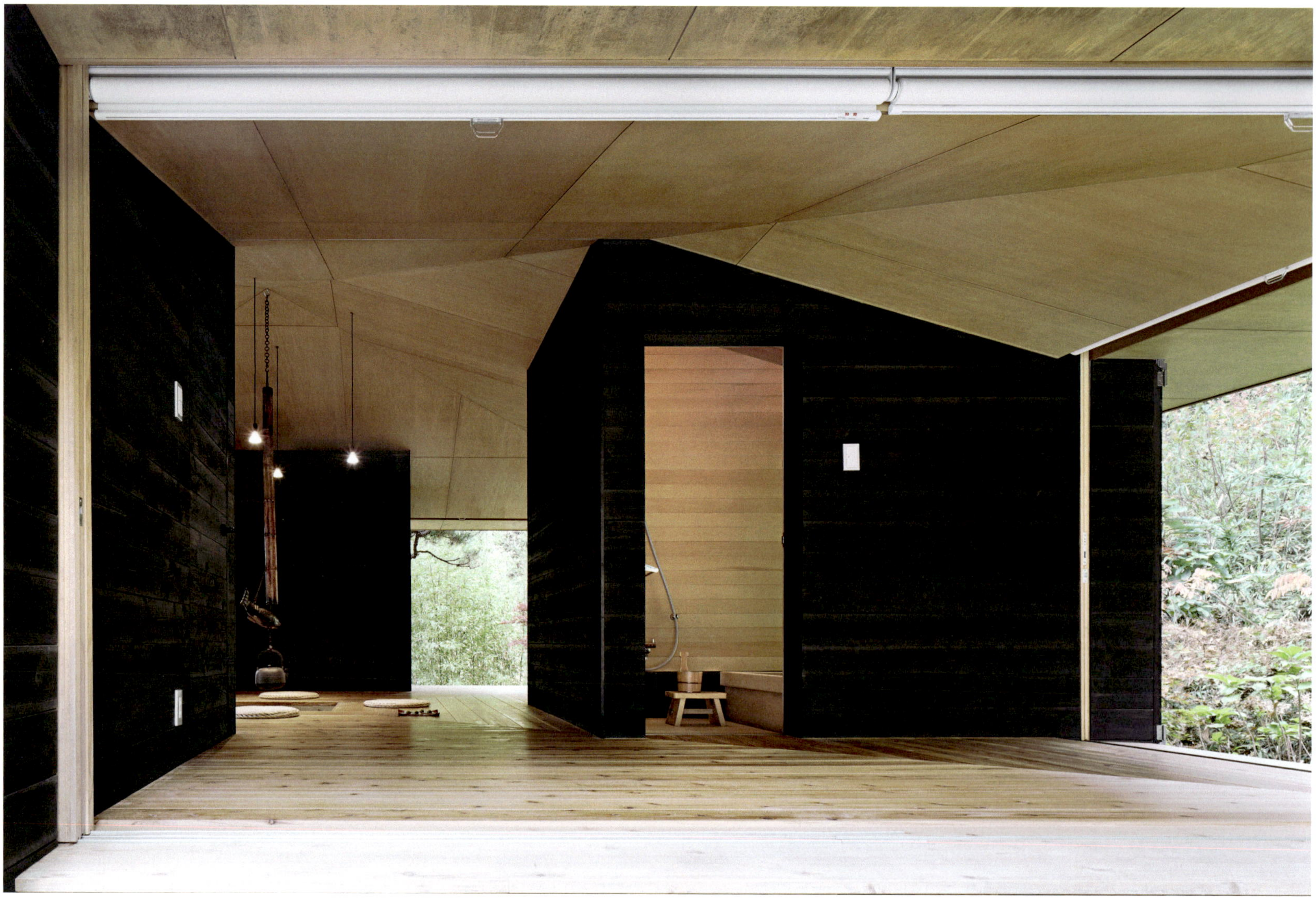

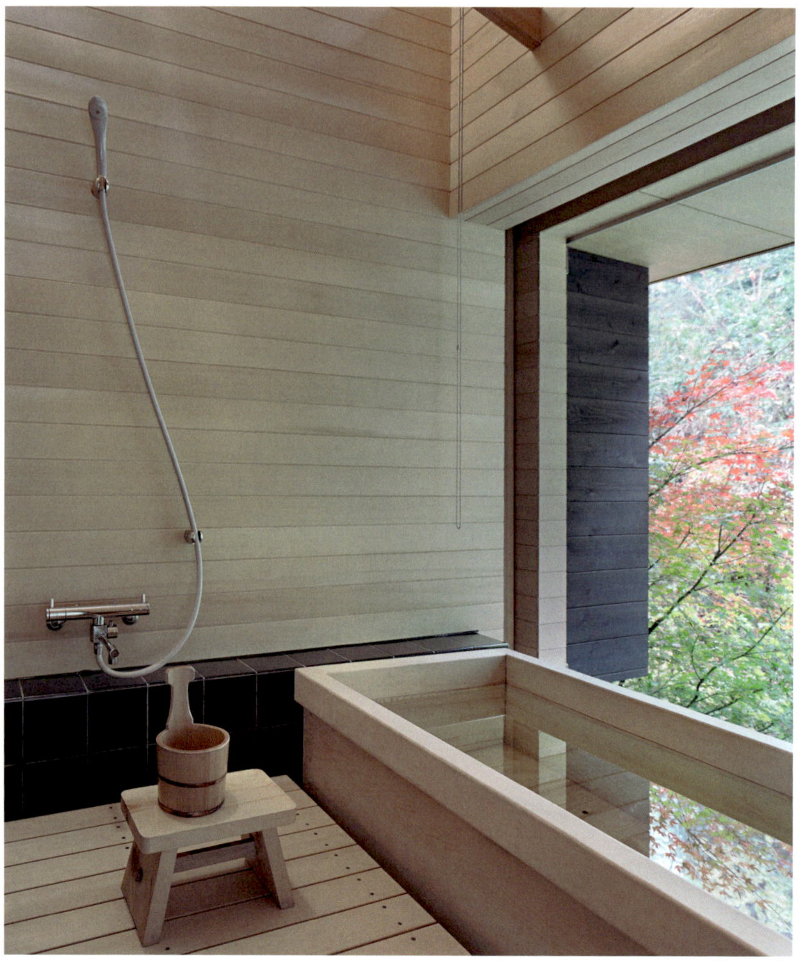

"There's nothing more relaxing than to sit here quietly, listening to the birds and the stream nearby. The Japanese maples and enkianthus treat us to a brilliant red display each fall, and winter brings its own show of colors that we enjoy from the warmth of the hearth. Watching the transition from flowers to fruit is one of the great joys of having a garden, and this building puts us right in the middle of it."
— *Shoichi Itoh*

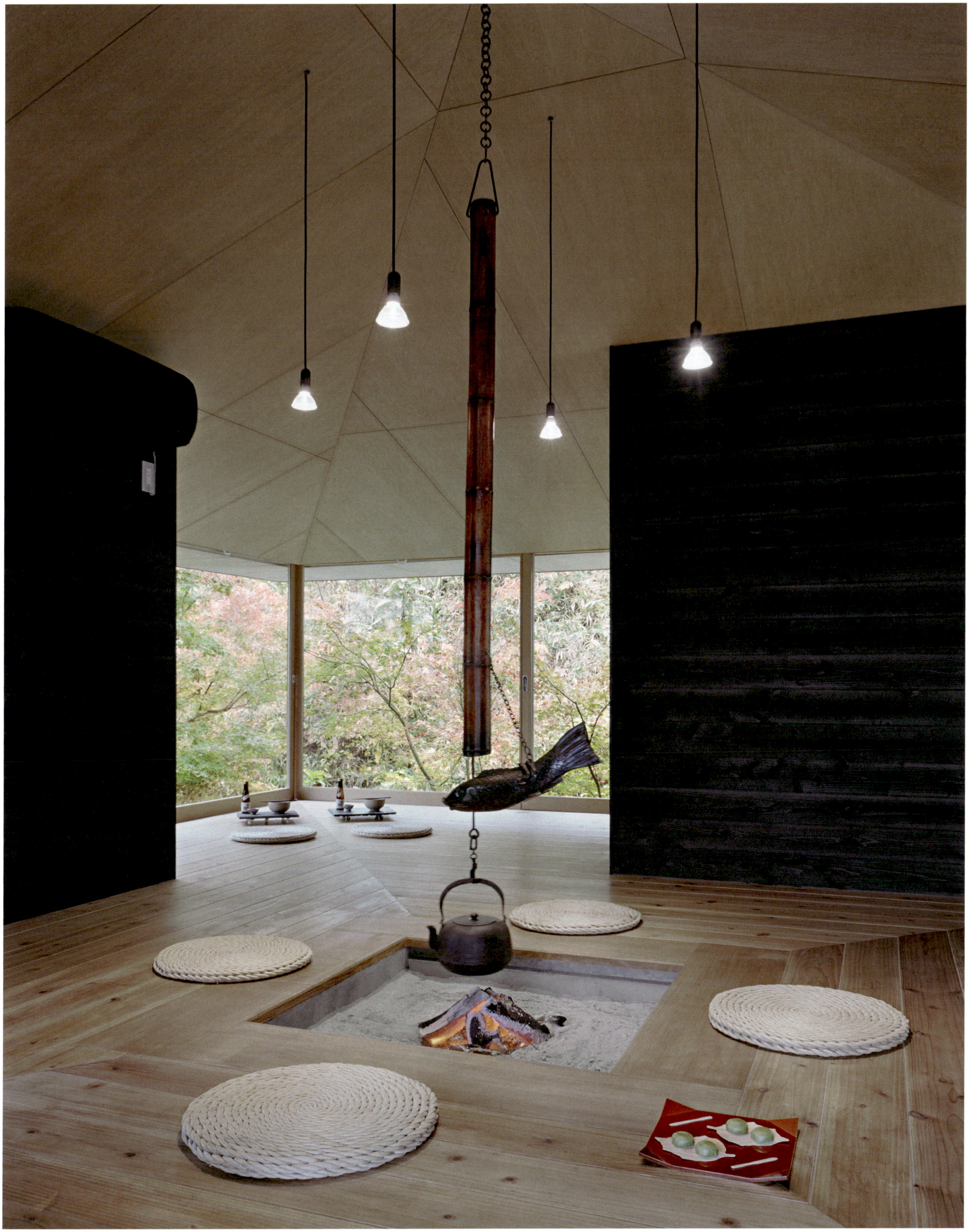

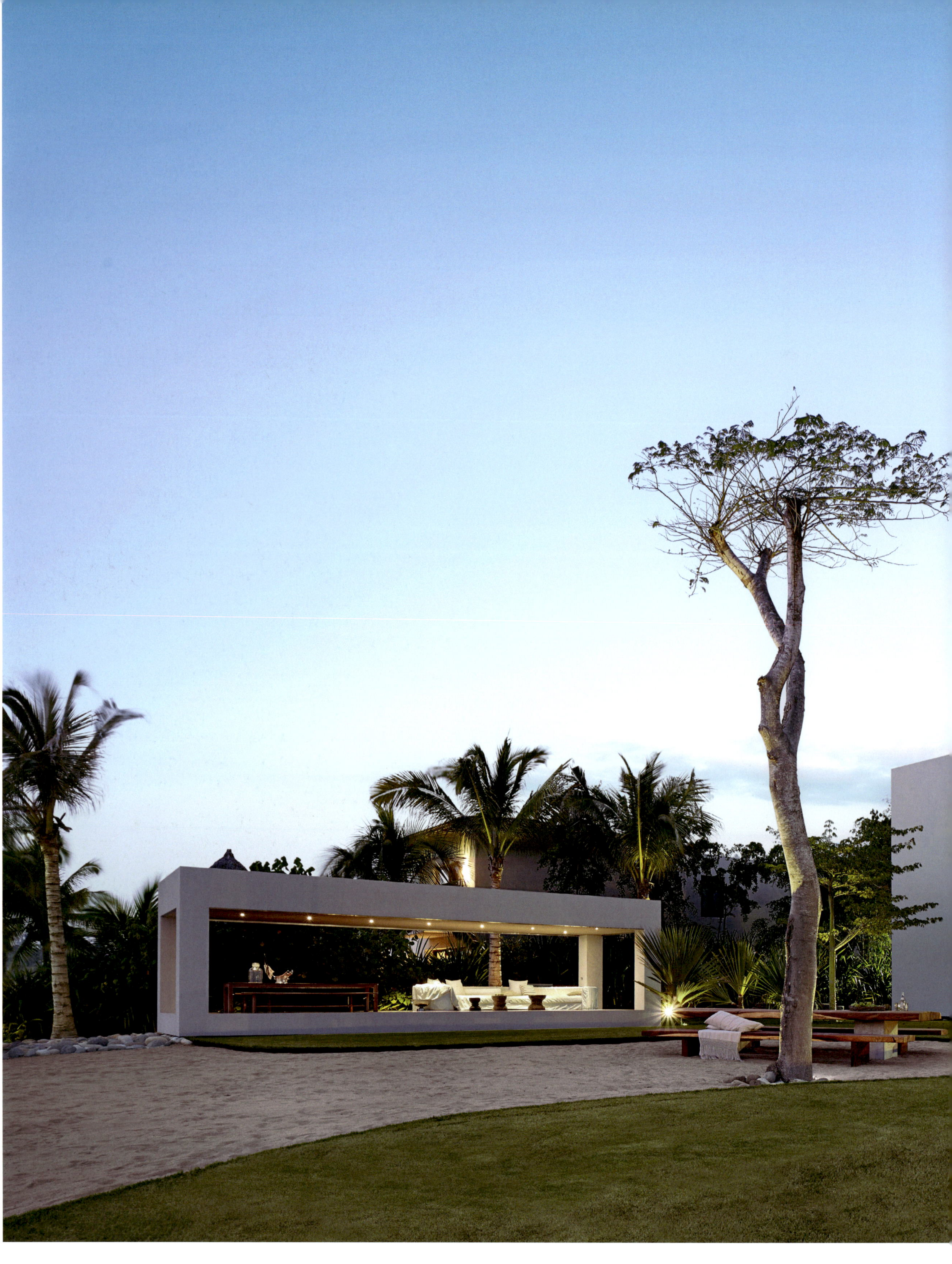

PUNTA DE MITA, MEXICO

CASA LA PUNTA

ELÍAS RIZO
OF ELÍAS RIZO ARQUITECTOS

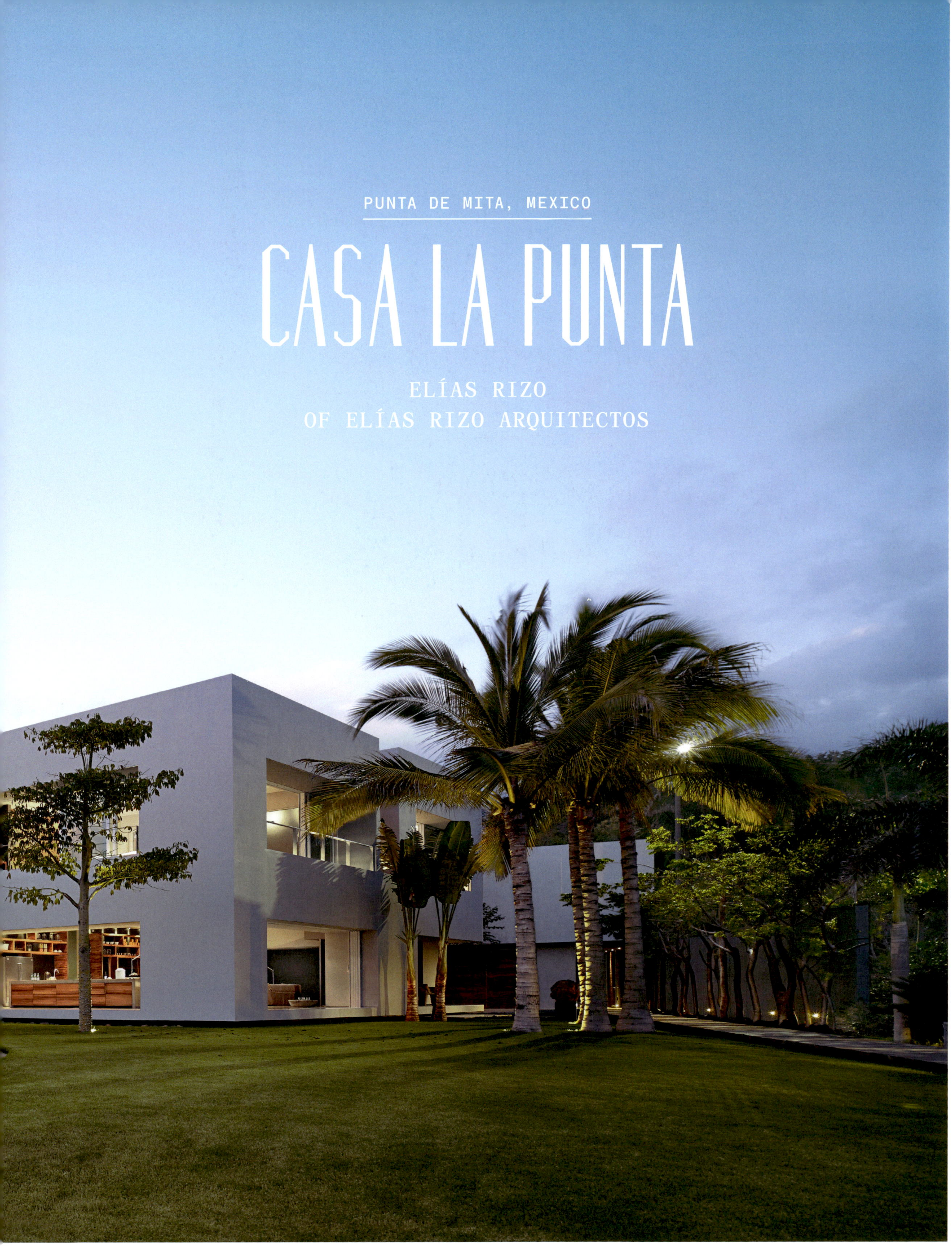

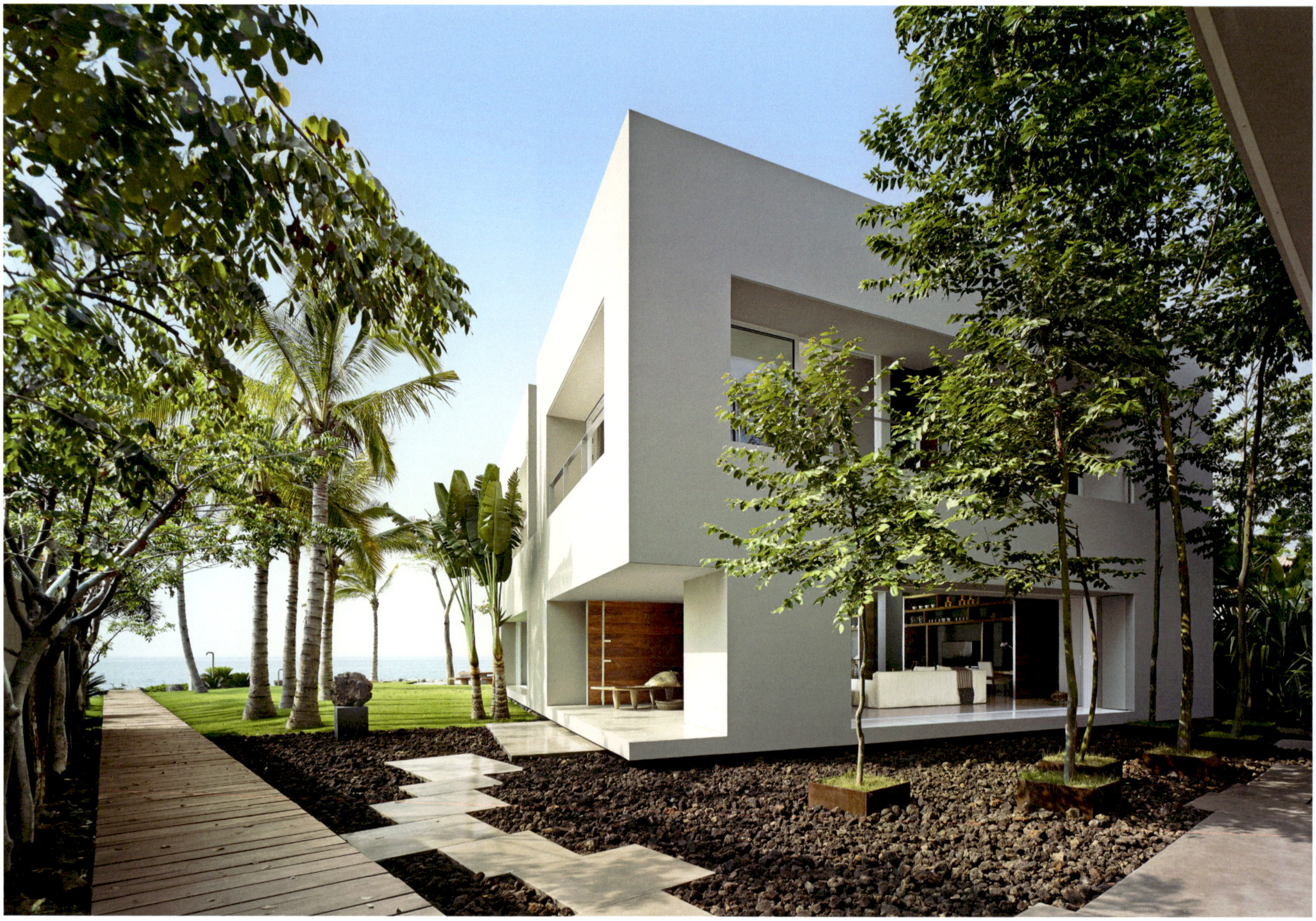

CASA LA PUNTA is centered on its beachside location. Working backward from that serene point, the beauty of the site has worked its way into every facet of the modular structure. The three volumes are orthogonal yet unobtrusive, and, in their openness, create an effortless and hospitable space.

Simple lines and neutral colors are all that Casa La Punta needs in order to capture the beauty of its location. Situated on a cusp of the Riviera Nayarit coastline in Mexico's Punta de Mita region, a clear ocean view bends around the site, echoing through the impressive open modules. As owner Karimia Dipp says, "What you see is the sea, the sea, the sea—that's all."

Dipp, an interior designer who juggles her time between busy work and social lives, owns the beachside property. She wanted a home that could cater to guests in a laid-back and carefree manner. It had to be a place that would be "easy to be in," she explains. To this end, she employed her friend Elías Rizo for the project. In describing his task, he says, "The spot is extraordinarily beautiful—really, we only had to create something that didn't interfere."

Rizo designed Casa La Punta in a modular arrangement where three separate structures define the site. The principal module consists of an expansive living space and kitchen on the lower floor, with the master bedroom and two guest bedrooms tucked away upstairs. Parota hardwood was used in the kitchen to counterbalance the severity of the stainless steel accents and appliances. Continuing this tonal balancing act, parota also forms the walkways that cut through the chilly gray modules, warming the property and grounding it in the majestic setting.

A double garage, a studio, and an apartment for the caretaker make up the smaller service module, which sits near the road. Resting at the edge of the beach, a third module protrudes from the manicured lawn, providing an outdoor dining and seating area that features a long table and benches made from lapacho wood. A flowing social area that expresses Dipp's desire for informal ease, this ~

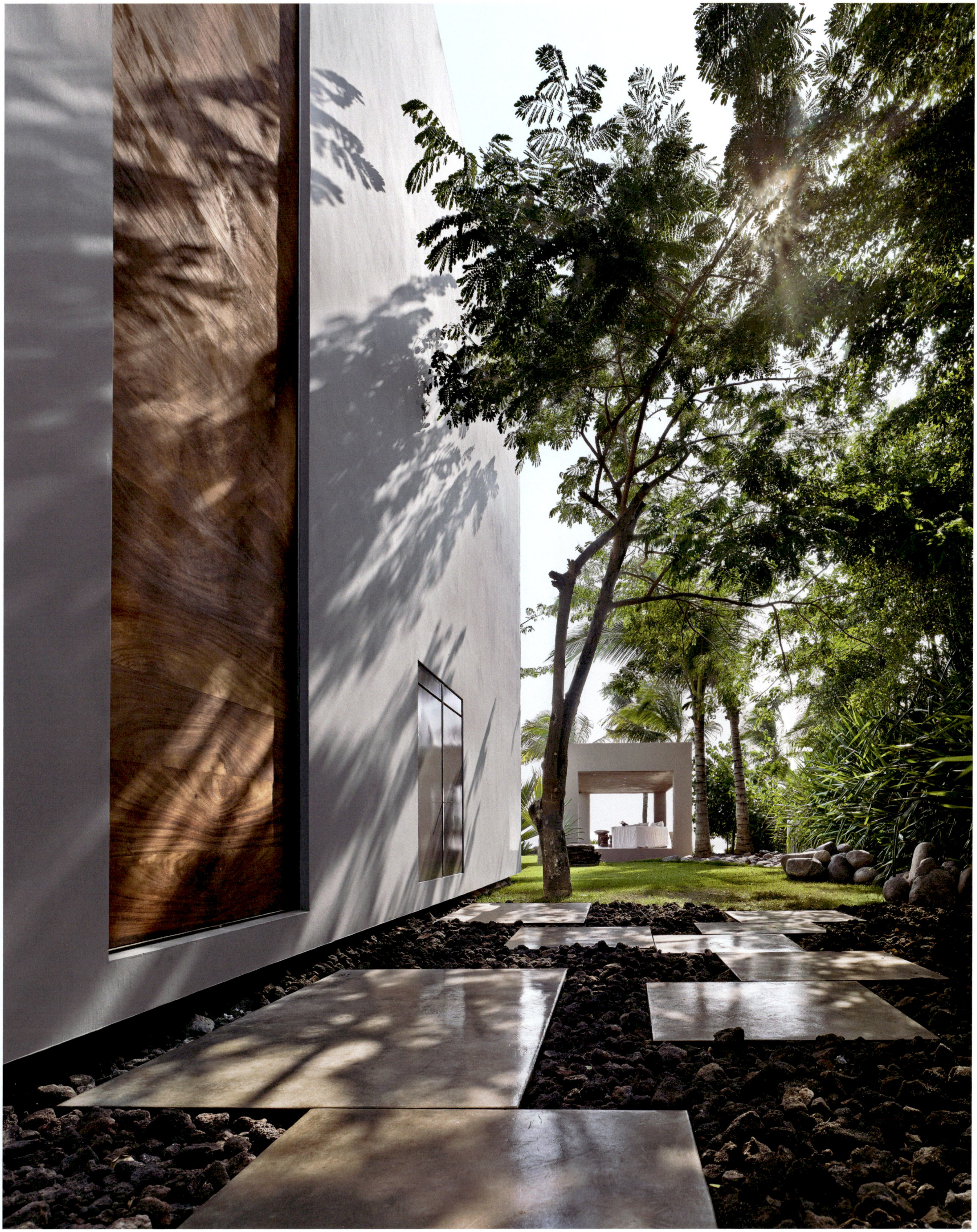

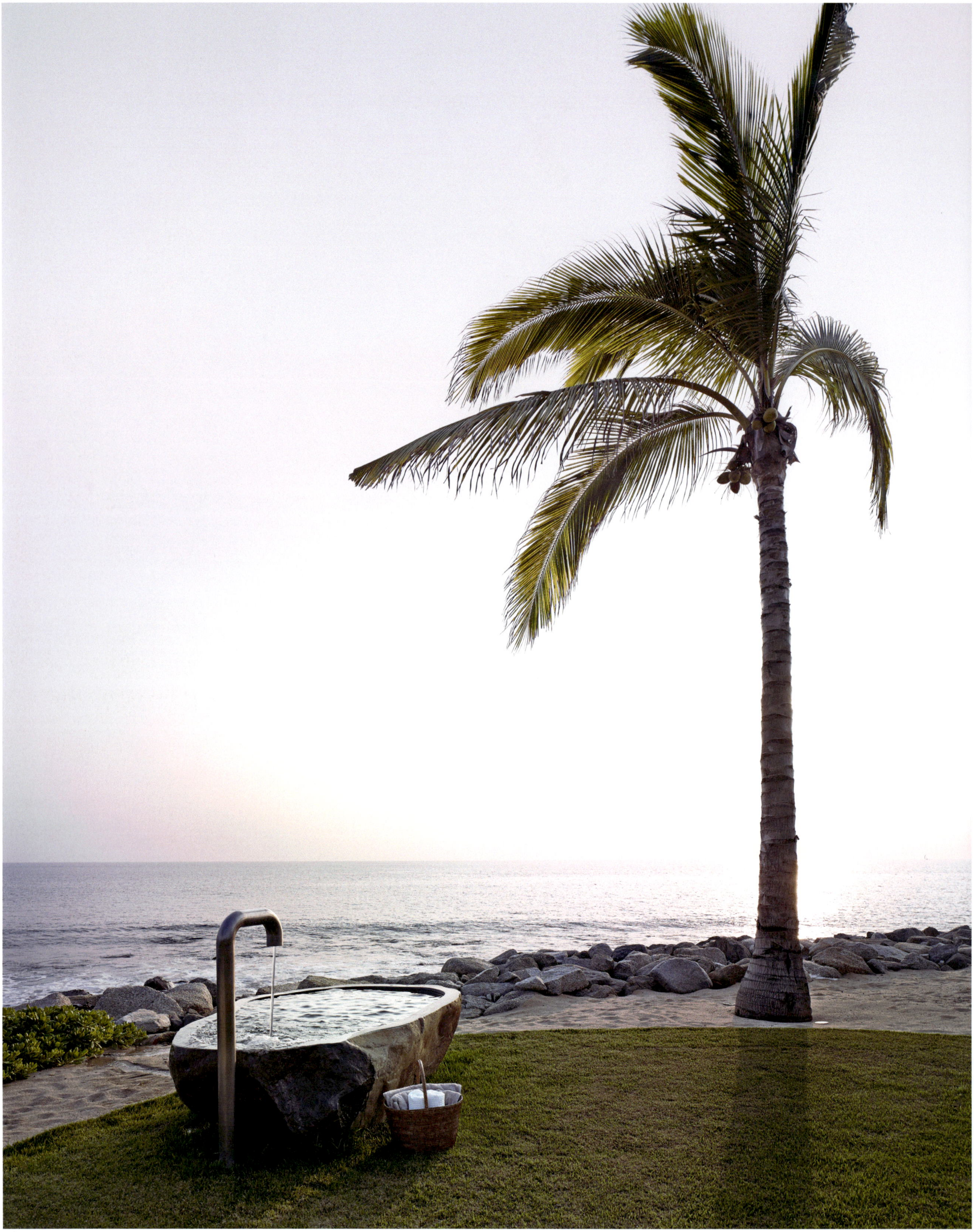

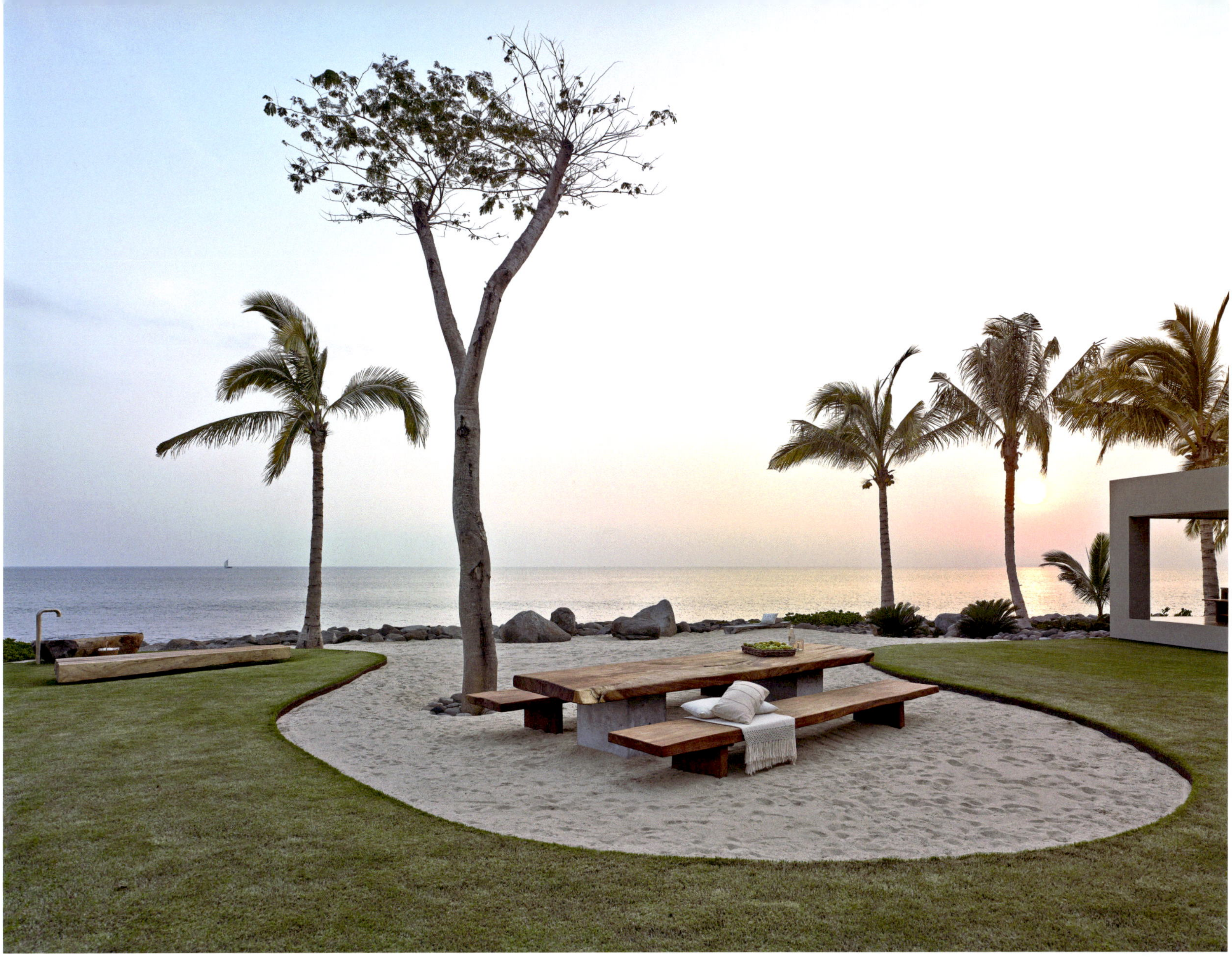

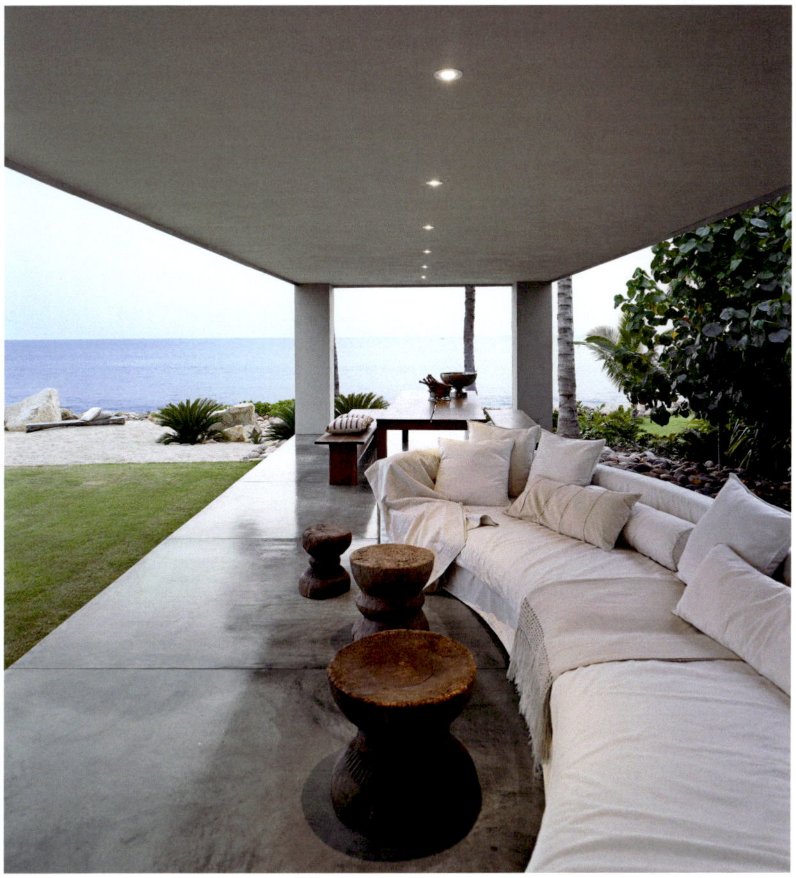

"The spot is extraordinarily beautiful—really, we only had to create something that didn't interfere."
— *Elias Rizo.*

volume transitions seamlessly between relaxation space and casual dining area.

Casa La Punta is as subtle as it is imposing, the realization of the goal to "create a sculptural place." The blend of natural materials and geometrical forms results in a restful space where guests can relax and enjoy unbroken views of the ocean. ◆

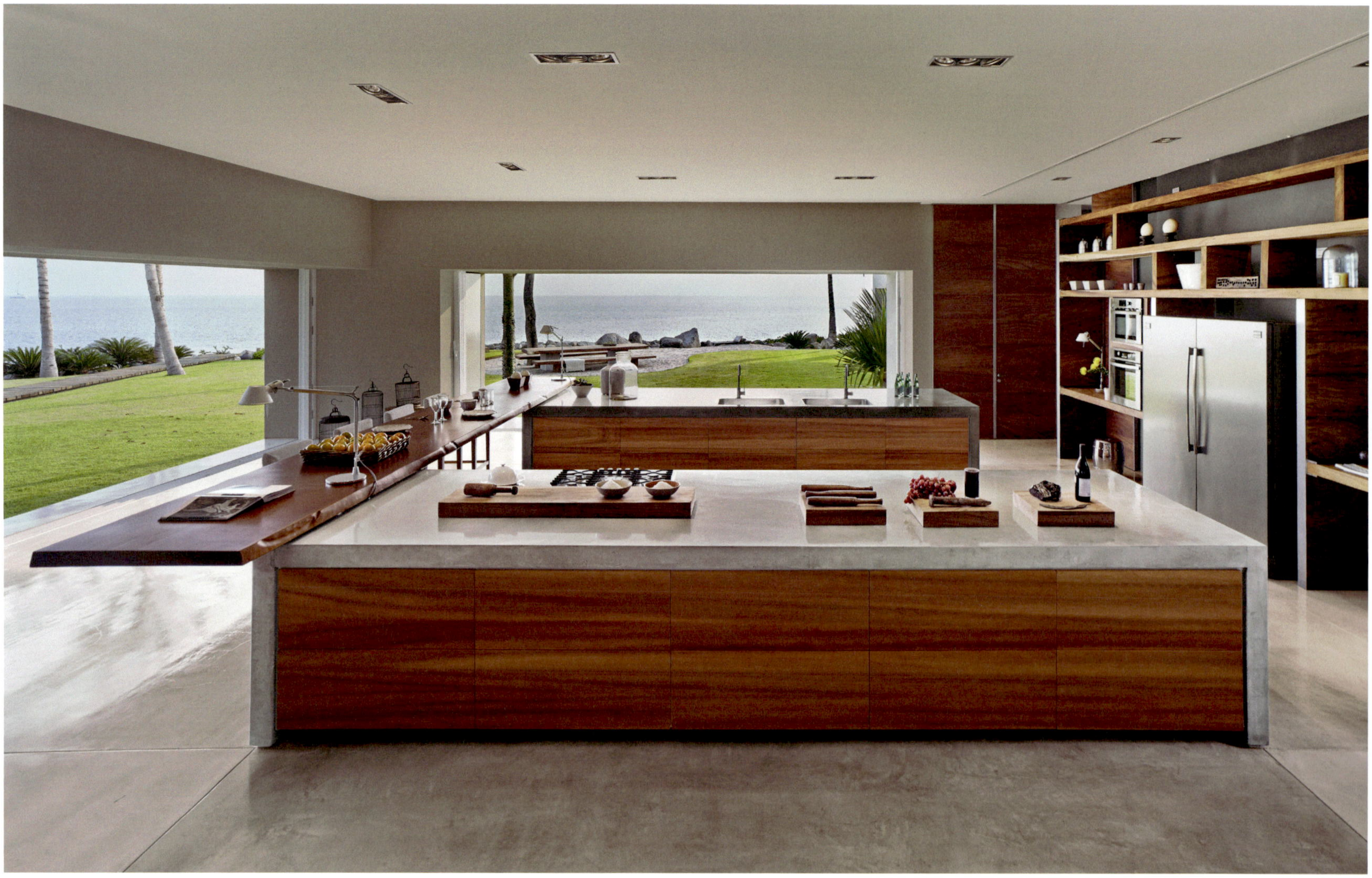

"PAROTA FORMS THE WALKWAYS THAT CUT THROUGH THE CHILLY GREY MODULES, WARMING THE PROPERTY AND GROUNDING IT IN THE MAJESTIC SETTING."

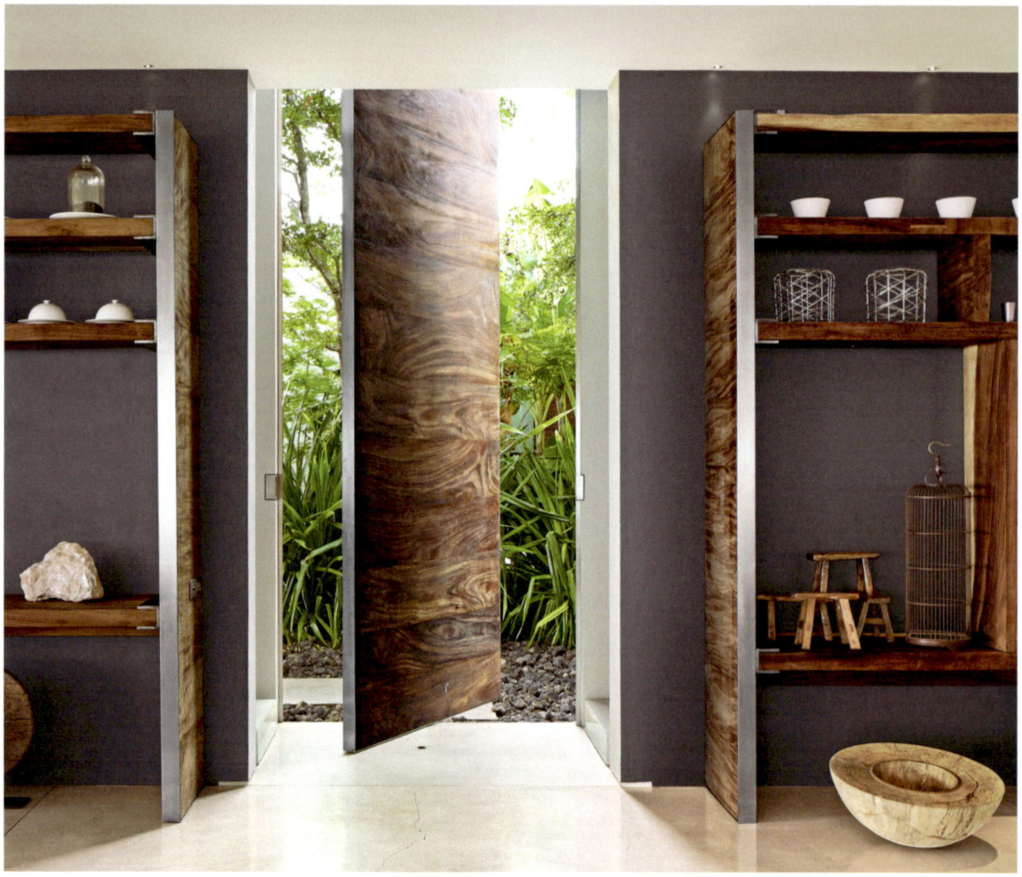

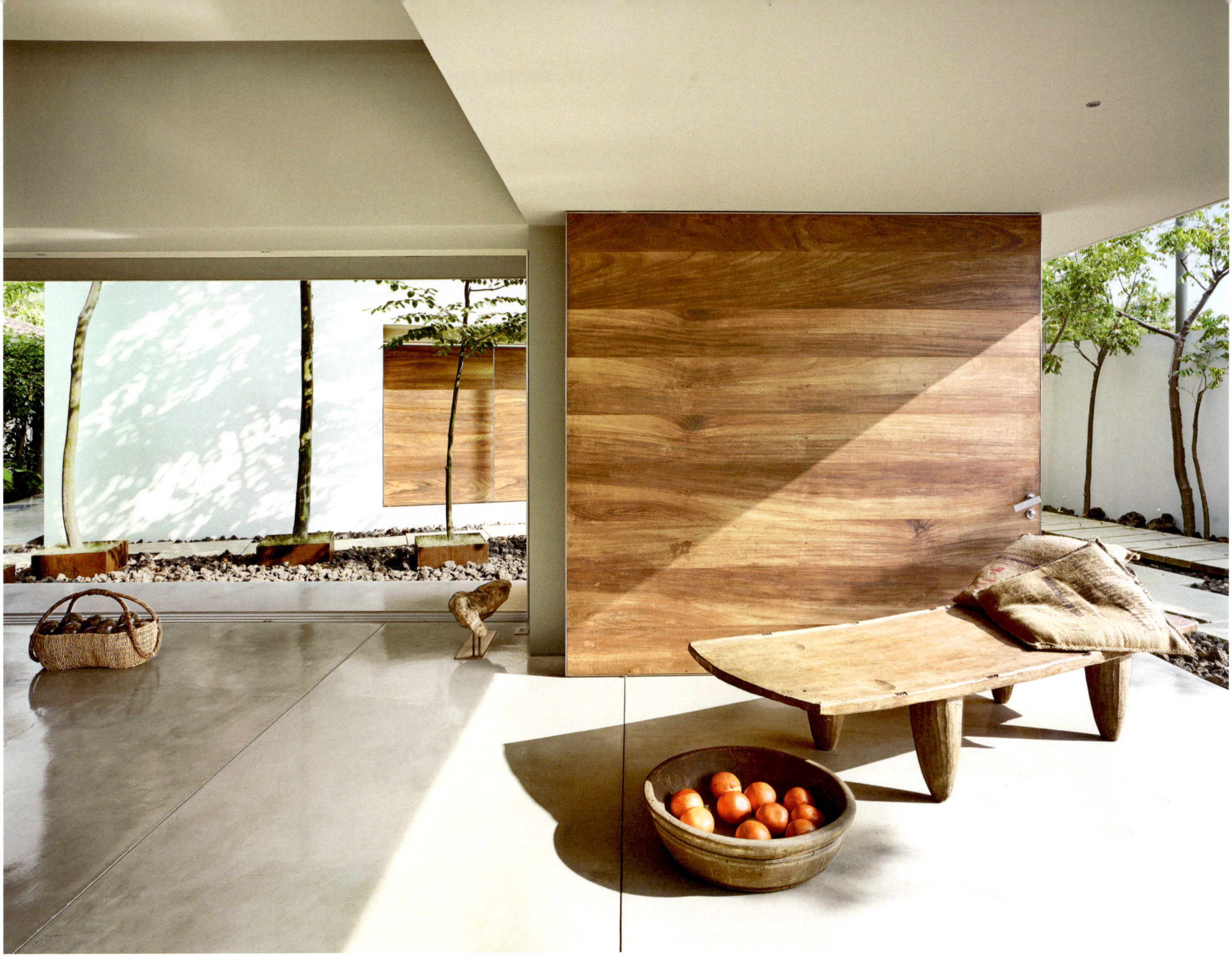

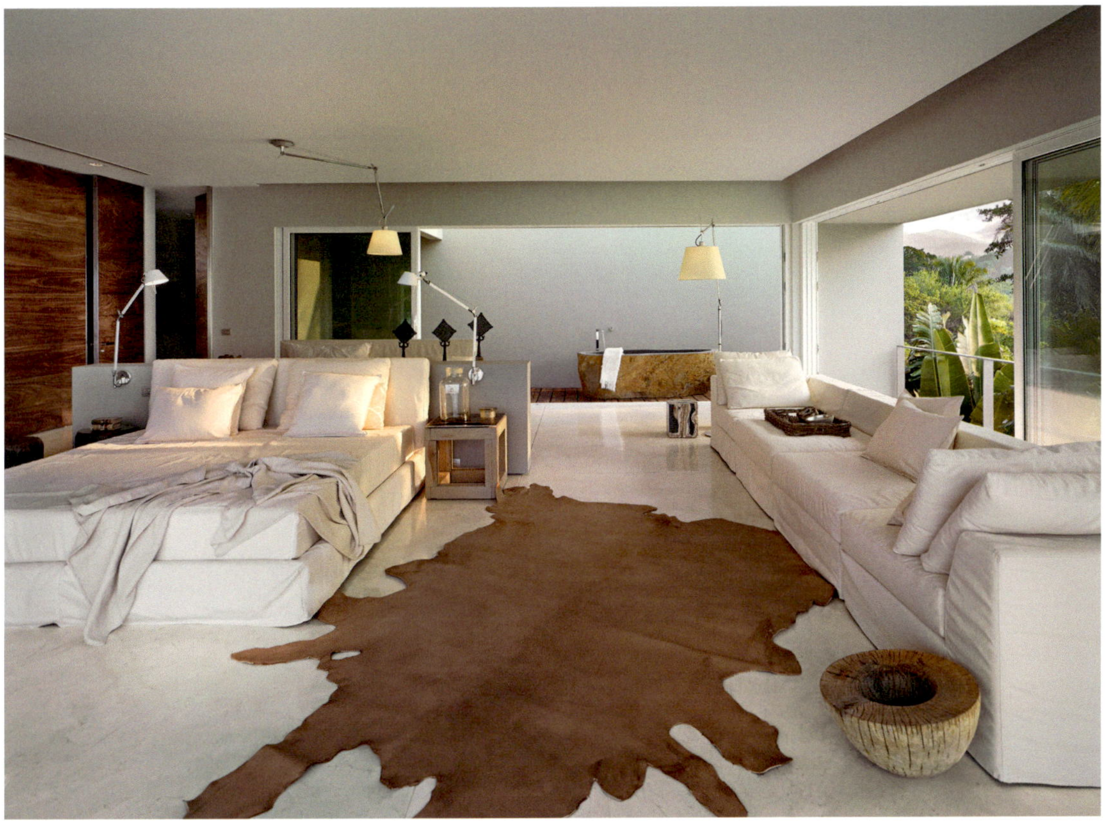

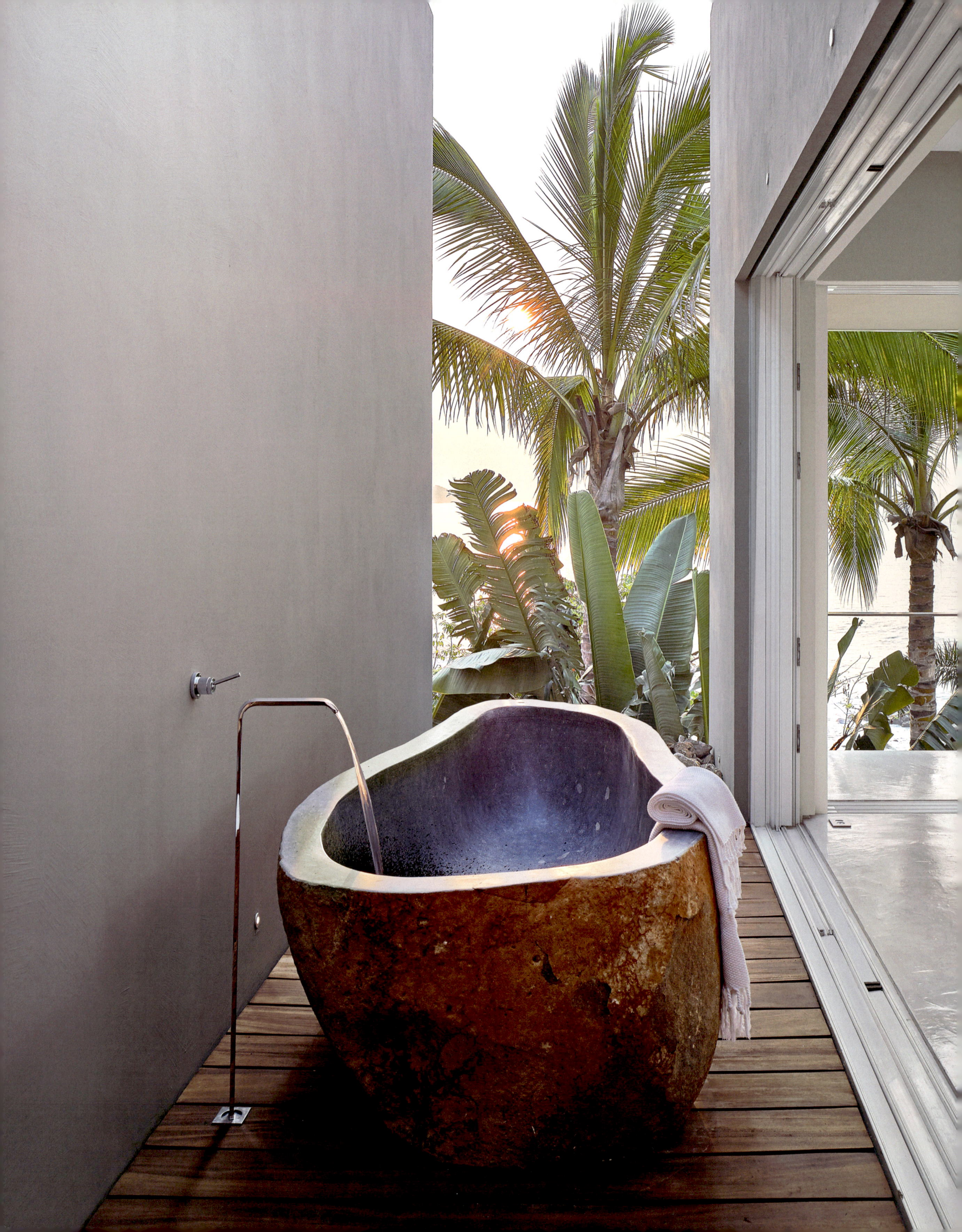

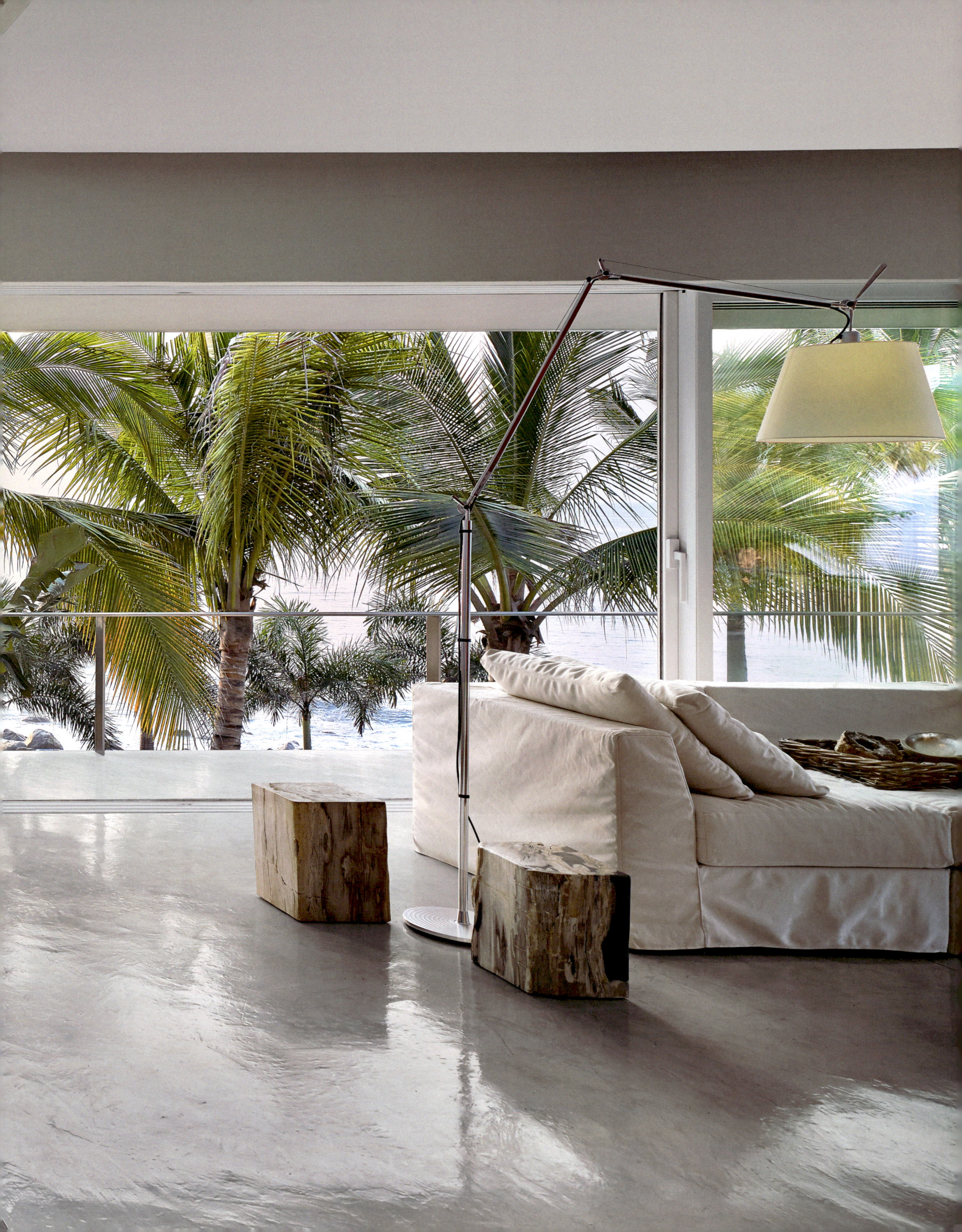

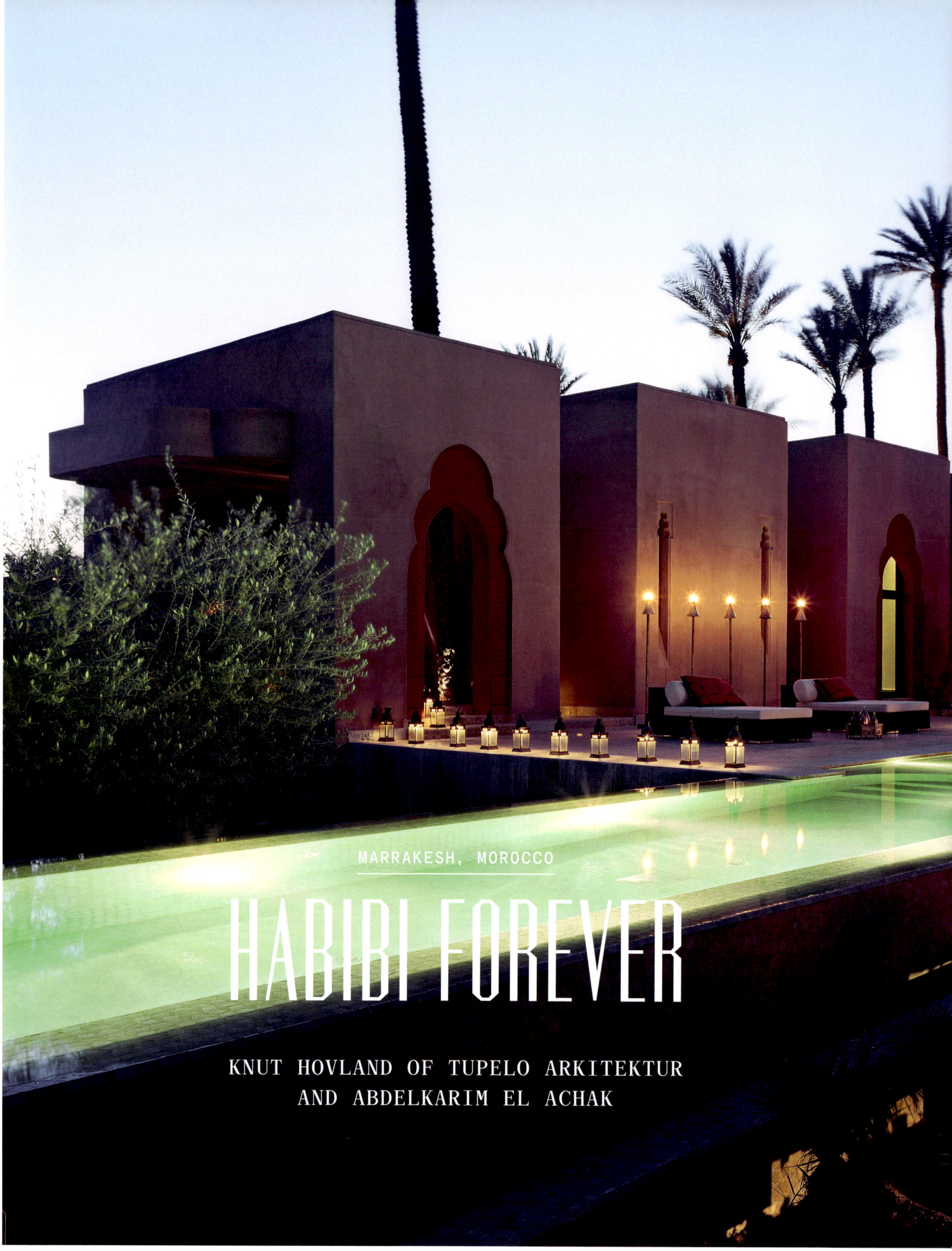

MARRAKESH, MOROCCO

HABIBI FOREVER

KNUT HOVLAND OF TUPELO ARKITEKTUR
AND ABDELKARIM EL ACHAK

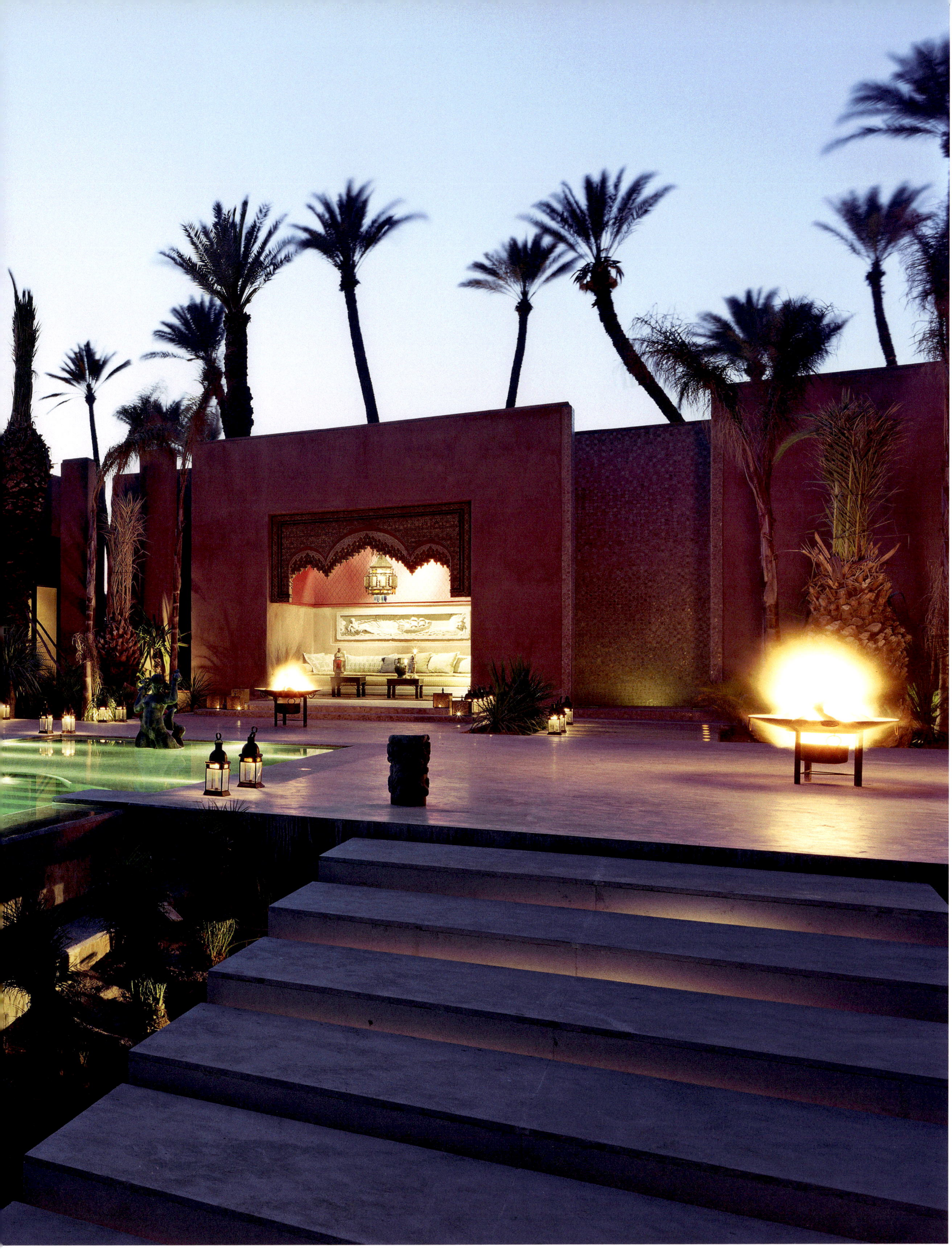

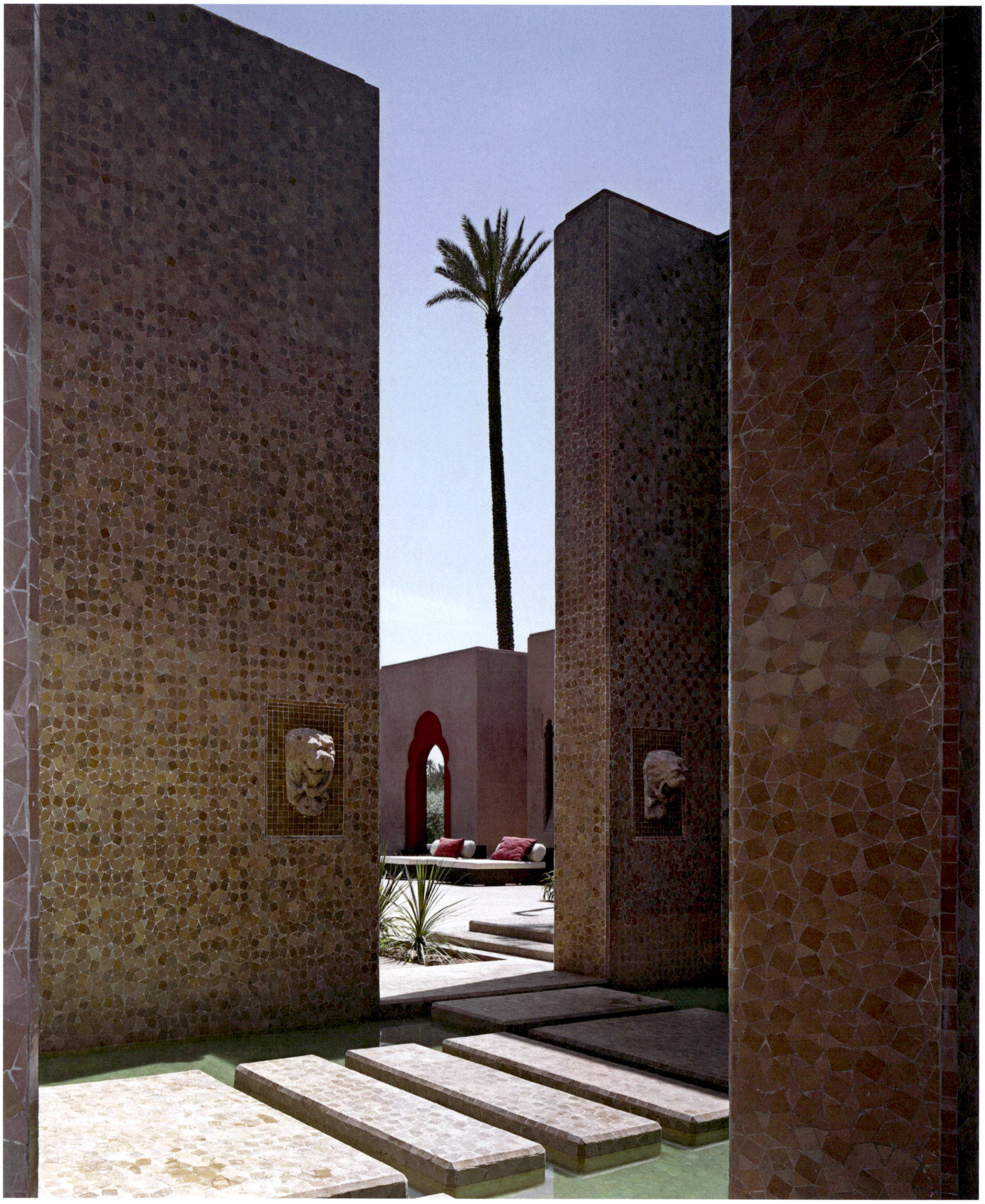

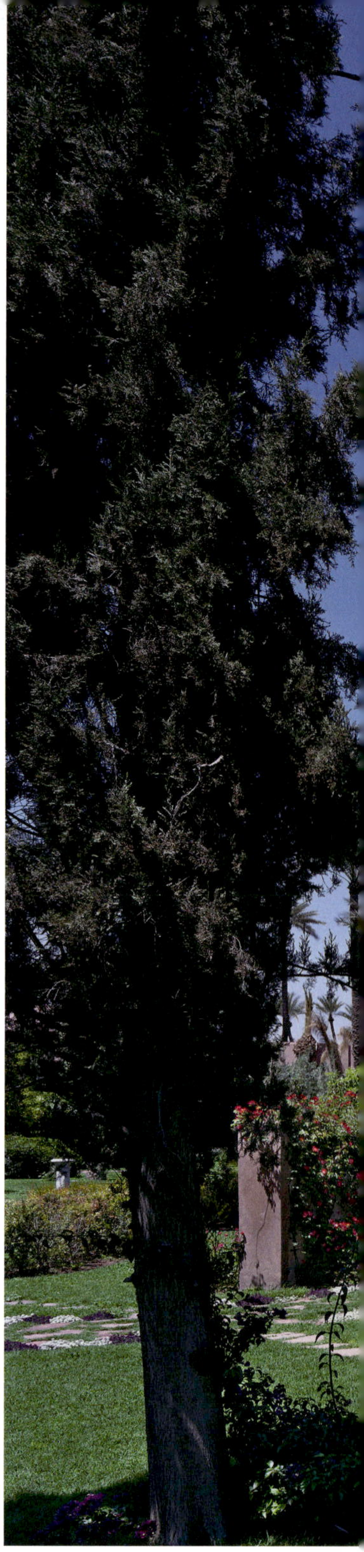

HABIBI FOREVER At first glance, the architecture of Morocco and Norway seem to have very little in common. But if one looks closer, as the Arabic and Nordic architects who designed this urban escape have done, distinct similarities reveal themselves.

Between the architecture of Morocco and Norway there exist many differences. Norway is known for simplicity, functionality, and refined craftsmanship, while at the other end of the spectrum, Moroccan aesthetics are vibrant, sensual, and decorative. It was an interesting decision, then, when the owners of this refuge asked the Norwegian Knut Hovland and the Moroccan Abdelkarim El Achak to collaborate on their home.

However, as Hovland points out, there is an underlying relationship between the two forms of architecture: "Both Moroccan and Scandinavian architecture place great emphasis on the dialogue between internal and external spaces."

The most apparent modification to traditional Moroccan architecture is the position and shape of the buildings. Three separate buildings constitute the property—Villa Principale, Villa Secondaire, and La Tour. Instead of being organized around one public courtyard ~

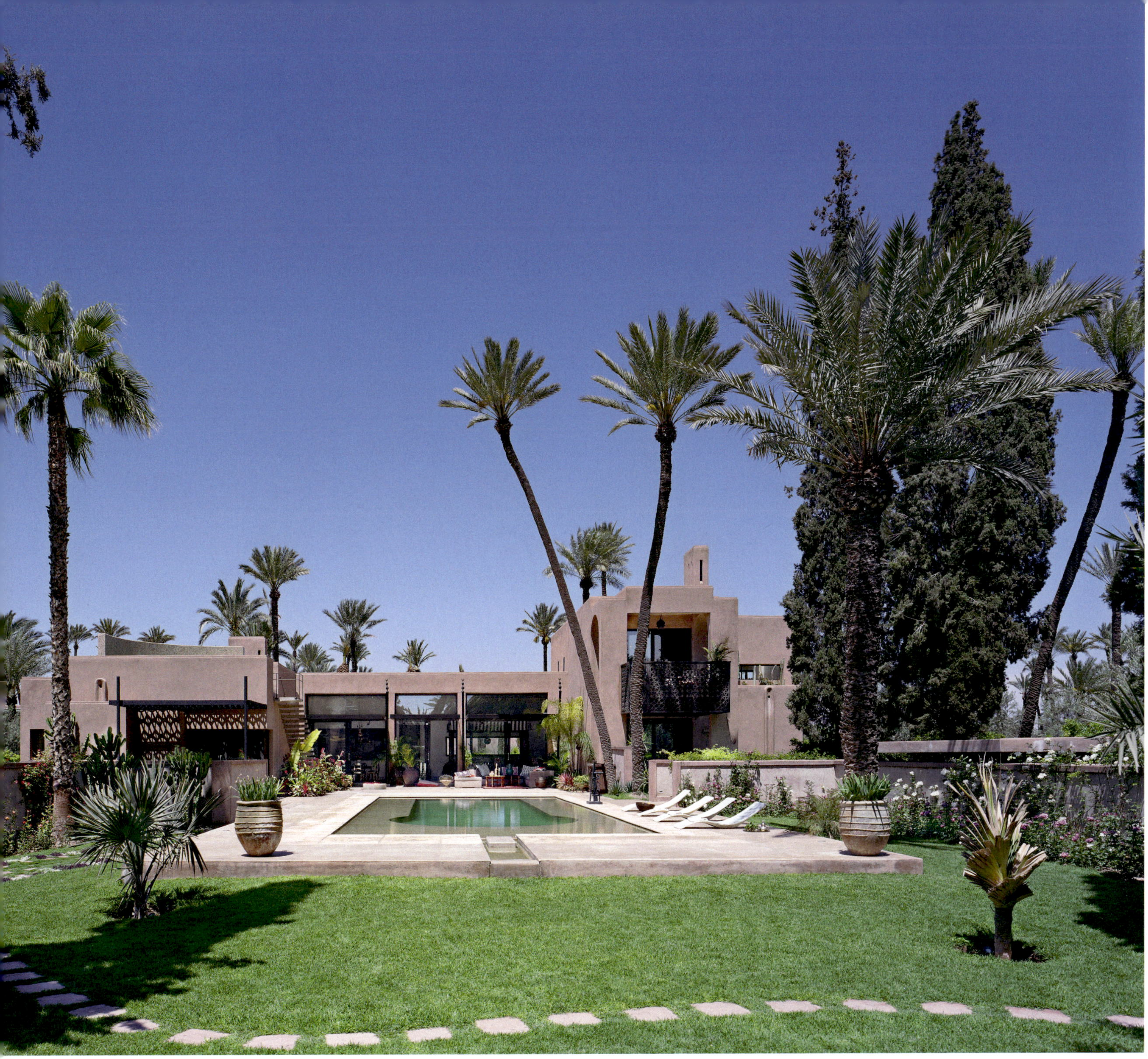

"Both Moroccan and Scandinavian architecture place great emphasis on the dialogue between internal and external spaces."
— *Knut Hovland*

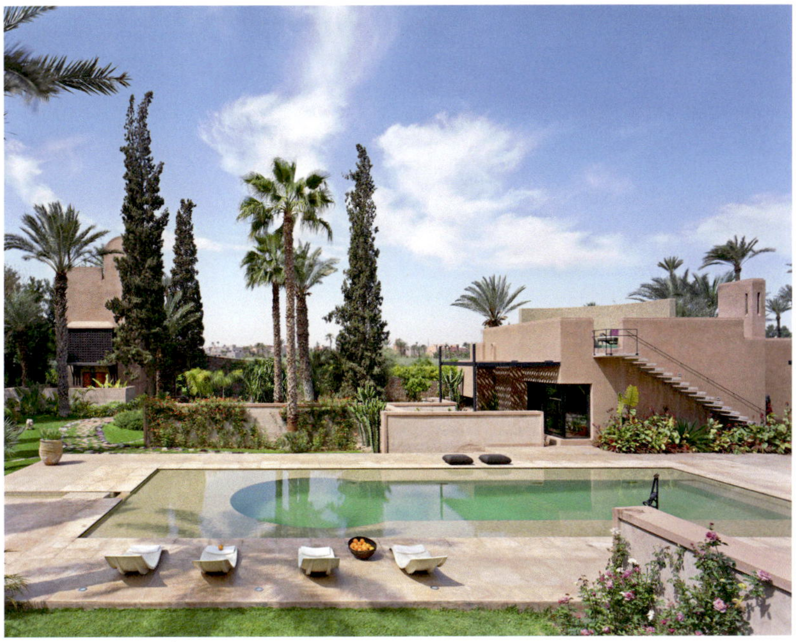

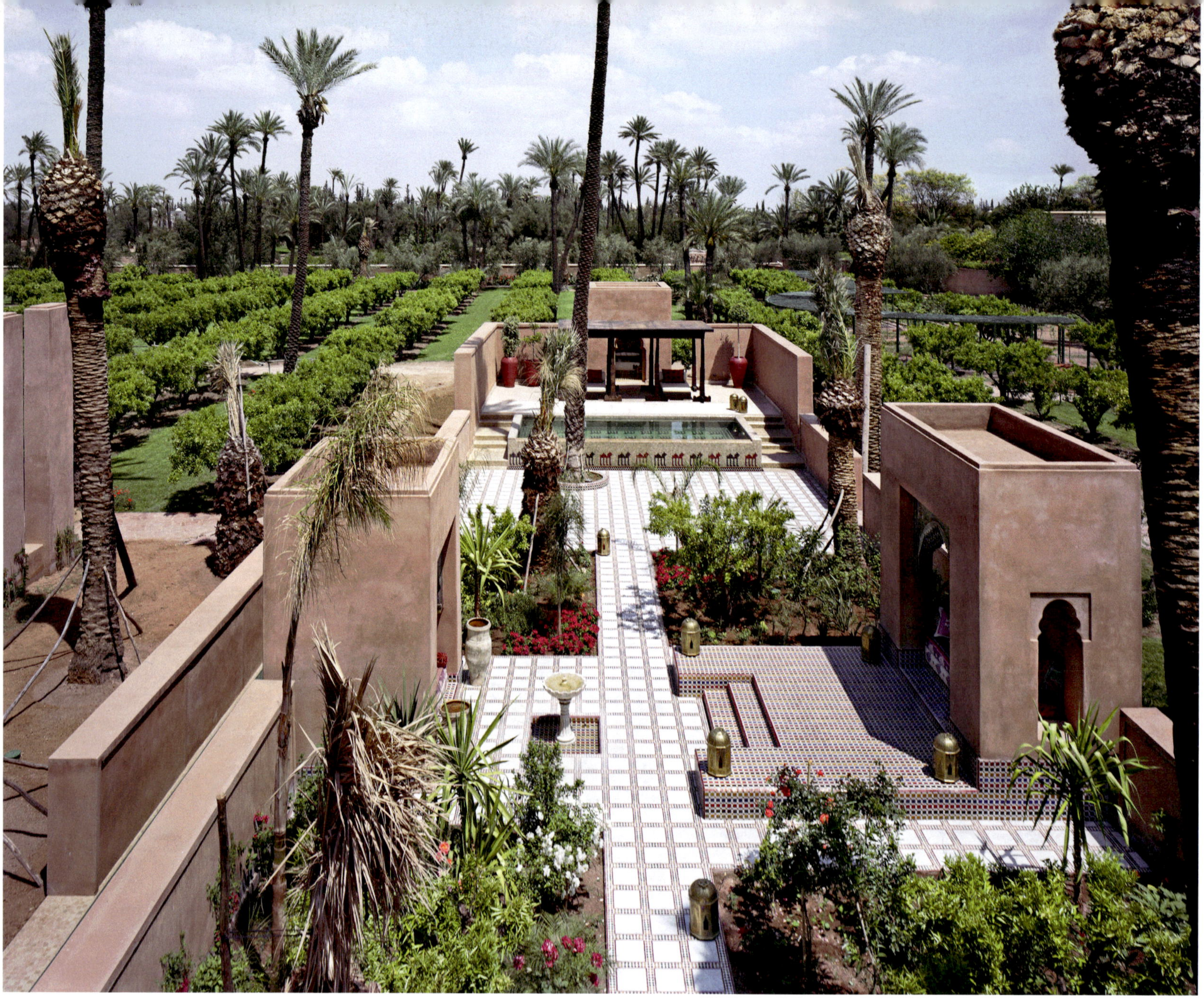

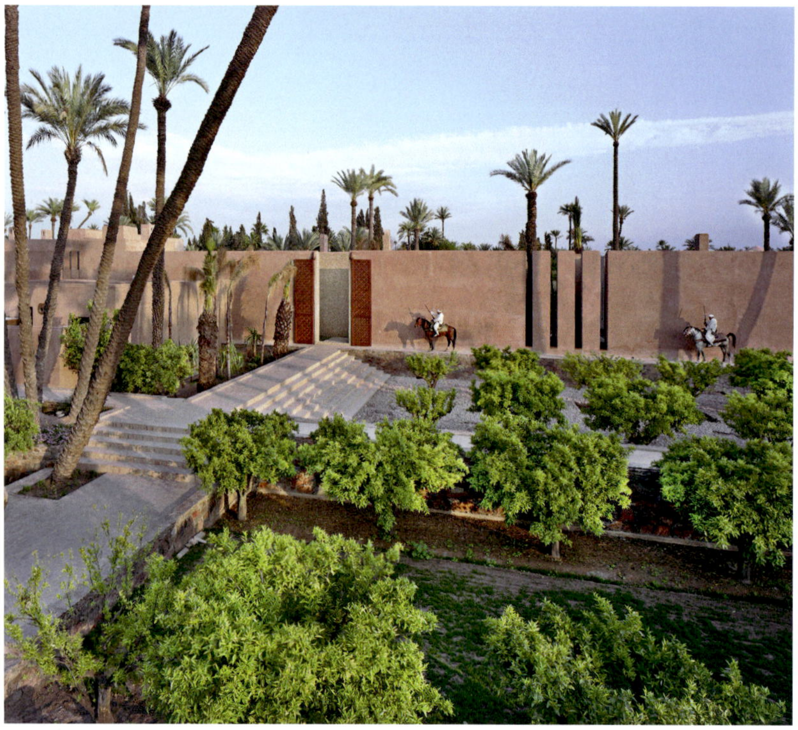

"INSTEAD OF BEING ORGANIZED AROUND ONE PUBLIC COURTYARD ACCORDING TO LOCAL CONVENTION, EACH RESIDENCE HAS ITS OWN OUTDOOR AREA OFFERING A SPACE OF SECLUSION."

according to local convention, each residence has its own outdoor area offering a space of seclusion.

With regard to the buildings' shapes, the square Moroccan geometry remains but loses its enclosed quality. Each dwelling has one glass face that opens out to views of the olive and orange trees that surround the expansive property. With the inclusion of this typical Nordic openness, a fine balance is achieved between in- and outside. ~

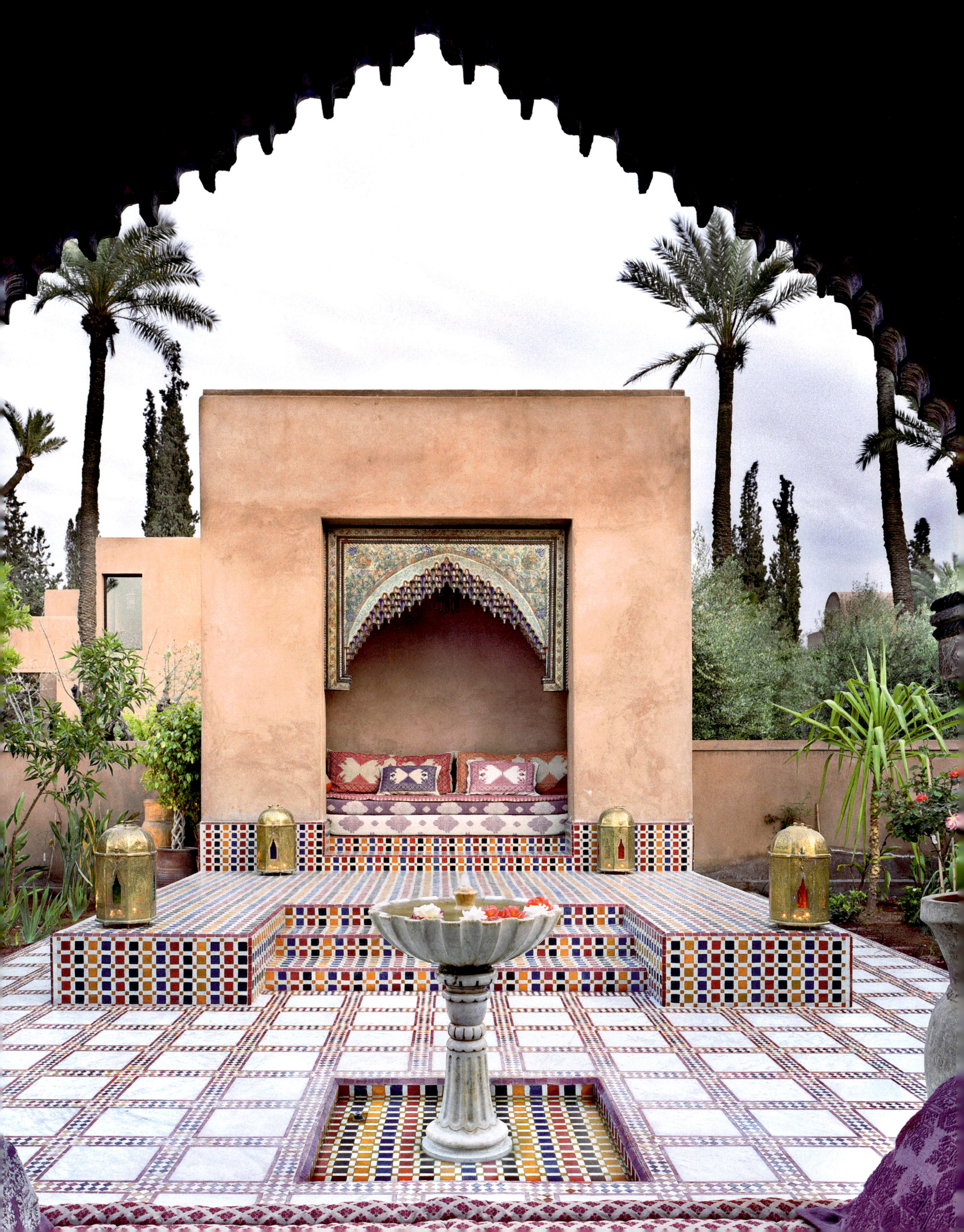

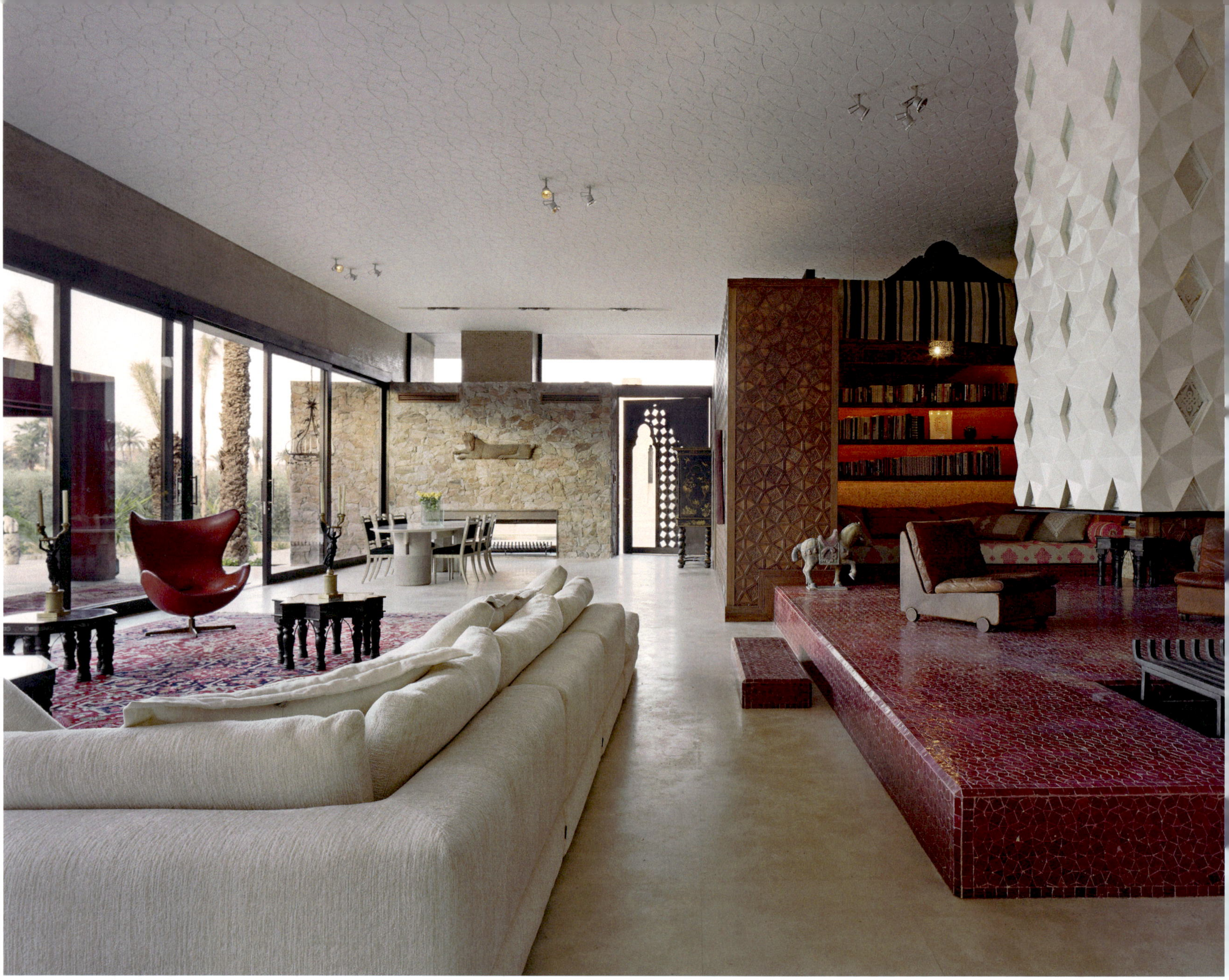

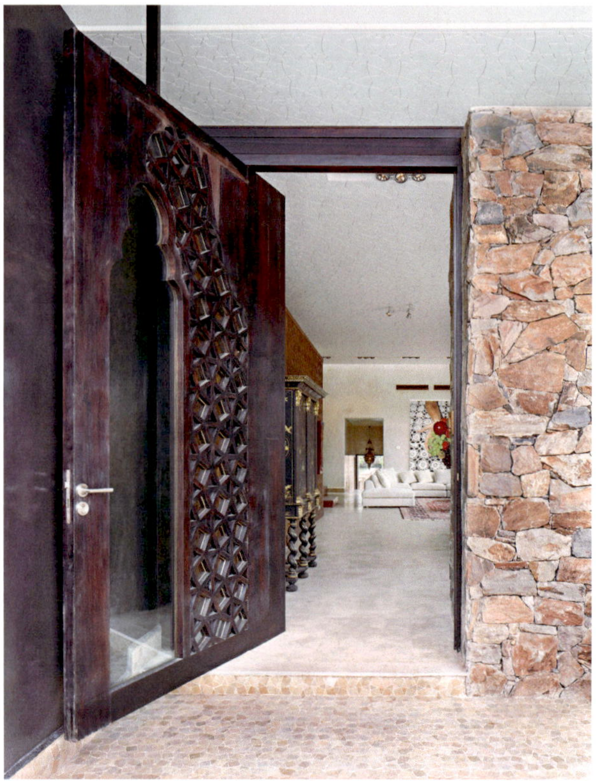

The Norwegian influence undergoes a unique transformation inside each house. Strong and simple lines meet minute detailing and decorative motifs—a contrast articulated most succinctly by Villa Principale's fireplace. Over a metal brassier, a white chimney made from lacquered wood hangs from the ceiling. Sculpted into a complex geometric pattern and inlaid with engraved mirrors, the mix of decadent detailing and simple coloration creates a distinctive harmony of both architectural worlds.

Through a careful negotiation of two different perspectives, this property evokes the timeless characteristics of each while creating new forms in the exchange. ◆

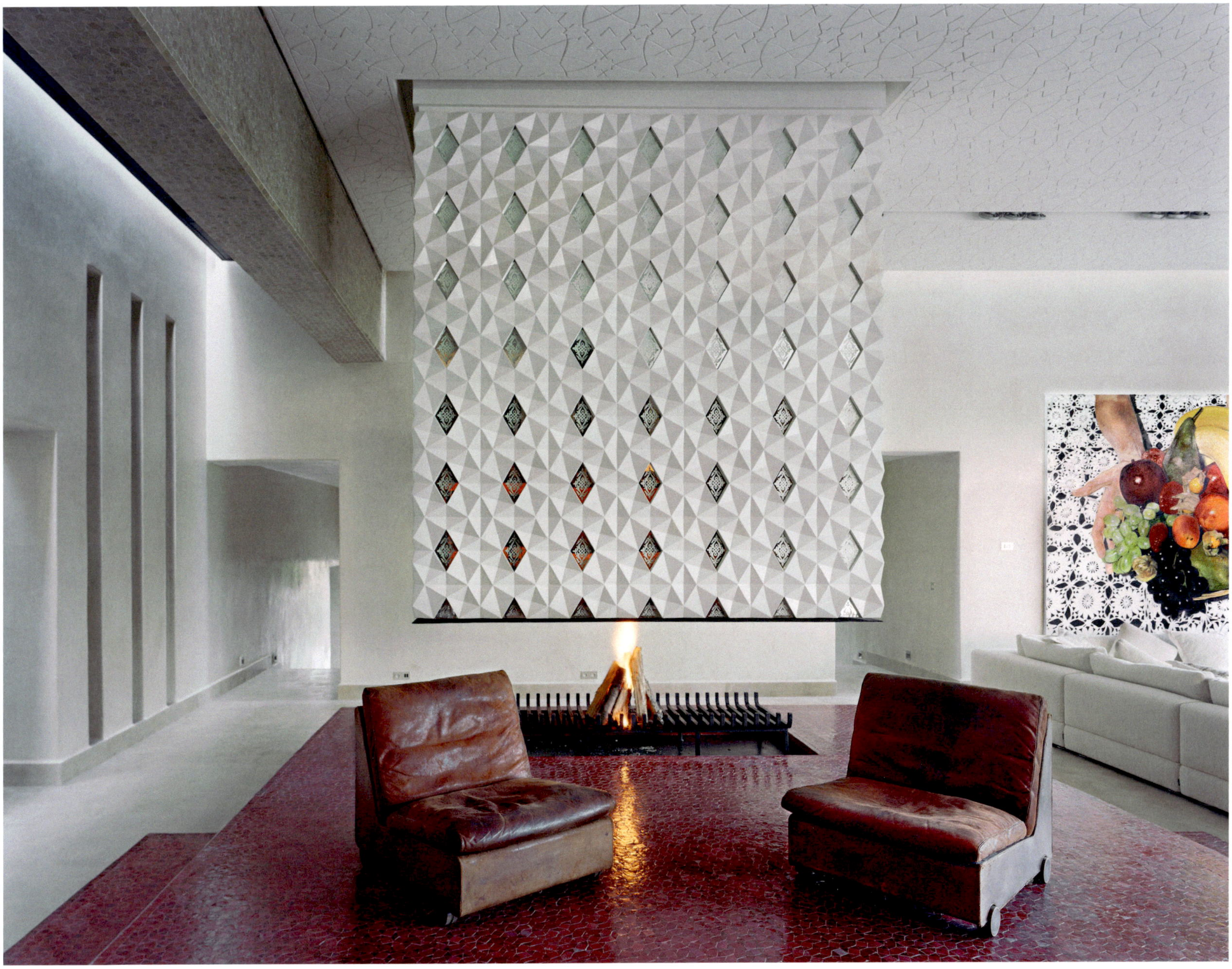

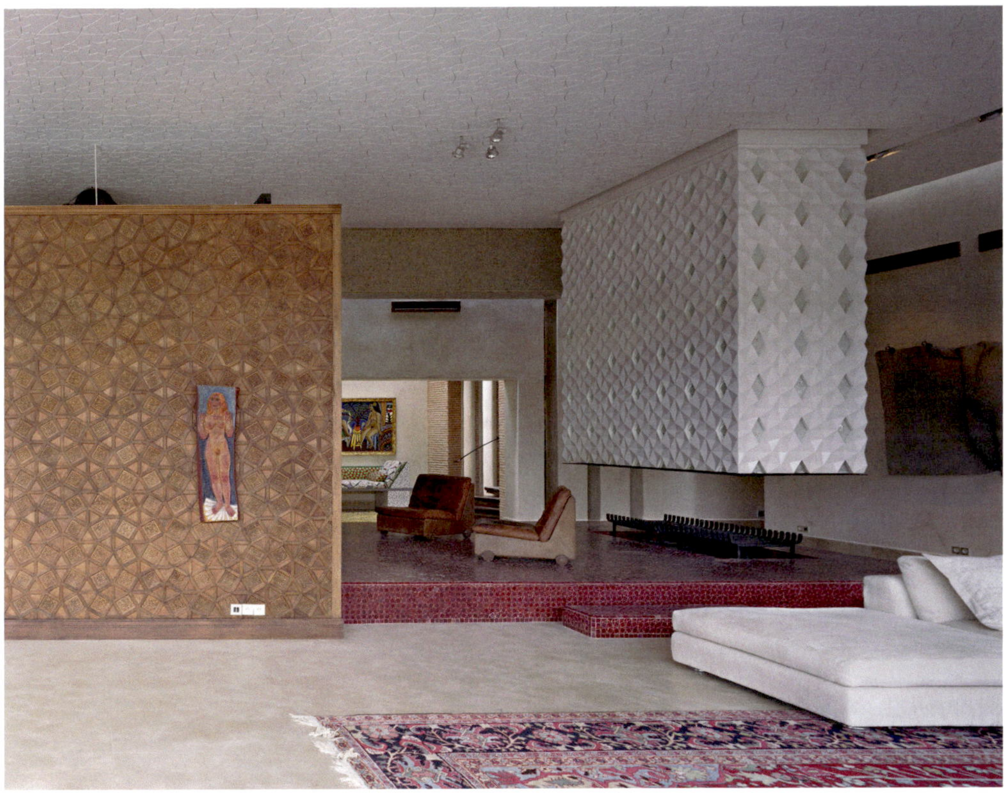

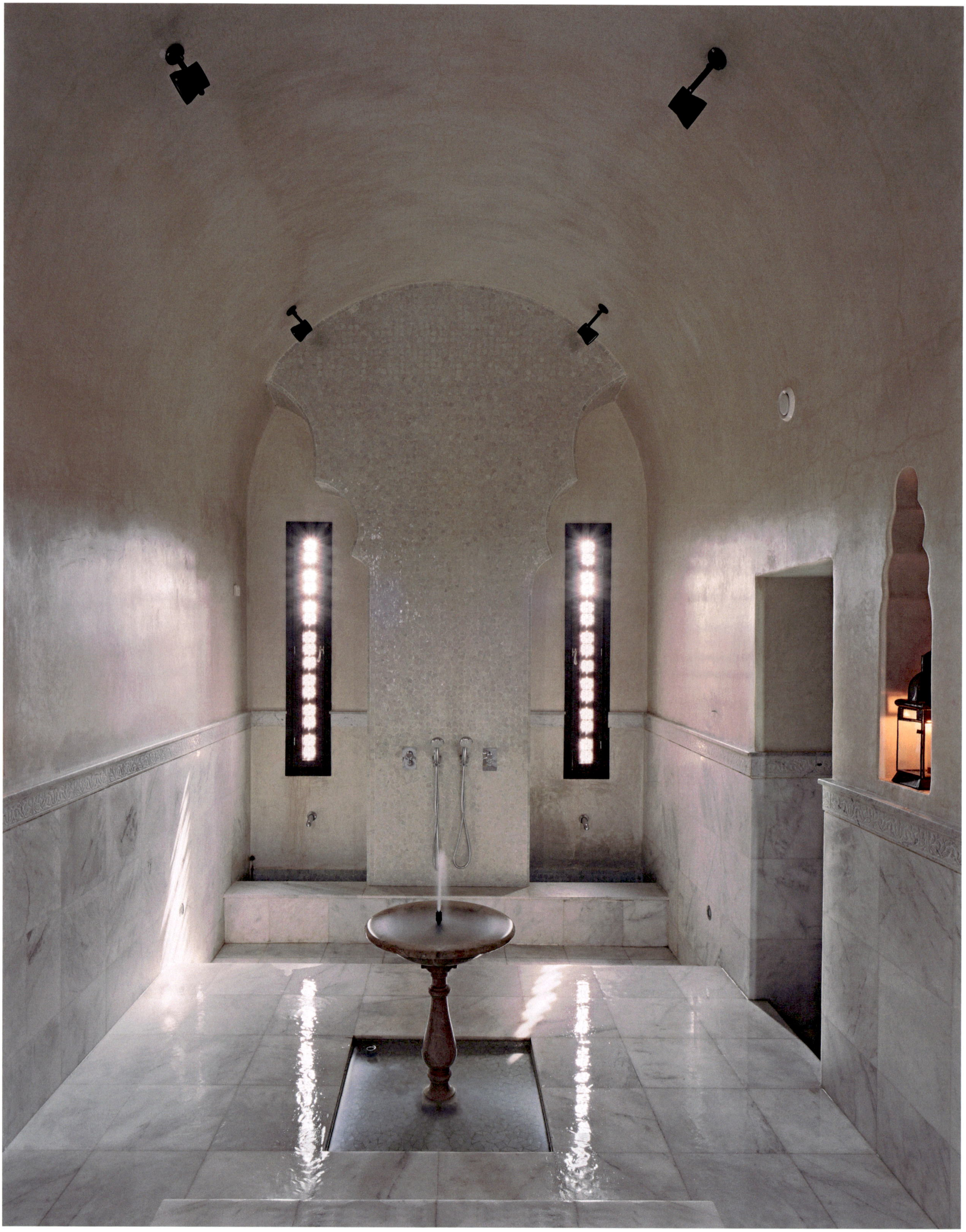

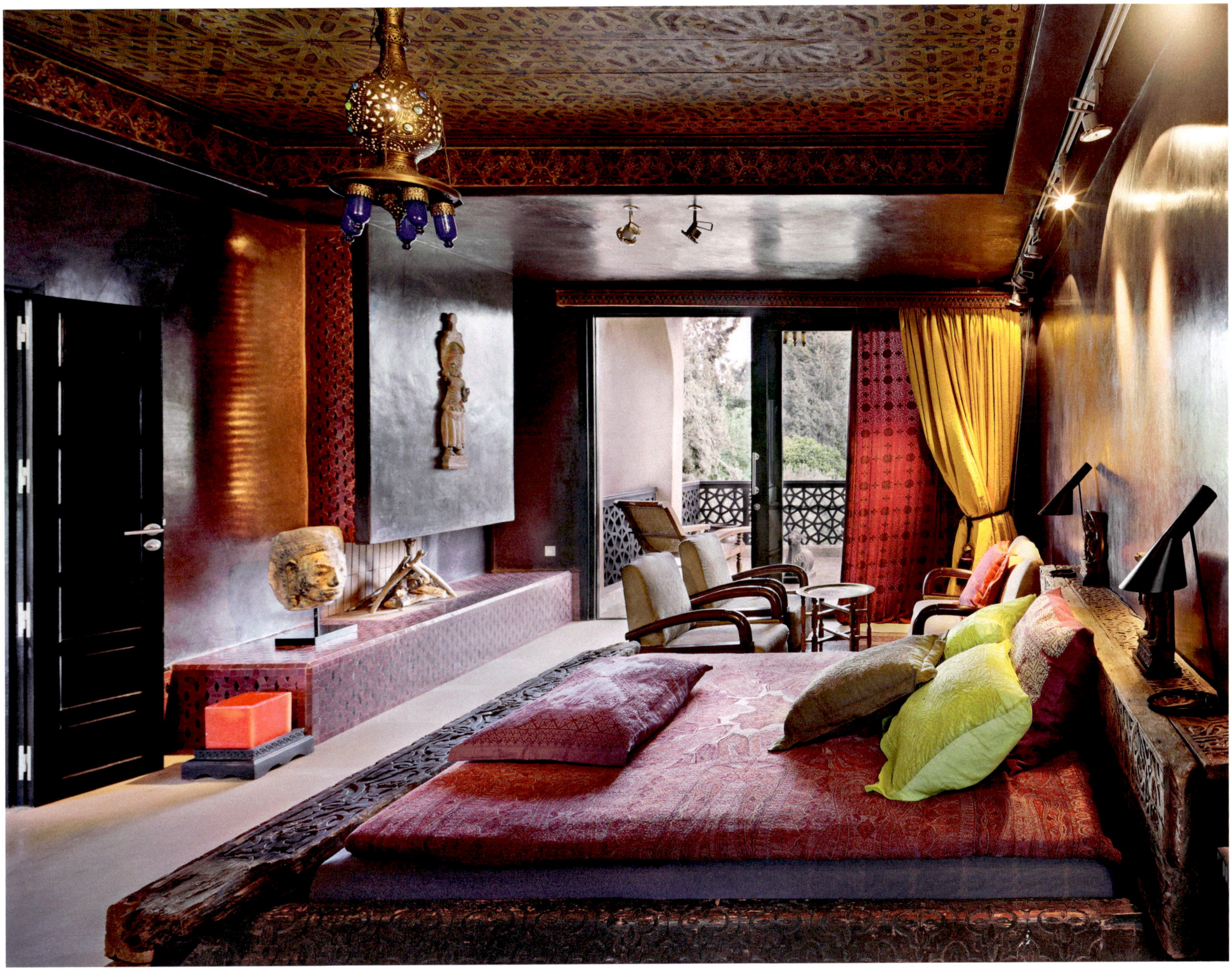

"STRONG AND SIMPLE LINES MEET MINUTE DETAILING AND DECORATIVE MOTIFS."

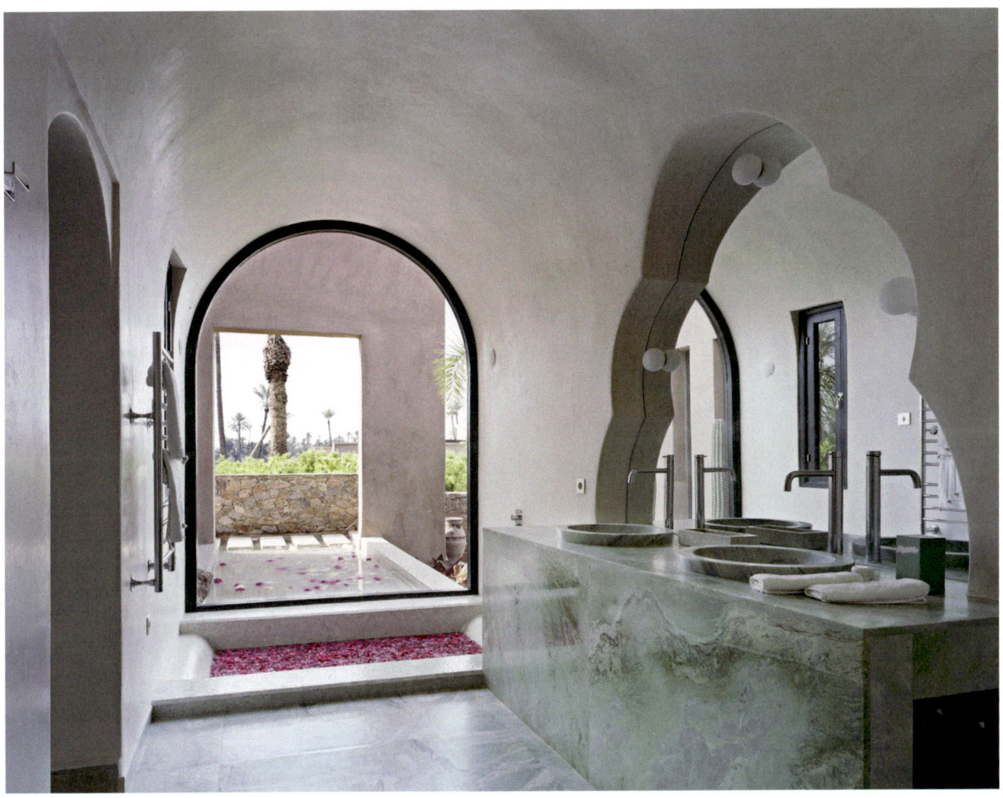

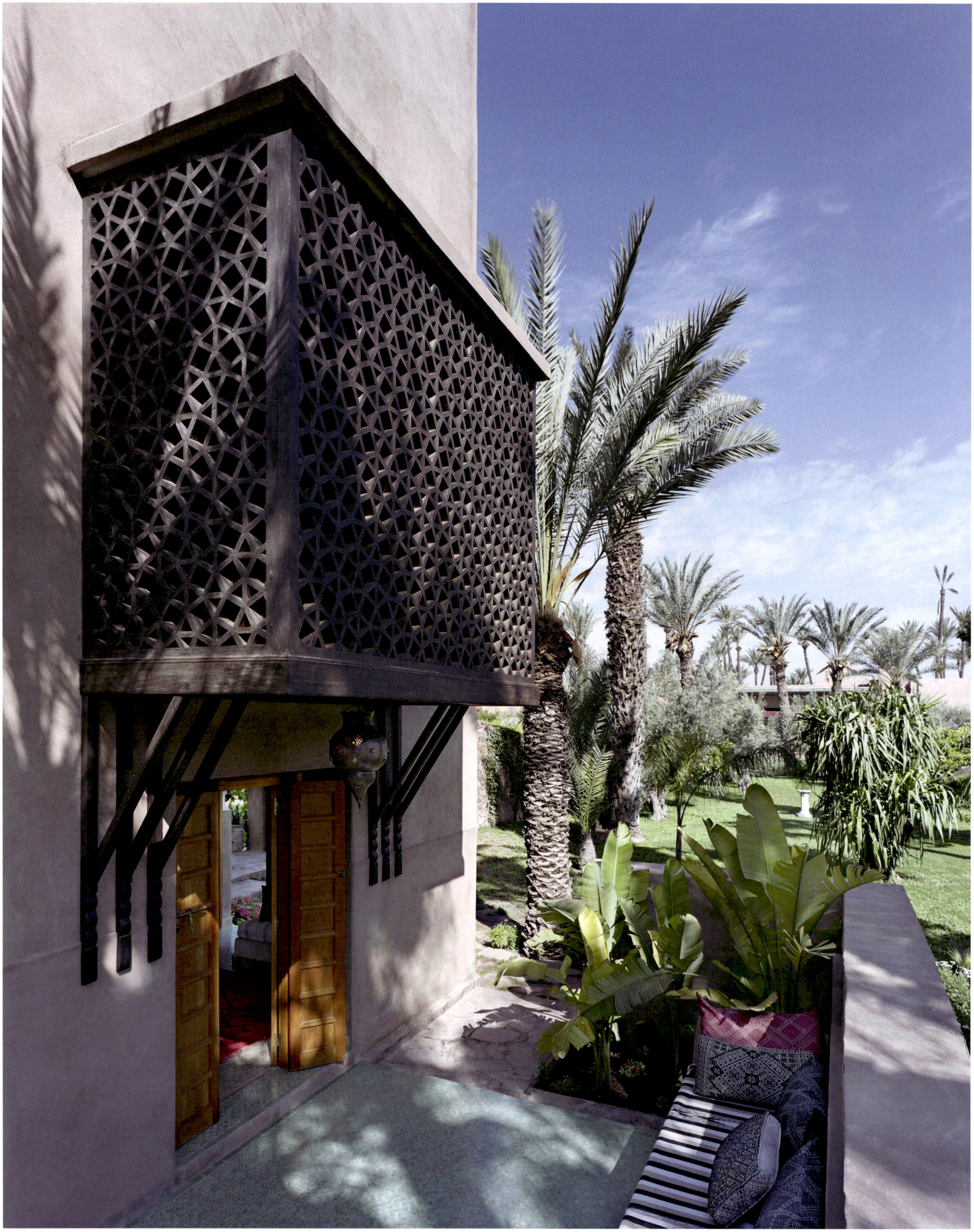

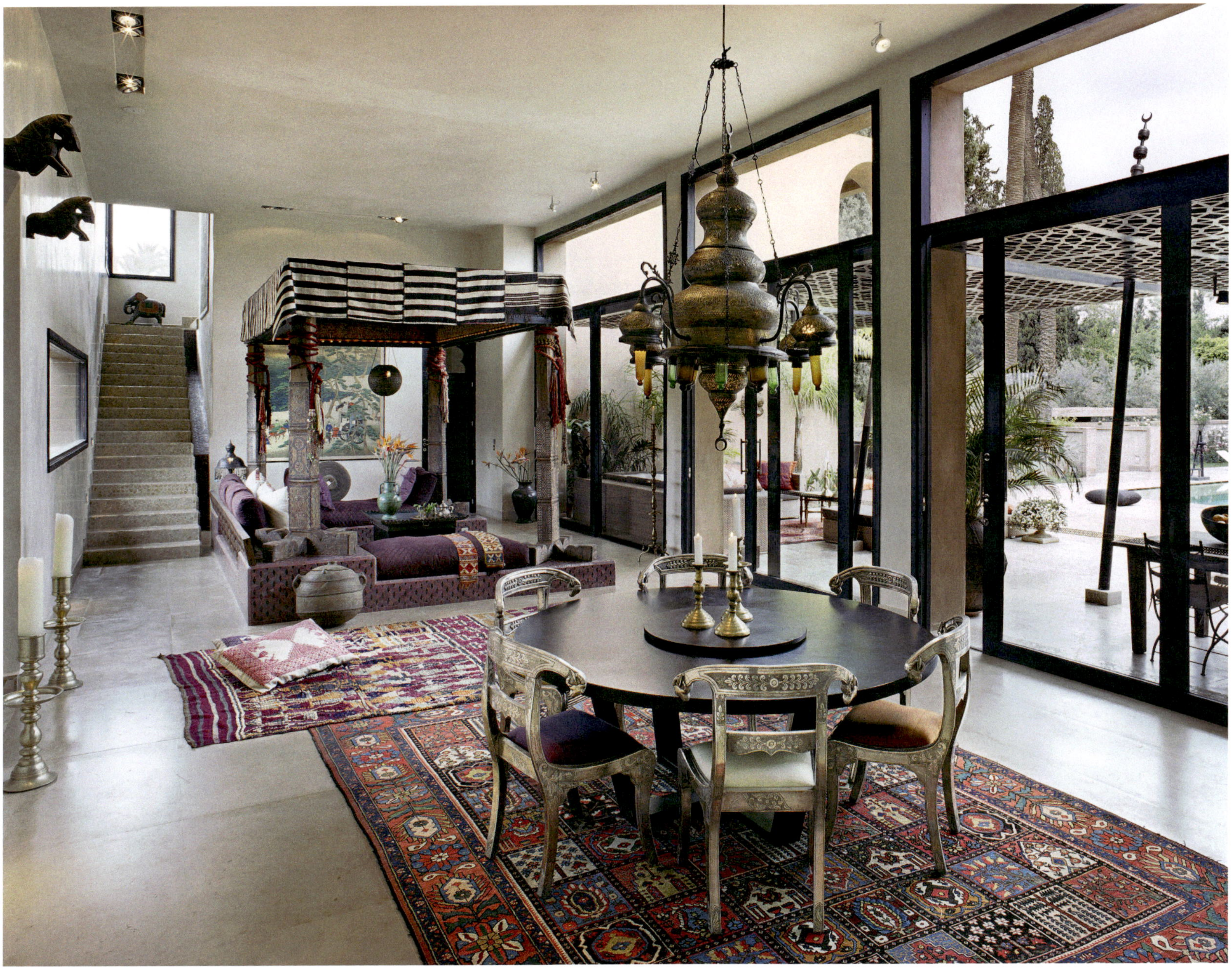

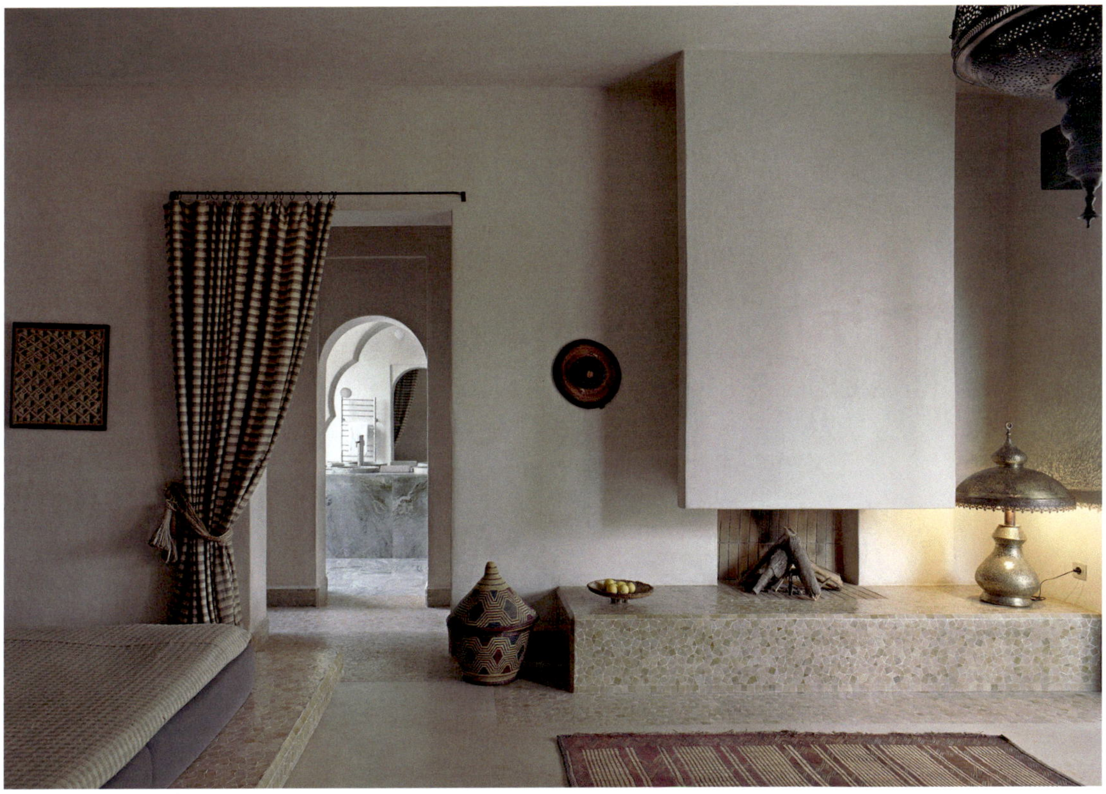

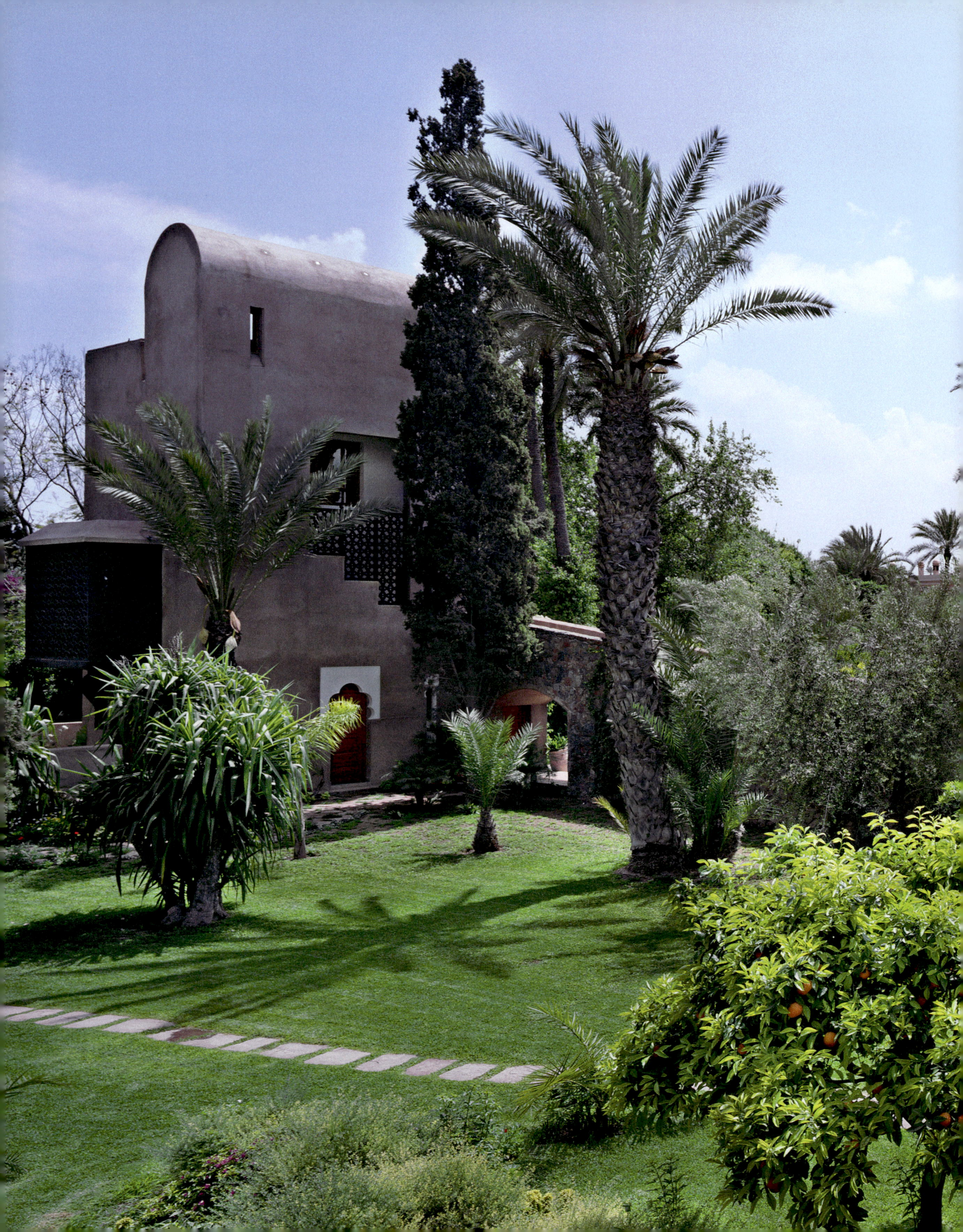

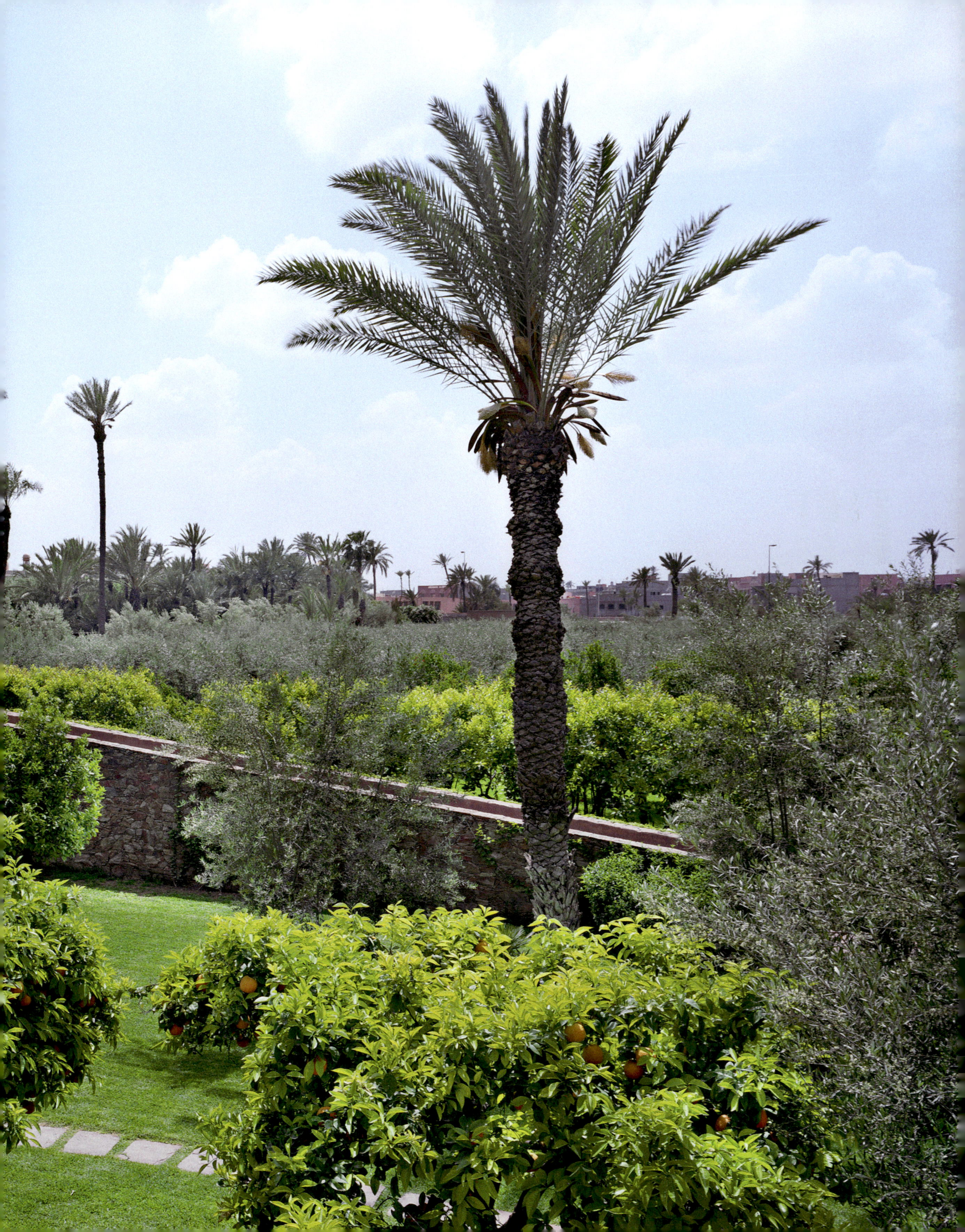

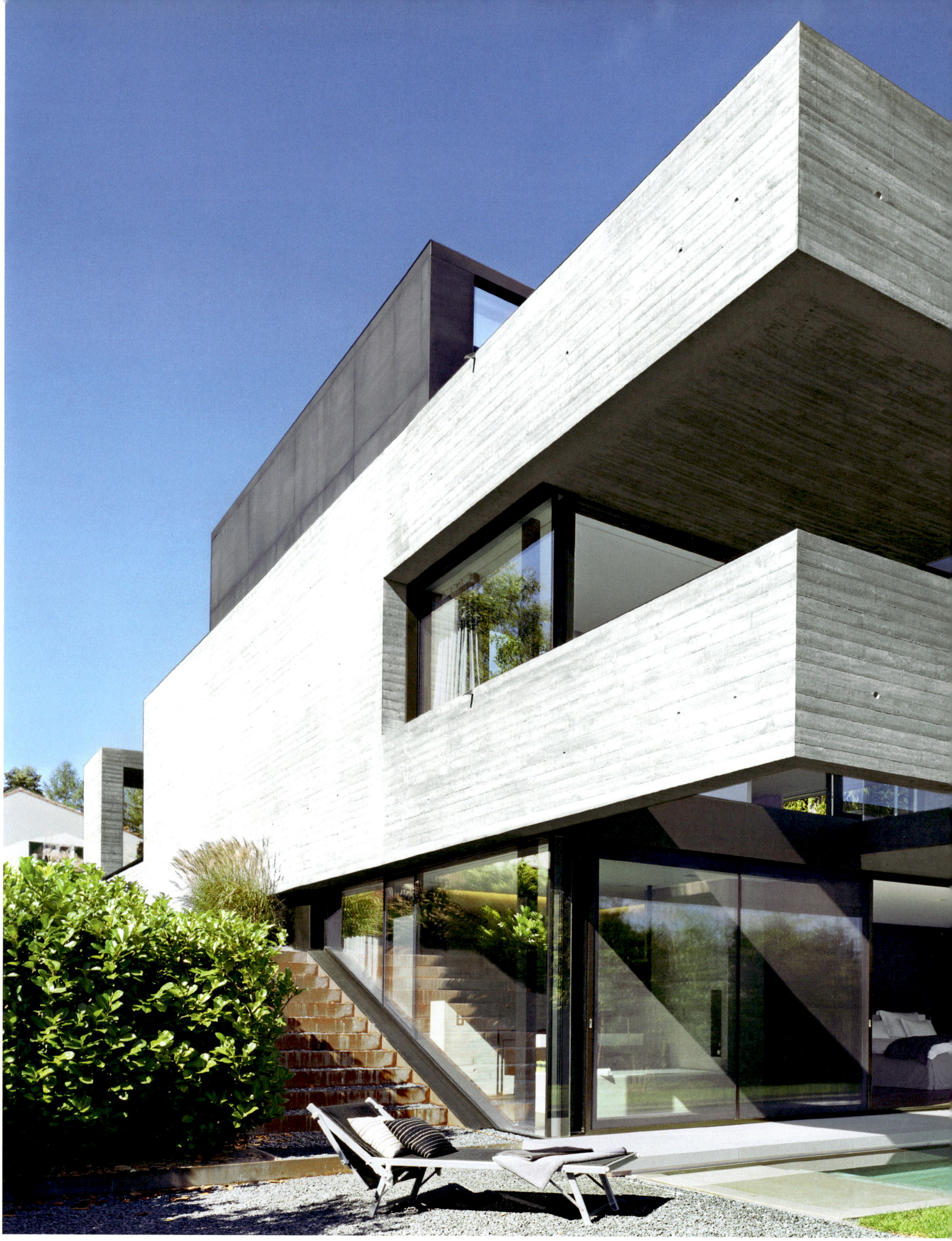

WÖRTHSEE, GERMANY

HOUSE N

BEMBÉ DELLINGER ARCHITECTS

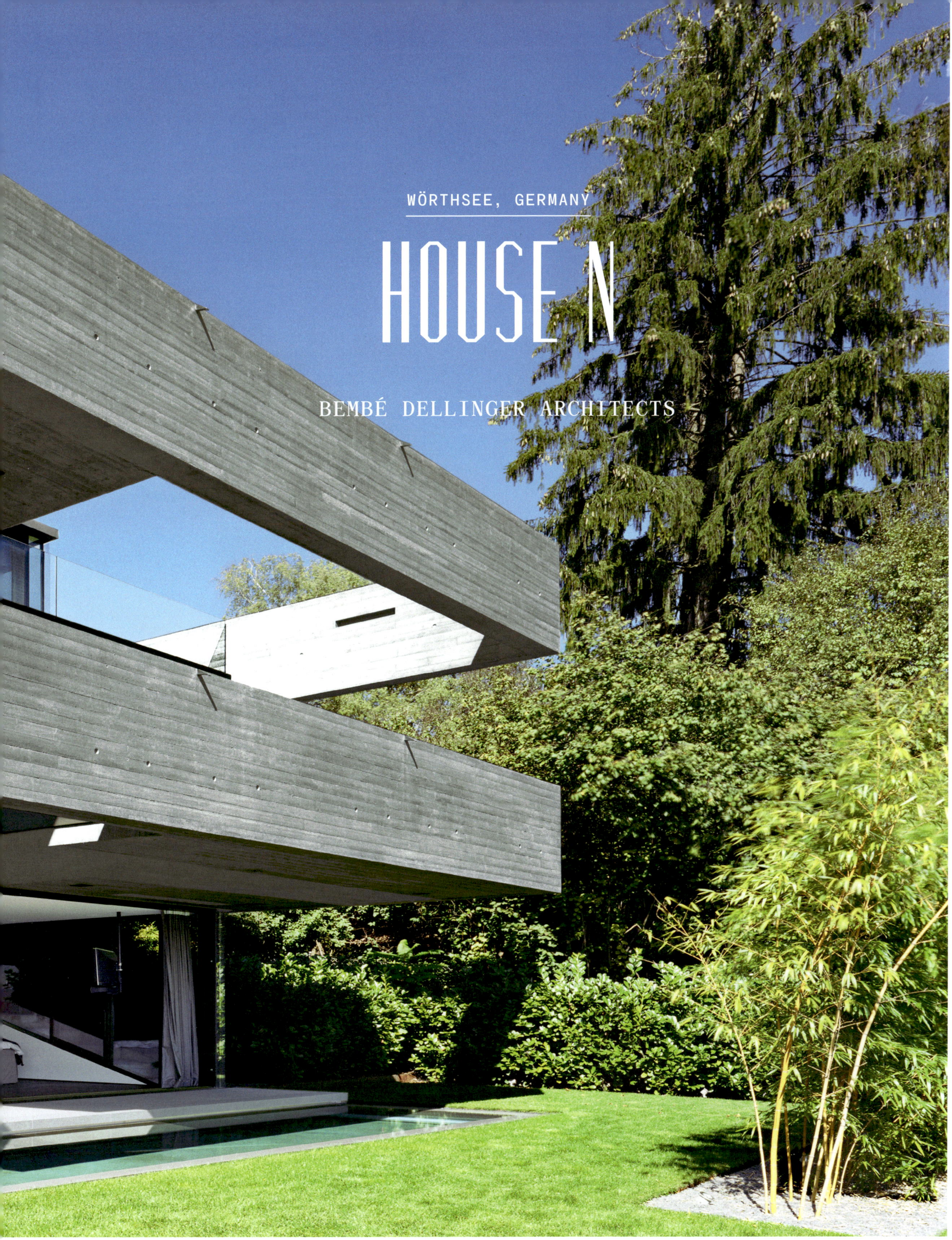

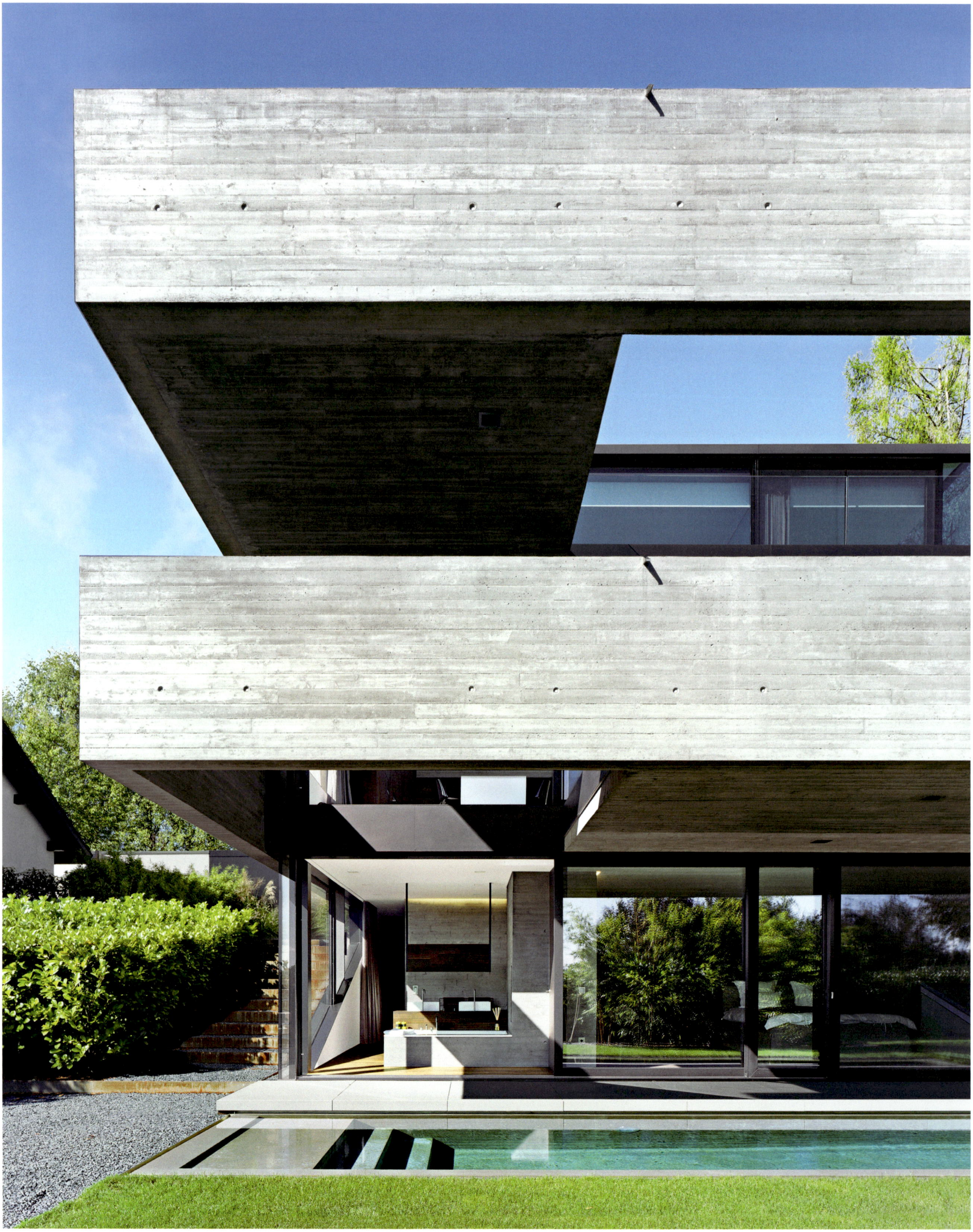

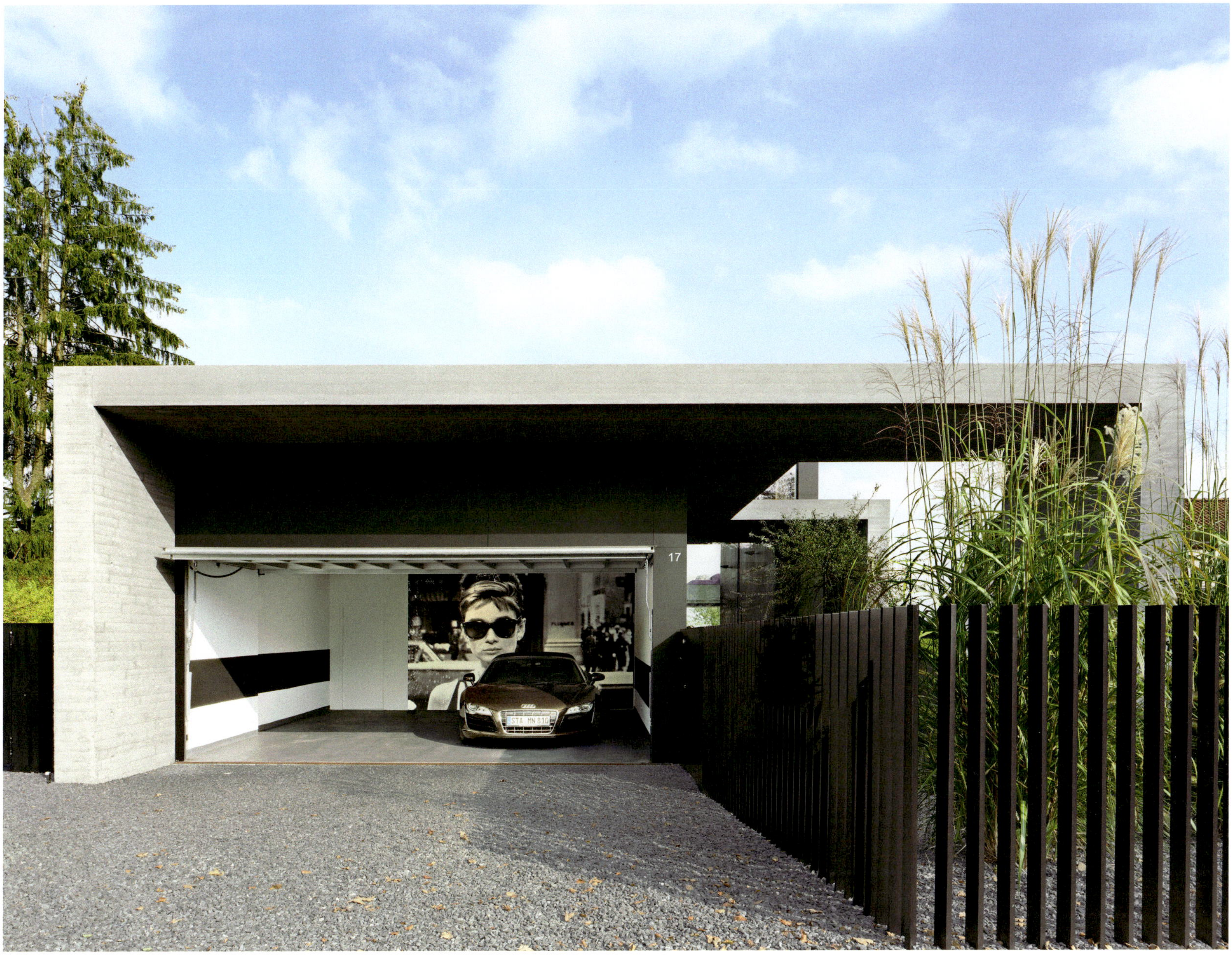

HOUSE N Bembé Dellinger Architects have completed yet another exceptional house in Germany's Five Lakes region. House N is a polished composition of concrete and steel, and its cutout style offers tranquil vistas that alternate between concealment and revelation as walls suddenly appear and drop away.

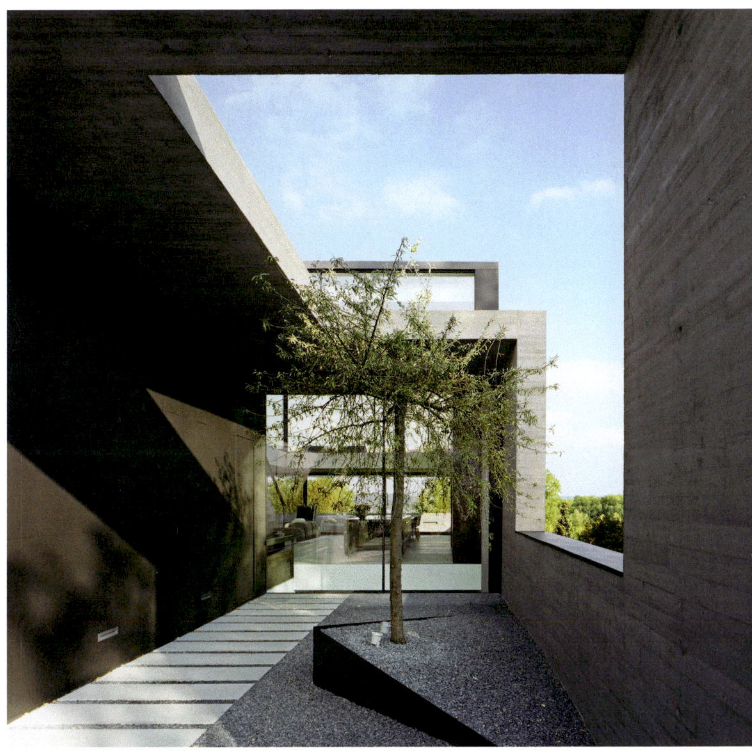

Starnberg is a district in southern Germany that contains five lakes—Starnberger See, Ammersee, Pilsensee, Weßlinger See, and Wörthsee. Colloquially known as the Five Lakes region, the verdant forests and profusion of water make the area a supremely beautiful location. And since it is only a short drive or train ride from Munich, it is also a practical holiday location for people with demanding schedules. Considered as a whole, the beauty and convenience of the region make it an almost unsurpassable getaway destination. ~

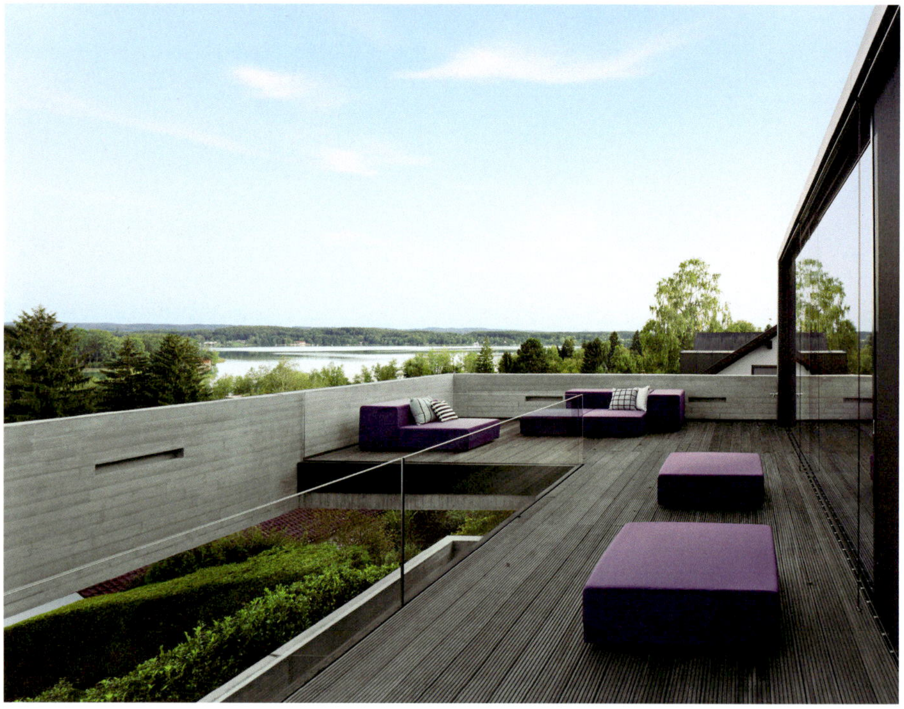

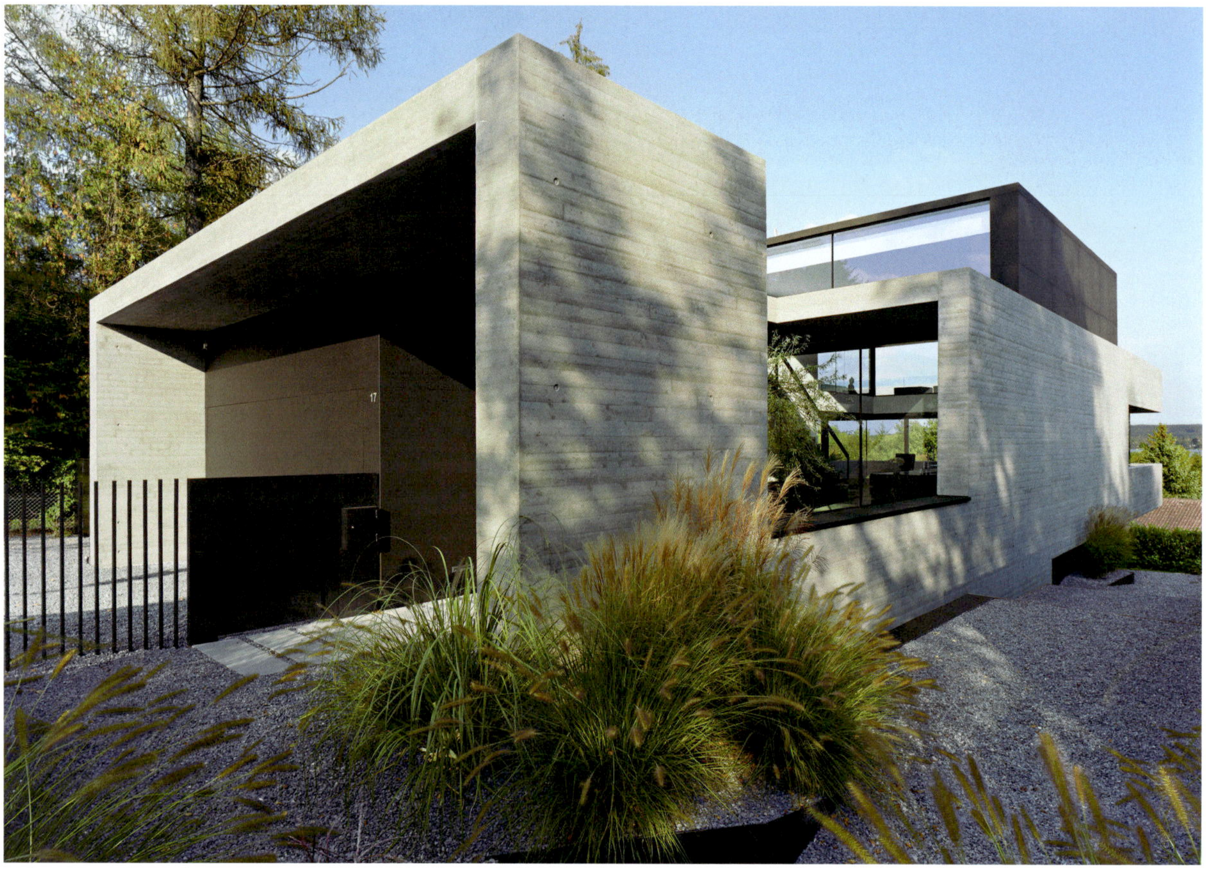

The two young professionals who own House N were attracted to Starnberg for these very reasons. When it came time to build, they went to Bembé Dellinger Architects. The Bavarian firm was the natural choice, considering the large number of houses that they have designed in the Five Lakes region. Speaking of his clients' wishes, Bembé says, "They asked for an honest building and clean use of materials. They were interested in holistic design, so all the secondary rooms had to be equally as well designed as the main living areas."

"THE CUTOUT METHOD, WHICH LEAVES THE HOUSE LOOKING AS IF ENTIRE SECTIONS OF WALL HAVE BEEN SNIPPED AWAY, IS DECISIVE IN IMBUING HOUSE N WITH ITS PLAYFUL QUALITY."

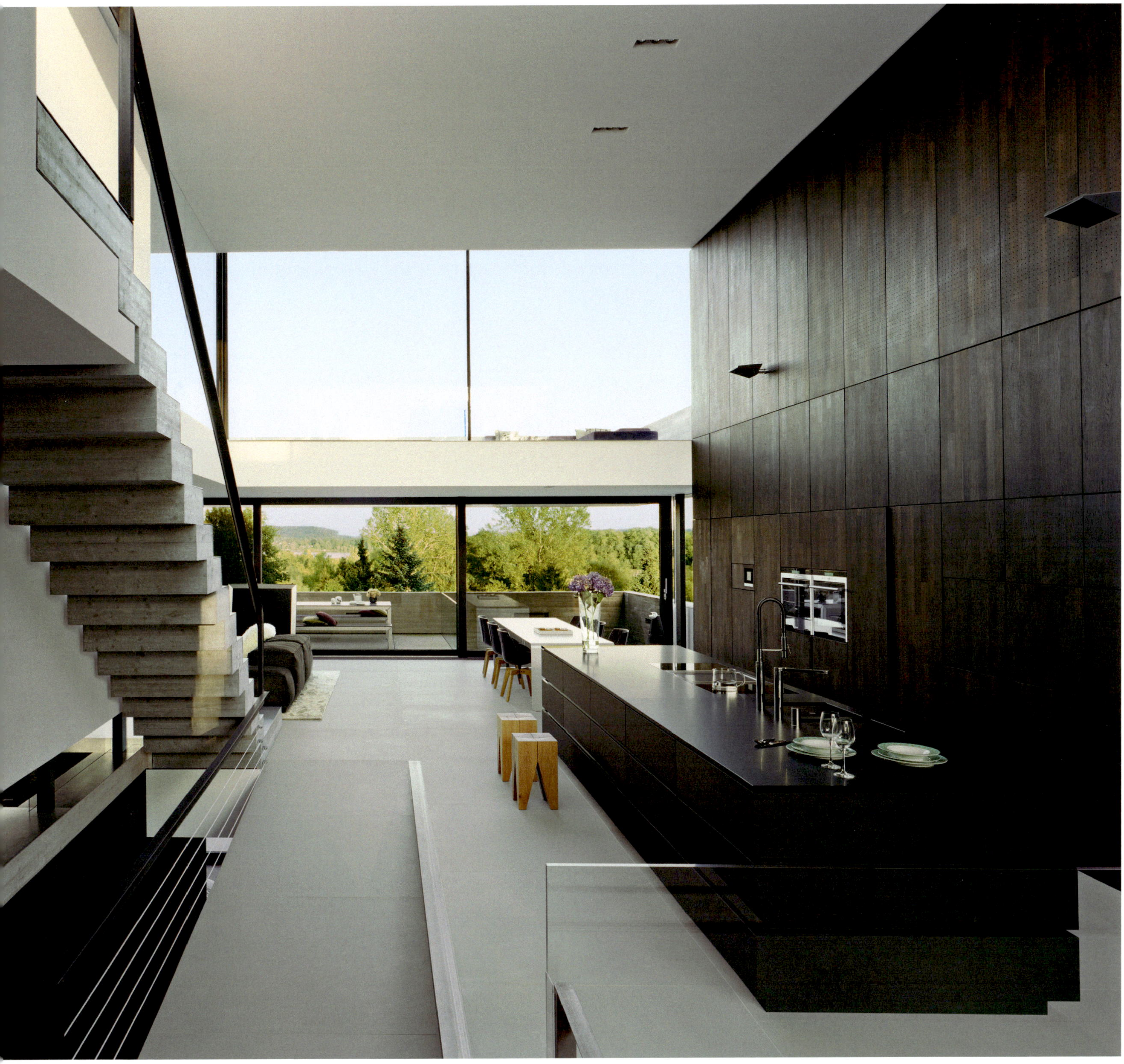

Encompassing three levels—the ground-floor master bedroom and second-floor office are separated by first-floor living spaces—the house achieves wide and open internal areas through reinforced concrete floors and steel framing. The use of concrete for the interior also creates a simple and coherent atmosphere, which is mirrored on the house's exterior, where concrete is employed as well. Here, juxtaposed against dense vegetation, concrete walls first tantalize visitors by obscuring the sweeping vista and then suddenly drop away to reveal all. The cutout method, which leaves the house looking as if entire sections of wall have been snipped away, is decisive in imbuing House N with its playful quality. At night, the bespoke lighting system, designed by the architects, emphasizes the sculptural aspects of the house. Ensconced on a forested hilltop and built with a real feeling for the picturesque landscape, House N is a sophisticated marvel. ◆

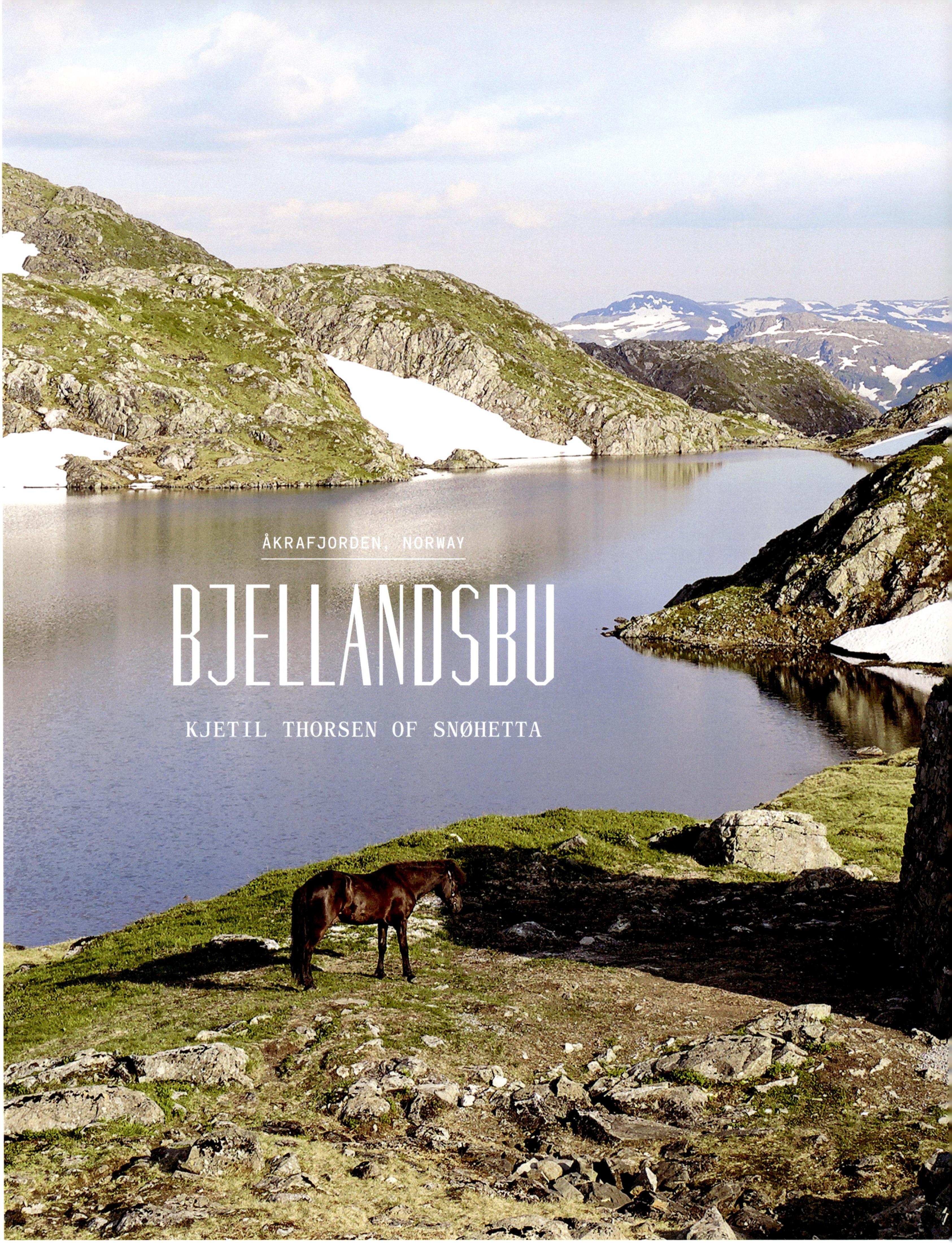

ÅKRAFJORDEN, NORWAY

BJELLANDSBU

KJETIL THORSEN OF SNØHETTA

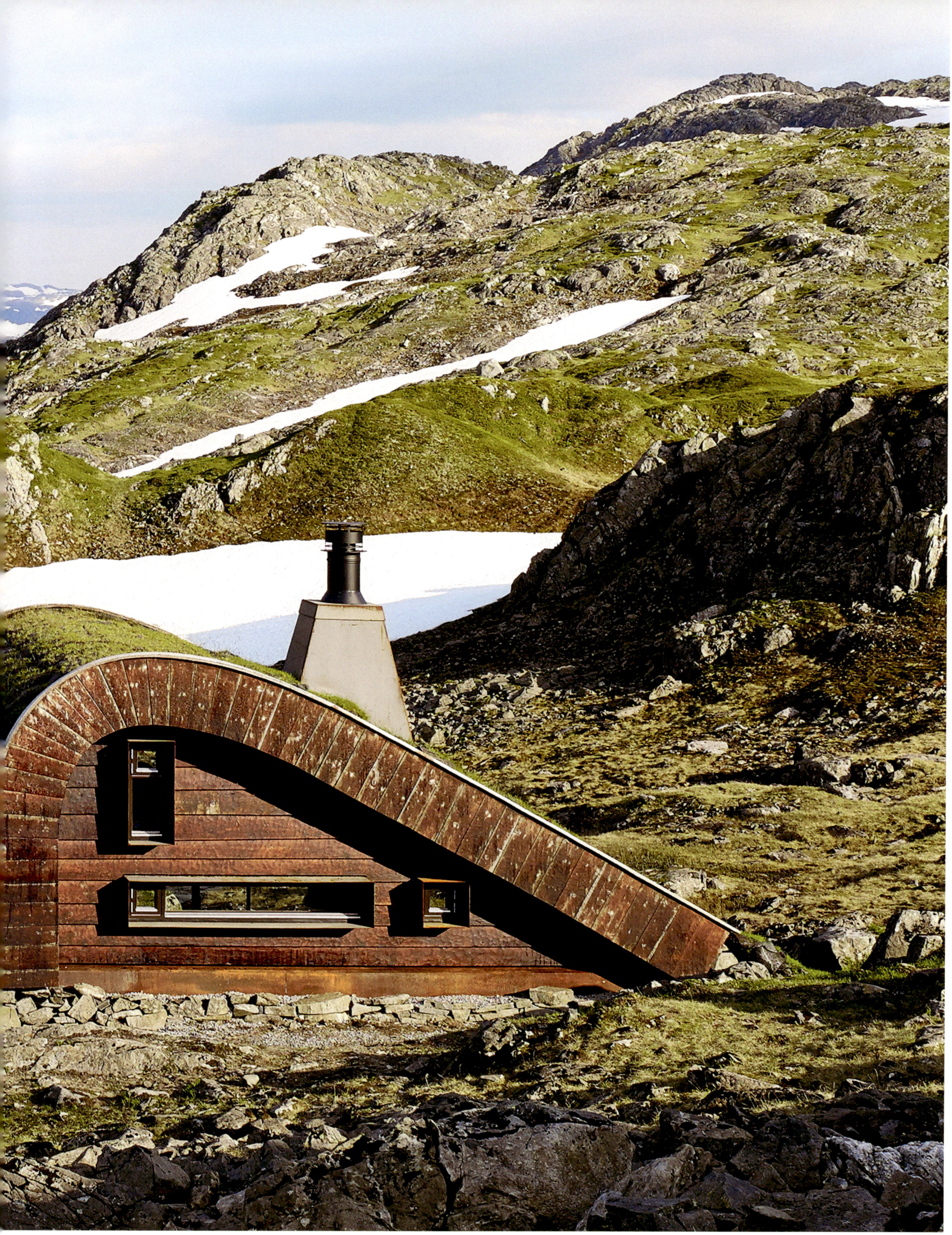

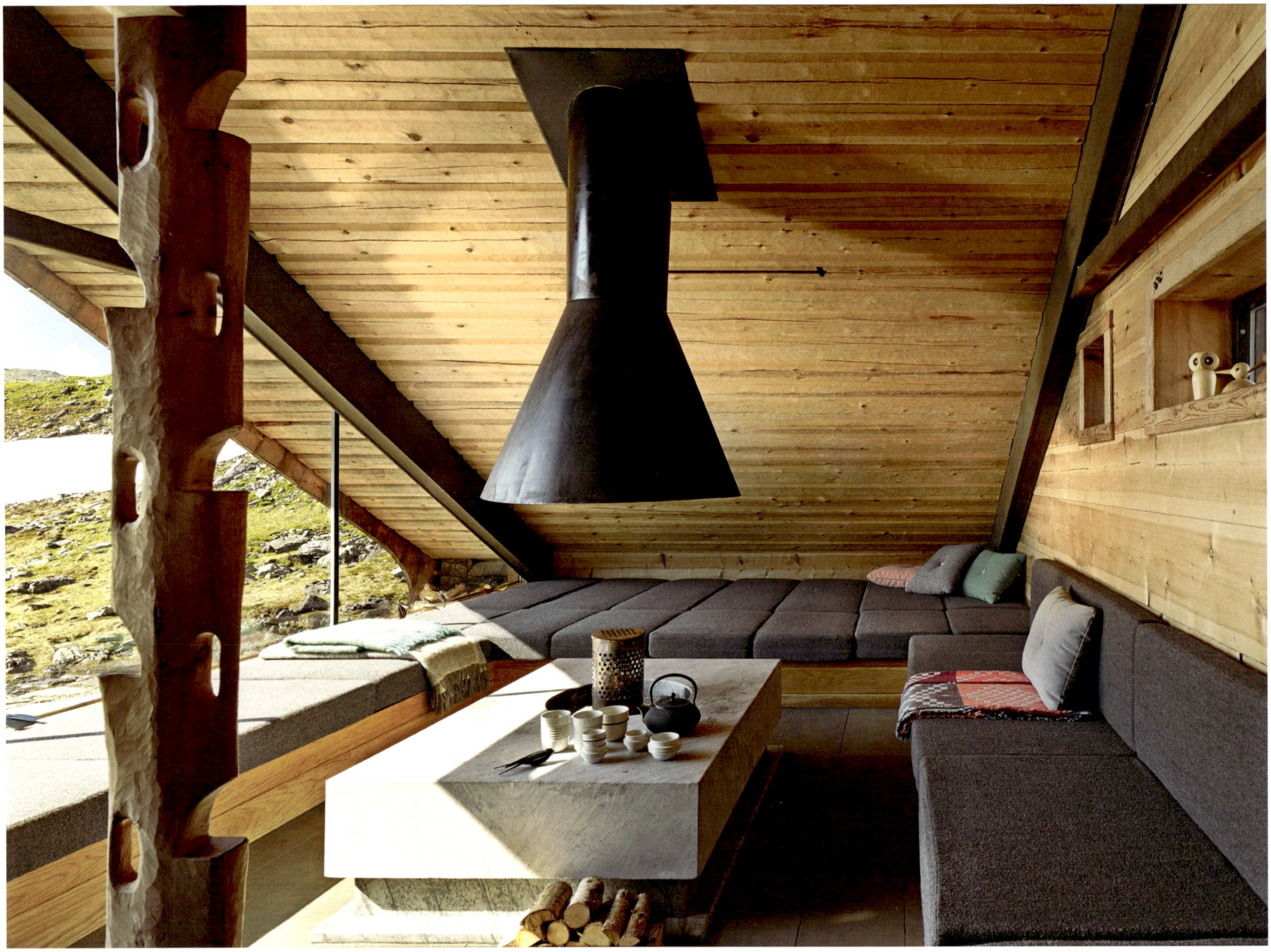

BJELLANDSBU Situated on a Norwegian fjord, this cabin contends with extremes of snow, wind, and subzero temperatures. From the rolling shape to the grass roof, nearly every feature is a response to the harsh environment. It is an example of a seamless synthesis of form and function that succeeds without sacrificing beauty.

For this build, architect Kjetil Thorsen of Snøhetta had to consider severe weather conditions before anything else. Speaking of decisions made in collaboration with owner Osvald Bjelland, he says, "We chose a form that distributes the snow loads effectively, because at certain times of the year you can't even see the building for snow."

Snow was not the only factor that influenced the cabin's design. Strong gales also whip across this wilderness. Acting as a wind barrier, a stacked stone wall meets the crest of the structure and extends to the rocky ground. Providing further protection, grass grows over the sloping roof, which helps to absorb vibrations.

In addition to excessive wind and snow, Bjelland and Thorsen faced the added challenge of securing the cabin to a rocky foundation. In response, a steel beam supports the pine roof and anchors the 35-square-meter structure to the inhospitable ground. Another interesting innovation is the southern wall—its surface is a glazing that warms the cabin, helping to melt accumulated snow. Attentive to the hostile environment, the cabin mirrors the rugged and unshakable terrain not only visually, but structurally as well. The emphasis on function carries through to the cabin's interior. Thorsen says he was asked to design the cabin so that "21 people could stay in it at the same time, and that it could provide warmth and an area to cook a basic meal." It is a small space to sleep 21, but the architect's efforts were a success: "It was comfortable. It's like being on a sailing boat."

A limestone fireplace sits in the center of the cabin, doubling as a basic kitchen and heater. Bench seats ~

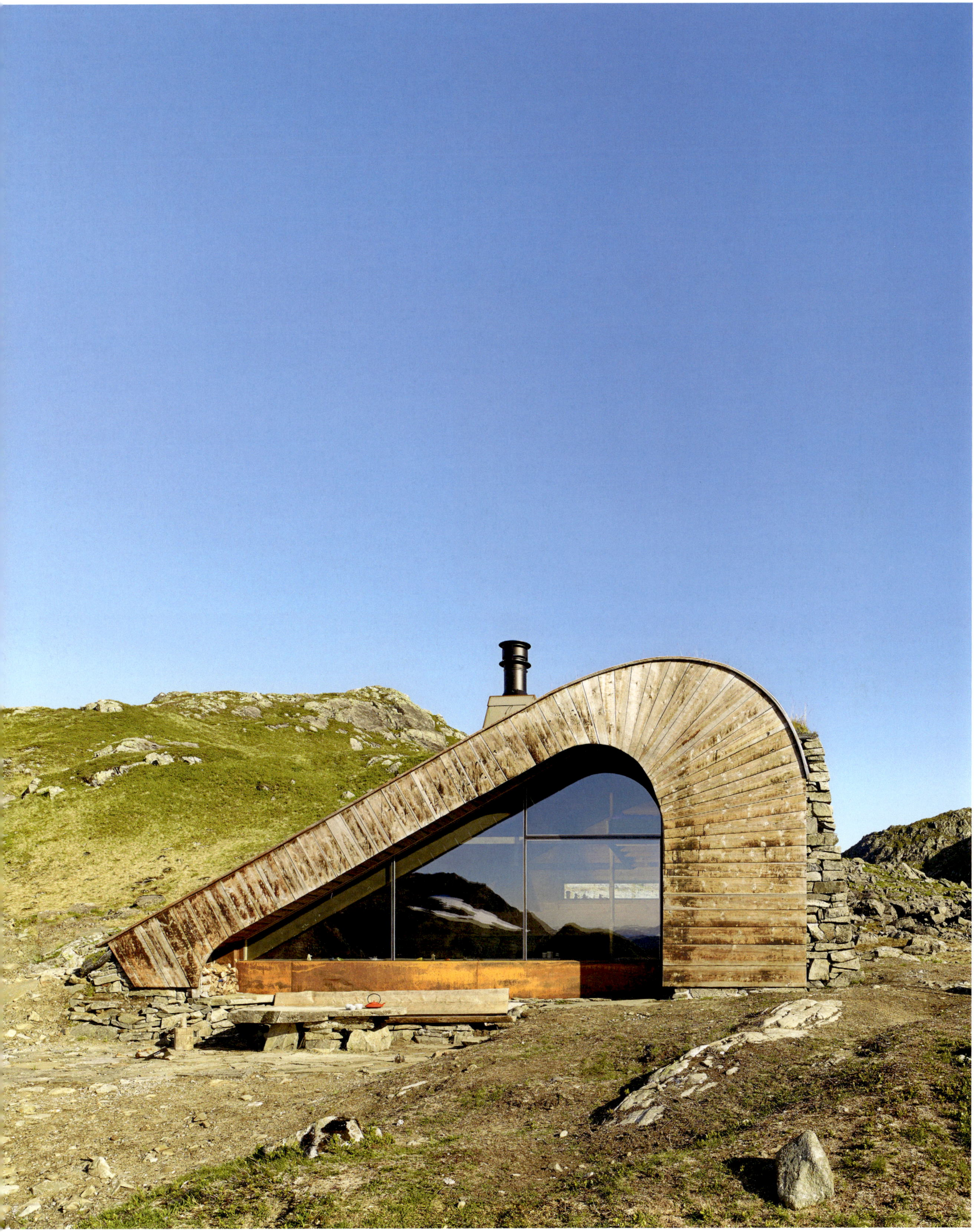

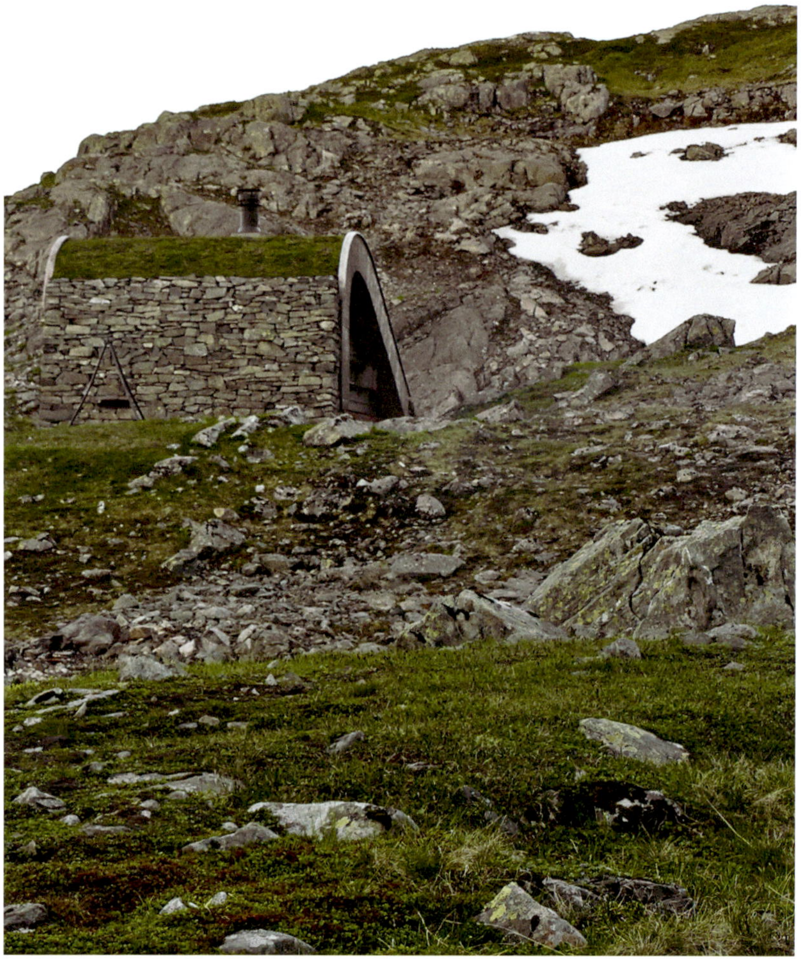

"I have been thinking about this specific spot for the last 40 years. I roamed these mountains with my father and uncles, just as they had done with my grand-father. For generations we've always had the little dream we would have a place to rest be-fore we carried on." — *Osvald Bjelland*

circle the large stone table, framing the open space, and a loft is tucked up overhead. With just these few necessities inside, the space is left open for people to move about and tell stories. There is no doubt that future generations of the Bjelland family will enjoy this robust cabin as the setting of many memories to come. ◆

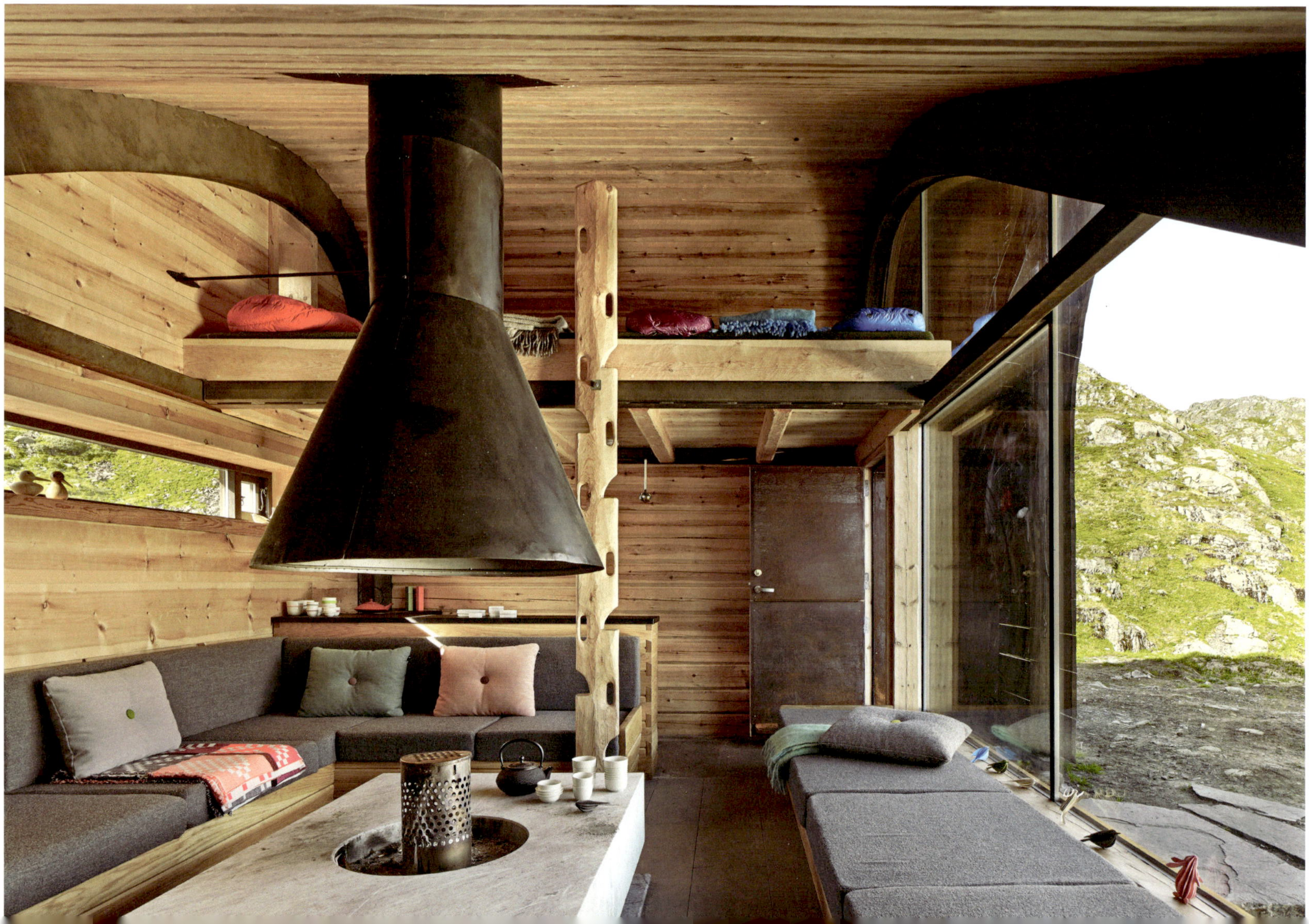

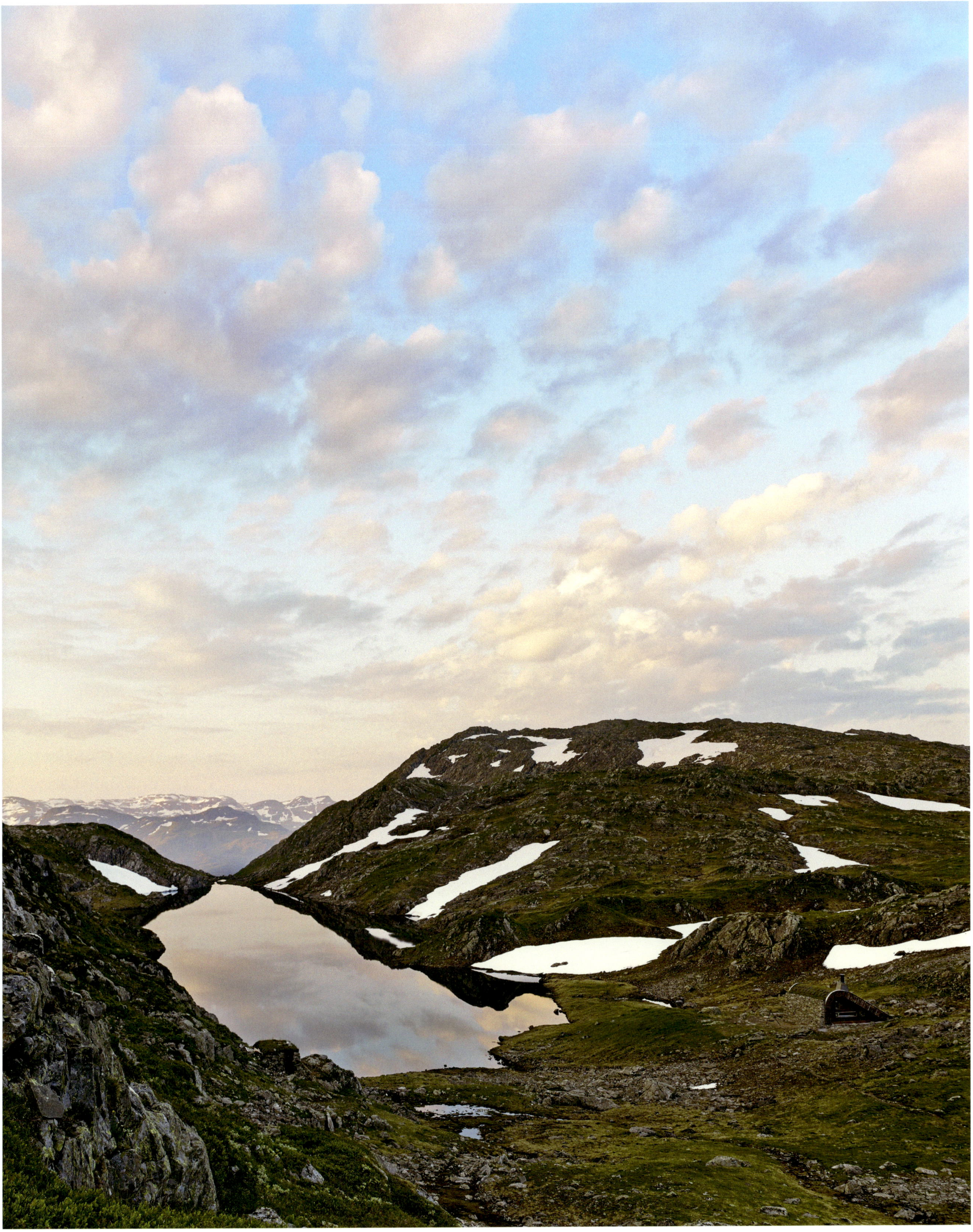

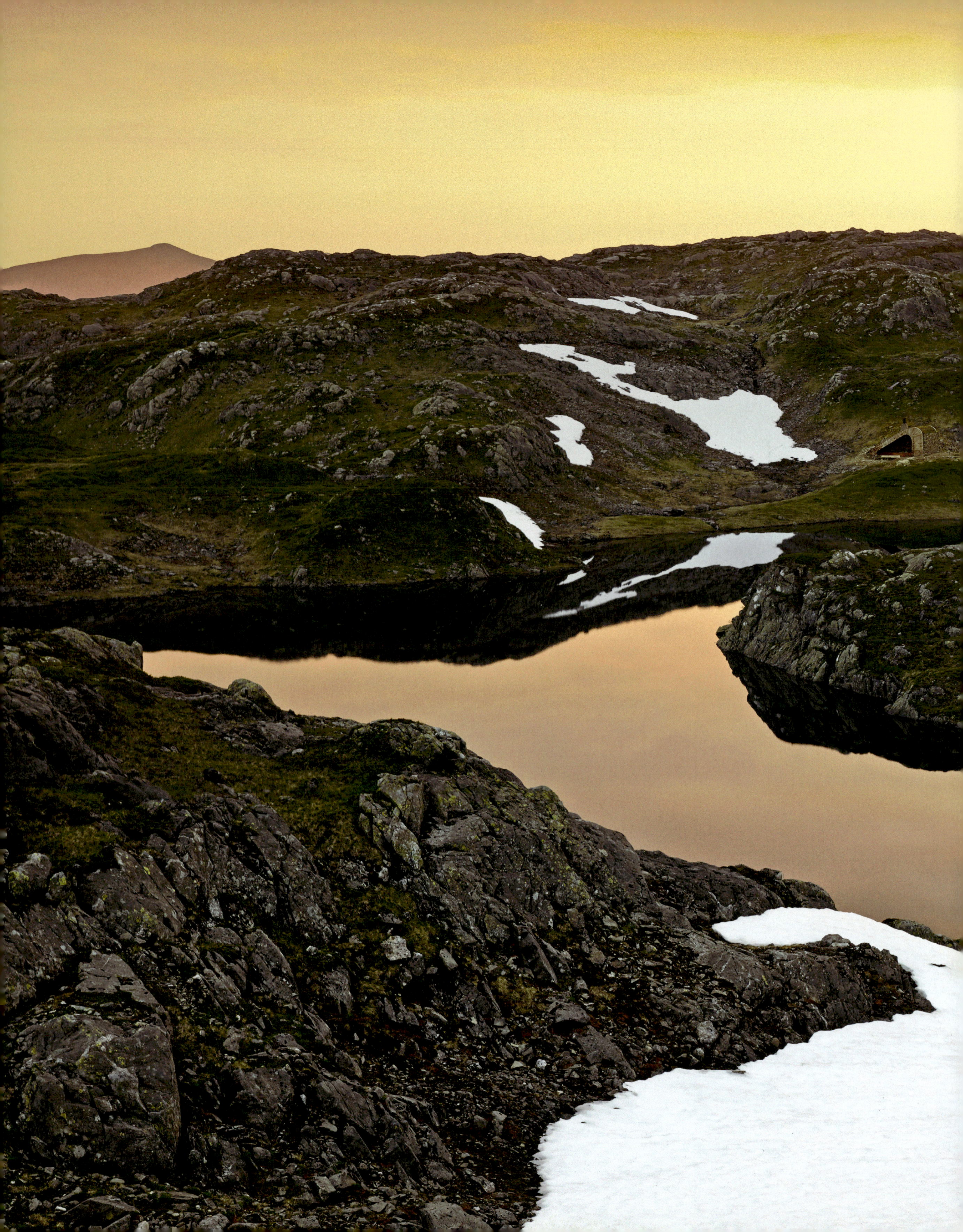

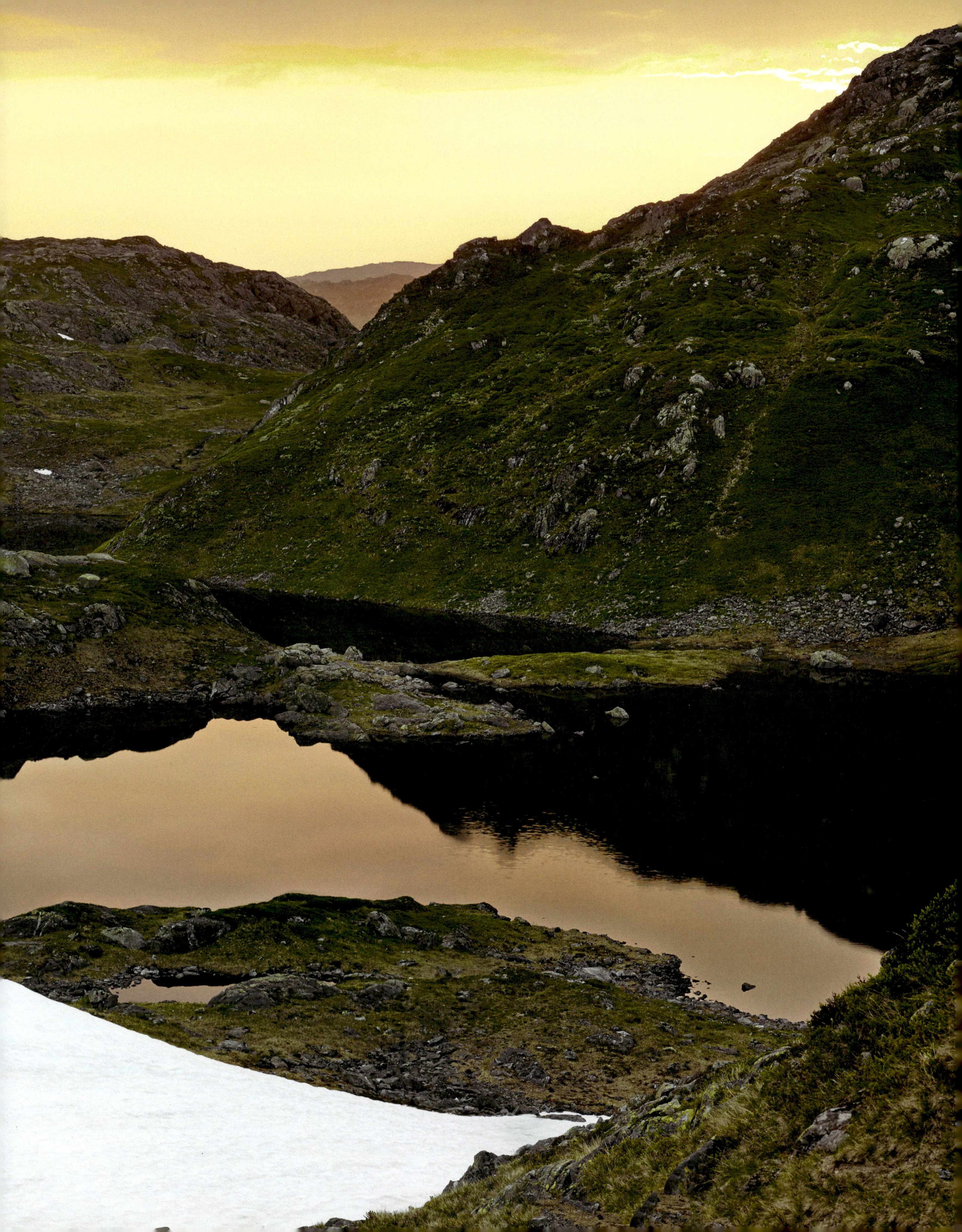

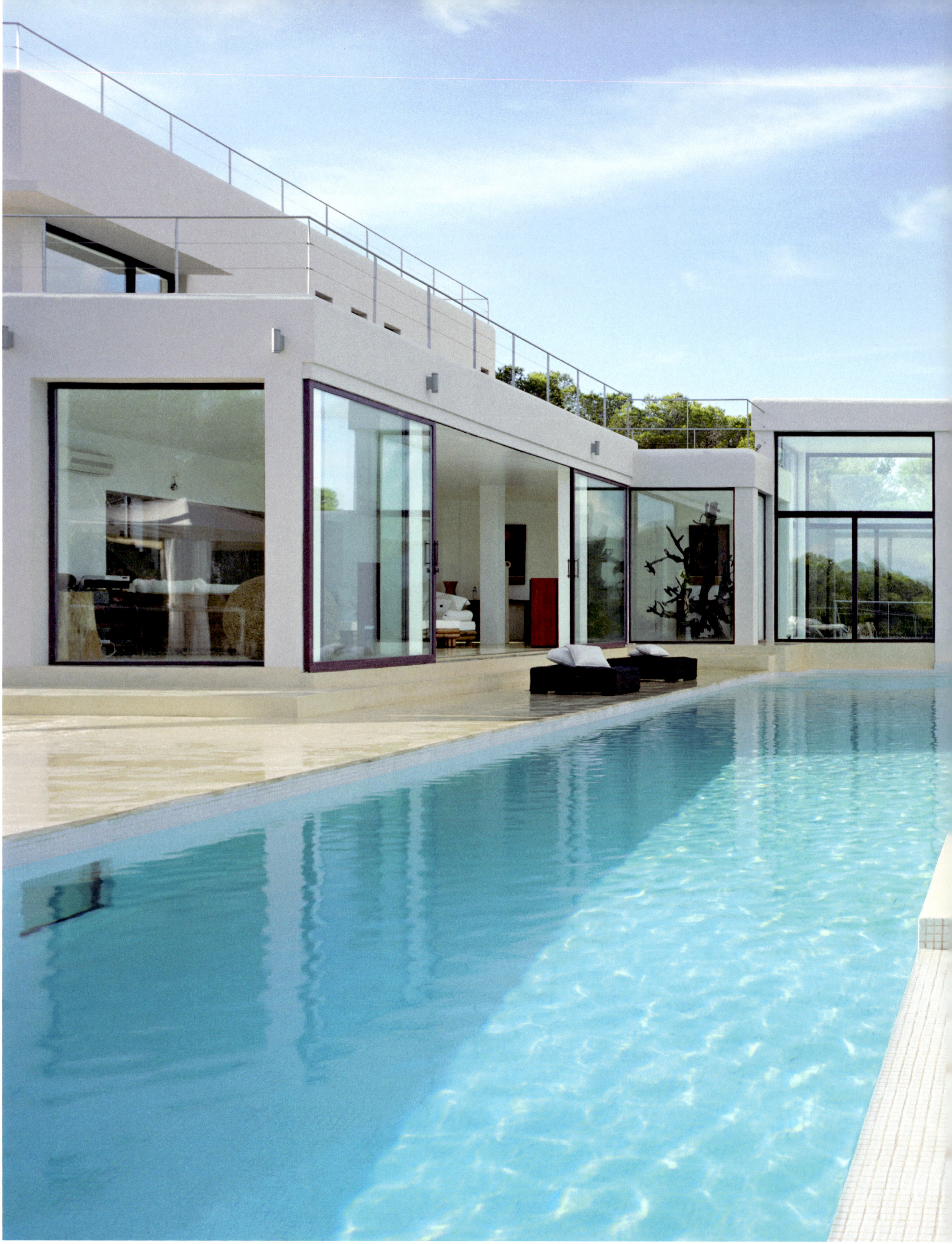

IBIZA, SPAIN

CASA JONDAL

JAIME SERRA OF ATLANT DEL VENT

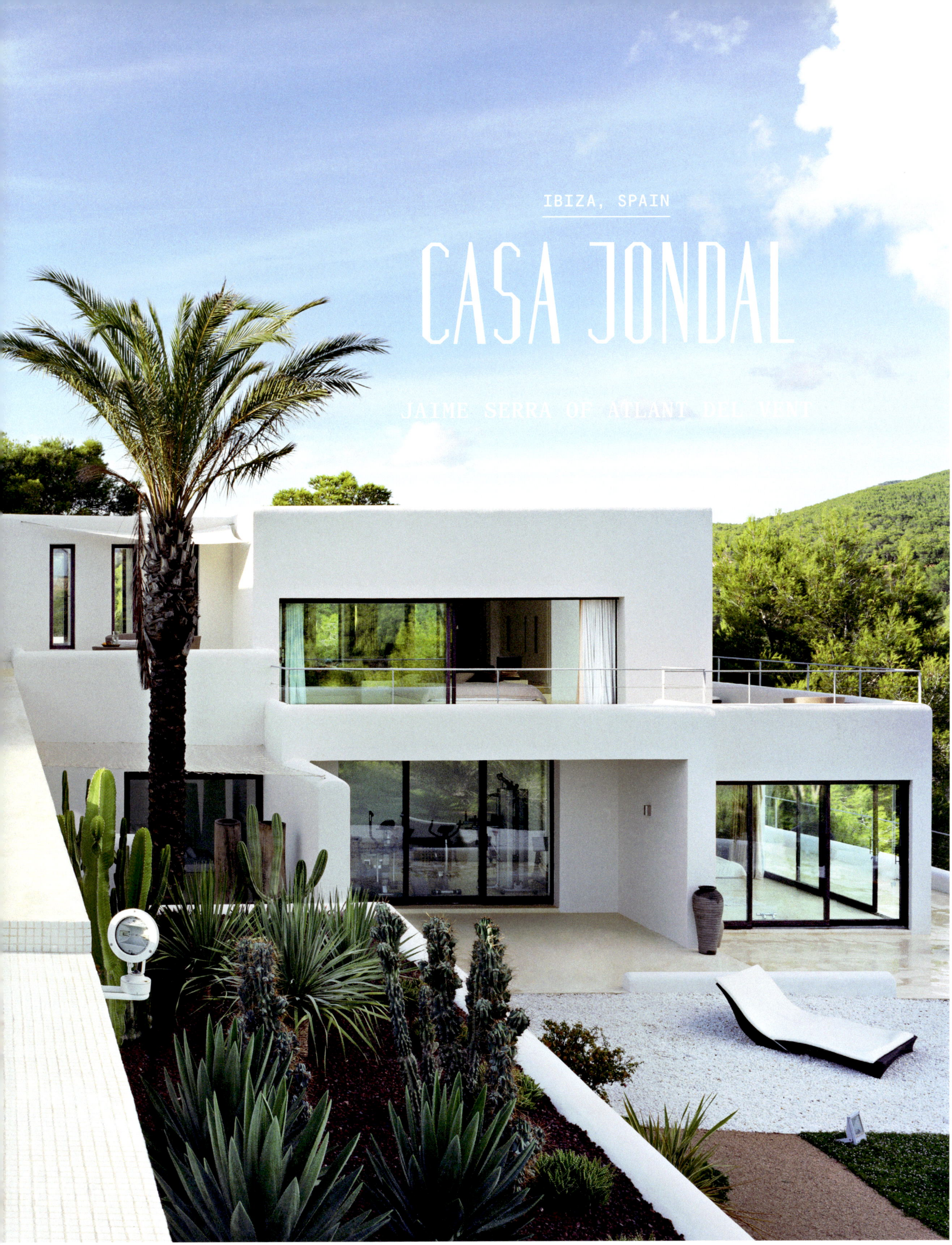

"TEMPERING THE BRIGHTNESS OF THE EXTERIOR WITH SOLID STONE, THE INTERIOR ACTS AS AN ANCHOR FOR THE STRUCTURE."

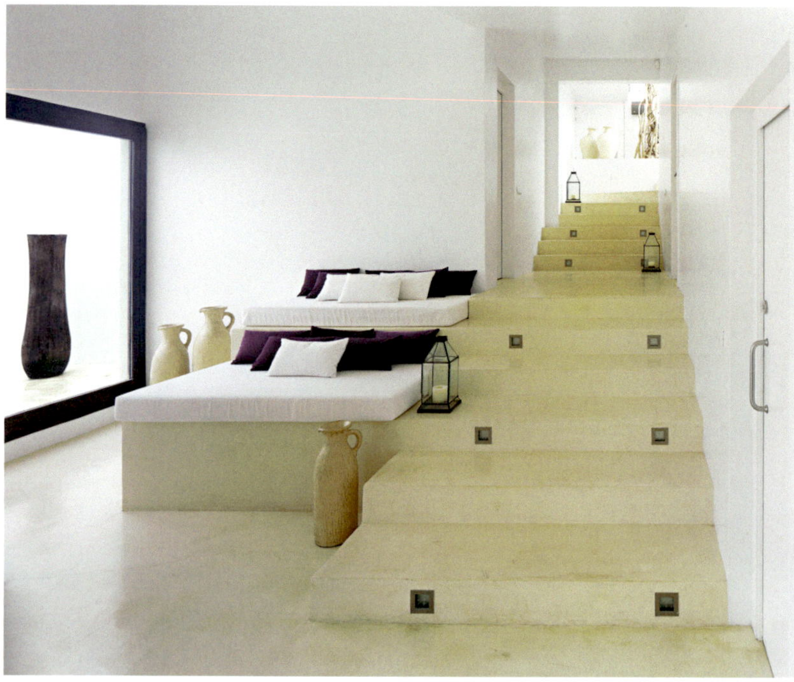

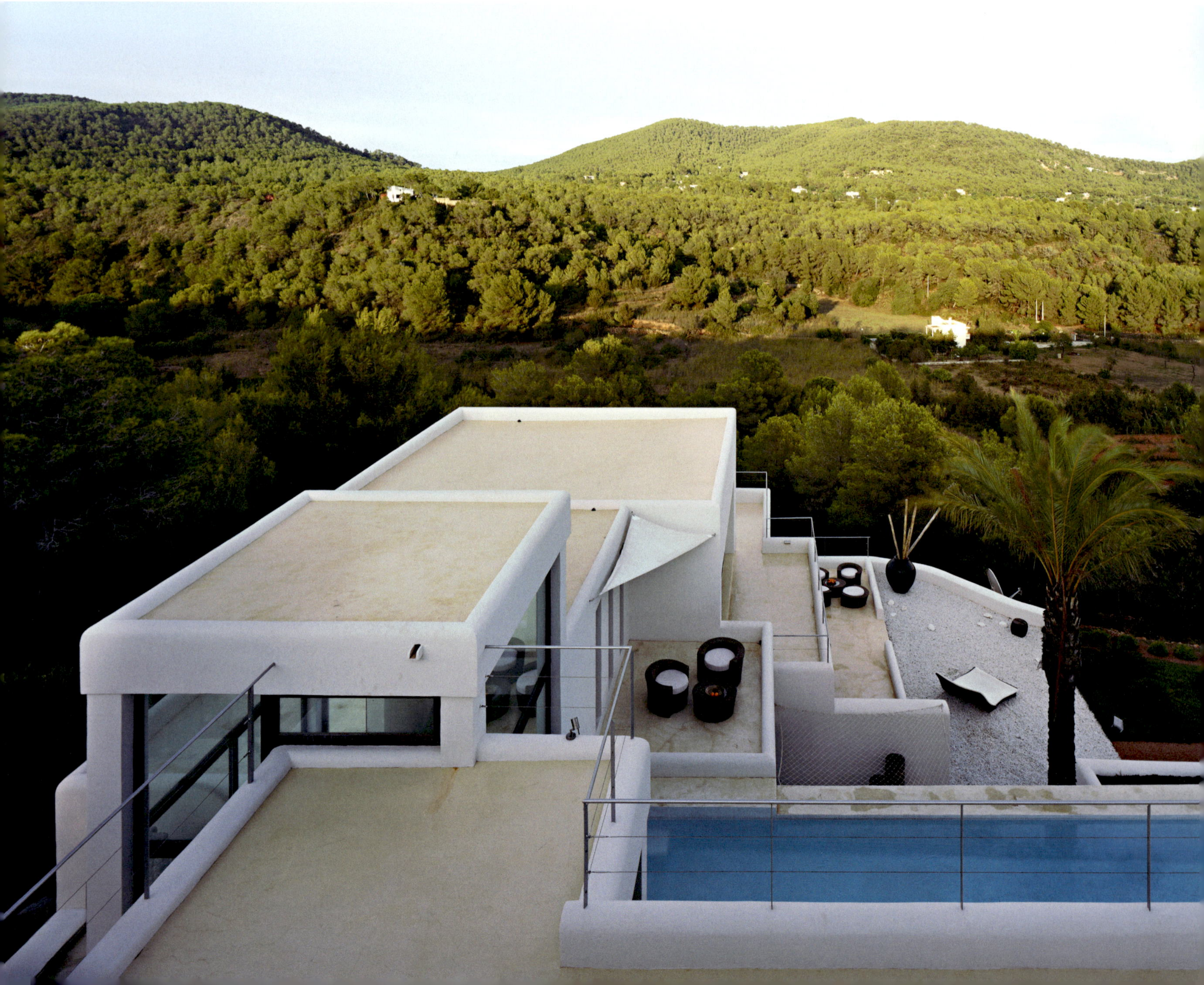

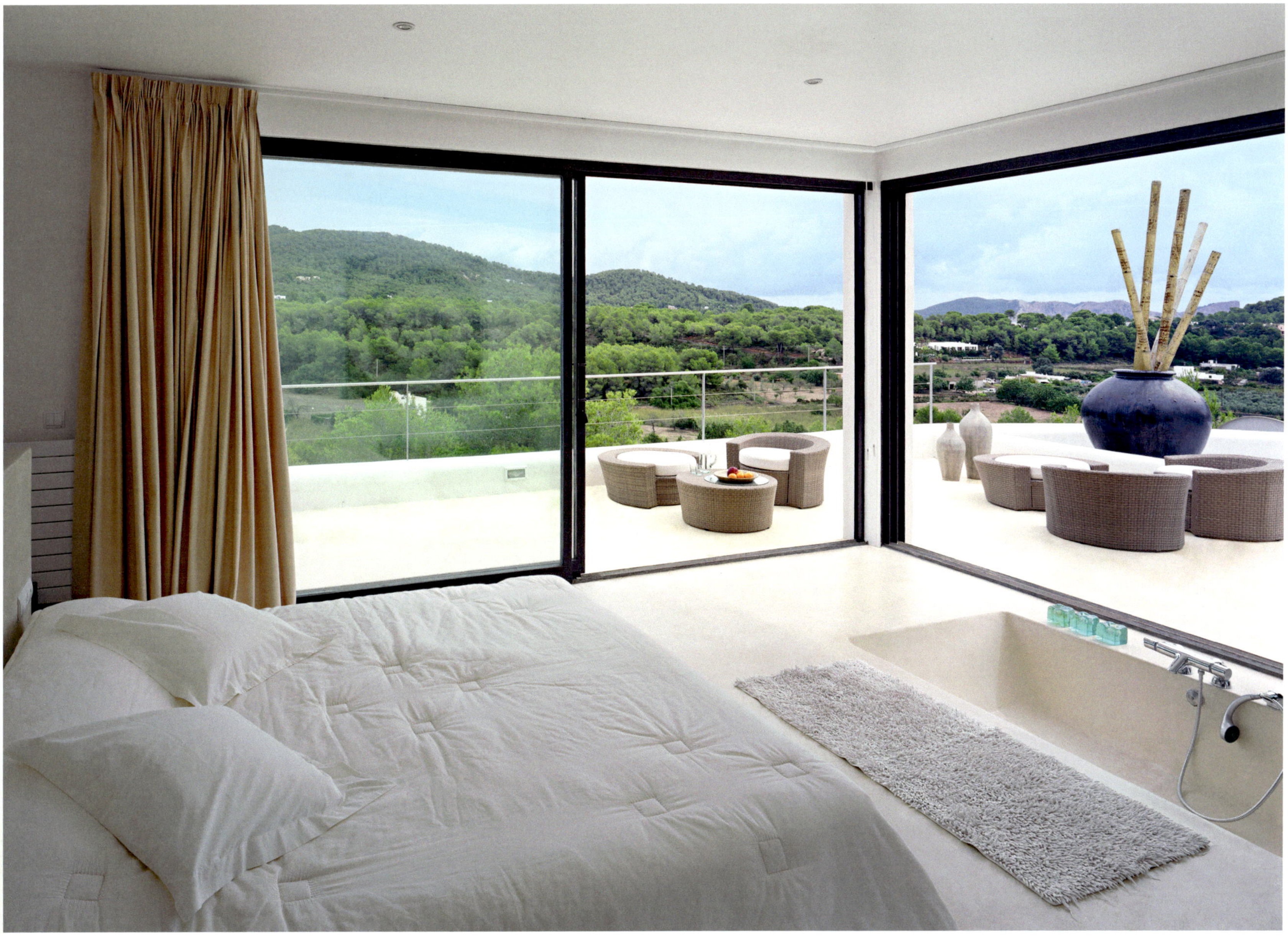

CASA JONDAL is a modern update of traditional Ibizan architecture. The charm of the house lies in its brilliant manipulation of light and its creative partitioning of space. A sprawling, luminous summer getaway quickly transforms into a cozy refuge in winter months.

Casa Jondal stands on the site of an old Ibizan farmhouse. Jaime Serra of Atlanta del Vent says, "Traditionally, farmers placed their houses on the best site on their land in order to benefit from natural sunlight, good ventilation, and views." Like those old houses, Casa Jondal is open to sun-drenched views of the sea and sheltered from harsh westerly winds.

The similarity to traditional housing does not stop there. Compartmentalized in its structure and sheltered by flat roofs, the home echoes older Ibizan building practices in which additions were stacked and slotted against one another as families grew. The house itself has been split into two areas: a summer area with four en-suite bedrooms and a small living space, and a winter area with a master bedroom, primary living area, and kitchen.

A tall glass room mediates between these spaces, sealing the summer quarters in the winter to preserve warmth, yet still allowing easy access to that wing when the house is full of guests. The glass tower also harmonizes with the steel-framed windows that reappear throughout the design.

The white plastered exterior reflects the Mediterranean sunshine, turning the home into a glimmering mountaintop gem. Inside, concrete flooring and furnishings such as the bath in the master bedroom have been cast in-situ. Tempering the brightness of the exterior with solid stone, the interior acts as an anchor for the structure.

Summing up the house, Serra says, "It takes advantage of natural light and views of the valley and sea, whereas the mixed volumes and their interrelations mean that the house is fully integrated into the contours of the ancient site." ◆

COSTA CAREYES, MEXICO

CASA TIGRE DEL MAR

GIAN FRANCO BRIGNONE

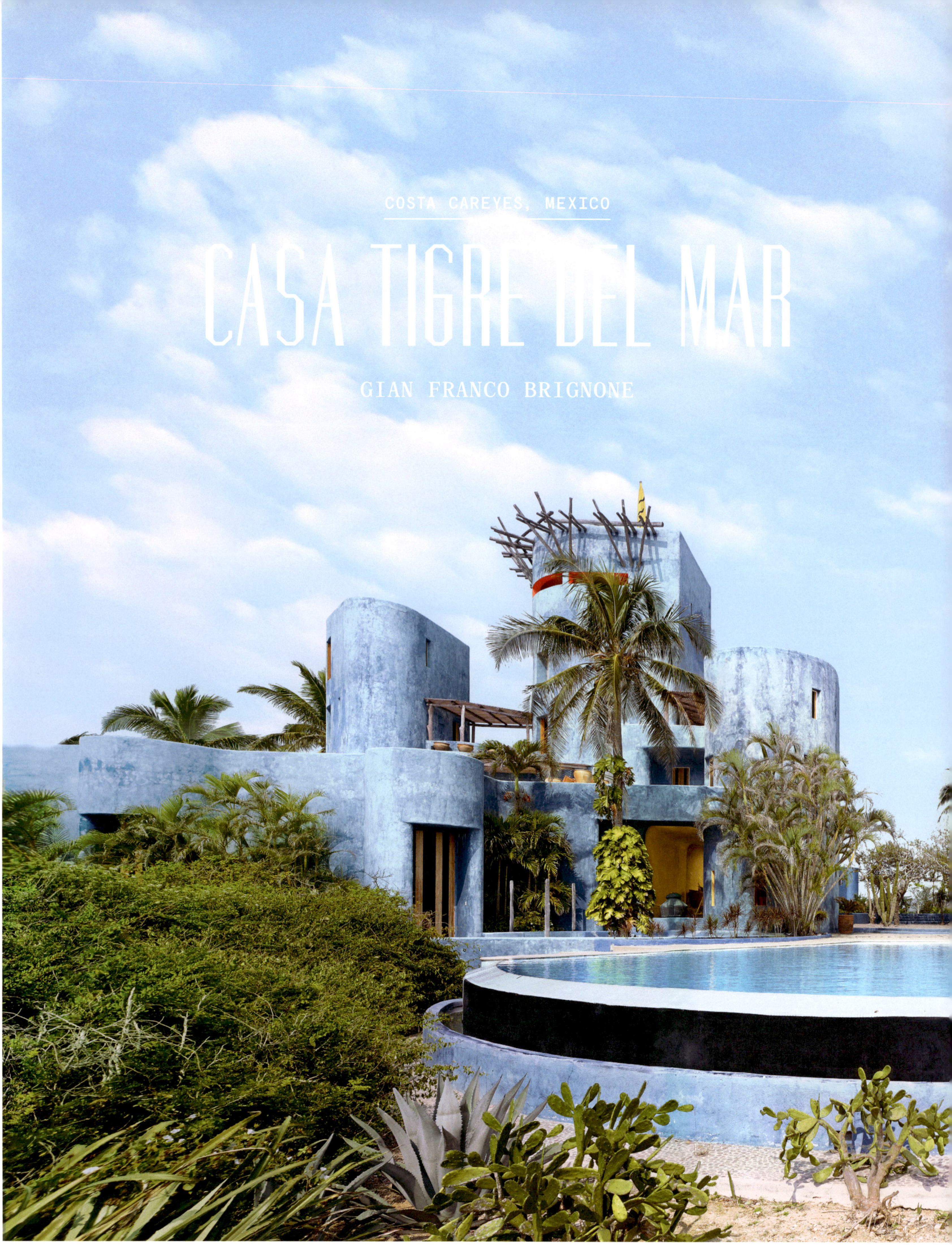

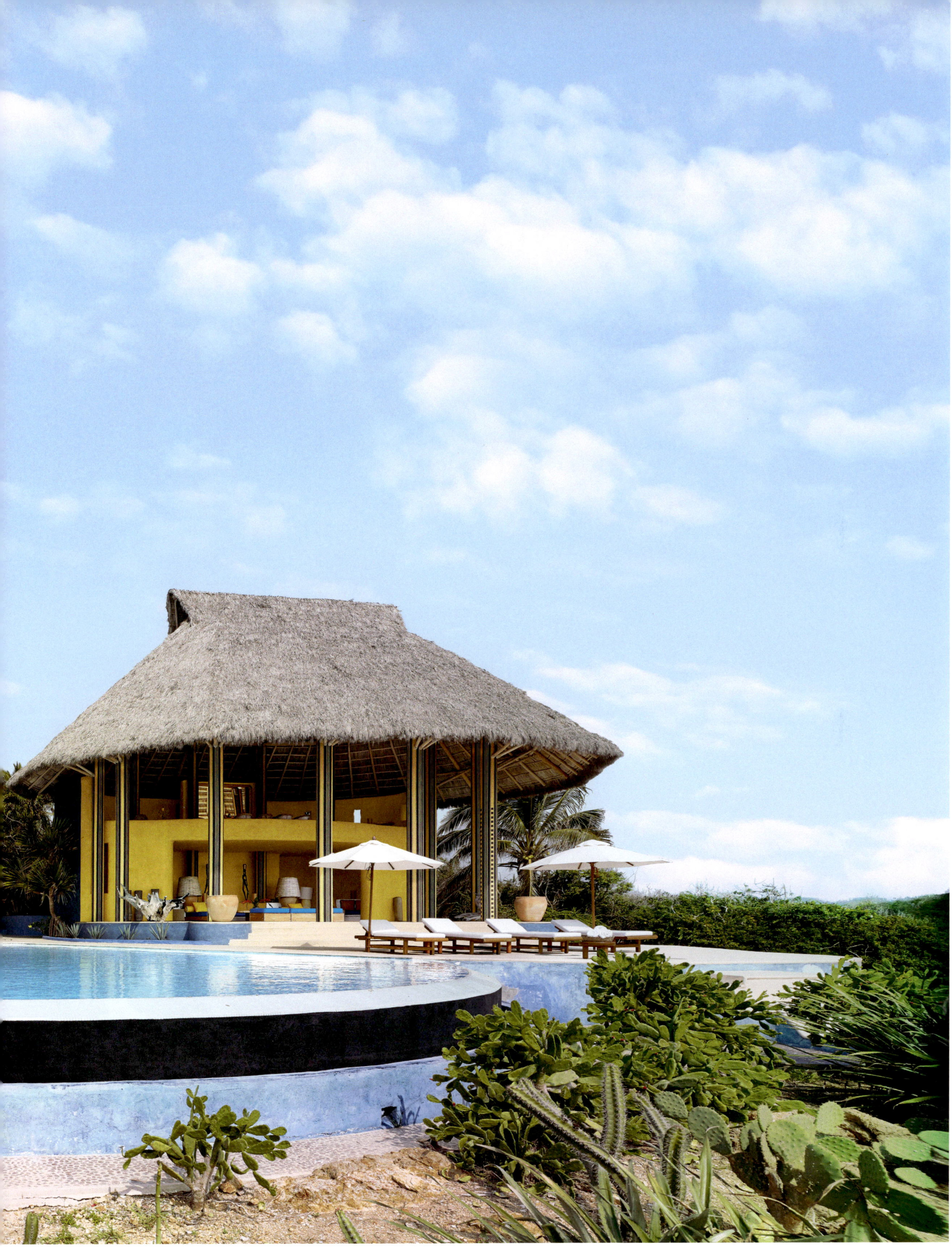

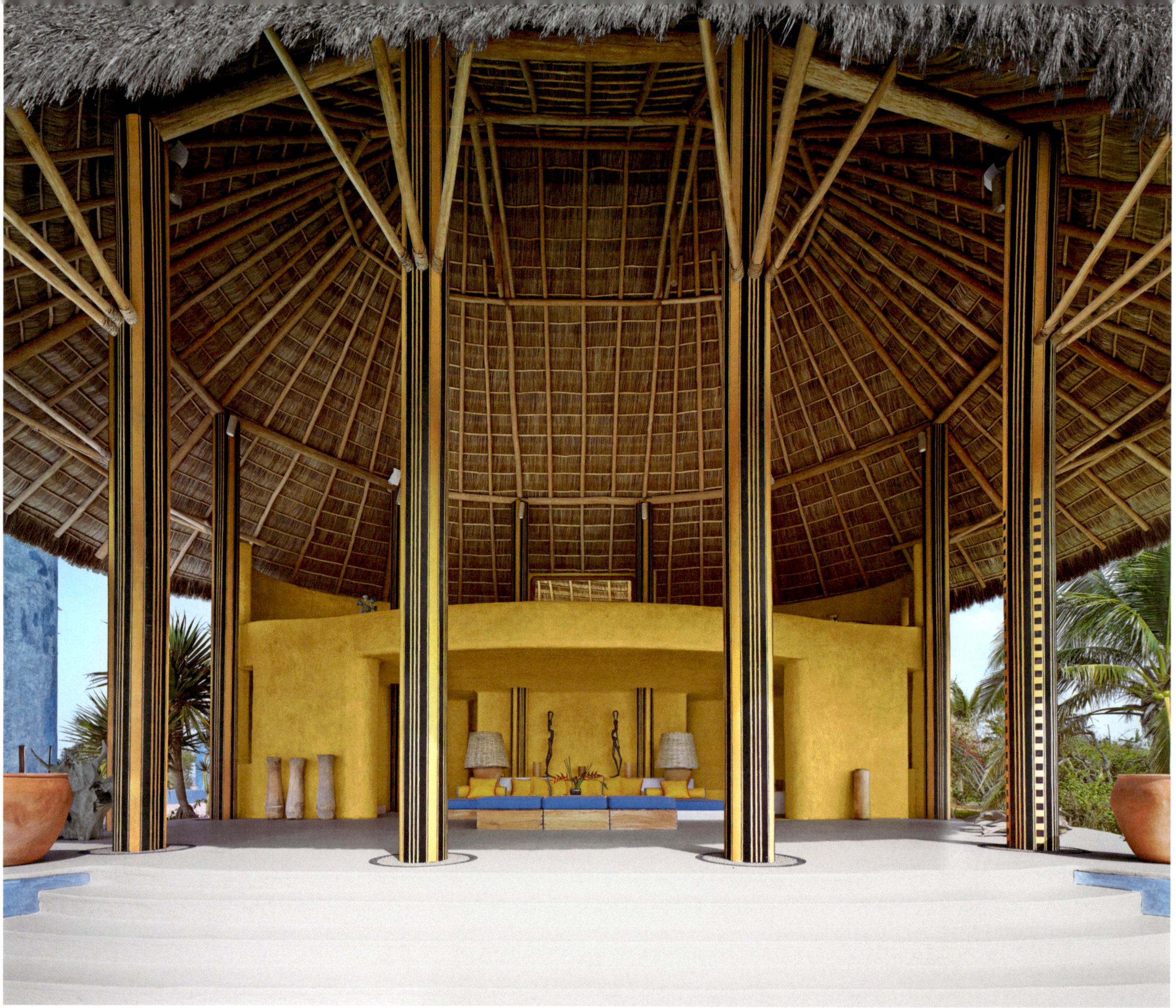

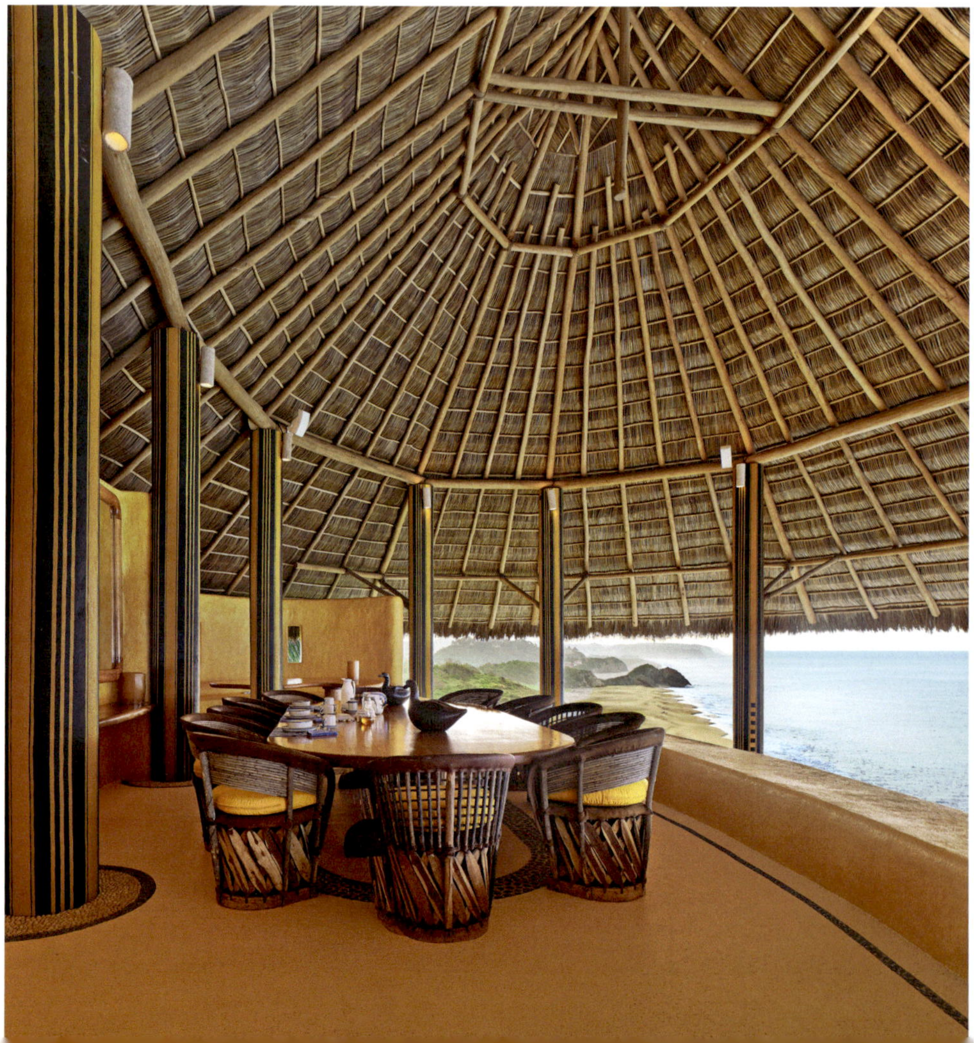

"VIEWS ARE FRAMED LIKE PAINTINGS AND INTERIOR DECORATION IS USURPED BY THE PRESTIGE GIVEN TO THE OUTSIDE WORLD, LEAVING EVEN THE MAIN HOUSE LARGELY DEVOID OF FURNITURE."

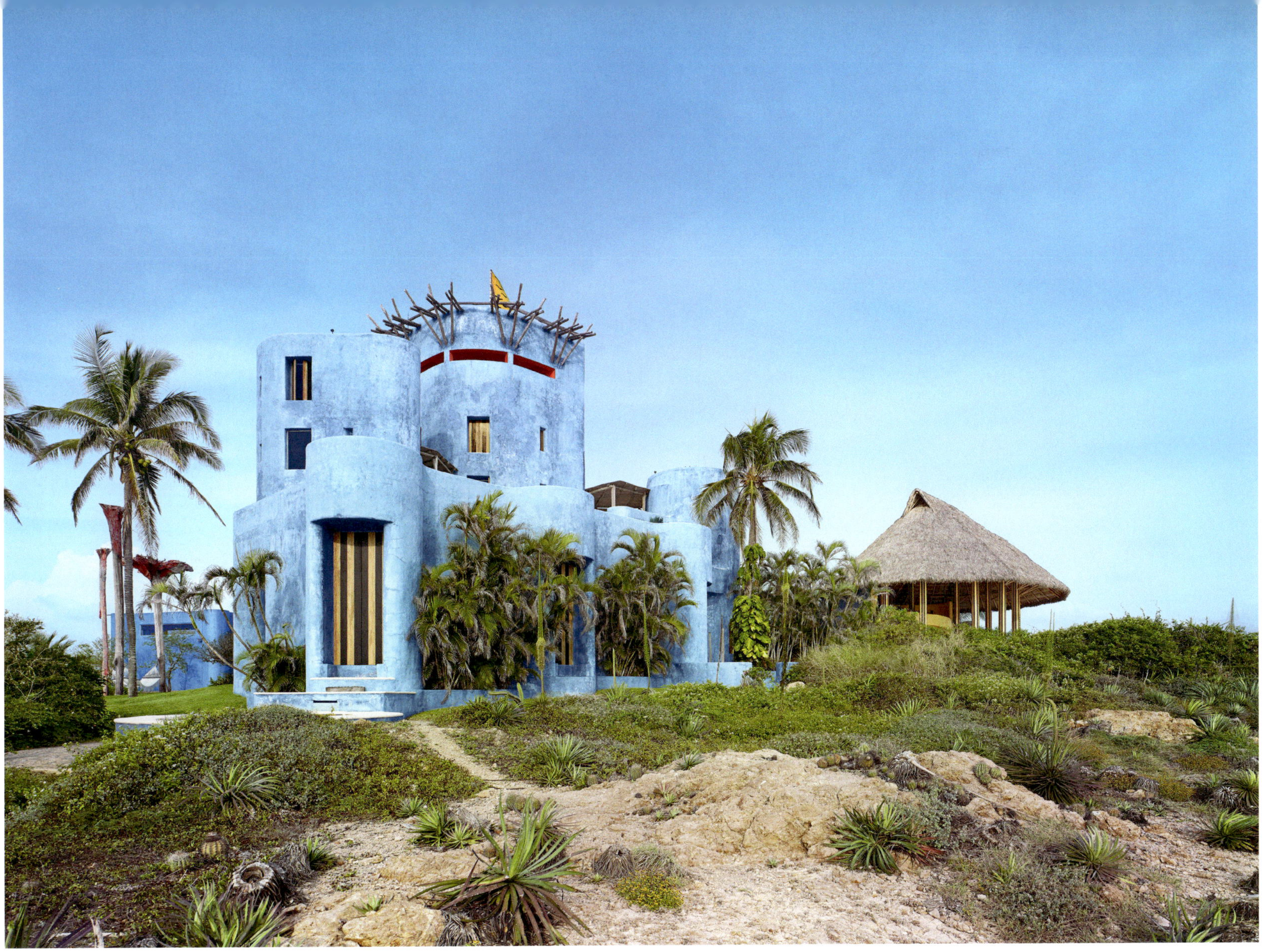

CASA TIGRE DEL MAR Contemplating the apparent idiosyncrasies of Casa Tigre del Mar is a fruitful exercise. Ancient architectural forms, universal language, reverence for nature, and a strange mixture of eccentricity and austerity collide to form these impressive buildings that merge with the Mexican landscape.

1968 was a formative year in Mexican architecture. Gian Franco Brignone, at the time an Italian banker flying over part of Mexico's west coast, was mesmerized by the resplendent landscape and decided to settle there, building on a patch of land that would become Costa Careyes. Today, more than 50 houses and 40 casitas enliven the community, one of which is home to Brignone and his son Filippo.

Casa Tigre del Mar, and the Careyes style in general, is anchored in an otherworldly and futuristic ethos that translates into concise bohemian structures on the ground. Rather than planning uniform relationships between buildings, Filippo Brignone says that the focus is on creating "a collection of disparate volumes assembled around the landscape." Views are framed like paintings and interior decoration is usurped by the prestige given to the outside world, leaving even the main house, La Torre, largely devoid of furniture. Polished concrete floors and walls transition to the exterior, where three layers of paint–white, green, and blue—participate in a dynamic play with the elements, changing color with the light of the sun and sea.

The guesthouse Casa del Tres Mil—its name reflects an ambition to reach the year 3,000—gives further expression to Casa Tigre del Mar's mystical foundations. The structure takes a library as its focal point, which communicates the importance of knowledge in the progression of ideal forms. Outside, a ladder stretches into the sky—when climbed, it reveals a question mark and an exclamation point etched on the roof. The swimming pool, meanwhile, features a labyrinth design from Chartres Cathedral. Brignone says, "These strange signs exist in all the languages of the world," and have been chosen to represent Casa Tigre del Mar because of their universal values. ~

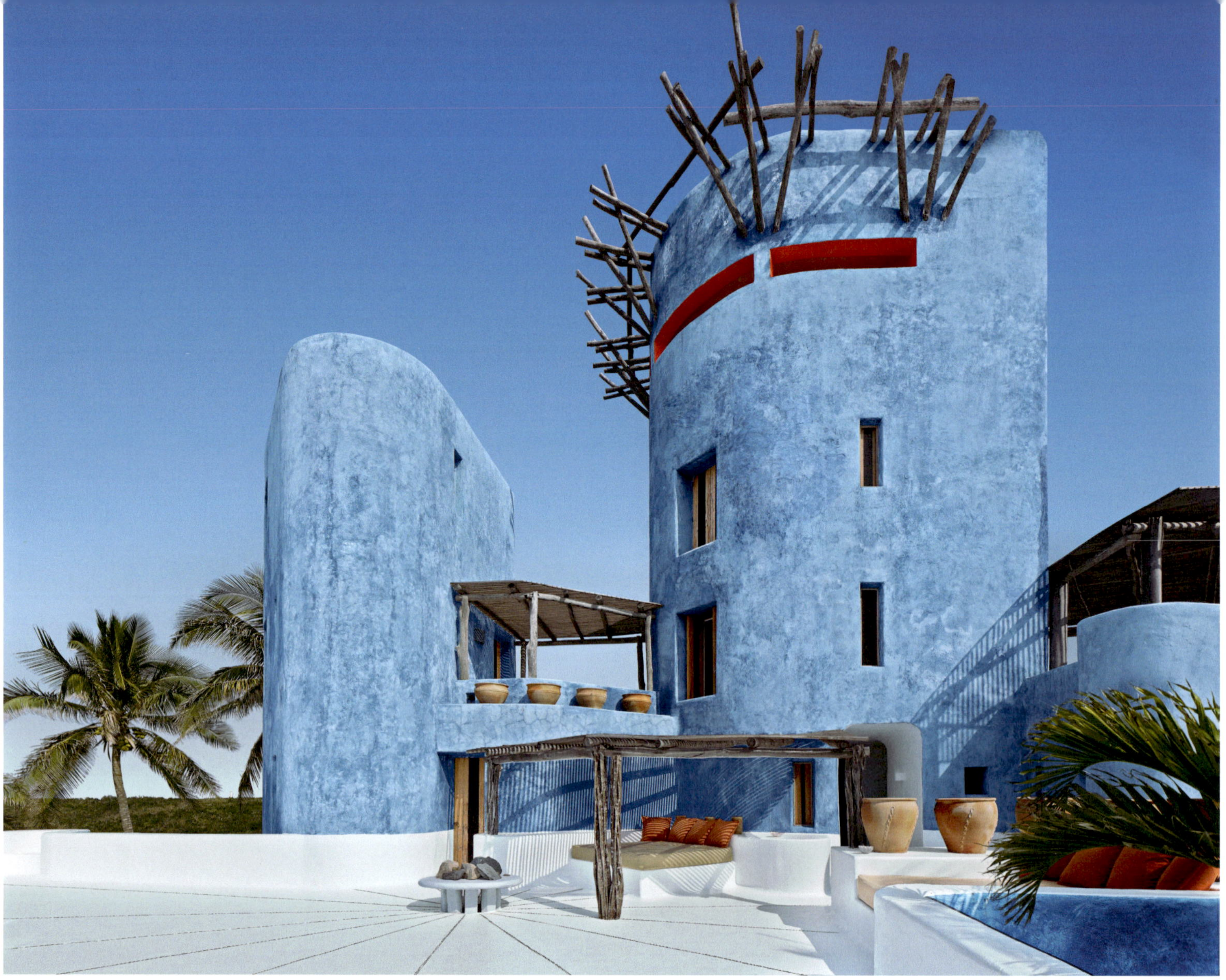

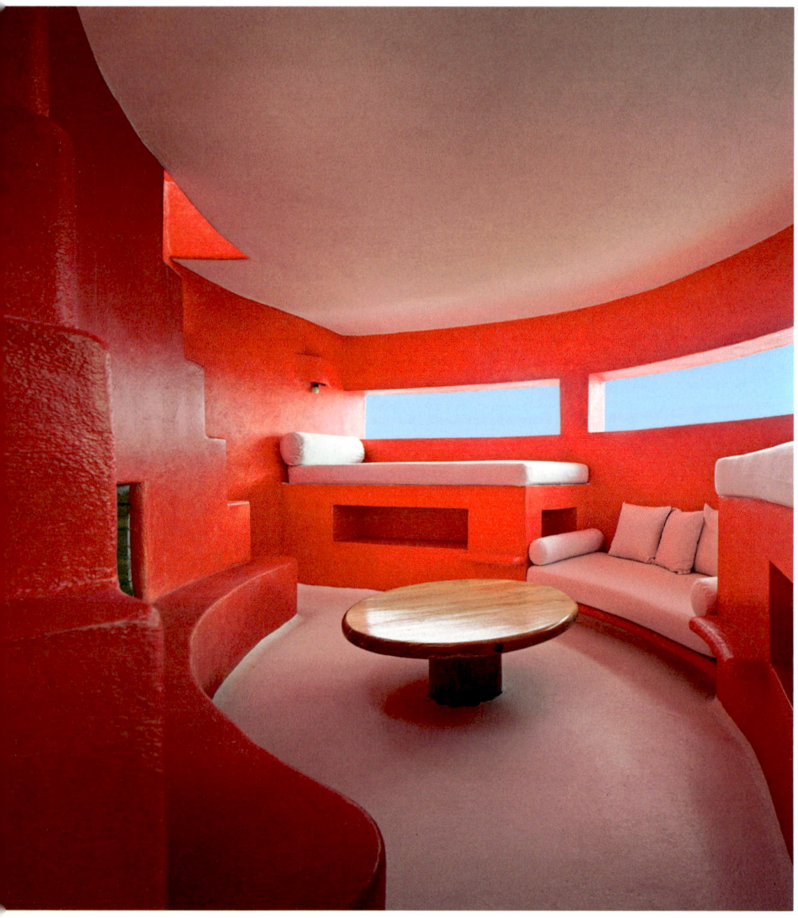

"CASA TIGRE DEL MAR, AND THE CAREYES STYLE IN GENERAL, IS ANCHORED IN AN OTHERWORLDLY AND FUTURISTIC ETHOS THAT TRANSLATES INTO CONCISE BOHEMIAN STRUCTURES ON THE GROUND."

The giant two-story palapa that occupies the center of the property is a precise statement of the kind of universality that the property seeks. Though greatly modified in form, it was built with traditional methods. As Brignone explains, Casa Tigre del Mar obtains a form that has "matured from that of a small Mexican village to an enlightened retreat where the ideals and creative impulses of the world thrive." Even though it might look like an alien invention, this compound respects ancient forms of building as much as it does nature. ◆

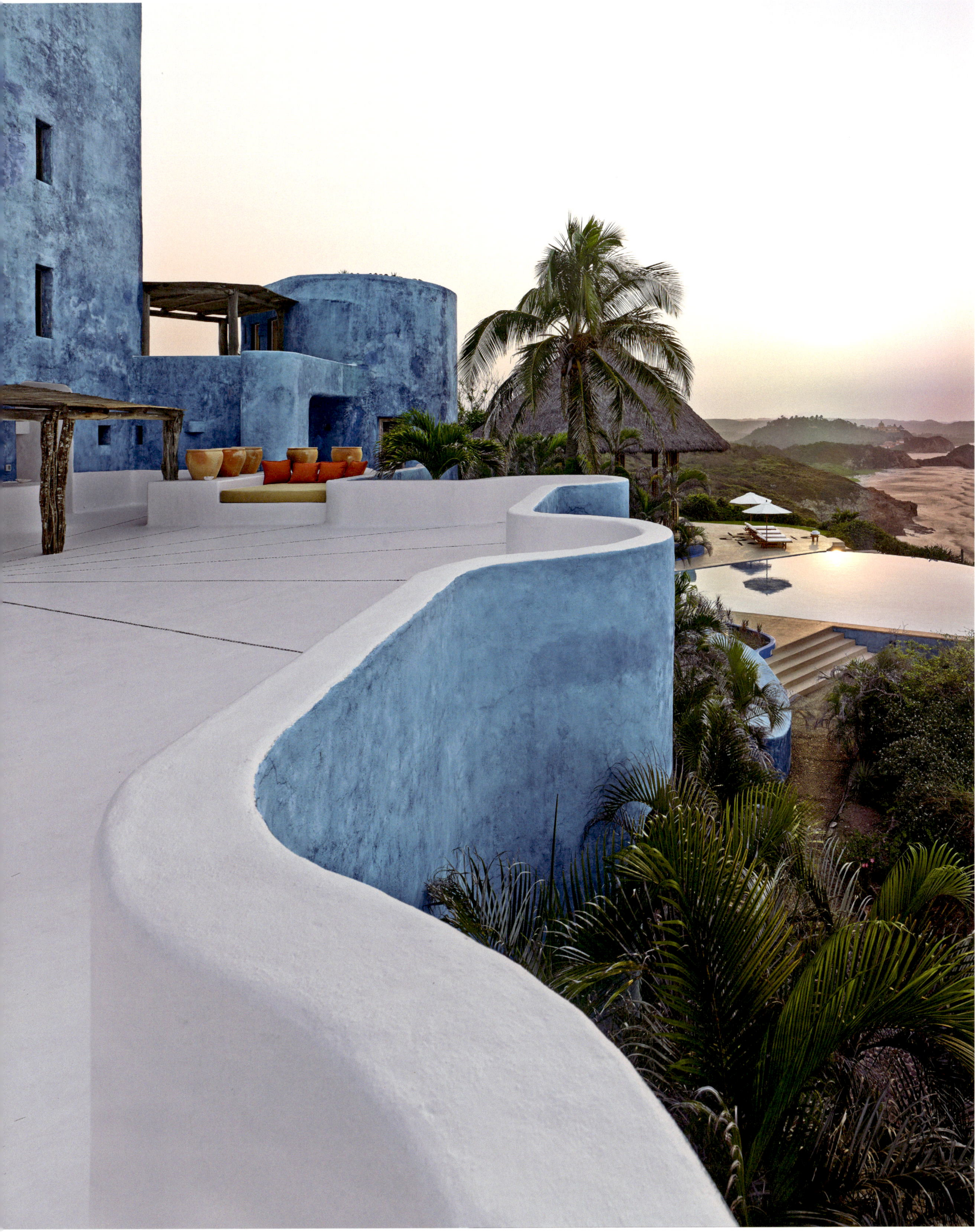

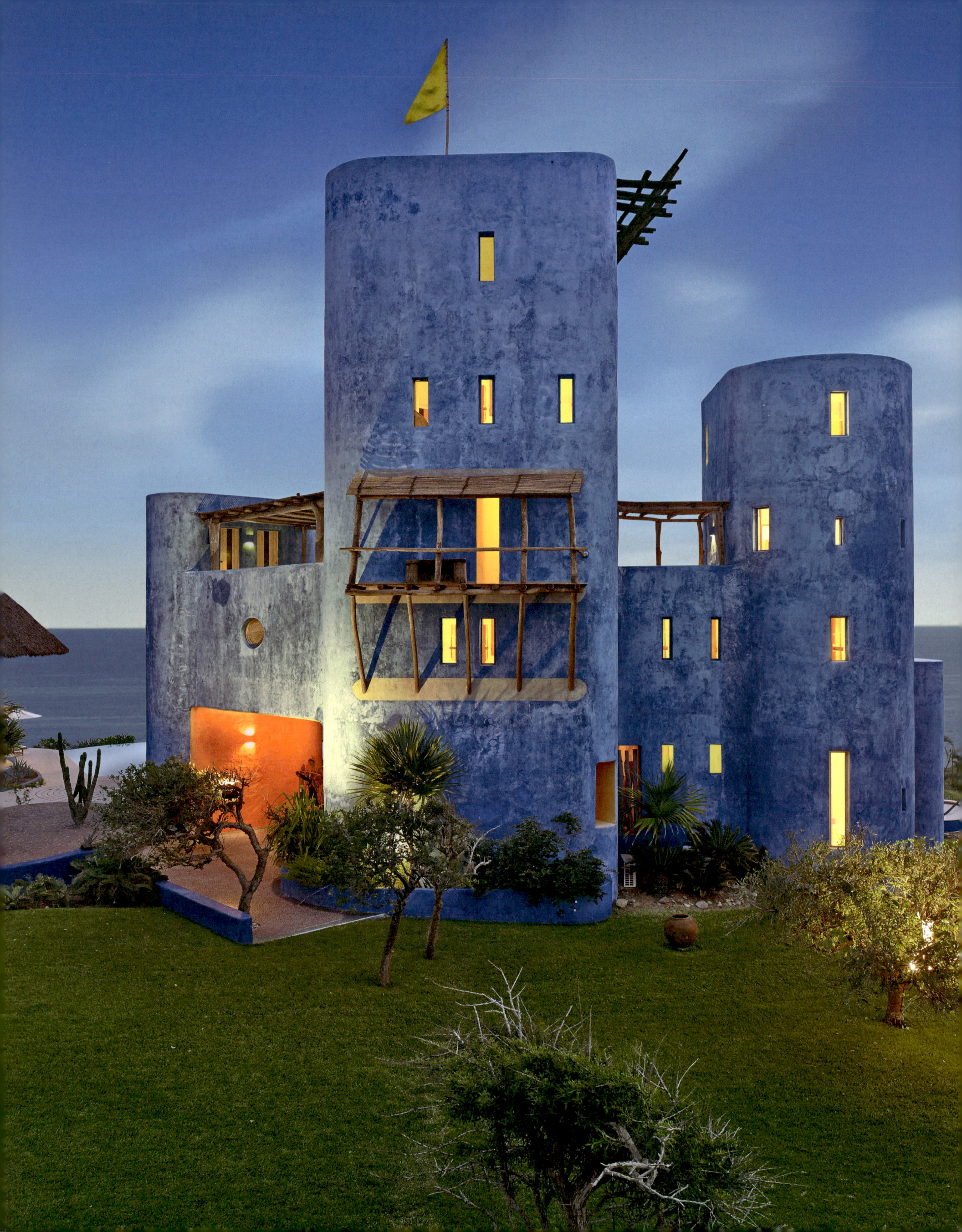

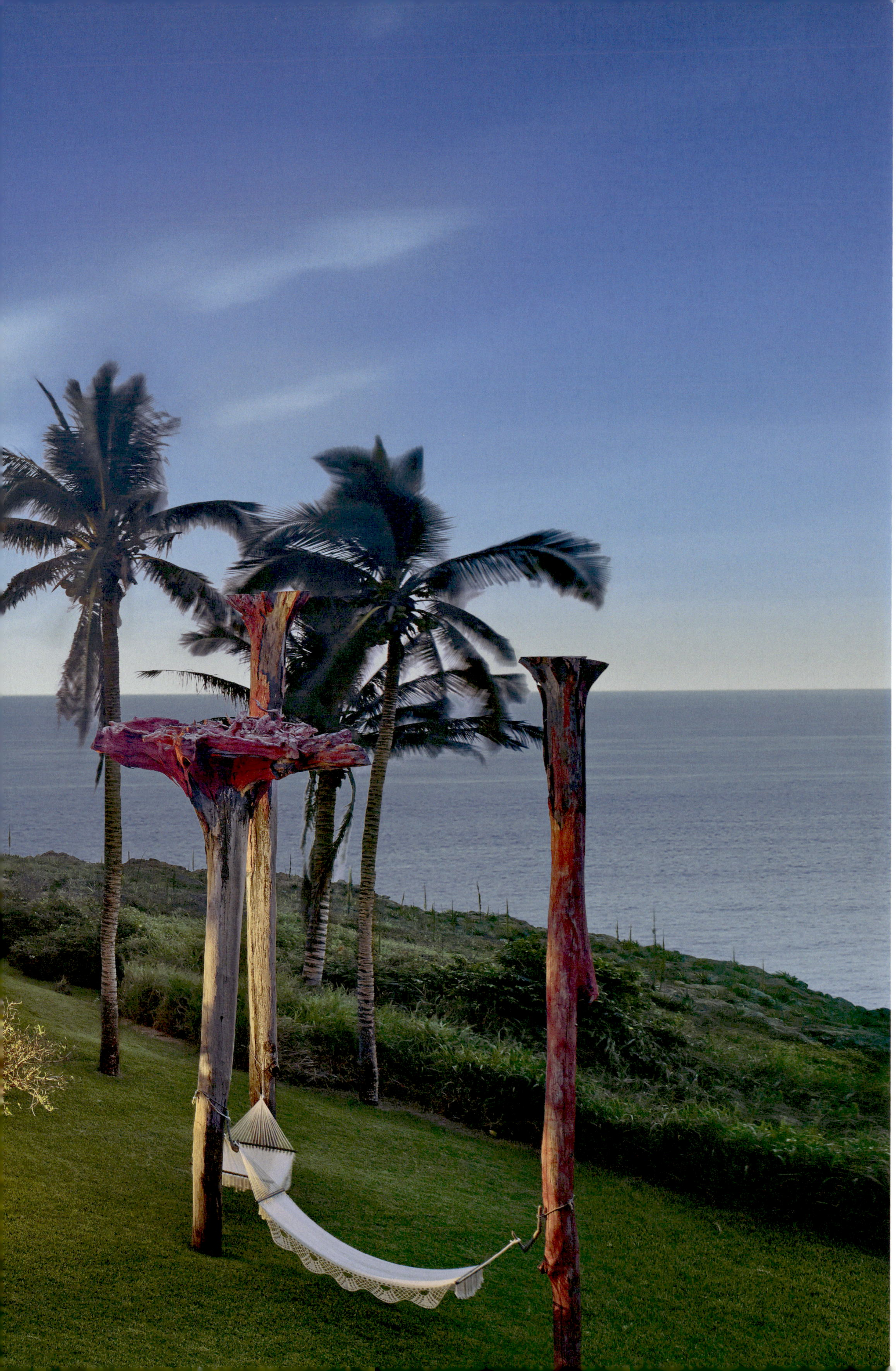

"Casa Tigre del Mar obtains a form that has 'matured from that of a small Mexican village to an enlightened retreat where the ideals and creative impulses of the world thrive.'"
— *Filippo Brignone*

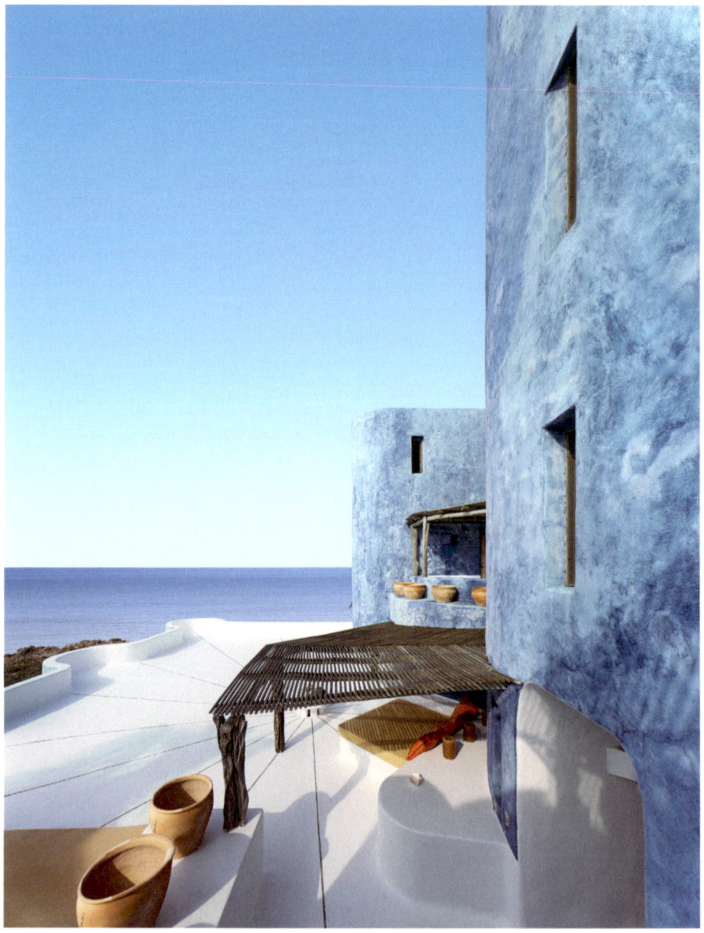

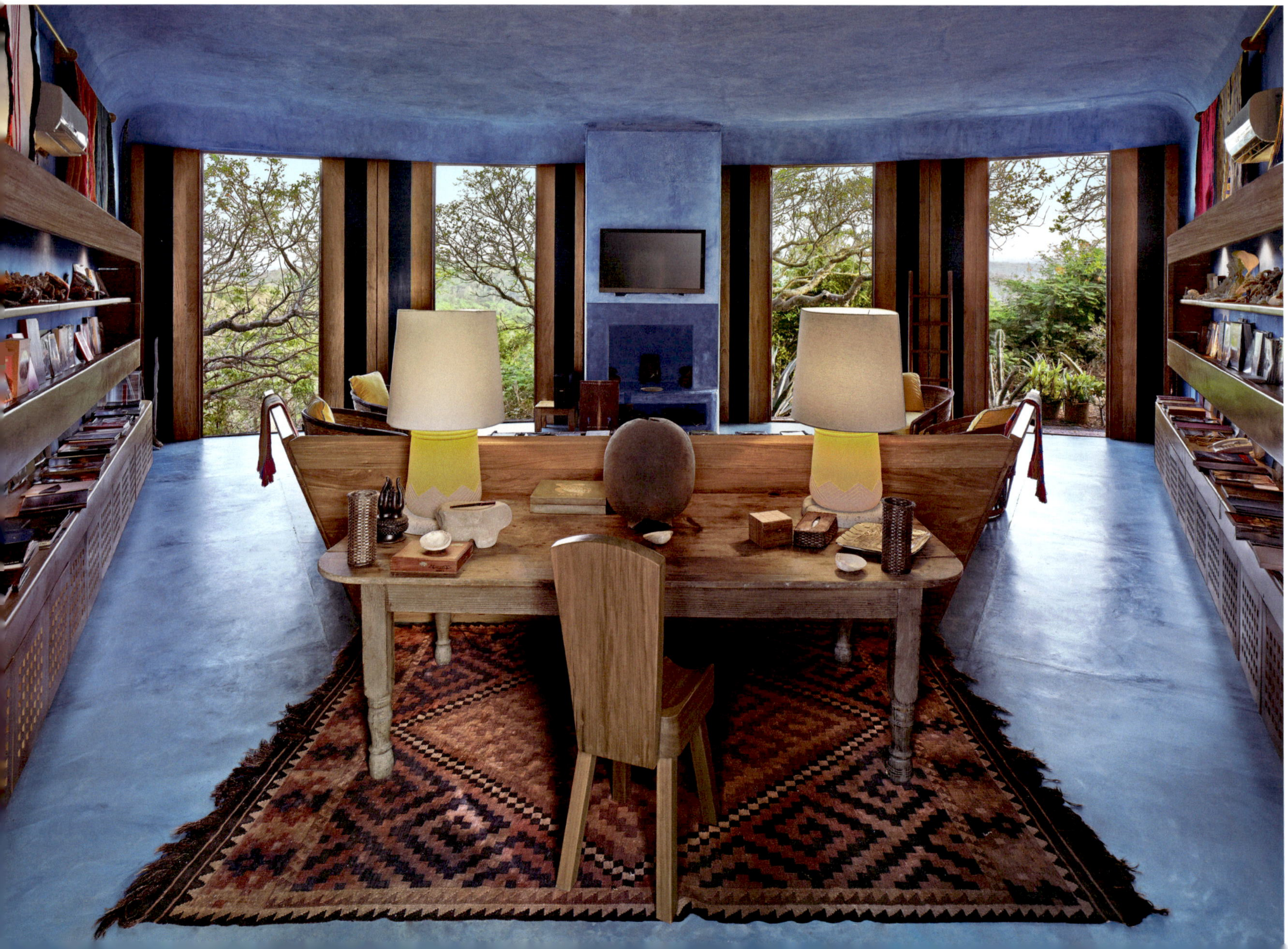

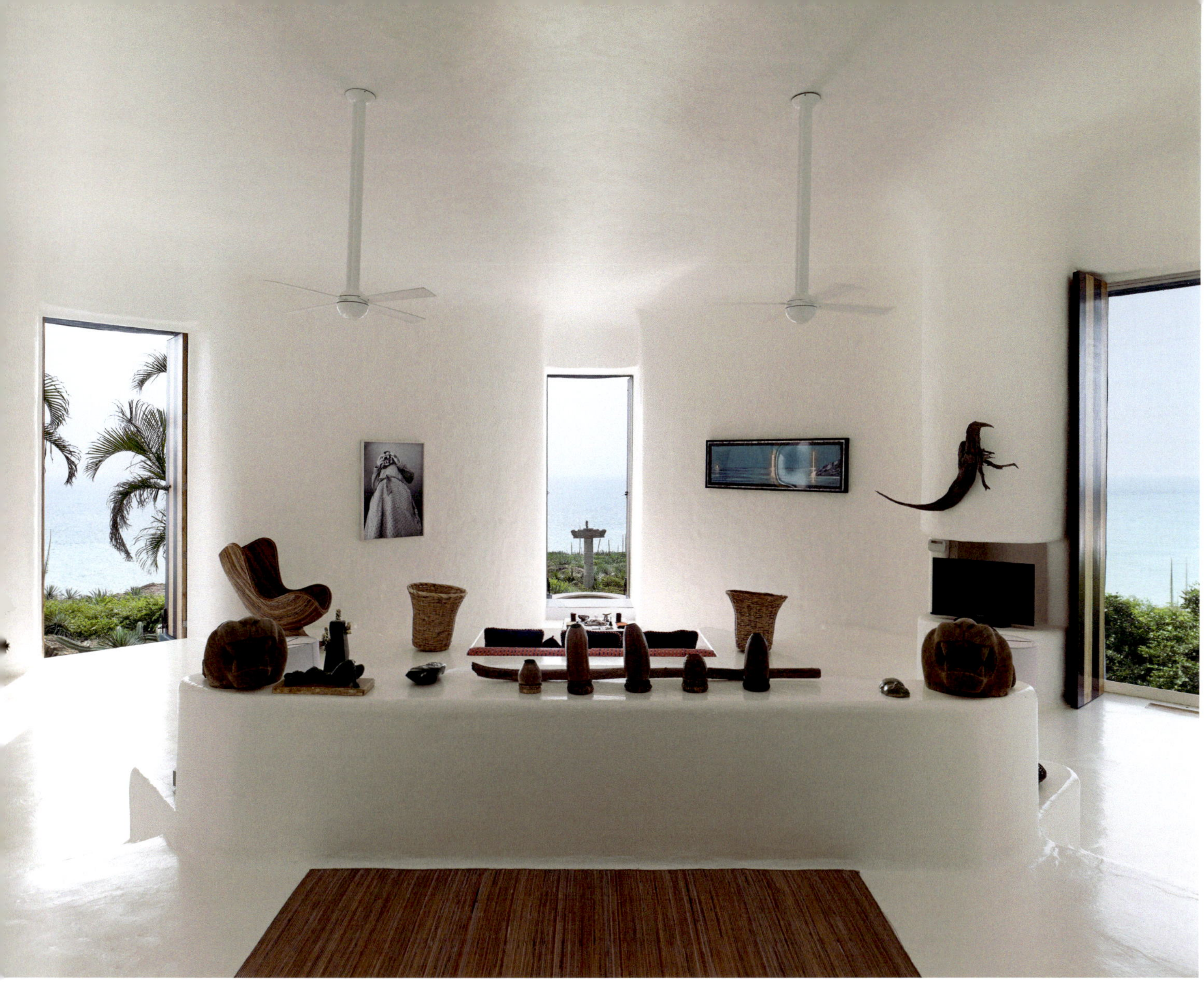

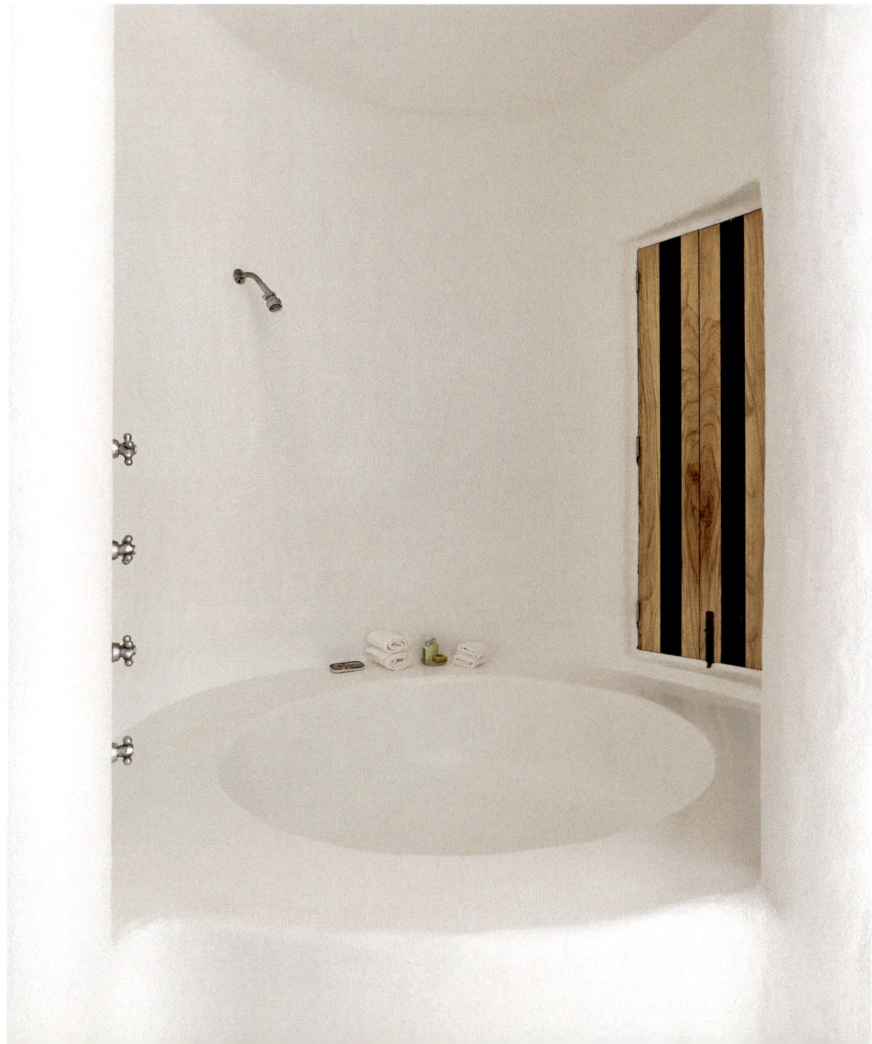

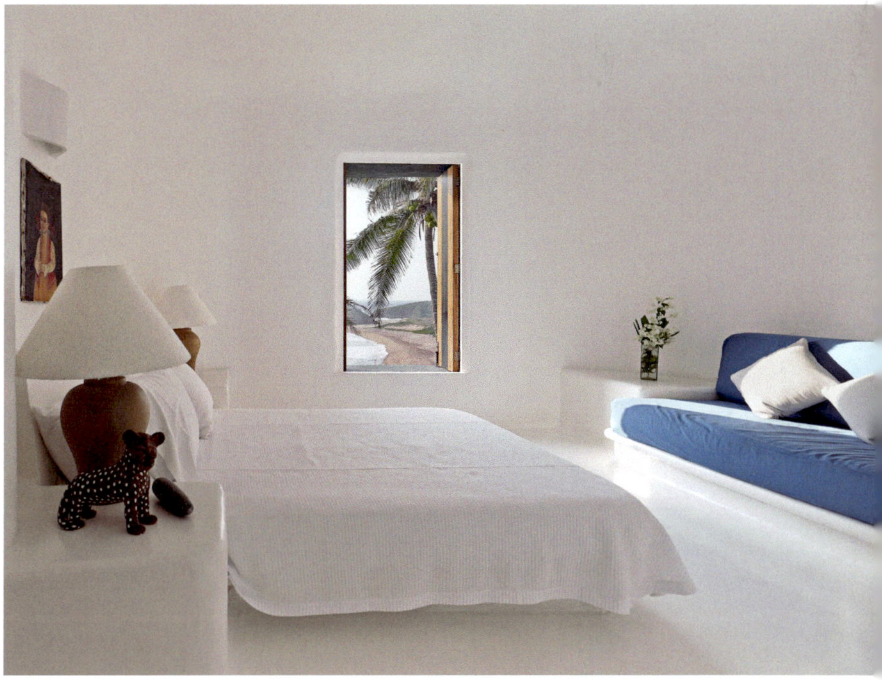

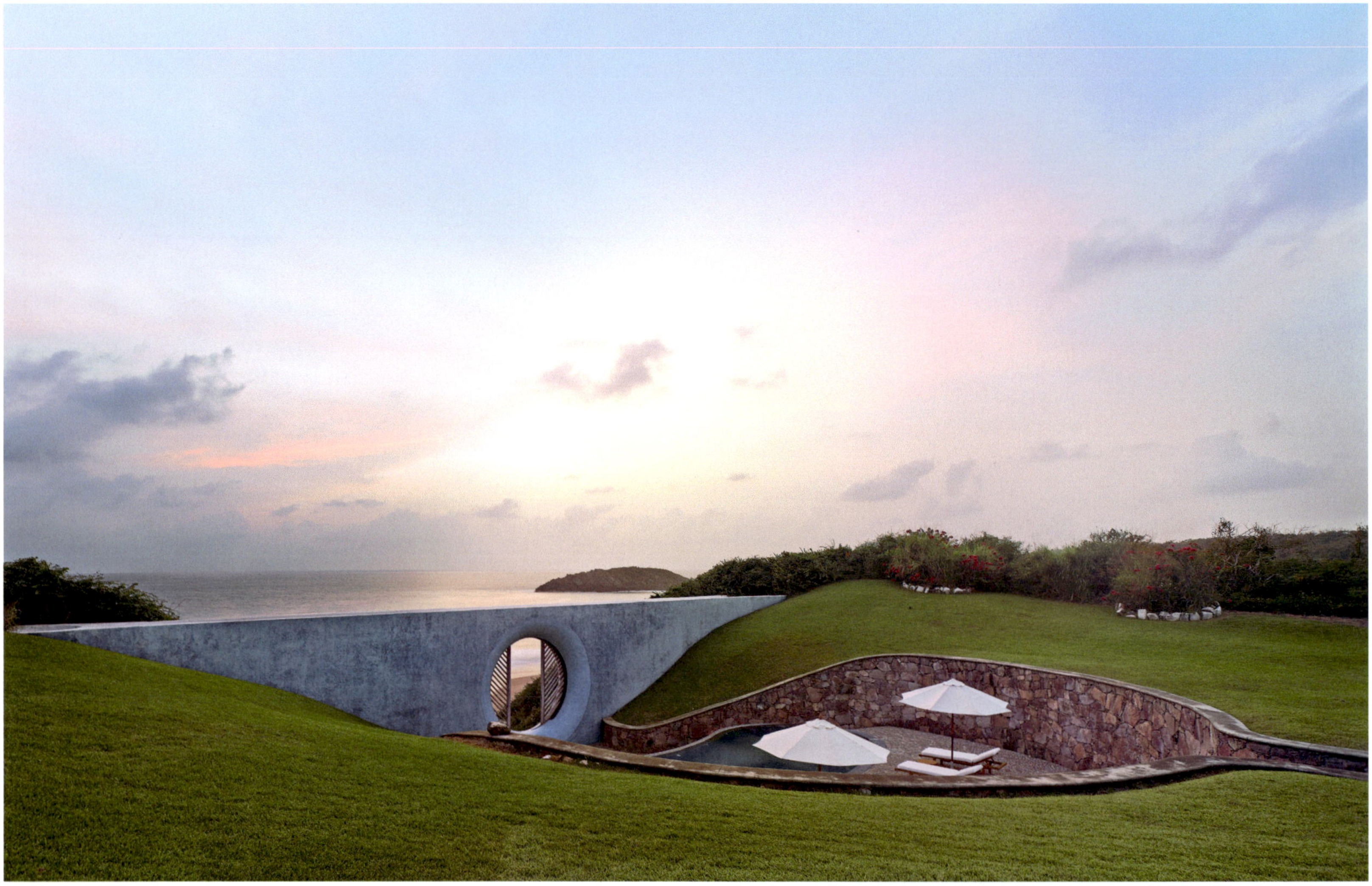

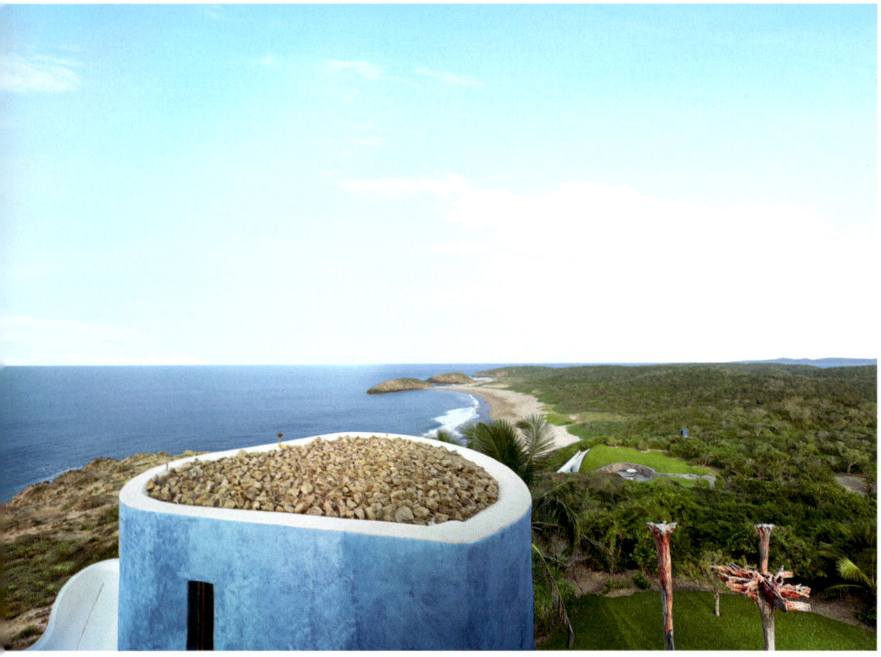

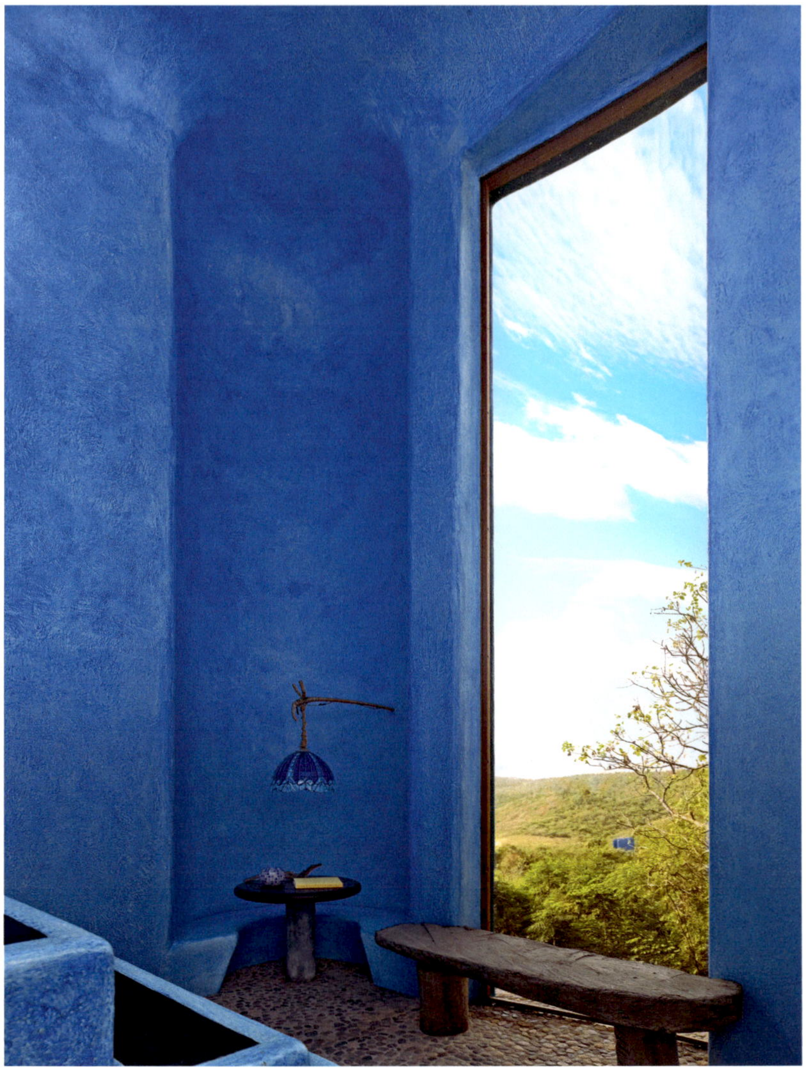

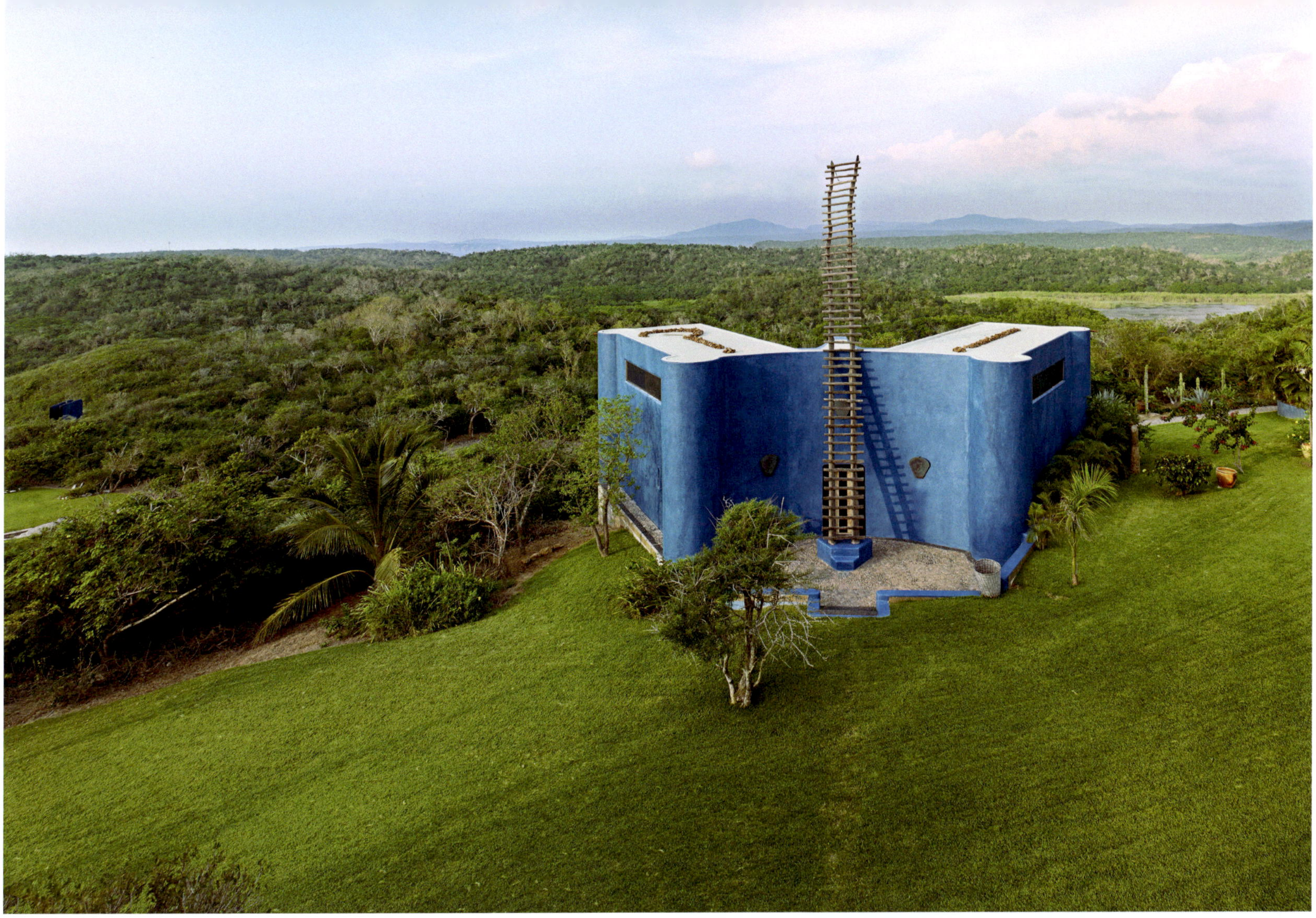

"OUTSIDE, A LADDER STRETCHES INTO THE SKY—WHEN CLIMBED, IT REVEALS A QUESTION MARK AND AN EXCLAMATION POINT ETCHED ON THE ROOF. THESE SYMBOLS ENCAPSULATE THE IDEA OF COSTA CAREYES."

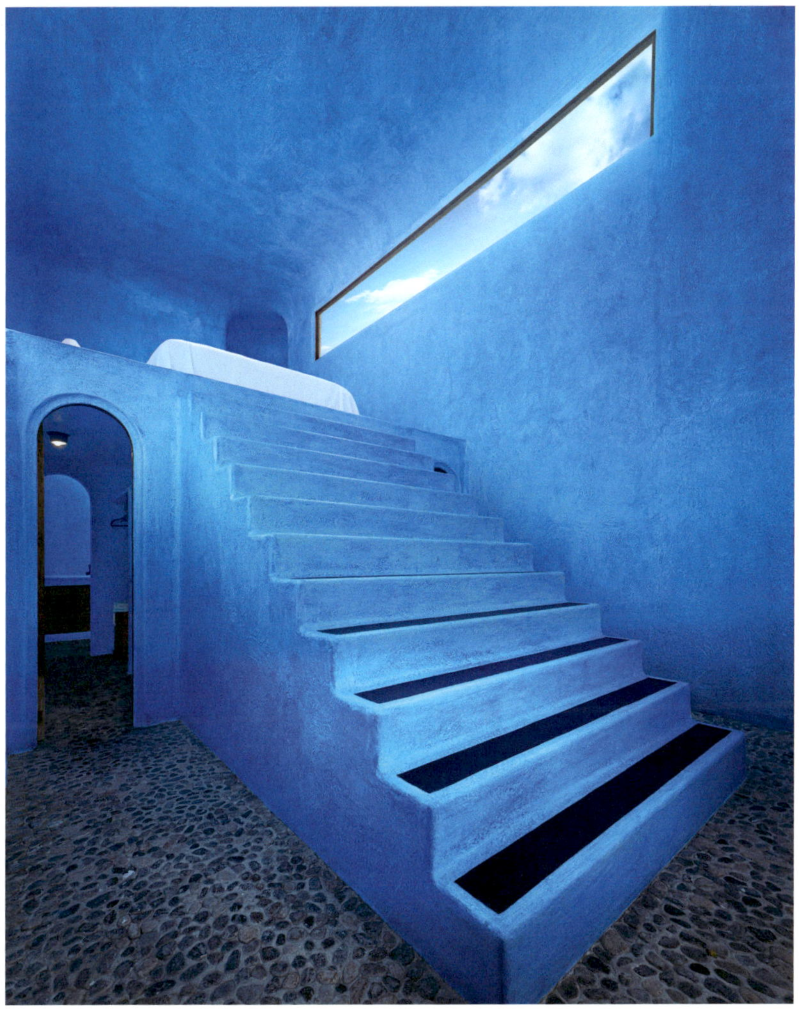

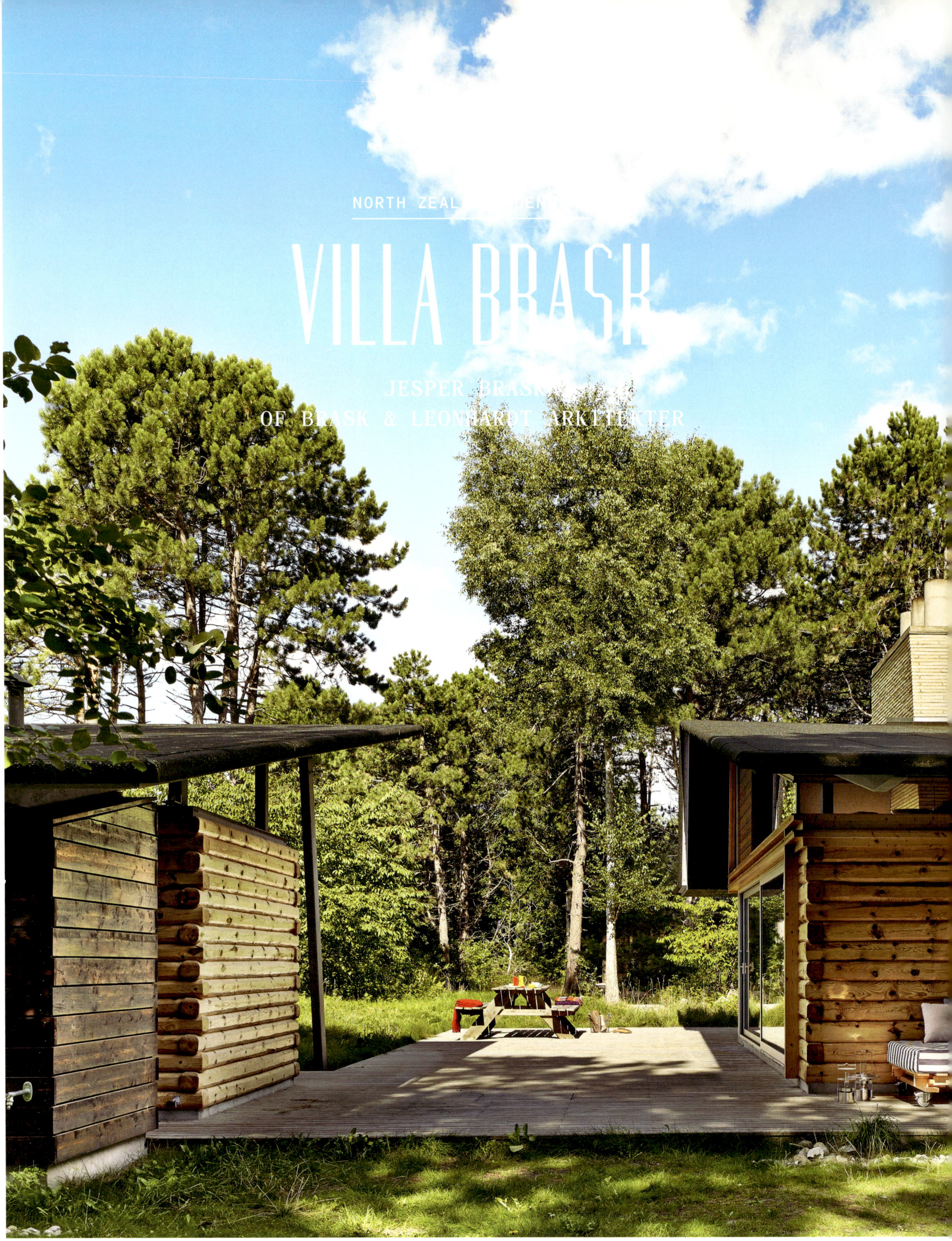

NORTH ZEALAND, DENMARK

VILLA BRASK

JESPER BRASK
OF BRASK & LEONHARDT ARKITEKTER

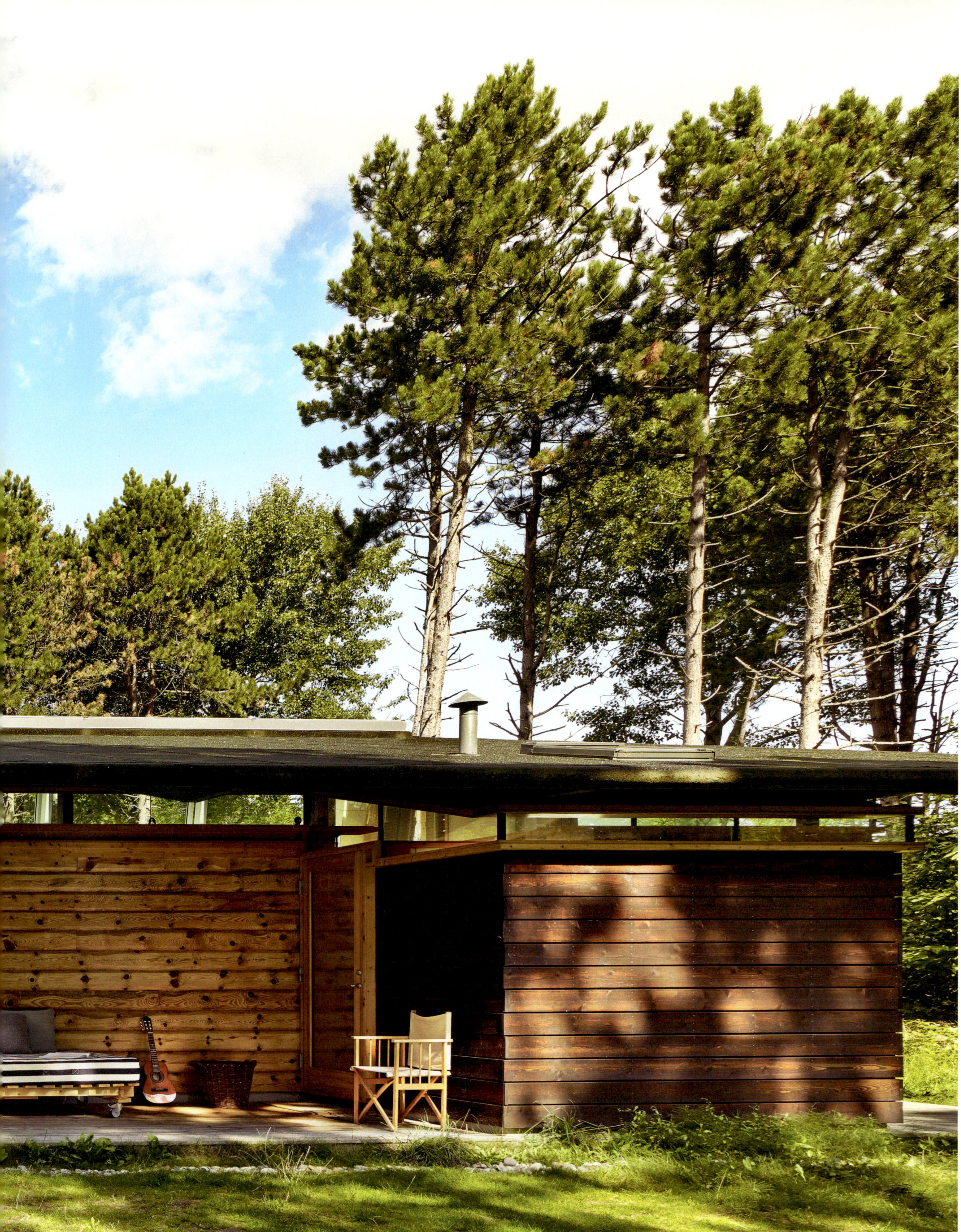

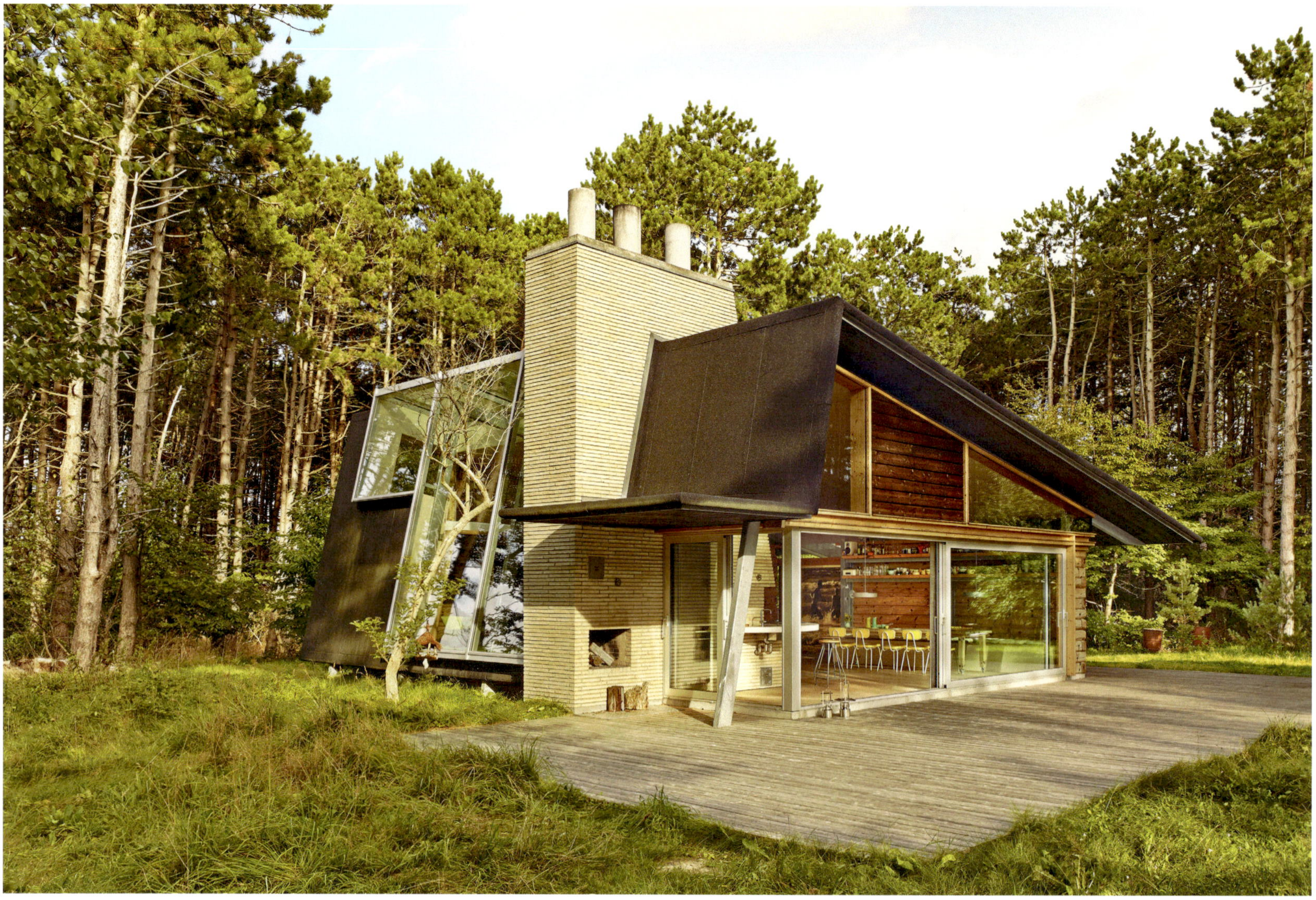

VILLA BRASK is a cabin that interacts with its environment in more ways than one. Featuring massive glass windows on one side, it removes barriers to the flora and fauna. But in a sustainable turn, the very trees that were felled to create a clearing for the cabin were also used in its construction.

Villa Brask begins and ends with its site and the materials found within it. After architect and owner Jesper Brask chanced upon the plot of land in North Zealand, Denmark, he decided to utilize the 150 pine trees that needed to be cleared in the actual construction of the house. After cutting the large pines down to workable logs, he left them to sit, dry, and harden for three years before construction began. With so much time on his hands to come up with a plan, he did not find the process as easy as one might imagine. "Designing for yourself is very difficult," he says, "because you feel that nothing can go wrong! It's important not to want too much and get too carried away with ideas. Eventually, though, I felt sure that we had a good idea."

At its most essential, that idea was to build a wooden cabin around a central fireplace. Assembled from narrow blonde bricks, the towering chimney is used to heat the 93-square-meter house, while also acting as an outdoor fireplace and heat source for the kitchen stove. In terms of aesthetics, the chimney interrupts the continuity of the black felted canopy roof, allowing one side to angle into an eave that shelters the entrance, and the other to continue down to the ground. Large windows are inlaid on this extended side, affording a view of the dense forest that surrounds the cabin.

A minimal galvanized steel frame, thin enough to leave the natural landscape unblemished, supports the family home. Its silver coloration mediates between the black roof and the lighter timber. The rest of the house is constructed of the original 150 pine trees that were felled in the initial stages of the project.

Unsurprisingly, he was pleased with the result. As he explains, "What I like about the house is that we have succeeded in creating a lovely natural atmosphere and environment. We wanted a house where we felt almost like being in the heart of nature and I believe the construction and material finishes are harmonious with this setting." ◆

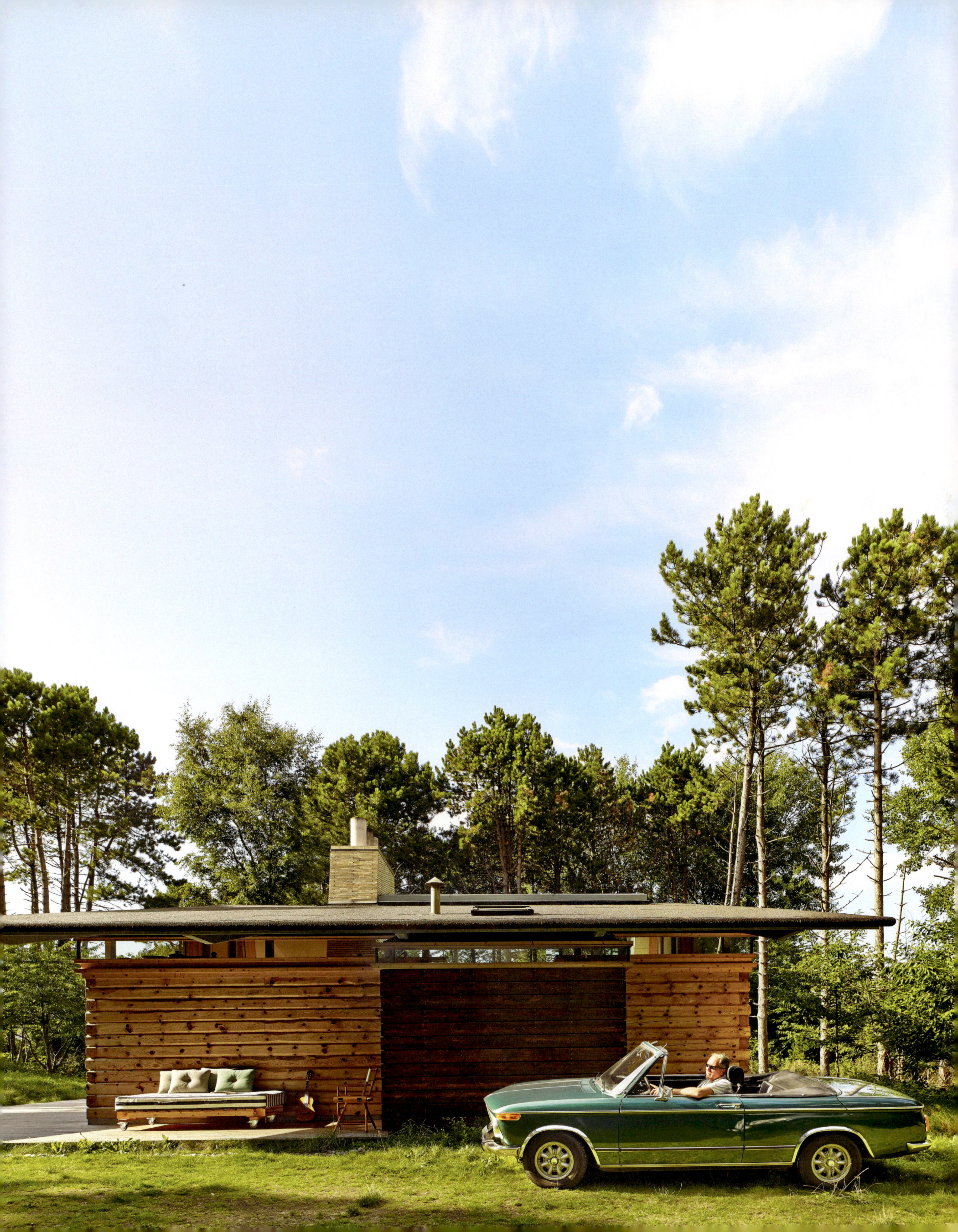

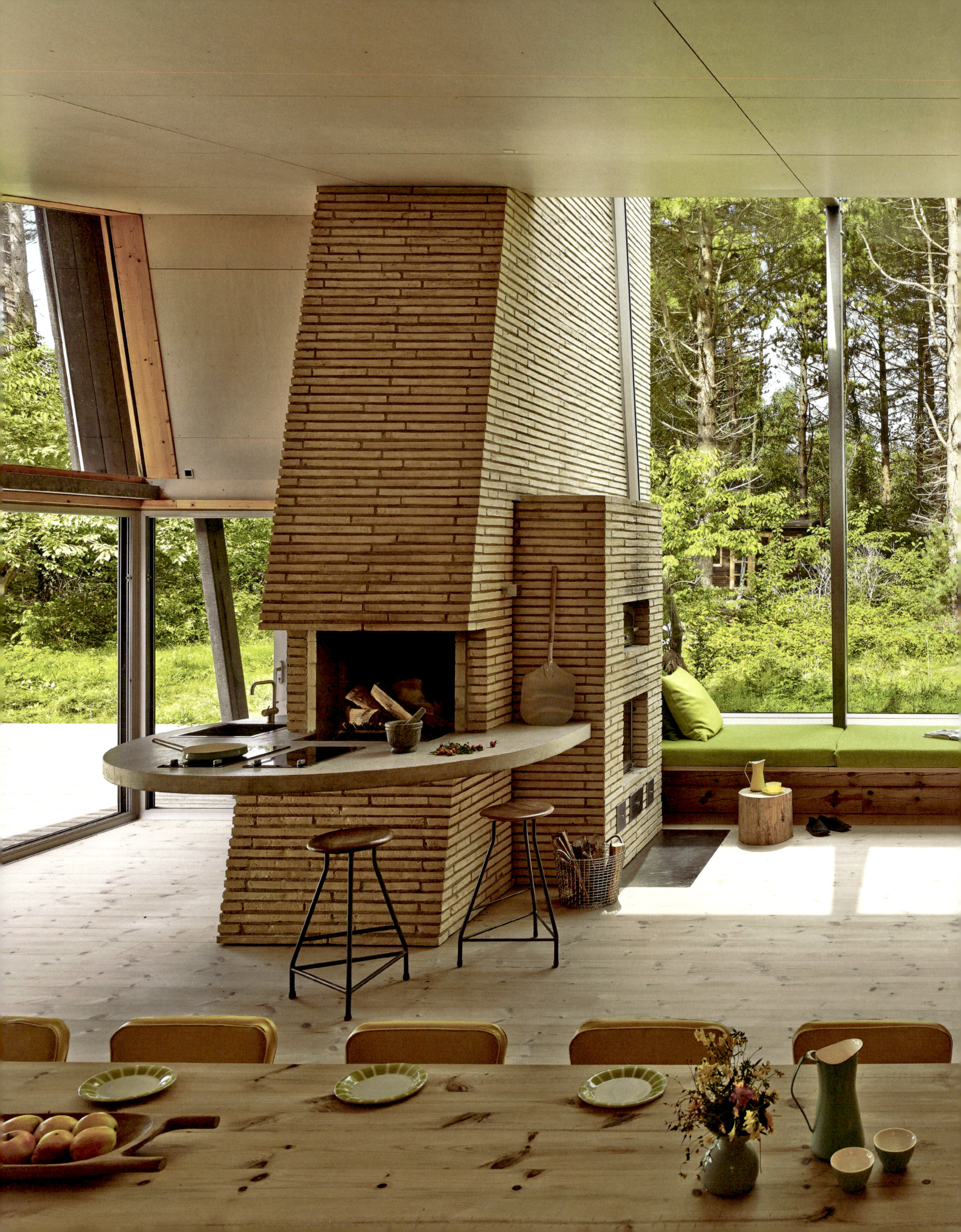

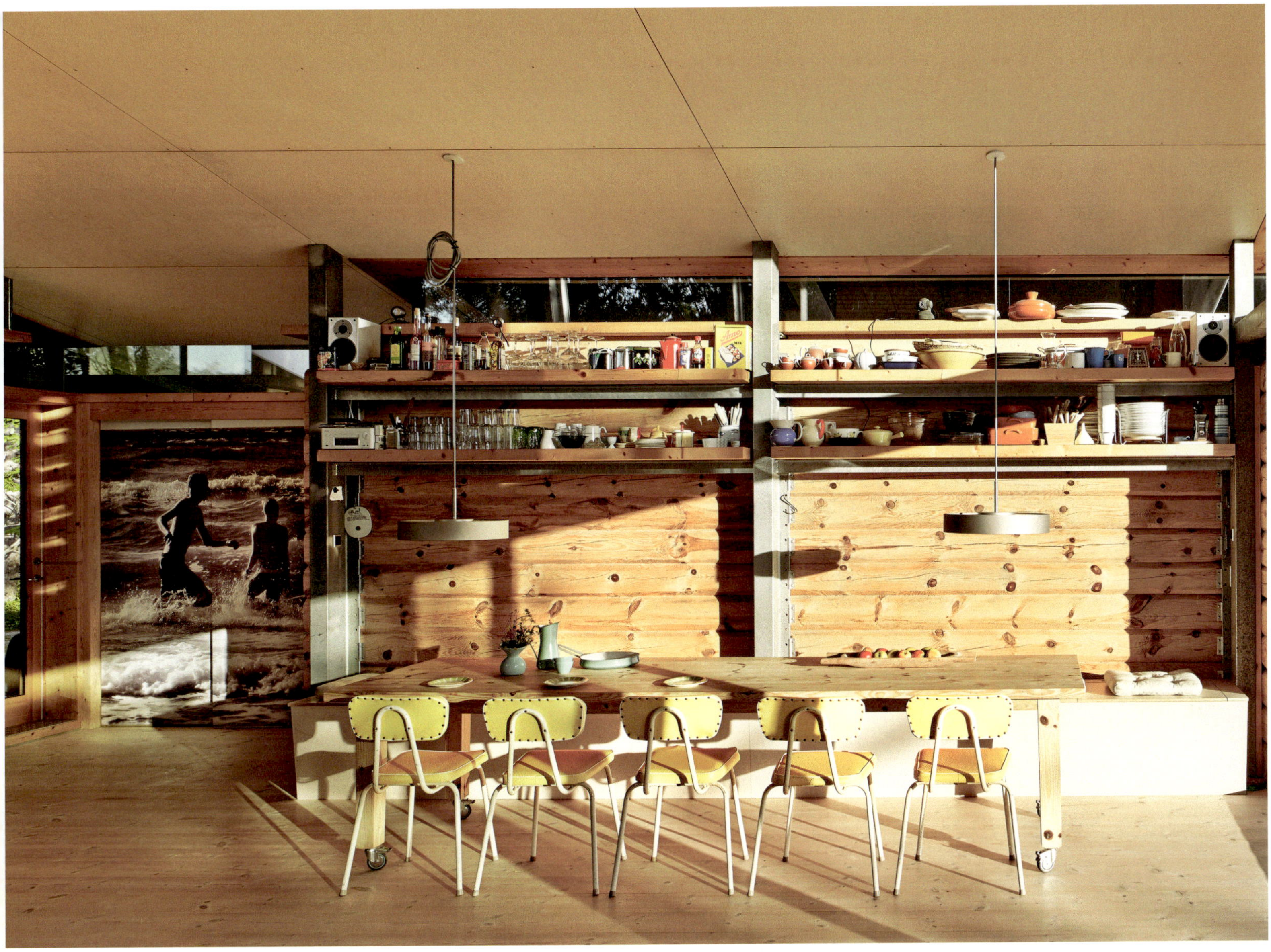

“THE HOUSE IS CONSTRUCTED OUT OF TIMBER BEAMS MADE FROM THE 150 PINE TREES THAT WERE FELLED TO MAKE A CLEARING FOR THE HOUSE.”

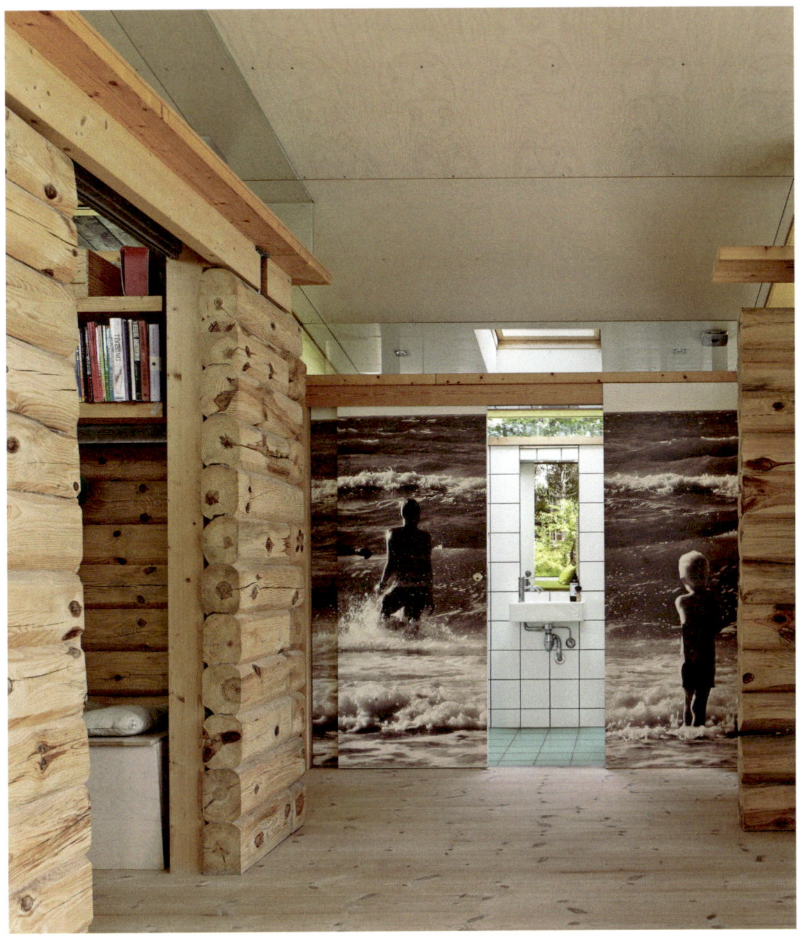

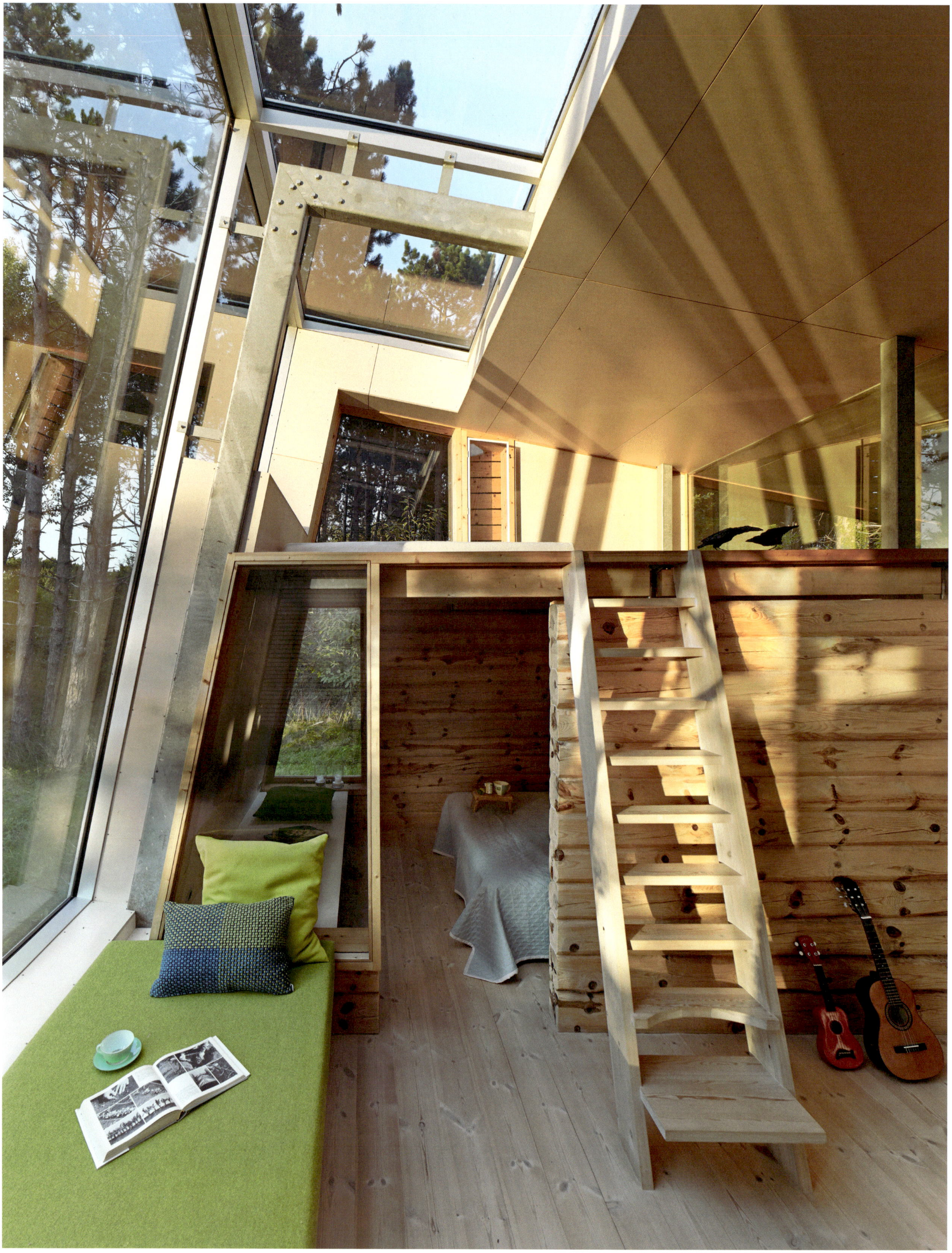

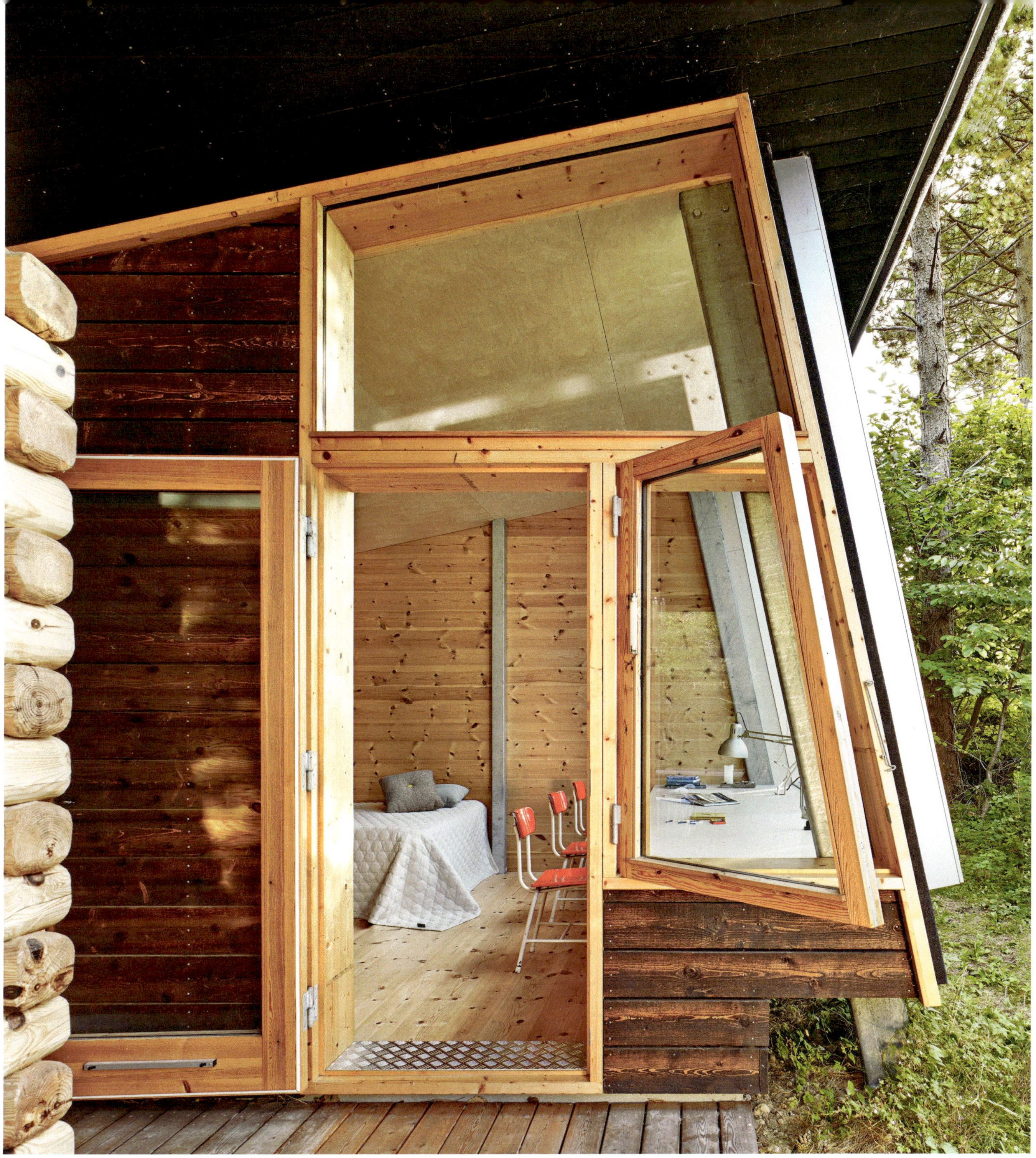

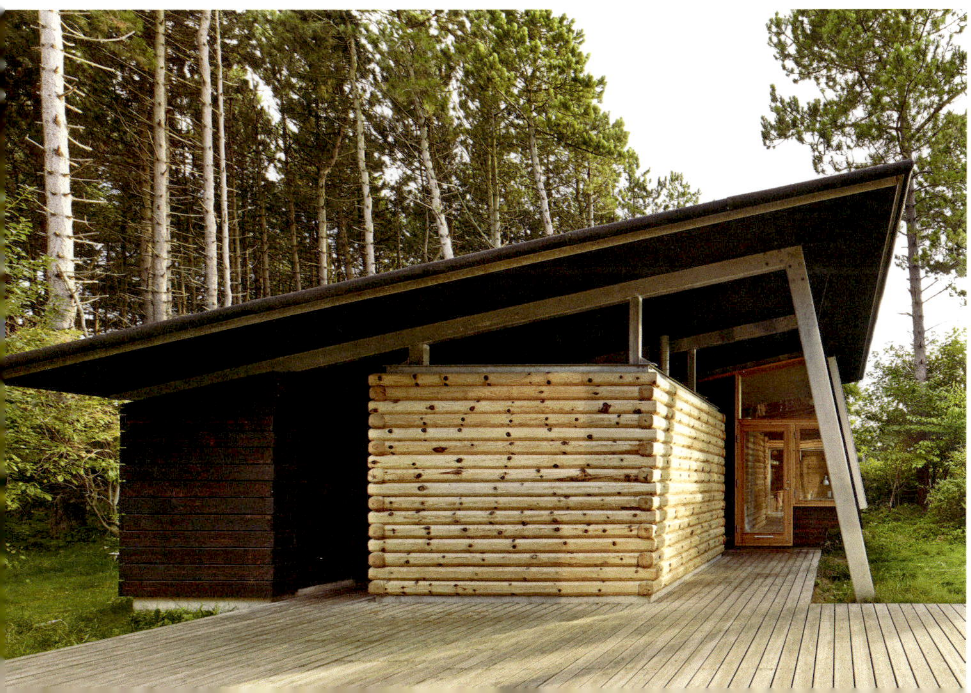

"Designing for yourself is very difficult because you feel that nothing can go wrong! It's important not to want too much and get too carried away with ideas."
— Jesper Brask

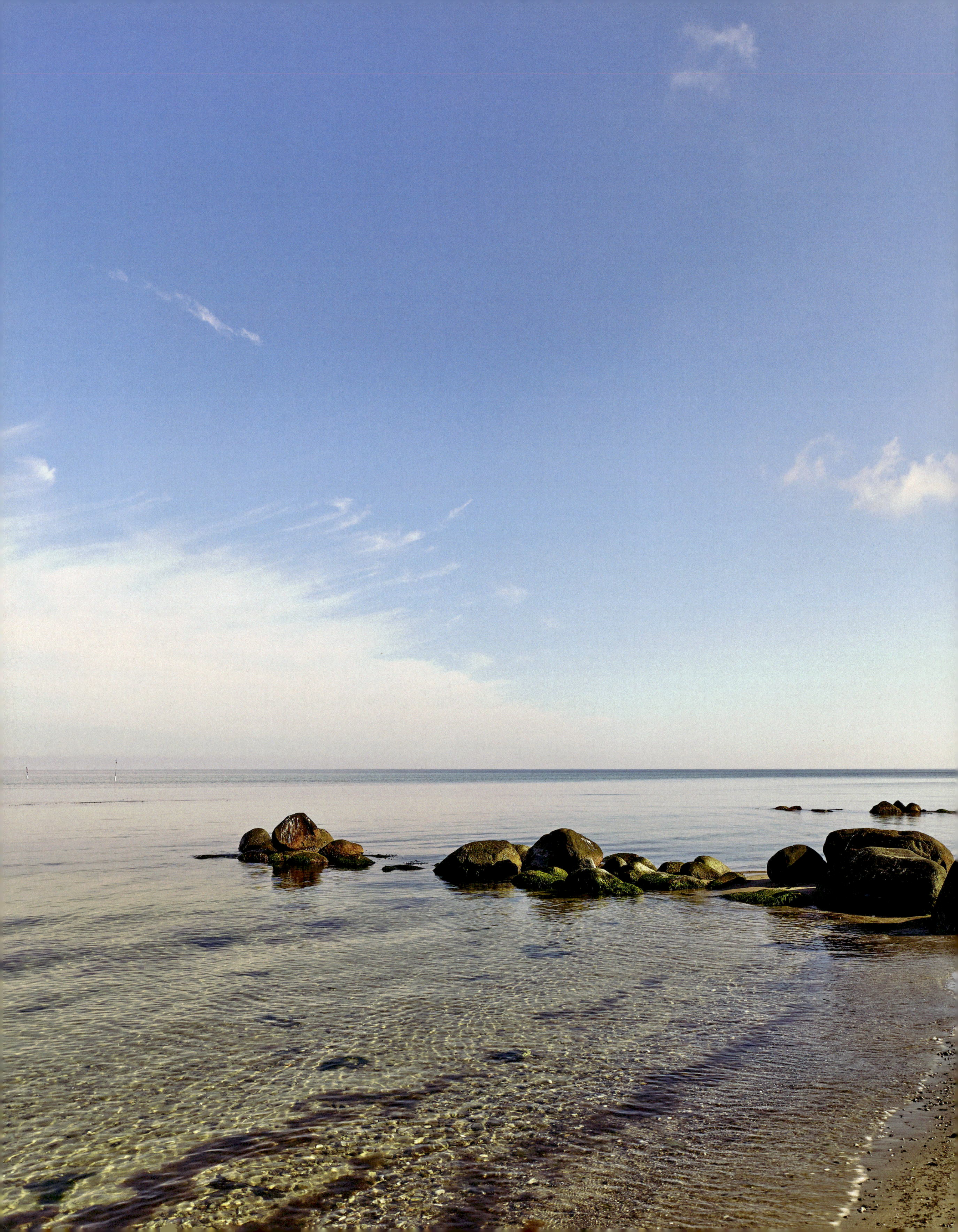

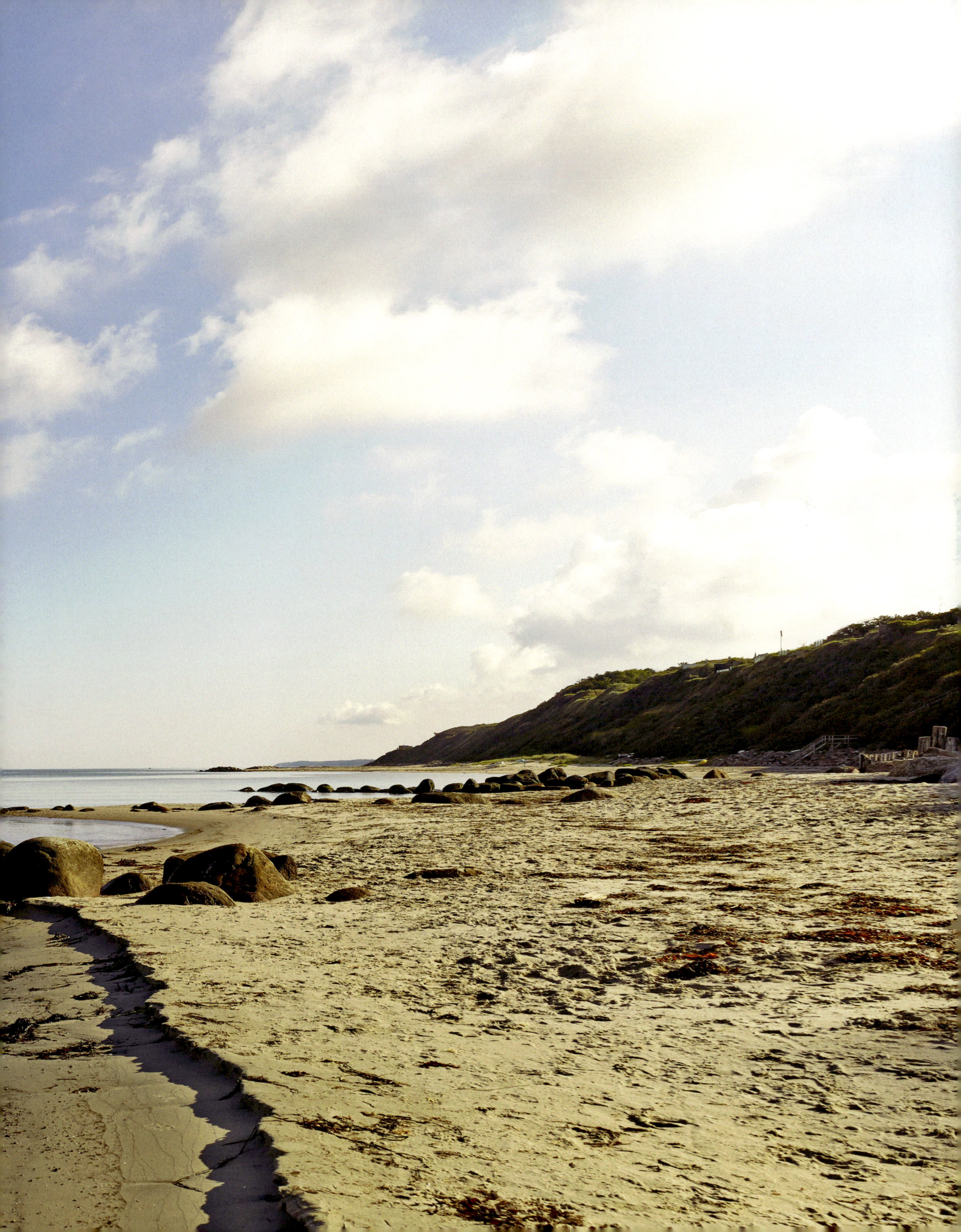

VALLE DE BRAVO, MEXICO

CASA LOS TECORRALES

VICTOR AND RICCARDO LEGORRETA
OF LEGORRETA + LEGORRETA

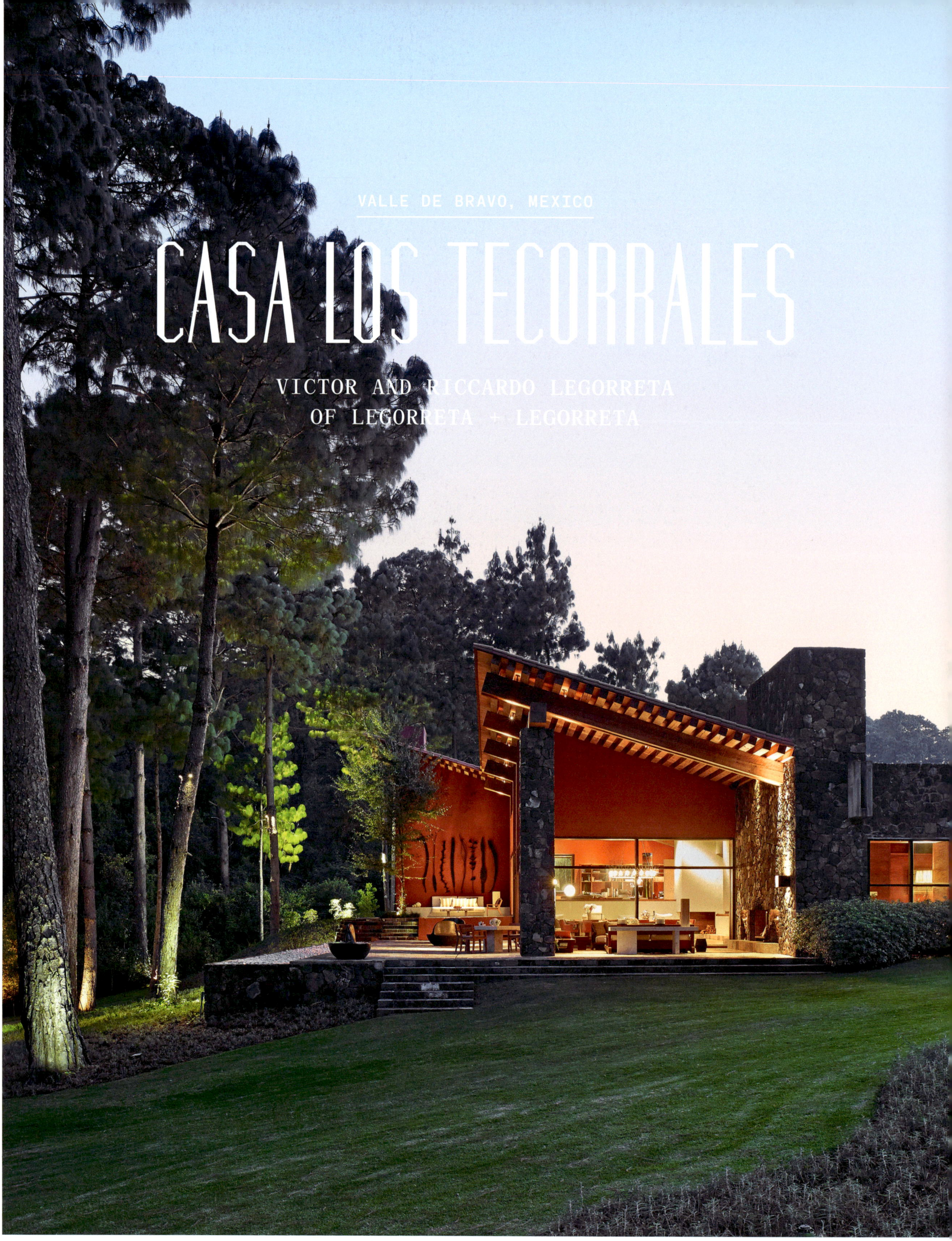

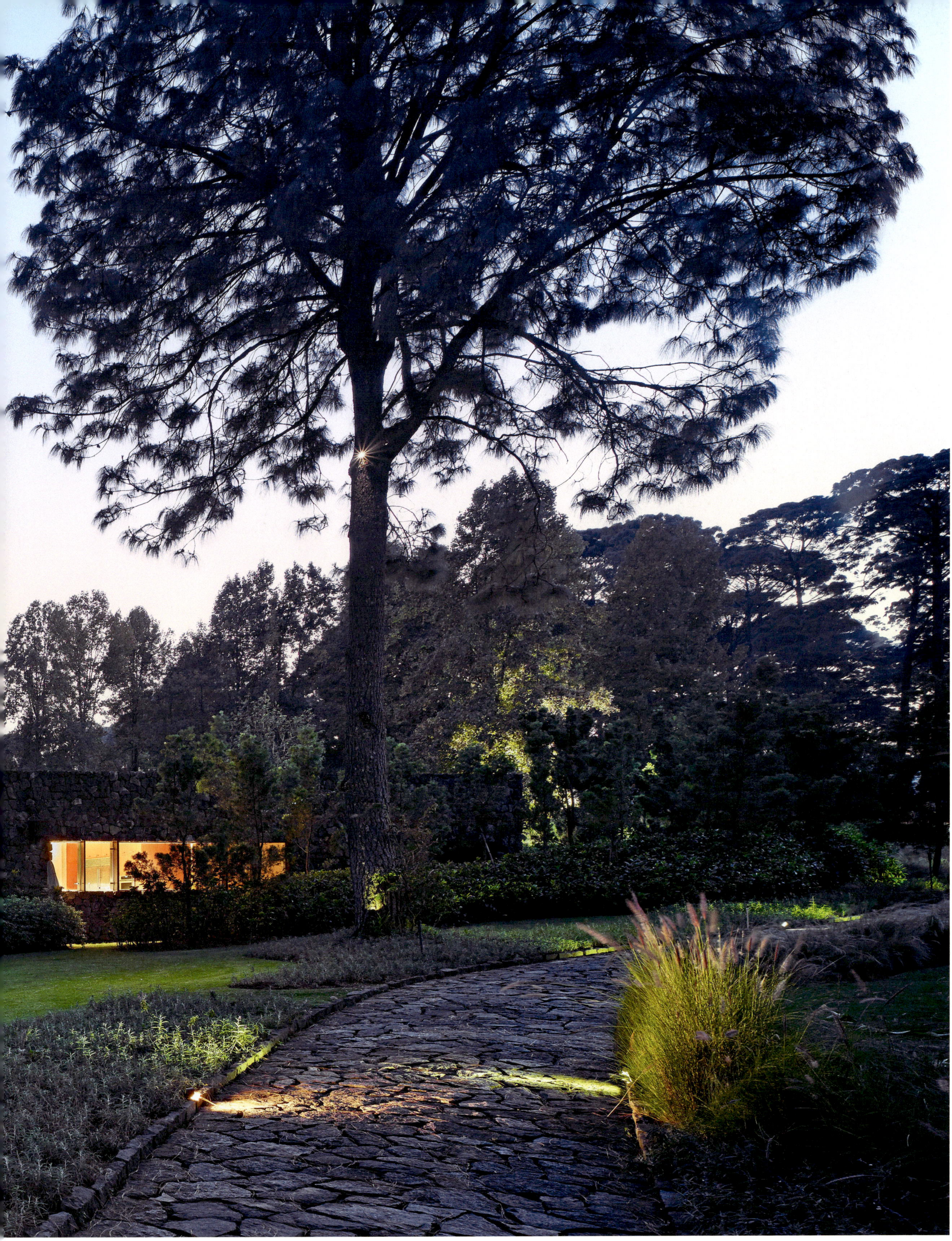

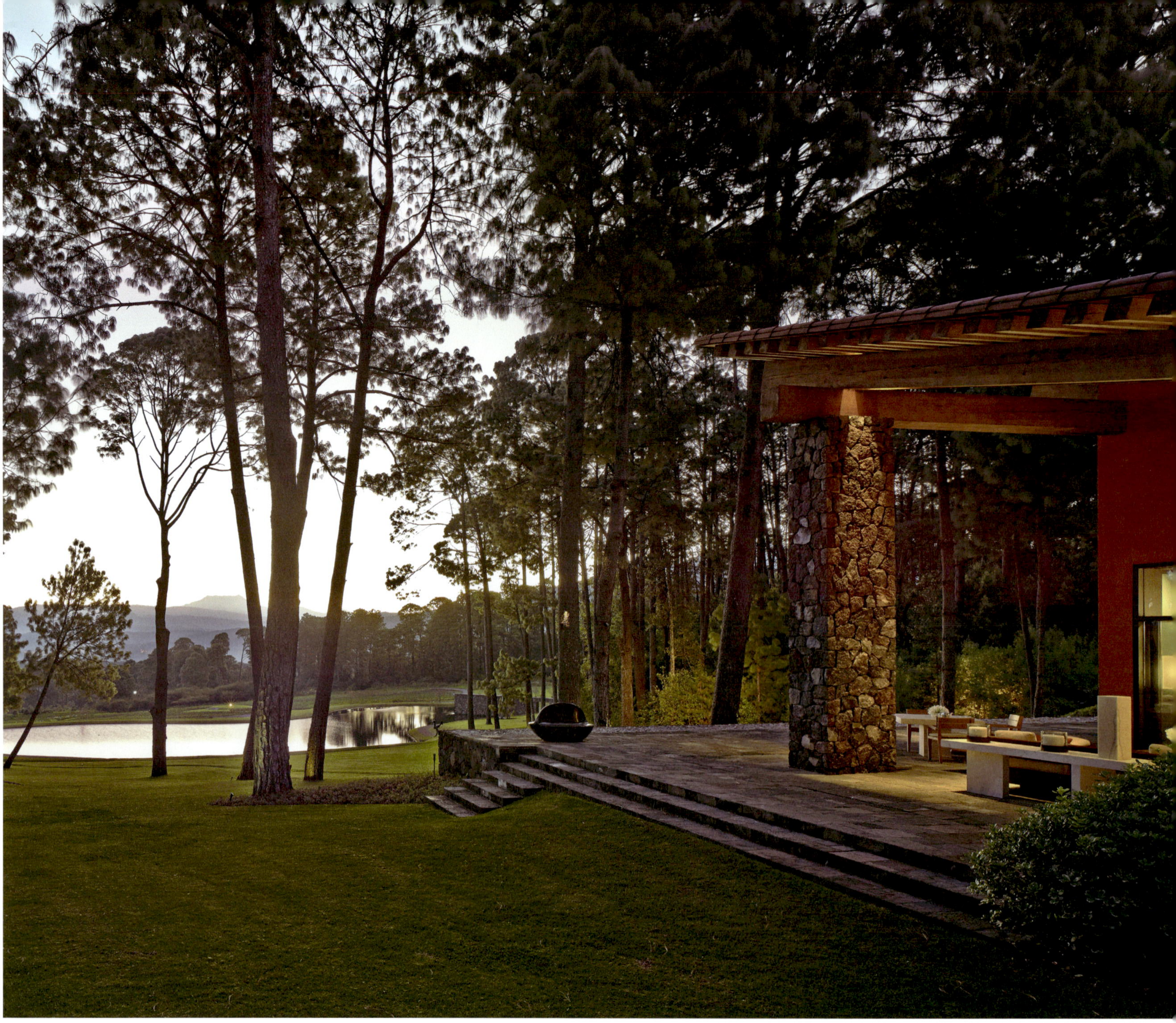

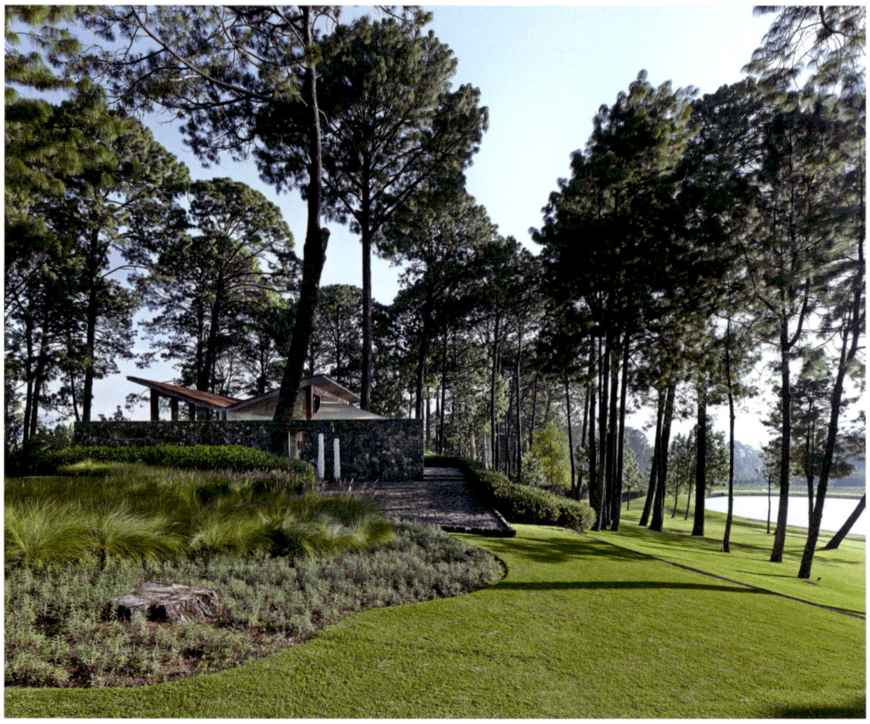

"ORTHOGONAL SCULPTURES BY THE ARTIST JORGE YAZPIK PIERCE THE SURFACE OF A SHALLOW POOL THAT TRACES THE PATH TO THE MAIN ENTRANCE."

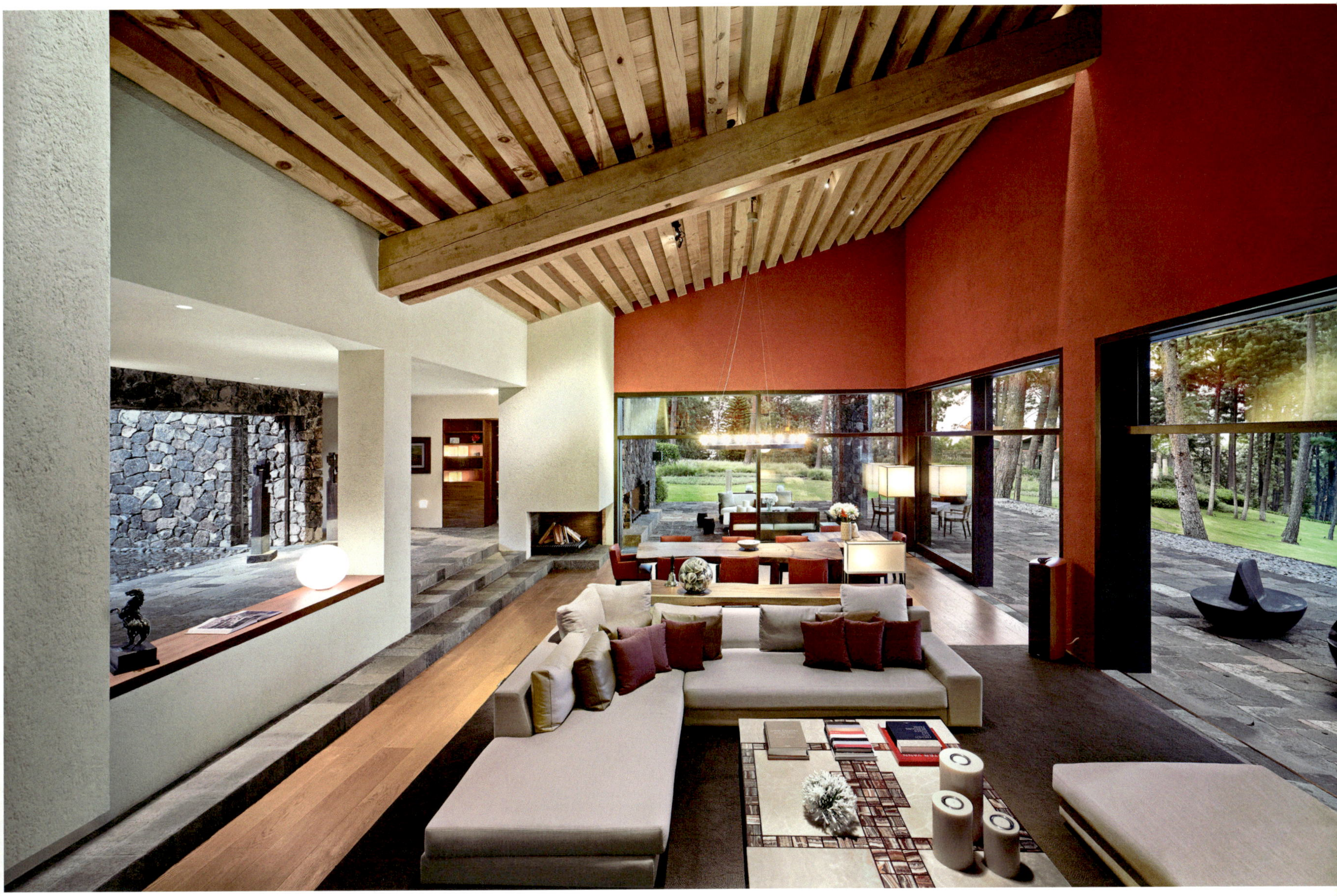

CASA LOS TECORRALES The conceptual foundation of Casa Los Tecorrales is rooted in a place between nature and art. It welcomes nature inside with its use of stone and water, and it relays art outdoors through sculpture. This interplay achieves a fine balance between the two worlds that results in a general coherency.

It took the owners of Casa Los Tecorrales four years to acquire the separate lots in Valle de Bravo that make up the 2,300-square-meter property. The businessman and his wife then turned to the Mexican architecture firm Legorreta + Legorreta and requested a design that incorporated their passions for nature and art in their new home.

This project was one of the last that Victor Legorreta worked on with his father—the esteemed architect Riccardo Legorreta—before he passed away in 2011. The father and son duo faced what Victor describes as "a beautiful challenge": choosing the site of the house from a multitude of possible locations. Overwhelmed by the beauty of each spot, they made a sensible choice to scatter separate buildings throughout. As a result, the expansive property comprises a main residence, guest quarters, a stable, a gatekeeper's residence, and a pool house. Stone and terracotta-colored plaster recur in each building, as do the steeply angled roofs, which lends coherency to the site.

The 850-square-meter main residence features an open living and dining area, a cinema, a master bedroom, a library, and a guest bedroom. The combined living and dining room opens onto a stone terrace that provides additional seating and affords a view of the manmade lake to the east. At 6,700-square-meters, the lake was a significant addition to the property, but it serves more than an aesthetic purpose. Since the climate of Valle de Bravo is one of dramatic contrasts, alternating between six months of rain and six months of drought, the artificial lake also acts as an irrigation system.

Just as the pool house draws water into the home, some of the art that adorns the interior also makes its way outside. Orthogonal sculptures by the artist Jorge Yazpik ~

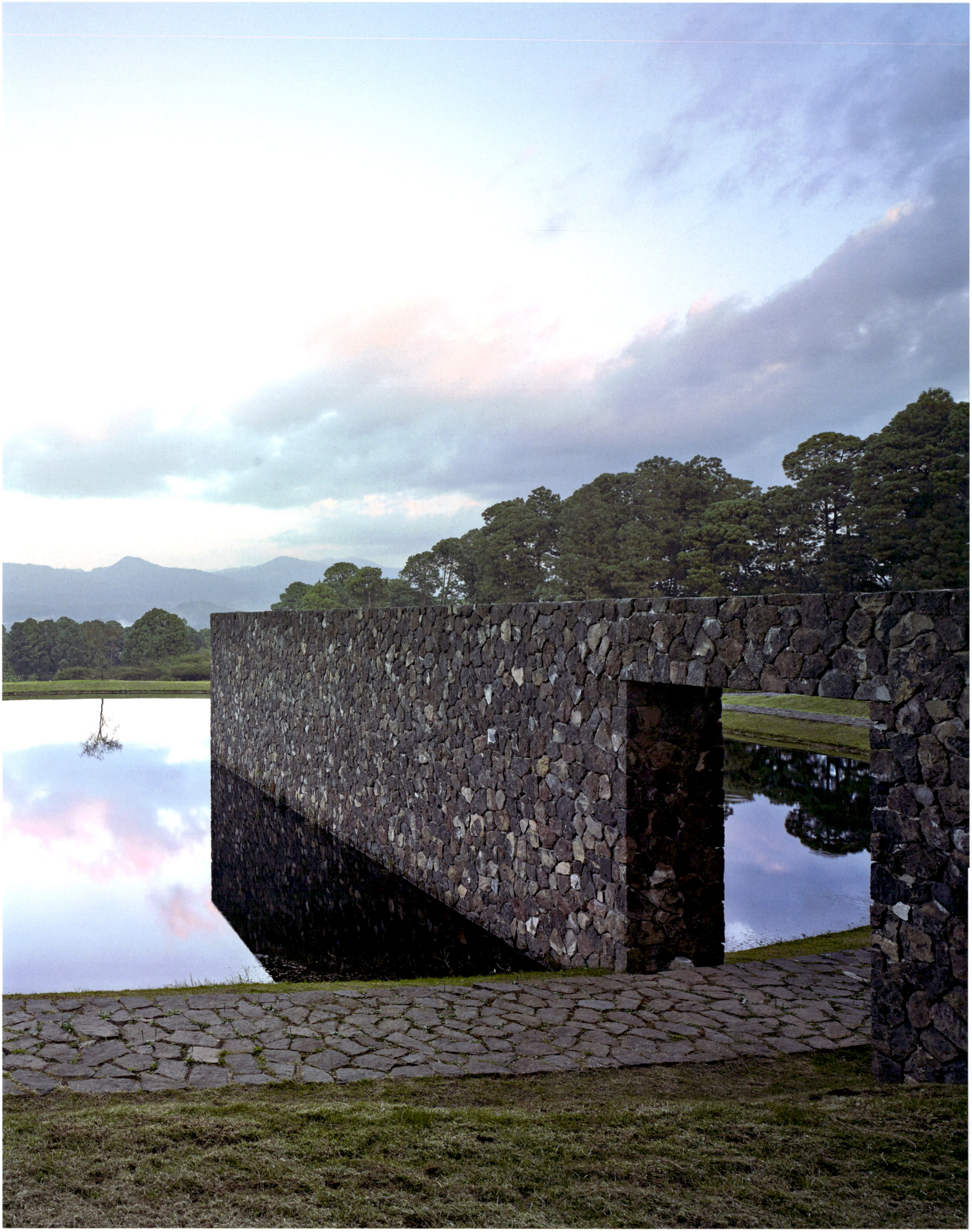

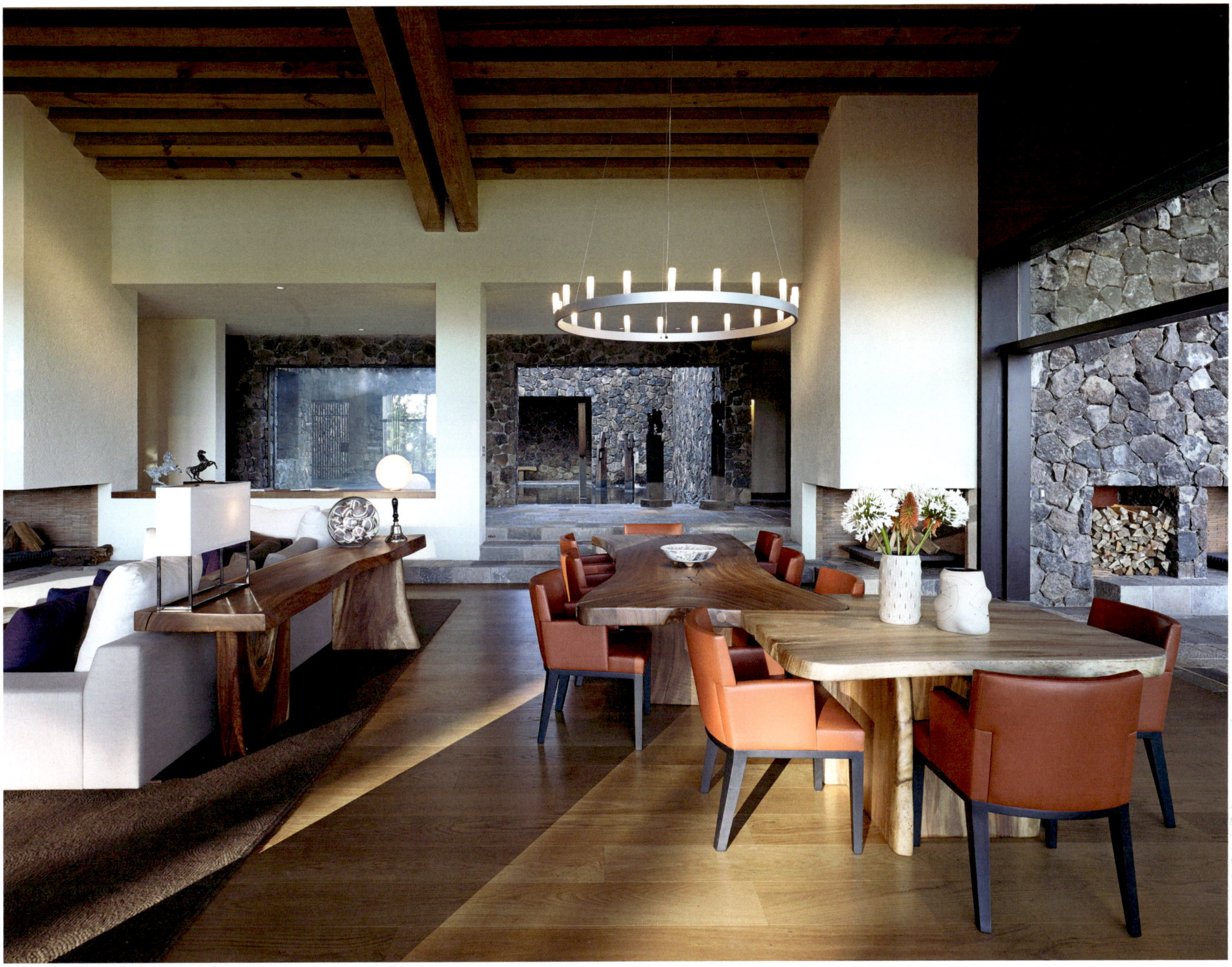

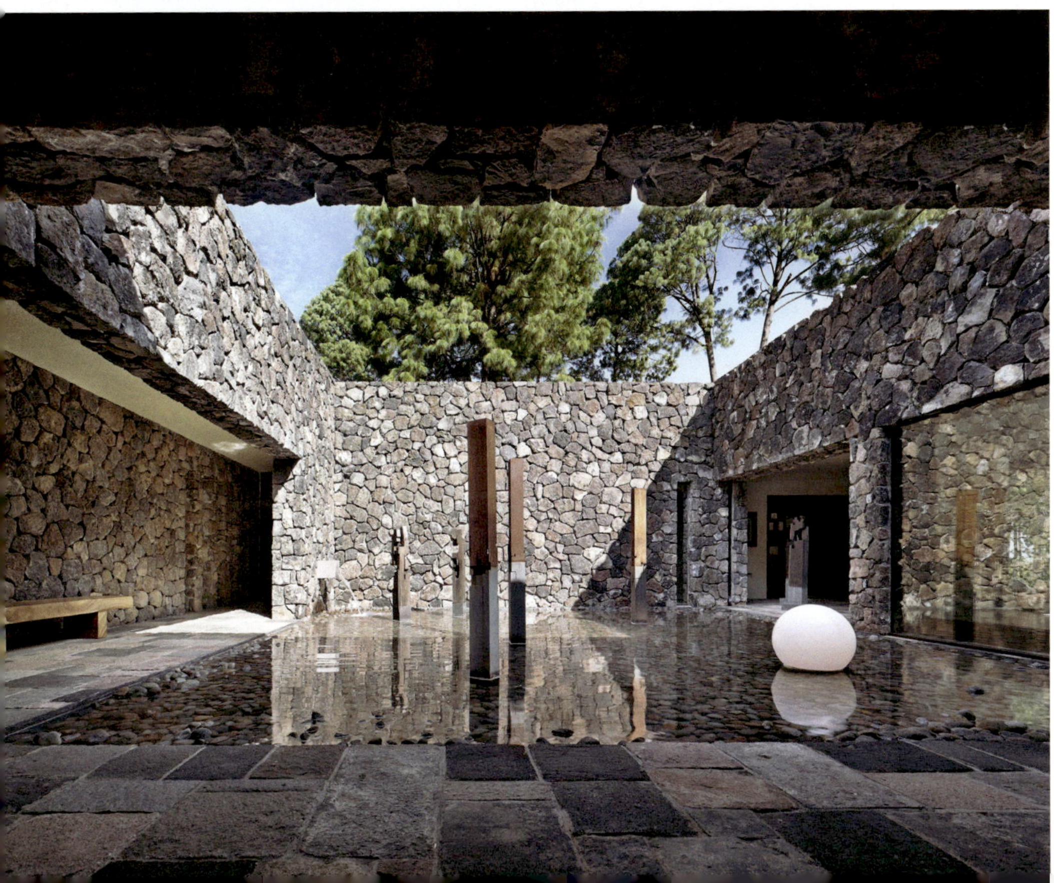

THE FATHER AND SON DUO FACED WHAT VICTOR LEGORRETA DESCRIBES AS "A BEAUTIFUL CHALLENGE."

pierce the surface of a shallow pool that traces the path to the main entrance. Nature and art achieve a comfortable balance in the house and throughout the property, reflecting both the identity of its owners and the skill of the architects. ◆

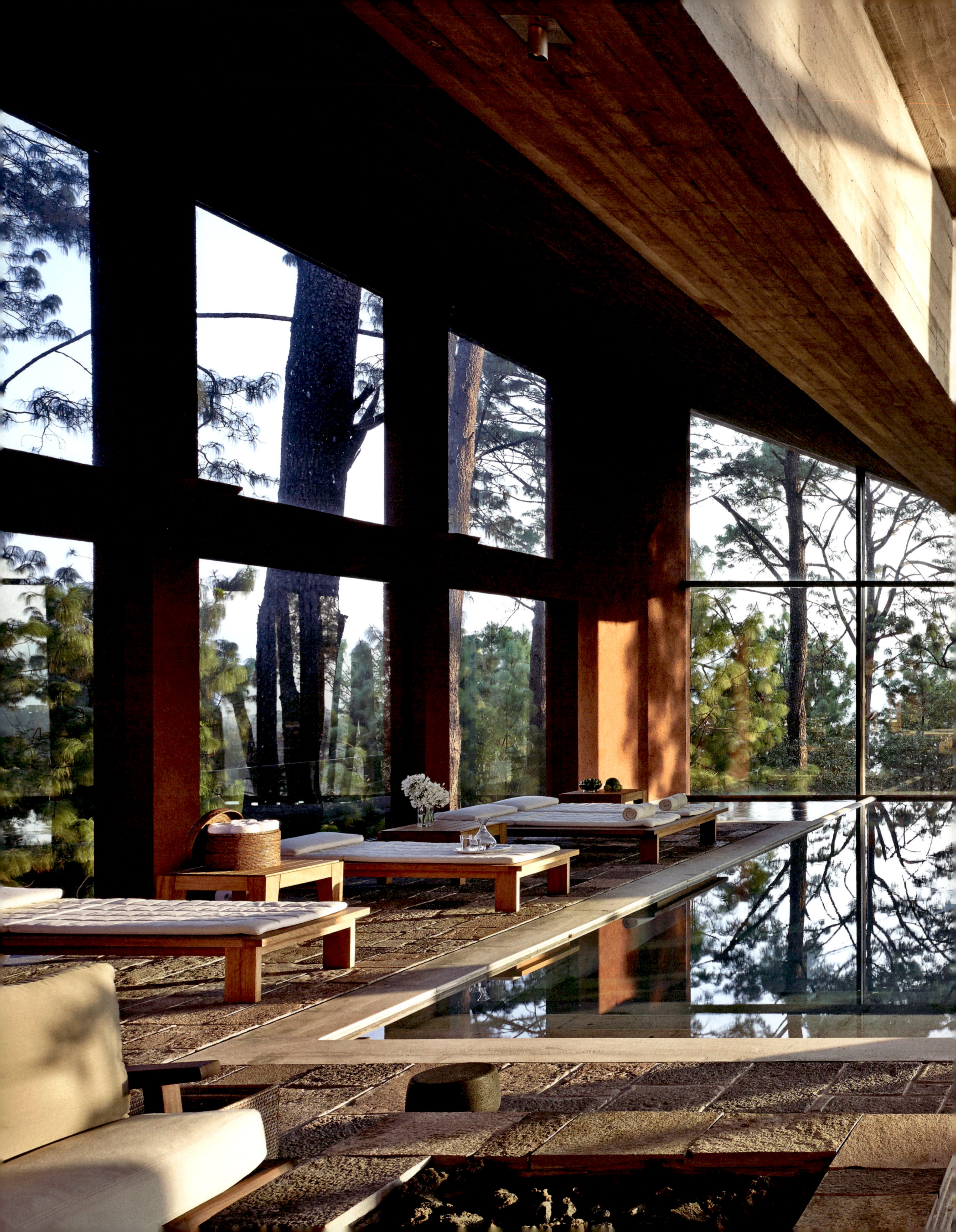

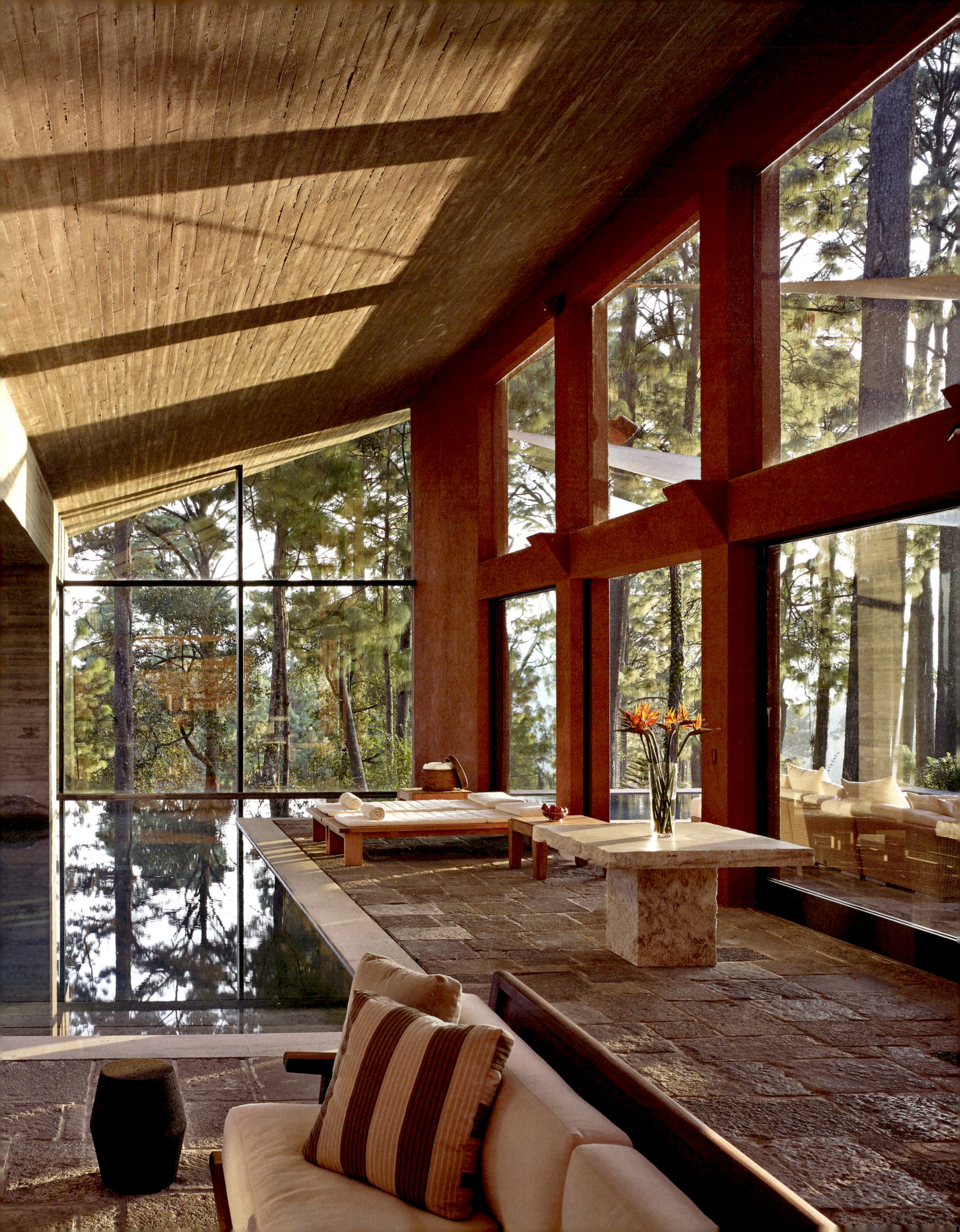

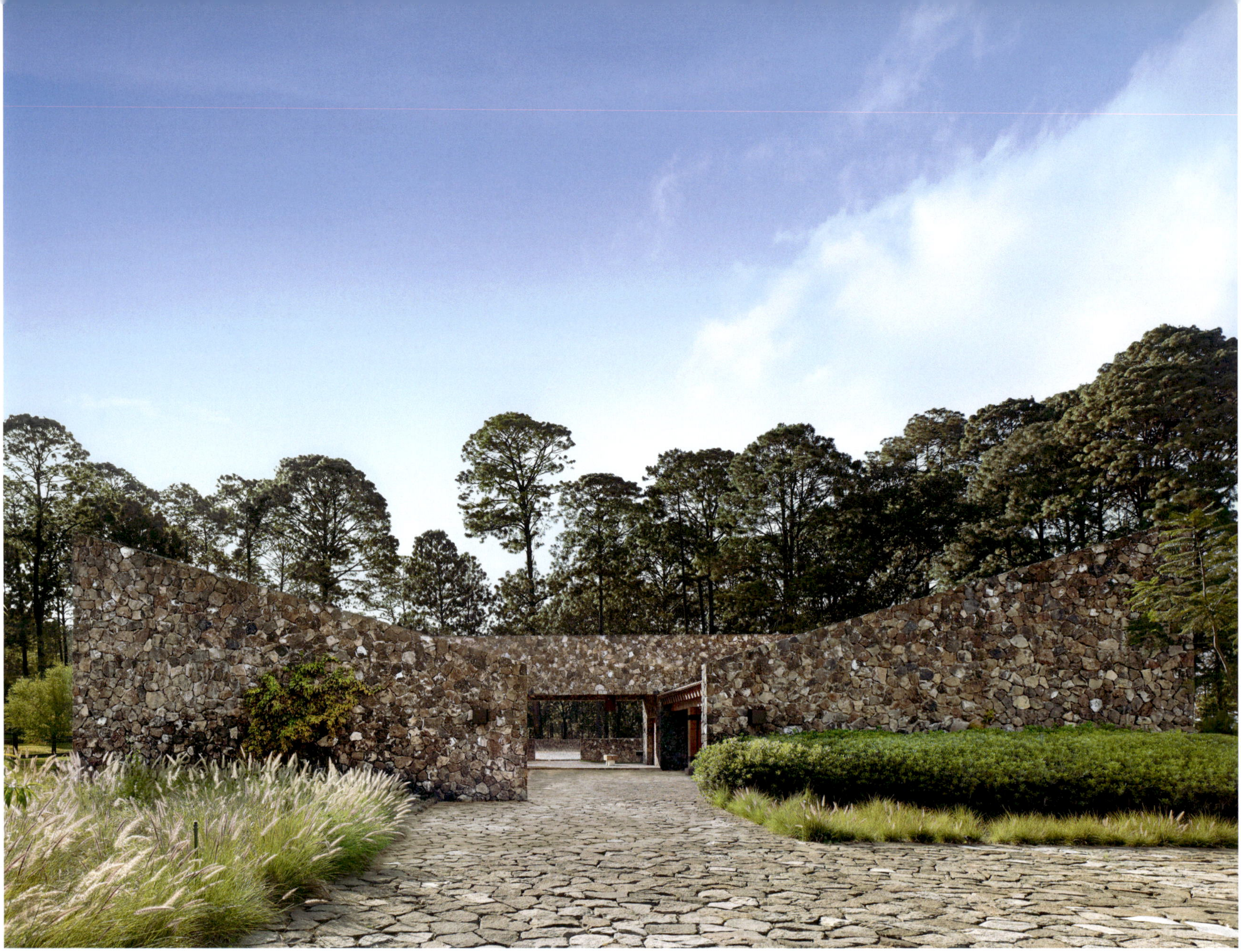

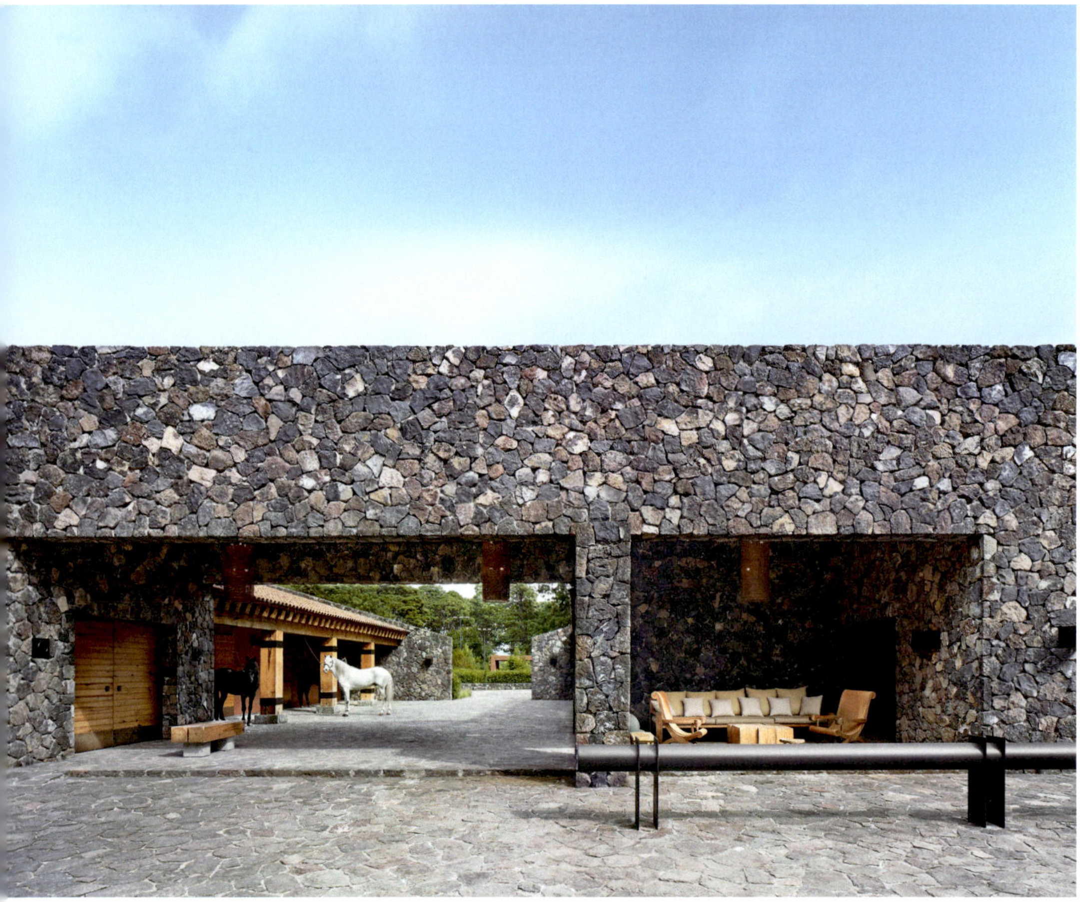

"NATURE AND ART ACHIEVE A COMFORTABLE BALANCE IN THE HOUSE AND THROUGHOUT THE PROPERTY, REFLECTING BOTH THE IDENTITY OF ITS OWNERS AND THE SKILL OF THE ARCHITECTS."

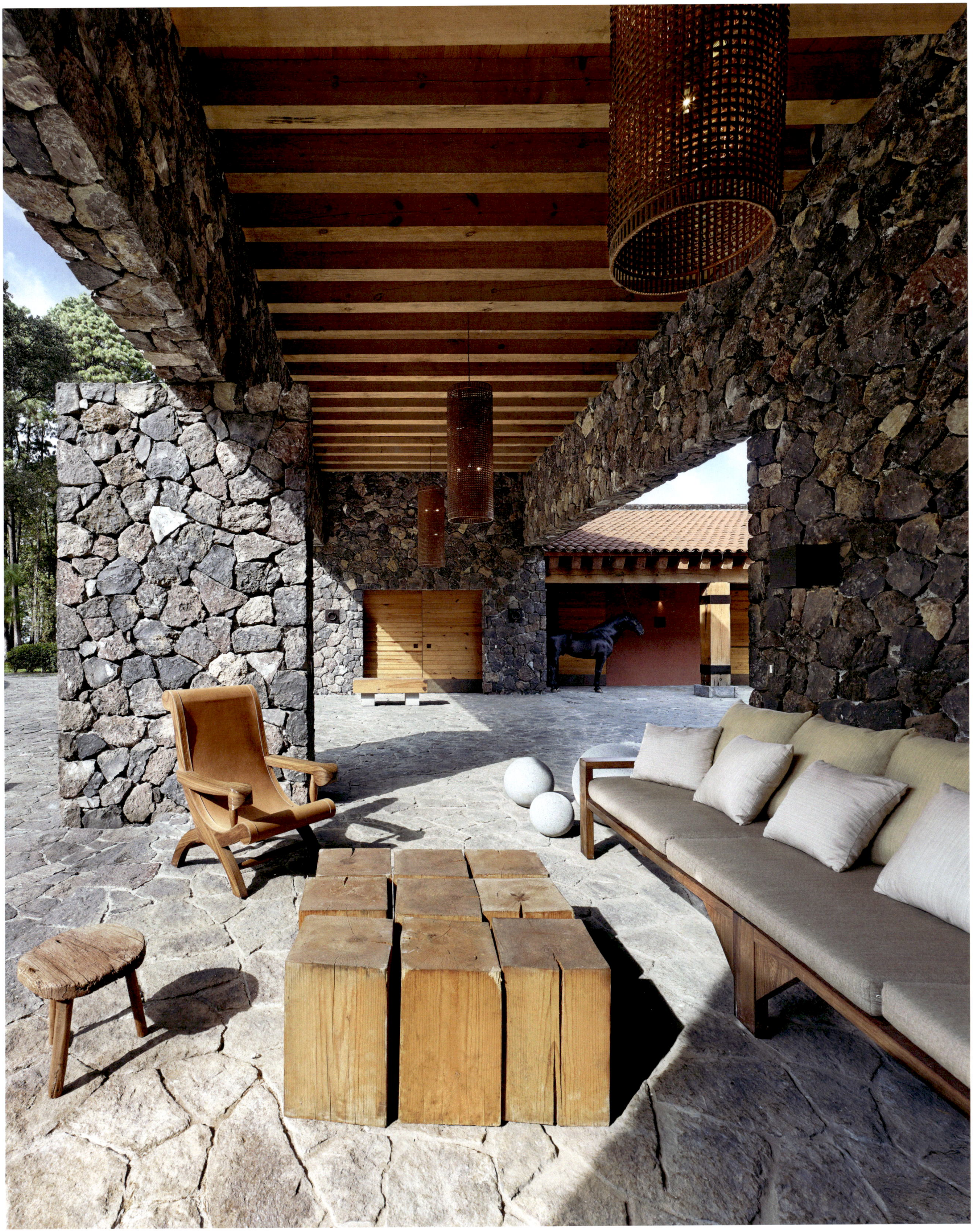

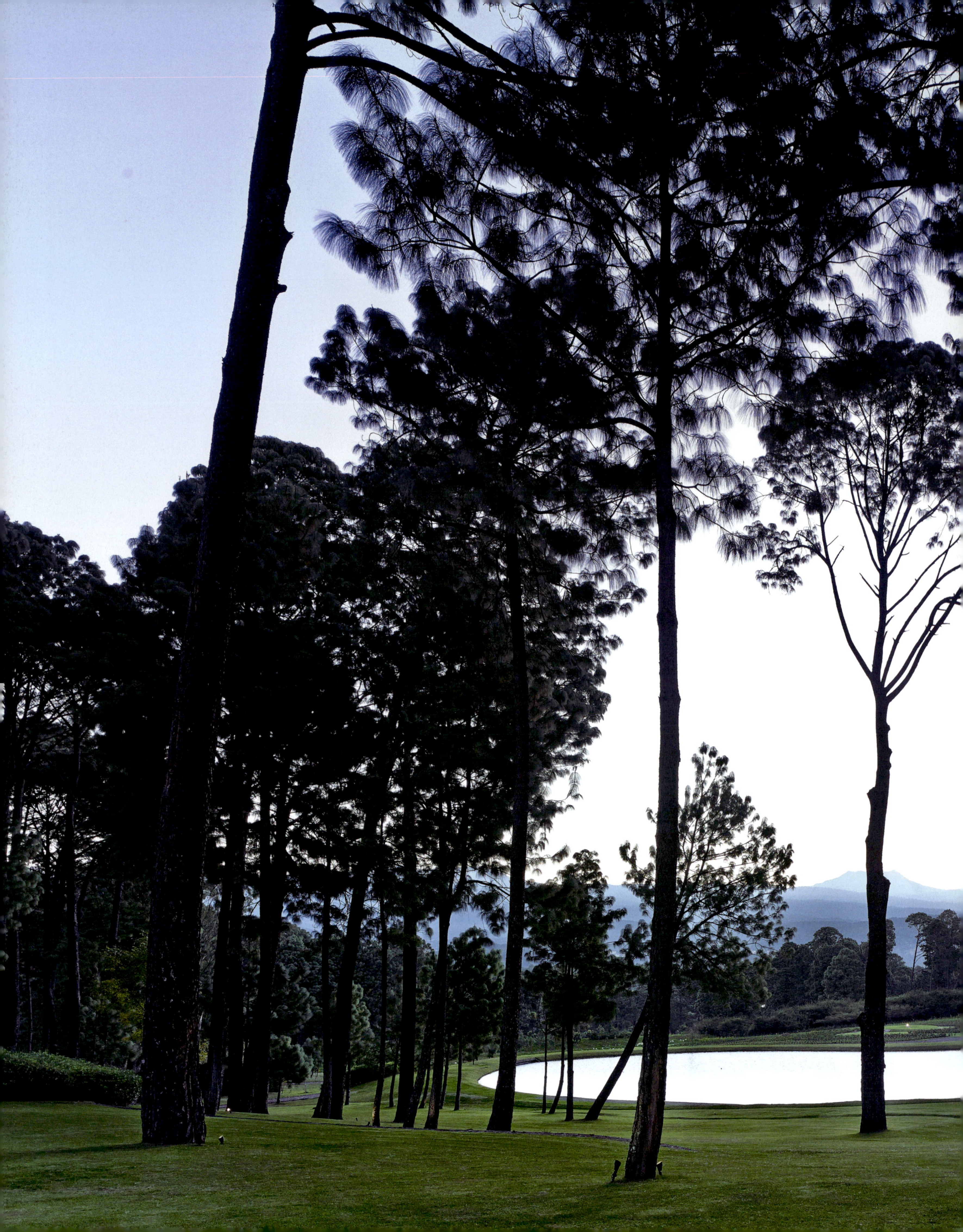

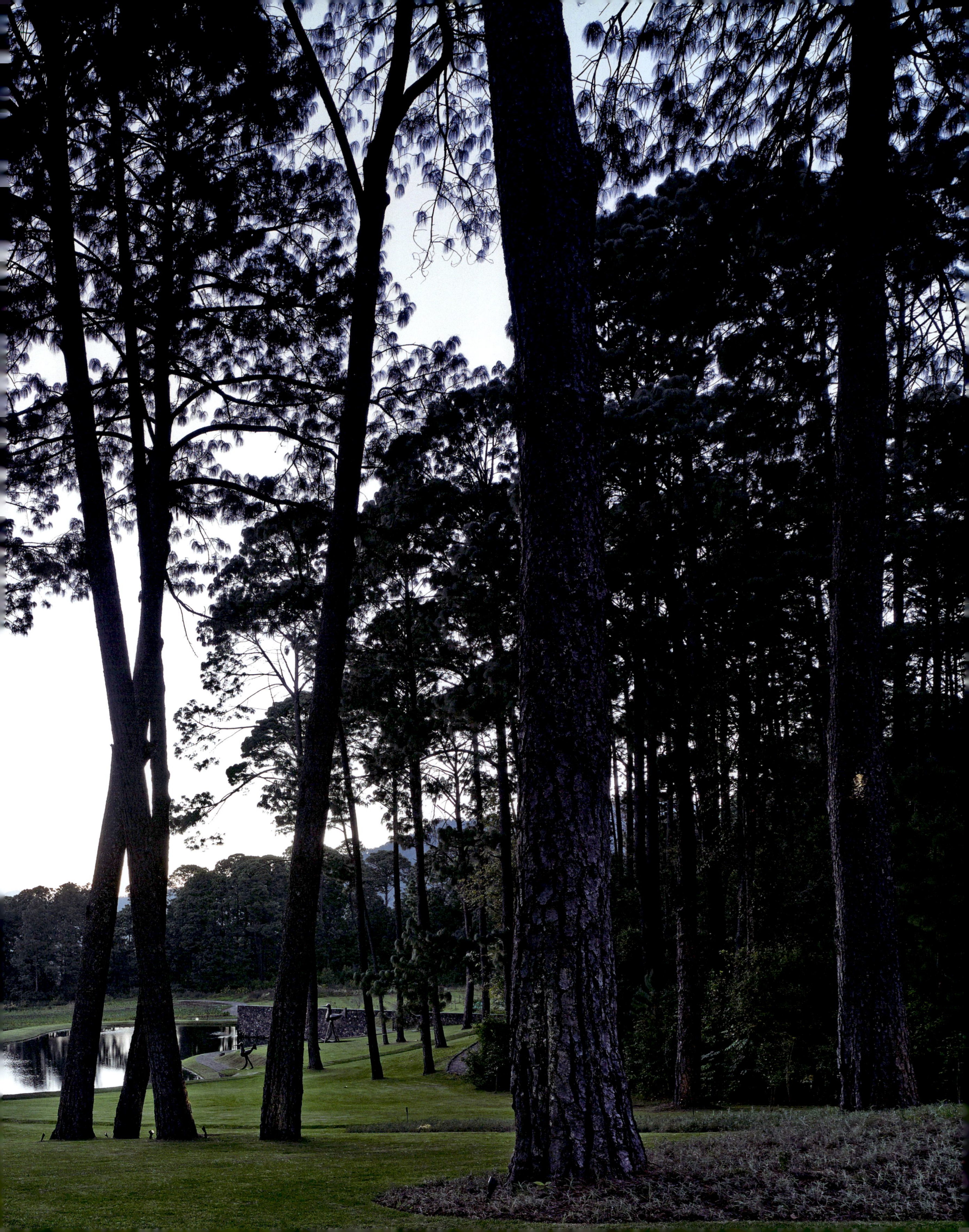

BRISSAGO, SWITZERLAND

CASA BRISSAGO

JÉRÔME DE MEURON
OF WESPI DE MEURON ROMEO ARCHITETTI

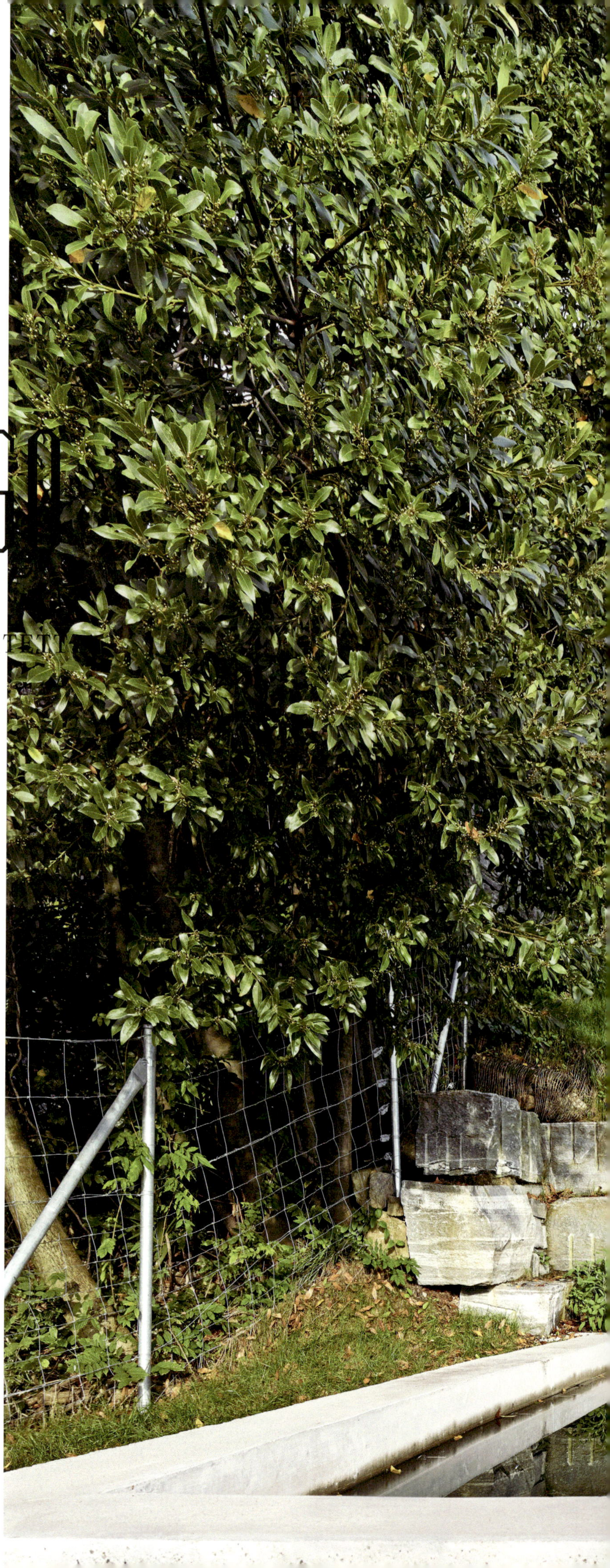

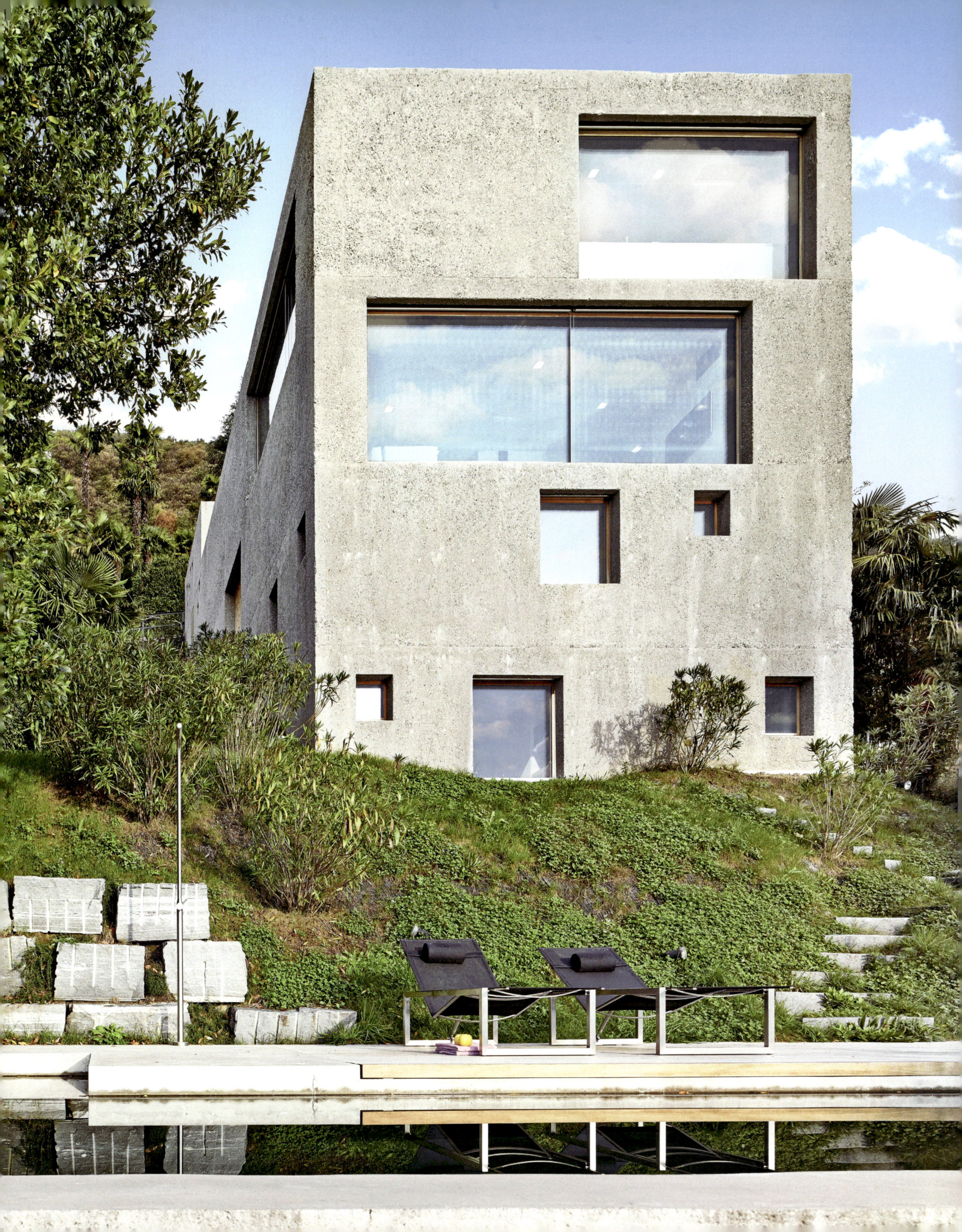

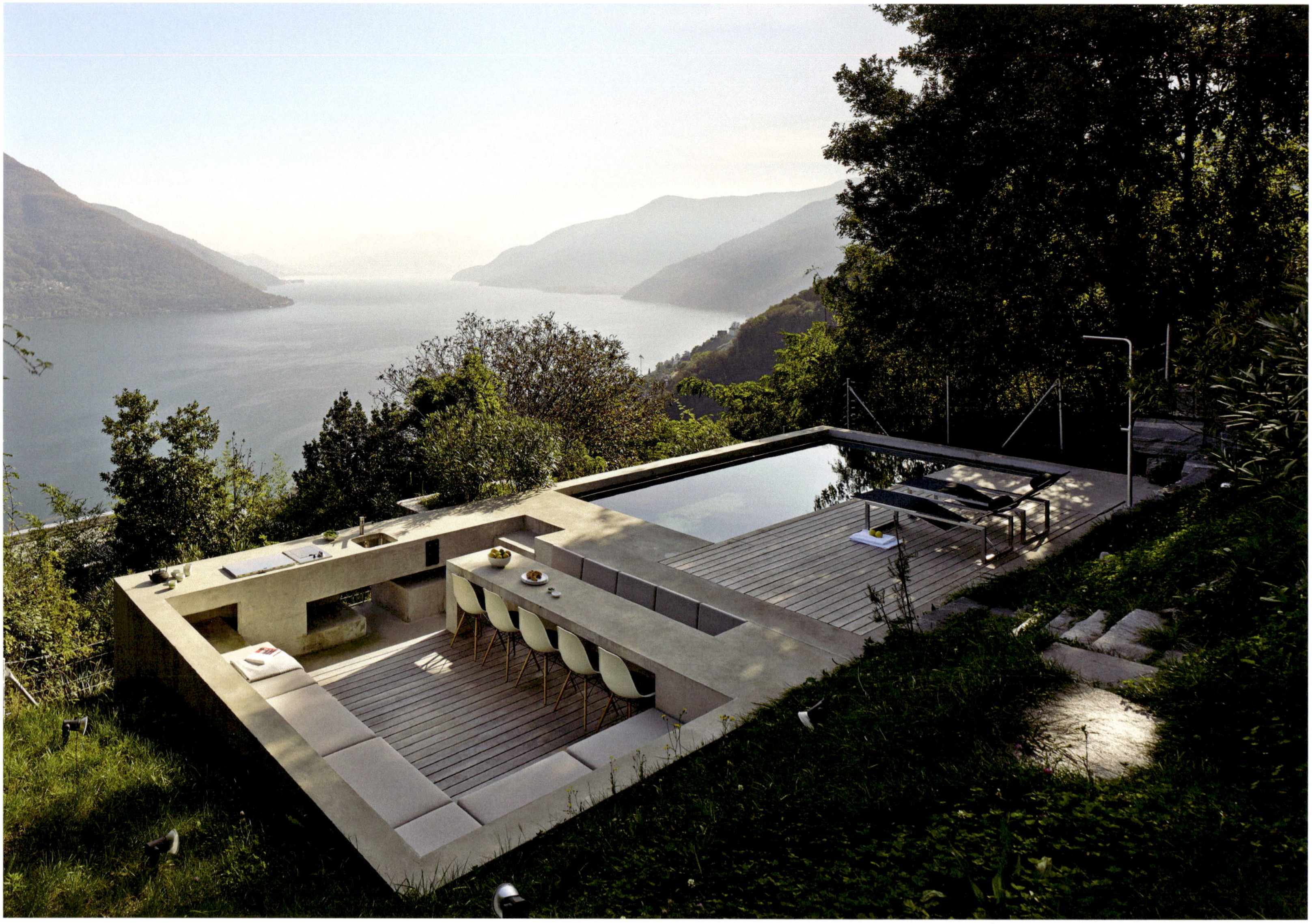

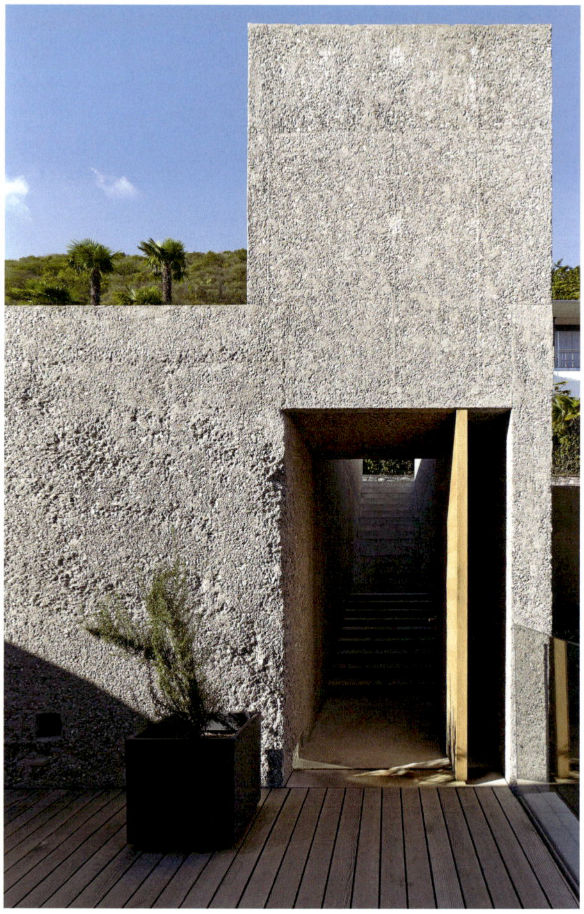

CASA BRISSAGO This hideaway looms on a Swiss hillside. A concrete monolith, its simple shape conceals an interior complexity. From the outside, the seemingly arbitrary placement of windows hints at its labyrinth-like interior—a sprawling mix of pathways, nooks, courtyards, and corners.

The exterior of this Swiss home yields none of its secrets. From its highest point by the roadside, one can enjoy a view of Lake Maggiore totally unobscured by the modernist block below it. Capped by a simple carport and enclosed by severe concrete walls, the structure appears to be absolutely clandestine while promising an interior complexity.

From the road, the concrete monolith extends four stories down the hillside. Downstairs from the carport is an interior courtyard with an adjoining kitchen and dining room. Above the kitchen counter, an uninterrupted windowpane negotiates a clear southward view of the lake. Nearby, a bespoke oak dining table rests on a polished concrete floor. ~

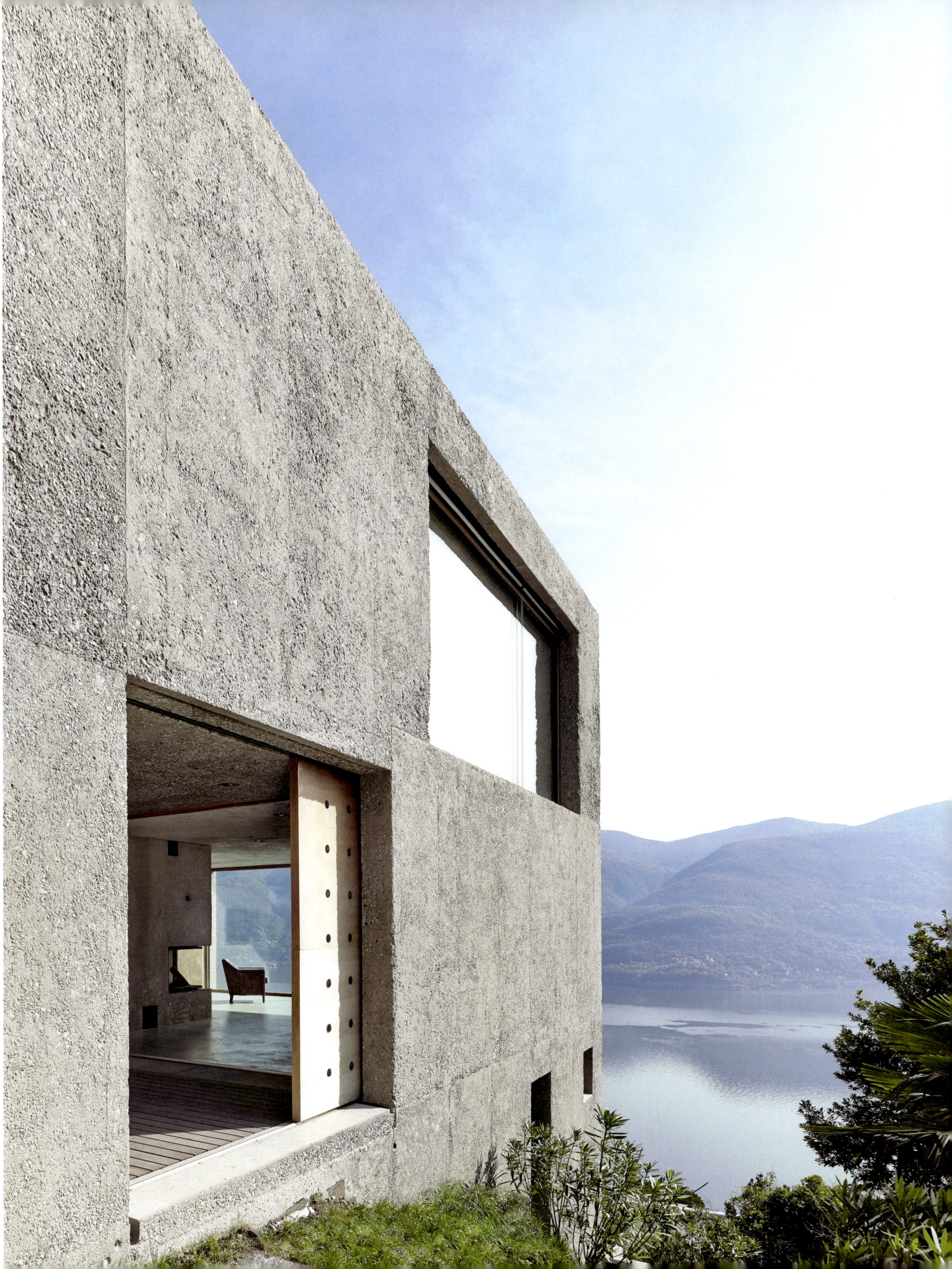

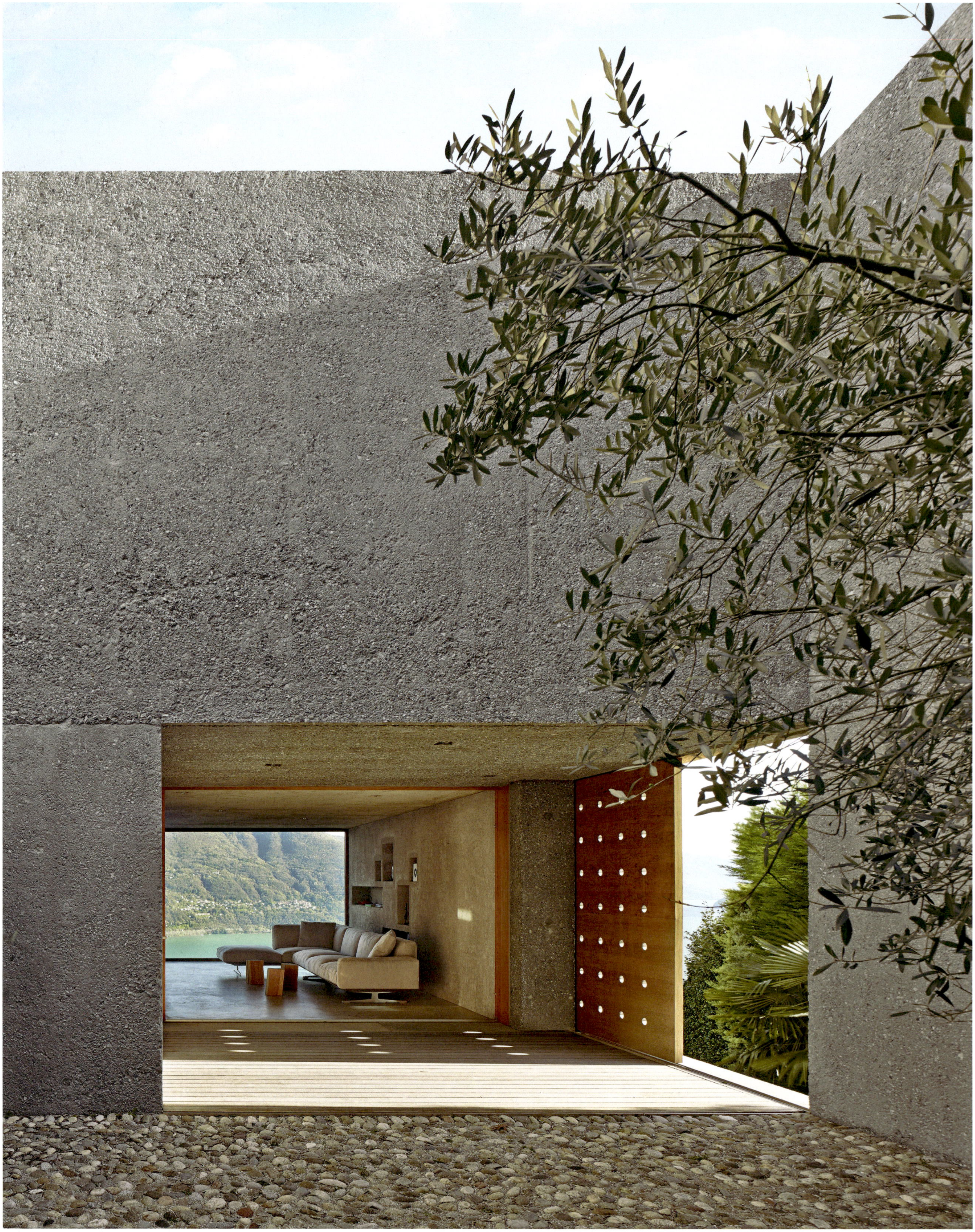

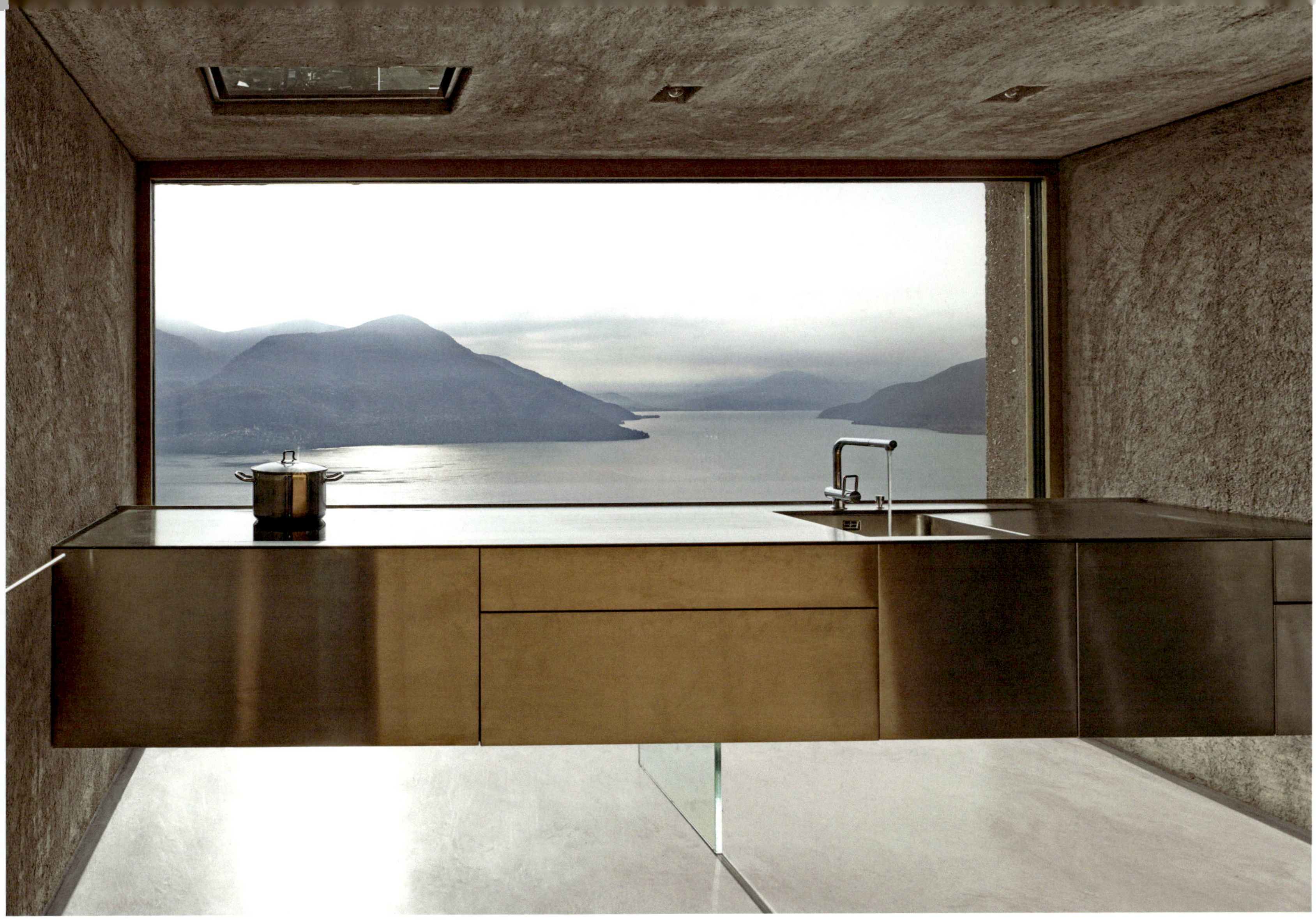

"A JUXTAPOSITION OF RAMBLING CONTENT WITH CLEAN SURFACES, THE HOUSE MELDS AN INTERIOR LABYRINTH WITH A STRICT EXTERIOR SIMPLICITY."

A lift and staircase join the fourth level to the main living area below. A corner sofa sits in front of a set of tall windows, while a unique glass-enclosed fireplace occupies an interior corner. Little nooks scattered throughout the living room's walls mirror the non-linear placement of windows in the concrete exterior. A wood-paneled corridor leads to the main courtyard, designed by architect Jérôme de Meuron to be "the heart of the house." As he explains, "It's where different paths join together, like in a historic village." To the side of the courtyard, a wooden door slides open to reveal a pathway leading to a lakeside refuge, complete with a pool and sunken kitchen area.

Two bedrooms, a bathroom, and an exercise area comprise the next level, while the first floor is home to the master bedroom, which has its own bathroom and sauna. Pathways run off these lower levels as well, snaking away to the outdoor area. A juxtaposition of rambling content with clean surfaces, the house melds an interior labyrinth with a strict exterior simplicity. ◆

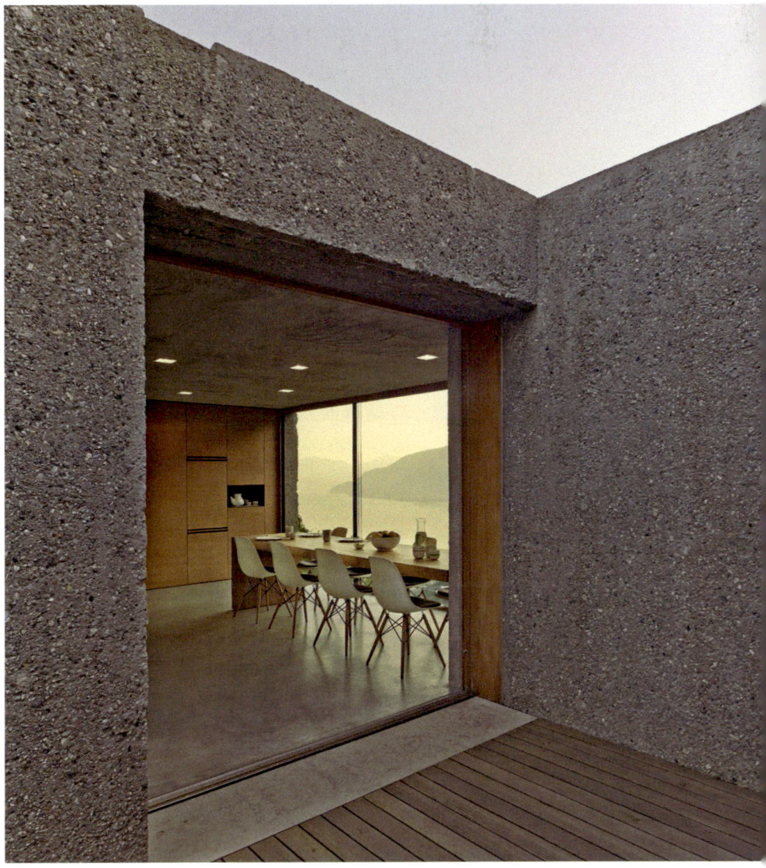

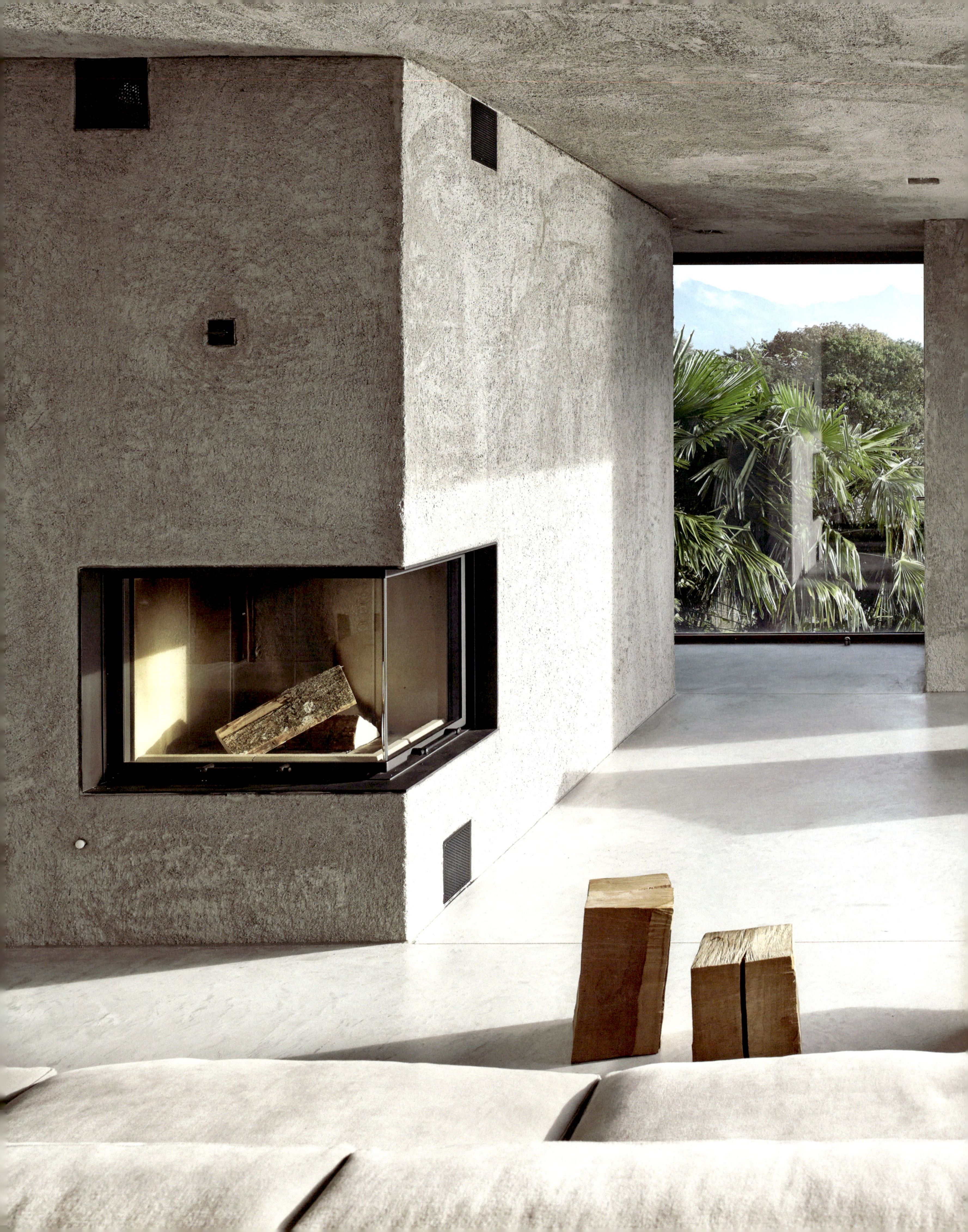

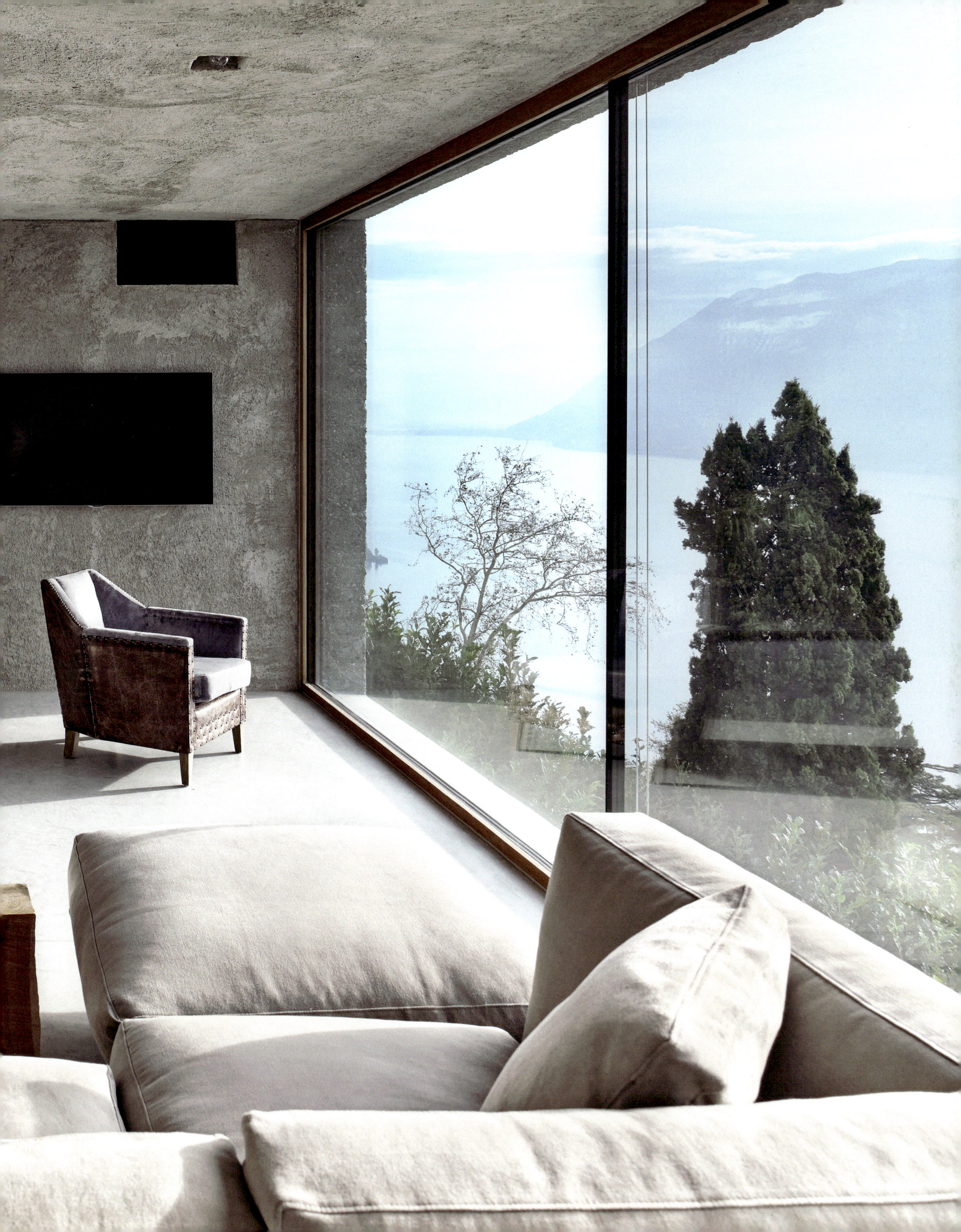

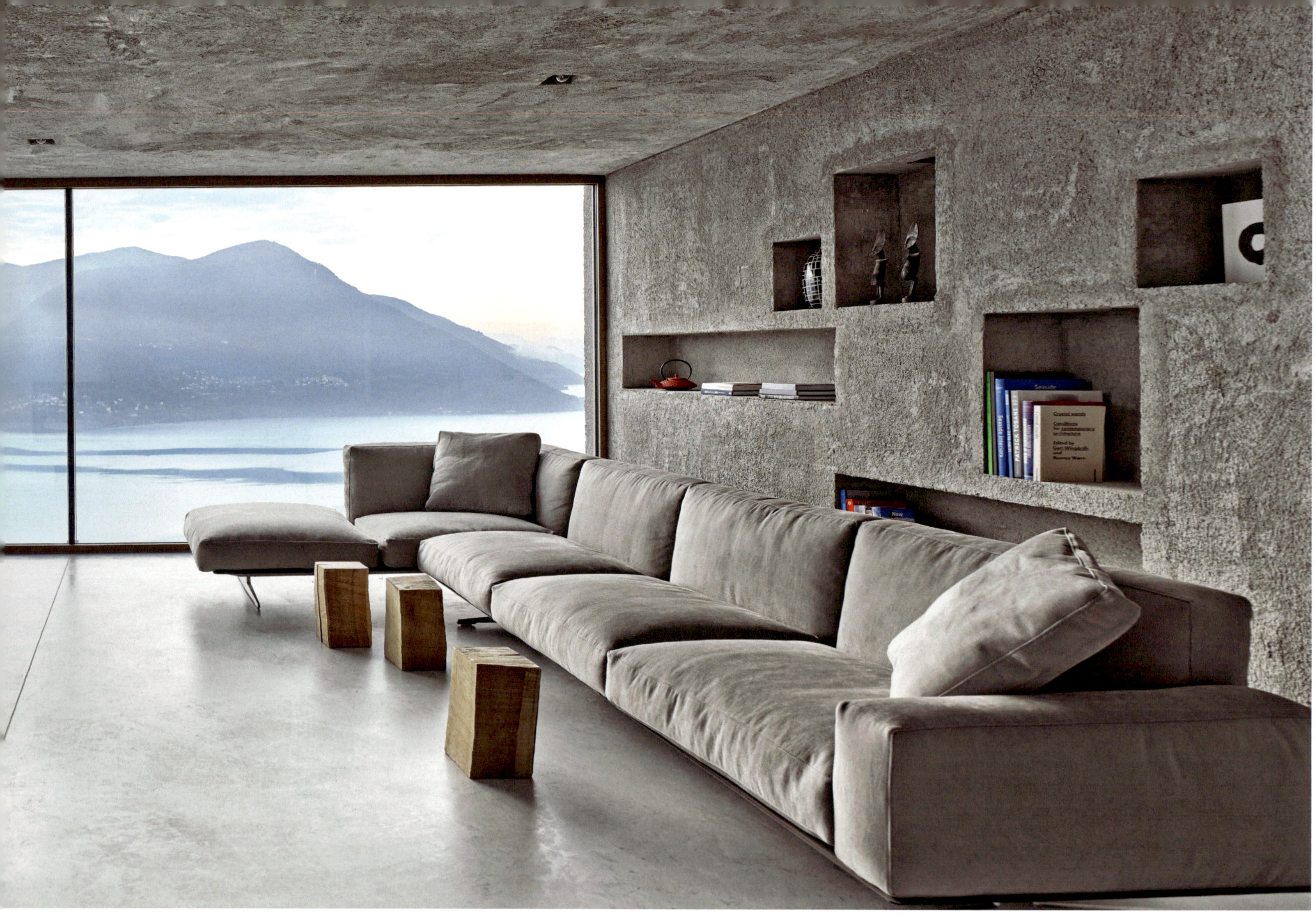

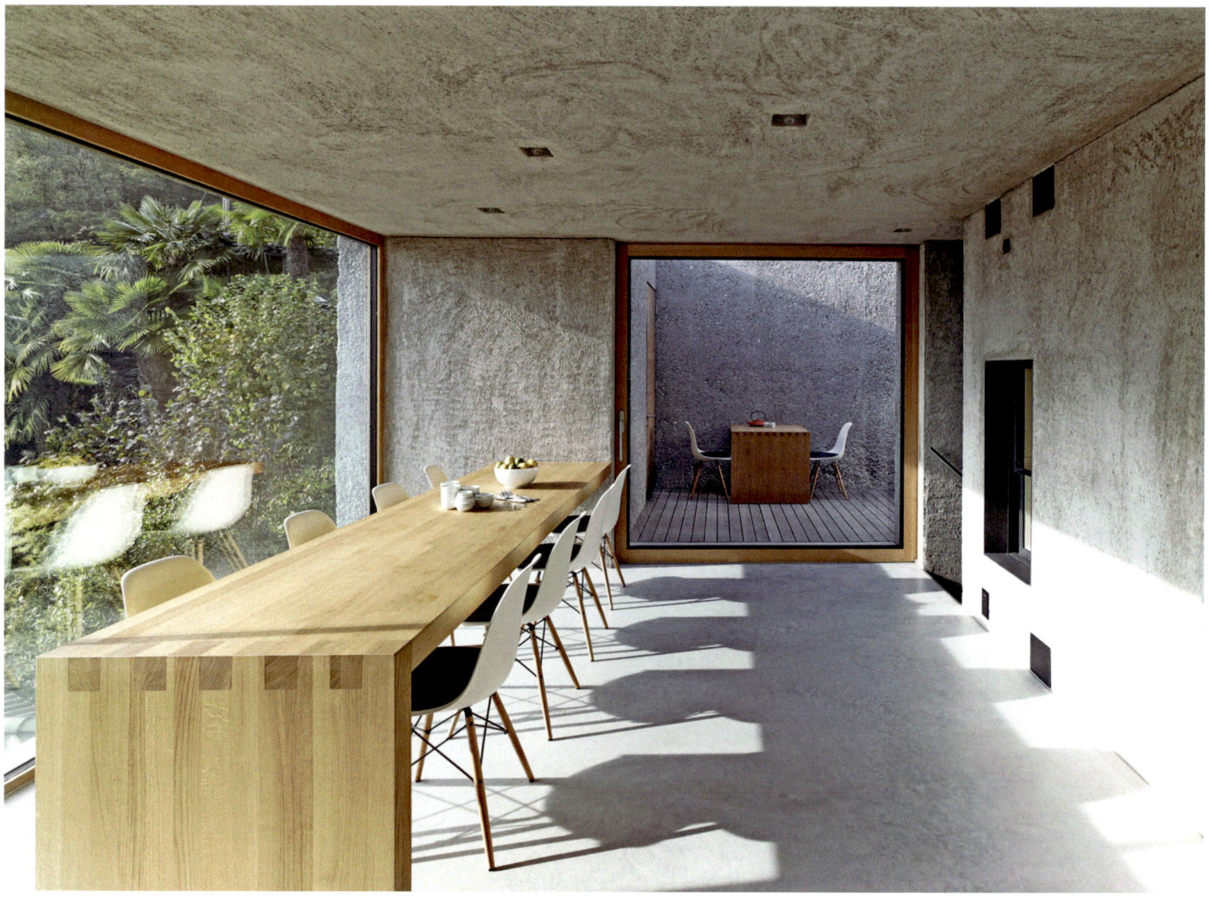

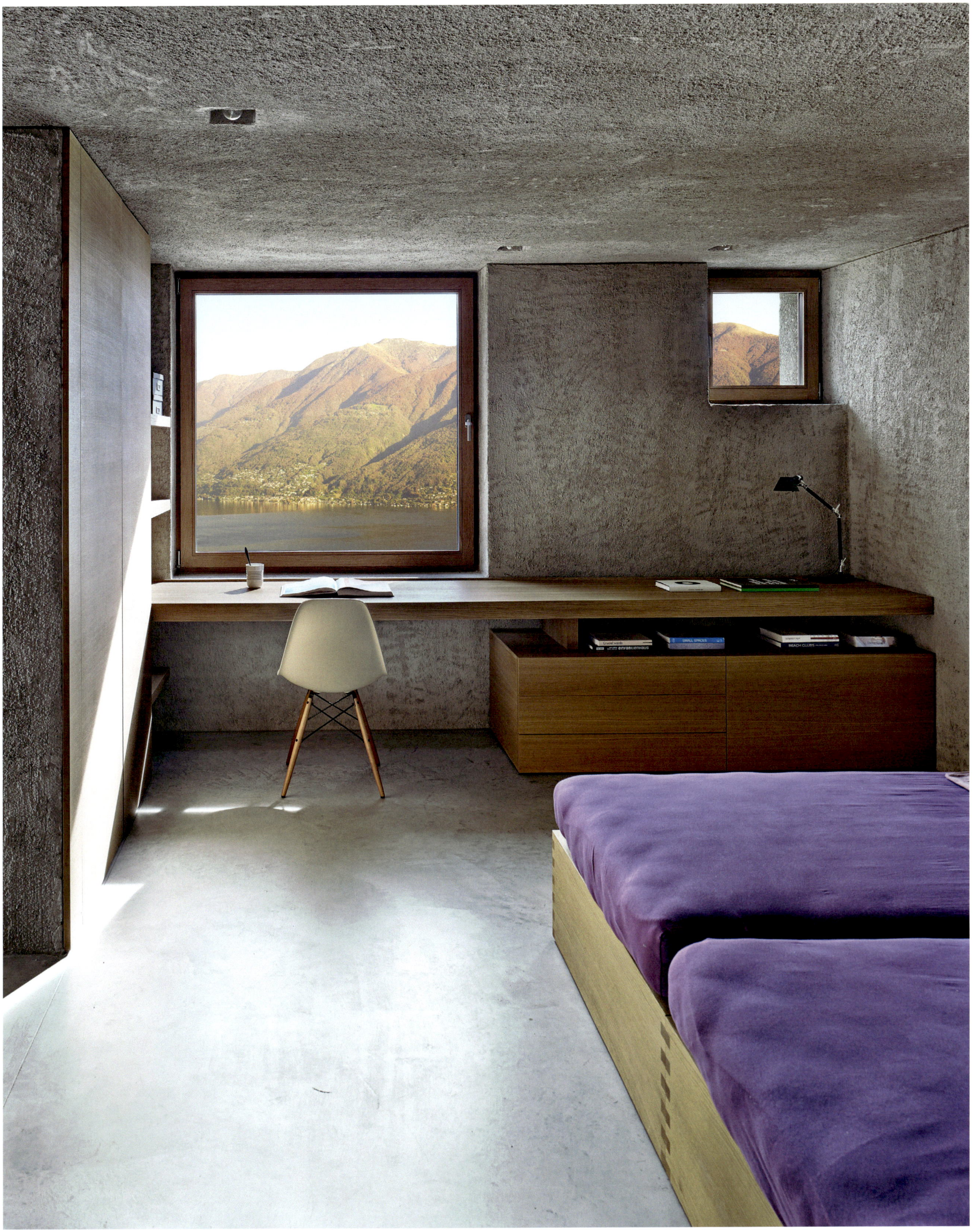
SMALL SPACES
BEACH CLUBS

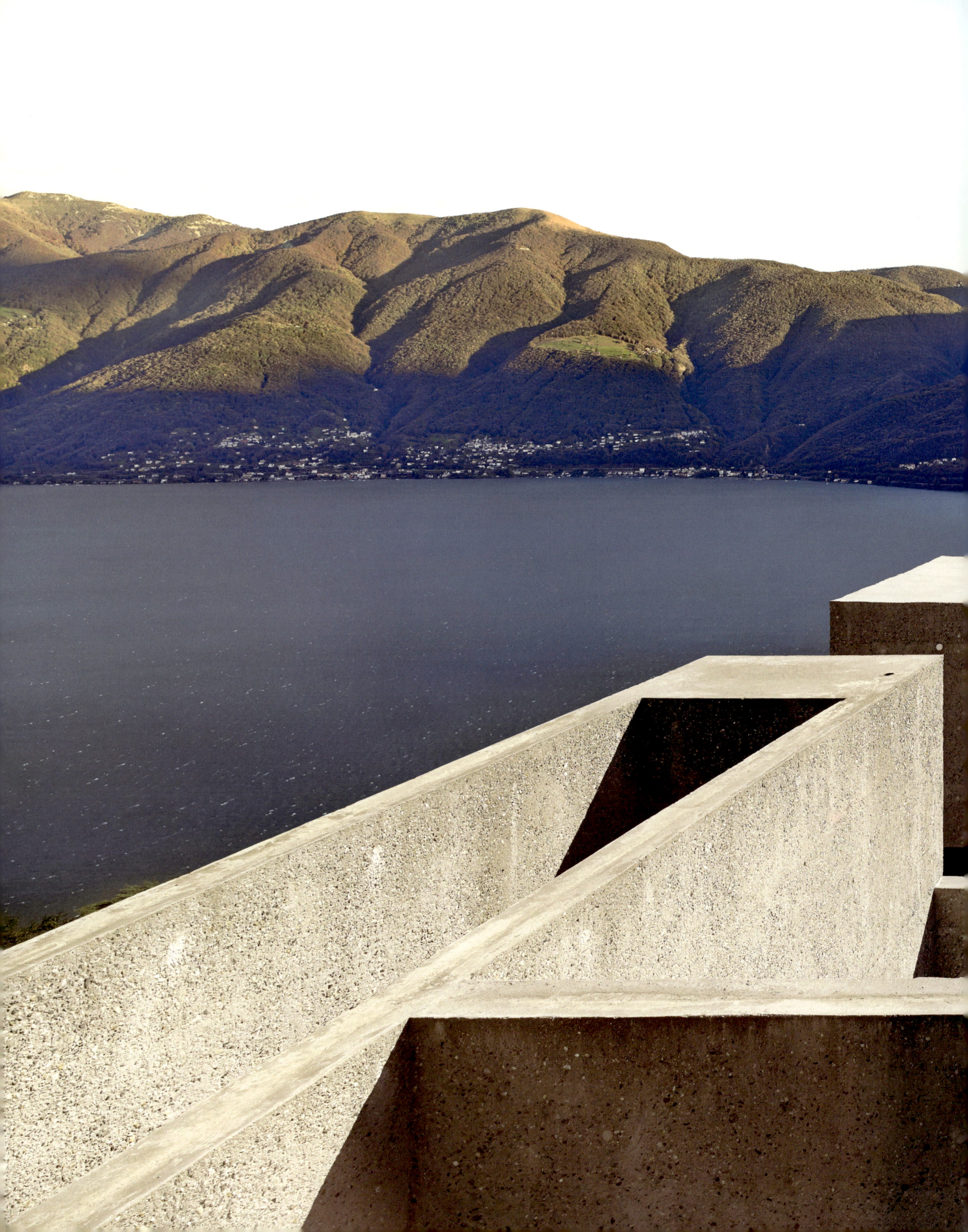

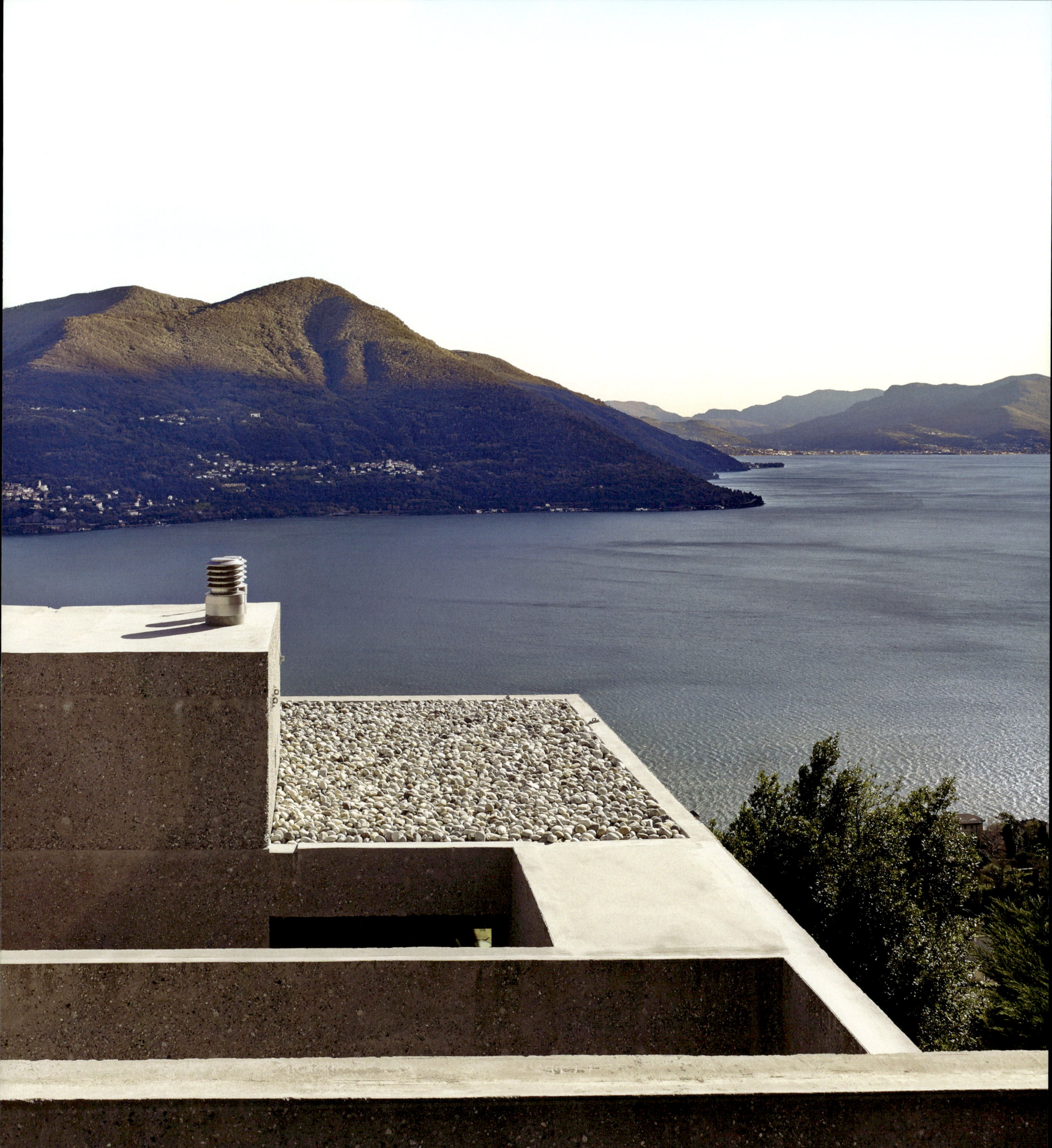

GÄVLE, SWEDEN

SKOGSSAUNA TOMTEBO

BENGT MATTIAS CARLSSON
OF METER ARKITEKTUR

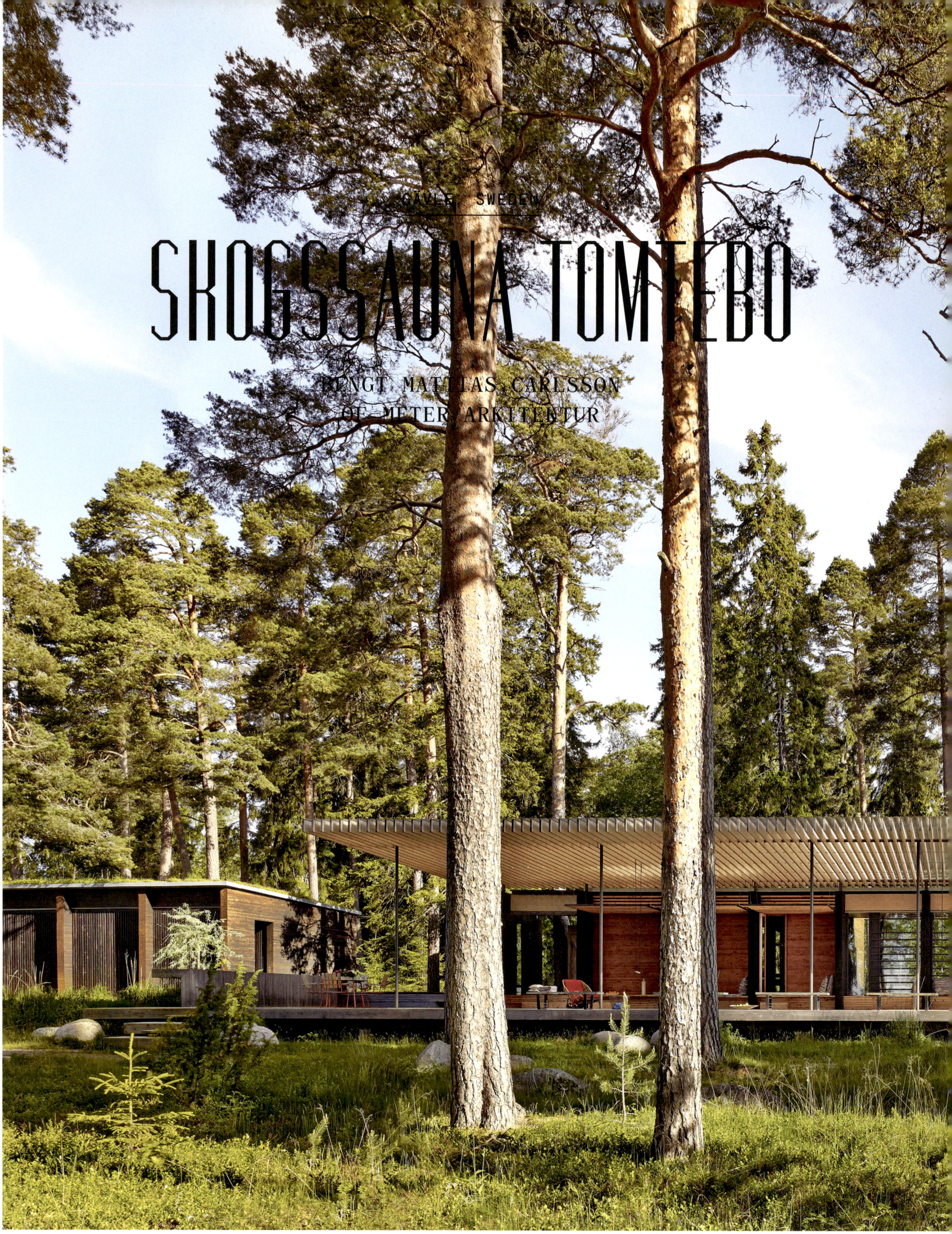

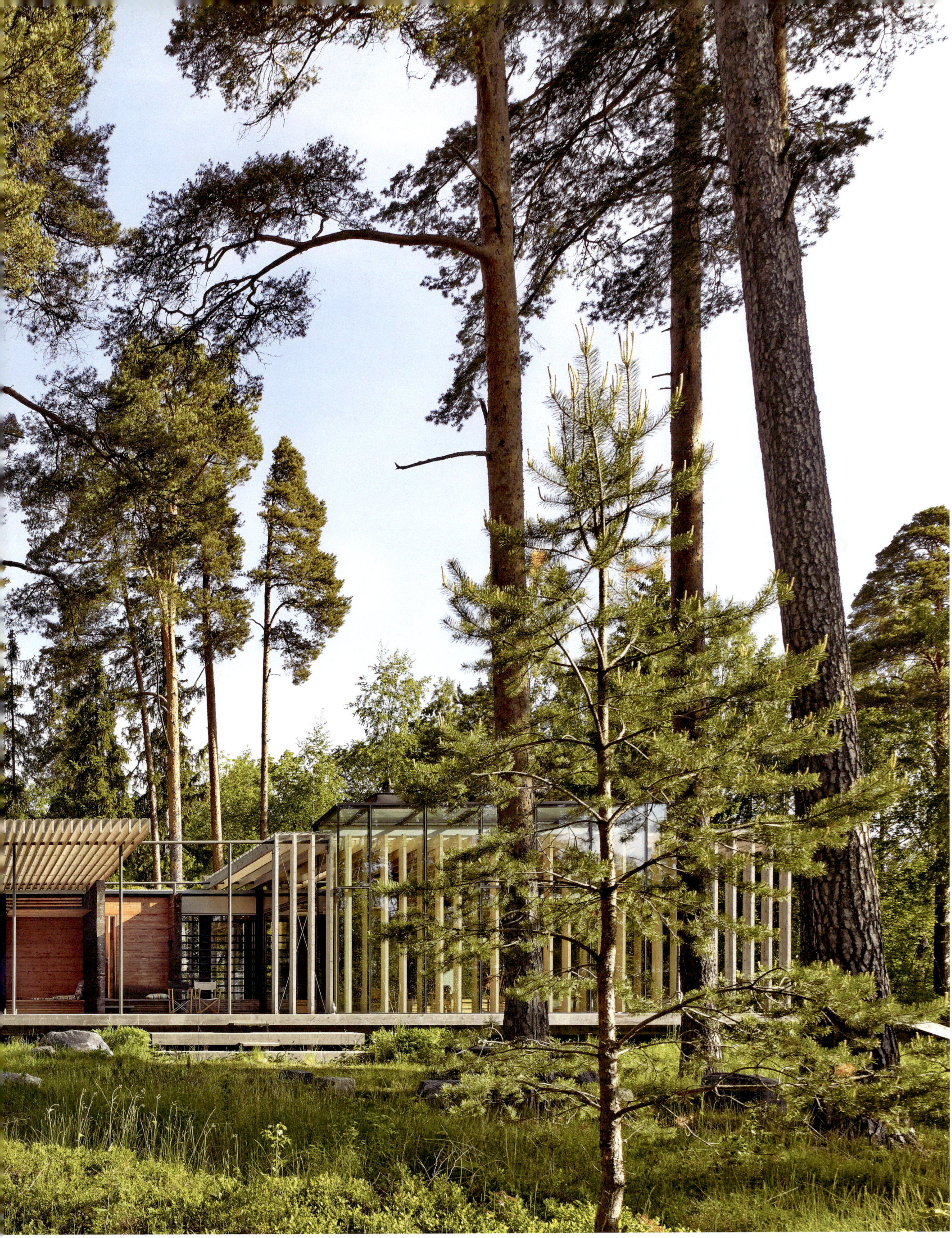

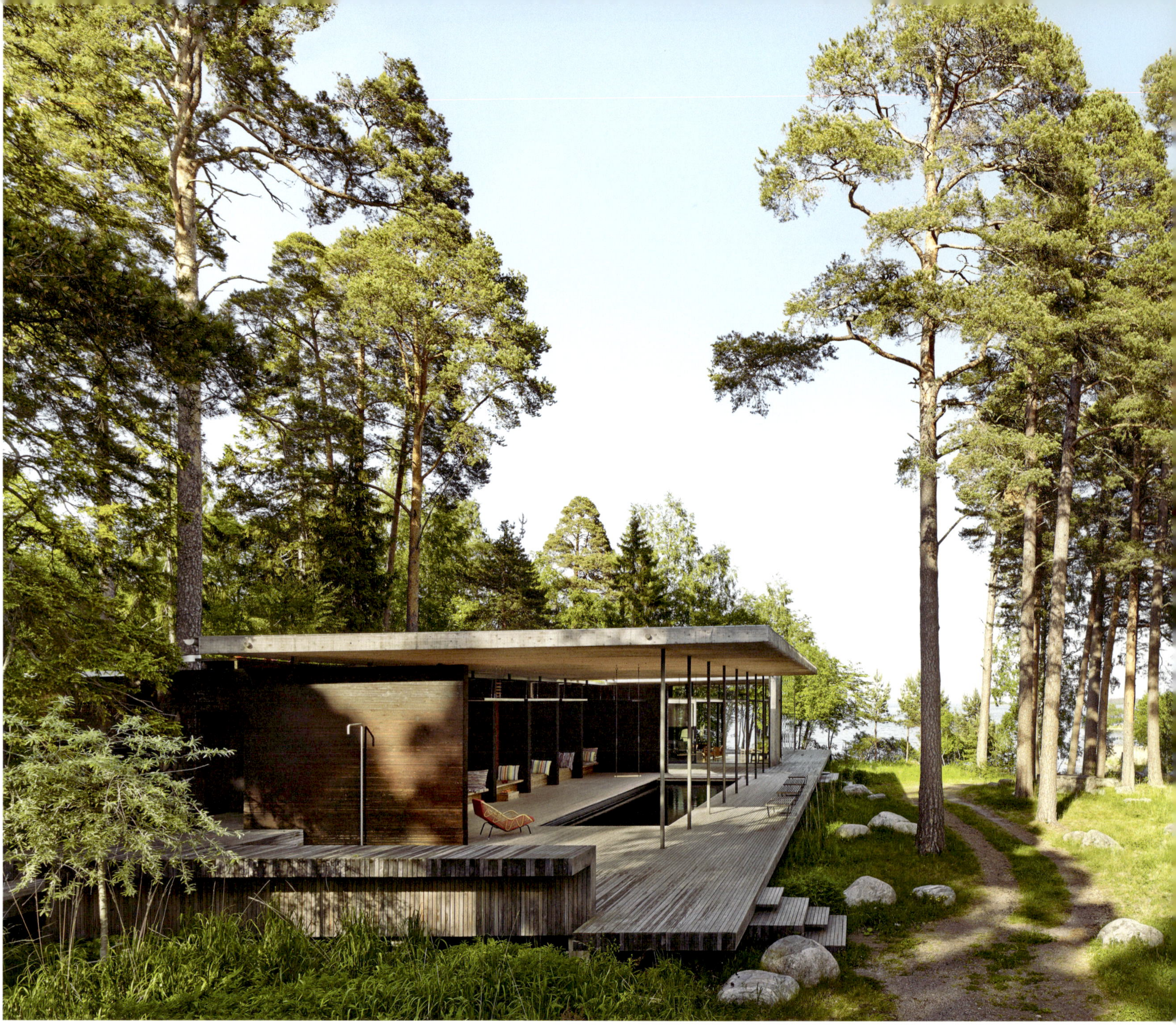

“ALTHOUGH EACH AREA IS PARTITIONED, THE PERSISTENCE OF WOOD THROUGHOUT LENDS THE BATHHOUSE A SENSE OF UNITY AND COHERENCE.”

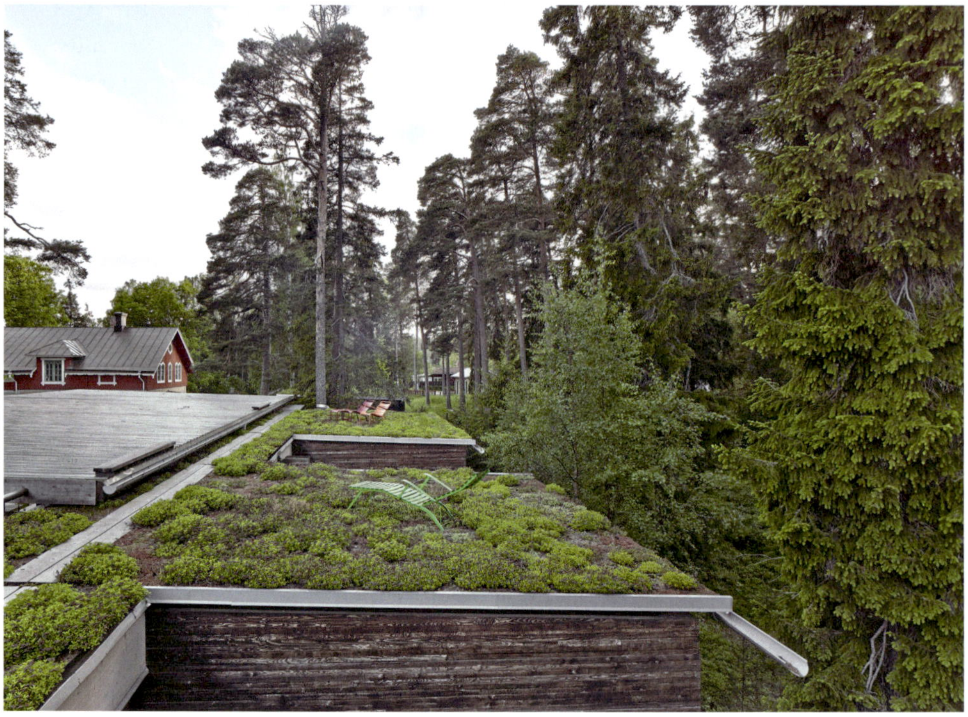

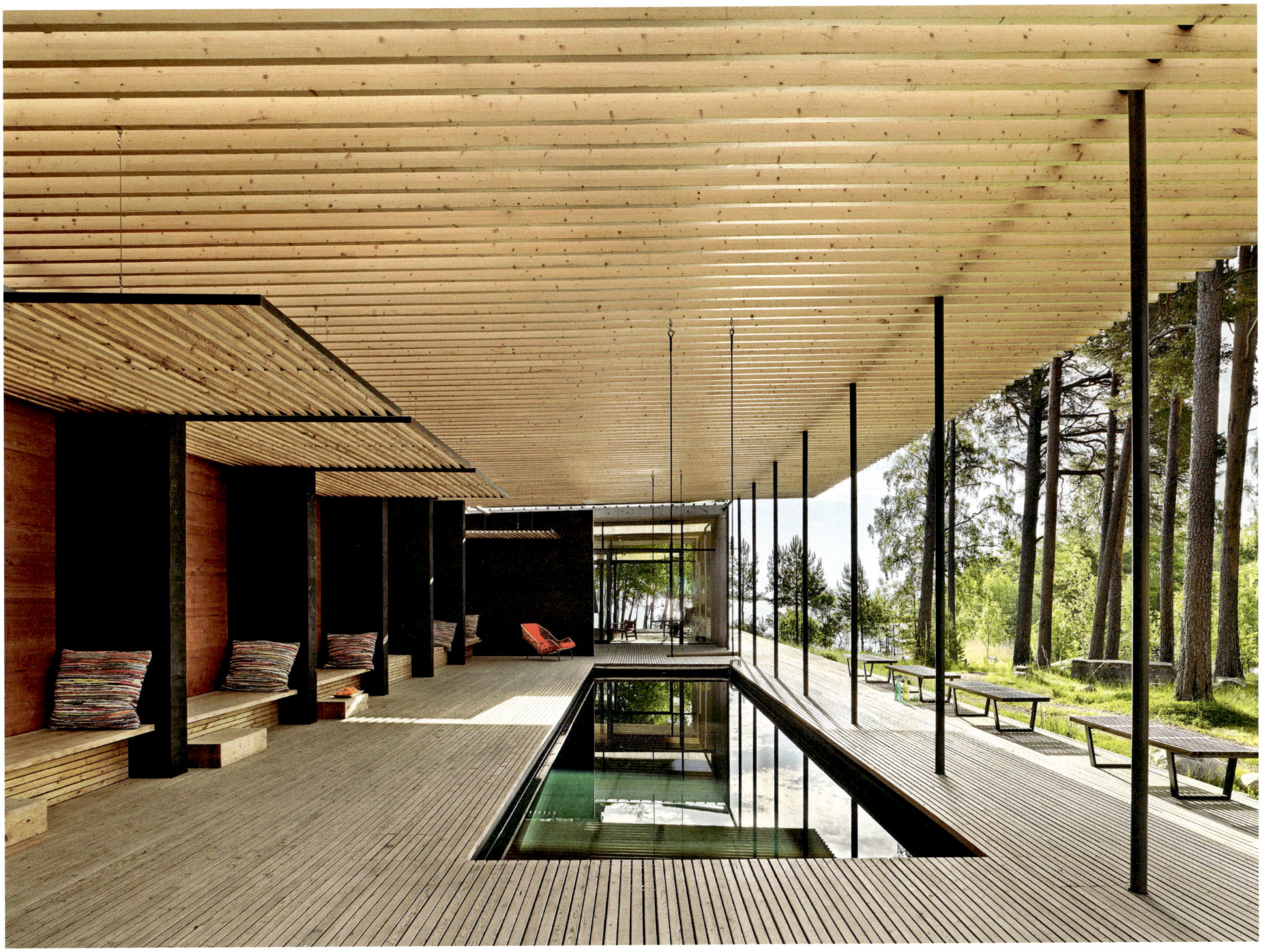

SKOGSSAUNA TOMTEBO Sweden has an ancient and entrenched fascination with carpentry. Employing these methods of construction, Skogssauna pays homage to the past while highlighting the emergent possibilities that lie within traditional techniques. Clean lines remain, but the creative play of angles adds a modern touch.

The ancient techniques of Nordic carpentry form the basis of this hammer-and-chisel structure. In a telling coinage, the building bears the name Skogssauna Tomtebo, which simply means "forest sauna"—a sign of its practical and modest heritage.

The bathhouse is structured in a modular layout. A 60-meter-long corridor spans the length of the building, connecting the sauna and bathing facilities to a laundry, guest rooms, and social areas. Although each area is partitioned, the persistence of wood throughout lends the bathhouse a sense of unity and coherence. Skogssauna Tomtebo also acts as both a border to the dense woodlands and as a transitional space. The outside sweeps into the building, delivering residents and guests into an intimate closeness with nature.

The framework is composed of rough-sawn glulam logs. The resulting 19-ply boards clad both the interior and exterior walls and are treated with only a protective coating of tar on the outside and a linseed oil glaze on the inside. A floor of spruce heartwood extends between each space and forms a solid platform for the pool and the communal area that overlooks Gävle Bay. Recalling the history of Nordic carpentry, the precise placement of the lengths of timber reflects the kind of craftsmanship that is developed over the course of many lifetimes.

The bathhouse's sense of heritage extends beyond an age-old respect for the value of good wood. The Swedish site is home to a building dating from 1880, and Skogssauna Tomtebo itself is built on top of a carefully preserved gun emplacement. However, the contrast between timbers, the angles of the joins, and the polished ⁓

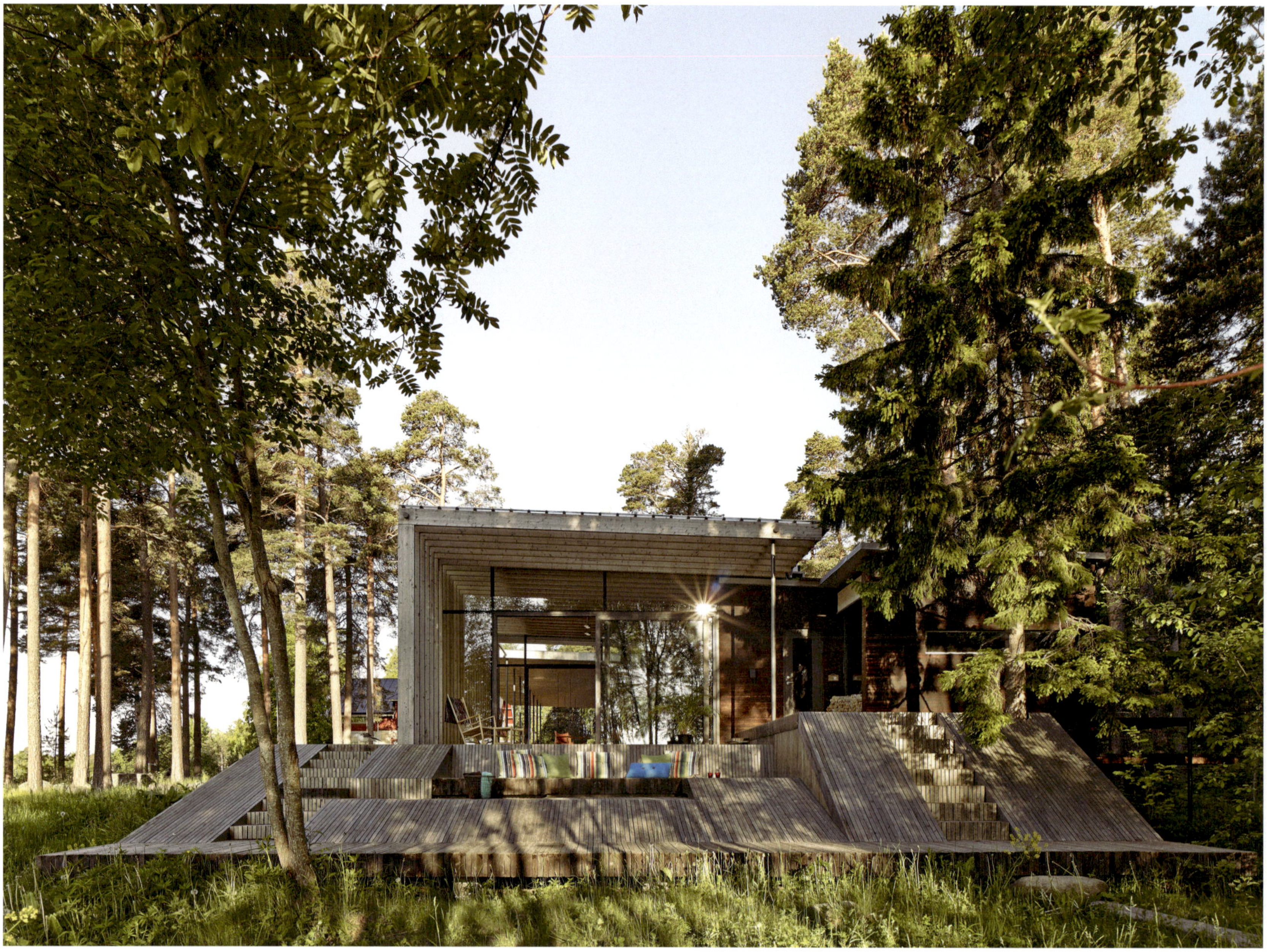

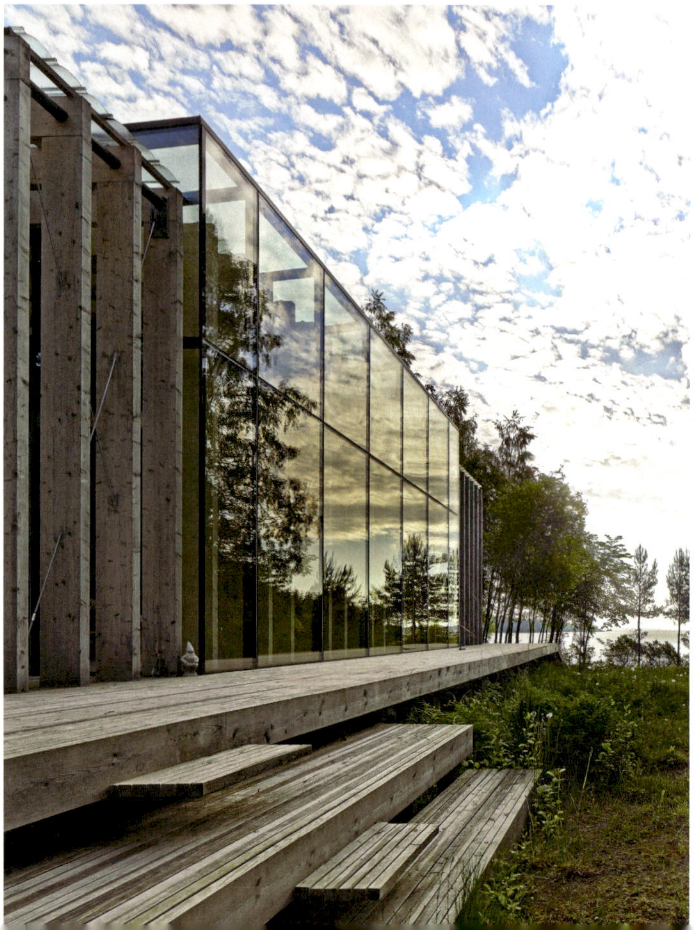

concrete floor in the living space all add a modern aspect to the structure. Yet it is the kind of modernism that results from careful refinement and progression, from staying within the limits of tradition and embracing them. ◆

"RECALLING THE HISTORY OF NORDIC CARPENTRY, THE PRECISE PLACEMENT OF THE LENGTHS OF TIMBER REFLECTS THE KIND OF CRAFTSMANSHIP THAT IS DEVELOPED OVER THE COURSE OF MANY LIFETIMES."

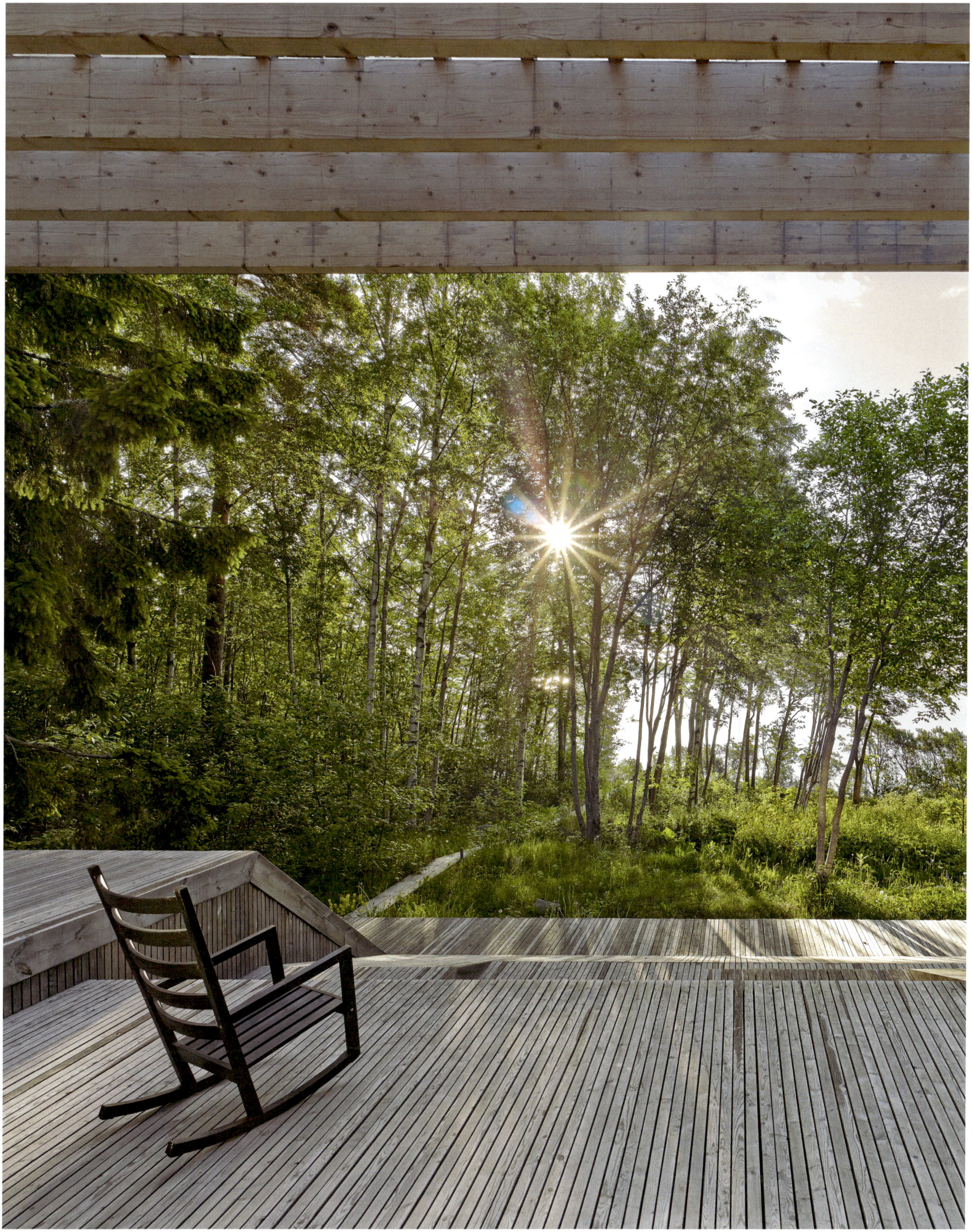

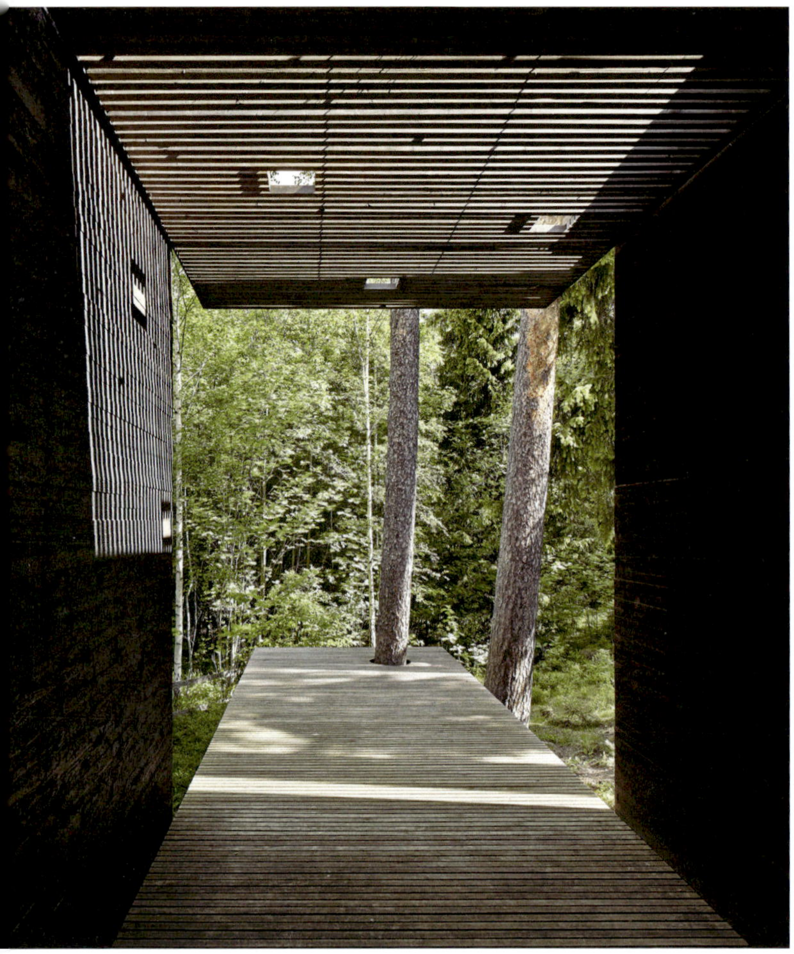

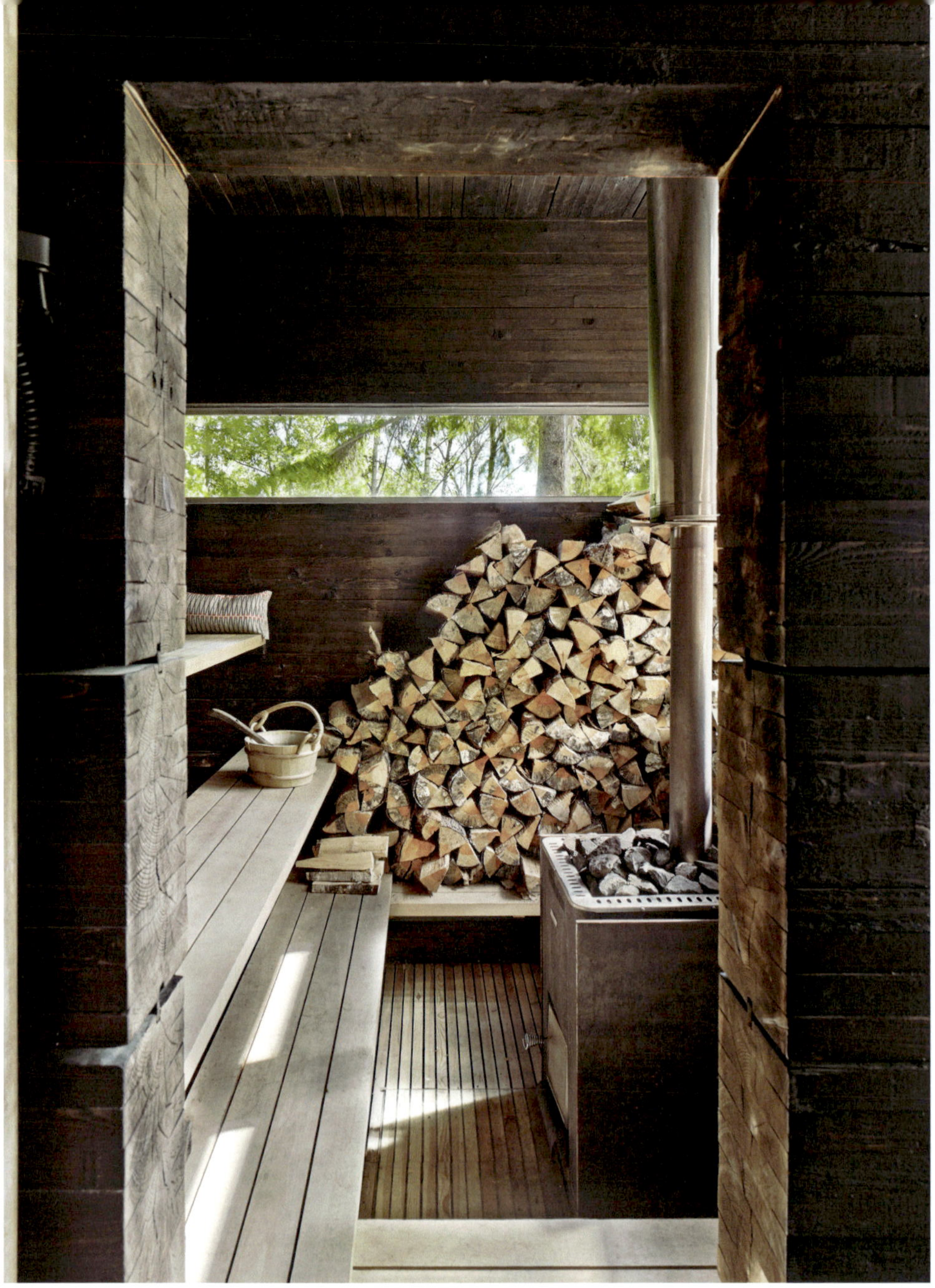

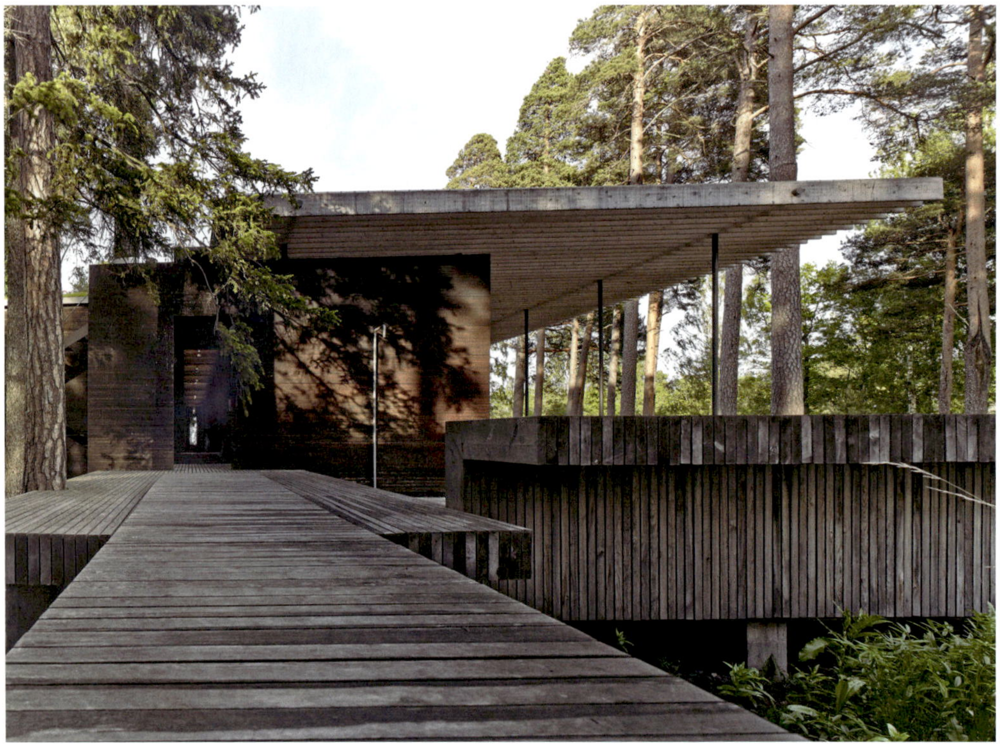

"THE OUTSIDE SWEEPS INTO THE BUILDING, DELIVERING RESIDENTS AND GUESTS INTO AN INTIMATE CLOSENESS WITH NATURE."

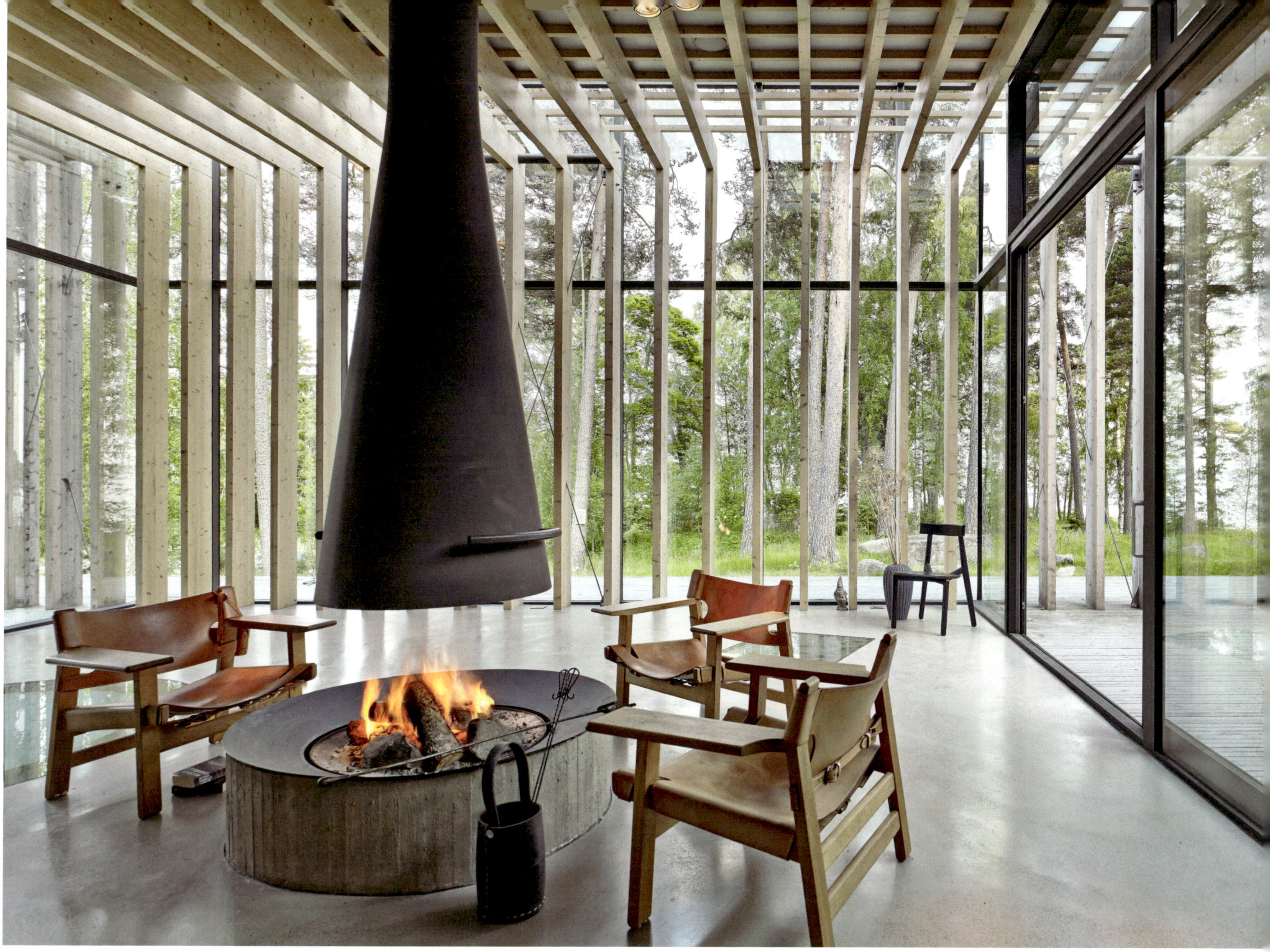

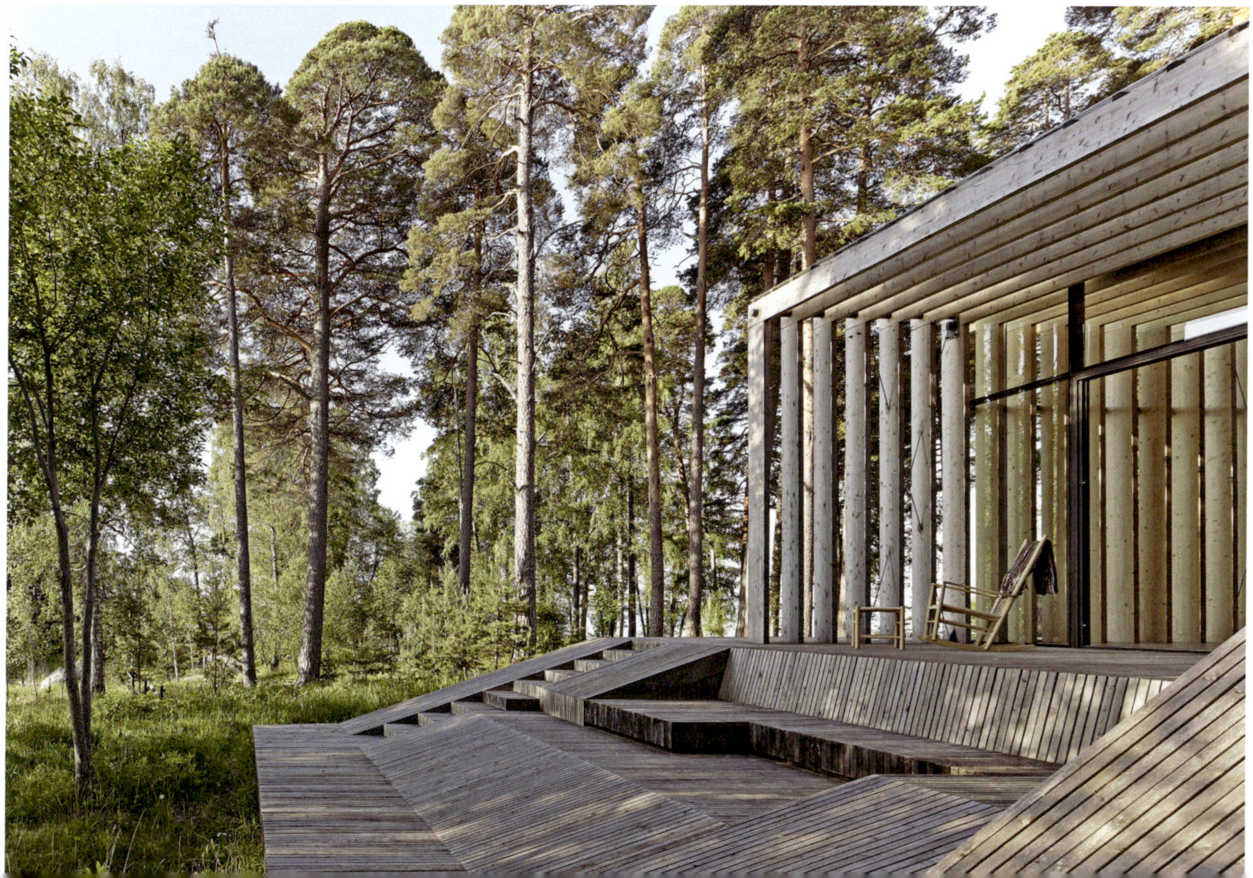

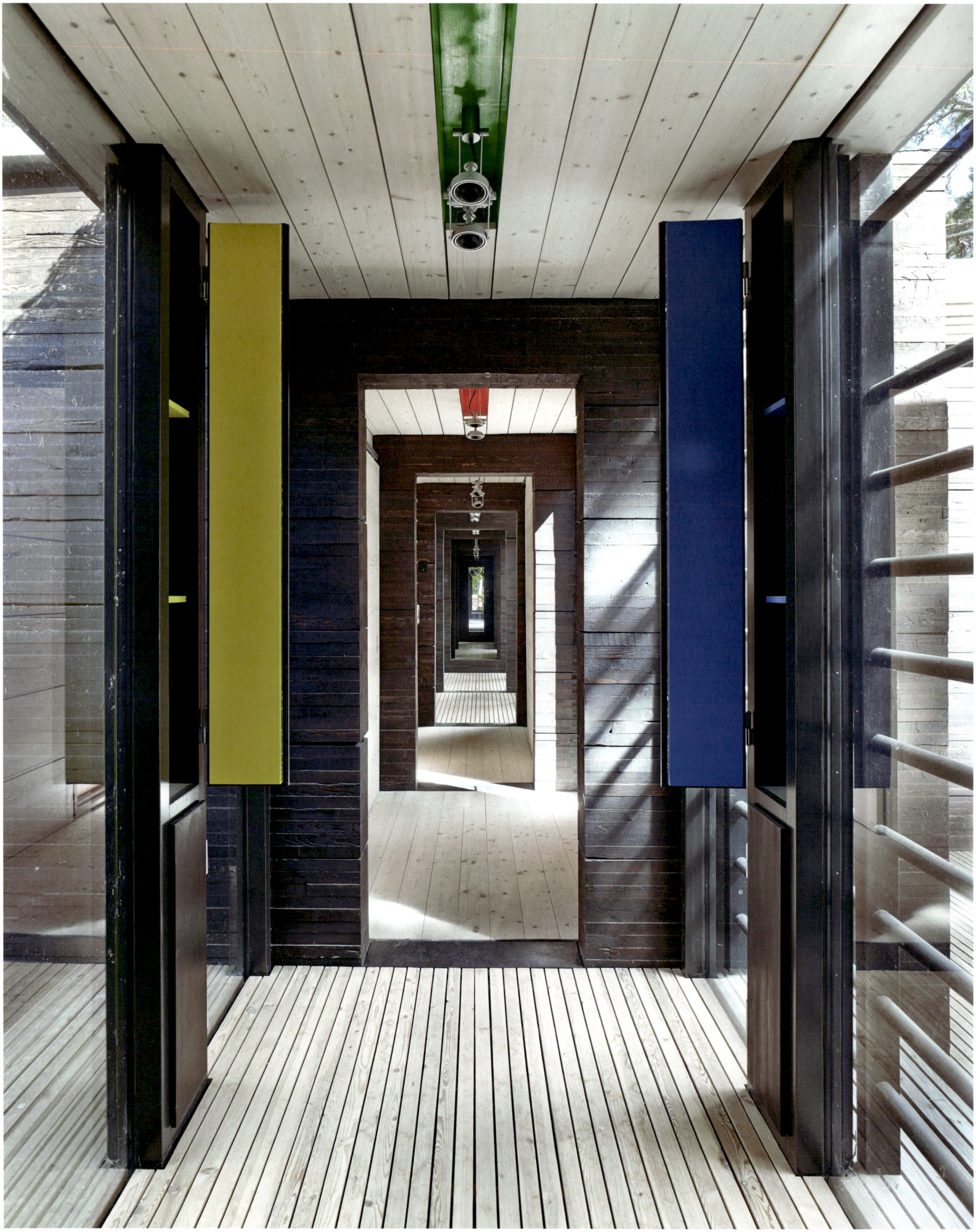

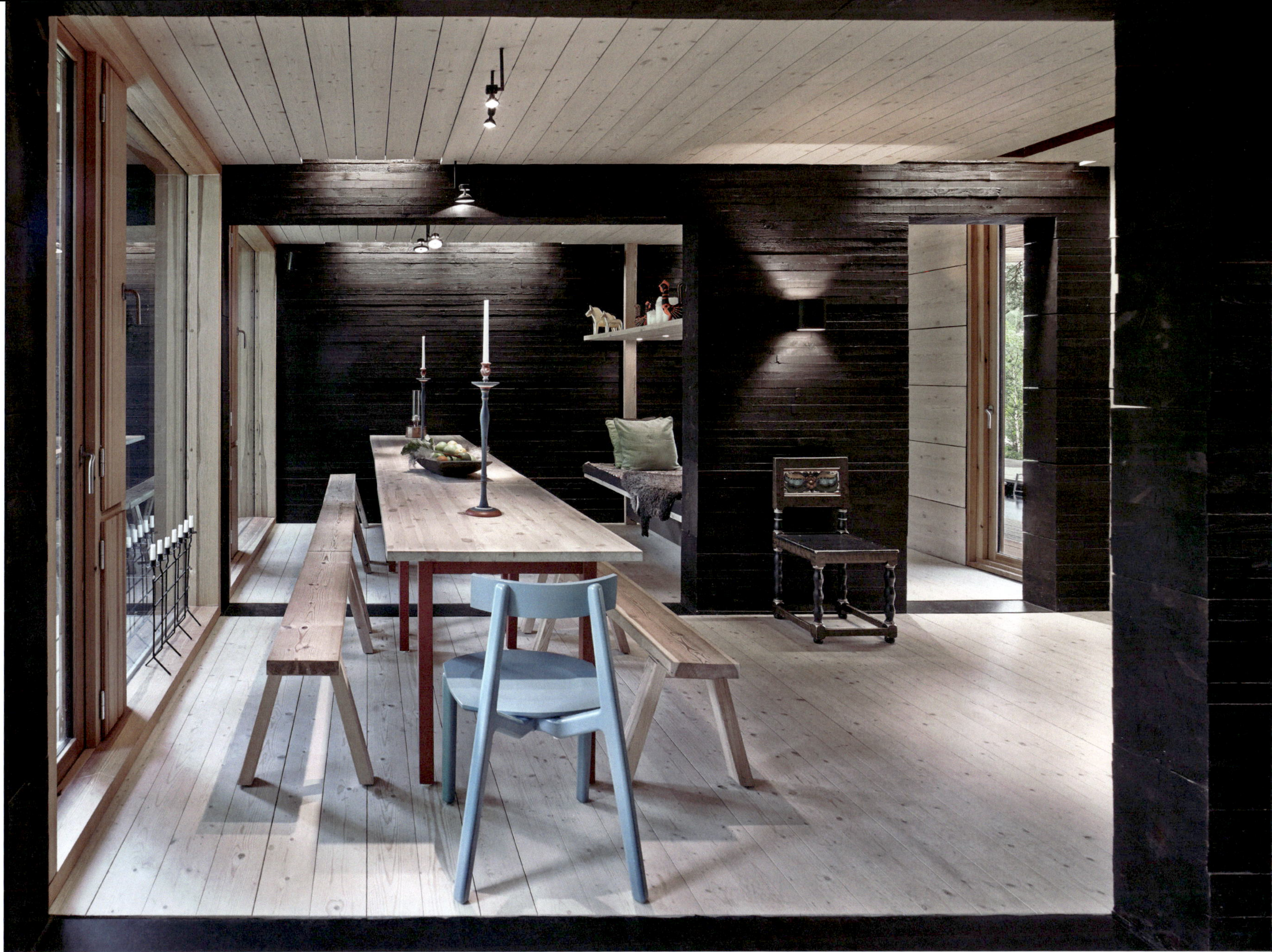

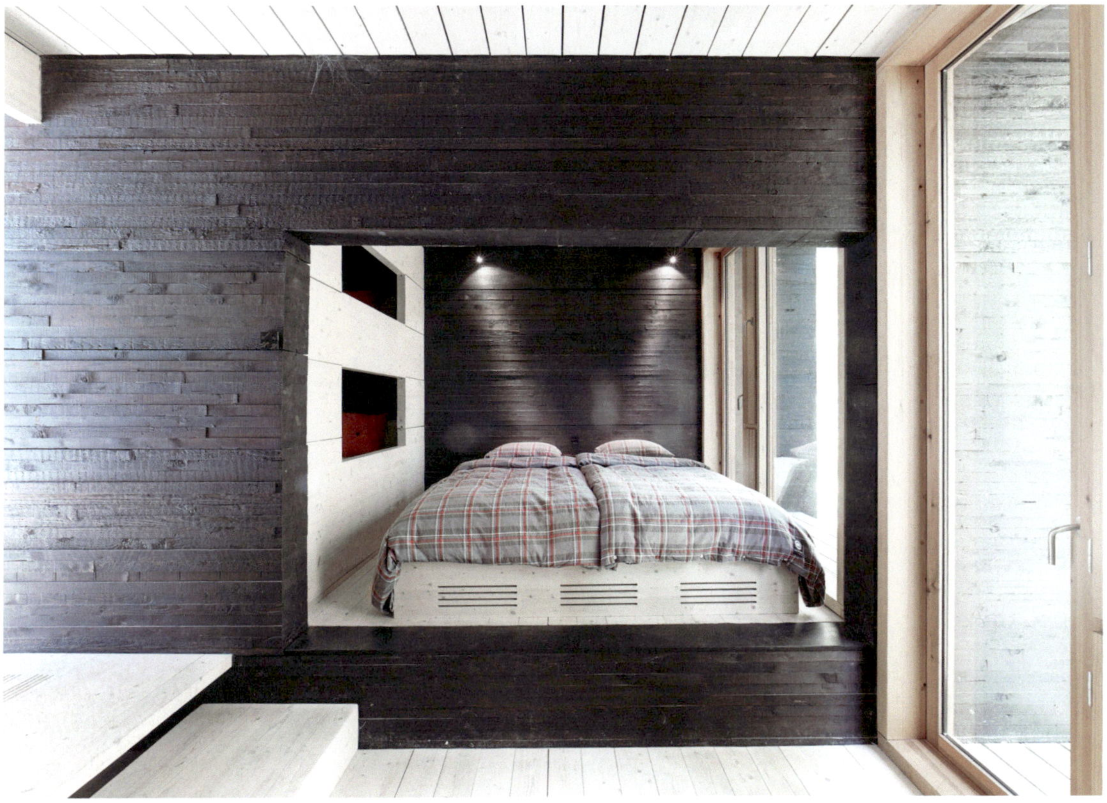

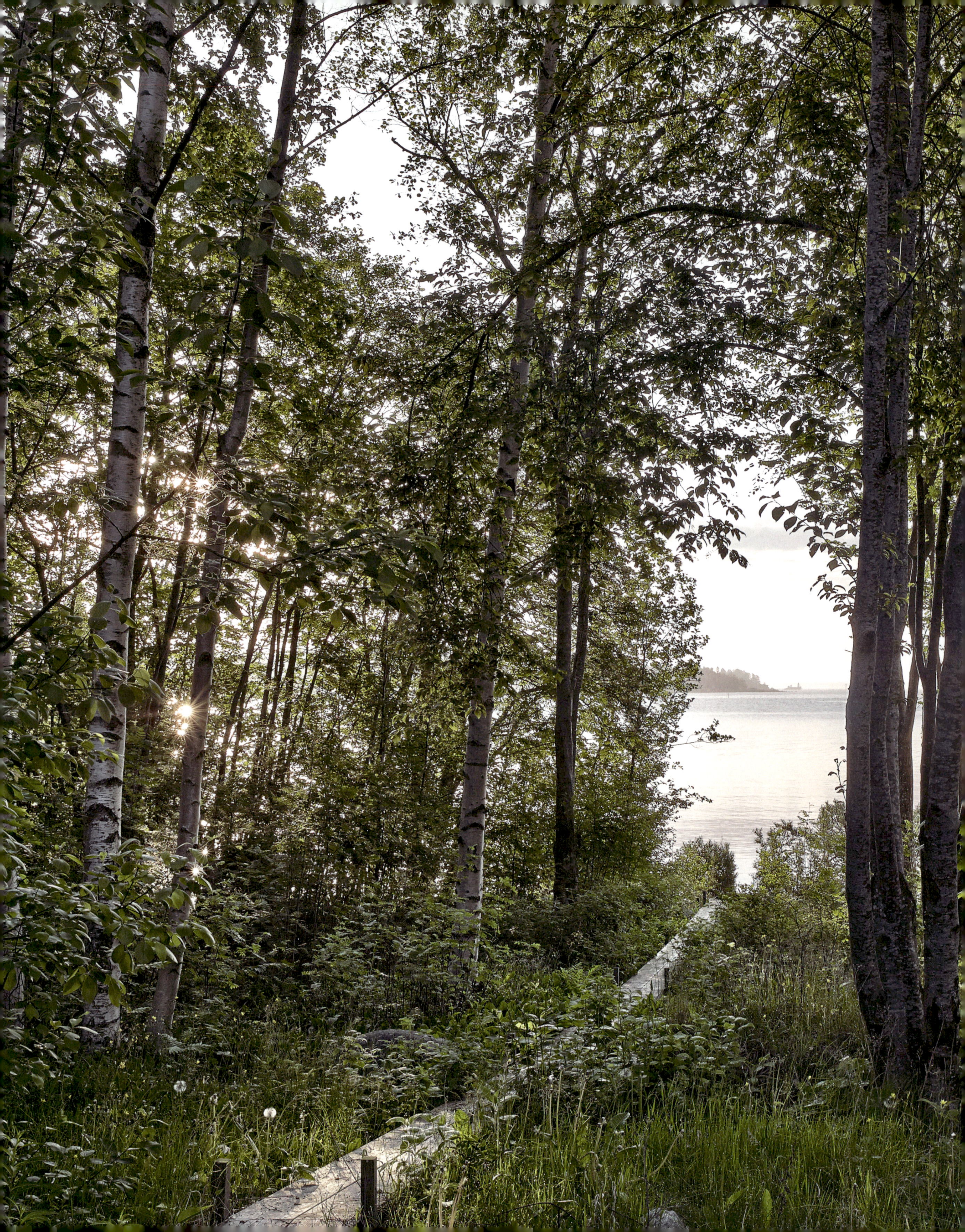

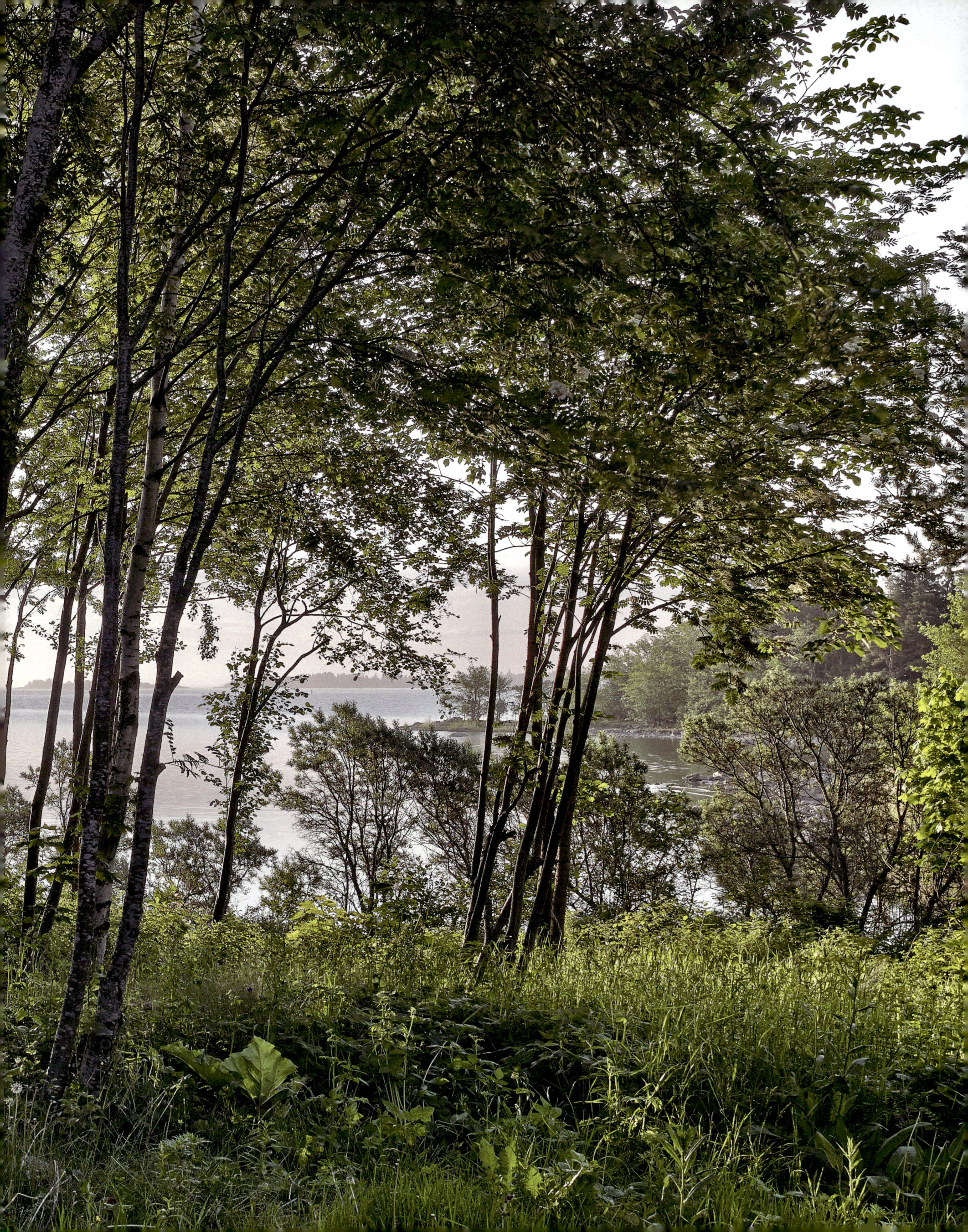

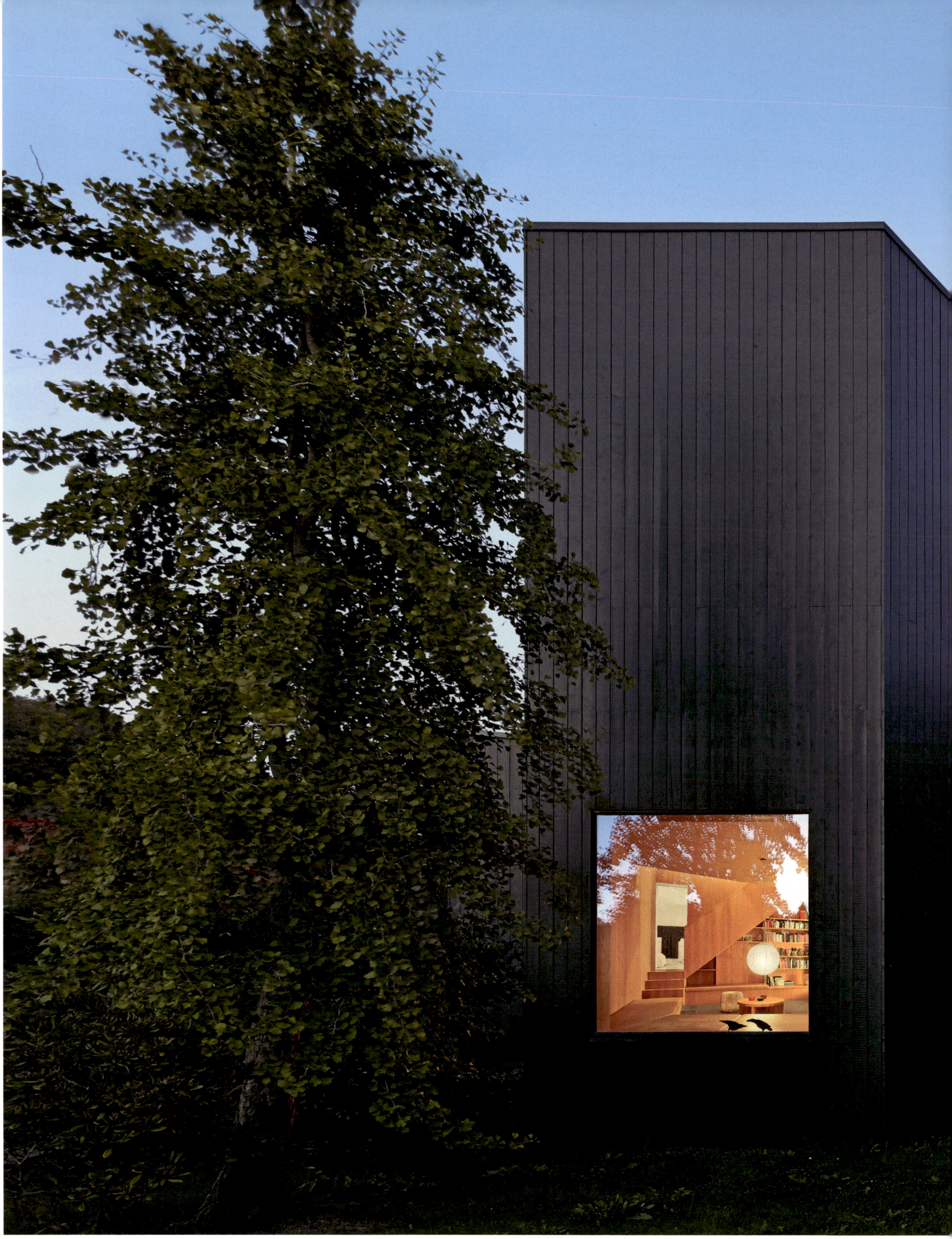

ÅRHUS, DENMARK

VILLA WIENBERG

MARTIN AND METTE WIENBERG

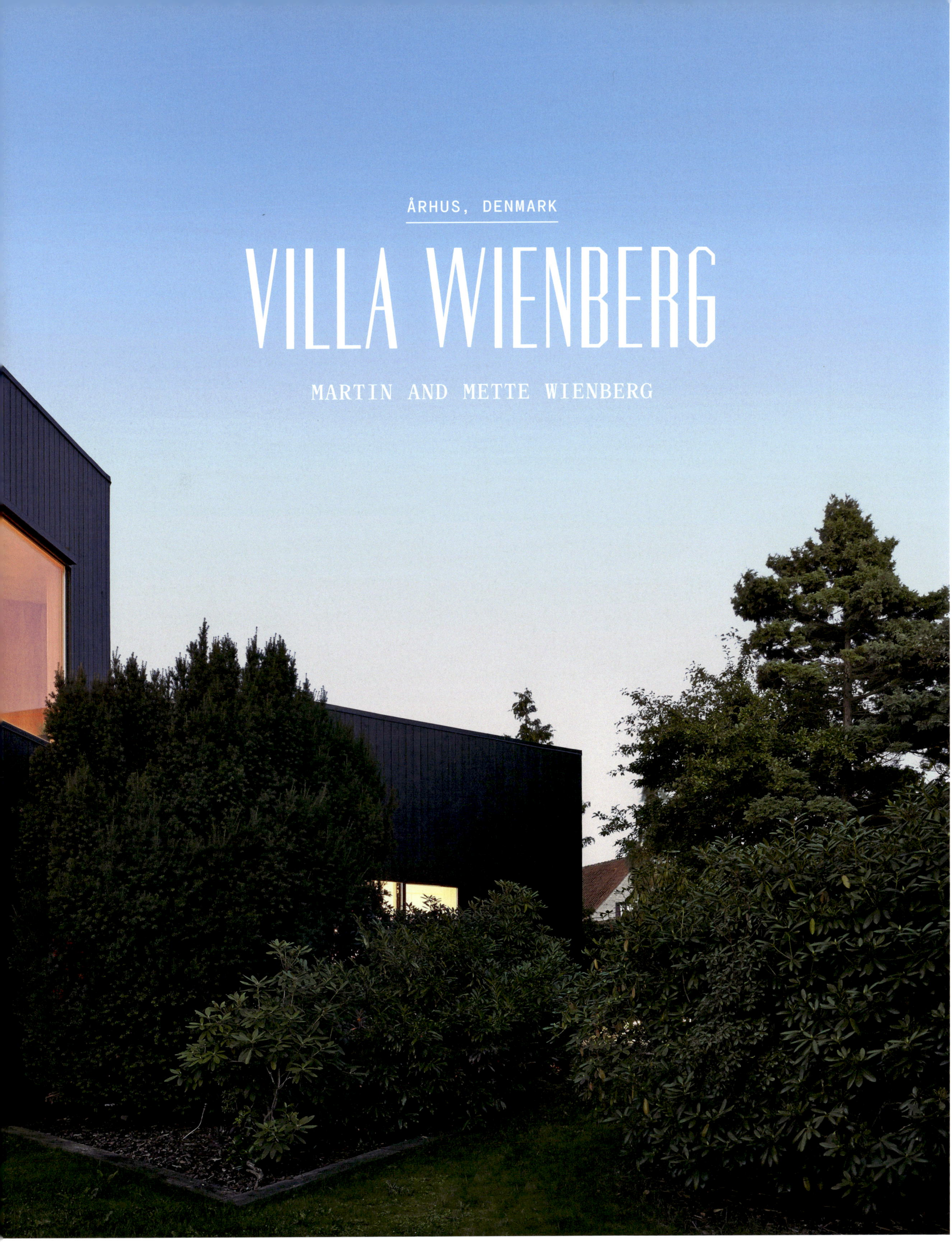

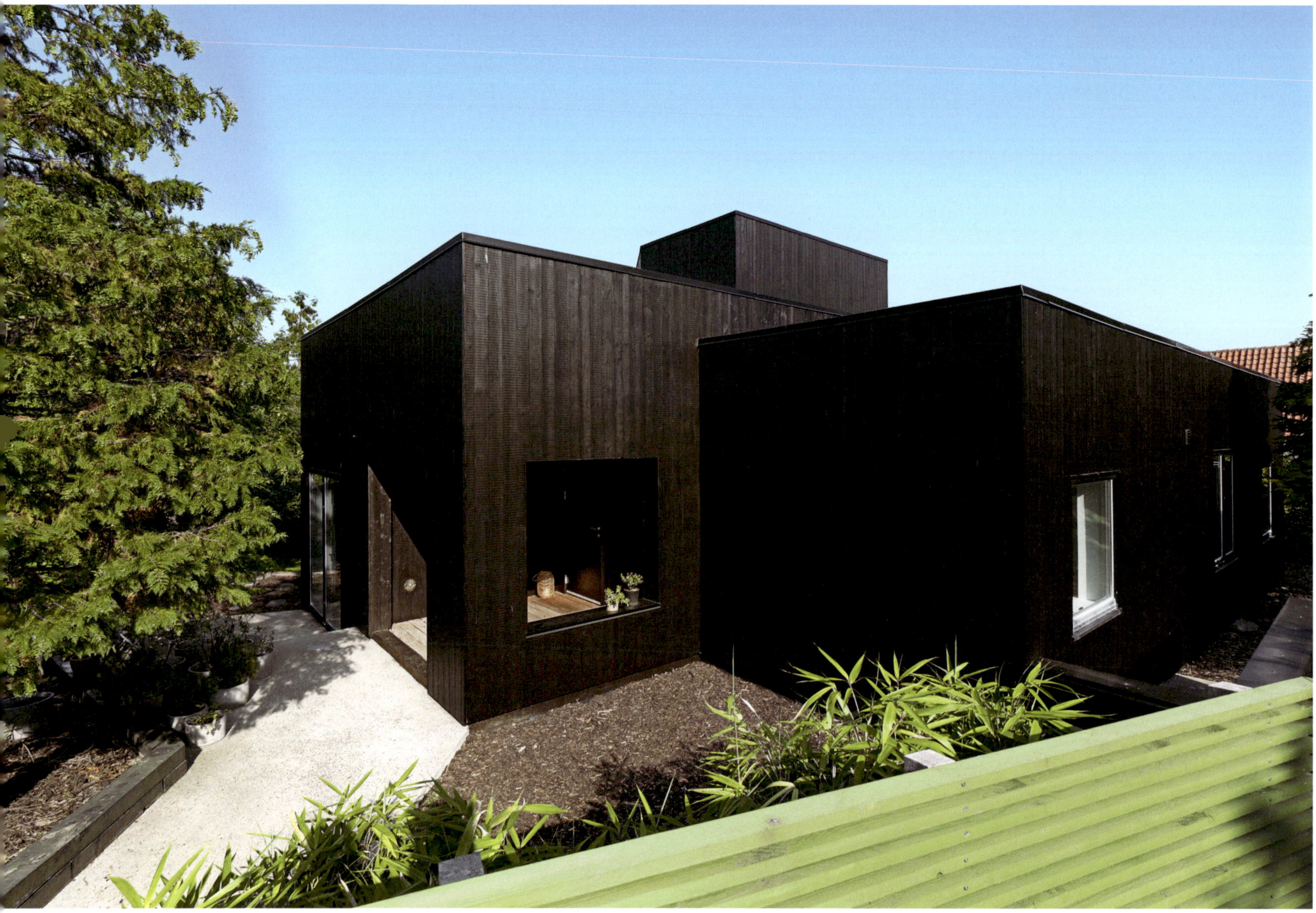

VILLA WIENBERG Architects Martin and Mette Wienberg had dreamt of their home long before its construction. The fruit of such careful consideration, Villa Wienberg negotiates fluid transitions in spite of the markedly different spaces that comprise the home, creating a warm and easy atmosphere in the process.

Martin and Mette Wienberg met in architecture school. In the years that followed, the couple traveled together and settled in Copenhagen, where they both established careers in architecture. But when it came time to think about designing their home, Denmark's urban capital was found to be lacking in one key element—nature. Located across the Kattegat, Århus seemed to be the perfect compromise, offering a blend of urbanite buzz and natural stillness. "The atmosphere of the site is so special," says Mette Wienberg. "We're surrounded by pine trees and we wanted to embrace these and create the feeling that we're living deep in the woods."

Speaking of their creative process, Wienberg says, "We've spent years discussing our thoughts on the design of our own home. So when we started sketching, we agreed on all the main values about the design and the materiality. There were no fights!" The ease of the process is reflected in Villa Wienberg's warm atmospherics and the thoughtful contrast between the separate areas of the home. And considering that Martin and Mette decided to extend and renovate an existing 1940s cabin on the site, the latter was no easy feat.

"We aren't creating contrasts within each space, just between each space," Wienberg explains, adding that "it was very important to us that the existing structure and the new extension should co-exist together seamlessly." And while the spaces of this home are certainly different, they do work together and transition smoothly. The kitchen and dining room have kept the low ceilings of the original home, with the space taking on a modern functionality via white walls. Providing a contrast without being out of place, the living room, like the rest of the bedrooms on the ground floor, has a bare wood finish, ⁓

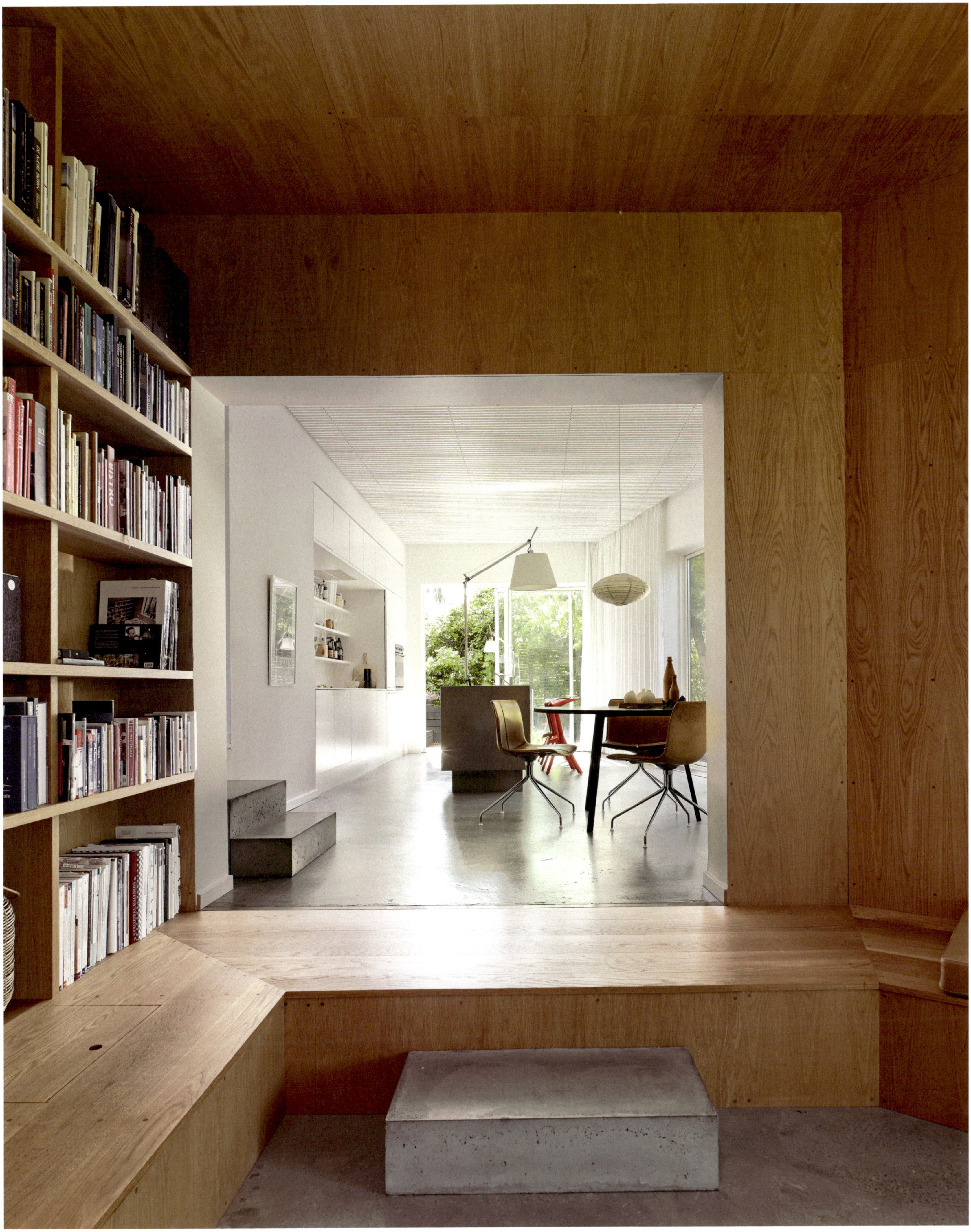

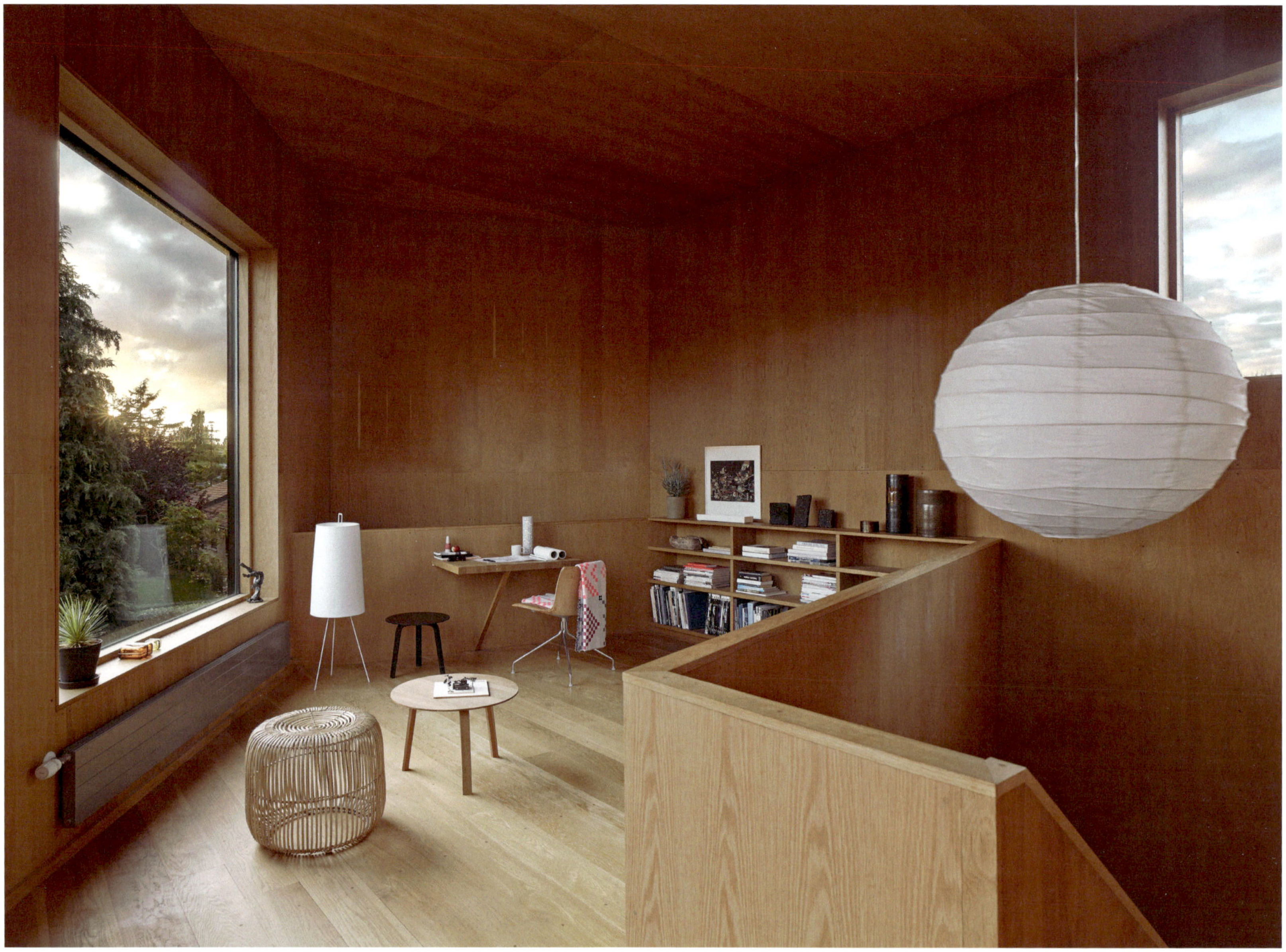

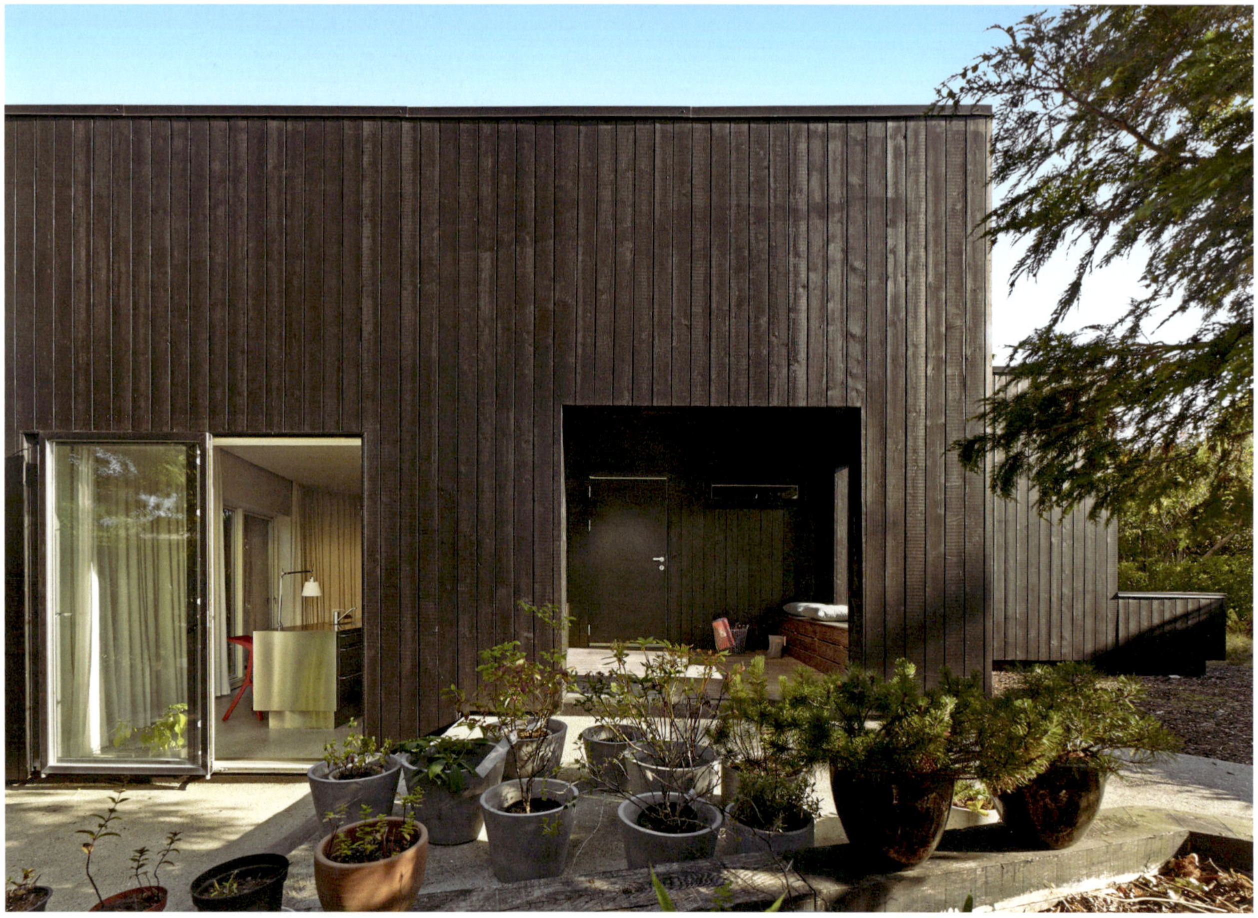

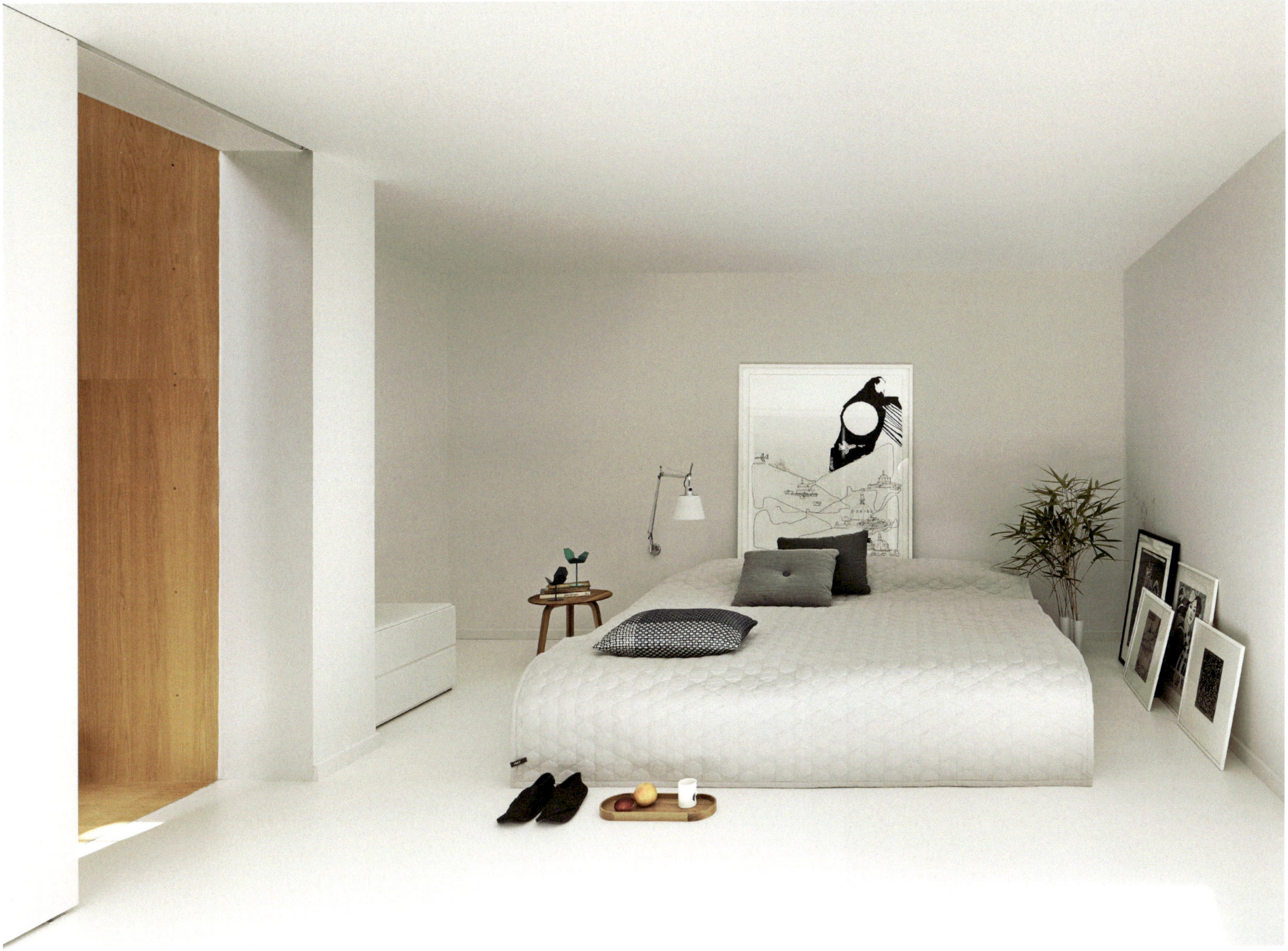

and the exposed oil-treated oak boards blanket the room with a welcoming and relaxing atmosphere. The ceilings open up to doubleheight here, and an angular stairway

> "It was very important to us that the existing structure and the new extension should co-exist together seamlessly."
> — *Mette Wienberg*

leads to a study and terrace upstairs. Much of the furniture is built-in. Wienberg is especially pleased with the hospitable quality Villa Wienberg has achieved, saying that guests "make themselves at home right away, which is a real compliment." ◆

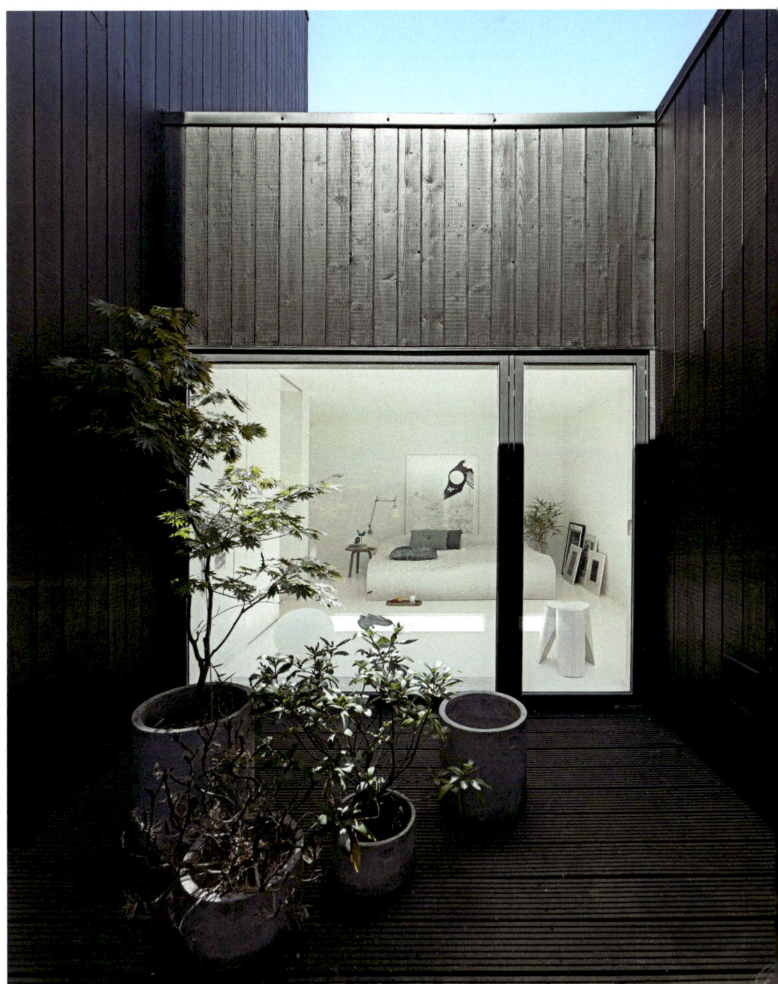

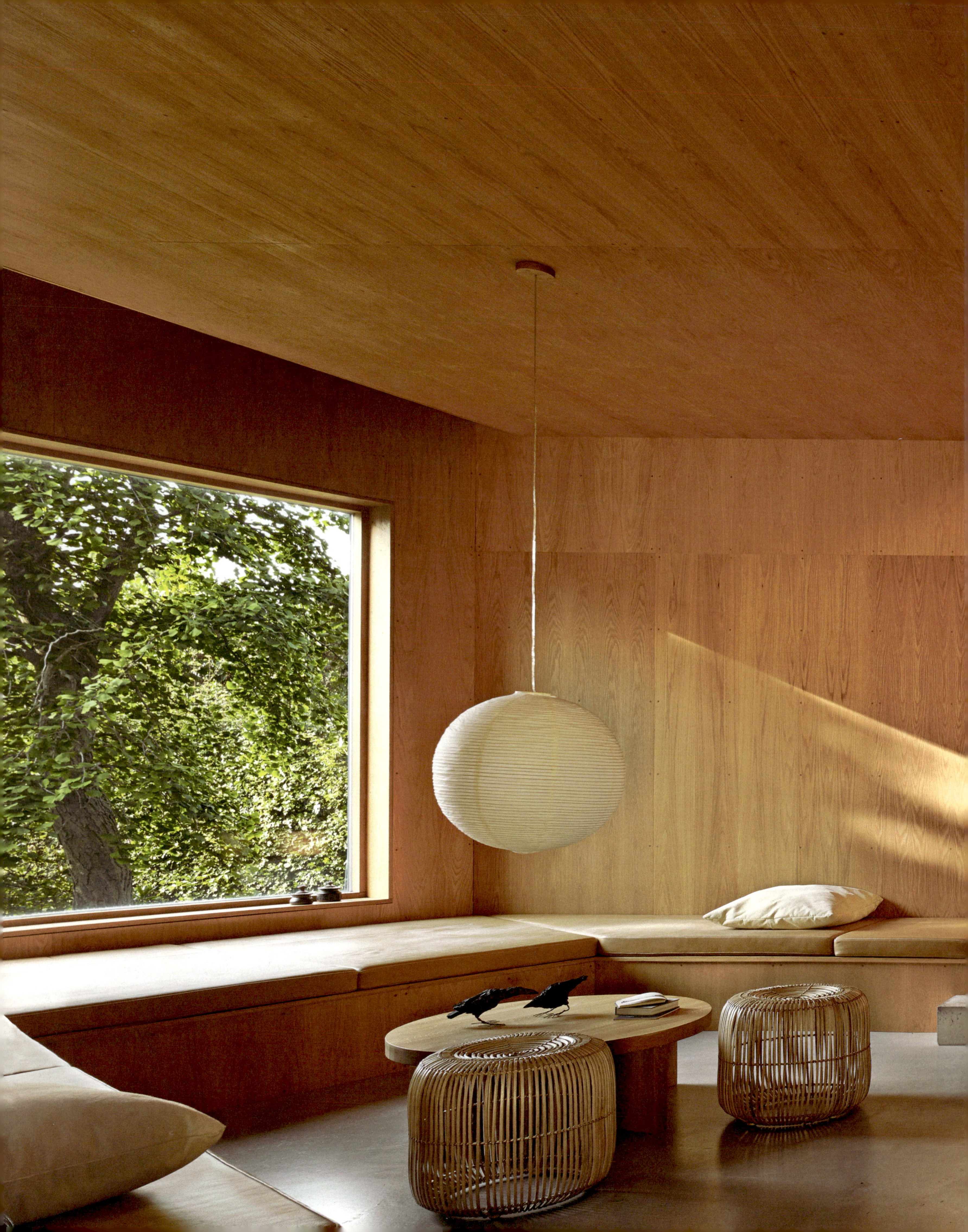

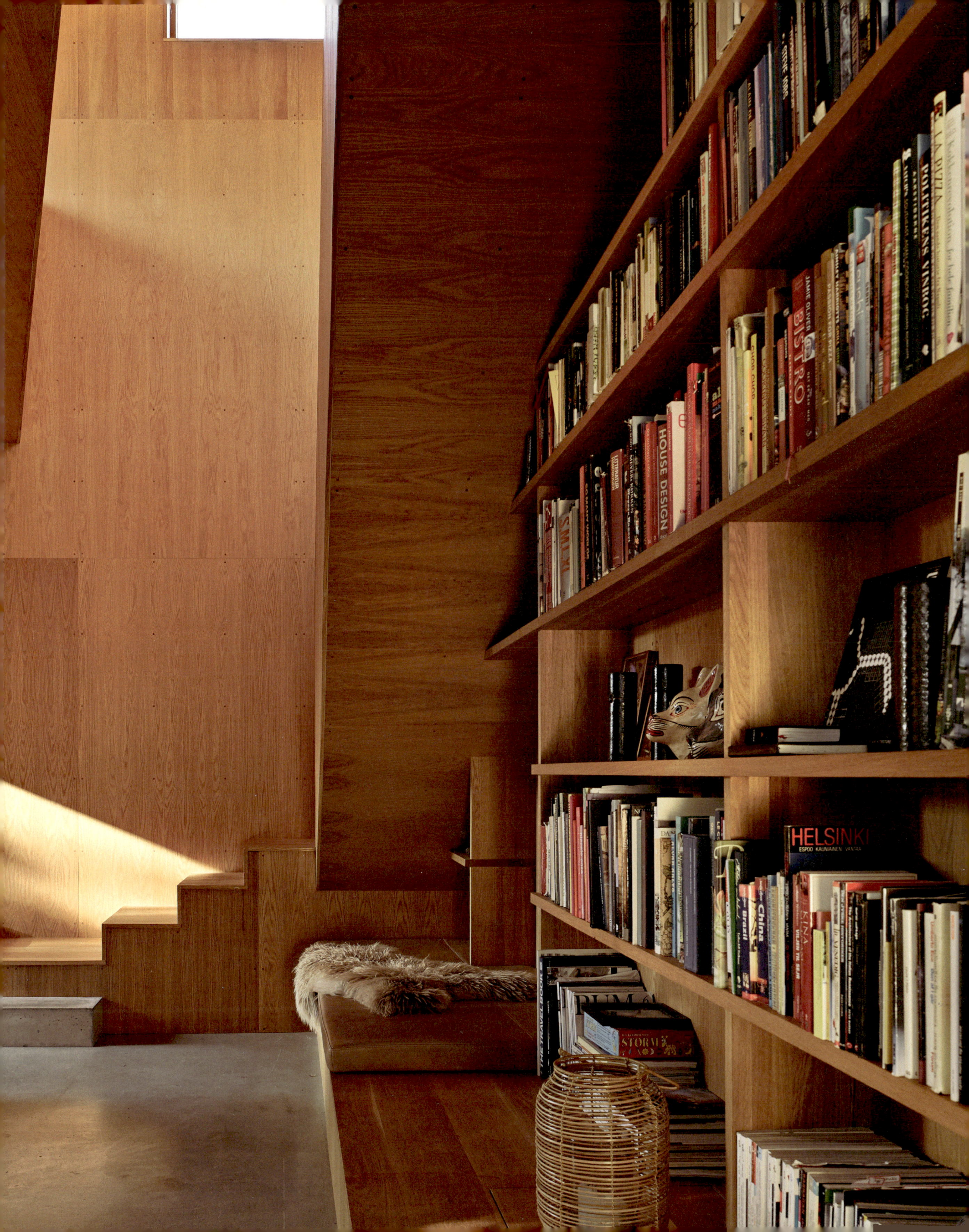
HELSINKI
ESPOO KAUNIAINEN VANTAA
HOUSE DESIGN
BISTRO
JAMIE OLIVER
POLITIKENS VINBOG
China
Brasil
STORM

INDEX A–Z

DEDICATION

This book is dedicated to my mother, Angela Silverman (22 July 1949–9 January 2015), who was taken from us so tragically and suddenly. From when I was a young boy, you gave me support, encouragement, and guidance to follow my passion in the arts. You were my inspiration and role model, incredibly talented and yet modest. In your earlier years you were known for being the first fashion designer of the young St Michael range for Marks and Spencer. You are the determination on every page. My love for you is eternal and I miss you deeply.

ACKNOWLEDGEMENTS

Big thanks to all those who accompanied me on the photo shoots, helping with styling and lending a hand with everything from blocking airplane trails and praying for sun when faced with constant rain to building vantage points for views and running around turning lights on and off: Alice Van, Julia Landgren, Colm Keller, Kurt Lightner, Patrick Geshel, Andrew Gauld, Kayo Aoyama, Agnes Gidenstam, Jodi Kelly, Louise Willet, Jenny Liv Ulander, Anna Elola, Stella Pilback, Lotta Alexius, and Johanna Sparf.

Thanks to all my retouchers: Daniel Samuelsson, Simon Fageus, Robert Westin, Lisa Kindberg, Agnes Myrehed, Joe Kendrick, and Anton Nordfeldt.

Thanks to all the editors who have selected my work over the years to be printed in fabulous magazines and to the team at Gestalten for publishing this book.

Special thanks to my fiancée Christel and my two beautiful daughters, Amber and Scarlet, and to my father Stanley, sister Amanda, brother-in-law Gideon, and my two nieces, Jasmine and Amelia, who have all been so supportive over the years.

THE PHOTOGRAPHER

James Silverman is one of the foremost photographers of architecture and interiors in the world today. A Briton residing in Sweden, he travels the globe for his projects. Images by Silverman have appeared in magazines such as *Architectural Digest, Dwell, Wallpaper*,* and *Vogue Living.*

More often than not, Silverman composes straight on, placing the viewer in the space as directly as possible. However, what is seen on the page is in stark contrast with the reality of what goes on behind the lens: missed flights, deported assistants, flights delayed by erupting volcanoes, misguided “guides,” exploding vehicles, attempts to communicate in unknown languages, sketchy cab drivers, cultural barriers, killer guard dogs, unannounced festivals, and inclement weather. Still, these obstacles all become part of his journey as he reaches for the next frame of the architect’s vision.

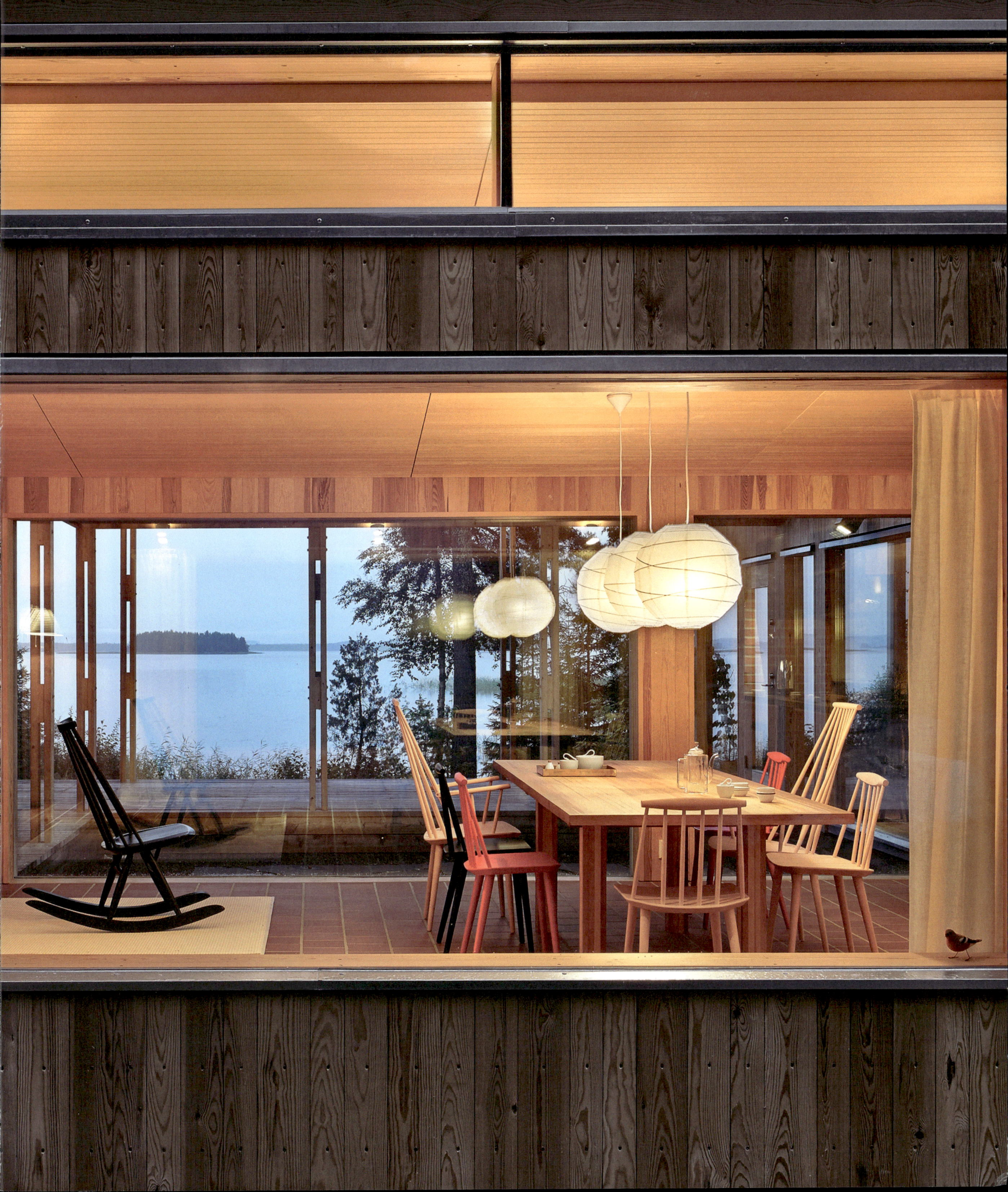

INFINITE SPACE

CONTEMPORARY RESIDENTIAL ARCHITECTURE
AND INTERIORS
PHOTOGRAPHED BY JAMES SILVERMAN

This book was conceived, edited and designed by GESTALTEN.

Edited by JAMES SILVERMAN, SVEN EHMANN, and ROBERT KLANTEN
All photographs by JAMES SILVERMAN

Preface by ALAN RAPP
Profile texts by BEN BARLOW

Editorial management by VANESSA OBRECHT
Copy-editing by KEVIN BROCHET-NGUYEN
Proofreading by TRANSPARENT LANGUAGE SOLUTIONS

Layout and design by JEANNINE MOSER
Cover by LUDWIG WENDT
Cover Photography: HOUSE LEHTIKIVI by JAMES SILVERMAN
Typefaces: ARCHIVE by COLOPHON FOUNDRY, GRACE JONES by HUGO HOPPMANN, and SEQUENCIA by MATT BURVILL (Gestalten Fonts)

Printed by Eberl Print GmbH, Immenstadt im Allgäu
Made in Germany

Published by Gestalten, Berlin 2016
ISBN: 978-3-89955-598-1

For more information, please visit www.gestalten.com.

Bibliographic information published by the Deutsche Nationalbibliothek. The Deutsche Nationalbibliothek lists this publication in the Deutsche Nationalbibliografie; detailed bibliographic data are available online at http://dnb.d-nb.de.

None of the content in this book was published in exchange for payment by commercial parties or designers; Gestalten selected all included work based solely on its artistic merit.

This book was printed on paper certified by the FSC®.

MIX
Paper from responsible sources
FSC® C002727